Web Standards

Mastering HTML5, CSS3, and XML

Leslie F. Sikos, Ph.D.

Apress®

Web Standards—Mastering HTML5, CSS3, and XML

ISBN-13 (pbk): 978-1-4302-4041-9

ISBN-13 (electronic): 978-1-4302-4042-6

President and Publisher: Paul Manning
Lead Editor: Ben Renow-Clark
Technical Reviewer: Charles Brown
Editorial Board: Steve Anglin, Mark Beckner, Ewan Buckingham, Gary Cornell, Morgan Engel, Jonathan Gennick, Jonathan Hassell, Robert Hutchinson, Michelle Lowman, James Markham, Matthew Moodie, Jeff Olson, Jeffrey Pepper, Douglas Pundick, Ben Renow-Clarke, Dominic Shakeshaft, Gwenan Spearing, Matt Wade, Tom Welsh
Coordinating Editor: Annie Beck
Copy Editor: Kim Wimpsett
Compositor: Bytheway Publishing Services
Indexer: SPI Global
Artist: SPI Global
Cover Designer: Anna Ishchenko

Distributed to the book trade worldwide by Springer Science+Business Media, LLC., 233 Spring Street, 6th Floor, New York, NY 10013. Phone 1-800-SPRINGER, fax (201) 348-4505, e-mail orders-ny@springer-sbm.com, or visit www.springeronline.com.

For information on translations, please e-mail rights@apress.com, or visit www.apress.com.

Apress and friends of ED books may be purchased in bulk for academic, corporate, or promotional use. eBook versions and licenses are also available for most titles. For more information, reference our Special Bulk Sales–eBook Licensing web page at www.apress.com/bulk-sales.

The source code for this book is available to readers at www.apress.com and at the companion website of the book at www.masteringhtml5css3.com. You will need to answer questions pertaining to this book in order to successfully download the code.

All names, companies and domains provided in the sample codes are fictitious. No identification with actual persons, companies, and websites is intended or should be inferred.

Contents at a Glance

Contents

About the Author

 **Leslie F. Sikos, Ph.D.** is an IT professional, hand coder, web standardista and multimedia expert. He is a computer scientist and senior web developer specializing in web quality assurance—including, but not limited to, website standardization in development and redesign, the Open Web Platform, XML technologies and XML serializations, the Semantic Web and metadata technologies, web accessibility, and multimedia. A comprehensive assessment of his achievements and activities can be found on his fully standards-compliant website at LeslieSikos.com.

About the Technical Reviewer

 **Charles Brown** is one of the most noted author, consultant, and trainers in the industry today. His books about Dreamweaver and Fireworks have received critical acclaim and used worldwide as teaching tools. In addition to his work in the IT industry, Charles is also a noted concert pianist, organist, and guitarist appearing in major concert centers world-wide. He began his musical studies at age 4 and went on to study with famed pianist Vladimir Horowitz. At age 14, he made his debut with Leonard Bernstein and later studied at the famed Juilliard School. Eventually he went to Paris to study with the 20th century legend, Igor Stravinsky. While working with Stravinsky, Charles developed a close friendship with one of the most powerful artistic forces of the 20th century: Pablo Picasso. What he learned about creativity from Picasso he uses today in his writings and training work. Charles is a certified Macromedia/Adobe trainer who is in heavy demand worldwide. He frequently speaks at major conferences such as MAX and NAB. You can see his blog at blog.charlesebrown.net and his website can be found at CharlesEBrown.net.

Preface

From its earliest stage at the beginning of the 1990s, the Web has been attracting all kinds of content authors. Anybody with minimal know-how can publish on the Web from anywhere, anytime. This easy access has allowed billions of web sites to appear on the "network of networks," in any form. However, this approach caused serious problems that affect both the present and the future of the Web.

Because of the rapidly growing number of Internet services (beyond WWW), such as Voice over Internet Protocol (VoIP), IPTV, and instant messaging, the number of users has also been increasing gradually. Among this growing popularity the need for web development is also increasing. More and more people want to develop and maintain their own web sites and provide online services, but they are often reluctant to pay for the services of an IT professional. However, these tasks can be rather complex and often require much more technical know-how than many people have.

In the era of modern content management systems, many people think that there is no need for qualified professionals anymore to develop web sites. Although these software tools are good options in many cases, neither non-IT people nor computer software will ever replace professional web site developers. However, the possibility exists for everyone to develop and maintain professional-like web sites on their own with user-friendly software tools. The problem is that these tools often produce invalid code and don't follow web standards.

Web developers are constantly pushed to address inconsistency problems of appearance and behavior of the same site in various rendering engines and browser versions, and this is something that nonprofessionals generally find very difficult to address. Web standards should be used to completely eliminate these problems.

Common development approaches do not consider more than just a few basic principles, such as design and user interface, or the behavior in the most popular browsers. Some developers who read about emerging technologies try to apply these approaches as soon as possible to compete with other web studios. Other developers keep using the same technologies, techniques, and practices for as long as possible even if better technologies and new trends appear. Unfortunately, the proper implementation of web standards is not a major concern in most cases.

Even though there have been more and more standards for web development and configuration practices, many of them take years before achieving widespread adoption or are completely ignored. Some examples are news feeds, SVG, Web Fonts, MathML, the namespace mechanism, accessibility techniques, and RDFa.

From the standardization point of view, it is not an exaggeration that nearly all web sites (even the ones that are constantly evolving) apply obsolete technologies and practices and are not optimal. The growing number of Internet users leads to growing demands for online services, appearance, presence, and overall functionality. As a result of the new trend of wide-screen monitors, for example, new resolution and aspect ratio standards have appeared. How can web site developers deal with that? And how can web content be prepared for both large-resolution monitors and small handheld devices at the same time? How can the latest Web 3.0 services be provided in a way that they can be used across most browsers? How can web site appearance and functionality be guaranteed on a variety of platforms?

How can the length of the markup and styling rules be minimized while preserving site information, functionality, and behavior?

Although there is no ultimate solution for these problems to date, the application of web recommendations and standards may be the one and only option. Applying new recommendations and standards provides impressive potential for addressing those issues that make the lives of both web site developers and Internet users more difficult.

Browsers are capable of ignoring incorrect code blocks and annotations. They are capable of rendering even incorrect documents by supplying missing end tags. Web browsers keep communication channels alive because the browsers are extremely error tolerant. Browsers can render not only standardized documents but also the ones full of errors, which is what makes the Web work. Most people, however, are prone to forget this fact or simply do not even know about it. Furthermore, many do not know anything about the issues arising with web site development practices that do not comply with standards. The needs of Internet users form the Web and introduce the need for new approaches and constant evolution of new technologies. Before such technologies are standardized, there is no formal way to implement them. After they are standardized, developers should apply them according to the corresponding standards. Standard compliance issues considerably affect the daily life of millions of people around the world. Even if users do not know the real reason why web sites fall apart, contain unreadable elements, are hard to use, and look completely different in various browsers, or do not work at all, these problems occur and reoccur.

It is the responsibility of web site developers to create and maintain a better, well-formed Web for everyone. Similarly, browser vendors should also contribute to standardization by providing proper standards support in their products.

This book is a comprehensive collection of state-of-the-art information on current and future standards for the World Wide Web. In fact, it is written to be the most complete reference of web standardization resources ever published. Since standard compliance is, in many cases, not a straightforward process, web developers should evaluate numerous standardization issues before achieving some kind of routine to be able to develop fully functional standard-compliant web sites. User-friendly descriptions and precise technical documents can also be presented beautifully. After all, web standardization is not a sacrifice!

Covering all major web standards, this book focuses on syntax, formal grammar, recommended annotations, and other standardization concerns rather than providing full technology descriptions.

The aim of this book is to provide a guide on standard web site creation for web developers. The chapters include both theoretical technology discussions and practical sample code for step-by-step programming. Beyond the basics and the short review of technologies, the book enumerates the most important practices and resources in standard web site development.

PART 1

Web Standards

In this part of the book, you will become familiar with the theoretical background behind web standards. You will learn the fundamental concepts of web site standardization, along with the standardization bodies that develop standards and the most influential web sites that announce, promote, and distribute them. You will learn about the importance of web standards and understand the reasons for incorrect implementations, along with techniques to correct or eliminate them. You will learn the web standards by category, from server configuration and internationalization settings to standard-compliant markup, style sheets, object embedding, metadata annotations, and news feeds. After reading these chapters, you will have a solid foundation of web standards and will be able to select the most appropriate standards for your projects.

CHAPTER 1

Introduction to Web Standards

Technical standards are widely used in various fields of life—think of the standards of paper size and the standard envelopes that fit them. *Web standards*, similar to other standards, are normative specifications of technologies and methodologies. In other words, they are well-defined sets of requirements to be satisfied. They are not only ideal from the technical point of view but also represent user needs. However, web standards are often ignored; the World Wide Web consists of billions of documents that do not consider proper restrictions or regulations, causing serious problems. This is because the Web is a "free forum" where everyone can publish even without a technical background. Unfortunately, this approach comes at a price: you will often encounter sites that download slower, have an inadequate appearance, or have poor functionality. Further, in spite of the benefits of standard compliance, not only content authors but also web developers find it difficult to implement web standards. One of the major reasons for that is the lack of widespread distribution. Even the most popular web sites can be very confusing, and in contrast to the common misconception, developers cannot use them as references to learn from. Moreover, many developers ignore standards because they think incorrectly that developing with standards means an additional workload. People have a limited knowledge about web standards, and they generally know neither the reason nor the optimal method for applying them.

In this chapter, you will learn about the significance of web standards and the reliable resources you should know in order to make the best use of web standards in your own applications. Web standards are often ignored, causing serious problems that are described in the "Problem Statement" section later in this chapter. This chapter sets out the major benefits of web standards. It will also give you a solid understanding of the diversity and status of standards. After reading the chapter, you will be able to recognize finalized specifications and select the most appropriate ones for any project.

The Basic Concepts

Web standards are applicable to the World Wide Web (for short, the Web). These formal standards define and describe various aspects of the Web. According to the Web Standards Project, a major standards promoter, "Web standards are carefully designed to deliver the greatest benefits to the greatest number of web users while ensuring the long-term viability of any document published on the Web. Designing and building with these standards simplifies and lowers the cost of production, while delivering sites that are accessible to more people and more types of Internet devices. Sites developed along these lines will continue to function correctly as traditional desktop browsers evolve, and as new Internet devices come to market" [1].

Web standards are often *de facto* (in practice) standards. Since there is no law that enforces them, web standards are ignored by a large share of web developers. The Recommendations published by the World Wide Web Consortium (W3C), the largest web standardization body in the world, are not exceptions either. However, in November 2010, W3C made a big step forward when it became an ISO/IEC JTC 1 PAS Submitter because any stable core web technologies produced by W3C are also in the scope of ISO. The International Standards Organization (ISO) and the International Electrotechnical

Commission (IEC) can efficiently contribute to the wider, and, if possible, global, adoption of W3C standards by changing the status of de facto standards to *de jure* (in principle) [2].

Web site standardization refers to the development process of standard web sites or the correction of nonstandard sites to fulfill the requirements to become standard sites. This phrase has been recently associated with the philosophy of web design and programming that includes the application of widely accepted technologies, techniques, and best practices. The list also includes various tricks, as well as CSS and JavaScript hacks used by many developers, most of whom are not aware that these techniques should not be used.

The main goals of standardization are functionality, interoperability, and browser and resolution independence in order to ensure user experience, access to content, menu usability, and predictable behavior.

The Role of Standardization

As you will see, there are several goals in web development, and they cannot be achieved without a standardized approach. How is it possible to use printers on a daily basis without paper-size standards? How could anyone use electric devices without standardized voltage? Why should web developers expect that standards are not essential to quality assurance?

The grammar and other rules defined by web standards should be followed when authoring on the Web. Although browsers have strong built-in error-handling features capable of eliminating problems on the user side, web developers should not misuse these features.

Overall, designing costs are lower because fewer design decisions need to be made. Routine design should be based on standards. A further advantage is that developers can use their knowledge again when designing.

Users switch to other web sites within a few seconds if the content is not provided in an appropriate manner. As a result, poor functionality and usability might have a severe impact on web site traffic and business revenue.

Furthermore, various browsers interpret bad or broken markup in different ways. This could be a reason for inconsistencies, bad layout, style problems, and unexpected script behavior. The best way is to fulfill all the requirements of structure, syntax, and other rules described by the appropriate Document Type Definition and W3C Recommendation (see the "W3C" section).

Applying up-to-date web technologies is difficult, but it's vital for providing powerful features that are expected by most users. Web authors should choose the right technologies to compete with other developers. Standard compliance is an essential feature of web site development that guarantees general quality [3].

Using web standards is, therefore, a promising way to improve the overall usability of the Web.

The Cost of Nonstandardized Markup

All Internet users encounter web sites from time to time that break apart and show elements in evidently wrong places that are partly overlapped with unreadable content.

The cause is, in most cases, the nonstandard or browser-specific source code or the lack of standard support of the web browser used to render the pages.

The majority of web sites are obsolete from the standardization point of view. Even the largest and most well-known companies publish nonstandard documents constantly.

The major drawbacks of nonstandardized documents are the following:

- Inadequate search engine indexing. Crawlers cannot index incorrectly coded documents, which can cause visitor loss.[1]

- Longer download time.

- Longer rendering.

- Incorrect rendering (one of the most significant drawbacks).

- Easier development.

- Low level of accessibility.

- Low level of backward compatibility.

- Lost traffic, fewer visitors, and fewer sales. Because of the inconveniences and problems listed earlier, web sites that are not standard-compliant have a higher risk of losing functionality, popularity, and productivity.

- Additional bandwidth load and hosting cost. Numerous needless characters in the source code increase both file size and complexity.

- Difficult updating and maintenance.

Benefits of Standard-Compliant Markup

Valid, standard-compliant markup has several advantages. Here are the most important ones:

- Search engine crawlers can index documents more adequately, and the content is basically search engine optimized.

- Compared to those websites that violate standards, standard-compliant websites can be downloaded faster.

- Well-structured markup provides faster rendering.

- Web documents that apply standards properly are rendered accurately.

- More users are accommodated, and they probably stay longer because of correct appearance and layout.[2]

- Lower development costs (only in case of well-qualified developers and carefully selected software tools).

- Standard-compliant markup serves as the basis for website accessibility.

- Backward compatibility is ensured as browsers evolve.

- Optimal content lengths and file size (no unnecessary characters are listed in the source code), as well as cost-optimal storage (potential for cheaper hosting).

---

[1] However, there are several additional factors that affect search engine indexing.
[2] Thanks to correct rendering rather than design.

- Standard-compliant markup is easier to maintain and update than the markup that violates standards.

- Standard-compliant source codes become obsolete later, and upgrading is much easier when new standards are introduced.

- Compatibility with current and future browsers is guaranteed (at least from a developer's point of view).

- Inspire implementation and force web browsers to support standards progressively.

It should be evident that standard-compliant, clean code has many advantages over nonstandard source code. Consequently, it is not only highly recommended but vital to consider standards during web site development.

Development and Announcement of Standards

Generally, web standards are *technical specifications of web technologies* released by standardization bodies. Most web standards are published by W3C [4]. Its *Recommendations* are vital when designing with standards.[3] W3C publishes specifications on markup languages, style sheets, metadata, XML technologies, semantic markup, mathematical notation, and graphical formats, just to mention the most important categories. However, there are also other influential standards organizations on the web standardization scene (Table 1-1).

Table 1-1. Influential Organizations on Web Standardization

Organization	Abbreviation	Web Site	Major Specifications and Standards
Dublin Core Metadata Initiative	DCMI	www.dublincore.org	Dublin Core Metadata
ECMA International (formerly ECMA)	ECMA	www.ecma-international.org	ECMAScript [5]
International Organization for Standardization	ISO	www.iso.org	Web site engineering and other IT standards [6], for example, user interface standards, PNG functional specification
Internet Assigned Numbers Authority	IANA	www.iana.org	Domain names, IP address coordination, protocol assignments [7]

---

[3] The term recommendation refers to the lack of legal status. This is one of the reasons why they are applied so rarely.

Organization	Abbreviation	Web Site	Major Specifications and Standards
Internet Engineering Task Force	IETF	`www.ietf.org`	Internet standard (STD) documents [8], Request for Comments (RFC) documents [9], for example, proper use of HTTP, MIME, and URI
Unicode Consortium	Unicode	`www.unicode.org`	Unicode Standard, Unicode Technical Reports (UTRs) [10]
Web Hypertext Application Technology Working Group	WHATWG	`www.whatwg.org`	HTML5, Microdata, Web Applications, Web Forms, Web Workers [11]
World Wide Web Consortium	W3C	`www.w3.org`	Recommendations, for example, (X)HTML, CSS, DOM, XForms, SVG, RDF, GRDDL, OWL

W3C

Founded and directed by Tim Berners-Lee ("the inventor of the Web"[4]), the *World Wide Web Consortium* is the largest international organization for developing standards for the World Wide Web. It has several local offices throughout the world. The members of W3C are mainly universities and research groups that are keen to participate in the development of web standards. W3C works as an open forum.

Efforts are made to ease contributions to web standards. In fall 2010, W3C released the Draft Proposal "Making W3C the place for new standards" [12]. Openness could be the key to new, easier contributions from the web community, including independent web developers without W3C membership. It also contributes to the maximization of knowledge reuse [13]. Important standards such as HTML5, CSS, SVG, MathML, various APIs, RDFa, and Microdata are summarized in a suite of technical standards called the *Open Web Platform*, which is open for contributions from external organizations and the public [14]. W3C is now "an open platform for web standardization" [15].

In fact, many problems web developers face every day have already been solved and published in earlier W3C Recommendations, sometimes several years ago. Some technologies are based on ideas that were originally created elsewhere but later shared with W3C to achieve wider support and popularity.

News feeds, for example, are not as new as one might think. They were described many years earlier when they first appeared on the Web and became supported by major browsers, operating systems, and office suites [for example, 16]. Surprisingly, RSS 0.9 was published as early as 1999 [17]! A similar trend holds for markup languages, vector graphics, equations, and other specifications.

Mathematical notations are published as GIF image files all over the Internet, although the markup language for this purpose became a Recommendation in 1999 (with updates soon following).

---

[4] Although he is often referred this way, he does not call himself so.

Vector graphics are seldom used on the Web, although W3C started to develop the SVG standard in 1998, and it became a Recommendation in 2001.[5] High-resolution bitmap graphics are used instead. But why? They should be replaced by SVG whenever possible, and raster graphics should be applied for publishing photographs only. SVG is supported by Amaya, the free web editor/browser of W3C, and popular graphic suites like Adobe Illustrator and CorelDraw. From 2010, SVG has also been indexed by Google [18]. SVG 1.2 supports animation too. Editing SVG is not more complicated than editing bitmaps, but SVG files are generally smaller in size, can be downloaded faster, and have incomparable quality compared to bitmaps.

WHATWG

The Web Hypertext Application Technology Working Group (WHATWG) is a professional yet unofficial community founded by individuals in 2004. It was a response to the relatively slow standards development at W3C and its decision to abandon HTML in favor of XHTML and other XML-based standards. The WHATWG has an invitation-only committee, which controls the editors of specifications. Anyone can contribute to the efforts of WHATWG by joining one of its open mailing lists [19].

ERCIM

The *European Research Consortium for Informatics and Mathematics* assembles researchers to work in cooperation on various fields of ICT and applied mathematics including, but not limited to, information system applications, information storage and retrieval, information interfaces and presentation, data encryption, and database management [20]. The scientific approach is ensured by 19 organizations from different countries across Europe. ERCIM has played a major role in the formulation of standards such as SMIL and SVG [21].

IETF

The Internet Engineering Task Force (IETF) is a standardization group within the nonprofit organization Internet Society (ISOC) along with the Internet Architecture Board (IAB). IETF focuses mainly on Internet protocols. IETF standards are generally on lower levels than web site developers are interested in; however, even the well-known TCP/IP has been developed by IETF. "The mission of the IETF is make the Internet work better by producing high quality, relevant technical documents that influence the way people design, use, and manage the Internet [22]." Technical documents are listed on the Requests for Comments (RFC) web site [23].

Ecma International

Ecma International is a nonprofit standards organization that develops and promotes standards for information and communication systems [24]. One of its most important standards from a web developer's point of view is the standardized scripting language ECMAScript (which JavaScript is based on; see the section "JavaScript" for more).

Unicode Consortium

The *Unicode Consortium* coordinates the development, maintenance, and promotion of Unicode and other internationalization standards [25]. The nonprofit organization defines the behavior and

---

[5] In contrast, Internet Explorer supports SVG natively from 2011 only.

relationship between Unicode characters. The consortium works in close collaboration with W3C and ISO. The most important part of the cooperation is the maintenance of ISO/IEC 10646, the International Standard synchronized with the Unicode Standard.

DCMI

The *Dublin Core Metadata Initiative* is a registered company in Singapore [26]. The open organization develops and maintains interoperable metadata standards. DCMI provides annual conferences and workshops, standards liaison, and standards promotion. A worldwide community of users and developers is supported by DCMI through collaborative work in discussion forums, communities, and task groups.

IANA

The *Internet Assigned Numbers Authority* is the organization that oversees global IP address and top-level domain allocations, root zone management in the Domain Name System (assignments of ccTLDs and gTLDs), MIME types, and other Internet Protocol–related symbols and numbers [27]. IANA is operated by the nonprofit corporation Internet Corporation for Assigned Names and Numbers (ICANN) [28].

OASIS

The *Organization for the Advancement of Structured Information Standards* (OASIS) works on open standards for web services, interoperability, security, and ebusiness. Its slogan is "Advancing open standards for the information society" [29]. The consortium maintains influential information portals on web services as well as on XML [30, 31].

ISO

Founded in 1947, the *International Organization for Standardization* is an international standardization body that represents various standards organizations from all over the world [32]. ISO provides both industrial and commercial standards. ISO has developed more than 18,500 international standards on a variety of subjects, many of which are also used on the Web (for example, country codes, date/time, and time duration annotations).

Standards Promotion and Distribution

Many web standards are optional only and not enforced by law (which is the only way to achieve worldwide application). However, there is a new trend that might change the situation within a few years (for example, there are accessibility standards that are enforced by law in some countries—see the section "Defining Web Accessibility"). Until then, web standards are not present everywhere, and it can be difficult for web developers to maintain up-to-date knowledge and learn new technologies. However, people can use a variety of events and resources to inform themselves as individuals or through affiliations, including conferences, printed or online documents, and books.

Groups and Associations

There are numerous groups among enthusiastic web developers that distribute and expedite standards and harmonize them with best practices. Membership fees are generally much lower than those of standardization bodies. Some of them are open, and anyone can join free of charge.

Note that many technical groups and associations focus mainly on technologies rather than standards. Their members are usually informed about the latest technology news only. The following sections provide a quick overview of influential groups related to web standardization.

The Web Standards Project

The Web Standards Project (WaSP) was founded in 1998 by professional web developers to spread the application of web standards published mainly by W3C. "The Web Standards Project is a grassroots coalition fighting for standards which ensure simple, affordable access to Web technologies for all" [33]. The organization focuses on standard support, accessibility, and easier development.

WaSP's major contributions to web standard support are known as *task forces*. Its aim is to attract the attention of the most considerable companies and organizations of the world and persuade them to become standard-compliant as much as possible. WaSP task forces include the following:

- Accessibility Task Force

- Adobe Task Force (former Dreamweaver Task Force)

- Education Task Force

- International Liaison Group

- Microsoft Task Force

- The Street Team

The Acid tests used to compare standard support of browsers (see the section "Standard Compliance Tests") were introduced by the Web Standards Project.

Web Standards Group

As a web designer/developer community, the *Web Standards Group* (WSG) focuses on web standards and best practices to achieve standard codes. Thousands of IT professionals from around the world are members of WSG [34].

Guild of Accessible Web Designers

The *Guild of Accessible Web Designers* (GAWDS) is a worldwide association of professional organizations, individual web designers, and developers. GAWDS works on promoting accessibility standards [35].

International Webmasters Association

The *International Webmasters Association* is a W3C member that "provides and fosters professional advancement opportunities among individuals dedicated to or pursuing a Web career, and to work diligently to enhance their effectiveness, image, and professionalism as they attract and serve their clients and employers" [36].

Web Industry Professionals Association

The *Web Industry Professionals Association* is a technical association in Australia. WIPA assembles professional individuals working in the web industry to "exchange ideas, participate in debate, advance education and promote ethical practice" [37]. WIPA is a major organizer of web courses in Australia.

Open Digital Rights Language Initiative

The *Open Digital Rights Language* (ODRL) *Initiative* is an international organization that develops and promotes the ODRL vocabulary [38], which is an open standard for policy expressions (see the section "DC, IMS, and ODRL").

Staying Informed: Events and Courses

Beyond online resources such as official news feeds, there are several types of appearances and events that contribute to the worldwide distribution of web standards. The list includes press releases, scientific and professional conferences, talks, workshops, meetings, discussion forums, symposiums, and tutorials. Many of the documents associated with these events are available online. Web standardistas can use these documents to maintain up-to-date knowledge and keep abreast of the latest specifications.

The primary resource for major events related to web standards such as workshops and conferences as well as announcements of recommendations and presentations is the W3C web site at www.w3.org [39]. Events are classified as "Talks and appearances" and "Events." Past events are available in the News Archive [40].

The World Wide Web Consortium also offers online training courses on standards such as SVG through a dedicated portal [41]. The courses consist of weekly modules with instructions (*lectures*), link collection, activities, and a discussion forum. The quality is guaranteed by the instructors since they are either co-authors or editors of the relevant W3C standard or internationally recognized experts in the field. Participants can expect to spend two to three hours per week on these courses.

The *Internationalization & Unicode Conference* (IUC) has been organized annually since 1977. It covers the latest industry standards and best practices on software and web application internationalization. Up-to-date information is available at www.unicodeconference.org [42].

IETF meetings are held three times a year. Information on upcoming meetings, requests, materials, proceedings, and sponsoring are published on the IETF web site [43].

The Dublin Core Metadata Initiative has held the International Conference on Dublin Core and Metadata Applications annually since 2001 [44].

WIPA provides up-to-date information on up-coming events such as Australian training courses and workshops on the WIPA web site [45]. The association also has two RSS channels, publishing general news [46] and industry events [47], respectively.

The Association for Computing Machinery (ACM) maintains an up-to-date calendar on IT conferences and events, some of which are related to web technologies [48].

World Standards Day has been celebrated since 1970 by ISO, IEC, and ITU each year on 14 October in Geneva, Switzerland. The message of World Standards Day 2010 clearly indicated a major aim of standardization: "Standards make the world accessible for all" [49].

Not all prominent events have a long track history, though. Many promising conferences and workshops are good initiatives such as the popular conference Future of Web Apps [50]. Carsonified also organizes online conferences on the latest technologies [51].

There are web sites that are collections of events and articles of a given topic. A good example is www.semanticmetadata.net, which is a comprehensive site for Semantic Web developers [52].

Resources

One of the easiest ways to keep up-to-date with web standards is to subscribe to the news feeds of standardization bodies and organizations. News is often published on the home pages of the related web sites. Course materials, conference proceedings, and presentation slides are also available in many cases. An endless variety of further resources are also available.

W3C provides a weekly newsletter [53]. Its latest news is available in both Atom [54] and RSS [55] news feeds. The vast majority of W3C documents are public and freely available.

General news on Unicode is available through the news feed of the Unicode Consortium [56].

The Dublin Core Metadata Initiative publishes news on the home page of its web site and provides a news feed [57]. The proceedings of the International Conference on Dublin Core and Metadata Applications are available at the DCMI Conference Papers page [58].

Scientific journal papers with Digital Object Identifier (DOI) can also be found throughout the Web, although many of these documents are not free of charge. Still, most of them provide at least an abstract in PDF.

Types, Stages, and Status of Standards

The Web is a highly innovative medium where constant changes and improvements necessitate continuous standard development. This results in different document *maturity levels*. For example, W3C Recommendations progress through five such levels, also known as the *W3C process flow* [59]:

- Working Draft (WD)

- Last Call Working Draft

- Candidate Recommendation (CR)

- Proposed Recommendation (PR)

- W3C Recommendation (REC)

The last version is considered by developers as the *(de facto)* standard to be applied. W3C Recommendations are sometimes updated by separately published *erratum*. After a considerable amount of changes, new editions are published that supersede the current version. However, their URIs generally remain constant. The *document status* determines which version is the most up-to-date one and which one should be applied. The list of current W3C publications and the latest revision of technical reports can be found in the W3C technical reports folder [60].

Other standardization bodies use different status conventions. The Internet Engineering Task Force, for example, applies document status such as *Internet draft, informational,* and *proposed standard.* The latter one is defined as a "generally stable specification which has resolved known design choices, is believed to be well-understood, has received significant community review, and appears to enjoy enough community interest to be considered valuable. However, further experience might result in a change or even retraction of the specification before it advances [61]." The IETF RFCs are designated as *standards, draft standards, proposed standards, best current practices, informational documents, experimental documents,* and *historic standards* [62].

The Microformat Community uses the status *draft specification* for those documents that are "somewhat mature in the development process" and whose stability is not guaranteed [63]. Implementers of such documents are warned to keep abreast of future developments and changes.

ISO applies the following conventions:

- *Preliminary work item* (PWI)

- *New work item proposal* (NP or NWIP, NP Amd/TR/TS/IWA)

- *Working draft(s)* (AWI, AWI Amd/TR/TS, WD, WD Amd/TR/TS)

- *Committee draft(s)* (CD, CD Amd/Cor/TR/TS, PDAmd (PDAM), PDTR, PDTS)

- *Enquiry draft* (DIS, FCD, FPDAmd, DAmd (DAM), FPDISP, DTR, DTS)

- *Final draft International Standard* (FDIS, FDAmd (FDAM), PRF, PRF Amd/TTA/TR/TS/Suppl, FDTR)

- *International Standard* (ISO TR, TS, IWA, Amd, Cor)

Many web standards are *open standards*, meaning that the development has been open to individual contributors; they are publicly available, and certain copyright licenses might apply.

The Variety of Rendering Engines

Web documents and files associated with style sheet files, script files, images, and XML files are processed and displayed (that is, rendered) or printed by *rendering engines* (*layout engines*). They are usually embedded in web browsers and e-mail clients.

Although the statistics of usage share of web browsers [64, 65, 66, 67, and so on] are either overestimated or underestimated, and thus generally not accurate, one thing is certain: no user agent can be claimed as "the most popular" or the "most widely used" one. Consequently, browser independence is more important than ever. Because of the differences in rendering and standards support, the features of rendering engines should be considered in web site development for the sake of interoperability and functionality.

No browser is perfect from the standards point of view. All have some problems with markup, styles, ECMAScript, or accessibility. However, most browser developers realized that standards support should be boosted; otherwise, they cannot compete with others.

From a web developer's point of view, it is a rather complex task to achieve a similar (and not pixel-by-pixel identical) appearance in various browsers. Because of different functioning and features, various browsers might render even standard-compliant web sites differently. In practice, various tricks and hacks are used to address the problem. However, these should be eliminated whenever possible.

In contrast to Internet Explorer (IE), updates of other browsers are released frequently, and this is how they provide new features prior to IE (Figure 1-1). Anti-IE developers often overlook this simple fact.

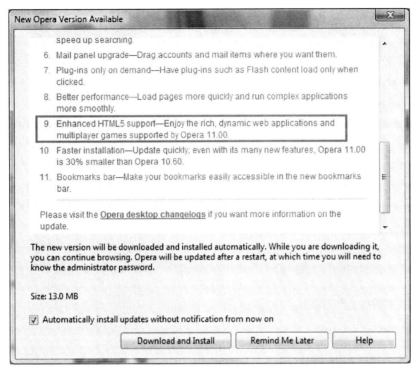

Figure 1-1. Browser updates provide new features such as advanced support of the latest standards.

Supporting SVG can serve as a good example. The specification was published in 1999, and no one cared for it until the growing popularity of HTML5, which natively supports the format. Browsers such as Firefox, Opera, or Safari have adopted the standard lately, although before IE. However, this is not a big achievement because none of them supported SVG for many years. In the early 2000s, one (if not the only one) that did was Amaya. Until recently, most people used the Adobe SVG Viewer plug-in to display SVG images in their browsers.

The implementation of elements and attributes does not necessarily mean proper, full support for a markup language. For example, some browser vendors claimed for years that their product supported MathML; however, MathML could not be rendered in many cases because of the lack of support for embedding mechanisms and external files. Even the appropriate MIME type was missing from the implementation.

Standards support, especially of CSS, has been incorrect and/or incomplete in most browsers for years. Moreover, the latest version of CSS, CSS3, was introduced before the previous one, CSS 2.1, could have gained complete support in browsers.

Trident

Used by Internet Explorer (since version 4) and IE shells, Outlook Express, Maxthon, and various media players, *Trident* is one of the most widely used rendering engines. Windows Internet Explorer (formerly Microsoft Internet Explorer) is a series of graphical web browsers developed by Microsoft. IE has been implemented in the Microsoft Windows operating systems since 1995.

Although Internet Explorer has been continuously improved in each version, even the most important standards, that is, the ones that describe the markup and style sheets, are implemented in an incomplete fashion. The limited standards support, incorrect floating positions, the expanding box problem, and especially the implementation of the individual box model of Internet Explorer 6, have caused serious problems in web design for years.

The standard-compliant mode was introduced in version 6; however, it did not solve the problem. Even some of the well-known HTML 4.01 elements (for example, abbr) were not supported prior to IE8. Several DHTML objects did not comply with standards. When web pages are rendered in IE8 mode, however, the methods and attributes updated in IE8 might cause problems with web sites that expect the rendering functionality of earlier IE versions [68].

For years Trident has supported HTML 4.01, XML 1.0, XSLT 1.0, and DOM Level 1 with minor implementation gaps. CSS Level 2 and DOM Level 2 have been provided with major implementation gaps and conformance issues. The CSS support in Windows Internet Explorer has constantly been evolving. Internet Explorer 6 was the first version with full CSS Level 1 compliance. However, some selectors such as min-height were missing. Internet Explorer 8 is the first IE version with nearly complete CSS 2.1 and partial CSS3 support. It is important to keep in mind that the CSS features introduced in Internet Explorer 8 will work only if the web pages are rendered in *IE8 mode* (or higher). This can be ensured by adding the meta tag described in Listing 1-1 to the head section of web pages.

Listing 1-1. *Version Targeting for Internet Explorer 8 (Should not Be Used)*

```
<meta http-equiv="X-UA-Compatible" content="IE=8" />
```

However, avoiding version targeting is strongly recommended, as mentioned earlier.

Since Trident version 4 (used by IE8), a built-in RSS/Atom news feed reader is also available through a dedicated button with the RSS logo in gray, which changes to orange after activation (if applicable).

Microsoft recently recognized the importance of standards support and is beginning to take it seriously. First, Microsoft became an active participant in standards development in the CSS3 and SVG Working Groups at W3C. Second, it is a co-chair of the HTML5 Working Group and a leader in the HTML5 Testing Task Force.

Trident 5 applied in Internet Explorer 9 introduced support for modern web standards, including HTML5, CSS3, ECMAScript5, DOM Levels 2 and 3, ICC Color Profiles, and SVG [69]. In contrast to earlier versions that can render only "HTML-compatible" XHTML documents served incorrectly with the text/html MIME-type, Trident 5 provides full XHTML support.

Gecko

Firefox, Camino, the Mozilla Application Suite, Netscape, Thunderbird, SeaMonkey, and other software apply the rendering engine Gecko (originally NGLayout) [70]. Netscape released the first version in 1997. In 1998, the Mozilla project was launched, and the source code was released under an open source license. Gecko is now developed by the Mozilla Foundation/Corporation. It is written in C++[6] as a cross-platform layout engine under three licenses: Mozilla Public License (MPL), GNU General Public License (GPL), and GNU Lesser General Public License (LGPL).

Gecko was originally designed to support web standards and is constantly improving. Beyond conventional standards such as markup, CSS, JavaScript, ECMAScript 3 and 5, DOM Levels 1/2/3, and XML 1.0; less commonly used standards such as MathML, RDF, XSLT, XPath, and SVG; and Animated PNG (APNG) images with alpha transparency are also supported. Firefox, which applies Gecko, supports

---

[6] The Mozilla Firefox browser has parts written in C/C++, JavaScript, CSS, XUL, and XBL.

not only W3C Recommendations but also proposals and standards from other standardization bodies, such as WHATWG.

To provide wide interoperability, Gecko supports DOCTYPE switching, which makes it possible to render correctly nonstandard web sites designed for older browsers and their variants (such as Netscape Communicator 4.*x*). Nonstandard Internet Explorer features such as the incorrect implementation of the document.all property or the marquee element are also supported to some extent. The Quirks Mode of Firefox is not perfect, but it's similar to other browsers.

Firefox also provides the Google protocol Safebrowsing to improve the security of data exchange.

Firefox does not support ActiveX controls by default. Although third-party plug-ins are available, they do not work safely in all versions or on all platforms.

KHTML

KHTML is the layout engine used by Konqueror. It supports HTML 4.01 and partially supports HTML 5. Both screen and paged media support is provided for CSS 2.1. Beyond the full implementation of CSS 3 selectors (from KDE 3.5.6 [71]), KHTML supports other CSS3 features, for example, multiple backgrounds, box-sizing, and text-shadow. KHTML supports DOM 1 and 2 fully and DOM 3 partially. ECMA-262 (JavaScript 1.5) can be used in KHTML, along with the graphic formats PNG, MNG, JPEG, GIF, and SVG (partial support).

WebKit

The forked (adopted) version of KHTML is the open source WebKit layout engine. The most well-known browsers that use WebKit are Apple Safari and Google Chrome. However, there are other browsers that apply WebKit, for example, Arora, Midori, OmniWeb, Shiira, iCab (4+), Epiphany, SRWare Iron, and Maxthon (3+). WebKit is used on several mobile devices such as the Apple iPad, iPhone, and iPod touch, as well as the browser on Android, Palm webOS, and Symbian S60. The desktop version of Safari is available for Mac and Windows computers.

Being one of the first implementers of the latest standards (which have also been proved by the Acid2 and Acid3 tests), Safari has always been considered as one of the most innovative web browsers. Safari 5, for example, supports not only HTML 4.01 and XHTML 1.0 but also several features of HTML5 such as Media Support, full-screen playback for the video element, canvas, Geolocation, structuring elements, Ajax history, the draggable attribute, forms validation, the sandbox attribute, and Ruby annotation. Safari 5 handles CSS animations, CSS effects, and Web Fonts. Moreover, it provides JavaScript support (ECMAScript 262 version 3), JSON, XML 1.0, and SVG 1.1. Advanced accessibility features are also provided in Safari 5 such as VoiceOver Screen Reader, ARIA Support, enhanced keyboard navigation, full-page zoom, content zoom, closed captions for HTML5 video, custom style sheets, and minimum font size. It also has a built-in news feed reader [72].

The first version of the other popular browser that use the WebKit rendering engine, Google Chrome, passed the Acid1 and Acid2 tests. Chrome passes the Acid3 test from version 4. Chrome is a leader in HTML5 implementation, which is constantly evolving because of the continuing development of the HTML5 specifications. Chrome also provides an impressive CSS3 selector support and fast JavaScript execution.

Presto

Presto is the rendering engine used primarily by the Opera Desktop browser (from version 7), the Opera Devices SDK, and the Opera Mobile and Mini variants. Opera is used as the basis for other browsers such as Nintendo DS and DSi, Nokia 770, and Wii Internet Channel, as well as the browser for Sony Mylo COM-1.

Similar to the developer of Trident (Microsoft), the developer of Presto, Opera Software, is a W3C member [73]. As a consequence, Opera has a high level of standard support. Opera 11, for example, supports HTML5 elements such as video, audio, web forms, contentEditable, and the input attribute or the input type. CSS 2.1 and CSS3 selectors have been completely implemented, along with SVG, SMIL, and canvas. Web Workers, Geolocation, Selectors API, Touch Events, the Viewport meta element, and other technologies and standards are also available in Presto [74].

Amaya

Unlike other browsers that are typically used exclusively to display web documents, Amaya is a free, open source web browser and a WYSIWYG web developer environment in one. Managed by W3C, Amaya supports HTML 4.01, XHTML 1.0, XHTML Basic, XHTML 1.1, HTTP 1.1, MathML 2.0, CSS2 (partially), and SVG [75]. Distributions are available for Windows, Linux, and Mac.

Testing the Standard Support of Browsers

Web browsers can be tested from two different aspects: supported standards and supported technologies. The development of browser tests depends on the approach and aim.

Automatic *layout tests* are difficult to perform on mobile devices. Typically, layout tests apply a screenshot-based approach that compares a screenshot to a reference.

An imperative feature should be a test format that can be run on as many platforms and browsers as possible. For example, the browser tests developed by Mozilla are not cross-browser tests.

Two different versions of the same web page supposed to result in exactly the same rendering can be compared using *ref-tests* [76]. Mozilla also provides an automated testing framework using *MochiKit* JavaScript libraries [77]. The test applies JavaScript function calls. These browser-specific tests cannot be used for general browser comparisons.

The World Wide Web Consortium provides HTML tests [78], CSS test suites [79], mobile tests [80], a MathML test suite [81], SVG test suites [82], and internationalization tests [83]. W3C is open to contributions as well [84].

Most browser tests require human evaluation to identify bugs with full certainty. Incomplete or incorrect standard support is usually tested with complex tests, many of which are public.

Standard Compliance Tests

The most well-known browser tests for standard compliance are the *Acid tests*. This name refers to the acid tests used for gold assessment. Instead of gold purity, however, these Acid tests provide a fast and easy-to-understand indication of the standard compliance of rendering engines. In spite of that, the Acid tests have always been criticized for testing a set of rarely used features, along with those without a finalized specification.

The first version of the Acid test, *Acid1*, was written in HTML 4.0 Strict in late 1998 to check interoperability issues between earlier web browsers. Acid1 tests several features with stress on compliance with the CSS1 specification on a page against a reference image [85]. According to the document title, Acid1 is a "display/box/float/clear test."

Acid2 is a test page published by the Web Standards Project in 2005. Again, a reference image is provided that should be compared with the rendered version. Note that the nose should change to blue when the mouse hovers over the face [86]. Beyond this hovering effect, Acid2 tests the paint order, the object element, data URIs, alpha transparency of PNG images, and several CSS features (absolute, relative, and fixed positioning, the CSS box model, CSS table formatting, CSS generated content, and CSS parsing). Safari was the first among the widely used browsers that passed Acid2 in late 2005. Others followed two to three years later. For example, Firefox passed the test from version 3.0.

Acid3 has been launched in 2008. The 100 subtests grouped in 6 "buckets" cover various parts of the following standards: data URI scheme, HTTP 1.1 Protocol, HTTP status codes, Unicode 5.0 UTF-8 and UTF-16, the image/png and text/plain content types, the HTML 4.0 Transitional, HTML 4.01 Strict, and XHTML 1.0 Strict markup languages, DOM Level 2 (Core, HTML, Events, Style, Views, Traversal, Range), the object element, ECMAScript (including garbage collection), CSS selectors, SVG 1.1 (including fonts), and SMIL 2.1. Not only those browsers fail the test that cannot achieve the score 100/100, but also the ones that cannot render the animation smoothly or render it differently than what is presented in the reference (Figure 1-2 [87]).

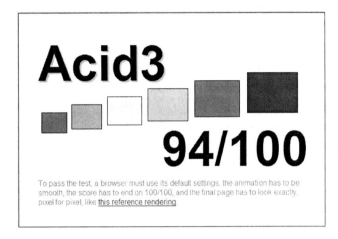

Figure 1-2. The Acid3 test in a browser that failed to pass

The following were the first stable, public browser releases that passed the Acid3 test:

- Apple Safari 4.0 (the very first web browser to pass Acid3 [88])
- Opera 10.6 [89]
- Google Chrome 4.0.249.78 [90]
- Epiphany 2.28.0 [91]
- iPhone[7] 3.1
- Iris Browser[7] 1.1.4
- Bolt browser[7] 1.6 [92]
- Opera Mobile[7] 9.7 [93]

---

[7] Mobile browsers

Comprehensive Tests

There are several other considerations in rendering engines beyond standard compliance, for example, security or CSS Selectors API94 support.

Layout tests, Mochi tests, and RefTests can be performed by BrowserTests, a repository of browser test cases and test suites [95].

A comprehensive comparison and evaluation of overall browser functionality are provided by BrowserScope. It is a "community-driven project for profiling Web browsers" [96]. The site provides up-to-date information on recent tests performed on the latest browser versions. Browsers can be compared, and tests can be run on the browser used for rendering the site.

Standards vs. Quirks Modes, DOCTYPE Switching

Standard-compliance problems of web browsers are not recent. The situation has been constantly improved, however. After partially supporting the W3C Recommendations, browser users and web site developers faced a serious problem. Millions of web sites developed earlier for older browsers looked fine in obsolete rendering engines but had serious issues in the latest ones. In other words, compliance with W3C Recommendations became a problem.

Todd Fahrner from the Web Standards Project invented the solution known as *DOCTYPE switching* in 1998 [97]. Older, nonstandard documents with a missing DOCTYPE might produce different results in various rendering engines. Modern browsers check the DOCTYPE, and if the expected behavior follows W3C standards, the document is rendered in *Standards Mode* (*Strict Mode*). If the Document Type Definition is missing, browsers switch to a mode known as *Quirks Mode* [98] that can deal with the nonstandard, unexpected behavior of older browsers (Figure 1-3).

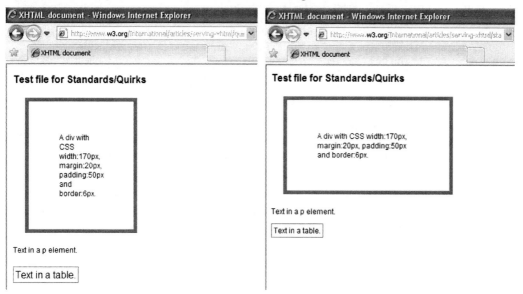

Figure 1-3. W3C test file in Standards Mode [99] and Quirks Mode [100]

One of the most famous browser bugs was the *Internet Explorer box model bug* that made identical pixel-by-pixel rendering in various browsers impossible. It occurred as its own implementation of a box model instead of the W3C CSS box model [101] in earlier versions of Microsoft Internet Explorer. (Some web developers, however, think that the box model implemented in IE5 was more logical than that of W3C's [102]; still, it was not standard.) IE6 and newer versions eliminate the problem in Standards Mode. For the sake of compatibility, however, the bug is still present in Quirks Mode. (Internet Explorer for Mac, which was discontinued in 2006, was not affected.) According to the W3C CSS1 specification, released in 1996 (revised later several times), determining the width and height attributes of all block-level elements should affect the width and height of visible elements only while the padding, borders, and margins should be applied later. Internet Explorer 5 wrapped the content, padding, and borders within a predetermined width/height. As a result, the rendering box was different from what was expected. The box model is present in newer versions of the Cascading Style Sheets specification too, including CSS 2.1 [103] and CSS3 [104].

Standard-compliant web pages can be opened faster since browsers can use Standards Mode instead of figuring out nonstandard markup in Quirks Mode.

Modern browsers render all pages providing a DOCTYPE in Standards Mode, whether they are served with or without an XML declaration. However, Internet Explorer 6 renders all pages in Quirks Mode if anything other than a byte-order mark appears before the DOCTYPE declaration.

Problem Statement

Most people think that web standardization is a well-regulated, exact process. In fact, there is no clear set of rules to follow. Those who are slightly familiar with web standards might believe that the World Wide Web Consortium provides standards for the Web. Although W3C develops web technologies for markup, annotation, styles, and so on, that will sooner or later obtain an official mandate, their implementation is an expectation only. Because of the lack of official status, these developments are recommendations instead of standards. Unlike the standards announced by standardization organizations, for example, the ISO, web recommendations are applied rather seldom because of the lack of an official status [105]. Individual vendors and web site developers *might* decide to follow some of the recommendations, but there is no enforcement. This is definitely not the way they should be treated. Efforts should be made to make the recommendations widely adopted; in fact, 99.9 percent of web sites are obsolete from the technology point of view [106]. The situation is not much better in standardization either: a large share of web sites provide invalid code.

A comprehensive validation test series was conducted in 2011 on the 350 most popular web sites in the world (selected by Alexa index[8] [107]). The test found 94 percent of those web sites failed the web standards validation tests that covered character encoding, markup, and styles.

There is no reason at all to apply 13 different character encodings, namely, UTF-8, ISO-8859-1, GB2312, Shift_JIS, GBK, Windows 1251, EUC-JP, Windows 1256, ISO-8859-15, ISO-8859-2, ISO-8859-7, ISO-8859-9, and Windows 874. The same holds for markup languages. Nine (X)HTML versions and variants have been identified. At the time of the test, 14 percent of web sites had applied HTML5 before the specification had been finalized, 23 percent used the obsolete HTML 4.01 Transitional, 45 percent the XHTML 1.0 Transitional, 8 percent the XHTML 1.0 Strict, 5 percent the HTML 4.01 Strict, and 5 percent other languages such as HTML 4.0 Transitional, HTML 4.0 Strict, and XHTML 1.1 (Figure 1-4). Although two versions, XHTML 1.0 Strict and HTML5, can be considered modern markup languages, they are applied incorrectly: the markup is full of errors in most cases. This situation is clearly indicated by the average number of markup errors, which was 6. The number of style sheet errors was even higher, with an incredible high maximum of 738 errors (!) in a single CSS file. The average number of CSS errors

---

[8] Naturally, the list of web sites changes constantly, but it does not have any impact on the conclusion.

was 45. And these numbers represent the index files only; a similar order of magnitude can be expected for all other pages as well.

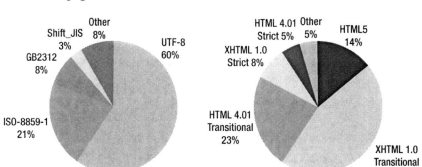

Figure 1-4. Share of character encodings and markup languages

Evidently, not all content authors are web developers, and the share of Web standardistas is even lower. The majority of web content authors do not even know the underlying technologies and standards, not to mention their application. Expectations do not force people to implement web technologies and standards correctly. The lack of consensus makes the Web chaotic. Compared to programming languages such as C, the Web is a very error-tolerant environment. This feature makes it possible for millions to create web pages without proper knowledge, but at the same time this is the reason for the incorrect markup Internet users face every day [108].

Companies desire a professional appearance to sell their products and often focus on design and marketing exclusively. In most cases, designers know little if anything about web standardization. Everyone should know at least the potential inherent in web standards.

Inadequate and incomplete standard implementations of web browsers also contribute to the problem of standardization and recommendations. Then again, even standardized web sites might look inadequate in browsers that are created with the lack of full standard support. Reasonable rendering can be expected only if standards are followed on both the user agents' and the web developers' sites.

Web publishing is often oversimplified, and only a very limited number of developers become hand coders, which is a major key to standardized web development. Since content authors need content management via graphical interfaces and dynamic content, proper standards implementations in authoring tools could also contribute to web standardization significantly. However, standards compliance has not been a major concern in content management systems and bloggers until recently.

After a certain point, web documents full of errors should not and cannot be tolerated. Such documents contain several improperly nested elements, malformed tags, and other errors often referred to as *tag soup*. Tables should be used for organizing data, not for layout or design. Missing tags should not be tolerated. Bad markup extends download time, not to mention rendering time. Efficiency can be boosted by reduced markup. It is evident that source code full of errors is much more complicated to render than error-free, standard code. Accessibility can also be increased, along with cross-browser compatibility and forward compatibility.

Server-Side Technologies and Content Management

Server-side technologies, such as PHP, ASP, or Ruby on Rails, are popular because of their powerful assistance in creating dynamic web sites.

Although server-side technologies and content management systems provide more dynamic web sites than static markup, they generally come with a lack of structure and semantics that would make web sites work better [109]. Thus, the most advanced, standard, accessible markup that also provides semantic content can still be generated manually. However, a slight improvement is noticeable in this area. The popular open source content management system Drupal, for example, supports some standards, such as semantic annotations with RDFa[9] [110].

Limited Standards Support in Development Tools

Nonprofessional authors using WYSIWYG software, such as Adobe Dreamweaver, produce a large share of web sites. Until recently, many of them provided nonstandard output. Modern versions of web development authoring tools support W3C standards. The same is true for open source environments providing dynamic content such as social networking sites, blog portals, and so on.

Still, these software tools are responsible for billions of web sites published on the Net without considering standard compliance. In most cases, complex web sites differ from the ones that are stored in the templates of authoring environments. To achieve this, users often try to modify or extend some parts of the source code, also leading to nonstandard code.

The standard compliance of markup and styles provided by WYSIWYG authoring tools is extremely important because of the large number of authors applying them. However, many aspects of standardization cannot be used fully without understanding the source code.

Major Concerns

Similar to documents, books, or movies, perfect web sites that meet every criteria and all user requirements cannot be created—what's suitable for one audience might not be for another, and even if you try to adhere absolutely to every standard published, you will find that certain standards cannot be used in combination with others. However, that doesn't mean you shouldn't strive to adhere to the most important standards. Several features contribute to a certain level of quality assurance. Most of them are basic requirements for standard compliance and lead to proper development practices. Moreover, they provide adequate and more expectable functionality and behavior, usability, and stability, as well as faster downloading and rendering.

Bad Practices

While proper coding practice is widely applied in programming, web developers and people without proper background do not take markup practices seriously. "It also works this way—why bother with standard compliance?" This is the approach serious web developers would be best to forget. Bad markup including, but not limited to, browser-specific code fragments, heavily nested table layouts, structure mixed with layout, locally applied style attributes, attribute minimization, missing attribute values, and other anomalies significantly increase code length, complexity, download, and rendering time.

Lack of Support

Web standards support is not adequate. There are no ultimate practical guidelines on web standards for the less experienced. Although free access is provided to standard specifications, most people find them too difficult to understand and apply in practice.

---

[9] From version 7

Where standard compliance is an official requirement, such as on government portals or EU project web sites, the best solution is to hire *web standardistas* to develop suitable web sites. Many web designers are not really interested in markup or style sheets. Their only concern is appearance; for example, with creative Flash animations, the focus is usually fully on the SWF itself, and very little thought is given to how it is to be embedded in the web page. Company leaders focus mainly on the content. It is extremely difficult for people to realize that standard compliance could be the solution for many of their problems, such as browser-dependent web pages, incorrect rendering, or poor functionality.

Unconcern

One of the major problems with web standards is that free access to them is not sufficient to convince people to use them. Standard implementations of authoring tools are limited, and the web sites produced by them seldom follow standards. Standard support of web browsers is partial only, although they are constantly evolving.

Many people "develop" web sites without a proper IT background. For some it is just a hobby; for others it is profit source. Unless the importance of web standards is emphasized by the most influential companies throughout the world, they will not catch on. On the other hand, some developers do not even know these technologies. The trends are forced by business and marketing to achieve popularity or to fulfill business requirements. For example, because of the lack of support for Flash on Apple iPhone, early HTML5 implementations appeared that applied unfinished specifications but at the same time expedited standards evolution and application. Everyone interested in web site design/development, whether a professional or not, should become familiar with web standards, because they are vital in web development and worth learning (instead of copying bad practices from others).

Without several years of expertise, no one can understand the choices. Which markup language is the most modern one? It is not possible to answer the question without knowing HTML, XHTML, XML, the Semantic Web, and the maturity levels of web standards.

Fortunately, there is a recent trend to apply web standards more frequently; however, this trend is far from worldwide use. There are very few hand coders, and only some of them develop web sites the standard way. Thus, there is a potential in content management systems to help web developers comply with standards. If they could reliably generate standard-compliant markup, it would be ensured by default. Most advanced markup codes are written by hand coders; however, they should take the responsibility of standards compliance completely by themselves. Even if there are many useful tools that might help them, hand coders cannot rely on automatic error checking (see Chapter 11). Since web standardistas manipulate not only the content but also the entire markup and style sheets character by character, along with all files of a web site, they should ensure standard compliance through frequent revision and tests.

Influential Sites

Developers often have the logical idea to follow the practices of the most popular and widely used web sites in the world. However, these web sites cannot serve as references in standardization simply because they often have serious problems with standard compliance.

It might be even more disappointing that top web designers also make serious mistakes. Believe it or not, the personal web sites of the most famous web standardistas in the world might also suffer from markup errors. Most of them are also afraid to provide W3C conformance icons on their pages linking to W3C validators.

It might be a good starting point to find modern web sites that are also standard-compliant at the same time. However, it can be very confusing for beginner standardistas. Evidently, it is impossible to fulfill all user requirements, but web sites that focus on standards adherence and are labeled with the logo "Valid XHTML" or "Valid CSS" often come with a lack of design and exhibit limited use of technologies. Good examples are the web sites of web standardization bodies or web accessibility designers. Even if the source code is valid and free of errors, the code often has other issues. Expected components such as news feeds or favorites icons (favicons) are missing, semantic markup is not present, and so on. These features do not affect the validity of such web documents, which cannot be used exclusively as starting points for developing modern, standard-compliant web sites. Not only personal web sites and blogs but also precise technical documents can be presented beautifully. Remember, web standardization is not a sacrifice! Some of the largest and most popular web sites in the world apply standards successfully.

But not all. Take a closer look at a code fragment from one of the largest web sites in the world (Listing 1-2).

Listing 1-2. High-Traffic Web Sites Do Not Necessarily Apply Standard Code

```
<body class="ego_page home hasLeftCol fbx ie8 win Locale_en_US">
<input type="hidden" id="post_form_id" name="post_form_id"
value="b053066a05f482d5739d31c033b5fd90" autocomplete="off" /><div
id="pagelet_presence"></div><div id="FB_HiddenContainer" style="position:absolute; top:-
10000px; width:0px; height:0px;" ></div><div id="blueBar" class=""></div><div
id="globalContainer"><div id="dialogContainer"></div><div id="c4d06220d5f2c97d20912236"><div
class="ptm clearfix" id="pageHead"><h1 id="pageLogo">
```

Evidently, this is a software-generated markup, and even the most experienced hand-coder web standardista could hardly interpret such codes. There are problems with virtually every element and attribute. The class attribute has an empty value. Identifiers are unreasonably long and not descriptive at all, such as c4d06220d5f2c97d20912236. There is inline style in the source, which should be in an external style sheet. Obviously, the layer positioning with -10.000 pixels is a trick (probably used for a technique such as image replacement) that could be eliminated by proper implementation of standards. Empty attributes should be eliminated, especially if they are intended to be used for identification (a class without a name cannot be used to identify an element class). Even for these few lines, the error list is long.

The Popularity of Flash

Design is one of the major concerns in web site production. Adobe Flash is an ideal technology to provide a stunning appearance and catch attention. Full Flash sites, however, have several disadvantages. Unless the web document is a single-page, brochure-style home page that provides contact data, it is far better to develop (X)HTML content, because textual markup has several benefits over binary files. It is especially true with the exploitation of the new, interactive HTML5 elements and CSS3 properties, which are good alternatives for Flash content.

Graphic designers are not necessarily web developers. As a consequence, Flash movies are often embedded incorrectly. Although Flash files can theoretically work in any browser with an appropriate plug-in, markup codes controlling them can be browser-dependent, which should be eliminated.

There is nothing wrong with Flash, but it is probably better used for headers and inline animations only. The combination of XHTML and CSS can provide a similar, if not more advanced, user experience, but without the need to download large files in full before showing the content of the index page. While it is not a problem for fast connections, there are millions of users around the world who might wait for half a minute to download such content. Even if the Flash files are streamed in certain browsers, the menus and content are unusable until downloading is completed. Furthermore, they can be indexed/searched more effectively, are smaller in size, and have full control over the browser window by default. Text content is much more robust to render than any other format. Even if some images fail to download or there are some styling problems, the content is still there (if not absolutely positioned outside the window or written in the color identical to the background). Unlike that of Flash contents,[10] (X)HTML text sharpness, font size, and other features can be changed upon user request directly from the browser.

Some software companies recognized the advantages of markup languages over Flash and released tools to convert Flash files to HTML (for example, *FlashKeeper* [111]). Even Adobe has an FLA-HTML converter called Wallaby [112]. However, similar to other automated markup generators, extended care must be taken with them because the result is often invalid and, therefore, not optimal.

Well-formedness

A basic requirement for XML documents and a desired one for all web documents is *well-formedness*. It is vital in standardization, because it guarantees that the list of syntax rules defined in the corresponding specifications are satisfied.

To achieve well-formedness in SGML languages such as HTML, elements should be opened and closed properly. Empty elements must also be terminated. Elements should be nested properly so that overlapping does not occur. The root element of the document should contain all other elements.

Since SGML parsers are extremely error-tolerant, these rules are rarely followed completely by HTML developers, which results in markup errors. Thus, the lack of well-formedness leads directly to incorrect, nonstandard markup.

In XML languages such as XHTML, well-formedness has additional requirements. The element tags are case sensitive; that is, start and end tags must match exactly. Well-formed XML documents should contain properly encoded and legal Unicode characters only. These characters, however, can also be used directly in element names and attributes, not just in character data (document text). Characters with special meaning in XML can be used for markup instructions only, for example, <, >, or &. If they are intended to be represented as text, their entity codes should be applied (see the section "Entity references").

Characters that go against well-formedness rules can cause certain XML parsers to be unable to process XML files (XHTML documents, RDF metadata, RSS feed channels, and so on). Such special characters might also result in error messages. A single (not well-formed) character can make the whole file impossible to process. For example, the XML file of a valid RSS feed opened locally in Internet Explorer 8 is presented as a tree structure. The same file retrieved from a server is represented as a news feed. If the file, however, contains one illegal character, IE8 gives the error message The XML page cannot be displayed. Similar error messages exist in all browsers (Figure 1-5).

---

[10] Although there are advanced font manipulation possibilities in Flash Player from version 10, too.

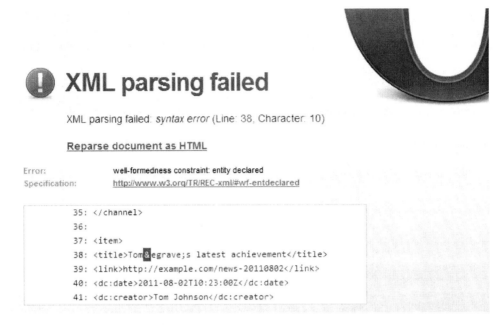

Figure 1-5. *An XML parsing error in Opera*

Interoperability

There is an endless variety of platforms, operating systems, and browsers available on the market. Every manufacturer and developer tries to provide additional features; thus, products are constantly competing with each other. This diversity results in different operations and functionalities. The functionality and behavior of web sites across the different systems are not guaranteed by default but can be achieved by the proper application of the latest standards. Naturally, users want to apply various systems in a combination that allows communication with each other and that exchanges data adequately. Data access cannot be restricted, and implementation-specific solutions should be avoided.

Web interoperability ensures that standard-compliant web pages can be viewed in any browser under various operating systems, from Windows to Mac OS and Linux, and not only on desktop computers but also on mobile devices, including tablet PCs and smartphones such as the Samsung Galaxy Tab, the Apple iPhone, or the HTC Sensation.

Several technologies support interoperability and should be used in web development, including, but not limited to, UTF-8 character encoding, XML documents, structural and semantic markup with XHTML or HTML5 [113], DOM scripting, ECMAScript, CSS-based layout, separated structure, presentation and behavior, equations described in MathML, and semantic metadata.

Browser Independence

"One page, many views" has always been a nightmare for web developers. Although it is a natural expectation from users for all web sites to look and behave the same way in various browsers, it is far from straightforward to fulfill.

Anyone who slaps a "this page is best viewed with Browser X" label on a Web page appears to be yearning for the bad old days, before the Web, when you had very little chance of reading a document written on another computer, another word processor, or another network.

—Tim Berners-Lee [114]

Nowadays the freedom of browser choice is more real than ever. People use a wide variety of software for browsing the Internet. However, the majority uses only a few browsers, namely, Internet Explorer, Mozilla Firefox, Google Chrome, Opera, and Safari. Hence, focusing on these flagships is sufficient in most cases. The four major rendering engines behind these desktop browsers—Trident, Gecko, Presto, and WebKit—are also used in mobile browsing (Internet Explorer Mobile, Firefox for mobile, Opera Mobile, and Safari). WebKit is also used by a variety of other mobile browsers (Android Browser, BlackBerry Browser, Iris Browser, Myriad Browser, Nokia Series 40 and Series 60 browsers, Obigo Browser, Polaris Browser, Skyfire Mobile Browser, and HP webOS Browser). In the mobile browsing scene, NetFront is also worth mentioning; it is used by Kindle Basic Web, NetFront, and the Sony PlayStation Portable Web Browser. Statistics show that only very few visitors use browsers powered by other rendering engines.

No one wants to drive potential customers away, so it is very important to avoid browser-specific web site development. Probably the best solution is to create pages that are *best viewed with any browser*. Sometimes this web site feature is also indicated clearly by a logo of the "Viewable with any browser" campaign [115].

The major problem for developers creating web sites to be identical in all browsers is that various tricks need to be applied in many cases to ensure functionality. However, these codes do not work under all browsers, so more and more different hacks have to be added for different browsers (and older versions of those browsers), resulting in a mass of extra code. The only option is to create standard-based web sites. Even if some standards are not completely supported by today's browsers (which is actually a headache for developers), these codes are at least ready for the future [116]. Moreover, they serve as excellent starting points for development.

A very bad practice associated with the problem of the different rendering behavior of browsers is *code forking*. Code forking is the development of multiple versions of the same content for various browsers. Code forking should not be applied because the resulting code cannot be used in the long term.

Web standardistas also agree that web sites cannot be expected to look exactly the same way in every browser, but the information published on web pages should be legible and all functionalities should be available in all major browsers [117, 118].

Eliminated Version Targeting

Since rendering engines are constantly evolving, even the various versions of the same browser support standards differently. To avoid losing users and potential customers who use older browser versions, web developers often apply various browser- and version-specific solutions in the markup or style sheets. In other words, *version targeting* means a considerable amount of additional work for developers, and the result works only in a certain version of a certain browser.

Furthermore, because of the improved standard support of current browser versions, these codes are actually threats to either functionality or code optimality, or both. Thus, version targeting should be eliminated, which, on the other hand, can cause problems with backward compatibility [119]. Although there are some techniques that can be used together with standard compliance to maximize version independence (for example, resetting the style sheets of the browser), creating web pages that work properly under all browsers and browser versions is unfeasible.

Standard-compliant web development should be adequate, and browsers ought to have full standard compliance by now. However, this is still not the case.

Browsers to be used for rendering version targeted web documents can be easily defined by a simple meta declaration in the document head (Listing 1-3).

Listing 1-3. Version Targeting Example (Should Not Be Used)

```
<meta http-equiv="X-UA-Compatible" content="IE=8;FF=3;OtherUA=4" />
```

The most up-to-date Internet Explorer version can be targeted by adding the IE=edge attribute value to the content attribute of the meta element [120] (Listing 1-4).

Listing 1-4. Version Targeting for the Latest IE Version (Should Not Be Used)

```
<meta http-equiv="X-UA-Compatible" content="IE=edge" />
```

Although targeted browsers might decide more quickly between old, backward-compatible and new, standard-compliant rendering modes when such data are provided, version targeting should be totally eliminated. Creating multiple versions of nonstandard markup for the same web page is not only costly but also unsustainable. Moreover, version targeting and browser detection scripts are not reliable and cannot target the correct browsers in many cases, because browsers often identify themselves as other browsers or other versions of the same browser.

Backward Compatibility

Standard-compliant web sites that work well under the currently used browser versions are also ready for the future but might be rendered incorrectly in older browsers because of the incorrect standards implementations of their rendering engines. Consequently, even with proper implementation, web standards do not work under all browsers. The support for old rendering engines, *backward compatibility*, should be within reasonable limits. Why bother with browsers that are no longer in use or the "very old" versions of major browsers? Netscape, for example, is "not widely used anymore" just like Internet Explorer 1.0 or Mozilla Firefox 0.9. The major problem with this question is how to define *browser obsoletion*. Can IE5.5 be labeled as "very old" and IE6 as "old"? The choice of supported browsers has a large impact on the traffic and popularity of a web site, and the lack of support for older—even obsolete—browsers can lead to loss of visitors. In fact, there is no ultimate decision regarding backward compatibility.

One of the biggest agonies regarding backward compatibility is the support for IE6. Its market share decreased slowly up to 2007 when it lost its popularity considerably, probably because of the new versions of Windows, Vista, and later Windows 7, and their new Explorer versions, 7, and later versions 8, 9, and 10,[11] as well as the growing popularity of competitors such as Mozilla Firefox, Apple Safari, and Google Chrome. Upgraders have taken several major concerns into account. First, serious security holes have been pointed out during the years that have been partially covered by later patches. However, thanks to growing needs, new functions have been introduced in other browsers and in Internet Explorer overtaking the market. All modern browsers support XML technologies, RSS feeds, and tabbed browsing, for example. IE8 and especially IE9 were big steps toward standard compliance and modern functions. Even Microsoft has recommended IE6 users to upgrade [121, 122]. Software giants like Google

---

[11] Internet Explorer 6 was shipped with Windows XP. Versions 7 and 8 can be used on XP, too, while IE9 requires Windows Vista or Windows 7. IE10 will run exclusively under Windows 7.

have started to reduce support for older browsers, which is another reason to do so [123]. Last but not least, it will be a great relief for developers when users stop using Internet Explorer 6.

The major drawback of backward compatibility is that it hinders the widespread use of new technologies at some point. Still, web standardistas should maximize backward compatibility whenever possible. Satisfied users cannot be pushed to upgrade their browsers every time a new version is released.

Because of the incomplete or deficient standard support of older browsers, backward compatibility is often equal to the application of browser-targeted hacks and code fragments, as well as to nonstandard and even deprecated markup that should be eliminated. A useful tool to achieve or maximize backward compatibility is the JavaScript library "Modernizr," which detects browser support for the latest web standards, such as HTML5 or CSS3 modules [124]. This software determines whether a currently used browser has implemented a given feature, which makes it possible for developers to apply new features in the browsers that support them and create a fallback mechanism for those browsers that do not.

Forward Compatibility

While a new browser release can be a problem for developers of nonstandard and especially browser-specific web sites, web standardistas do not have to worry. *Forward compatibility* accompanies standard compliance. Standardized web documents can be easily turned into newer ones that apply the most up-to-date markup language, style sheet, and other technologies.

Functionality

Beyond content, functionality is one of the most important web site features. Without it, all other efforts would be useless, including even popular design.

Standards should be supported on both the developers' and browsers' sides. For web standardistas, development the standard way often seems like some kind of sacrifice. For example, certain CSS selectors, which can be used for various web site features, are not supported by some rendering engines (generally either Trident or Gecko). In such cases, the developer should make a decision: either follow the guidelines of recommendations and standards and do not support some browsers (which cannot be tolerated) or provide nonstandard, fully functional code. It is unfortunate that developers sometimes face these choices.

Device Independence

Internet access is no longer restricted to desktop computers. Mobile devices such as laptops, netbooks, PDAs, smartphones, and e-book readers are also connected to browse web sites. However, some devices—especially the handheld ones—have limited screen size, scrollability, and computing power. Care must be taken to provide code that works on a variety of devices. The concept also contributes to web site accessibility and partly overlaps with internationalization.

There is a wide choice of computer monitors, screens, TVs, and projectors. All of them come with different sizes, aspect ratios, resolutions, contrast ratios, and color fidelity, for example. One of the basic requirements in this respect is *resolution independence*. Functionality should be available on a variety of devices regardless of different hardware controls, such as keyboards, touchscreens, or customizable control buttons of mobile devices. Device independence provides support for different access mechanisms and different modes of use (for example, visual and auditory modes of use). The aim of device independence is to "match Web content to the needs, capabilities, and limitations of the delivery environment" [125]. Especially the increasing interest in mobile browsing makes device independence a major concern in web site development.

Markup languages such as HTML and XHTML are good examples for device independence standards. CSS can be used to provide device independence through additional style sheets for devices other than desktop computers including but not limited to mobile phones, projectors, and printers.[12] Java applets can be executed on a variety of devices under different platforms, because Java is a cross-platform programming language. Image file formats such as JPEG, TIFF, or GIF are also device-independent files. In document publishing and sharing, PDF is a classic example for device independence.

Separating Content from Presentation

In the early period of the Web, the only concern about web publishing was the web presence itself. At that time, web documents were limited mainly to the mixture of lightly formatted text content and images. When the possibilities widened, the Web soon became a full multimedia platform.

Since more and more people (not just web developers) tried to publish on the Web, there was a need to make the process easier. As a result, nearly everyone became capable of publishing on the Web even if they were not competent to do so. To maintain the functions of the Web, browser developers made their products foolproof and error-tolerant. People began to think that what was beneath the surface did not matter.

It has been proved over the years that formatting should be separated from structure. This is one of the major concepts of Cascading Style Sheets. This approach leads to centralized style control, which makes it possible to change the styles of the entire web site from a single location. Moreover, the markup becomes shorter, less redundant, clearer, less complicated, and easier to interpret and render. Beyond syntax, semantic annotations can also be provided in web documents. In contrast to styling rules, semantics are logically related to the markup and the content.

Usability

Usability can be defined as "setting clear and concise goals for a web site, determining a correct and exhaustive set of user requirements, ensuring that the web site meets user's expectations, setting usability goals, and providing useful content" [126]. It is a measure of how easily a system can be used. Usability can be achieved by optimizing the user experience, providing browser independence and accessibility, providing an appropriate home page and site structure, and providing reliable layout. Usability should not be confused with accessibility, which means access to all, regardless of user disabilities or device limitations.

Web sites should provide useful content that is relevant and appropriate to the audience. Web content should be written properly. There are numerous requirements for the appearance of texts, links, lists, controls, graphics, and multimedia. Beyond content, the navigation and site structure should be organized in a way that meets user expectations. This can be achieved by involving users in testing sites. The primary goals of any web site should precede the designing and developing processes. User interface issues as well as multiple designs should be considered during design.

Solutions that are highly likely to confuse or disturb users should be avoided. Pop-up windows should be eliminated. Web sites should be developed in accordance with standards so that users can perform tasks in the sequence and manner in which they are accustomed.

---

[12] The same web site without background image, ensured width that does not exceed US Letter paper width, and so on.

Reliable Layouts

Reliable positioning of web site elements has always been a major concern in web site development. Because of the enormous number of factors to consider, some elements should be positioned absolutely while others relatively. There are elements that are meant to be fixed, even if the content exceeds the browser window and the content is scrolled (see the section "Reliable Positioning").

In CSS there are several measurement units for defining element dimensions, lengths, and distances. Units can be relative to the relevant font or the viewing device (em, ex, px) as well as absolute (in, cm, mm, pt, pc). Percentages can also be applied. However, units should be chosen reasonably (see the section "Sizes and Proportions"). Unreliable or browser-dependent positioning and improperly combined units can result in unreadable content or limited functionality. The overlapping order of layers might also be a problem since the order can cause unreadable content in various environments.

Layout is in strong correlation with device, resolution, and browser independence.

Code Optimality

Web standards provide a way to develop reliable, fully functional, interoperable, device-independent web sites. However, they cannot guarantee *optimal code length* by default. Even if each character in the source code has its meaning, that is, none of them is unnecessary, code length might still be far from optimal. Long identifiers in the markup and especially the ignored inheritance in CSS (see the section "Ignored Inheritance") can increase complexity and length, resulting in larger file size, slower downloads, and longer rendering time (see the section "Nonoptimal Code Length").

Summary

In this chapter, you learned that web standards are not fixed sets of rules but a constantly evolving list of finalized specifications. You are well aware by now that there are several web sites where open standards are published and that web standardization also involves best practices. Proper standards implementation is independent from site popularity and the trends content authors and developers try to pursue. There is no best way to design and develop web sites; however, following standards is highly beneficial, and it is the only way to provide the highest level of interoperability and secure your web sites for the future.

In the next chapter, I will discuss language and character settings on servers and in markup to ensure proper character representation and provide advanced hints for software agents that search and process web documents. The internationalization settings of web documents typically precede the development process and thus are described as one of the first steps in standard web site development.

References

1. Gustafson A, Casciano C, Walter A et al (2010) www.webstandards.org. The Web Standards Project. Accessed 26 April 2010

2. Dardailler D (2010) W3C PAS FAQ. World Wide Web Consortium. www.w3.org/2010/04/pasfaq. Accessed 06 November 2010

3. Hazaël-Massieux, D (2002) Buy standards compliant Web sites. World Wide Web Consortium. www.w3.org/QA/2002/07/WebAgency-Requirements. Accessed 24 October 2010

4. W3C (2010) All standards and drafts. World Wide Web Consortium. www.w3.org/TR/#Recommendations. Accessed 26 April 2010

5. ECMA (2010) Formal publications. www.ecma-international.org/publications/index.html. ECMA International. Accessed 26 April 2010

6. ISO (2010) World Wide Web standards at the ISO website. www.iso.org/iso/search.htm?qt=world+wide+web&published=on&active_tab=standards. International Organization for Standardization. Accessed 26 April 2010

7. IANA (2010) Website of IANA. www.iana.org. Internet Assigned Numbers Authority. Accessed 26 April 2010

8. IETF (2010) IETF website. www.ietf.org. The Internet Engineering Task Force. Accessed 26 April 2010

9. IETF (2010) RFC pages. www.ietf.org/rfc.html. The Internet Engineering Task Force. Accessed 26 April 2010

10. Unicode Consortium (2010) Technical Reports. www.unicode.org/reports/index.html. Unicode, Inc. Accessed 26 April 2010

11. WHATWG (2011) WHATWG community website. www.whatwg.org. Web Hypertext Application Technology Working Group. Accessed 29 July 2011

12. Jacobs I (2010) Making W3C the place for new standards. W3C Draft Proposal. www.w3.org/2010/07/community. Accessed 14 September 2010

13. Dardailler D (2010) Open Standards Policies. In: W3C: An Open Platform for Web Standardisation. Future Internet Conference - Standardization Workshop. World Wide Web Consortium. www.w3.org/2010/12/dd-w3c.html#(3). Accessed 03 December 2010

14. Dardailler D (2010) W3C Exec Summary. In: W3C: An Open Platform for Web Standardisation. World Wide Web Consortium. www.w3.org/2010/06/dd-diplo.html#(7). Accessed 10 October 2010

15. Dardailler D (2010) W3C: An Open Platform for Web Standardisation. World Wide Web Consortium. www.w3.org/2010/12/dd-w3c.html. Accessed 12 December 2010

16. Guha RV, Bray T (1997) Meta Content Framework using XML. World Wide Web Consortium. www.w3.org/TR/NOTE-MCF-XML/. Accessed 07 October 2009

17. Netscape Communications (1999) My Netscape Network: Quick Start. Netscape. http://web.archive.org/web/20001208063100/http://my.netscape.com/publish/help/quickstart.html. (archived version accessed 02 September 2010, original version is no longer available)

18. Stanescu B, Sarapata J (2010) Google now indexes SVG. Google Inc. http://googlewebmastercentral.blogspot.com/2010/08/google-now-indexes-svg.html. Accessed 27 September 2010

19. WHATWG (2011) WHATWG Mailing List. Web Hypertext Application Technology Working Group. www.whatwg.org/mailing-list. Accessed 01 Aug 2011

20. ERCIM (2010) ERCIM website. www.ercim.org. The European Research Consortium for Informatics and Mathematics. Accessed 23 September 2010

21. Jeffery K (2009) Twenty Years of ERCIM: History and Outlook. European Research Consortium for Informatics and Mathematics. http://ercim-news.ercim.eu/en77/joint-ercim-actions/twenty-years-of-ercim-history-and-outlook. Accessed 29 July 2011

22. IETF (2011) The Internet Engineering Task Force (IETF). www.ietf.org. Accessed 14 March 2011

23. IETF (2010) RFC-Editor Webpage. www.rfc-editor.org. The Internet Engineering Task Force. Accessed 23 September 2010

24. ECMA (2010) ECMA Website. www.ecma-international.org. ECMA International. Accessed 23 September 2010

25. Unicode (2011) The Unicode Consortium. Unicode Inc. www.unicode.org. Accessed 14 February 2011

26. DCMI (2011) The Dublin Core Metadata Initiative. Dublin Core Metadata Initiative Limited. http://dublincore.org. Accessed 13 February 2011

27. IANA (2010) Internet Assigned Numbers Authority. www.iana.org. Accessed 13 February 2011

28. ICANN (2010) Internet Corporation for Assigned Names and Numbers. www.icann.org. Accessed 13 February 2011

29. OASIS (2010) OASIS: Advancing open standards for the global information society. www.oasis-open.org. OASIS. Accessed 23 September 2010

30. OASIS (2010) The Cover Pages. http://xml.coverpages.org. OASIS. Accessed 23 September 2010

31. OASIS (2010) XML.org. www.xml.org. Accessed 23 September 2010

32. ISO (2011) International Organization for Standardization. www.iso.org. Accessed 13 February 2011

33. WaSP (2011) The Web Standards Project. www.webstandards.org. Accessed 15 February 2011

34. WSG (2010) WSG website. http://webstandardsgroup.org. Web Standards Group. Accessed 23 September 2010

35. Byrne J, Pedley M, Millen B, Allard N, Henley C (2010) The Guild of Accessible Web Designers. GAWDS. www.gawds.org. Accessed 27 September 2010

36. IWA (2011) The International Webmasters Association website. International Webmasters Association. www.iwanet.org. Accessed 15 February 2011

37. WIPA (2011) The Web Industry Professionals Association website. Web Industry Professionals Association Incorporated. www.wipa.org.au. Accessed 15 February 2011

38. ODRL Initiative (2011) ODRL website. Open Digital Rights Language Initiative. http://odrl.net. Accessed 15 February 2011

39. W3C (2011) World Wide Web Consortium. www.w3.org. Accessed 13 February 2011

40. W3C (2011) News Archive. World Wide Web Consortium. www.w3.org/News/. Accessed 13 February 2011

41. W3C (2011) World Wide Web Consortium. www.w3techcourses.com. Accessed 14 February 2011

42. OMG (2011) Internationalization & Unicode Conference. Object Management Group. www.unicodeconference.org. Accessed 13 February 2011

43. IETF (2011) IETF Meetings. The Internet Engineering Task Force. www.ietf.org/meeting/. Accessed 13 February 2011

44. DCMI (2011) International Conference on Dublin Core and Metadata Initiatives. Dublin Core Metadata Initiative. http://dcevents.dublincore.org/index.php/index/index/index. Accessed 14 February 2011

45. WIPA (2011) Web Industry Professionals Association. http://wipa.org.au. Accessed 14 February 2011

46. WIPA (2011) WIPA News. Web Industry Professionals Association. http://wipa.org.au/newsfeed.cfm. Accessed 14 February 2011

47. WIPA (2011) Industry Events from WIPA. Web Industry Professionals Association. http://wipa.org.au/eventfeed.cfm. Accessed 14 February 2011

48. ACM (2011) Calendar. Association for Computing Machinery. www.acm.org/calendar-of-events. Accessed 14 February 2011

49. Gasiorowski-Denis E (ed) (2010) Standards make the world accessible for all – 41st World Standards Day. International Organization for Standardization. www.iso.org/iso/pressrelease.htm?refid=Ref1356. Accessed 13 February 2011

50. Carsonified (2011) The Future of Web Apps Conference. Carsonified. http://futureofwebapps.com. Accessed 14 February 2011

51. Carsonified (2011) Online conferences. http://thinkvitamin.com/online-conferences/. Carsonified. Accessed 14 February 2011

52. Lux M (2010) SemanticMetadata.net. Mathias Lux. www.semanticmetadata.net. Accessed 14 February 2011

53. W3C (2011) Weekly newsletter. World Wide Web Consortium. www.w3.org/News/Public/. Accessed 13 February 2011

54. W3C (2011) W3C News (Atom new feed). World Wide Web Consortium. www.w3.org/News/atom.xml. Accessed 13 February 2011

55. W3C (2011) W3C News (RSS new feed). World Wide Web Consortium. www.w3.org/News/news.rss. Accessed 13 February 2011

56. Unicode (2011) The Unicode Blog (news feed). Unicode Consortium. http://unicode-inc.blogspot.com/feeds/posts/default?alt=rss. Accessed 13 February 2011

57. DCMI (2011) News feed of the Dublin Core Metadata Initiative. Dublin Core Metadata Initiative. http://dublincore.org/news.rss. Accessed 15 February 2011

58. DCMI (2011) DCMI Conference Papers. Dublin Core Metadata Initiative. http://dcpapers.dublincore.org/ojs/pubs. Accessed 15 February 2011

59. Dardailler D (2010) W3C Process Flow. In: W3C: An Open Platform for Web Standardisation. Future Internet Conference - Standardization Workshop. World Wide Web Consortium. http://www.w3.org/2010/12/dd-w3c.html#(7). Accessed 03 December 2010

60. W3C (2011) All Standards and Drafts. World Wide Web Consortium. www.w3.org/TR/. Accessed 13 February 2011

61. Bradner S (1996) The Internet Standards Process – Revision 3. The Internet Engineering Task Force. http://tools.ietf.org/html/rfc2026. Accessed 01 December 2010

62. IETF(2008) RFC overview. The Internet Engineering Task Force. www.rfc-editor.org/overview.html. Accessed 03 May 2011

63. TMC (2010) Drafts. In: The microformats wiki. The Microformats Community. http://microformats.org/wiki/Main_Page. Accessed 13 November 2010

64. Net Apps (2011) Browser Market Share. Net Applications. www.netmarketshare.com/browser-market-share.aspx?qprid=0. Accessed 09 February 2011

65. STAT OWL (2011) Web Browser Market Share. STAT OWL. http://statowl.com/web_browser_market_share.php. Accessed 09 February 2011

66. StatCounter (2011) StatCounter Global Stats. StatCounter. http://gs.statcounter.com/#browser-ww-monthly-201101-201101-bar. Accessed 09 February 2011

67. W3Counter (2011) Global Web Stats. Awio Web Services LLC. www.w3counter.com/globalstats.php?year=2011&month=1. Accessed 09 February 2011

68. Microsoft Developer Network (2010) Standards Compliance Updates in Internet Explorer 8. Microsoft Corporation. http://msdn.microsoft.com/library/dd433047(VS.85).aspx. Accessed 31 December 2010

69. Microsoft (2010) www.beautyoftheweb.com/#/highlights/html5. Microsoft Corporation. Accessed 31 December 2010

70. Scholz F et al (2010) Gecko. Mozilla Developer Network. https://developer.mozilla.org/en/Gecko. Accessed 31 December 2010

71. KDE Webmasters (2011) KDE 3.5.6 Changelog. KDE e.V. www.kde.org/announcements/changelogs/changelog3_5_5to3_5_6.php. Accessed 09 February 2011

72. Apple (2011) Safari features. Apple Inc. www.apple.com/safari/features.html. Accessed 09 February 2011

73. W3C (2011) Current members. World Wide Web Consortium. www.w3.org/Consortium/Member/List. Accessed 09 February 2011

74. Opera Software (2011) Web specifications support in Opera products. Opera Software ASA. www.opera.com/docs/specs/productspecs/. Accessed 09 February 2011

75. Quint V (ed) (2010) Amaya.W3C's editor/browser. World Wide Web Consortium. www.w3.org/Amaya/. Accessed 10 February 2011

76. Baron LD (2006) Layout Engine Visual Tests (reftest). Mozilla Corporation. http://mxr.mozilla.org/mozilla-central/source/layout/tools/reftest/README.txt. Accessed 10 February 2011

77. Shepherd E (ed) (2011) Mochitest. Mozilla Developer Network. https://developer.mozilla.org/en/Mochitest. Accessed 10 February 2011

78. W3C (2011) HTML Testing area. World Wide Web Consortium. http://test.w3.org/html/. Accessed 10 February 2011

79. Bos B (ed) (2010) Official W3C Test Suites. World Wide Web Consortium. www.w3.org/Style/CSS/Test/. Accessed 10 February 2011

80. Hazael-Massieux D (ed) (2011) Mobile Tests. World Wide Web Consortium. http://test.w3.org/m/. Accessed 10 February 2011

81. Ion, PDF (ed) (2010) MathML Test Suite. World Wide Web Consortium. www.w3.org/Math/testsuite/. Accessed 10 February 2011

82. W3C (2010) SVG test suites. World Wide Web Consortium. www.w3.org/Graphics/SVG/WG/wiki/Test_Suite_Overview. Accessed 10 February 2011

83. Ishida R (ed) (2010) Internationalization tests. World Wide Web Consortium. www.w3.org/International/tests/. Accessed 10 February 2011

84. Le Hégaret P (2010) How do we test a Web browser? World Wide Web Consortium. www.w3.org/QA/2010/09/how_do_we_test_a_web_browser_o.html. Accessed 10 February 2011

85. Fahrner T (1998) The Acid1 test. World Wide Web Consortium, the National Insititue of Standards and Technology, Case Western Reserve University. www.w3.org/Style/CSS/Test/CSS1/current/test5526c.htm. Accessed 23 September 2010

86. Hickson I (2005) The Acid2 test. Web Standards Project. http://acid2.acidtests.org. Accessed 10 February 2011

87. Hickson I (2008) The Acid 3 test. Web Standards Project. http://acid3.acidtests.org. Accessed 10 February 2011

88. Apple (2010) Safari – Learn about the features available in Safari. Apple Inc. www.apple.com/safari/features.html. Accessed 23 September 2010

89. Opera Software (2009) Turbocharge your Web experience with Opera 10. Opera Software ASA. www.opera.com/press/releases/2009/09/01/. Accessed 23 September 2010

90. Laforge A (2010) Google Chrome Releases: Stable Channel Update. Google Inc. http://googlechromereleases.blogspot.com/2010/01/stable-channel-update_25.html. Accessed 23 September 2010

91. Ryan P (2009) Linux garden gets a new GNOME with version 2.28. Ars Technica. http://arstechnica.com/open-source/news/2009/09/linux-garden-gets-a-new-gnome-with-version-228.ars. Accessed 23 September 2010

92. Scott (2009) Bolt Browser gets Updated to Version 1.6 – Brings New Features! Smartphone Blogs Network. http://blackberrysync.com/2009/12/bolt-browser-gets-updated-to-version-1-6-brings-new-features/. Accessed 23 September 2010

93. Engebø HL (2009) Opera Mobile 9.7 with Opera Turbo. Opera Software ASA. http://my.opera.com/operamobile/blog/2009/03/26/opera-mobile-9-7-beta-for-windows-mobile. Accessed 23 September 2010

94. Van Kesteren A, Hunt L (2009) Selectors API Level 1, W3C Candidate Recommendation. World Wide Web Consortium. http://dev.w3.org/2006/webapi/selectors-api/. Accessed 23 September 2010

95. Pasche S (2010) BrowserTests. Cross-browser automated tests. Google Inc. http://code.google.com/p/browsertests/wiki/StartPage. Accessed 10 February 2011

96. Simon L et al (2011) Browserscope. www.browserscope.org. Accessed 10 February 2011

97. Fahrner T (2002) Geocrawler.com - mozilla-layout - NG layout and 5.0 Navigator. An e-mail of Todd Fahrner archived by archive.com. Open Source Development Network. http://web.archive.org/web/20030212115103/http://www.geocrawler.com/archives/list-name.mbox/123/1998/7/0/1037920/. Accessed 16 September 2010

98. Ishida R (2010) Serving HTML & XHTML. 'Standards' vs 'Quirks' modes. World Wide Web Consortium. www.w3.org/International/articles/serving-xhtml/. Accessed 15 September 2010

99. Ishida R (2010) XHTML test document for Standards Mode. In: Serving HTML & XHTML. 'Standards' vs 'Quirks' modes. World Wide Web Consortium. www.w3.org/International/articles/serving-xhtml/standards.html. Accessed 15 September 2010

100. Ishida R (2010) XHTML test document for Quirks Mode. In: Serving HTML & XHTML. 'Standards' vs 'Quirks' modes. World Wide Web Consortium. www.w3.org/International/articles/serving-xhtml/quirks.html. Accessed 15 September 2010

101. Lie HW, Bos B (2008) Formatting model. In: Cascading Style Sheets, level 1. W3C Recommendation, revised version. www.w3.org/TR/REC-CSS1/#formatting-model. World Wide Web Consortium. Accessed 16 September 2010

102. Bowman D (2005) Douglas Bowman declares his love to CSS ... Vorsprung durch Webstandards. http://www.vorsprungdurchwebstandards.de/interviews/fallinginlovewithcss/douglas-bowman/. Accessed 16 September 2010

103. Bos B, Çelik T, Hickson I, Lie HW (2009) CSS 2.1 Box model. In: Cascading Style Sheets Level 2 Revision 1 (CSS 2.1) Specification, W3C Candidate Recommendation. World Wide Web Consortium. www.w3.org/TR/CSS2/box.html. Accessed 16 September 2010

104. Bos B (2007) CSS basic box model, W3C Working Draft. World Wide Web Consortium. www.w3.org/TR/css3-box/. Accessed 16 September 2010

105. Gertner M (2008) Is Web Standardization Obsolete? Just Browsing. http://browsing.justdiscourse.com/2008/01/22/is-web-standardization-obsolete/. Accessed 09 September 2010

106. Zeldman J, Marcotte E (2009) 99.9% of websites are obsolete. In: Designing with Web standards, 3rd edn. New Riders, Berkeley

107. Alexa (2011) Alexa Top 500 Global Sites. Alexa Internet, Inc. www.alexa.com/topsites. Accessed 14 March 2011

108. Anderson E, DeBolt V, Featherstone D, Gunther L, Jacobs DR, Jensen-Inman L, Mills C, Schmitt C, Sims G, Walter A (2010) InterACT With Web Standards – A Holistic Approach to Web Design. New Riders, Berkeley

109. Zeldman J, Marcotte E (2009) Core forking can be hazardous to your site's long-term health. In: Designing with Web standards, 3rd edn. New Riders

110. Herman I, Corlosquet S, Clark L (2010) Combine the Web of Data and the Web of Documents (RDFa and Drupal 7). Proceedings of the International Semantic Web Conference 2010, 8 November 2010, Shanghai. www.w3.org/2010/Talks/RDFa-Drupal-Tutorial/. Accessed 22 September 2010

111. Sparkle Media (2010) Publishing Flash Animations to HTML format. Sparkle Media Systems. www.flashkeeper.com/publishhtml.htm. Accessed 12 January 2011

112. Adobe Labs (2011) Convert Adobe Flash FLA files into HTML and reach more devices. Adobe Systems Incorporated. http://labs.adobe.com/technologies/wallaby/. Accessed 22 June 2011

113. Çelik T (2010) HTML5 Now: A Step-by-Step Video Tutorial for Getting Started Today. New Riders Publishing, Berkeley

114. Berners-Lee T (1996) Technology Review, July 1996. http://en.wikiquote.org/wiki/Tim_Berners-Lee. Accessed 14 April 2011

115. Burstein CD (2008) Viewable with Any Browser: Campaign. Cari D. Burstein. www.anybrowser.org/campaign/. Accessed 25 September 2010

116. Kyrnin J (2006) Browser Specific Web Designs – Why Should You Care. The New York Times Company. http://webdesign.about.com/od/browsers/a/aa111797.htm. Accessed 26 September 2010

117. Allsopp J (2009) It doesn't have to look the same in every browser. In: Developing with Web standards. New Riders, Berkeley

118. Zeldman J (2010) Gentle persuasion. In: Designing with Web standards. New Riders, Berkeley

119. Gustafson A (2008) Beyond DOCTYPE: Web Standards, Forward Compatibility, and IE8. A List Apart Magazine. www.alistapart.com/articles/beyonddoctype. Accessed 26 September 2010

120. Microsoft Developer Network (2010) Standards by Default: What Does It Mean? Microsoft Corporation. http://msdn.microsoft.com/en-us/library/cc817575.aspx. Accessed 31 December 2010

121. Shankland S (2009) Microsoft actively urges IE 6 users to upgrade. CNET News. http://news.cnet.com/8301-30685_3-10406468-264.html. Accessed 25 September 2010

122. Microsoft (2011) The Internet Explorer 6 Countdown – Moving the world off Internet Explorer 6. Microsoft Corporation. http://ie6countdown.com. Accessed 14 Mar 2011

123. Protalinski E (2010) Google to send Internet Explorer 6 users packing come March. Ars Technica. http://arstechnica.com/microsoft/news/2010/01/google-to-send-internet-explorer-6-users-packing-come-march.ars. Accessed 25 September 2010

124. Ateş F, Irish P, Sexton A (2011) Modernizr — Front-end development done right. Faruk Ateş, Paul Irish, and Alex Sexton. www.modernizr.com. Accessed 01 Aug 2011

125. Gimson R, Finkelstein SR, Maes S, Suryanarayana L (eds) (2003) Device Independence Principles. World Wide Web Consortium. www.w3.org/TR/di-princ/. Accessed 31 Jul 2011

126. Leavitt MO, Shneiderman B, Bailey RW, Barnum C, Bosley J, Chaparro B, Dumas J, Ivory MY, John B, Miller-Jacobs H, Koyani SJ, Lewis JR, Page S, Ramey J, Redish J, Scholtz J, Wigginton S, Wolfson CA, Wood LE, Zimmerman D (eds) (2006) Research-based Web Design & Usability Guidelines. Department of Health & Human Services (HHS), U.S. Government. http://usability.gov/guidelines/guidelines_book.pdf. Accessed 12 February 2011

CHAPTER 2

Internationalization

Web authors publish in all languages of the world, and several technologies support this multilingual Web. A key factor of correct character representation on the Web is applying the appropriate character encoding. Although this depends on server settings as well, web developers can effectively contribute to proper internationalization of the physical and syntactic structures of web documents. One of the very first steps in standard web site development is to apply national settings on both the file and document content level. Unicode can be considered as the ultimate encoding and is described from the standardistas' point of view. The use of Unicode byte-order marks, which provide information about the ordering of individually addressable subcomponents within the representation of this multibyte character encoding, can be confusing. Special characters and symbols can often be provided in various ways, including entity sets, escape codes, and hexadecimal notation.

In this chapter, you will learn how to secure character rendering on web sites that makes it possible to properly display any character or ideogram of natural languages. Characters can be represented in several ways, determined by the character encoding being chosen. Although there is a variety of character encoding systems, Unicode can be used for almost all scenarios. The character encoding can be set in many ways, from meta tags to the HTTP header. Most characters can be added directly to the markup; however, there are some exceptions you should keep in mind. You will also learn the proper application of character entities and whitespace characters that can be used to add special characters to web sites, such as invisible, unprintable control characters.

The Importance of Character Encoding

Until the 1990s, computers mainly supported the characters of the English alphabet only (partly because of the American dominance on the computer market), and the need for international characters has been satisfied with hardware code pages, such as CP852 or CP1252, supported by the then-used operating systems (for example, DOS, Windows 3.1, Windows 95). The proper display of Central-European characters, for example, was dependent on the hardware configuration, the operating system, and its settings. A few years later, with the introduction of the Web, such limitations could not be accepted any longer. In 1997, HTML 4.0 introduced advanced support for international characters.

The American Standard Code for Information Interchange (ASCII) has been the most widely supported character encoding scheme, which stores 128 characters on 7 bits. Additional characters have been provided by 8-bit character sets, such as the ISO/IEC 8859 series of ASCII-based standard character encodings (informally referred to as Latin-1). They were first published in 1987 and supported most Western European languages and partly supported some other languages.

Most modern character encoding systems are based on ASCII; however, they support many more characters.

If anything other than the most basic Latin characters is needed, text on your web site might be unreadable unless an appropriate *character encoding* is specified. These standards define not only the identification of each character and the associated numeric value (*codepoint*[1]) but also the way this value is represented in the bits of the file being encoded.

If the character encoding is declared properly, browsers can use the appropriate encoding to render web documents. Consequently, all special characters will be displayed correctly. Browsers usually have an automatic character encoding recognition feature as well, which is activated in case the character encoding of a document is not declared. Based on the setting of the file, the browser might identify the character encoding being used. Users can also select an encoding scheme manually in most browsers, which is a forced method and should not be used if all server and document settings are correct.

As an example, let's assume Christmas greetings are to be published in several languages on a web page, as in Table 2-1.

Table 2-1. Christmas Greetings in Different Languages

Language	Greetings
Albanian	Gëzuar Krishtlindjet e Vitin e Ri
Arabic	أجمل التهاني بمناسبة الميلاد و حلول السنة الجديدة (Ajmel altehani bemonasebt almīlad wa helol alseneh aljedīdah)
Bulgarian	Честита Коледа! (Čestita Koleda!)
Dutch	Prettige kerstdagen en een Gelukkig Nieuwjaar!
English	Merry Christmas and a Happy New Year!
Finnish	Hyvää joulua ja onnellista uutta vuotta
French	Joyeux Noël et bonne année
German	Frohes Fest und guten Rutsch [ins neue Jahr]
Hindi	नये साल की हार्दिक शुभकामनायें (Naye sāl kī hārdik śubhkāmnaye ṅ)
Hungarian	Kellemes karácsonyi ünnepeket és boldog új évet!
Italian	Buon Natale e felice anno nuovo
Persian	مبارک جهان مردم تمامی بر میلادی نو سال (Sale noe miladi bar tamami marodme jahan mobarak!)
Russian	С Рождеством Христовым и С наступающим Новым Годом
Urdu	Sale No Mobarak

---

[1] Codepoints are code positions that can be any of the numerical values that form the codespace of a character encoding.

This content intends to satisfy localization requirements that cannot be encoded by all character encoding schemes; that is, not all character encoding systems are appropriate for representing such a character variety. The correct rendering of such characters is not as natural as one might think. It could easily happen that undesirable characters, such as squares (□) or question marks (◆), appear instead of the correct form of nonbasic characters. Inappropriate character encoding (or its declaration) can cause additional problems too; for example, text might become impossible to search. Even if there might be legible characters from the overlapping part of the appropriate and the inadequate character encoding, a large share of the text would contain meaningless characters. Wrong encoding causes not just inappropriate rendering but also further processing problems; for example, databases might become inaccessible.

Beyond inadequate encoding information, other reasons can spoil text readability, too. Missing fonts are only one of them.

The possibility of encoding special characters depends on the character encoding and character set used.

There are a variety of character sets. The most well-known ones can be grouped as follows:

- *UTF*: UTF-8/UTF-16/UTF-32 (Unicode, worldwide)

- *ISO standards*: ISO-8859-1 (Western Europe), ISO-8859-2 (Central Europe), ISO-8859-3 (Southern Europe), ISO-8859-4 (Northern Europe), ISO-8859-5 (Cyrillic), ISO-8859-6-i (Arabic), ISO-8859-7 (Greek), ISO-8859-8 (Hebrew, visual), ISO-8859-8-i (Hebrew, logical), ISO-8859-9 (Turkish), ISO-8859-10 (Latin 6), ISO-8859-11 (Latin/Thai), ISO-8859-13 (Latin 7, Balic Rim), ISO-8859-14 (Latin 8, Celtic), ISO-8859-15 (Latin 9), ISO-8859-16 (Latin 10), ISO-2022-jp (Japanese, e-mail), ISO-ir-111 (Cyrillic KOI-8)

- *US-ASCII (basic English)*

- *Windows*: Windows-1250 (Central Europe), Windows-1251 (Cyrillic), Windows-1252 (Western Europe), Windows-1253 (Greek), Windows-1254 (Turkish), Windows-1255 (Hebrew), Windows-1256 (Arabic), Windows-1257 (Baltic Rim)

- *Encodings for eastern languages*: EUC-JP (Japanese, Unix), Shift_JIS (Japanese, Win/Mac), EUC-kr (Korean), gb2312 (Chinese, simplified), gb18030 (Chinese, simplified), big5 (Chinese, traditional), Big5-HKSCS (Chinese, Hong Kong), tis-620 (Thai)

- *Other*: koi8-r (Russian), koi8-u (Ukrainian), Macintosh (MacRoman), and so on.

In spite of this wide variety, only the variants of a single character encoding—Unicode—should be used unless there is a very good reason not to do so. The following section describes that character encoding.

Unicode

Unicode is a standard for universal character encoding. It provides the capacity to encode all characters used for the written languages of the world [1]. Beyond the characters of natural languages and widely used notations, all historic scripts of the world are also covered. Unicode provides codes for approximately 109,000 characters covering 93 scripts (even historic ones such as Egyptian hieroglyphs), including alphabets, ideograph sets, and symbols. Moreover, the Unicode codespace supports more than a million codepoints. The Unicode Character Code Charts provide quick access to any characters and their codepoints [2]. These classifications also give an insight into the wonderful richness of languages and fields supported by Unicode:

- Scripts
  - *European scripts*: Armenian (including ligatures), Coptic (including Coptic in Greek block), Cypriot syllabary, Cyrillic, Georgian, Glagolitic, Gothic, Greek, Latin (extended, including ligatures and fullwidth Latin letters), Linear B (with syllabary and ideograms), Ogham, Old Italic, Phaistos Disc, Runic, and Shavian
  - *Phonetic symbols*: IPA extensions, phonetic extensions, modifier tone letters, spacing modifier letters, superscripts and subscripts
  - *Combining diacritics*: Combining diacritical marks and combining half marks
  - *African scripts*: Bamum, Egyptian hieroglyphs, Ethiopic, N'Ko, Osmanya, Tifinagh, and Vai
  - *Middle Eastern scripts*: Arabic, Imperial Aramaic, Avestan, Carian, Cuneiform (including numbers and punctuation, Old Persian, and Ugaritic), Hebrew, Lycian, Lydian, Mandaic, Old South Arabian, inscriptional Pahlavi, inscriptional Parthian, Phoenician, Samaritan, and Syriac
  - *Central Asian scripts*: Mongolian, Old Turkic, Phags-Pa, and Tibetan
  - *South Asian scripts*: Bengali, Brahmi, Devanagari, Gujarati, Gurmukhi, Kaithi, Kannada, Kharoshthi, Lepcha, Limbu, Malayalam, Meetei Mayek, Ol Chiki, Oriya, Saurashtra, Sinhala, Syloti Nagri, Tamil, Telugu, Thaana, and Vedic extensions
  - *Southeast Asian scripts*: Batak, Balinese, Buginese, Cham, Javanese, Kayah Li, Khmer (with symbols), Lao, Myanmar (extended), New Tai Lue, Rejang, Sundanese, Tai Le, Tai Tham, Tai Viet, and Thai
  - *Philippine scripts*: Buhid, Hanunoo, Tagalog, and Tagbanwa
  - *East Asian scripts*: Bopomofo (extended), CJK unified ideographs (Han, extended), CJK compatibility ideographs (with supplement), CJK / KangXi radicals, Hangul Jamo (extended) and syllables, Hiragana, Katakana (with phonetic extensions, Kana supplement, and half-width Katakana), Kanbun, Lisu, and Yi (with syllables and radicals)
  - *American scripts*: Cherokee, Deseret, and Unified Canadian Aboriginal Syllabics
  - *Other scripts*: Alphabetic presentation forms, half-width and full-width forms, and ASCII characters
- Symbols and punctuation
  - *Punctuation*: General punctuation (ASCII punctuation, Latin-1 punctuation, small form variants), supplemental punctuation (CJK symbols and punctuation, CJK compatibility forms, full-width ASCII punctuation, and vertical forms)

- *Alphanumeric symbols*: Letterlike symbols (including Roman symbols), mathematical alphanumeric symbols, enclosed alphanumerics, enclosed CJK letters and months, CJK compatibility symbols (including additional squared symbols)

- *Numbers and digits*: Aegean numbers, Ancient Greek numbers, ASCII digits (including fullwidth ASCII digits), common Indic number forms, counting Rod numerals, Cuneiform numbers and punctuation, number forms, Rumi numeral symbols, superscripts, and subscripts

- *Mathematical symbols*: Arrows, mathematical alphanumeric symbols, mathematical operators, and geometric shapes

- *Other symbols*: Alchemical symbols, ancient symbols, Braille patterns, and currency symbols, dingbats, emoticons, game symbols, miscellaneous symbols, musical symbols (including Ancient Greek musical notation and Byzantine musical symbols), transport and map symbols, and Yijing symbols

- *Special characters*: Layout controls, invisible operators, tags, and variation selectors

The standard supports three encoding forms (UTF-8, UTF-16, UTF-32) that use a common repertoire of characters. They support the same data transmission but in 8, 16, or 32 bits per code unit format, respectively (byte, word, or double word). They can even be transformed into one another. All three encoding forms need a maximum of 4 bytes (32 bits) of data for each character. Depending on the encoding form chosen (UTF-8, UTF-16, or UTF-32), each character is represented as a sequence of either one to four 8-bit bytes, one or two 16-bit code units, or a single 32-bit code unit. Since UTF-8 and UTF-16 are variable-width encodings, UTF-8 results in smaller file size for English text. However, UTF-8 requires 3 bytes for an Asian character for which UTF-16 requires only 2 bytes. UTF-32 codepoint calculations can be performed quickly, but all codepoints require 4 bytes (fixed-width encoding).

For web content, UTF-8 is recommended, which provides interoperability and backward compatibility with US-ASCII[2] and has further advantageous characteristics [3]. UTF-8 supports *internationalized resource identifiers* (IRIs, multilingual web addresses) [4, 5]. UTF-8 uses one byte at the minimum in encoding the characters, while UTF-16 uses two, so a UTF-8 encoded file tends to be smaller than a UTF-16 encoded file. UTF-8 is byte oriented, while UTF-16 and UTF-32 are not; in other words, the byte order should be declared for UTF-16 and UTF-32 files by the byte-order mark (BOM—will be described in the corresponding section under "Special Characters"). UTF-8 is better in recovering from errors than the other Unicode flavors.

There are further variants of UTF-16 and UTF-32, depending on the *endianness*, which is the order of individually addressable subcomponents within the character set. If the most significant byte is the first byte (lowest address) and the least significant byte is the last byte (highest address), the file is called *big-endian* (UTF-16BE, UTF-32BE). If these bytes are reversed, the file is referred to as *little-endian* (UTF-16LE, UTF-32LE). Table 2-2 summarizes the differences between UTF-8 and the variants of UTF-16 and UTF-32.

---

[2] All US-ASCII characters use exactly the same bytes in UTF-8 as in US-ASCII; i.e., a UTF-8 file that contains only ASCII characters is identical to an ASCII file.

Table 2-2. Comparison of Unicode Encoding Schemes

Encoding	UTF-8	UTF-16	UTF-16BE	UTF-16LE	UTF-32	UTF-32BE	UTF-32LE
Smallest code point	0000	0000	0000	0000	0000	0000	0000
Largest code point	10FFFF	10FFFF	10FFFF	10FFFF	10FFFF	10FFFF	10FFFF
Code unit size	8 bits	16 bits	16 bits	16 bits	32 bits	32 bits	32 bits
Byte order	Not provided	*BOM*	Big-endian	Little-endian	*BOM*	Big-endian	Little-endian
Fewest bytes per character	1	2	2	2	4	4	4
Most bytes per character	4	4	4	4	4	4	4

According to the HTML5 specification, "authors are encouraged to use UTF-8. Conformance checkers may advise authors against using legacy encodings [6]. Authoring tools should default to using UTF-8 for newly-created documents [7]."

Characters That Should Be Avoided in Markup Contexts

Some Unicode characters should not be applied in the context of markup in HTML or XML documents (Table 2-3) because of one or more of the following reasons:

- They are deprecated in the Unicode standard.
- They cannot be supported without additional data.
- They are difficult to handle because they are stateful.[3]
- They can be handled more efficiently with markup.
- They should be avoided because of the potential conflict they could cause with equivalent markup.

---

[3] A character represented by a particular value in the text depends on values provided earlier in the text stream, e.g., escape sequences or bidirectional embedding controls.

Table 2-3. Unicode Characters Not Suitable for Use with Markup [8]

Codepoint(s)	Description	Comment
U+0340..U+0341	Clones of grave and accent	Deprecated in Unicode.
U+17A3, U+17D3	Obsolete characters for Khmer	Deprecated in Unicode.
U+2028..U+2029	Line and paragraph separator	`<xhtml:br />`, `<xhtml:p></xhtml:p>`, or equivalent should be used instead.
U+202A..U+202E	BIDI (bidirectional) embedding controls (LRE, RLE, LRO, RLO, PDF)	Strongly discouraged in HTML 4.01.
U+206A..U+206B	Activate/Inhibit Symmetric swapping	Deprecated in Unicode.
U+206C..U+206D	Activate/Inhibit Arabic form shaping	Deprecated in Unicode.
U+206E..U+206F	Activate/Inhibit National digit shapes	Deprecated in Unicode.
U+FFF9..U+FFFB	Interlinear annotation characters	Ruby markup should be used instead.
U+FEFF	As ZWNBSP	U+2060 word joiner should be used instead.
	As Byte Order Mark	Use only at the start of a file, not as part of markup.
U+FFFC	Object replacement character	Markup should be used instead, e.g., `<object>`, `<img>`.
U+1D173..U+1D17A	Scoping for Musical Notation	An appropriate markup language should be used instead.
U+E0000..U+E007F	Language Tag code points	`xhtml:lang` or `xml:lang` should be used instead.

Formatting Characters Suitable Also for Markup

There are special formatting characters in Unicode that can also be used for markup (Table 2-4). They affect text and can be applied for markup simultaneously. These formatting characters are interpreted by rendering engines.

Table 2-4. *The Most Important Formatting Characters That Can Also Be Used for Markup [9]*

Codepoint(s)	Name or Function	Comment
U+00A0	Nonbreakable space	Line break control.
U+00AD	Soft hyphen	Line break control.
U+200B	Zero-width space	Line break control.
U+200C..U+200D	Zero-width join controls (ZWJ and ZWNJ)	Required for Persian and many Indic scripts.
U+200E..U+200F	Implicit directional marks (LRM and RLM)	LRM and RLM are allowed.
U+2011	Nonbreaking hyphen	Line break control.
U+2044	Fraction slash	Alternatively, MathML markup can be used.
U+2060	Word joiner	This should be used for word joiner instead of U+FEFF (ZWNBSP).
U+2061..U+2064	Invisible mathematical operators	Mathematical use.
U+2FF0..U+2FFB	Ideographic character description	Graphic characters (not controls).
U+303E	Ideographic variation indicator	Graphic character (not a control).
FE00..FE0F	Variation selectors	Modify graphic characters.
E0100..E01DF	Variation selectors	Modify graphic characters.

Special Characters

Certain Unicode characters deserve extended attention because they should be used with caution.

The Byte-Order Mark (BOM)

Unicode files can contain special bytes at the very beginning known as the *byte-order mark* (BOM). This codepoint is the U+FEFF (Zero-width non-breaking space, ZWNBSP). As mentioned earlier, the byte order of UTF-16 and UTF-32 encoded files should be declared, and the BOM provides this information.

In UTF-16, the 2 or 4 bytes of characters can be ordered in two ways (little-endian or big-endian—essentially just defining the direction the bytes should be read in). To choose from the two, documents encoded in UTF-16 should always start with the BOM. In UTF-8, it is optional since there are no alternate byte sequences in characters. If the BOM is still provided in UTF-8, it is called the *UTF-8 signature*. According to the I18N Activity Group at W3C, the byte-order mark should be omitted in UTF-8 [10]. This byte-order mark can cause display problems in some browsers. For example, it produces an extra line or unwanted characters at the top of the page [11]. An advanced text editor or Richard Ishida's *UTF-8 BOM tester* [12] can be used to check the presence of UTF-8 signatures.

Whitespace Characters

A small subset of Unicode characters are considered *whitespace* characters that have different line-breaking properties, different ligating properties, and different widths. These characters are used to separate different parts of the document with line breaks, tabulators, and spaces. They represent horizontal or vertical spaces on web pages and thus contribute to the appearance and layout of blocks of content or the entire page. Whitespace characters are typically nonvisual marks but reserve some space when rendered. The list of whitespace characters varies from context to context. For example, the form feed control character is considered as whitespace in HTML but not in XML. Moreover, each markup language defines those few whitespace characters that can be applied as part of the markup syntax. The XML specification defines whitespace as a combination of one or more of the following characters: space (U+0020), carriage return (U+000D), line feed (U+000A), or tab (U+0009). HTML 4.01 also supports the form feed character (U+000C); however, that character cannot be used in XHTML.

Not all whitespace characters can be typed in from the keyboard, although the most common ones, such as a blank space (the basic word divider in Western languages) or a single tabulator, can be typed using the spacebar and the Tab key, respectively. Advanced text editors usually provide inserting options for all the others (see the later section "Development Tools").

A very bad practice from the 1990s is to provide whitespaces by embedding blank images, such as `spacer.gif` files, instead of whitespace characters. This approach still exists, although it has only disadvantages. For example, the content of a web page using space-holder images loses its structure and provides elements without semantic or structural meaning. As a result, the length of the source code of such documents is not optimal. Even the slightest modification in the content might result in disrupted layout. Such images might also have a negative effect on searchability. Moreover, the page content of such documents is not accessible for text browsers and screen readers (that would read aloud "spacer.gif" repeatedly).

NFC Normalization Is Recommended

In Unicode the same text can be provided with different character sequences. The accentuated a (in other words, á), for example, can be represented either as the *pre-composed* U+00E1 (Latin small letter a with acute) or as the *decomposed* sequence of U+0061 (Latin small letter a) and U+0301 (Combining acute accent).

Unicode Standard supports four *normalization forms*: *NFC, NFD, NFKC,* and *NFKD*. The *C* stands for composed (precomposed), *D* for decomposed, while *K* represents compatibility.

The normalization form being used is especially important when accents or other diacritics are used in (X)HTML identifiers or CSS selectors and class names. If such a word is used in precomposed form in the HTML (for example, `<div id="hangsúlyos">`), but in decomposed form in the CSS (for example, `#hangsúlyos { color: red; }`), then the selector won't match the class name. This problem can be eliminated by avoiding accented characters in markup attributes and CSS properties, which is strongly recommended.

W3C recommends NFC normalization—which is supported by advanced text editors by default—on the Web to improve interoperability [13].

Unicode Should Be Preferred

Web documents should use one character encoding at a time. Different parts of the same document should not be encoded with different encoding schemes.

UTF-8 character encoding can significantly reduce the complexity of multilingual sites. Unicode allows more languages to be used on a single page than any other encoding system. In most cases, it is ideal for content, forms, scripts, and databases. Consequently, Unicode should be used wherever possible [14]. Fortunately, there is a good tendency toward this use on the Web. According to a Google report released in August 2010, approximately 50 percent of web sites apply UTF-8. The universal use of an ultimate character encoding can eliminate incorrect assumptions made by user agents while rendering documents that contain special characters.

However, the application of Unicode does not guarantee that texts will be displayed correctly in browsers. Several scripting languages such as Arabic require additional techniques to ensure the appropriate character sequence of glyphs.

Declaring Character Encoding for the Markup

Character encoding of web documents can be determined in many ways:

- Using the HTTP header
- Using in-document declarations
    - Using the *pragma directive* (HTML 4, XHTML, (X)HTML5)
    - Using the `meta charset` attribute (HTML5)
    - Using the XML declaration[4] (XHTML)

The last three options are used in the markup, but not the first one, which is applied by the web server to indicate the character encoding. As indicated earlier, not all in-document declarations can be used in any markup languages, but the pragma directive can be used in most. Since all of these techniques provide information about the encoding to rendering engines on how to interpret the file, it is vital to ensure that these declarations correspond to the actual character encoding of the file.

If multiple encoding declarations are inconsistent or contradictory, the following precedence rules determine which declaration to apply:

1. HTTP `Content-Type` header
2. Byte-order mark[5]

---

[4] The character encoding declaration, if provided exclusively using the XML declaration, is ignored by some rendering engines.

3. XML declaration

4. The `meta` element

5. The `link charset` attribute

Encoding Declaration in the HTTP Header

One of the options for declaring character encoding is to provide the appropriate data in the HTTP header. Listing 2-1 shows an example.

Listing 2-1. Setting the Character Encoding in the HTTP Header

```
HTTP/1.1 200 OK
Date: Tue, 02 Aug 2011 14:18:05 GMT
Server: Apache/2.2.3 (Oracle)
...
Content-Type: text/html; charset=UTF-8
Content-Language: en
```

As mentioned earlier, these declarations have the highest precedence. They should be consistent with in-document declarations.

Documents using UTF-16 should be declared as UTF-16 rather than UTF-16BE or UTF-16LE and provide a byte-order mark in the file.

HTTP headers are used for other purposes too. For more information on the HTTP header, see Chapter 4.

In-Document Declarations

In HTML 4, the *pragma directive* should be used at the top of the head element in the form shown in Listing 2-2.

Listing 2-2. Declaring the Character Encoding with the Pragma Directive

```
<meta http-equiv="Content-type" content="text/html;charset=UTF-8">
```

The previous declaration can be used in HTML5 as well, which also provides a newly specified meta charset attribute (Listing 2-3). Either of them could be used but only one at a time. The whole declaration must fit within the first 512 bytes of the page.

Listing 2-3. HTML5 meta charset

```
<meta charset="UTF-8">
```

The encoding declaration of XHTML documents depends on which MIME type they are served with. If they are served as text/html, the *pragma directive* in Listing 2-2 can be used at the top of the head element.

XHTML documents served as XML can use the encoding declaration of the XML declaration (Listing 2-4) in the first line of the document (see Chapter 3).

---

[5] The BOM has been added to the hierarchy by the HTML5 specification, but this is not implemented in all browsers yet.

Listing 2-4. Setting the Character Encoding in XML Documents

```
<?xml version="1.0" encoding="utf-8"?>
```

An XML declaration is required for any XML documents that use character encoding other than UTF-8 or UTF-16 as well as in case the encoding is not provided by the HTTP header (see later in Chapter 3).

Declaring Character Encoding for CSS

Generally, there is no need to declare character encoding for style sheets. However, the encoding of external CSS files should always be declared if and only if any non-ASCII content is provided within the CSS. Alternatively, descriptive names of selectors or other CSS content written in languages requiring non-Latin characters can be provided without accents, totally eliminating the need for CSS encoding declarations.

HTTP Header Declarations

CSS encoding can also be declared in the HTTP Content-Type header. For example, if the character encoding is UTF-8, the HTTP declaration looks like Listing 2-5.

Listing 2-5. Declaring the Character Encoding for CSS (Rarely Used)

```
Content-Type: text/css; charset=UTF-8
```

Beyond the HTTP declaration, it is always recommended to use an in-document declaration as well (see the next section). This can guarantee that the encoding of the external CSS file can be determined even if the file is moved or used locally.

The character encoding declared in the HTTP header should coincide with the one declared in the CSS file. Naturally, the first one has higher precedence.

In-Document Declarations

Character encoding can be set by the @charset *at-rule* with the syntax shown in Listing 2-6.

Listing 2-6. Syntax of the @charset At-Rule

```
@charset "<charset-name>";
```

Only one @charset rule can be used per CSS file. It should be declared at the very beginning of the file. No characters should precede the declaration (only BOM if the CSS file is Unicode encoded[6]).

The charset-name can be one of the character sets defined by IANA [15]. Some encodings have multiple names in the IANA registry (in these cases the one denoted as preferred should be applied). Listing 2-7 shows a typical example for character encoding declaration of external CSS files.

Listing 2-7. Setting the Character Encoding of CSS with an At-Rule

```
@charset "UTF-8";
```

---

[6] External CSS files are usually encoded in US-ASCII.

These rules can be used exclusively for external style sheets. In-document style sheet declarations should avoid @charset rules.

The HTML 4.01 specification defines a charset attribute to the link element, which could be used for identifying the character encoding of the target document. In HTML5, however, this attribute of the link element is considered obsolete (partly because it is not supported fully by browsers); thus, it should be avoided.

Escape Codes, Special Characters, and Symbols

In HTML and XHTML documents, each character can be represented directly or by a character sequence (also known as a *character reference*). Two types of character sequences exist: *numeric character references* and *character entity references*.

Assume a document fragment contains an a character with an accent. It can be declared by either the á or á numeric character references or by the á entity reference in (X)HTML documents (see the following sections for details). However, the direct use of the character á should be applied instead. The same is true for the copyright sign (© instead of ©), the registered trademark sign (® instead of ®), and so on.

Characters should always be preferred to escape codes except when those characters that should be represented have syntactic meaning in (X)HTML or XML are invisible or ambiguous. However, in those cases, using entities is mandatory [16]. In other words, markup characters used in text or attribute values must be *escaped*. For example, when an (X)HTML source code should be represented as document content without processing, the < and > characters should be provided by their entity names in the source code. Analogously, if an & character is needed as text within an RSS feed or an RDF file, the & entity should be used instead (see the "Entity References" section for more information).

Numeric References

Numeric character references identify characters by *Universal Character Set* or *Unicode codepoints* in the form &#*nnnn*; where *nnnn* is the codepoint in decimal form.

Both HTML and XHTML support *hexadecimal references* as well. In HTML, they can be applied in either the &#X*hhhh*; or &#x*hhhh*; form. Since XML is case sensitive, in XHTML they must be in lowercase (&#x*hhhh*;) [17].

The nnnn or hhhh can be any number of digits and may include leading zeros.

Numeric references should be eliminated in favor of direct character use. In most cases, there is no reason to insert a single apostrophe in the markup as ’ rather than the ' character itself. The same holds true for other characters too. If a character, such as a Japanese ideograph, cannot be typed in with the keyboard, the corresponding character can be inserted with advanced software tools or copy and pasted from other applications, codecharts, or web sites via the clipboard. Note that even advanced text editors display many of these directly inserted characters incorrectly during development; however, browsers will display them correctly if the character encoding of the containing file has been set properly and the file is being served correctly.

Entity References

Character entity references refer to characters by the name of the appropriate entity that has the desired character as its replacement text in the form &*name*;.

HTML supports 252 character entities [18]. In XHTML, there are 253 entities (including the 5 predefined entities of XML 1.0) [19]; however, their application is affected by the way XHTML documents are processed. It should be kept in mind that XHTML documents, if served correctly, are processed by XML parsers instead of SGML parsers that interpret HTML documents. Those characters that have a meaning in XML, such as the less-than sign (<), cause parsing errors if they are provided directly rather than using entities. There are only four character entities whose processing is guaranteed in all XML environments: &, >, <, and " (&, >, <, and " respectively). Fortunately, this short list contains those very important character entities that can be used for syntactic notation (ampersand, greater than, less than). W3C recommends the use of ampersand characters in href attributes of XHTML documents [20]. Particular attention should be paid to URIs that include parameters. Single ampersand characters in these URIs should be replaced by the & entity [21].

Although the ' entity (apostrophe, U+0027) is among the five predefined entities of XML, it should not be used in XHTML [22].

Since virtually all characters can be represented directly in Unicode including, but not limited to, all letters and ideograms of natural languages, accentuated letters, special characters, mathematical signs, and symbols, character references should be eliminated [23]. Direct character use is easier to interpret, maintain, and modify than numeric or entity references (Listing 2-8). Texts with references are more difficult to extend and almost impossible to search. Many characters cannot be represented by references, which often resulted in incorrect characters on web pages in the 1990s. For example, the small o with tilde, õ, has been displayed instead of o with the double acute accent (also known as the Hungarumlaut), ő, which is a different character.

Listing 2-8. Three Versions of the Same Central-European Text with Characters, Numeric and Entity References

```
<h1>Áttekintés</h1>
<p>
A HTML5 a HTML teljes megújulása, új funkciókkal felvértezve.
</p>

<h1>&#193;ttekint&#233;s</h1>
<p>
A HTML5 a HTML teljes meg&#250;jul&#225;sa, &#250;j funkci&#243;kkal felv&#233;rtezve.
</p>

<h1>&Aacute;ttekint&eacute;s</h1>
<p>
A HTML5 a HTML teljes meg&uacute;jul&aacute;sa, &uacute;j funkci&oacute;kkal
felv&eacute;rtezve.
</p>
```

Checking I18N

Those settings and content that support internationalization can be checked by the *W3C Internationalization Checker* [24]. It can determine whether the HTML/XHTML documents contain non-NFC class names and identifiers, the language settings of pages, and so on. The validator is described in detail in the "Validating I18N" section in Chapter 14.

Summary

In this chapter, you learned the importance of internationalization settings that enable properly displayed characters to be rendered on web sites or processed in databases. You know by now that there is a wide choice of character encoding systems, many of which have been used for decades but became obsolete in recent years. There is an ultimate variable-width character encoding, called UTF-8, which is a flavor of Unicode, omits the BOM, and is backward compatible with the once most widely used encoding scheme, ASCII.

The next chapter will describe the markup, where most standardization efforts take place. The markup not only provides the document structure and content but also serves as the basis for accessibility support and semantic annotations. As you will see, there is a wide choice of markup languages, not just HTML5, the one most developers talk about these days. You will learn the HTML and XHTML elements and attributes that can be safely applied in a variety of documents while maintaining standard compliance. The chapter will also make you understand why strict markup should always be preferred.

References

1. The Unicode Consortium (2010) The Unicode Standard: A Technical Introduction. Unicode, Inc. www.unicode.org/standard/principles.html. Accessed 29 September 2010

2. Unicode (2011) Unicode 6.0 Character Code Charts. Unicode Consortium. www.unicode.org/charts/. Accessed 03 Aug 2011

3. Yergeau F (2003). UTF-8, a transformation format of ISO 10646 [RFC3629]. The Internet Society. www.ietf.org/rfc/rfc3629.txt. Accessed 29 September 2010

4. Duerst M, Suignard M (2005) Internationalized Resource Identifiers (IRIs). The Internet Society. www.ietf.org/rfc/rfc3987. Accessed 30 September 2010

5. Ishida R (2010) An Introduction to Multilingual Web Addresses. World Wide Web Consortium. www.w3.org/International/articles/idn-and-iri/. Accessed 30 September 2010

6. Hickson I (ed.) (2010) HTML5 (Edition for Web Authors) revision 1.4439. A vocabulary and associated APIs for HTML and XHTML. Editor's Draft. World Wide Web Consortium. http://dev.w3.org/html5/spec-author-view/semantics.html. Accessed 29 September 2010

7. Hickson I (ed.) (2010) HTML5 (including next generation additions still in development). Draft Standard. Apple Computer, Inc., Mozilla Foundation, and Opera Software ASA. www.whatwg.org/specs/web-apps/current-work/multipage/semantics.html. Accessed 29 September 2010

8. Dürst M, Freytag A (2007) Characters not suitable for use with markup. In: Unicode in XML and other Markup Languages. Unicode Technical Report #20. W3C Working Group Note. World Wide Web Consortium. www.w3.org/TR/unicode-xml/#Suitable. Accessed 30 September 2010

9. Dürst M, Freytag A (2007) Format Characters Suitable for Use with Markup. In: Unicode in XML and other Markup Languages. Unicode Technical Report #20. W3C Working Group Note. World Wide Web Consortium. www.w3.org/TR/unicode-xml/#Format. Accessed 30 September 2010

10. Ishida R (2010) What do I need to know about the BOM? In: The byte-order mark (BOM) in HTML. World Wide Web Consortium. www.w3.org/International/questions/qa-byte-order-mark#bomhow. Accessed 30 September 2010

11. Cawkwell D, Ishida R (2010) Display problems caused by the UTF-8 BOM. World Wide Web Consortium. www.w3.org/International/questions/qa-utf8-bom. Accessed 30 September 2010

12. Ishida R (2007). UTF-8 BOM tester. Richard Ishida. http://rishida.net/utils/bomtester/. Accessed 30 September 2010

13. Ishida R (2010) Normalization in HTML and CSS. World Wide Web Consortium. www.w3.org/International/questions/qa-html-css-normalization. Accessed 30 September 2010

14.   Ishida R (2010) Use UTF-8, if you can. In: Choosing & applying a character encoding. World Wide Web Consortium. www.w3.org/International/questions/qa-choosing-encodings#useunicode. Accessed 30 September 2010

15.   Simonsen K et al (2010) Character sets. The Internet Assigned Numbers Authority. www.iana.org/assignments/character-sets. Accessed 30 September 2010

16.   Ishida R (2010) When to use escapes. In: Using character escapes in markup and CSS. World Wide Web Consortium. www.w3.org/International/questions/qa-escapes#use. Accessed 30 September 2010

17.   Pemberton S et al (2002) Entity references as hex values. In: XHTML 1.0 – The Extensible HyperText Markup Language (2nd edn). A Reformulation of HTML 4 in XML 1.0. W3C Recommendation. World Wide Web Consortium. www.w3.org/TR/xhtml1/#h-4.12. Accessed 29 September 2010

18.   Le Hors A, Jacobs I (ed.) (1999) Character entity references in HTML 4. In: HTML 4.01 Specification. W3C Recommendation. World Wide Web Consortium. www.w3.org/TR/html4/sgml/entities.html. Accessed 29 September 2010

19.   Pemberton S et al (2002) Entity Sets. In: XHTML 1.0 – The Extensible HyperText Markup Language (2nd edn). A Reformulation of HTML 4 in XML 1.0. W3C Recommendation. World Wide Web Consortium. www.w3.org/TR/xhtml1/#h-A2. Accessed 29 September 2010

20.   Pemberton S et al (2002) Using Ampersands in Attribute Values (and Elsewhere). In: XHTML 1.0 – The Extensible HyperText Markup Language (2nd edn). A Reformulation of HTML 4 in XML 1.0. W3C Recommendation. World Wide Web Consortium. www.w3.org/TR/2002/REC-xhtml1-20020801/#C_16. Accessed 30 September 2010

21.   Ishida R (2010) By the way. In: Using character escapes in markup and CSS. World Wide Web Consortium. www.w3.org/International/questions/qa-escapes#bytheway. Accessed 30 September 2010

22.   Pemberton S et al (2002) The Named Character Reference '. In: XHTML 1.0 – The Extensible HyperText Markup Language (2nd edn). A Reformulation of HTML 4 in XML 1.0. W3C Recommendation. World Wide Web Consortium. www.w3.org/TR/2002/REC-xhtml1-20020801/#C_16. Accessed 30 September 2010

23.   Ishida R (2010) When not to use escapes. In: Using character escapes in markup and CSS. World Wide Web Consortium. www.w3.org/International/questions/qa-escapes#not. Accessed 30 September 2010

24.   W3C I18N Activity Group (2010) W3C Internationalization Checker. World Wide Web Consortium. http://qa-dev.w3.org/i18n-checker/. Accessed 30 September 2010

CHAPTER 3

Markup Languages: More Than HTML5

Since markup is the essence of web documents, it provides the largest place for standardization efforts. The popularity of HTML has not decreased since the birth of the Web; thus, becoming familiar with the versions and variants of that language is important. On the other hand, the application of XML languages has been increasing significantly. The differences between HTML and XHTML are crucial for understanding the techniques for migrating from one document type to another. The general structure of all web documents follows the same logic; however, HTML5 introduced new structuring elements that can be used to create rather sophisticated document structures. By examining well-structured document examples with limited content, you will be able to create well-structured web documents on your own. To achieve well-structuredness, the block-line and inline-level elements should be differentiated, which is also important in understanding how to embed elements into each other (element nesting). You should also know how to use Formal Public Identifiers and Document Type Definitions for creating standard-compliant documents. The strict rules of XML declarations are vital for XHTML authoring.

In this chapter, you will learn about the most important standards in web site development. This chapter covers the most advanced markup languages along with mixed-namespace document types. I provide sample HTML and XHTML documents for the sake of easier understanding. You will understand how to distinguish deprecated elements and attributes that should not be used from the ones that can be used in almost all versions and variants of markup languages available on the Web today. Beyond the most popular versions of markup languages, you will learn the power of XML through mixed-namespace documents where not only general-purpose texts but also vector graphics and mathematical annotations can be provided by textual markup. After reading the chapter, you will be able to apply semantically meaningful markup elements and attributes, eliminate obsolete markup, and create web documents with proper element nesting and DOM structure.

■ **Note** The detailed description of markup basics is beyond the scope of this book. Several resources are available for both beginner and intermediate developers. One of them is "Getting started with HTML," a very short overview written by the author/editor of HTML specifications, Dave Raggett [1]. Another—strongly recommended—W3C document is the "HTML: The Markup Language Reference" by Michael Smith [2]. There are also many books on HTML5 [e.g., 3, 4, 5, 6] and XHTML.[1] However, extended care must be taken to consider changes and obsoletion of documents about HTML5. If a short summary is required for a certain element during development, the W3C Cheatsheet can be more than helpful too [7].

SGML Languages

Standard Generalized Markup Language (SGML) is a markup language family. It has been used since the mid-1980s. One of the major features of SGML is flexibility.

The most important SGML language for web developers is HTML, which has been the core language of the World Wide Web from the very beginning.

■ **Caution** Despite the similarities in the markup syntax of earlier HTML versions and HTML5, the latest version is no longer based on SGML; however, it is backward-compatible with conventional HTML parsing.

HTML

The idea behind *Hypertext Markup Language (HTML)* was born at the European Laboratory for High-Energy Physics (CERN) in Geneva, Switzerland, as early as 1989 [8]. One year later, the World Wide Web project was also started there. In the beginning, HTML was used to share information between scientists. The major elements of the language were formed at that time, including headings, paragraphs, and hyperlinks. However, the semantics of these documents were limited [9]. New elements and multimedia capabilities were also added later that caused interoperability problems for documents across different platforms.

The relatively simple syntax and vocabulary of the language made rapid and wide distribution possible. However, it is also the reason for invalid markup found in more than 90 percent of HTML documents. The error tolerance of browsers is constantly being misused. People should appreciate the value of quality web documents, accessibility, good presentation, and functionality in various browsers.

---

[1] XHTML hand coders can write HTML markup with ease.

XML Languages

Extensible Markup Language (XML) is a universal format for structured documents and data on the World Wide Web. Since XML has been extended from SGML, it can also be considered as a restricted, machine-readable form of SGML. In this context, it removes those features of SGML that might result in loose source code.

In contrast to most computer languages, XML has no fixed, predefined set of tags. With XML, individual markup formats can be defined. Some of the most well-known and frequently used XML formats and/or XML serializations on the Web are XML, XHTML, SVG, MathML, XSL, RDF, Atom, and RSS.

Many markup languages have primarily been designed for text documents; however, the need for representing other types of information is constantly growing. Music, video, playlists, vector graphics, content syndication, and various web services are some typical examples. One of the big advantages of XML is that it is strict, well-defined, and extensible. XML also makes it possible to combine multiple markup languages into single profiles, such as XHTML + MathML + SVG or XHTML + SMIL. The additional vocabularies (elements, attributes, and further components) of other XML applications can be used through the namespace mechanism declared by the `xmlns` attribute. This is one of the major advantages of XHTML over HTML.

XHTML

Extensible Hypertext Markup Language (XHTML) is an XML language family that can be used as an alternative to HTML. XHTML is an application of XML and thus more restrictive than HTML. In contrast to HTML, for XHTML documents it must be ensured that they are properly written; otherwise, rendering engines give error messages instead of rendering the content. They require an XML parser rather than an SGML parser.

Documents served with an XML MIME type, such as `application/xhtml+xml`, are treated as XML documents by browsers; in other words, they are parsed by an XML processor. Consequently, XML and HTML are processed differently. In fact, even minor syntactic errors will prevent an XML document (or the ones that claimed to be XML) from being rendered correctly. In contrast, the errors of such documents would be ignored in the HTML syntax. A parsing error of XML documents can easily result in the "Yellow Screen of Death."

Version Overview

Understanding the major differences and capabilities of the different markup language versions and variants and analyzing sample documents with minimum content known as *skeleton documents* is useful. They will be provided throughout the following sections. These documents can serve as the basis for hand-coder development from scratch. Note that indentation is used for providing clear, easy-to-understand code. Naturally, tabulators can be omitted to obtain complete code optimality. Furthermore, all provided documents are valid from character to character on an as-is basis, so they must be extended with valid markup only to maintain validity. All these documents can be downloaded from the book's web page at `www.apress.com`, as well as from the companion web site of the book at `www.masteringhtml5css3.com`.

HTML Versions and Variants

This section will highlight certain versions of HTML for two reasons. First, some have made a significant impact on the evolution of the Web and are used as the basis of future standards. Second, some are still in use more than 10 years after their introduction.

Although most of the early HTML versions are not used any longer, their milestones and the evolution of HTML are important to know.

The formal specification of HTML was created in 1992, and this specification has evolved constantly in the form of an SGML Document Type Definition. HTML soon became the *lingua franca* of web publishing. HTML documents can be created manually in plain-text editors as well as in WYSIWYG environments.[2]

HTML 2.0 was created by the HTML Working Group of the Internet Engineering Task Force in 1995. It is also denoted as RFC 1866 [10]. HTML 2.0 is the first standardized form of the core HTML elements. HTML 2.0 was used for platform-independent hypertext documents. The document type is obsolete and currently stated as historic. More details can be found in the W3C archives [11].

HTML 3.2 is the first HTML Recommendation of W3C. This is the version in which new elements have been introduced for creating tables, applets, superscripts, and subscripts, as well as for text flows around images [12]. HTML 3.2 was backward-compatible with version 2.0. The code in Listing 3-1 is a fragment of an HTML 3.2 document.

Listing 3-1. Bad Practices in an Old HTML Document (Just Demonstration, Should Not Be Used)

```
<!DOCTYPE HTML PUBLIC "-//W3C//DTD HTML 3.2//EN">
<title>An HTML 3.2 example</title>
<body bgcolor="#FFF6F0"
 text="#000000"
 link="#C00000">
<h1 align=center>Example header</h1>

 <p><A HREF=http://www.example.com/><img align=left border=0 alt="Example:"
width=102 height=52
src=http://www.example.com/images/author.jpg></A> <i>The Author</i>
</body>
```

You can see that this markup is not case-sensitive. The previous example is loose code; in fact, it is a bad example for web developers, because some of the attributes are not quoted (for example, `width=102` instead of `width="102"`), strictly presentational attributes (`bgcolor`, `align`) are used that should be eliminated by using CSS, the paragraph is not closed (the `</p>` tag is missing), and so forth.

■ **Tip** Although HTML allows both capitalized and lowercase letters in element and attribute names, it is better to become accustomed to using lowercase letters, which are allowed in every markup (including XHTML, which is case-sensitive).

---

[2] For web standardistas the first one is the real choice.

HTML 4 is an ISO-conforming version (ISO 8879) that was the *de facto* standard, the "publishing language of the World Wide Web," for many years [13]. The specification was released in 1997 and revised in 1998. HTML 4 was superseded by HTML 4.01.

Listing 3-2 shows a fragment of a typical HTML 4.0 document.

***Listing 3-2.** A Typical HTML 4 Document (Obsolete)*

```
<!DOCTYPE HTML PUBLIC "-//W3C//DTD HTML 4.0 Transitional//EN">
<html>
<head>
<title>An HTML 4.0 example</title>
</head>
<body>
 …
</body>
</html>
```

Undoubtedly, similarity can be noticed between the structure of this document and the previous one. Markup languages are constantly evolving, and most versions rely on earlier versions and variants.

One of the most well-known previously used HTML versions was HTML 4.01. It was the primary markup language of the Web for more than a decade. The W3C Recommendation was released in late 1999. It has three variations: the Strict, the Transitional, and the Frameset [14]. In the HTML 4 era, the real choice was the Strict flavor, because it contained those elements only that had been selected for inclusion in future versions. The Transitional variant was created to make it easier for developers to stop using deprecated tags and provided time to learn how to write markup without these obsolete tags (hence the name). Since frames have been considered obsolete for many years now, Frameset documents should not be used at all. There were many problems with frames. If you accessed a web site with a broken frameset, for example, missing contents would take up the whole window. If a visitor arrived through a direct link to a framed page, the context would be missed. Search engines could not index frameset documents effectively. There were linking and bookmarking issues, and further problems such as the Back button did not work in browsers. Frames also reduced the amount of usable space on a web page and caused problems with printing.

XHTML Versions and Variants

XHTML is a document type family that is the reformulation of HTML in XML rather than SGML. Typical XHTML *file extensions* are .html, .htm, .xhtml, .xht, and .xml. XHTML documents generally apply the application/xhtml+xml *Internet media type*; however, there are occasional exceptions (as you'll see in the next chapter).

***Table 3-1.** Core XHTML Versions*

Version	Descriptive Name	Site	Status	Date
XHTML 1.0	A reformulation of HTML 4 in XML 1.0	www.w3.org/TR/xhtml1/	R	2000-01-26 r. 2002-08-01
XHTML 1.1	Module-based XHTML	www.w3.org/TR/xhtml11/	R	2001-05-31 r. 2010-10-07

Version	Descriptive Name	Site	Status	Date
XHTML 2.0 (XHTML2)	–	`www.w3.org/TR/xhtml2/`	WD[3]	2006-07-26
XHTML5	A vocabulary and associated APIs for XHTML	`www.w3.org/TR/html5/`	WD	2008-01-22

R: W3C Recommendation   WD: W3C Working Draft   r: revised

Beyond the core versions of XHTML (Table 3-1), several compounds, extensions, and special profiles are known (Table 3-2), and further ones can also be defined. The additional mechanisms allow XHTML subsets or supersets. XHTML 1.1 + MathML 2.0 + SVG 1.1 and XHTML+RDFa documents are typical examples of supersets of XHTML. Because of the additional (external) element sets applied in them, they have a wider variety of markup elements than simple XHTML documents.

Table 3-2. Special and Mixed-Namespace XHTML Document Types

Version	Descriptive Name	Status	Date
XHTML 1.1 + MathML 2.0 + SVG 1.1	An XHTML + MathML + SVG Profile [15]	WD	2002-08-09
XHTML-MP 1.2	XHTML Mobile Profile	R[4]	2008-07-29
XHTML-Print	XHTML for Printing	R	2006-09-20
XHTML-Print 2nd ed.		R	2010-11-23
XHTML+RDFa 1.0	RDFa in XHTML [16]	R	2008-10-14
XHTML+RDFa 1.1	Support for RDFa via XHTML Modularization [17]	WD	2010-08-03

R: W3C Recommendation   WD: W3C Working Draft

XHTML 1.1 + MathML 2.0 + SVG 1.1 documents can be written in any of the compounds, all of which have their own document format. The selected language is the *host language* (see the "XHTML + MathML + SVG" section later in the chapter).

XHTML 1.0

According to the subtitle of its specification released in 2000 (and revised in 2002), XHTML 1.0 is "a reformulation of HTML 4 in XML 1.0" [18]. Similar to the three flavors of HTML 4.01, XHTML 1.0 also defines the Strict, Transitional, and Frameset variants, respectively. XHTML 1.0 Strict includes those

---

[3] It has been suspended.
[4] Defined by Open Mobile Alliance not W3C.

elements and attributes only that have not been deprecated in HTML 4.01. Every "missing" element and attribute can be substituted by their CSS equivalents.

XHTML 1.0 Transitional provides the presentational elements such as center or font that are not allowed in the Strict variant. Listings 3-3 and 3-4 show an example.

Listing 3-3. An Element Deprecated a Long Time Ago Is Still Used in XHTML 1.0 Transitional Documents

```
<center>
  <p>
  A paragraph aligned to center.
  </p>
</center>
```

Listing 3-4. The Code of Listing 3-3 Written in XHTML 1.0 Strict and Styled by CSS

```
.center {
  text-align: center;
}

<p class="center">
A paragraph aligned to center.
<p>
```

XHTML 1.0 also has a Frameset variant, although, as we saw earlier, eliminating framesets is strongly recommended even if they were a common feature of web documents in the first decade of the Web.

Listing 3-5 presents an XHTML 1.0 Strict skeleton document.

Listing 3-5. An XHTML 1.0 Strict Skeleton Document

```
<?xml version="1.0" encoding="UTF-8"?>
<!DOCTYPE html ↵
 PUBLIC "-//W3C//DTD XHTML 1.0 Strict//EN" ↵
 "http://www.w3.org/TR/xhtml1/DTD/xhtml1-strict.dtd">
<html xmlns="http://www.w3.org/1999/xhtml" xml:lang="en" lang="en">
  <head>
    <title>Minimal XHTML 1.0 Document</title>
    <meta http-equiv="Content-Type" content="application/xhtml+xml; charset=utf-8" />
  </head>
  <body>
    <p>
    This is a minimal XHTML 1.0 document.
    </p>
  </body>
</html>
```

■ **Tip** This is the best starting point for any kind of XHTML documents, because this document type contains fundamental markup elements only that have been derived from HTML and are still current in most markup languages. This markup also serves as the basis to be extended using external vocabularies (doing so, the document type will change). If you want to use new markup elements introduced in HTML5 and migrate from XHTML 1.0 Strict, minimal changes are needed (such as removing the DTD, changing the character encoding declaration to the new one, and adding new elements).

XHTML 1.1

Over the years it has been realized that there are presentational components in markup languages that can be handled more efficiently with style sheets. Moreover, web documents developed for handheld devices can use limited resources more effectively if a subset of selected elements is applied in a document rather than the whole set of elements. This is the basic idea behind *XHTML modularization,* and these element subsets are called *element modules.*

XHTML 1.1, the "module-based XHTML," contains exclusively those elements that are defined by the "Modularization of XHTML" [19]. Consequently, elements deprecated in HTML 4 and XHTML 1.0 cannot be used in XHTML 1.1. The modules of XHTML 1.1 are the following [20]:

- Structure Module: body, head, html, title

- Text Module: abbr, acronym, address, blockquote, br, cite, code, dfn, div, em, h1, h2, h3, h4, h5, h6, kbd, p, pre, q, samp, span, strong, var

- Hypertext Module: a

- List Module: dl, dt, dd, ol, ul, li

- Object Module: object, param

- Presentation Module: b, big, hr, i, small, sub, sup, tt

- Edit Module: del, ins

- Bi-directional Text Module: bdo

- Forms Module: button, fieldset, form, input, label, legend, select, optgroup, option, textarea

- Table Module: caption, col, colgroup, table, tbody, td, tfoot, th, thead, tr

- Image Module: img

- Client-side Image Map Module: area, map

- Server-side Image Map Module: ismap attribute on img

- Intrinsic Events Module: event attributes

- Metainformation Module: meta

- Scripting Module: `noscript`, `script`

- Stylesheet Module: `style` element

- Style Attribute Module (deprecated): `style` attribute

- Link Module: `link`

- Base Module: `base`

The description of the previous modules, their elements and attributes, and their minimal content are defined by the "Modularization of XHTML" [19].

Listing 3-6 presents an XHTML 1.1 skeleton document.

Listing 3-6. *An XHTML 1.1 Skeleton Document*

```
<?xml version="1.0" encoding="utf-8"?>
<!DOCTYPE html PUBLIC "-//W3C//DTD XHTML 1.1//EN" ↩
 "http://www.w3.org/TR/xhtml11/DTD/xhtml11.dtd">
<html xmlns="http://www.w3.org/1999/xhtml" xml:lang="en">
  <head>
    <title>XHTML 1.1 sample document title</title>
    <meta http-equiv="Content-Type" content="application/xhtml+xml; charset=utf-8" />
  </head>
  <body>
    <p>
    XHTML 1.1 sample document body
    </p>
  </body>
</html>
```

XHTML 1.1 can also be used in mixed-namespace documents to support mathematical markup and vector graphics (see "XTHML+MathML+SVG").

XHTML 2.0

XHTML 2.0 (also denoted as XHTML2) could have been the next-generation markup language and the successor of XHTML 1.0 and 1.1. However, it remained on the Working Draft level and never became a Recommendation.

Although XHTML 2.0 has several elements from earlier versions of markup languages, it has issues with backward compatibility. In spite of that, coders familiar with XHTML 1.0 and 1.1 can easily develop XHTML 2.0 documents.

The "Modularization of XHTML" refers to XHTML 2.0 as not just another markup language but as an *XHTML host language* [19]. It consists of modules with elements and attributes. However, there are several updated modules in XHTML 2.0 compared to the "Modularization of XHTML."

After its suspension, several features (beyond the vital text and hyperlinking modules) that were originally intended to be enclosed in XHTML 2.0 are being developed by independent working groups within W3C. Such technologies are Access, RDFa, Role, XForms, or XML Events.

HTML5

HTML5 was initially proposed by individuals from Apple, Mozilla Foundation, and Opera Software, known as the *Web Hypertext Application Technology Working Group* (*WHATWG*) [21]. Later, W3C took notice of the WHATWG proposal and announced a restart of an HTML specification effort [22]. WHATWG found XHTML 2.0 too document-centric and thus inappropriate for blogs, forums, web stores, and multimedia sites. Their major concern was to create a platform for dynamic web applications [23].

In spite of the tricky name, *HTML5* is not just another HTML language. It is often used in the context of web applications. It is the complete reformulation of HTML with new capabilities. Still, HTML5 is designed to be backward-compatible with older browsers. Moreover, HTML5 uses an HTML syntax that is compatible with both HTML and XHTML documents. However, processing instructions are not supported. Beyond the well-known `text/html` media type, a new media type called `text/html-sandboxed` can also be used, which makes it possible to interpret a file without giving the content access to the rest of the web site. Because of a new approach that separates authoring and rendering conformance requirements, deprecated tags are not needed anymore.

During the upcoming years when earlier browser versions will still be present, HTML5 support can be critical. There are services such as the "HTML5 test" that checks HTML5 support in the browser they are opened [24]. As for the markup contributors, several tests are available on the W3C testing web page, where current tests can be reviewed, and new tests submitted [25].

HTML5 focuses strongly not only on structural and multimedia elements in the markup but also on application programming interfaces (APIs); thus, web developers with some programming knowledge can develop applications for their web sites. HTML5 applications are accessible and device-independent, and codes can be reused easily. Additionally, these web applications need declarative programming (and thus much less coding) compared to traditional procedural programming [26]. However, a large share of HTML5 functionalities can be achieved through the use of additional technologies, including CSS3, server-side scripts, JavaScript transformations, Java, or XSLT.

Listing 3-7 shows an HTML5 skeleton document.

Listing 3-7. *An HTML5 Skeleton Document*

```
<!DOCTYPE html>
<html>
  <head>
    <title>Sample HTML5 document</title>
    <meta charset="UTF-8" />
  </head>
  <body>
    <header>
      <h1>Document sample</h1>
    </header>
    <section>
      <article>
        <h2>Article1</h2>
          The first article of the document.
      </article>
      <article>
        <h2>Article2</h2>
          The second article of the document.
      </article>
    </section>
```

```
    <footer>
      Copyright © 2011 John Smith. All rights reserved.
    </footer>
  </body>
</html>
```

HTML5 also supports external vocabularies, such as Scalable Vector Graphics (SVG) and MathML, both of which can be embedded directly into the HTML5 markup. For example, an SVG image can be embedded between the <svg> and </svg> tags such as in Listing 3-8.

Listing 3-8. Directly Embedded SVG in HTML5

```
<svg xmlns="http://www.w3.org/2000/svg">
    <rect stroke="black" fill="blue" x="50px" y="50px" width="300px" height="150px" stroke-
    width="2">
</svg>
```

MathML equations can be embedded similarly. These elements can also be nested for more complex content [27].

■ **Caution** In contrast to the common misconception, HTML5 is not a standard yet! The different modules of the specification are in various stages of development, and you might see misleading labels such as "living standard," most of which refer to the corresponding module only. According to the W3C expectation, HTML5 will probably become a W3C Recommendation in 2014 [28].

XHTML5

In HTML5 developers have the freedom of choice of flavor since HTML5 can be written either in HTML or in XML syntax. In the latter case, the markup is called XHTML5. XHTML5 is the XML serialization of HTML5. The syntax is described by the HTML5 specification. However, one should not be confused since XHTML5 is an application of XML. In other words, HTML5 and XHTML5 have identical vocabulary but different parsing rules.

Documents using elements and attributes defined by the HTML5 specification might be written as valid XML documents. This markup is often referred as a *polyglot language*, which is the *overlap language* of documents that are HTML5 and XML documents at the same time. Markup of a web document can be considered polyglot markup if the document is a valid HTML document and a well-formed XML document and if it produces an identical DOM when processed as HTML and when parsed as XML[5] [29]. HTML5 and XHTML5 serializations are cross-compatible. However, XHTML5 has a stricter syntax. Furthermore, some parts of XHTML5 such as processing instructions are not valid in HTML5.

Listing 3-9 shows an XHTML5 skeleton document.

---

[5] Except for those xml, xmlns, and xlink attributes for which HTML and XML parsers generate different DOMs, e.g., xml:lang, xml:space, xml:base, xmlns="", xmlns:xlink="", and xlink:href.

Listing 3-9. An XHTML5 Skeleton Document

```
<?xml version="1.0" encoding="utf-8"?>
<!DOCTYPE html>
<html xmlns="http://www.w3.org/1999/xhtml">
  <head>
    <title>An XHTML5 example</title>
    <meta charset="UTF-8" />
  </head>
  <body>
    <header>
      <h1>Document sample</h1>
    </header>
    <section>
      <article>
        <h2>Article1</h2>
          The first article of the document.
      </article>
      <article>
        <h2>Article2</h2>
          The second article of the document.
      </article>
    </section>
    <footer>
      Copyright © 2011 John Smith. All rights reserved.
    </footer>
  </body>
</html>
```

Markup Syntaxes

Although similar, there are some considerable differences in the markup of HTML (until version 5) and XHTML. We'll examine the major ones here.

The HTML Syntax

The individual markup components are called *elements*. In HTML, keywords provided in angle brackets called *tags* delimit document fragments to which they are applied. Elements should have a starting tag and an ending tag in the form shown in Listing 3-10.

Listing 3-10. Pseudocode of Starting and Closing Tags

```
<element_name> element_content </element_name>
```

The *start tag* contains the name of the element, surrounded by angle brackets (in the form `<element>`). Element features such as appearance, behavior, or functioning are determined by the optional *attributes* specified on the start tag (Figure 3-1). They are separated by spaces.

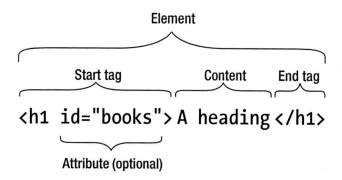

Figure 3-1. *HTML element structure*

To distinguish the *end tag* from the start tag, the end tag has a slash after the opening angle bracket (in the form `</element>`). For example, a simple HTML paragraph looks like Listing 3-11.

Listing 3-11. *A Simple Paragraph in HTML*

```
<p>A simple paragraph.</p>
```

The elements can provide the structure and meaning to web documents through the indication of coherent sections such as headings, paragraphs, lists, tables, image embeddings, forms, and so on.

The default style sheet of the browser used to render the document determines the default appearance. However, the default appearance can be arbitrarily overridden by external style sheets as will be discussed later when we look at Cascading Style Sheets (CSS).

Two special tags in HTML are different from all the others. Comments can be added by the `<!-- … -->` tag. The document type can be defined by the `<!DOCTYPE>` tag (see the "Document Type Declaration" section later in the chapter).

The XHTML Syntax and Restrictions

The element and attribute sets of the HTML and XHTML languages largely overlap, and most HTML elements can be used in the corresponding XHTML 1.0 flavor (HTML 4.01 Transitional elements in XHTML 1.0 Transitional, and HTML 4.01 Strict elements in XHTML 1.0 Strict). However, some elements introduced in the XHTML specifications can be applied in XHTML exclusively (compare the elements of the various markup language versions in Table 3-7). The major difference between earlier HTML and XHTML versions is that XHTML is stricter than HTML and it is extensible while HTML is not.[6] The difference between the HTML and XHTML vocabularies completely disappeared with the introduction of the latest markup versions, HTML5 and XHTML5, since HTML5 has exactly the same elements and attributes as XHTML5.

By understanding the difference between valid HTML and XHTML markup, you take the first major step toward web site standardization. In fact, these are vital points that can serve as the basis for not just valid XHTML markup but also accessibility and semantic notations. These rules are the keys for authoring web documents that are both backward- and forward-compatible at the same time.

---

[6] Up to version 4.01. From HTML5, external vocabularies, such as SVG and MathML, can be used in HTML, too, as you will see later.

Well-formedness

Well-formedness is a basic concept in XHTML. All elements must be closed. Nesting should be done in the proper order (Listing 3-12). Overlapping elements are incorrect in XHTML (Listing 3-13).

Listing 3-12. Properly Nested Elements

```
<p>Part of this <strong>bold text should be <em>italic as well</em></strong>.</p>
```

Listing 3-13. Overlapping Elements (Incorrect)

```
<p>Part of this <strong>bold text should be <em>italic as well</strong></em>.</p>
```

Names Are in Lowercase

Since XML is case-sensitive, all XHTML element and attribute names must be in lowercase.

Required End Tags

In HTML, the end tag of several elements can be omitted, which is not allowed in XHTML (Listings 3-14 and 3-15).

Listing 3-14. Properly Closed Elements

```
<p>This is the first paragraph.</p>
<p>This is the second one.</p>
```

Listing 3-15. Unterminated Elements Are Incorrect in XHTML

```
<p>This is the first paragraph. <p>This is the second one.
```

All elements that are declared in the DTD as *empty elements* (meta, link, br, hr, img, input) can be closed either by an end tag (similar to nonempty elements) or by the shorthand notation; in other words, a space and a slash character are inserted prior to the end of the declaration, as shown in Listing 3-16

Listing 3-16. Pseudocode of Element Closing with Shorthand Notation (Self-closing)

```
<element_name attrib1="value1" … attribn="valuen" />
```

which provides shorter code. Although the space is optional, it should be preferred because the result is easier to read (Listing 3-17). Tags without a closing tag are also known as *self-closing tags*.

Listing 3-17. Terminated Empty Element

```
<br />
```

In XHTML, all unterminated elements are incorrect, including unterminated empty elements (Listing 3-18).

Listing 3-18. Unterminated Empty Elements Are Incorrect in XHTML

```
<br> unterminated elements are incorrect in XHTML <hr>
```

The script element applies either to the full form (with the end tag) or to the shorthand notation, depending on the number of parameters and the behavior of the element.

Quoted Attribute Values

All attributes must include values in XHTML. All attribute values must be quoted (Listing 3-19). Unquoted attribute values are not allowed in XHTML (Listing 3-20).

Listing 3-19. Defining XHTML Attributes Correctly

```
<input type="checkbox" name="checkbox" id="checkbox" value="True" checked="checked" />
```

Listing 3-20. Unquoted and Minimized Attributes (Incorrect in XHTML)

```
<input type=checkbox name=checkbox id=checkbox value=True checked />
```

No Attribute Minimization

Attribute-value pairs must be written in full (Listing 3-21). Attribute minimization is not supported by XHTML (Listing 3-22). Attribute names such as compact and checked cannot be used in elements without specifying their values (Table 3-3).

Listing 3-21. Attributes Should Be Written in Full

```
<option value="eng" selected="selected">English</option>
```

Listing 3-22. Minimized Attribute (Incorrect in XHTML)

```
<option value="eng" selected>English</option>
```

Table 3-3. Attributes That Can Be Minimized in HTML, but Not in XHTML.

Minimized Attribute (HTML)	Full Form (HTML/XHTML)
compact	compact="compact"
checked	checked="checked"
declare	declare="declare"
readonly	readonly="readonly"
disabled	disabled="disabled"

Minimized Attribute (HTML)	Full Form (HTML/XHTML)
selected	selected="selected"
defer	defer="defer"
ismap	ismap="ismap"
nohref	nohref="nohref"
noshade	noshade="noshade"
nowrap	nowrap="nowrap"
multiple	multiple="multiple"
noresize	noresize="noresize"

Whitespace Handling

Leading and trailing whitespace characters are stripped in XHTML.

In contrast to HTML, whitespace characters in XHTML attribute values are normalized to single spaces. According to the XML specification, a single interword space (#x20) is appended to whitespace character sequences (#x20, #xD, #xA, #x9) [30].

Using Script and Style Elements

While the content type of the script and style HTML elements is character DATA (CDATA), it is processed character DATA (#PCDATA) in XHTML. The script and style elements are defined with #PCDATA content; in other words, < is handled as the beginning of markup code, while < is recognized as an entity (Listing 3-23).

Listing 3-23. Unescaped Script Content

```
<script type="text/javascript">
  <![CDATA[
  unescaped script content
  ]]>
</script>
```

XML processors recognize these CDATA sections. They are represented as nodes in the Document Object Model.

Alternatively, external script files/styles sheet files can be used, eliminating the need for unescaped script or style contents.

Identifiers

Instead of the name attribute defined in HTML 4, the id attribute should be used in XHTML for identifiers.

XHTML documents must use the id attribute when defining fragment identifiers on the elements a, applet, form, frame, iframe, img, and map. This ensures the well-structuredness required by XML.

Element Prohibitions

In XHTML, elements cannot be nested arbitrarily. Those who are not familiar with XHTML often commit nesting errors. The nesting rules should not be confused with overlapping, which is strictly forbidden in XHTML. The nesting rules of XHTML 1.0 are similar to those of HTML 4.01. However, there are some differences. The table element can contain a tr element directly in XHTML, which is not allowed in HTML. In such cases, a tbody element is implied in HTML but not in XHTML. This behavior is important in some cases, such as if tbody is used as a selector in the CSS of the web page. Table 3-4 summarizes those parent-child element relationships that are not allowed in XHTML.

Table 3-4. XHTML Elements with Prohibitions

Element	Prohibition(s)
a	Cannot contain other a elements
pre	Cannot contain img, object, big, small, sub, or sup elements
button	Cannot contain input, select, textarea, label, button, form, fieldset, iframe, or isindex elements
label	Cannot contain other label elements
form	Cannot contain other form elements

Additionally, some nesting restrictions are defined by descriptions in the XHTML specifications. As a result, some nesting violations are not recognized by validators when applying XHTML document types, while errors can be clearly identified when using HTML.

Unlike in HTML, texts cannot be provided directly in the XHTML body without wrapping them in container elements (such as p). Such attempts usually lead to the error message "character data is not allowed here" in the W3C Markup Validator (Chapter 14).

Invalid Characters

Older HTML documents, especially the ones that were written in the first decade of the Web, are often full of character entities. This holds true not only for those documents that used to represent non-Latin characters but also for the ones containing special characters such as the copyright sign (©) or the registered trademark sign (®). These entities should be eliminated in XHTML (except in the case of a few special characters, as discussed earlier). Using characters directly with UTF-8 encoding is strongly recommended.

Dashes in Comments Are Limited

Double dashes can be provided only at the beginning and end of XHTML comments (Listing 3-24).

Listing 3-24. A Comment in XHTML

```
<!-- Comment -->
```

Avoid Using Deprecated Elements

Although a large set of HTML elements can also be used in certain XHTML versions and variants (as discussed earlier), the blackface, blockquote, embed, layer, noembed, and shadow deprecated elements cannot. All of them can be replaced by style sheets except embed and noembed whose contents can be provided with object. Moreover, there are elements that are allowed in XHTML 1.0 Transitional and XHTML 1.0 Frameset but cannot be used in XHTML 1.0 Strict (Table 3-5).

Table 3-5. Elements Not Allowed in XHTML 1.0 Strict Must Be Avoided

Element	Deprecated in Favor of
applet	object
basefont	Style sheets
center	Style sheets
dir	ul
font	Style sheets
isindex	input element, CGI forms
menu	ul, nl
s	Style sheets
u	Style sheets

Although menu elements are replaced by ul elements in XHTML 1.0 Strict and XHTML 1.1 (or nl in XHTML2), they can be used again in XHTML5.

The most arguable elements are i and b that are not deprecated and can be used in every XHTML version to create italic and bold texts, respectively. However, they are purely presentational elements without structural meaning. Although most user agents render the appropriate structural elements (em and strong) similarly if not identically to the basic character formatting elements i and b, em and strong are preferred.

Applying the strictest set of XHTML elements supported by most or all XHTML versions and variants is a good practice. Certainly, new elements introduced in newer versions such as XHTML5 can also be used, but only if the browser support becomes adequate and proved.

As a general rule, XHTML 1.0 Strict hand coders can easily learn and apply other XHTML document types too, simply because they eliminate obsolete elements.

Avoid Deprecated Attributes

Several HTML attributes have been deprecated in XHTML in favor of other attributes or style sheets (Table 3-6).

Table 3-6. Attributes Deprecated in XHTML

Attribute	Deprecated in Favor of
alink	Style sheets
align	Style sheets
background	Style sheets
border	Style sheets
color	Style sheets
compact	Style sheets
face	Style sheets
height	Style sheets
language	type attribute
link	Style sheets
name	id attribute
noshade	Style sheets
nowrap	Style sheets
size	Style sheets
start	Style sheets

Attribute	Deprecated in Favor of
`text`	Style sheets
`type`	Style sheets
`value`	Style sheets
`version`	DTDs
`vlink`	Style sheets
`width`[7]	Style sheets

Data Types

The data types that can be used in element contents and attribute values are defined by DTDs and specifications of the markup language being used. While many elements and attributes allow most Unicode characters (such as the `p`, `div`, and `section` elements), there are elements and attributes that have specific restrictions. Evidently, a link in the `href` attribute of an `a` element must contain a valid URL or file path (Listing 3-25). Knowing the allowed values is important to provide valid attribute values. For example, the `width` attribute of an `img` element should be a value expressed by a number, with or without the unit `px` or `%`, and cannot be in any unit (Listing 3-26).

Listing 3-25. *Correct and Incorrect URLs in the `href` Attribute Value*

```
<a href="http://www.example.com/about/"> <!-- correct -->
<a href="contact.htm"> <!-- correct -->
<a href="a;b.html"> <!-- incorrect (contains an illegal character) -->
```

Listing 3-26. *Correct and Incorrect Width Attribute Values*

```
<img src="images/logo.png" width="128" height="128" alt="logo" /> <!-- correct -->
<img src="images/logo.png" width="100px" height="100px" alt="logo" /> <!-- correct -->
<img src="images/logo.png" width="78pt" height="64pt" alt="logo" /> <!-- incorrect (not
allowed unit) -->
```

Characters might be illegal in certain data types because of many reasons, such as if they are reserved or unsafe.

HTML elements and attributes can contain a variety of data types, such as case information, SGML basic data types, text strings, URIs, colors, lengths, content types, language codes, character encodings, single characters, dates and times, link types, media descriptors, script data, and style sheet data [31].

The syntax of the core markup element content values and attribute values are derived from SGML tokens such as the following:

- *PCDATA*: Parsed Character Data. Mixed content; in other words, an element can contain any number of character data and/or child elements in arbitrary order.

---

[7] It is deprecated on certain elements only (e.g., cannot be used on `td`, but allowed on `img`).

- *CDATA*: Character data. A sequence of characters from the document character set and may include character entities. CDATA attribute values should not contain leading or trailing whitespace characters. User agents replace character entities with characters, replace carriage returns and tabs with a single space, and ignore line feeds when interpreting CDATA attribute values. For script and style elements, CDATA sections are treated as raw text and passed forward as is. The end tag open delimiter </ is considered as the terminator of the element content.

- *NAME, ID*: Identifier tokens that must begin with a letter (A–Z, a–z) and may be followed by any number of letters, digits (0–9), hyphens (-), underscores (_), colons (:), and periods (.)

- *NUMBER*: Tokens containing a minimum of one digit (0–9).

They have been introduced in the ISO 8879 standard [32], and they determine the allowed values of the data types to be used in markup attributes such as URLs, text, numbers, and so on.

The PCDATA and CDATA data types are used mainly in XML applications and serialization, including XHTML, RSS, Atom, and so on (Chapter 7). SGML and XML Document Type Definition files also use PCDATA and CDATA for markup declarations.

▨ **Caution** In HTML, <![CDATA[...]]> is a *bogus comment*; that is, the sequence of characters]]> is considered as regular character data. In XHTML, <![CDATA[...]]> is a CDATA section; in other words, the sequence of characters]]> should be the mark for the end of the CDATA section. Otherwise, it will result in a well-formedness error.

Naturally, there are many more data types in modern markup languages. The fundamental data types of HTML5 are the following:

- *Text*: A sequence of Unicode characters that does not contain U+0000 characters, control characters other than space characters, or any permanently undefined Unicode characters.

- *String*: An arbitrary mixture of text and character references.

- *Token*: A string without space characters.

- *Browsing-context name*: A string that does not start with an underline (_) character and is at least one character long.

- *Browsing-context name or keyword*: A string that is either a browsing-context name or one of the following literal strings: _blank, _self, _parent, or _top.

- *ID*: A string without space characters that is at least one character long.

- *Name*: A string without space characters that is at least one character long.

- *Hash-name reference*: A string that starts with a # character.

- *Number*: Integer, positive integer, non-negative integer, floating-point number, positive floating-point number, or non-negative floating-point number.

- *Date and time*: A date-time as defined in RFC 3339, with the additional constraints that the literal letters *T* and *Z* must always be uppercase and that the date + full year is described as four or more digits representing a number greater than 0.

- *URL*: A valid IRI reference as defined in RFC 3987.

- *MIME type*: A string identifying a valid MIME media type defined by RFC 2046.

- *Character encoding name*: A character encoding a name or alias from the IANA registry.

- *Meta-charset string*: A string with the following parts (in that order): the literal string `text/html;`, one or more optional space characters, the literal string `charset=`, and a character encoding name (HTML5) or the string `UTF-8` (XHTML5).

- *Refresh value*: Either a non-negative integer or a string containing a non-negative integer, a `;` character, one or more space characters, the string `url=`, and finally a URL (in that order).

- *Default-style name*: A string.

- *Media-query list*: A media query list as defined in the W3C specification "Media Queries" [33].

- *Language tag*: A language tag as defined in BCP 47 [34].

- *List of key labels*: An ordered set of unique space-separated tokens, each of which is exactly one Unicode codepoint in length.

- *Dropzone value*: An unordered set of unique space-separated tokens, each of which is one of the values `copy`, `move`, or `link`, or any string with a minimum of three characters, beginning with the literal string `s:` (Plain Unicode string) or `f:` (File items). The default value is `copy`.

- *Functionbody*: Any JavaScript code that is a FunctionBody production according to ECMA 262.

- *Coordinates*: Rectangle coordinates (four integers), circle coordinates (two integers and a non-negative integer number), or polygon coordinates (minimum six integers).

- *Sandbox allow keywords list*: An unordered set of unique space-separated tokens that can be the literal string `allow-forms`, `allow-scripts`, `allow-top-navigation`, or `allow-same-origin`.

- *Pattern*: A regular expression that is a JavaScript pattern production according to ECMA 262.

- *E-mail address*: Any string that matches the ABNF production `1*( atext / "." ) "@" ldh-str 1*( "." ldh-str )`, where `atext` is as defined in RFC 5322, and `ldh-str` is as defined in RFC 1034.

- *Color.* A string exactly seven characters long, starting with a # character, followed by six characters in the range 0–9, a–f, and A–F.

Markup Elements

The various versions and variants of HTML provide a different set of elements; in other words, they have different vocabularies, although there is a large degree of overlapping (Table 3-7, historic versions not included).

Fundamental markup elements have been introduced in the early versions of HTML, and later versions gradually extended the set of elements. Some elements become *obsolete* over time and are *deprecated,*[8] removed, or replaced. Additionally, new specifications often introduce new elements. There are 70 elements listed in the HTML 3.2 specification [35], 91 in HTML 4.01 [36], and more than 100 in HTML5 [37].

There is a large similarity between the elements of the Transitional, Frameset, and Strict flavors of HTML and that of their XHTML counterparts. XHTML 1.0 Frameset is the XML equivalent of HTML 4.01 Frameset, the document type that provides the definition of frameset documents, which was a common web feature of the late 1990s. XHTML 1.0 Transitional is the XML equivalent of HTML 4.01 Transitional, the document type that includes the presentational elements, such as center and font, that are excluded from the Strict variant. XHTML 1.0 Strict is the XML equivalent of HTML 4.01 Strict, which includes strictly those elements that have not been deprecated.

The various XHTML versions and variants provide a different set of elements. There are 89 elements in XHTML 1.0 Transitional, 92 in XHTML 1.0 Frameset, 78 in XHTML 1.0 Strict, 83 in XHTML 1.1, 99 in XHTML 2.0, and more than 100 in XHTML5 (the same as in HTML5) [38]. The applet, basefont, center, dir, font, isindex, menu, s, strike, and u elements have been deprecated in XHTML 1.0. Consequently, they can be used in XHTML 1.0 Transitional or XHTML 1.0 Frameset but not in XHTML 1.0 Strict or above.[9] This important fact has not been understood by many developers who applied the Transitional variant of HTML4 or XHTML 1.0 for more than a decade. A Transitional variant, even if it is written free of errors, is allowed to contain obsolete elements that have been deprecated in the specification with the intention to indicate that these elements will be removed from future markup versions and thus should not be used. In other words, millions of web sites have used a markup until recently that allowed elements already obsoleted in HTML 4.01!

XHTML 1.0 Strict and XHTML 1.1 have a very similar set of elements. The most important differences are that XHTML 1.1 introduced the *Ruby elements* and removed the access element. Prior to XHTML 1.1, the lang attribute was used (instead of xml:lang, which is preferred today). The name attribute for anchors and client-side maps was used until XHTML 1.0, which should be replaced by the id attribute from XHTML 1.1. The essence of XHTML 1.1 is that elements are collected to *modules,* making it possible to apply subsets of the full element set in environments with limited resources (for example, mobile devices), known as *XHTML modularization* (as mentioned earlier in the chapter).

XHTML 2.0 has several elements that are not found in any other markup language, namely, action, delete, di, dispatch, ev:listener, group, h, handler, insert, l, load, message, model, nl, output, range, rebuild, recalculate, refresh, repeat, reset, revalidate, secret, section, select1, send, bseparator, setfocus, setindex, setvalue, standby, submit, summary, switch, trigger, and upload. These elements have been introduced in XHTML 2.0 but discontinued in (X)HTML5. A few XHTML 2.0 elements have been defined in XHTML 1.1, some of which have been included in (X)HTML5, such as ruby, while others have been excluded, such as rtc. The fundamental elements have been derived from earlier versions.

---

[8] Prior to HTML5
[9] The only exception is menu that has become allowed again in HTML5 although with a new meaning.

The latest version of XHTML, XHTML5, has the same set of elements as HTML5, as mentioned earlier. The most significant extension of markup elements and attributes in the past decade have been realized in (X)HTML5, especially because of the new structuring and multimedia elements that cannot be used in any earlier versions.

Table 3-7. Overview of Markup Elements

Element	HTML 4.01			XHTML					(X)HTML	Meaning
	T	F	S	1.0 T	1.0 F	1.0 S	1.1	2.0	5	
a	+	+	+	+	+	+	+ + +			Hyperlink anchor
abbr	+	+	+	+	+	+	+ + +			Abbreviation
access	–	–	–	–	–	+	+	– +		Accessibility mapping
acronym	+	+	+	+	+	+	+	–	–	Acronym
action	–	–	–	–	–	–	–	+	–	Action
address	+	+	+	+	+	+	+ + +			Author information
applet	+	–	–	+	+	–	– – –			Java applet
area	+	+	+	+	+	+	+	–	+	Client-side image map
article	–	–	–	–	–	–	– –		+	Logically separate section
aside	–	–	–	–	–	–	– –		+	Additional content section
audio	–	–	–	–	–	–	– –		+	Audio stream
b	+	+	+	+	+	+	+	–	+	Bold text style
base	+	+	+	+	+	+	+	–	+	Document base URI
basefont	+	–	–	+	+	–	– – –			Base font size
bdo	+	+	+	+	+	+	+	–	+	Writing direction
big	+	+	+	+	+	+	+	–	–	Large text style
blockcode	–	–	–	–	–	–	– –		+	Code block

Element	HTML 4.01			XHTML					(X)HTML	Meaning
	T	F	S	1.0 T	1.0 F	1.0 S	1.1	2.0	5	
blockquote	+	+	+	+	+	+	+ + +			Long quotation
body	+	+	+	+	+	+	+ + +			Document body
br	+	+	+	+	+	+	+ + +			Line break ("break row")
button	+	+	+	+	+	+	+	–	+	Push button
canvas	–	–	–	–	–	–	– –		+	Bitmap canvas
caption	+	+	+	+	+	+	+ + +			(Table/figure) caption
center	+	–	–	+	+	–	– – –			Content alignment to center
cite	+	+	+	+	+	+	+ + +			Citation
code	+	+	+	+	+	+	+ + +			Code fragment
col	+	+	+	+	+	+	+ + +			Table column
colgroup	+	+	+	+	+	+	+ + +			Table column group
command	–	–	–	–	–	–	– –		+	User command
datalist	–	–	–	–	–	–	– –		+	Data list
dd	+	+	+	+	+	+	+ + +			Definition description
del	+	+	+	+	+	+	+	–	+	Deleted text
delete	–	–	–	–	–	–	–	+	–	Delete
details	–	–	–	–	–	–	– –		+	Detailed information
dfn	+	+	+	+	+	+	+ + +			Definition
di	–	–	–	–	–	–	–	+	–	Definition item
dir	+	–	–	+	+	–	– – –			Directory list

Element	HTML 4.01			XHTML				(X)HTML		Meaning
	T	F	S	1.0 T	1.0 F	1.0 S	1.1	2.0	5	
dispatch	–	–	–	–	–	–	–	+	–	Dispatch
div	+	+	+	+	+	+	+ + +			Generic (block) container ("division")
dl	+	+	+	+	+	+	+ + +			Definition list
dt	+	+	+	+	+	+	+ + +			Definition term
em	+	+	+	+	+	+	+ + +			Emphasized text style
embed	–	–	–	–	–	–	– –		+	Embedded content
ev:listener	–	–	–	–	–	–	–	+	–	Event listener
fieldset	+	+	+	+	+	+	+	–	+	Form control group
figcaption	–	–	–	–	–	–	– –		+	Legend
figure	–	–	–	–	–	–	– –		+	Paragraph with embedded content and caption
font	+	–	–	+	+	–	– – –			Font properties (local)
footer	–	–	–	–	–	–	– –		+	(Document or section) footer
form	+	+	+	+	+	+	+	–	+	Interactive form
frame	–	+	–	–	+	–	– – –			Subwindow (frame)
frameset	–	+	–	–	+	–	– – –			Window subdivision
group	–	–	–	–	–	–	–	+	–	Element group
h	–	–	–	–	–	–	–	+	–	Heading
h1	+	+	+	+	+	+	+ + +			Level 1 heading
h2	+	+	+	+	+	+	+ + +			Level 2 heading

Element	HTML 4.01				XHTML				(X)HTML	Meaning
	T	F	S	1.0 T	1.0 F	1.0 S	1.1	2.0	5	
h3	+	+	+	+	+	+	+ + +			Level 3 heading
h4	+	+	+	+	+	+	+ + +			Level 4 heading
h5	+	+	+	+	+	+	+ + +			Level 5 heading
h6	+	+	+	+	+	+	+ + +			Level 6 heading
handler	–	–	–	–	–	–	–	+	–	Handler definition
head	+	+	+	+	+	+	+ + +			Document head
header	–	–	–	–	–	–	– –		+	Section header
hgroup	–	–	–	–	–	–	– –		+	Section heading
hr	+	+	+	+	+	+	+	–	+	Horizontal rule
html	+	+	+	+	+	+	+ + +			Document root
i	+	+	+	+	+	+	+	–	+	Italic text style
iframe	+	–	–	+	+	–	– –		+	Inline frame
img	+	+	+	+	+	+	+ + +			Embedded image
input	+	+	+	+	+	+	+ + +			Form input
ins	+	+	+	+	+	+	+	–	+	Inserted text
insert	–	–	–	–	–	–	–	+	–	Insert
isindex	+	–	–	+	+	–	– – –			Keyword index that can be searched by entering keywords
kbd	+	+	+	+	+	+	+ + +			Text to be entered by the user ("keyboard")
keygen	–	–	–	–	–	–	– –		+	Key generator
l	–	–	–	–	–	–	–	+	–	Line of text

Element	HTML 4.01			XHTML					(X)HTML	Meaning
	T	F	S	1.0 T	1.0 F	1.0 S	1.1	2.0	5	
label	+	+	+	+	+	+	+	+	+	Form field label
legend	+	+	+	+	+	+	+	−	+	Fieldset legend
li	+	+	+	+	+	+	+	+	+	List item
link	+	+	+	+	+	+	+	+	+	Media-independent link
load	−	−	−	−	−	−	−	+	−	Load
map	+	+	+	+	+	+	+	−	+	Client-side image map
mark	−	−	−	−	−	−	−	−	+	Marked text
menu	+	−	−	+	+	−	−	−	+	Menu list
message	−	−	−	−	−	−	−	+	−	Message
meta	+	+	+	+	+	+	+	+	+	Generic metadata
meter	−	−	−	−	−	−	−	−	+	Scalar measurement
model	−	−	−	−	−	−	−	+	−	Model
nav	−	−	−	−	−	−	−	−	+	Navigation links section
nl	−	−	−	−	−	−	−	+	−	Navigation list
noframes	−	+	−	+	+	−	−	−	−	Alternate content for frames
noscript	+	+	+	+	+	+	+	−	+	Alternate content for scripts
object	+	+	+	+	+	+	+	+	+	Generic embedded object (Flash, applet, inline frame)
ol	+	+	+	+	+	+	+	+	+	Ordered list

Element	HTML 4.01			XHTML					(X)HTML	Meaning
	T	F	S	1.0 T	1.0 F	1.0 S	1.1	2.0	5	
optgroup	+	+	+	+	+	+	+	−	+	Option group
option	+	+	+	+	+	+	+	−	+	Select box item
output	−	−	−	−	−	−	−	+	+	Output
p	+	+	+	+	+	+	+ + +			Paragraph
param	+	+	+	+	+	+	+ + +			Named property value ("parameter")
plaintext	−	−	−	−	−	−	− − −			Plain (nonformatted) text
pre	+	+	+	+	+	+	+ + +			Preformatted text
progress	−	−	−	−	−	−	− −		+	Task progress
q	+	+	+	+	+	+	+ + +			Short (inline) quotation
range	−	−	−	−	−	−	−	+	−	Range definition
rb	−	−	−	−	−	−	+	+	−	Ruby base
rbc	−	−	−	−	−	−	+	+	−	Ruby base container
rebuild	−	−	−	−	−	−	−	+	−	Rebuild
recalculate	−	−	−	−	−	−	−	+	−	Recalculate
refresh	−	−	−	−	−	−	−	+	−	Refresh
repeat	−	−	−	−	−	−	−	+	−	Repeat
reset	−	−	−	−	−	−	−	+	−	Reset
revalidate	−	−	−	−	−	−	−	+	−	Revalidate
rp	−	−	−	−	−	−	+	+	+	Ruby parentheses
rt	−	−	−	−	−	−	+	+	+	Ruby text

Element	HTML 4.01			XHTML				(X)HTML		Meaning
	T	F	S	1.0 T	1.0 F	1.0 S	1.1	2.0	5	
rtc	–	–	–	–	–	–	+	+	–	Ruby text container
ruby	–	–	–	–	–	–	+	+	+	Ruby markup
s	+	–	–	+	+	–	– – –			Strike-through text style
samp	+	+	+	+	+	+	+ + +			Sample output
script	+	+	+	+	+	+	+	–	+	Script statements
secret	–	–	–	–	–	–	–	+	–	Secret input
section	–	–	–	–	–	–	–	+	+	Document section
select	+	+	+	+	+	+	+ + +			Option selector
select1	–	–	–	–	–	–	–	+	–	Single select
send	–	–	–	–	–	–	–	+	–	Send
separator	–	–	–	–	–	–	–	+	–	Separator
setfocus	–	–	–	–	–	–	–	+	–	Set focus
setindex	–	–	–	–	–	–	–	+	–	Set index
setvalue	–	–	–	–	–	–	–	+	–	Set value
small	+	+	+	+	+	+	+	–	+	Small text style HTML5: small print
source	–	–	–	–	–	–	– –		+	Media resource
span	+	+	+	+	+	+	+ + +			Generic (inline) container
standby	–	–	–	–	–	–	–	+	–	Message (while loading)
strike	+	–	–	+	+	–	– – –			Strike-through text

Element	HTML 4.01			XHTML					(X)HTML	Meaning
	T	F	S	1.0 T	1.0 F	1.0 S	1.1	2.0	5	
strong	+	+	+	+	+	+	+ + +			Strong emphasis, importance
style	+	+	+	+	+	+	+ + +			Style information
sub	+	+	+	+	+	+	+ + +			Subscript
submit	–	–	–	–	–	–	–	+	–	Submit
summary	–	–	–	–	–	–	–	+	+	Table summary
sup	+	+	+	+	+	+	+ + +			Superscript
switch	–	–	–	–	–	–	–	+	–	Selection
table	+	+	+	+	+	+	+ + +			Table
tbody	+	+	+	+	+	+	+ + +			Table body
td	+	+	+	+	+	+	+ + +			Table data cell
textarea	+	+	+	+	+	+	+ + +			Multiline text field
tfoot	+	+	+	+	+	+	+ + +			Table footer
th	+	+	+	+	+	+	+ + +			Table header cell
thead	+	+	+	+	+	+	+ + +			Table header
time	–	–	–	–	–	–	– –		+	Date and/or time
title	+	+	+	+	+	+	+ + +			Document title
tr	+	+	+	+	+	+	+ + +			Table row
track	–	–	–	–	–	–	– –		+	Timed track
trigger	–	–	–	–	–	–	–	+	–	Trigger
tt	+	+	+	+	+	+	+	–	–	Teletype (monospace) text style

Element	HTML 4.01			XHTML				(X)HTML	5	Meaning
	T	F	S	1.0 T	1.0 F	1.0 S	1.1	2.0	5	
u	+	–	–	+	+	–	– – –			Underlined text style
ul	+	+	+	+	+	+	+ + +			Unordered list
upload	–	–	–	–	–	–	–	+	–	File upload
var	+	+	+	+	+	+	+ + +			Variable
video	–	–	–	–	–	–	– –		+	Video
wbr	–	–	–	–	–	–	– –		+	Conditional line break
xmp	–	–	–	–	–	–	– – –			Preformatted text

Block vs. Inline Elements

To provide full control over different document sections, HTML elements are on different levels. Similar to the character, paragraph, and document formatting levels used in word processors, HTML provides tags with different scopes. Certain elements, known as *inline elements*, can be applied both on individual characters and on strings, such as font features, italic or bold texts, subscripts, and superscripts.[10] They are usually placed in paragraphs (p) or divisions (div) that contain text and/or inline elements. These containers are the block elements that form the basic structure of web documents. These elements can also be the containers of other block elements. Block-level elements have their own block margins, width, and height properties that can be set independently from other parts of the document (see Chapter 5). Block-level elements are usually rendered on a new line. In contrast, inline elements are treated as parts of the text flow and cannot have margins, cannot have width or height properties, and do break across lines.

In Listing 3-27, the paragraph below the heading begins in a new line, because both h1 and p are block-level elements. The emphasized text in the paragraph (between <em> and </em>) is rendered continuously and does not begin in a new line, because em is an inline element. While the div might have margins (set from CSS), the em cannot.

Listing 3-27. Block vs. Inline Elements

```
<div>
  <h1>Attention</h1>
  <p>View our <em>special offers</em> now!</p>
</div>
```

Most HTML elements that can be used within the document body are classified as either block-level elements or inline elements. There are some elements that can be used in both contexts (such as buttons, objects, and scripts).

---

[10] Obsolete HTML elements used exclusively for character formatting should be substituted by CSS. (These styling elements have been removed from the Strict variants, and later from all other versions.)

Block-Level Elements

The following elements are handled as block-level elements in HTML5: article, aside, blockcode, blockquote, body, button, canvas, caption, col, colgroup, dd, div, dl, dt, embed, fieldset, figcaption, figure, footer, form, h1, h2, h3, h4, h5, h6, header, hgroup, hr, li, map, object, ol, output, p, pre, progress, section, table, tbody, textarea, td, tfoot, th, thead, tr, ul, and video.

Inline Elements

Generally, inline elements can contain text or other inline elements only. They are usually rendered within the current line. The inline elements of HTML5 are a, abbr, address, area, b, cite, code, del, details, dfn, command, datalist, em, font, i, iframe, img, input, ins, kbd, label, legend, link, mark, meter, nav, optgroup, option, q, samp, small, select, source, span, strong, sub, summary, sup, textarea, tt, u, time, and var.

Elements That Can Be Either Block or Inline Elements

Elements such as button, del, iframe, ins, map, object, and script can be used as either block-level elements or inline elements. If used as inline elements (e.g., within another inline element or a paragraph), these elements should not contain any block-level elements.

Attributes

The HTML5 element attributes are summarized in Table 3-8 [39].

Table 3-8. HTML5 Attributes

Attribute	Element(s)	Description	Value
accept	input	Hint for expected file type in file upload controls	Set of comma-separated tokens
accept-charset	form	Character encodings (form submission)	Ordered set of unique space-separated tokens (ASCII case-insensitive)
accesskey	HTML elements	Keyboard shortcut to activate or focus element	Ordered set of unique space-separated tokens (case-sensitive; one Unicode codepoint)
action	form	URL (form submission)	URL
alt	area, img, input	Alternate text for images or input fields	Text

Attribute	Element(s)	Description	Value
async	script	Execute script asynchronously	Boolean attribute
autocomplete	form, input	Prevent autocompletion for form control(s)	on | off
autofocus	button, input, keygen, select, textarea	Gives focus to form control automatically when the page is loaded	Boolean attribute
autoplay	audio, video	Media playback starts automatically	Boolean attribute
challenge	keygen	String to package with the generated and signed public key	Text
charset	meta	Character encoding declaration	Preferred MIME name of an encoding
charset	script	Character encoding of external script file	Preferred MIME name of an encoding
checked	command, input	Determines whether the command or control is checked	Boolean attribute
cite	blockquote, del, ins, q	Link to quotation source or additional information	URL
class	HTML elements	Element class	Set of space-separated tokens
cols	textarea	Maximum number of characters per line	Non-negative integer greater than zero
colspan	td, th	Number of columns that the cell is to span	Non-negative integer greater than zero
content	meta	Meta content	Text
contenteditable	HTML elements	Determines whether the element is editable	true | false

Attribute	Element(s)	Description	Value
contextmenu	HTML elements	Context menu of the element	ID
controls	audio, video	Playback controls	Boolean attribute
coords	area	Shape coordinates (image map)	List of integers
data	object	Resource URL	URL
datetime	del, ins	Date and (optionally) time of modification	Date string with optional time
datetime	time	Time value	Date or time string
default	track	Enable the track if there is no more suitable track	Boolean attribute
defer	script	Defers script execution	Boolean attribute
dir	HTML elements	Text directionality	ltr | rtl
dirname	input, textarea	Form field name to send directionality (form submission)	Text
disabled	button, command, fieldset, input, keygen, optgroup, option, select, textarea	Determines whether the form control is disabled	Boolean attribute
draggable	HTML elements	Determines whether the element is draggable	true | false
dropzone	HTML elements	Accepted item types for Drag & Drop	Unordered set of unique space-separated tokens (ASCII case-insensitive)
enctype	form	Encoding type (form submission)	application/x-www-form-urlencoded | multipart/form-data | text/plain

Attribute	Element(s)	Description	Value
for	label	Associates the label with a form control	ID
for	output	Specifies controls from which the output was calculated	Unordered set of unique space-separated tokens (case-sensitive)
form	button, fieldset, input, keygen, label, meter, object, output, progress, select, textarea	Associates the control with a form element	ID
formaction	button, input	URL to use for form submission	URL
formenctype	button, input	Encoding type to use for form submission	application/x-www-form-urlencoded | multipart/form-data | text/plain
formmethod	button, input	HTTP method to use for form submission	GET | POST
formnovalidate	button, input	Bypass form control validation for form submission	Boolean attribute
formtarget	button, input	Browsing context for form submission	Browsing context name or keyword
headers	td, th	Header cells for the cell	Unordered set of unique space-separated tokens (case-sensitive)
height	canvas, embed, iframe, img, input, object, video	Vertical dimension	Non-negative integer
hidden	HTML elements	Hides element	Boolean attribute
high	meter	Low limit of high range	Floating-point number
href	a, area, link	Hyperlink URL	URL

Attribute	Element(s)	Description	Value
href	base	Document base URL	URL
hreflang	a, area, link	Language of the linked resource	BCP 47 language tag
http-equiv	meta	Pragma directive	Text
icon	command	Command icon	URL
id	HTML elements	Element identifier	Text
ismap	img	Determines whether the image is a server-side image map	Boolean attribute
keytype	keygen	The type of cryptographic key to generate	Text
kind	track	The type of text track	subtitles | captions | descriptions | chapters | metadata
label	command, menu, optgroup, option, track	Label	Text
lang	HTML elements	Element language	BCP 47 language tag or empty string
list	input	List of autocomplete options	ID
loop	audio, video	Determines whether to loop the media	Boolean attribute
low	meter	High limit of low range	Floating point number
manifest	html	Application cache manifest	URL
max	input	Maximum value	Varies
max	meter, progress	Upper bound of range	Floating-point number
maxlength	input, textarea	Maximum length of value	Non-negative integer

Attribute	Element(s)	Description	Value
media	a, area, link, source, style	Applicable media	Media query
method	form	HTTP method to use for form submission	GET ∣ POST
min	input	Minimum value	*Varies*
min	meter	Lower bound of range	Floating-point number
multiple	input, select	Whether to allow multiple values	Boolean attribute
name	button, fieldset, input, keygen, output, select, textarea	Name of form control (form submission or form.elements API)	Text
name	form	Form name (document.forms API)	Text
name	iframe, object	Name of nested browsing context	Browsing context name or keyword
name	map	Image map name to reference from the usemap attribute	Text
name	meta	Metadata name	Text
name	param	Parameter name	Text
novalidate	form	Bypasses form control validation for form submission	Boolean attribute
open	details	Determines whether the details are visible	Boolean attribute
optimum	meter	Optimum value in gauge	Floating-point number
pattern	input	Pattern to be matched by the value of the form control	Regular expression matching the JavaScript pattern production

Attribute	Element(s)	Description	Value
placeholder	input, textarea	Visible label placed within the form control	Text
poster	video	Poster frame displayed prior to video playback	URL
preload	audio, video	Buffering hint for media	none | metadata | auto
pubdate	time	Determines whether the element value represents a publication time for the nearest article or body	Boolean attribute
radiogroup	command	Radio button group consists of commands	Text
readonly	input, textarea	Determines whether the value is editable	Boolean attribute
rel	a, area, link	Relationship between the document containing the hyperlink and the destination resource	Set of space-separated tokens
required	input, select, textarea	Determines whether the control is required for form submission	Boolean attribute
reversed	ol	List with reversed numbering	Boolean attribute
rows	textarea	Number of lines to show	Non-negative integer greater than zero
rowspan	td, th	Number of rows that the cell is to span	Non-negative integer
sandbox	iframe	Security rules for nested content	Unordered set of unique space-separated tokens consisting of allow-same-origin, allow-forms, and allow-scripts (ASCII case-insensitive)

Attribute	Element(s)	Description	Value
spellcheck	HTML elements	Specifies the need for spelling and grammar check	true | false
scope	th	Specifies header cell scope	row | col | rowgroup | colgroup
scoped	style	Specifies style scope (entire document or parent subtree)	Boolean attribute
seamless	iframe	Determines whether to apply the document styles to the nested content	Boolean attribute
selected	option	Option selected by default	Boolean attribute
shape	area	Shape type in an image map	circle | default | poly | rect
size	input, select	Control size	Non-negative integer greater than zero
sizes	link	Icon size for rel="icon"	Unordered set of unique space-separated tokens (ASCII case-insensitive)
span	col, colgroup	Number of columns spanned by the element	Non-negative integer greater than zero
src	audio, embed, iframe, img, input, script, source, track, video	Resource URL	URL
srcdoc	iframe	A document source of the inline frame	An iframe srcdoc resource
srclang	track	Text track language	BCP 47 language tag
start	ol	Ordinal value of the first item	Integer
step	input	Granularity to be matched by the form control value	Floating-point number greater than zero, or any
style	HTML elements	Styles (formatting and presentation)	CSS declarations

Attribute	Element(s)	Description	Value
summary	table	Table summary	Text
tabindex	HTML elements	Focus order	Integer
target	a, area	Hyperlink target	Browsing context name or keyword
target	base	Default browsing context (hyperlink navigation, form submission)	Browsing context name or keyword
target	form	Browsing context for form submission	Browsing context name or keyword
title	HTML elements	Additional visible information	Text
title	abbr, dfn	Reveals abbreviation or definition	Text
title	command	Command hint	Text
title	link	Link title	Text
title	link, style	Alternate style sheet set name	Text
type	a, area, link	Hint for resource type	MIME type
type	button	Button type	submit | reset | button
type	button, input	Form control type	Input type keyword
type	command	Command type	command | checkbox | radio
type	embed, object, script, source, style	Resource type	MIME type
type	menu	Menu type	context | toolbar
usemap	img, object	Image map to use	Hash-name reference
value	button, option	Value to be used for form	Text

Attribute	Element(s)	Description	Value
		submission	
value	input	Form control value	*Varies*
value	li	Ordinal value of the list item	Integer
value	meter, progress	Current value of the element	Floating point number
value	param	Parameter value	Text
width	canvas, embed, iframe, img, input, object, video	Horizontal dimension	Non-negative integer
wrap	textarea	Wrap type of the form control (form submission)	soft I hard

The global attributes and event handlers are described in the following sections by category.

Global attributes

Table 3-9 summarizes those attributes that can be applied to most elements.

Table 3-9. Global HTML Attributes

Attribute	Value
accesskey	List of unique space-separated key labels
class	Set of space-separated tokens (class name)
contenteditable	true I false I "" I empty
contextmenu	Menu identifier
dir	ltr I rtl
draggable	true I false I auto
hidden	hidden I "" I empty
id	Identifier

Attribute	Value
lang	Language code
spellcheck	true | false | "" | empty
style	String (style definition)
tabindex	Integer
title	Normal character data (text)

Although the accesskey, class, dir, id, lang, style, tabindex, and title attributes can also be used in HTML 4, their context and the set of allowed values are changed in HTML5.

Window Event Attributes

HTML5 added several attributes to the body element that are used to perform an action on the browser window. They are summarized in Table 3-10. In HTML 4, only the attributes onblur, onfocus, and onload can be applied.

Table 3-10. Window Event Attributes

Attribute	HTML 4	5	Runs the Script …
onafterprint	–	+	After the document is printed
onbeforeprint	–	+	Before the document is printed
onbeforeonload	–	+	Before the document is loaded
onblur	+	+	When the window loses focus
onerror	–	+	When an error occurs
onfocus	+	+	When the window gets focus
onhaschange	–	+	When the document has changed
onload	+	+	When the document is being loaded
onmessage	–	+	When the message is activated
onoffline	–	+	When the document goes offline

Attribute	HTML 4	5	Runs the Script ...
ononline	–	+	When the document comes online
onpagehide	–	+	When the window is hidden
onpageshow	–	+	When the window becomes visible
onpopstate	–	+	When the window history changes
onredo	–	+	When the last action is repeated
onresize	–	+	When the window is resized
onstorage	–	+	When loading
onundo	–	+	When the last action is undone
onunload	–	+	When the user leaves the web page

All window event attributes have a script as the attribute value.

Form Event Attributes

Several actions are associated with HTML forms. Users might add incorrect data, miss required rows, and so on. Table 3-11 summarizes the event handlers used on forms.

Table 3-11. Form Event Attributes

Attribute	HTML 4	5	Runs the Script When ...
onblur	+	+	An element loses focus
onchange	+	+	An element changes
oncontextmenu	–	+	A context menu is activated
onfocus	+	+	An element receives focus
onformchange	–	+	A form changes
onforminput	–	+	a form receives user input

Attribute	HTML 4	5	Runs the Script When ...
oninput	–	+	An element receives user input
oninvalid	–	+	An element is invalid
onreset	+	–	A form is reset
onselect	+	+	An element is selected
onsubmit	+	+	A form is submitted

Note that the onreset attribute is not supported in HTML5.

Keyboard Event Attributes

Web page functions can also be activated from the keyboard with three attributes that can be applied to all elements (Table 3-12).

Table 3-12. Keyboard Event Attributes

Attribute	Runs the Script When...
onkeydown	A key is pressed
onkeypress	A key is pressed and released
onkeyup	A key is released

Mouse Event Attributes

In the era of graphical user interfaces, many user actions are triggered by a pointing device, which is usually a mouse. The mouse event attributes described in Table 3-13 apply to all HTML5 elements.

Table 3-13. Mouse Event Attributes

Attribute	Runs the Script...
onclick	On a single click
ondblclick	On a double-click
ondrag	When an element is dragged
ondragend	At the end of dragging
ondragenter	When an element has been dragged to a valid drop target
ondragleave	When an element leaves a valid drop target
ondragover	When an element is being dragged over a valid drop target
ondragstart	At the start of dragging
ondrop	When a dragged element is being dropped
onmousedown	When the mouse button is pressed
onmousemove	When the mouse pointer moves
onmouseout	When the mouse pointer moves out of an element
onmouseover	When the mouse pointer moves over an element
onmouseup	When the mouse button is released
onmousewheel	When the mouse wheel is being rotated
onscroll	When an element scrollbar is being scrolled

Touch Event Attributes

Table 3-14 summarize the touch events supported by HTML5.

Table 3-14. Touch Event Attributes

Attribute	Runs the Script When...
ontouchcancel	A touch point has been disrupted
ontouchend	The user removes a touch point from the touch surface, or the touch point physically left the touch surface
ontouchenter	A touch point moves onto the interactive area defined by a DOM element
ontouchleave	A touch point moves off the interactive area defined by a DOM element
ontouchmove	The user moves a touch point along the touch surface
ontouchstart	The user places a touch point on the touch surface

Media Event Attributes

Media event attributes apply to all HTML5 elements but are used most commonly on media elements such as audio, embed, img, object, and video. They are summarized in Table 3-15.

Table 3-15. Media Event Attributes

Attribute	Runs the Script...
onabort	On an abort event
oncanplay	When the media data can be started to play with potential buffering
oncanplaythrough	When the media data can be played to the end without buffering
ondurationchange	When the length of the media object is changed
onemptied	When the media resource becomes empty
onended	When the media object has reached the end
onerror	When a loading error occurs
onloadeddata	When the media data is loaded
onloadedmetadata	When media metadata such as duration is loaded
onloadstart	When the browser starts to load the media data

Attribute	Runs the Script...
onpause	When the media data is paused
onplay	When the media data is going to start playing
onplaying	When the media data has started playing
onprogress	When the browser is fetching the media data
onratechange	When the playing rate of the media data has changed
onreadystatechange	When the ready-state changes
onseeked	When the seeking attribute is no longer true and seeking has ended
onseeking	When the seeking attribute is true and seeking has begun
onstalled	When the media data cannot be fetched
onsuspend	When fetching media data has been started but stopped before the entire media file was fetched
ontimeupdate	When the media object changes its playing position
onvolumechange	When the media object changes the volume or when volume is set to mute
onwaiting	When the media content has stopped playing but is expected to resume

HTML Document Structure

HTML documents apply a platform- and language-independent interface known as the *Document Object Model* (*DOM*) that makes it possible to refer to HTML, XHTML, and XML elements as objects [40]. This model provides dynamic content access and updates as well as document styling for scripts [41]. The DOM can be considered a mechanism that makes web pages behave like applications [42]. The DOM can be visualized as a tree structure for the hierarchy of markup elements within a document (Listing 3-28, Figure 3-2).

Listing 3-28. A Well-Structured HTML Document

```
<!DOCTYPE html>
<html>
  <head>
    <title>A DOM example</title>
    <link rel="stylesheet"
     type="text/css"
     href="main.css">
```

```
    </head>
    <body>
        <p>Paragraph content</p>
    </body>
</html>
```

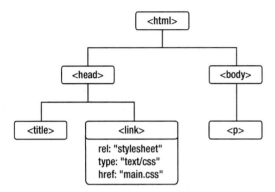

Figure 3-2. The DOM tree of Listing 3-28

Improperly closed elements—and in many cases the missing closing tags—destroy the DOM structure, which might have serious consequences, from disrupted layout to incorrect styling. Thanks to the built-in error-handling feature of web browsers, many of such errors might be corrected on-the-fly while rendering, but the intended structure can be presumed only. Developers should not rely on this error-handling feature!

An HTML document usually consists of a document type declaration, a Formal Public Identifier, and a link associating the document with the appropriate DTD in that order at the very beginning of the file (except HTML5 documents that usually omit the last one). All HTML documents must have an html root element[11] that contains the document head and the document body, respectively [43].

The document head provides processing information and metadata relating to the whole document. Background, font styles, margins, and other styles are generally defined here too.

The document body holds the content of the document. This can contain simple text, formatted text, images, videos, applets, or dynamic content, for example. Block elements can be grouped with div elements (Figure 3-3), while inline contents can be delimited with span. A text that has the semantic meaning of a paragraph should be provided by the p element.

In older versions of HTML, the usual structure looked like Listing 3-29.

Listing 3-29. The Document Structure Up to HTML 4.01

```
<!DOCTYPE HTML PUBLIC
"-//W3C//DTD HTML 4.01//EN"
"http://www.w3.org/TR/html4/strict.dtd">
<html>
    <head>
        <title>Sample HTML document structure</title>
    </head>
```

---

[11] Even if the HTML 4.01 specification denotes it as optional.

```
<body>
  <div class="section">
    <div class="article">
      <h2>Abstract</h2>
      <p>… first paragraph of main content …</p>
    </div>
    <div class="article">
      <h2>Overview</h2>
      <p>… second paragraph of main content …</p>
    </div>
  </div>
  <div id="footer">
    <p>
    Copyright © 2011 John Smith. All rights reserved.
    </p>
  </div>
</body>
</html>
```

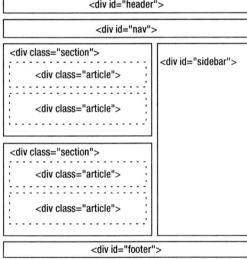

Figure 3-3. Typical document structure within the body up to HTML 4.01

In HTML5 there are additional, meaningful (semantic) structuring elements (Figure 3-4), so the typical structure of HTML5 documents is more sophisticated and logical (Listing 3-30).

Listing 3-30. Typical HTML5 Document Structure

```
<!DOCTYPE html>
<html>
  <head>
    <title>Sample HTML5 document structure</title>
  </head>
```

```
<body>
  <header>
    <h1>Document structure sample</h1>
  </header>
  <section>
    <article>
      <h2>Abstract</h2>
      <p>This sample document demonstrates the structure of HTML5 documents.</p>
    </article>
    <article>
      <h2>Overview</h2>
      <p>
      HTML5 adds more semantics to the document stucture. Instead of using general purpose
divisions, it provides meaningful elements.
      </p>
    </article>
  </section>
  <footer>
    <p>
    Copyright © 2011 John Smith. All rights reserved.
    </p>
  </footer>
  </body>
</html>
```

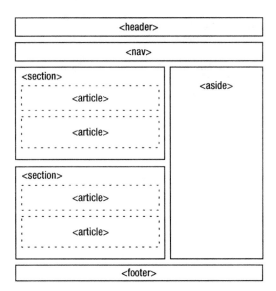

Figure 3-4. Document structure in HTML5

The new structuring elements of HTML5 can be summarized as follows:

- article: Articles, blog posts, forum posts, and so on

- `aside`: Sidebars, such as cross-references to an article

- `section`: Group of elements (typically with a `header` and a `footer`)

- `header`: The header of a section (usually with a title and maybe a short overview)

- `hgroup`: Heading group of `h1`–`h6` elements for subtitles, alternate titles, or taglines

- `footer`: Footer information of the entire page or a part of it (consequently, there might be more `footer` tags in a page)

- `nav`: Navigation elements

Naturally, not all these structuring elements can be used on all web pages, and they should be applied accordingly.

Document Type Declaration

Since there are various versions of markup languages with different features, they should be handled differently. As discussed earlier, elements of one document type are not necessarily allowed in others. Thus, the appropriate rendering strongly relies on the identification of the document type being used.

A straightforward solution is the declaration of the document type in the top of the document that associates it with a formally defined specification. The document type declaration can be defined by a *Formal Public Identifier* (*FPI*) and the URI of the so-called *Document Type Definition* (*DTD*). These URIs are used for identification, and they are not hyperlinks. This is a machine-readable way to express "this document is HTML" or "this document is XHTML." Most DTD driver files are provided by the World Wide Web Consortium.

An FPI is a human-readable, descriptive name that identifies the HTML version, while the DTD defines the location of the `.dtd` file (machine-readable grammar) on the W3C server (this file specifies the rules the document type should follow).

You can see the general syntax of the HTML document type declaration in Listing 3-31. Note that HTML5 has a streamlined `DOCTYPE`, as you will see.

Listing 3-31. *General Syntax of Document Type Declaration*

```
<!DOCTYPE root-element PUBLIC "FPI" ↩
  SYSTEM "URI"
>
```

The root element is `html` since it is the element opened first and closed last in HTML files (see "Core Structure Elements").

The various versions of HTML use similar syntax (except HTML5):

- HTML 2.0 (historical, not used anymore)

  ```
  <!DOCTYPE html PUBLIC "-//IETF//DTD HTML 2.0//EN">
  ```

- HTML 3.2 (historical, not used anymore)

  ```
  <!DOCTYPE html PUBLIC "-//W3C//DTD HTML 3.2 Final//EN">
  ```

- HTML 4.0 Transitional (should not be used)

  ```
  <!DOCTYPE HTML PUBLIC "-//W3C//DTD HTML 4.0 Transitional//EN" ↵
      "http://www.w3.org/TR/REC-html40/loose.dtd">
  ```

- HTML 4.0 Frameset (obsolete, should not be used)

  ```
  <!DOCTYPE HTML PUBLIC "-//W3C//DTD HTML 4.0 Frameset//EN" ↵
      "-//W3C//DTD HTML 4.0 Frameset//EN">
  ```

- HTML 4.0 Strict

  ```
  <!DOCTYPE HTML PUBLIC "-//W3C//DTD HTML 4.0//EN" ↵
      "http://www.w3.org/TR/REC-html40/strict.dtd">
  ```

- HTML 4.01 Transitional (should not be used)

  ```
  <!DOCTYPE HTML PUBLIC "-//W3C//DTD HTML 4.01 Transitional//EN" ↵
      "http://www.w3.org/TR/html4/loose.dtd">
  ```

- HTML 4.01 Frameset (obsolete, should not be used)

  ```
  <!DOCTYPE HTML PUBLIC "-//W3C//DTD HTML 4.01 Frameset//EN" ↵
      "http://www.w3.org/TR/html4/frameset.dtd">
  ```

- HTML 4.01 Strict

  ```
  <!DOCTYPE HTML PUBLIC "-//W3C//DTD HTML 4.01//EN" ↵
      "http://www.w3.org/TR/html4/strict.dtd">
  ```

- HTML 4.01+RDFa

  ```
  <!DOCTYPE HTML PUBLIC "-//W3C//DTD HTML 4.01+RDFa 1.1//EN" ↵
      "http://www.w3.org/MarkUp/DTD/html401-rdfa11-1.dtd">
  ```

- HTML5 (DOCTYPE without DTD). Unlike the former, SGML-based HTML versions, HTML5 requires neither an FPI nor a reference to a DTD. The document type can be defined by the DOCTYPE declaration <!DOCTYPE html>. Since the text/html serialization of HTML5 is not SGML-based, HTML5 applies the document type for mode selection only.

  ```
  <!DOCTYPE HTML>
  ```

Core Structure Elements

HTML documents must contain one element that is the parent of all other elements, that is, the html element. This element is called the *root element*. It has been standardized in the HTML 2.0 specification, along with the other two fundamental structure elements, head and body.

The html *root element* contains all other elements within the document; in other words, the <html> starting tag and the </html> closing tag delimit the document.

The HTML Head

The head section of HTML documents is the container of processing information and metadata. The document head should be provided between the <head> and </head> tags and precede the document body.

Common elements in the HTML head (with one example for each) include the following:

- title element (required)

  ```
  <title>Document title</title>
  ```

- meta elements[12] (optional, one or more)

  ```
  <meta name="keywords" content="web standardization, valid XHTML5, valid ↵
      XHTML+RDFa, tableless CSS layout, W3C validation, WCAG, semantic web, ↵
      accessibility">
  ```

- link elements (optional, one or more)

  ```
  <link rel="stylesheet" type="text/css" media="all" href="alt2.css" ↵
      title="Alternate style 2">
  ```

- script elements (optional, one or more)

  ```
  <script type="text/javascript" src="js/loading.js"></script>
  ```

The document body is the main content of a web document. It might contain both block and inline elements including, but not limited to, plain and formatted text, lists, headers, paragraphs, divisions, images, objects, forms, and tables. Certain prohibitions, however, determine which elements can be included in other elements.

Element Nesting

To maintain a logical document structure, certain HTML elements cannot contain all types of data or elements. For example, elements of a table such as table body and data cells should be within a table; the ins element cannot contain block-level content when it is used as an inline element, and so on. Some elements cannot contain other enclosed elements of the same kind (e.g., form, label). The content delimited by some elements can be a certain type of data only (e.g., script, style).

Certain nesting rules require the knowledge of content categories. In HTML5, the following kinds of content are differentiated [44]:

- *Metadata content*: Content that determines the presentation or behavior of the page content, sets up the relationship of the document with other documents, or provides additional information.

  base, command, link, meta, noscript, script, style, title

- *Flow content*: Most elements that are used in the document and application body are referred to as flow content.

---

[12] See Chapter 7 for details.

a, abbr, address, area (as a descendant of a map element), article, aside, audio, b, bdi, bdo, blockquote, br, button, canvas, cite, code, command, datalist, del, details, dfn, div, dl, em, embed, fieldset, figure, footer, form, h1, h2, h3, h4, h5, h6, header, hgroup, hr, i, iframe, img, input, ins, kbd, keygen, label, map, mark, math, menu, meter, nav, noscript, object, ol, output, p, pre, progress, q, ruby, s, samp, script, section, select, small, span, strong, style (only with the scoped attribute), sub, sup, svg, table, textarea, time, u, ul, var, video, wbr, and text

- *Sectioning content*: Content that defines the scope of headings and footers.

  article, aside, nav, section

- *Heading content*: Content that defines the header of a section.

  h1, h2, h3, h4, h5, h6, hgroup

- *Phrasing content*: The document text and elements in paragraphs.

  a (only with phrasing content), abbr, area (as a descendant of a map element), audio, b, bdi, bdo, br, button, canvas, cite, code, command, datalist, del (only with phrasing content), dfn, em, embed, i, iframe, img, input, ins (only with phrasing content), kbd, keygen, label, map (only with phrasing content), mark, math, meter, noscript, object, output, progress, q, ruby, s, samp, script, select, small, span, strong, sub, sup, svg, textarea, time, u, var, video, wbr, and text

- *Embedded content*: Imported content from external resources, or content from another vocabulary directly embedded into the document.

  audio, canvas, embed, iframe, img, math, object, svg, video

- *Interactive content*: Content dedicated to user interaction.

  a, audio (only with the controls attribute), button, details, embed, iframe, img (only with the usemap attribute), input (only if the type attribute is not set to hidden), keygen, label, menu (only if the type attribute is not set to toolbar), object (only with the usemap attribute), select, textarea, video (only with the controls attribute)

The most common elements can be nested as follows:

- html
  - head
    - title (required)
    - script, style
      - CDATA
    - base, meta, link (empty)
    - object
      - param (empty)
      - flow
  - body
    - ins, del

- flow
  - block
  - inline
- script
  - CDATA
- block
  - address
    - inline
  - article
    - header
    - sectioning (article, aside, section)
  - aside
    - header
    - sectioning (article, aside, section)
  - audio, video
  - blockquote
    - block
    - script
      - CDATA
  - div
    - flow
  - dl
    - dt
      - inline
    - dd
      - flow
  - fieldset
    - #PCDATA
    - inline
    - flow
    - legend
      - inline
  - form
    - block except an enclosed form
    - script
      - CDATA
  - footer
    - flow
  - h1, h2, h3, h4, h5, h6, p
    - inline

- ■ #PCDATA
- ■ a
  - ● inline except an enclosed a element
- ■ button
  - ● flow except a, button, fieldset, form, input, label, select, textarea
- ■ abbr, b, bdo, cite, code, dfn, em, i, kbd, q, samp, small, span, strong, sub, sup, var
  - ● inline
- ■ img, br (empty)
- ■ input (empty)
- ■ label
  - ● label except enclosed label
- ■ map
  - ● area (empty)
  - ● block
- ■ object
  - ● param (empty)
  - ● flow
- ■ script
  - ● CDATA
- ■ select
  - ● optgroup
    - ○ option
  - ● option
- ■ textarea
- ● header
  - ○ hgroup
    - ■ h1, h2, h3, h4, h5, h6 (minimum 2)
  - ○ h1, h2, h3, h4, h5, h6
  - ○ form
  - ○ img
  - ○ flow
- ● hr (empty)
- ● nav
  - ○ header
  - ○ sectioning (article, aside, section)
- ● noscript
  - ○ flow

- pre
  - inline except img, object, small, sub, sup
- section
  - header
    - hgroup
      - h1, h2, h3, h4, h5, h6 (minimum 2)
    - h1, h2, h3, h4, h5, h6
    - form
    - img
    - flow
  - footer
  - sectioning (article, aside, section)
- table
  - caption
    - inline
  - colgroup
    - col (empty)
  - col (empty)
  - thead, tbody
    - tr
      - th, td
        - flow
- ul, ol
  - li
    - flow

After understanding the difference between block-level and inline elements, nesting elements is rather straightforward. Empty elements, such as img or hr, cannot contain other elements. Some elements have restrictions for not only the elements but also the data types they can contain (for example, the contents of script elements should be CDATA). Violating the nesting order of element might destroy the DOM structure of the document, which makes rendering unreliable, risking the usability of the web page.

XHTML Document Structure

XHTML document structure is similar to that of HTML in the sense that there is a head and a body section; however, additional restrictions apply. Since XHTML documents are XML documents too, they begin with an XML declaration not known in HTML. Moreover, there are several document types and profiles to choose from, depending on the main purpose of the web document being developed.

XML Declaration

The very first line in XHTML documents is usually the optional XML prolog (its application is recommended by W3C). The most commonly used XML declaration looks like Listing 3-32.

Listing 3-32. The Most Commonly Used XML Declaration

```
<?xml version="1.0" encoding="utf-8"?>
```

No content is allowed to precede the declaration (except an optional byte-order mark). Although the character encoding is optional only, it is highly recommended.

Some older browsers cannot handle the XML declaration. The web page might become invisible, or the content is rendered incorrectly (for example, in IE6). IE7 ignores the XML prolog and correctly renders the content in Strict Mode (discussed in Chapter1).

Document Type Declaration

Similar to HTML, XHTML documents use a specific *document type declaration*[13] to identify the document type being used.

Generally, transforming an XHTML document into another XHTML document type is straightforward, especially if XHTML 1.0 Strict elements are applied exclusively. However, care must be taken when performing such an action because of the differences between the specifications. XHTML 1.0 Transitional is much more permissive, and changing the document type declaration of these documents will probably result in numerous errors that should be justified in order to obtain a valid XHTML 1.0 Strict, XHTML 1.1, or XHTML5 document.

Until recently, the former Quality Assurance Interest Group at W3C maintained a "Recommended list of Doctype declarations" [45]. Although it could be considered a "list of valid DTDs," it is not complete; thus, some of the newer as well as the most up-to-date document types are not listed (e.g., Mobile Profile, XHTML 2.0, or XHTML+RDFa), partly because the group closed in 2007. This does not affect the application or validation of such documents. Some non-W3C validators use the previous list and give warnings if a document type missing from that list is used.

Such warnings can be considered as false positives in many cases, because some of the less used, earlier DTDs as well as the latest document types are not on the list.

The document type declaration of the various XHTML versions and variants are summarized here:

- General documents

    - XHTML Basic 1.0

        ```
        <!DOCTYPE html PUBLIC "-//W3C//DTD XHTML Basic 1.0//EN"  ↵
          "http://www.w3.org/TR/xhtml-basic/xhtml-basic10.dtd">
        ```

    - XHTML Basic 1.1

        ```
        <!DOCTYPE html PUBLIC  ↵
          "-//W3C//DTD XHTML Basic 1.1//EN"  ↵
          "http://www.w3.org/TR/xhtml-basic/xhtml-basic11.dtd">
        ```

---

[13] Prior to XHTML5

- XHTML 1.0 Transitional (should not be used)

  ```
  <!DOCTYPE html PUBLIC "-//W3C//DTD XHTML 1.0 Transitional//EN" ↵
    "http://www.w3.org/TR/xhtml1/DTD/xhtml1-transitional.dtd">
  ```

- XHTML 1.0 Frameset (obsolete, should not be used)

  ```
  <!DOCTYPE html PUBLIC "-//W3C//DTD XHTML 1.0 Frameset//EN" ↵
    "http://www.w3.org/TR/xhtml1/DTD/xhtml1-frameset.dtd">
  ```

- XHTML 1.0 Strict

  ```
  <!DOCTYPE html PUBLIC "-//W3C//DTD XHTML 1.0 Strict//EN" ↵
    "http://www.w3.org/TR/xhtml1/DTD/xhtml1-strict.dtd">
  ```

- XHTML Basic 1.1

  ```
  <!DOCTYPE html PUBLIC "-//W3C//DTD XHTML Basic 1.1//EN" ↵
    "http://www.w3.org/TR/xhtml-basic/xhtml-basic11.dtd">
  ```

- XHTML 1.1

  ```
  <!DOCTYPE html PUBLIC "-//W3C//DTD XHTML 1.1//EN" ↵
    "http://www.w3.org/TR/xhtml11/DTD/xhtml11.dtd">
  ```

- XHTML 2.0 (XHTML2) (suspended [46])

  ```
  <!DOCTYPE html PUBLIC "-//W3C//DTD XHTML 2.0//EN" ↵
    "http://www.w3.org/MarkUp/DTD/xhtml2.dtd">
  ```

- XHTML5 (DOCTYPE without DTD)

  ```
  <!DOCTYPE html>
  ```

- XHTML+RDFa

  ```
  <!DOCTYPE html PUBLIC "-//W3C//DTD XHTML+RDFa 1.0//EN" ↵
    "http://www.w3.org/MarkUp/DTD/xhtml-rdfa-1.dtd">
  ```

- Mobile profiles
  - XHTML Mobile Profile 1.0

    ```
    <!DOCTYPE html PUBLIC "-//WAPFORUM//DTD XHTML Mobile 1.0//EN" ↵
      "http://www.wapforum.org/DTD/xhtml-mobile10.dtd">
    ```

  - XHTML Mobile Profile 1.1

    ```
    <!DOCTYPE html PUBLIC "-//WAPFORUM//DTD XHTML Mobile 1.1//EN" ↵
      "http://www.openmobilealliance.org/tech/DTD/xhtml-mobile11.dtd">
    ```

  - XHTML Mobile Profile 1.2

    ```
    <!DOCTYPE html PUBLIC "-//WAPFORUM//DTD XHTML Mobile 1.2//EN" ↵
      "http://www.openmobilealliance.org/tech/DTD/xhtml-mobile12.dtd">
    ```

- Mathematical markup
  - MathML 1.01

```
<!DOCTYPE math SYSTEM ↵
"http://www.w3.org/Math/DTD/mathml1/mathml.dtd">
```

- MathML 2.0

```
<!DOCTYPE math PUBLIC "-//W3C//DTD MathML 2.0//EN" ↵
 "http://www.w3.org/TR/MathML2/dtd/mathml2.dtd">
```

- MathML 3.0

```
<!DOCTYPE math PUBLIC "-//W3C//DTD MathML 3.0//EN" ↵
 "http://www.w3.org/Math/DTD/mathml3/mathml3.dtd">
```

- Graphical markup

  - SVG 1.0

```
<!DOCTYPE svg PUBLIC "-//W3C//DTD SVG 1.0//EN" ↵
 "http://www.w3.org/TR/2001/REC-SVG-20010904/DTD/svg10.dtd">
```

  - SVG 1.1 Tiny

```
<!DOCTYPE svg PUBLIC "-//W3C//DTD SVG 1.1 Tiny//EN" ↵
 "http://www.w3.org/Graphics/SVG/1.1/DTD/svg11-tiny.dtd">
```

  - SVG 1.1 Basic

```
<!DOCTYPE svg PUBLIC "-//W3C//DTD SVG 1.1 Basic//EN" ↵
 "http://www.w3.org/Graphics/SVG/1.1/DTD/svg11-basic.dtd">
```

  - SVG 1.1 Full

```
<!DOCTYPE svg PUBLIC "-//W3C//DTD SVG 1.1//EN" ↵
 "http://www.w3.org/Graphics/SVG/1.1/DTD/svg11.dtd">
```

- Compound documents

  - XHTML + MathML + SVG (using XHTML as the host)

```
<!DOCTYPE html PUBLIC ↵
 "-//W3C//DTD XHTML 1.1 plus MathML 2.0 plus SVG 1.1//EN" ↵
 "http://www.w3.org/2002/04/xhtml-math-svg/xhtml-math-svg.dtd">
```

  - XHTML + MathML + SVG (using SVG as the host)

```
<!DOCTYPE svg:svg PUBLIC ↵
 "-//W3C//DTD XHTML 1.1 plus MathML 2.0 plus SVG 1.1//EN" ↵
 "http://www.w3.org/2002/04/xhtml-math-svg/xhtml-math-svg.dtd">
```

The Root Element in XHTML

All XML documents must contain a root element with the syntax shown in Listing 3-33.

Listing 3-33. Pseudocode of the Root Element

```
<root>
  <child>
    <subchild>.....</subchild>
  </child>
</root>
```

The root element of XHTML documents must be `html`. Furthermore, the root element must contain an `xmlns` attribute to associate it with the XHTML namespace. The namespace URI is `http://www.w3.org/1999/xhtml` for XHTML 1.0 and XHTML5 documents, and it is `http://www.w3.org/2002/06/xhtml2/` for XHTML2 documents. Consequently, the most common XHTML namespace declaration looks like Listing 3-34.

Listing 3-34. The Most Common XHTML Namespace Declaration

```
<html xmlns="http://www.w3.org/1999/xhtml">
```

The natural language of XML documents is often identified by the `xml:lang` attribute of the `html` element[14] (Listing 3-35).

Listing 3-35. Common Use of the xml:lang Attribute

```
<html xmlns="http://www.w3.org/1999/xhtml" xml:lang="en">
```

Namespace Declaration

Beyond the default XHTML namespace `http://www.w3.org/1999/xhtml`, additional ones can also be used in XHTML documents. For example, XHTML+RDFa documents often use additional namespaces for semantic markup (for more details, see Chapter 7). In the example shown in Listing 3-36, the namespace of the FOAF Vocabulary Specification follows the default namespace declaration.

Listing 3-36. Additional Namespace Declaration

```
<html version="XHTML+RDFa 1.0" ↵
 xmlns="http://www.w3.org/1999/xhtml" xmlns:foaf="http://xmlns.com/foaf/0.1/" ↵
 xml:lang="en">
```

In mixed-namespace documents, such as XHTML + MathML + SVG, multiple namespace declarations occur throughout the document body (unlike the previous ones that are declared in the head section). Listing 3-37 shows an example.

Listing 3-37. Namespace Declarations in the body of a Compound Document

```
<!-- … XHTML content … -->
  <math xmlns="http://www.w3.org/1998/Math/MathML">
    <!-- … MathML notation … -->
```

---

[14] Although it is used frequently, this is just one of the many options to identify the XML document language (see Chapter 4).

```
    </math>
    <!-- … XHTML content … -->
    <svg:svg version="1.1" ↵
    xmlns:svg="http://www.w3.org/2000/svg" xmlns:xlink="http://www.w3.org/1999/xlink">
        <!-- … SVG graphic … -->
    </svg>
<!-- … XHTML content … -->
```

The XHTML Head

The title of XHTML documents can be written exactly the same way as in HTML, that is, between the start and end tags (Listing 3-38).

Listing 3-38. XHTML Document Title

```
<title>Title of the sample XHTML document</title>
```

The meta, link, and script elements can be provided in the head section of XHTML documents like in HTML documents. However, in XHTML these elements (along with all other elements) should be closed. These empty elements apply the XHTML shorthand notation (self-closing)(Listing 3-39).

Listing 3-39. A Self-closing Link Element in XHTML

```
<link rel="stylesheet" type="text/css" media="all" href="alt2.css" ↵
 title="Alternative style 2" />
```

In the following example, the title attribute is used to indicate search engines that show where to locate the German and Hungarian versions of the original English document (Listing 3-40). The xml:lang attribute declares the language of the target documents.

Listing 3-40. Links to Other Language Versions of the Same Document

```
<head>
  <title>The document in English</title>
  <link title="Das Dokument auf Deutsch" ↵
  rel="alternate" ↵
  href="http://example.com/german/" />
  xml:lang="de" ↵
  <link lang="hu" title="A dokumentum magyarul" ↵
  rel="alternate" ↵
  xml:lang="hu" ↵
  href="http://example.com/hungarian/" />
</head>
```

The character encoding of the page specified as the link target can be declared by the charset attribute.

The media attribute specifies the medium the link applies to. Table 3-16 summarizes the possible values.

Table 3-16. Values of the media Attribute on the link Element

Value	Description
screen	Computer screens (default)
tty	TeleTypes (fixed character width)
tv	Televisions and similar devices (low resolution, limited scrollability)
projection	Projectors
handheld	Mobile devices, smartphones, PDAs (small screens, limited bandwidth)
print	Print preview/printed pages
braille	Braille devices
aural	Speech synthesizers
all	Suitable for all devices

Listing 3-41 shows an example for three different style sheets written for three different media types (all, handheld, print).

Listing 3-41. CSS Files for Different Media Types

```
<link rel="stylesheet" type="text/css" media="all" href="main.css" ↵
 title="Default style" />

<link rel="stylesheet" type="text/css" media="handheld" href="mobile.css" ↵
 title="Styles for mobile devices" />

<link rel="stylesheet" type="text/css" media="print" href="print.css" ↵
 title="Styles for printing" />
```

The rel attribute (which stands for relationship) is a space-separated list of one or more values specifying the relationship between the current page and the target resource (Listing 3-42). Possible values are alternate, appendix, bookmark, chapter, contents, copyright, glossary, help, index, next, prev, section, stylesheet, and subsection.

Listing 3-42. Application Example for the rel Attribute

```
<link rel="alternate" type="application/rss+xml" title="New feed of example page" ↵
 href="http://www.example.com/rss.xml" />
<link rel="glossary" title="Glossary" href="glossary/" />
<link rel="copyright" title="Copyright" href="copy/" />
<link rel="bookmark" title="About" href="about/" />
```

```
<link rel="bookmark" title="Services" href="services/" />
<link rel="bookmark" title="Portfolio" href="portfolio/" />
<link rel="bookmark" title="Contact" href="contact/" />
```

The author of the document can be determined similarly (Listing 3-43).

Listing 3-43. A Link to the Author

```
<link rel="author"> href="http://www.example.com/" />
```

The favorites icon (favicon[15]), a 16x16 pixel square icon by default, can be determined by the shortcut icon or icon link (Listing 3-44). The first one is supported in all browsers; however, it is not declared in HTML specifications.

Listing 3-44. A Link to the Web Site Icon

```
<link rel="shortcut icon" href="favicon.ico" type="image/x-icon" />
```

Although the default image format is ICO, modern browsers support other formats too such as PNG, animated PNG, JPEG, GIF, animated GIF, and SVG. They can be used in the form shown in Listing 3-45.

Listing 3-45. Link Examples for rel="icon"

```
<link rel="icon" type="image/vnd.microsoft.icon"> href="http://www.example.com/image.ico" />
```

```
<link rel="icon" type="image/png"> href="http://www.example.com/image.pgn" />
```

```
<link rel="icon" type="image/gif"> href="http://www.example.com/image.gif" />
```

▓ **Tip** Since the attribute value icon was not standardized until HTML5 and browser support varies, it is a common practice to declare the same icon file with both the shortcut icon and icon attribute values.

The files can also be 32x32 or 48x48 pixels in size with 8-, 24-, or 32-bit color depth. However, because of the different browser support, the preferred format for favicons is the *de facto* file name and type (**favicon.ico**) provided in the root directory of the web site. Note that the larger the resolution and color depth, the longer the download time. File size should be kept within reasonable limits (see Chapter 9 for more on this).

The rel attribute is often used in other contexts as well. The microformats rel="license", rel="nofollow", and rel="tag", for example, provide various metadata on (X)HTML elements, most commonly on the a element. Generally they are parts of the document body but are used for specific purposes; thus, they are described later in Chapter 7.

In the head section of XHTML documents, further attribute values can also be used from namespaces other than the default XHTML namespace. Listing 3-46 shows an example for that.

---

[15] Also known as bookmark icon, URL icon, shortcut icon, or web site icon

Listing 3-46. Linking to an Additional Namespace

```
<link rel="foaf:primaryTopic" type="application/rdf+xml" title="FOAF" ↵
href="http://www.example.com/metadata/foaf.rdf" />
```

In this case, the FOAF namespace is also required to make the foaf:primaryTopic meaningful. The declaration of the additional namespace should be provided on the html element, as discussed in the previous section (Listing 3-36).

The XHTML Body

The XHTML document body is similar to the HTML body from the document structuring point of view. However, XHTML is case-sensitive. Consequently, the JavaScript event handler onload cannot be written with the same camel case notation onLoad used in HTML. It should be in lowercase (Listing 3-47).

Listing 3-47. Case-Sensitive Event Handler in XHTML

```
<body onload="function();">
```

Moving from HTML to XHTML

A common task for web standardistas is to convert HTML documents into XHTML. However, with the release of a brand new line of HTML, more and more web developers intend to use HTML5.[16] There are several reasons to use stricter markup. Although some changes to be made on HTML documents while upgrading to XHTML are straightforward, there are significant differences between the two formats in features and behavior that need to be considered. Since XHTML is the reformulation of HTML 4 as an application of XML, it can be used as an XML-conforming language with all of its attendant benefits:

- *Strict markup:* Unlike HTML, XHTML complies with strict conventions. As a result, there are no missing end tags, overlapping elements, or unnecessary attributes, just pure code. XHTML is well-formed and easy to write, interpret, and read. Content and styles are separated.

- *Easy introduction of new markup:* New elements and attributes can be added quite easily through XHTML modules.

- *XML conformance:* As such, they are readily viewed, edited, and validated with standard XML tools.

- *DOM choice:* Applets and scripts, and other applications can apply either the HTML Document Object Model or the XML Document Object Model.

- *Interoperability:* As web markup languages evolve, documents that conform to XHTML conventions will be more likely to interoperate within different user agents of the future.

Additionally, backward- as well as forward-compatibility can be ensured with appropriate markup.

---

[16] It is important to keep in mind that HTML5 can also be written in XML-style syntax, known as XHTML5, that use the same vocabulary, and provides well-formed XML files.

Specific Markup Languages

Beyond the general-purpose HTML and XHTML markup languages, there are more specific languages such as the ones that represent vector graphics (SVG), mathematical annotations (MathML), multimedia presentations (SMIL), or textual information synchronized with other media (TTML [47]). The vocabulary of such languages is used either in a specific file type or embedded in general-purpose markup. The following sections provide an overview of SVG and MathML.

SVG

In contrast to raster graphic formats such as GIF, PNG, or JPEG that have been handled by browsers for years, native support of vector graphics did not appear until the introduction of HTML5. Although the *Vector Markup Language* (*VML*) and the *Precision Graphics Markup Language* (*PGML*) appeared in 1998, they were soon followed by *Scalable Vector Graphics* (*SVG*) in 1999; however, implementers had to wait for a decade.

SVG is an XML-based markup for describing two-dimensional static and dynamic (animated or interactive) vector graphics [48]. The first version, SVG 1.0, became a W3C Recommendation in 2001, followed by SVG 1.1 in 2003. Beyond the full version, SVG also has a Tiny specification and a Basic specification optimized for mobile devices [49]. They are described as profiles of SVG 1.1. SVG Tiny 1.2 became a W3C Recommendation in 2008. The full version of SVG 1.2 has been stalled in the Working Draft stage and dropped in favor of SVG 2.0, which is a completely new version with advanced support for HTML5, CSS3, and Web Fonts (Chapter 9). Because of the native SVG support in (X)HTML5 along with the increasing browser support, the SVG format has gradually gained popularity.[17] Internet Explorer 9+, Firefox 3.5+, Safari 3.1+, and Opera 9.5+ have native SVG rendering and embedding support and do not require a plugin for SVG images.

■ **Caution** The browser support for SVG in modern browsers, which do not require a plug-in for displaying SVG, is different for each embedding method (inline, via `img`, via `object`) and feature (SVG effects, SVG in SMIL animation, SVG filters, SVG in CSS background, and SVG fonts).

Most browsers that support SVG do not render SVG files unless they are served as `image/svg+xml`. The most common rendering error with embedded SVG files is that they are served with an incorrect MIME type.

SVG is suitable for logos, graphs, geographical information systems, and so on. The major benefits of the SVG format can be summarized as follows:

- *Accessibility.* Images are often magnified by mobile users as well as for the visually impaired. SVG images are scalable without distortions or quality loss. Moreover, in SVG, text is rendered as text. Textual equivalents of objects can also be developed.

- *Optimal file size.* Although it depends on image content complexity, SVG files are generally smaller in size than their bitmap equivalents.

---

[17] Although it can be used in XHTML 1.x/2.0 too.

- *Scriptability.* All features of SVG images can be manipulated through JavaScript and the DOM.

- *Animation:* SVG elements and element groups can also be animated without scripting. This can be achieved by using Synchronized Multimedia Integration Language (SMIL) together with SVG.

■ **Note** SMIL is an XML markup language that defines markup for media synchronization, layout, animations, visual transitions, and media embedding. It supports presentations with text, images, audio, video, and links to other SMIL presentations. SMIL is a W3C Recommendation [50].

Syntax

The root element of both embedded and inline SVG images is svg. Listing 3-48 shows an example.

Listing 3-48. The svg Root Element

```
<svg xmlns="http://www.w3.org/2000/svg">
  <rect x="10" y="10" rx="0" ry="0" width="80" height="80" fill="#898989" />
</svg>
```

The namespace prefix can also be specified on the xmlns attribute. Doing so, the corresponding namespace is not the default namespace. Consequently, an explicit namespace prefix must be assigned to all elements such as in Listing 3-49.

Listing 3-49. Explicit Namespace Prefix

```
<svg:svg xmlns:svg="http://www.w3.org/2000/svg">
  <svg:rect x="10" y="10" rx="0" ry="0" width="80" height="80" fill="#898989" />
</svg:svg>
```

Both examples draw a rectangle using the rect element with a top-left positioning (x, y), dimensions (width, height), and optional horizontal and vertical corner radii (rx, ry). If length units are omitted, they are assumed to be in pixels. The default fill color for such objects is black, which can be overridden by the fill attribute.

Other geometrical shapes can be drawn in SVG similarly. Circles, for example, can be declared by a horizontal and vertical center and a radius (Listing 3-50).

Listing 3-50. A Circle in SVG

```
<circle cx="100" cy="100" r="90" stroke="#666" fill="#fff" />
```

For ellipses, a horizontal and a vertical center, as well as a horizontal and a vertical radius, are required (Listing 3-51).

Listing 3-51. An Ellipsis in SVG

```
<ellipse cx="100" cy="100" rx="120" ry="80" fill="blue" />
```

The svg element can contain any of the following elements, in any order [51]: animation elements (animate, animateColor, animateMotion, animateTransform, set), descriptive elements (desc, metadata, title), shape elements (circle, ellipse, line, path, polygon, polyline, rect), structural elements (defs, g, svg, symbol, use), gradient elements (linearGradient, radialGradient), a, altGlyphDef, clipPath, color-profile, cursor, filter, font, font-face, foreignObject, image, marker, mask, pattern, script, style, switch, text, and view.

Embedding

SVG images can be embedded in the markup by using the img or object element or by writing the SVG code directly into the markup (*inline SVG*).

The first approach applies the markup element img, which is used for other images such as JPEG or PNG (Listing 3-52).

Listing 3-52. Embedding SVG with the img Element

```
<img src="images/cover.svg" width="400" height="300" alt="Book cover" />
```

However, this embedding type has become supported in browsers with native SVG support only recently. In browsers and browser versions that do not support SVG embedding via the img element, the object element can be used (it cannot be ensured that users have an SVG plug-in installed). Listing 3-53 shows an example.

Listing 3-53. Embedding SVG Using object

```
<object type="image/svg+xml" data="images/cover.svg" width="400" height="300">
  <img src="images/cover.png" alt="Book cover" />
</object>
```

The disadvantage of the technique is that an image is provided as a general object rather than an image, which is not optimal from the semantic point of view: the meaning of an element representing an image is logically provided by the img element with more specific information about the content. The major advantage is that it displays the alternate (in this case PNG) version of the image in browsers that cannot display SVG. Moreover, object elements are included in the DOM, which allows the SVG image to be scripted.

The third option for providing SVG content is to write it directly into the XHTML or HTML5 markup. The major risk associated with the direct SVG embedding in XHTML is that XHTML documents containing inline SVG files should be valid, served as application/xml or application/xml+xhtml, and have an XHTML DOCTYPE. Otherwise, the SVG images are not displayed in the browser. Moreover, if XHTML documents are served correctly for browsers with a real XML parsing, Internet Explorer does not render the document at all (not only the SVG images).[18] This problem does not exist in HTML5, where direct SVG embedding is a native feature.

---

[18] This problem can be eliminated by specifying the MIME type text/html for Internet Explorer and application/xml for other browsers on the server.

Because of these issues, providing external SVG files is generally a better solution especially if the same file (such as a logo) is used throughout the site.

There are nonstandardized approaches called *SVG Support Libraries* such as the JavaScript API "Raphaël" [52]. It supports SVG and VML in a manner that all graphical objects are also DOM objects, with the potential to attach JavaScript event handlers. Raphaël provides a cross-browser solution; however, it requires JavaScript to be enabled and applies a programmer interface via JavaScript rather than SVG markup. The advantage of Raphaël is that it provides VML for IE8 or earlier and provides SVG for all browsers with SVG support.

MathML

The *Mathematical Markup Language (MathML)* is an XML application for describing mathematical annotations on the Web. It provides both content and structure, making it possible to index and process equations.

The first version of the Mathematical Markup Language, MathML 1.0, has become a W3C Recommendation in 1998 [53] and slightly modified in 1999 as MathML 1.01 [54]. After three years of development, MathML2 has obtained the Recommendation status in 2001, which has been further improved as the second edition until 2003 [55]. After recognizing the limitations of the second version, several new features have been introduced in MathML3, such as advanced line breaking and indentation, elementary math notation, alignment of Content MathML with OpenMath, support for bi-directional languages, new attributes for the math tag, semantic annotations, interaction with the host environment, linking, and new elements such as mglyph and mpadded [56].

MathML is supported by a variety of applications including web pages, e-books, screen readers, Braille displays, equation editors, ink input devices, and e-learning and computational software tools. However, the rendering engine implementation for MathML varies, and no browser provides full MathML support.

Internet Explorer has no native MathML support, and the MathPlayer plug-in has been used for versions up to IE8. Unfortunately, MathPlayer does not work under IE9. Native rendering support for MathML is available in Gecko-based browsers such as Firefox and Camino from the first versions and in Safari from version 5.1. Opera supports MathML since version 9.5. As of 2011, Chrome has no support for MathML, but WebKit support is in development.

Syntax

MathML has presentational, content, and mixing markup elements. There are two types of flavor for MathML markup. The first one focuses on the display of equations, known as *Presentation MathML*. The second, *Content MathML*, stresses the semantic meaning of the mathematical annotation.

Similar to XHTML, there are two types of elements in MathML: the ones with the start and end tags and the empty elements that are self-closing. However, the ratio of empty elements is much higher in MathML than in XHTML. Elements can have optional attributes that consist of a name and a value (the latter one is quoted in double or single quotes). The majority of MathML attribute values must be in a predetermined format such as a positive integer or the keyword true.

In MathML there are *container elements* such as mrow (a group of subexpressions) and *token elements* such as mi (identifier; i.e., a name of a constant, a variable, or a function). The element mo represents an operator (e.g., +), a fence (e.g., {), or a separator (e.g., ,). Numeric literals are specified by mn. The proper use of mi, mo, and mn is vital to provide adequate information for rendering engines to apply the correct typographic rules. Containers can contain other elements only while token elements delimit plain-text characters, special entity references, or symbols (the smallest units with meaning). Listing 3-54 shows an example.

Listing 3-54. A Simple Example for Container and Token Elements in MathML

```
<mrow>
  <mi>a</mi>
  <mo>+</mo>
  <mi>b</mi>
</mrow>
```

Entity references begin with an ampersand (&) and end with a semicolon (;). Beyond keywords such as α, a numeric format referring to the Unicode codepoint of the symbol is also allowed. More than 1,800 symbols are supported.

The MathML namespace is http://www.w3.org/1998/Math/MathML. It can be declared in two ways: using the xmlns attribute or an attribute with an xmlns prefix. In the first case, the default namespace applies to the element on which it is provided, as well as all child elements (Listing 3-55).

Listing 3-55. A Presentation MathML Document Fragment Applying the MathML Namespace

```
<math mode="display" xmlns="http://www.w3.org/1998/Math/MathML">
  <mrow>
  <mi>x</mi>
  <mo>=</mo>
  <mfrac>
    <mrow>
      <mrow>
        <mo>-</mo>
        <mi>b</mi>
      </mrow>
      <mo>&#xB1;<!--PLUS-MINUS SIGN--></mo>
      <msqrt>
        <mrow>
          <msup>
            <mi>b</mi>
            <mn>2</mn>
          </msup>
          <mo>-</mo>
          <mrow>
            <mn>4</mn>
            <mo>&#x2062;<!--INVISIBLE TIMES--></mo>
            <mi>a</mi>
            <mo>&#x2062;<!--INVISIBLE TIMES--></mo>
            <mi>c</mi>
          </mrow>
        </mrow>
      </msqrt>
    </mrow>
    <mrow>
      <mn>2</mn>
      <mo>&#x2062;<!--INVISIBLE TIMES--></mo>
      <mi>a</mi>
    </mrow>
```

```
      </mfrac>
    </mrow>
</math>
```

This is identical to the Content notation in Listing 3-56.

Listing 3-56. *The Content MathML Equivalent of Listing 3-55*

```
<math>
  <apply>
    <eq/>
    <ci>x</ci>
      <apply>
        <divide/>
      <apply>
        <plus/>
        <apply>
          <minus/>
          <ci>b</ci>
        </apply>
        <apply>
          <root/>
          <apply>
            <minus/>
            <apply>
              <power/>
              <ci>b</ci>
              <cn>2</cn>
            </apply>
            <apply>
              <times/>
              <cn>4</cn>
              <ci>a</ci>
              <ci>c</ci>
            </apply>
          </apply>
        </apply>
      </apply>
      <apply>
        <times/>
        <cn>2</cn>
        <ci>a</ci>
      </apply>
    </apply>
  </apply>
</math>
```

Both should be rendered as the following well-known quadratic formula in browsers that support MathML:

$$x = \frac{-b \pm \sqrt{b^2 - 4ac}}{2a}$$

In the second case, the prefix associates other elements and attributes with a particular namespace. For example, the namespace and the prefix are declared on the body element, as shown in Listing 3-57.

Listing 3-57. Namespace and Prefix Declaration on the body

```
<body xmlns:m="http://www.w3.org/1998/Math/MathML">
```

which adds meaning to mathematical notations such as the ones in Listing 3-58.

Listing 3-58. An Example for Using the MathML Prefix

```
<m:math>
  <m:mrow>
    <m:mi>x</m:mi>
    <m:mo>+</m:mo>
    <m:mn>y</m:mn>
  </m:mrow>
</m:math>
```

Embedding

Since MathML is an XML language, it can be directly embedded into XML files, including XHTML (see the next section). Because of the lack of support for namespaces, MathML embedding was not supported by HTML versions up to 4.01. HTML5 is the first version of HTML that supports MathML.

Combinations, Profiles, and Mixed-Namespace Documents

Several newly developed web site features are very useful but not required for basic documents. These technologies are defined by various specifications that can be used as the extensions of certain versions of (X)HTML. One of them combines markup and additional semantics, while another supports mathematical markup and vector graphics within (X)HTML documents. Some of these compound documents have their own DTDs they can be validated against and namespaces[19] that provide containers for the context of identifiers, including uniquely named elements and attributes.

(X)HTML+RDFa

The need for publishing semantically meaningful structured data, such as metadata in RDFa, is not recent. RDFa in XHTML became a World Wide Web Consortium (W3C) Recommendation on 14 October, 2008 [57]. XHTML+RDFa (Extensible Hypertext Markup Language + Resource Description Framework in attributes) is an extended version of the XHTML markup language for supporting RDF through a collection of attributes and processing rules in the form of well-formed XML documents. This

---

[19] By utilizing namespaces, XHTML documents can provide extensibility by including fragments from other XML-based languages such as SVG and MathML. This option was the privilege of XHTML languages, and was not supported by HTML before HTML5.

combination is one of the most advanced markup codes available today. XHTML+RDFa provides the option to develop Semantic Web content by embedding rich semantic markup. Version 1.1 of the language is a superset of XHTML 1.1, integrating the attributes according to RDFa Core 1.1. In other words, it is RDFa support through XHTML Modularization. The RDFa Core 1.1 specification describes how attributes can be used to express structured data in any markup language, with an emphasis on HTML (instead of XHTML), SVG, the Open Document Format, and other web-enabled document formats [58]. If the host language is XHTML, it is called XHTML+RDFa 1.1 [59].

The RDFa markup in XHTML+RDFa reuses the markup code, thus eliminating the need for unnecessary duplications. XHTML+RDFa can provide machine-readable metadata within the markup code, which makes additional user functionalities available. Most important of all, actions can be performed automatically that enable up-to-date publishing, structured searches, and sharing [60].

XHTML+RDFa is not widely distributed yet, probably because of the lack of support in authoring tools and content management systems [61]. However, there is a good tendency, especially because of the introduction of native RDFa support in (X)HTML5. Although the specification HTML+RDFa 1.1 is primarily an extension of HTML5, it describes rules and guidelines for applying RDFa, not only in HTML5 but also in HTML 4.01 and XHTML5 [62].

Listing 3-59 presents an XHTML+RDFa skeleton document.

Listing 3-59. *An XHTML+RDFa Skeleton Document with an Additional Namespace*

```
<?xml version="1.0" encoding="UTF-8"?>
<!DOCTYPE html PUBLIC "-//W3C//DTD XHTML+RDFa 1.0//EN" ↵
 "http://www.w3.org/MarkUp/DTD/xhtml-rdfa-1.dtd">
<html  version="XHTML+RDFa 1.0" ↵
 xmlns="http://www.w3.org/1999/xhtml" ↵
 xmlns:foaf="http://xmlns.com/foaf/0.1/" xml:lang="en">
  <head>
    <title>An XHTML+RDF example</title>
    <meta http-equiv="Content-Type" content="application/xhtml+xml; charset=utf-8" />
  </head>
  <body>
    <p>This is a paragraph with semantic content. It was written by ↵
     <span about="#smith" typeof="foaf:person" property="foaf:name">John Smith</span>.
    </p>
  </body>
</html>
```

The RDFa notation is described in Chapter 7.

XHTML-Print

XHTML-Print is defined in the W3C Recommendation "Modularization of XHTML" [19]. This profile can be used in printing environments without installing printer-specific drivers. XHTML-Print can also be useful for mobile devices and low-cost printers that often come with a lack of large (full-page) buffers and that generally print from top-to-bottom and left-to-right with portrait orientation.

The XHTML-Print document structure is based on the XHTML 1.0 specification. However, application and usage restrictions apply for images, styles, and forms.

XHTML + MathML + SVG

One of the easiest ways to demonstrate the power of XML is to create mixed-namespace documents. General and mathematical markup as well as vector graphics can be described within the same document by the XHTML + MathML + SVG profile. This profile combines XHTML 1.1, MathML 2.0, and SVG 1.1.

The *host language* of XHTML + MathML + SVG documents can be either XHTML or SVG.

XHTML as the Host Language

Listing 3-60 shows a typical XHTML + MathML + SVG document.

Listing 3-60. An XHTML + MathML + SVG Skeleton Document in XHTML

```
<?xml version="1.0" encoding="UTF-8"?>
<!DOCTYPE html PUBLIC•↵
 "-//W3C//DTD XHTML 1.1 plus MathML 2.0 plus SVG 1.1//EN" ↵
 "http://www.w3.org/2002/04/xhtml-math-svg/xhtml-math-svg.dtd">
<html xmlns="http://www.w3.org/1999/xhtml" xml:lang="en" dir="ltr">
  <head>
    <title>Sample XHTML 1.1 plus MathML 2.0 plus SVG 1.1 document</title>
    <meta http-equiv="Content-Type" content="application/xhtml+xml; charset=utf-8" />
    <link rel="stylesheet" type="text/css" href="style/style.css"/>
  </head>
  <body>
    <h2 id="math">MathML sample</h2>
    <p>Math expression
      <math xmlns="http://www.w3.org/1998/Math/MathML">
        <mrow>
          <mi>y</mi>
          <mo>=</mo>
          <mfrac>
            <mn>1</mn>
            <msqrt>
              <mrow>
                <msup>
                  <mi>x</mi>
                  <mn>2</mn>
                </msup>
                <mo>+</mo>
                <mn>1</mn>
              </mrow>
            </msqrt>
          </mfrac>
        </mrow>
      </math>
    inside an XHTML paragraph.</p>
    <h2 id="svg">SVG sample</h2>
    <p>
```

```
              <svg:svg xmlns:svg="http://www.w3.org/2000/svg" width="5em" height="4em" ↵
               viewBox="0 0 500 400" version="1.1">
                <svg:title>A star</svg:title>
                <svg:polygon style="fill:red; stroke:blue; stroke-width:10" ↵
                 points="210,46 227,96 281,97 238,129••
                 254,181 210,150 166,181 182,129••
                 139,97 193,97" />
              </svg:svg>
          </p>
        </body>
      </html>
```

Developers have the freedom to change the parameter entities of the DTD if required. Since MathML and SVG require additional support, the validity of the previous code does not guarantee that the document will be rendered correctly by all web browsers.

SVG as the Host Language

A mixed document can be created by inserting XHTML and MathML into SVG with `foreignObject` (Listing 3-61).

Listing 3-61. An XHTML+MahtML+SVG Skeleton Document in SVG

```
<?xml version="1.0"?>
<!DOCTYPE svg PUBLIC ↵
 "-//W3C//DTD XHTML 1.1 plus MathML 2.0 plus SVG 1.1//EN"•↵
 "http://www.w3.org/2002/04/xhtml-math-svg/xhtml-math-svg.dtd"[•↵
  <!ENTITY % SVG.prefixed "IGNORE" >
  <!ENTITY % XHTML.prefixed "INCLUDE" >
  <!ENTITY % XHTML.prefix "xhtml" >
  <!ENTITY % MATHML.prefixed "INCLUDE" >
  <!ENTITY % MATHML.prefix "math" >
]>
<svg version="1.1" xml:lang="en"•↵
 xmlns="http://www.w3.org/2000/svg"•↵
 xmlns:xlink="http://www.w3.org/1999/xlink">
  <desc>SVG as the host language</desc>
  <!-- ... SVG content ... -->
  <switch>
    <foreignObject width="800px" height="600px">
      <xhtml:p xmlns:xhtml="http://www.w3.org/1999/xhtml">
      <!-- ... XHTML content ... -->
        <math:math xmlns:math="http://www.w3.org/1998/Math/MathML">
        <!-- ... MathML content ... -->
        </math:math>
      <!-- ... XHTML content ... -->
      </xhtml:p>
    </foreignObject>
  </switch>
  <!--... SVG content ... -->
</svg>
```

Choosing a Markup Language

One of the most important aspects to be considered when choosing a markup language is browser support. Even if there are thousands of resources on the latest markup language and the browser support for its features are gradually growing, rendering web pages written in the most up-to-date markup always involves some risks.

The Transitional variants of HTML 4.01 and XHTML 1.0 have been developed to ease the work of web developers by providing features whose replacements have already been planned (tagged as deprecated elements). Their purpose was to give developers time to change obsolete markup, not to maintain them. The Traditional variants intended to provide a way to make the transition to modern web standards. Frameset documents are contradictory with the philosophy of XHTML. Consequently, the Frameset variant of XHTML 1.0 had a purpose similar to that of the Transitional variant. Both variants have been designed with backward compatibility in mind. In other words, XHTML 1.0 Strict should have been used exclusively after its introduction wherever possible. Although many content authors have done so, error-free markup has always been very rare. But what is the point of applying a strictly regulated markup in implementations full of errors? In fact, web developers are not entirely to blame. Web developers often have to deal with incorrect markup in the form of third-party and CMS-generated dynamic content based on templates that are not standard-compliant.

The potential for modularization in XHTML 1.1 has not been exploited either. XHTML 2.0 has been criticized by web developers, and W3C has been pushed to suspend the development of the specification.

Because of the new, advanced features introduced in (X)HTML5, HTML5 can be recommended but with the extended attention of gradually improving browser support. For conventional web documents, there is no reason to change a valid XHTML 1.0 Strict markup to HTML5 unless some new features introduced in the latter one would be essential for the content.

The Benefits of XHTML 1.*x* over HTML 4.*x*

In spite of the advantages of strict XML codes, it took several years for developers to realize the power of XHTML and to implement XHTML instead of HTML. Both HTML and XHTML have their advantages and disadvantages (Table 3-17).

Table 3-17. HTML vs. XHTML

Benefits of HTML	Benefits of XHTML
• Backward compatibility	• Strict XML syntax, well-formed markup
• Well-known syntax	• Easier maintenance
• Error-tolerance	• Direct integration with other XML vocabularies, e.g., SVG, MathML
• "Loose" syntax that might be convenient for some developers (permissive nesting, omission of certain tags and attributes)	• XML processing
	• Forced elimination of presentational markup

It is easy to see that some HTML features that claimed to be advantageous are not necessarily real benefits because precise, strict markup should always be considered better than loose markup.

The Benefits of HTML5 over HTML 4.*x* and XHTML

The latest version of HTML overcomes several limitations and inconsistencies of earlier HTML versions and XHTML. The new parsing rules of HTML5 are not based on SGML, which makes parsing more flexible and improves compatibility. The new elements provide more sophisticated document structuring (article, aside, audio, bdo, canvas, command, datalist, details, embed, figcaption, figure, footer, header, hgroup, keygen, mark, meter, nav, output, progress, rp, rt, ruby, section, source, summary, time, video, wbr) and new types of form controls (datetime, email, url, search, number, range, tel, color). Obsolete markup elements have been dropped, including acronym, applet, basefont, big, center, dir, font, frame, frameset, isindex, noframes, strike, and tt. New attributes have been introduced, such as the id, tabindex, and hidden global attributes, and the custom data attribute data-*. The charset attribute on the meta element and the async attribute on the script element have been improved. Inline SVG and MathML can be embedded in text/html documents.

HTML5 is recommended by a large share of developers as well as W3C since it fulfills all common user requirements and supports modern media that is suitable for most applications.

Alternatives to Web Markup

Although the lion's share of web documents are published in (X)HTML files, forms, brochures, flyers, posters, animations, source codes, presentations, and office documents are often provided in other formats such as in the ones indexed by Google [63]:

- Adobe Flash (.swf)

- Adobe Portable Document Format (.pdf)

- Adobe PostScript (.ps)

- Autodesk Design Web Format (.dwf)

- Basic source code (.bas)

- C/C++ source code (.c, .cc, .cpp, .cxx, .h, .hpp)

- Google Earth (.kml, .kmz)

- GPS eXchange Format (.gpx)

- Hancom Hanword (.hwp)

- Java source code (.java)

- Microsoft Excel (.xls, .xlsx)

- Microsoft PowerPoint (.ppt, .pptx)

- Microsoft Word (.doc, .docx)

- OpenOffice presentations (.odp)

- OpenOffice spreadsheet (.ods)

- OpenOffice text (.odt)

- Perl source code (.pl)

- Python source code (`.py`)

- Rich Text Format (`.rtf`, `.wri`)

- Text (`.ans`, `.asc`, `.cas`, `.txt`, `.text`)

Always use the appropriate file type for web publishing. (X)HTML documents are preferred for general contents and should be used whenever possible. With the introduction of HTML5, the share of documents published as markup has become larger. HTML5—especially empowered by CSS3 style sheets—has all the features to create animations instead of Flash, presentations instead of PowerPoint presentations, and so forth. Still, editable documents should not be converted into markup. Downloading a Word document and modifying it to fit your needs can be very convenient. Printable documents that need to be signed only are frequently provided in PDF. Special file types are confusing and cannot be processed by user agents.[20] It is the web author's responsibility to provide documents in the right file format.

Summary

In this chapter, you learned about the versions and variants of markup languages, which is beneficial for many reasons. First, it is required to know the history of markup languages to become capable of choosing the most suitable markup for your projects. Second, the relationship between these markup languages is vital when moving from one document type to another. Third, becoming familiar with the vocabulary of HTML and XHTML languages can be useful not only for comparison but also to ensure that you use only those elements and attributes that are allowed in the chosen document type.

Error-free markup code is among the most important features of standard-compliant web sites, but its full potential can be used only if it is served with proper settings. The next chapter will discuss the basics of server configuration, the most common content types, and the URIs used to query and link web sites.

References

1. Raggett D (2005) Getting started with HTML, revised version. World Wide Web Consortium. www.w3.org/MarkUp/Guide/. Accessed 11 September 2010

2. Smith M (2010) HTML: The Markup Language Reference. World Wide Web Consortium. http://dev.w3.org/html5/markup/. Accessed 21 January 2011

3. Pilgrim M (2010) HTML5: Up and Running. O'Reilly Media, Sebastopol

4. Meloni JC, Morrison M (2009) Teach Yourself HTML and CSS in 24 Hours (8th edn). Sams, Indianapolis

5. Lemay L, Colburn R (2010) Teach Yourself Web Publishing with HTML and CSS in One Hour a Day: Includes New HTML5 Coverage (6th edn). Sams, Indianapolis

6. Powell TA (2010) HTML & CSS: The Complete Reference (5th edn). McGraw-Hill Osborne

7. W3C (2010) W3C Cheat Sheet. World Wide Web Consortium. www.w3.org/2009/cheatsheet/. Accessed 01 October 2010

---

[20] Unknown file types that browsers cannot recognize by extension might still be processed or rendered (such as unknown formats provided in XML serialization are probably be represented as an XML tree).

8. Quittner J (1999) Tim Berners Lee – Time 100 People of the Century. Time Magazine. http://205.188.238.181/time/time100/scientist/profile/bernerslee.html. Accessed 11 September 2010

9. Lie HW, Saarela J (1998) Multi-purpose publishing using HTML, XML, and CSS. Association for Computing Machinery, Inc. www.w3.org/People/Janne/porject/paper.html. Accessed 11 September 2010

10. Berners-Lee T (1995) Hypertext Markup Language – 2.0, RFC 1866. Network Working Group, Internet Engineering Task Force. http://datatracker.ietf.org/doc/rfc1866/. Accessed 11 September 2010

11. Connolly D (1999) HTML 2.0 Materials. World Wide Web Consortium. www.w3.org/MarkUp/html-spec/. Accessed 11 September 2010

12. Raggett D (1997) HTML 3.2 Reference Specification, W3C Recommendation. World Wide Web Consortium. www.w3.org/TR/REC-html32. Accessed 11 September 2010

13. Raggett D, Le Hors A, Jacobs I (1998) HTML 4.0 Specification, W3C Recommendation. World Wide Web Consortium. www.w3.org/TR/1998/REC-html40-19980424/. Accessed 11 September 2010

14. Raggett D, Le Hors A, Jacobs I (1999) HTML 4.01 Specification, W3C Recommendation. World Wide Web Consortium. www.w3.org/TR/html401/. Accessed 01 October 2010

15. Masayasu I (ed) (2002) An XHTML + MathML + SVG Profile. W3C Working Draft. World Wide Web Consortium. www.w3.org/TR/XHTMLplusMathMLplusSVG/xhtml-math-svg.html. Accessed 17 February 2011

16. Adida B, Birbeck M, McCarron S, Pemberton S (2008) RDFa in XHTML: Syntax and Processing. A collection of attributes and processing rules for extending XHTML to support RDF, W3C Recommendation. World Wide Web Consortium. www.w3.org/TR/rdfa-syntax/. Accessed 10 September 2010

17. McCarron S (2010) XHTML+RDFa 1.1. Support for RDFa via XHTML Modularization, W3C Working Draft. World Wide Web Consortium. www.w3.org/TR/2010/WD-xhtml-rdfa-20100803/. Accessed 10 September 2010

18. Pemberton S et al (2002) XHTML 1.0 The Extensible HyperText Markup Language (2nd edn). A Reformulation of HTML 4 in XML 1.0. W3C Recommendation. World Wide Web Consortium. www.w3.org/TR/xhtml1/. Accessed 05 October 2010

19. Altheim M, Boumphrey F, Dooley S, McCarron S, Schnitzenbaumer S, Wugofski T (2001) Modularization of XHTML, W3C Recommendation. World Wide Web Consortium. www.w3.org/TR/2001/REC-xhtml-modularization-20010410/. Accessed 14 September 2010

20. Altheim M, McCarron S (eds) (2001) The XHTML 1.1 Document Type. W3C Recommendation. World Wide Web Consortium. www.w3.org/TR/xhtml11/doctype.html. Accessed 06 October 2010

21. Hickson I (2010) The HTML5 Draft Standard. Web Hypertext Application Technology Working Group. www.whatwg.org. Accessed 09 September 2010

22. Hickson I (2007) W3C restarts HTML effort. In: The WHATWG Blog, 07 March 2007. Web Hypertext Application Technology Working Group. http://blog.whatwg.org/w3c-restarts-html-effort. Accessed 09 September 2010

23. Hickson I (2008) Relationship to XHTML2. In: HTML 5. A vocabulary and associated APIs for HTML and XHTML, W3C Working Draft. World Wide Web Consortium. www.w3.org/TR/2008/WD-html5-20080122/#relationship0. Accessed 09 September 2010

24.   Leenheer N (2010) The HTML5 test – How well does your browser support HTML5? Niels Leenheer. www.html5test.com/. Accessed 19 January 2011

25.   W3C (2011) Testing – HTML Wiki. World Wide Web Consortium. www.w3.org/html/wiki/Testing. Accessed 19 January 2011

26.   Pemberton S (2010) XML and Applications. World Wide Web Consortium. www.w3.org/2010/Talks/11-11-steven-applications/. Accessed 11 November 2010

27.   Van Kesteren A (2010) HTML5 differences from HTML4. World Wide Web Consortium. www.w3.org/TR/2010/WD-html5-diff-20100624/. Accessed 23 September 2010

28.   Le Hégaret P, Jacobs I (2011) FAQ for HTML5 Last Call. World Wide Web Consortium. www.w3.org/2011/05/html5lc-faq.html. Accessed 14 Aug 2011

29.   Graff E (2011) Polyglot Markup: HTML-Compatible XHTML Documents. World Wide Web Consortium. www.w3.org/TR/html-polyglot/. Accessed 12 Aug 2011

30.   Bray T, Paoli J, Sperberg-McQueen CM, Maler E, Yergeau F (2008) Extensible Markup Language (XML) 1.0, Section 3.3.3 Attribute-Value Normalization. World Wide Web Consortium. www.w3.org/TR/REC-xml/. Accessed 23 September 2010

31.   Raggett D, Le Hors A, Jacobs I (eds) (1999) Basic HTML data types. In: HTML 4.01 Specification. World Wide Web Consortium. www.w3.org/TR/html4/types.html. Accessed 15 February 2011

32.   ISO (1996) "Information Processing — Text and Office Systems — Standard Generalized Markup Language (SGML)". ISO 8879:1986/Cor 1:1996. International Organization for Standardization. www.iso.org/iso/iso_catalogue/catalogue_tc/catalogue_detail.htm?csnumber=28557. Accessed 15 February 2011

33.   Lie H W, Çelik T, Glazman D, van Kesteren A (eds) (2010) Media Queries. World Wide Web Consortium. www.w3.org/TR/css3-mediaqueries/. Accessed 13 Aug 2011

34.   Phillips A, Davis M (eds) (2009) Tags for Identifying Languages. Internet Engineering Task Force. http://tools.ietf.org/html/bcp47. Accessed 13 Aug 2011

35.   Raggett D (1997) HTML 3.2 Reference Specification. W3C Recommendation. World Wide Web Consortium. www.w3.org/TR/REC-html32. Accessed 01 October 2010

36.   Raggett D, Le Hors A, Jacobs I (eds) (1999) Index of Elements. In: HTML 4.01 Specification. W3C Recommendation. World Wide Web Consortium. www.w3.org/TR/html401/index/elements.html. Accessed 01 October 2010

37.   Hickson I (ed) (2010) Index of elements. In: HTML5 - A vocabulary and associated APIs for HTML and XHTML. W3C Working Draft. World Wide Web Consortium. www.w3.org/TR/html5/index.html#elements-1. Accessed 01 October 2010

38.   Hickson I (ed) (2010) Index of elements. In: HTML5 - A vocabulary and associated APIs for HTML and XHTML. W3C Working Draft. World Wide Web Consortium. www.w3.org/TR/html5/index.html#elements-1. Accessed 01 October 2010

39.   Hickson I (ed) (2011) HTML5 attributes. In: HTML5. A vocabulary and associated APIs for HTML and XHTML. World Wide Web Consortium. www.w3.org/TR/html5/index.html#attributes-1. Accessed 16 February 2011

40.   Le Hégaret P (2009) Document Object Model (DOM). World Wide Web Consortium. www.w3.org/DOM/. Accessed 25 January 2011

41. Le Hors A, Le Hégaret P, Wood L, Nicol G, Robie J, Champion M, Byrne S (eds) (2004) Document Object Model (DOM) Level 3 Core Specification 1.0. W3C Recommendation. World Wide Web Consortium. www.w3.org/TR/2004/REC-DOM-Level-3-Core-20040407/. Accessed 01 October 2010

42. Zeldman J, Marcotte E (2010) A Standard Way to Make Web Pages Behave Like Applications. In: Designing with Web standards, 3rd Ed., New Riders, Berkeley

43. Raggett D, Le Hors A, Jacobs I (1999) The global structure of an HTML document. In: HTML 4.01 Specification. W3C Recommendation. World Wide Web Consortium. www.w3.org/TR/REC-html40/struct/global.html. Accessed 12 October 2010

44. Hickson I (ed) (2011) Kinds of content. In: HTML5 – A vocabulary and associated APIs for HTML and XHTML. World Wide Web Consortium. www.w3.org/TR/html5/content-models.html#kinds-of-content. Accessed 14 Aug 2011

45. Dubost K, Curran P (2007) Recommended Doctype Declarations to use in your Web document. Quality Assurance Interest Group, World Wide Web Consortium. www.w3.org/QA/2002/04/valid-dtd-list.html. Accessed 17 September 2010

46. Axelsson J, Birbeck M, Dubinko M, Epperson B, Ishikawa M, McCarron S, Navarro A, Pemberton S (2006) The XHTML 2.0 Document Type. In: XHTML 2.0, W3C Working Draft. World Wide Web Consortium. www.w3.org/TR/xhtml2/xhtml2-doctype.html#s_doctype. Accessed 23 September 2010

47. Adams G (ed), Dolan M, Freed G, Hayes S, Hodge E, Kirby D, Michel T, Singer D (2011) Timed Text Markup Language (TTML) 1.0. World Wide Web Consortium. www.w3.org/TR/ttaf1-dfxp/. Accessed 18 February 2011

48. W3C SVG Working Group (2011) What is SVG? Graphics Markup for the Web. World Wide Web Consortium. www.w3.org/Graphics/SVG/. Accessed 24 January 2011

49. Andersson O, Berjon R, Dahlström E, Emmons A, Ferraiolo J, Grasso A, Hardy V, Hayman S, Jackson D, Lilley C, McCormack C, Neumann A, Northway C, Quint A, Ramani N, Schepers D, Shellshear A (eds) et al (2008) Scalable Vector Graphics (SVG) Tiny 1.2 Specification. World Wide Web Consortium. www.w3.org/TR/SVGTiny12/. Accessed 24 January 2011

50. Bulterman D, Jansen J, Cesar P, Mullender S, Hyche E, DeMeglio M, Quint J, Kawamura H, Weck D, Pañeda XG, Melendi D, Cruz-Lara S, Hanclik M, Zucker DF, Michel T (eds) (2008) Synchronized Multimedia Integration Language (SMIL 3.0). World Wide Web Consortium. www.w3.org/TR/SMIL/. Accessed 14 Aug 2011

51. Dahlström E, Ferraiolo J, Fujisawa J, Grasso A, Jackson D, Lilley C, McCormack C, Doug Schepers D, Watt J, Dengler P((2010) The svg element. In: Scalable Vector Graphics (SVG) 1.1 (Second Edition). World Wide Web Consortium. www.w3.org/TR/SVG11/struct.html#SVGElement. Accessed 24 January 2011

52. Baranovskiy D (2011) Raphaël — JavaScript Library. Dmitry Baranovskiy. http://raphaeljs.com/. Accessed 23 January 2011

53. Ion P, Miner R (eds), Buswell S, Devitt S, Diaz A, Poppelier N, Smith B, Soiffer N, Sutor R, Watt S et al (1998) Mathematical Markup Language (MathML) 1.0 Specification. World Wide Web Consortium. www.w3.org/TR/1998/REC-MathML-19980407/. Accessed 09 February 2011

54. Buswell S, Devitt S, Diaz A, Ion P, Miner R, Poppelier N, Smith B, Soiffer N, Sutor R, Watt S et al (1999) Mathematical Markup Language (MathML) 1.01 Specification. World Wide Web Consortium. www.w3.org/TR/REC-MathML/. Accessed 09 February 2011

55. Ausbrooks R, Buswell S, Carlisle D, Dalmas S, Devitt S, Diaz A, Froumentin M, Hunter R, Kohlhase M, Poppelier N, Smith B, Soiffer N, Sutor R, Watt S et al (2003) Mathematical Markup Language (MathML)

Version 2.0 (Second Edition). World Wide Web Consortium. www.w3.org/TR/MathML2/. Accessed 09 February 2011

56. Carlisle D, Ion P, Miner R (eds), Ausbrooks R, Buswell S, Carlisle D, Chavchanidze G, Dalmas S, Devitt S, Diaz A, Dooley S, Hunter R, Kohlhase M, Lazrek A, Libbrecht P, Miller B, Rowley C, Sargent M, Smith B, Soiffer N, Sutor R, Watt S et al (2010) Mathematical Markup Language (MathML) Version 3.0. World Wide Web Consortium. www.w3.org/TR/MathML3/. Accessed 09 February 2011

57. Adida B, Birbeck M, McCarron S, Pemberton S (eds) (2008) RDFa in XHTML: Syntax and Processing. A collection of attributes and processing rules for extending XHTML to support RDF. W3C Recommendation. World Wide Web Consortium. www.w3.org/TR/2008/REC-rdfa-syntax-20081014/. Accessed 27 October 2010

58. Adida B, Birbeck M, McCarron S, Herman I (eds) (2010) RDFa Core 1.1. Syntax and processing rules for embedding RDF through attributes. W3C Working Draft. World Wide Web Consortium. www.w3.org/TR/2010/WD-rdfa-core-20101026/. Accessed 27 October 2010

59. McCarron S (ed) (2011) XHTML+RDFa 1.1 – Support for RDFa via XHTML Modularization. World Wide Web Consortium. www.w3.org/TR/2010/WD-xhtml-rdfa-20100422/. Accessed 03 May 2011

60. Pollock JT (2009) Semantic Web for Dummies. Wisley Publishing, Hoboken

61. Watson M (2009) Scripting Intelligence: Web 3.0 Information, Gathering and Processing. Apress, Berkeley

62. Sporny M, McCarron S (eds), Adida B, Birbeck M, Pemberton S (authors) (2010) HTML+RDFa 1.1. Support for RDFa in HTML4 and HTML5. World Wide Web Consortium. www.w3.org/TR/2010/WD-rdfa-in-html-20101019/. Accessed 26 October 2010

63. Google Inc. (2010) What file types can Google index? Google Webmaster Central. www.google.com/support/webmasters/bin/answer.py?hl=en&answer=35287. Accessed 15 January 2011

CHAPTER 4

Serving and Configuration

The correct appearance and handling of web documents cannot be guaranteed simply by applying strict, error-free markup. Web server configuration has a significant impact on web site appearance, operation, and behavior. Documents should be served with the proper media type and character encoding. Content negotiation can be used to serve various document versions to browsers supporting the corresponding media types. XHTML documents can be served as either HTML or XML, but there is a huge difference in processing. XML files are processed by XML parsers that are far more error sensitive than SGML parsers. XHTML served as XML involves the risk that the document cannot be rendered at all. On the other hand, backward-compatible serving cannot use the benefits of strict XML markup. There are several aspects of sending HTML and XHTML from the server to the rendering engine, all of which should be considered to achieve proper settings.

In this chapter, you will learn how to configure your web site, browser, and server in order to serve web documents correctly. Becoming familiar with the most important MIME types is crucial for properly serving web documents and the files used by them, for example, style sheets, images, audio and video files, ZIP archives, and office documents. Beyond Internet media types, you will also learn domain configuration; the difference between URIs, URLs, and URNs; the application of base directories; and practices to eliminate file extensions.

The HTTP Header

The foundation of data communication on the World Wide Web is the Hypertext Transfer Protocol (HTTP). It is a networking protocol that functions as a request-response protocol in a client-server computing model. In this model, a typical client is a web browser, while an application that runs on the host of a web site is a server. During each query, the client submits an HTTP request message to the server. In return, the server sends a response message to the client that contains additional data, such as completion status information about the request, which is sent along with web documents from the server to the user agent. These header fields form the *HTTP header*. The header fields determine the parameters of the HTTP communication. HTTP requests are used to indicate which content types and character sets are acceptable (`Accept`, `Accept-Charset`), the date and time the message was sent (`Date`), the domain name (`Host`), a string representing a user agent (`User-Agent`), and so on.

As you can see in Listing 4-1, HTTP responses provide the name of the server (`Server`), an alternate location for the returned data (`Content-Location`), and the date and time after which the response expires (`Expires`). The `Vary` field confirms whether the cached response can be used rather than repeat the request. The Platform for Privacy Preferences Project (P3P) policy can be set by the `P3P` field. An identifier of a specific version of the resource is provided by `ETag`. These are the most common HTTP header fields, but there are many more, all of which are described by RFC 4229 [1].

Listing 4-1. *HTTP Header Example*

```
HTTP/1.1 200 OK
Date: Fri, 10 Sep 2010 10:05:08 GMT
Server: Apache/2.2.16 (Unix) PHP/5.3.3
Content-Location: index.html
Vary: negotiate,accept-language,accept-charset
TCN: choice
P3P: policyref=http://example.com/p3p.xml
Cache-Control: max-age=21600
Expires: Fri, 10 Sep 2010 16:05:08 GMT
Last-Modified: Fri, 21 Aug 2009 22:18:49 GMT
ETag: "3668bab8;37e77d1c"
Accept-Ranges: bytes
Content-Length: 11537
Connection: close
Content-Type: text/html; charset=UTF-8
Content-Language: en
```

Internet Media Types (MIME)

Internet media types (also known as *MIME types* or *content-types*) determine the way browsers handle web documents. They are the file format identifiers of the Web. Thus, it is crucial to set the right media type for web site components and web pages.

The Multipurpose Internet Mail Extensions (MIME) specification was introduced in 1992 by the Internet Engineering Task Force (see Chapter 1 for more information on the IETF). Most specifications are available as an IETF/ISOC Request for Comments (RFCs). Although the original MIME concept was designed to format non-ASCII messages,[1] it is used in web browsers to make it possible to render or process files other than (X)HTML. The Internet media types are standardized by IANA registration (again, see Chapter 1 for more information on the IANA) [2]. Nonstandard MIME types and subtypes can be recognized by their prefix, since they all begin with x-. Vendor-specific subtypes begin with vnd., while personal subtypes begin with prs..

Media types consist of a minimum of two parts: a type, a subtype, and optional parameters.

XML data can be assigned to two MIME media types: application/xml and text/xml. They are defined by RFC 3023 [3]. Further, MIME types can be identified by the suffix +xml. The most important media type from a web standardista's point of view is the XML media type registered for XHTML, namely, application/xhtml+xml, which is defined in RFC 3236 [4]. Although XHTML documents could be served with the application/xhtml+xml, application/xml, or text/xml media type, W3C recommends serving XHTML as XML with its dedicated MIME type application/xhtml+xml [5]. However, using this media type cannot guarantee proper XML handling without a correct XML header (see Chapter 3 for more on XML headers). Furthermore, Internet Explorer 6 and earlier IE versions do not render the contents of documents served as application/xhtml+xml; instead, users are prompted to download the file.

---

[1] The advanced version, S/MIME, supports message encryption too.

■ **Caution** If the media type for an XHTML web page is set to `text/html`, it will be parsed as HTML. If the media type is set to `application/xhtml+xml`, browsers will parse the document as XML. This is a huge difference! XHTML files served with the proper MIME cannot contain a single error; otherwise, the document will not be rendered, and the XML parser will give an error, as already mentioned earlier in Chapters 1 and 3.

Another registered XML media type is `application/atom+xml`, which is used for the Atom Syndication Format (see Chapter 8) defined by the proposed standard RFC 4287 [6]. Other frequently used XML media types of this kind are `application/rss+xml` (RSS; see Chapter 8), `application/mathml+xml` (MathML; see Chapter 3), `image/svg+xml` (SVG; see Chapter 3), and `application/xslt+xml` (XSLT; see Chapter 5). The full list of MIME types is published on the IANA web site [7].

The `Content-Type` field of the HTTP header describes the data format as a MIME media type (Listing 4-2). Additionally, this entry can also provide the character encoding of the document (as discussed earlier in Chapter 2).

Listing 4-2. A Content-Type Example

```
Content-Type: application/xhtml+xml; charset=UTF-8
```

The MIME type of web pages can also be set on the document level with the `meta` element such as in Listing 4-3.

Listing 4-3. MIME Type Declaration with the `meta` Element

```
<meta http-equiv="Content-Type" content="application/xhtml+xml; charset=utf-8" />
```

Generally, the MIME type `text/html` is used for HTML documents, and the `application/xhtml+xml` is used for XHTML documents. However, XHTML documents can be served with both (as we'll see later in the chapter).

The wide variety of Internet media types is not fixed. Custom MIME types can also be registered at IANA [8].

Common Media Types

The most common media types are listed in the next sections. Note that this is not a full list by any means.

Application-Specific Media Types

Table 4-1 summarizes the most common application-specific MIME types.

Table 4-1. Common Application-Specific Media Types

Media Type	Specification	Description
application/atom+xml	RFC 4287 [9], RFC 5023 [10]	Atom news feed
application/ecmascript	RFC 4329 [11]	ECMAScript
application/javascript[2]	RFC 4329 [10]	JavaScript
application/json	RFC 4627 [12]	JavaScript Object Notation
application/mathml-content+xml	MathML 3.0, Appendix B [13]	Content MathML
application/mathml-presentation+xml	MathML 3.0, Appendix B [12]	Presentation MathML
application/mathml+xml	MathML 3.0, Appendix B [12]	MathML
application/octet-stream	RFC 2046 [14]	Nonspecified binary data
application/ogg	RFC 5334 [15]	Ogg multimedia container
application/pdf	RFC 3778 [16]	PDF document
application/postscript	RFC 2045 [17] RFC 2046 [18]	PostScript
application/rdf+xml	RFC 3870 [19]	RDF document
application/rtf	IANA registration [20]	RTF document
application/sgml	RFC 1874 [21]	SGML document
application/smil+xml	RFC 4536 [22]	SMIL document
application/soap+xml	RFC 3902 [23]	Simple Object Access Protocol

---

[2] Cannot be used in IE8 or earlier

Media Type	Specification	Description
application/sparql-query	In: SPARQL Query Language for RDF [24]	SPARQL
application/sparql-results+xml	In: SPARQL Query Results XML Format [25]	SPARQL Query Results
application/xhtml+xml	RFC 3236 [26]	XHTML document
application/xml	RFC 3023 [27]	XML document
application/xml-dtd	RFC 3023 [26]	DTD file
application/xslt+xml	In: XSLT 2.0 [28]	XSL Transformations
application/zip	IANA registration [29]	ZIP archive file

Vendor-Specific Media Types

Table 4-2 summarizes the most common vendor-specific MIME types.

Table 4-2. Common Vendor-Specific Media Types

Media type	Specification	Description
application/vnd.google-earth.kml+xml	IANA registration [30]	Google Earth file in XML
application/vnd.google-earth.kmz	IANA registration [31]	Google Earth file
application/msword	IANA registration [32]	Microsoft Word file
application/vnd.ms-excel	IANA registration [33]	Microsoft Excel file
application/vnd.ms-powerpoint	IANA registration [34]	Microsoft PowerPoint file
application/vnd.oasis.opendocument.graphics	IANA registration [35]	OpenDocument Graphics

143

Media type	Specification	Description
application/vnd.oasis.opendocument.presentation	IANA registration [36]	OpenDocument Presentation
application/vnd.oasis.opendocument.spreadsheet	IANA registration [37]	OpenDocument Spreadsheet
application/vnd.oasis.opendocument.text	IANA registration [38]	OpenDocument Text

It is highly probable that nonstandardized MIME types associated with widely used file formats will become registered in the near future. The application/x-dvi represents device-independent documents. The MIME type of LaTeX files, application/x-latex, is not standardized yet either. Adobe Flash files will probably have the already widely used media type, application/x-shockwave-flash. RAR archive files that could be associated with the application/x-rar-compressed MIME type are also still not standardized.

Audio Media Types

Table 4-3 summarizes the most common audio MIME types.

Table 4-3. Common Audio Media Types

Media Type	Specification	Description
audio/mpeg	RFC 3003 [39]	MPEG audio, for example, MP3
audio/ogg	RFC 5334 [14]	Ogg Vorbis, Flac, and other audio
audio/vorbis	RFC 5215 [40]	Vorbis Encoded Audio
audio/x-ms-wma	MS KB 288102 [41]	Windows Media Audio
audio/vnd.wave	RFC 2361 [42]	WAV audio

Image Media Types

Table 4-4 summarizes the most common image MIME types.

Table 4-4. Common Image Media Types

Media Type	Specification	Description
image/gif	RFC 2045 [16], RFC 2046 [17]	GIF image
image/jpeg	RFC 2045 [16], RFC 2046 [17]	JPEG image
image/png	RFC 2083 [43]; IANA registered [44]	PNG image
image/svg+xml	In: SVG Tiny 1.2 Appendix M [45]	SVG vector image
image/tiff	RFC 3302 [46]	TIFF image
image/vnd.microsoft.icon	IANA registered [47]	ICO image (icon)

Multipart Object Media Types

Table 4-5 summarizes the most common multipart object media types.

Table 4-5. Common Multipart Object Media Types

Media Type	Specification	Description
multipart/mixed	RFC 2045 [16], RFC 2046 [17]	MIME e-mail
multipart/alternative	RFC 2045 [16], RFC 2046 [17]	MIME e-mail
multipart/related	RFC 2387 [48]	MIME e-mail; used by MHTML (HTML mail)
multipart/form-data	RFC 2388 [49]	MIME web form
multipart/signed	RFC 1847 [50]	Digital signature
multipart/encrypted	RFC 1847 [49]	Encrypted message

Text Media Types

Table 4-6 summarizes the most common text media types.

Table 4-6. Common Text Media Types

Media Type	Specification	Description
text/css	RFC 2318 [51]	Cascading Style Sheets (CSS)
text/csv	RFC 4180 [52]	Comma-separated values
text/html	RFC 2854 [53]	HTML
text/javascript	RFC 4329 [54]	JavaScript; obsoleted in favor of application/javascript (RFC 4329)
text/plain	RFC 2046 and RFC 3676 [55]	Textual data
text/xml	RFC 3023 [26]	Extensible Markup Language

Video Media Types

Table 4-7 summarizes the most common video media types.

Table 4-7. Common MIME Types for Video

Media Type	Specification	Description
video/mpeg	RFC 2045 [16], RFC 2046 [17]	MPEG-1 video
video/mp4	RFC 4337 [56]	MP4 video
video/ogg	RFC 5334 [57]	Ogg Theora or other video
video/quicktime	IANA registered [58]	QuickTime video
video/x-ms-wmv	MS KB 288102 [59]	Windows Media Video

Serving XHTML

There are two approaches for serving XHTML, both of which have their advantages and disadvantages. They are described in the following sections.

Serving XHTML as HTML

In the early days of the Web, HTML was the exclusive markup language. After several years, new innovations appeared that could not have been covered by HTML. XML rules have been added to it, creating XHTML, a new line of markup languages. These rules are the ones that should also be applied when converting HTML documents to XHTML, as discussed earlier in Chapter 3.

However, the vocabulary of HTML 4.01 has been more or less preserved; thus, it is similar to that of XHTML 1.0. Consequently, XHTML documents can be served as HTML to rendering engines. This approach provides backward compatibility. Media types can be used to request browsers to handle XHTML as HTML instead of XML. If the media type of an XHTML document is defined as `text/html`, the rendering engine will parse the web page as if it were HTML. If the media type is given as `application/xhtml+xml`, browsers will process the document as XML.

Several server and server-side scripting platforms (PHP, ASP, and so on) apply the `text/html` media type for web content by default. The "dirty secret" of XHTML is that several browsers with an XML parser treat documents served as `text/html` with XHTML syntax and `DOCTYPE` as HTML.[3] But backward compatibility comes at a price: the impressive features of XML cannot be used at all in XHTML served this way. And what is the point of applying strict rules if documents cannot use their full potential? Where backward compatibility is not a major concern, the solution is to serve XHTML as XML.

Serving XHTML as XML

Errors are not accepted at all in many environments such as programming languages. Code reliability strongly depends on markup structure and correctness. The browsers' behavior of refusing to render invalid XHTML markup might seem annoying; however, the browsers have a really good reason to do so. HTML documents full of errors are being processed by guessing the intentions of the developers. Browsers cannot succeed with this task each time, and the results cannot be guaranteed. Furthermore, the error tolerance of rendering engines provides various results.

There are scenarios where errors cannot be tolerated. In scientific publishing, for example, the representation of mathematical equations should be reliable. If such documents are published on the Web with MathML embedded in XHTML, errors cannot be tolerated because the consequences can cost millions or be fatal. This is the main reason for the extreme error sensitivity of XML parsers.

Being an XML language family, XHTML was intended to be served as XML. This approach enjoys all the benefits of XML. However, it also involves a serious risk. Web documents served as `application/xhtml+xml` request browsers to process them according to the rules of XML. Since invalid XHTML markup is not rendered at all in web browsers, extended care should be taken when serving XHTML as XML. One simple character at the wrong location in the source code results in an XML parsing error message instead of the web page content (as already hinted in Chapter 1). Probably this is one of the reasons why HTML has always been preferred by a large share of content authors and developers. However, real web standardistas should not be afraid of authoring pure XHTML code. If you

---

[3] Real XML parsers such as that of Firefox or Safari consider the MIME type of documents (as sent by the server) rather than file syntax and DOCTYPE only.

learn how to use the practices described in the previous chapter, you will be able to create not only error-free XHTML documents but also any kind of structured markup.

Although modern browsers support the application/xhtml+xml MIME type, some older browsers do not. One of the options to preserve backward compatibility with older browsers and support advanced XML applications for modern ones is the technique called *content negotiation*. It can be done through .htaccess[4] settings or using server-side scripting languages.

The HTTP specification defines the mechanism for serving different versions of the same resource [60]. Document types, document languages, and image types are some examples [61]. The preferred and acceptable document format(s)—in our case, the preference between HTML and XHTML files—can be defined in the HTTP header, as shown in Listing 4-4.

Listing 4-4. Content Negotiation in the HTTP Header

```
Accept: text/html, application/xhtml+xml, application/xml; q=0.9, */*; q=0.8
```

Using the previous example, the browser can specify that HTML and XHTML are preferred to XML. The "relative quality parameter" (q) and its value (qvalue) are considered as follows. All items without a specified preference value get the default value 1 (in this case text/html and application/xhtml+xml). The specified value for application/xml is 0.9, and all the other formats 0.8. The precedence values ordered in descending order reveal the actual precedence, in other words, 1 for text/html and application/xhtml+xml, 0.9 for application/xml, and 0.8 for any other content types.

On Apache servers, the directive shown in Listing 4-5 should be added to your .htaccess (or httpd.conf) file to set the HTTP headers required for the correct MIME type.

Listing 4-5. Preference Between text/html and application/xhtml+xml

```
Options +Multiviews
AddType application/xhtml+xml;qs=0.8
AddType text/html;qs=0.9
```

The "quality of source" parameter (qs), set to 0.8 in our example, determines whether the AddType directive applies the specified MIME type. Since the qs value for application/xhtml+xml is smaller than that of text/html, application/xhtml+xml will be used by compliant browsers only; otherwise, the preferred version will be the MIME type text/html.

Content negotiation can also be implemented in server-side scripting languages. The most common implementations are summarized in Listing 4-6, 4-7, and 4-8.

Listing 4-6. Content Negotiation in PHP

```php
$accept = $_SERVER["HTTP_ACCEPT"];
$ua = $_SERVER["HTTP_USER_AGENT"];
if (isset($accept) && isset($ua)) {
  if (stristr($accept, "application/xhtml+xml") || stristr($ua, "W3C_Validator")) {
    header("Content-Type: application/xhtml+xml");
  }
}
```

---

[4] A common configuration file on web servers (note that it begins with a period and has no extension).

Listing 4-7. Content Negotiation in ASP

```
Dim strAccept, strUA
strAccept = Request.ServerVariables("HTTP_ACCEPT").Item
strUA = Request.ServerVariables("HTTP_USER_AGENT").Item
If InStr(1, strAccept, "application/xhtml+xml") > 0 Or InStr(1, strUA, "W3C_Validator") > 0
  Then Response.ContentType = "application/xhtml+xml"
End If
```

Listing 4-8. Content Negotiation in C# in ASP .NET

```
string accept = Request.ServerVariables["HTTP_ACCEPT"];
string ua = Request.ServerVariables["HTTP_USER_AGENT"];
if (accept != null && ua != null) {
  if (accept.IndexOf("application/xhtml+xml") >=0 || ua.IndexOf("W3C_Validator") >= 0) {
    Response.ContentType = "application/xhtml+xml";
  }
}
```

The previous codes perform content negotiation with their own syntax. In PHP, for example, the server variables contained in the $_SERVER array are used to evaluate the HTTP Accept header of the user agent and set the appropriate MIME type via the header function (Listing 4-6).

URIs, URLs, and URNs

A *Uniform Resource Identifier* (*URI*) is a character string that identifies a name or a resource on the Internet (RFC 2396 [62]). URIs can be classified as *Uniform Resource Locators* (*URLs*; RFC 1738 [63]), *Uniform Resource Names* (*URNs*), or both. A URN defines the identity of a resource, while the URL provides a method for finding it (including protocol and path). URIs are often used incorrectly as the synonym for URL, although URI is a wider term (RFC 3305 [64]). Both the URN and the URL are subsets of URI, but they are generally disjoint sets.

The best-known examples for URLs are the web site addresses on the World Wide Web. Listing 4-9 shows the general URL syntax.

Listing 4-9. URL Syntax

```
protocol://domain:port/path?query_string#fragment_identifier
```

The *protocol* (*scheme name*) is followed by a colon. The other parts of URLs depend on the scheme being used. Usually there is a domain name or an IP address, an optional port number, and an optional path to the resource or script. Programs such as PHP or CGI scripts might have a query string. The end of the URL can be an optional fragment identifier.

Since many of these sections are optional, one or more of them are omitted. Listing 4-10 shows an example, where http is the protocol, www.masteringhtml5css3.com is the domain, and the path leads to the shop directory.

Listing 4-10. A Typical URL

```
http://www.masteringhtml5css3.com/shop/
```

URI references are widely used in markup languages, for example, as the attribute value of the `href` attribute on the a element in HTML or as the system identifier after the `SYSTEM` keyword in an XML DTD.

Persistent URIs

All web users know how it looks when a web site address typed into the address bar of the browser cannot be retrieved. The same might happen when a user clicks a hyperlink of a web page.

There are many reasons for URIs to become disconnected. The simplest reasons are that files have been moved to another folder or they have removed from the server. Another reason is that technologies applied on the server have been changed. For example, a company used to apply CGI scripts but recently changed to Perl. In that case, the URIs of the files located in the `cgi-bin` directory have become obsolete.

There are only a few cases when discontinuing the maintenance of URIs is acceptable, such as if the company or organization have been closed. However, causeless changes should be eliminated.

Poorly designed URIs are responsible for a large share of dead links on the Web. It is a rather complex task to design URIs in a way that they will be usable in the next few decades.

Designing URIs

URIs can be designed persistently by minimizing the information provided in them [65]. The author of an updated document can be different from that of the original one, and thus the author should not be included. The subject should also be eliminated since it changes very fast. For example, a web technology blog should apply the directory name `markup` instead of the names of exact technologies that are currently the most up-to-date ones (`XHTML11`, `HTML5`). Directory names that indicate the status of documents such as `draft` or `latest` should not be used in URIs simply because document status changes over time. A persistent URI is required for the latest version of each document.

Some parts of a web site might be restricted to members only. The access should also be eliminated from URIs because documents might be moved from the private section to the public one, or vice versa.

The most frequently provided needless information in URIs is the file extension. Technologies and tools that are currently considered as the most advanced will probably change in the near future, or the developer might change the applied technologies. Changed URIs can affect not only the findability of web pages or web page components but also your maintenance tasks. Carefully selected directory names are logical and seldom should be changed in the references in the markup.

■ **Tip** Use the name `script` or `scripts` for the directory where you store the script files of a web site instead of `php` or `javascript`, because if you adopt further scripting languages later, the URIs in the files of the site will reflect a specific language rather than a common name. Similarly, the directory name `style` or `styles` is more practical than `css` or `xsl`, and the name `news` or `feed` is more fortunate than `rss` or `atom`. The name `images` is better than `jpg`, and a `doc` or `docs` directory can hold a variety of documents from PDF to Word documents, not just a certain type.

Directory names that indicate software mechanisms such as `cgi-bin` should also be eliminated from URIs. They might change. Topic names, company sections, access levels, or security levels are also inappropriate for URIs. Classifications can change. The creation date is constant so it can be provided.

Keep in mind that multiple web servers can be hidden inside an apparent server with proxying and redirection.

Beyond providing descriptive names for users and machines, URIs should be simple, stable, and manageable. Properly designed URIs are fundamental parts of the Semantic Web [66].

Domain Names

Web resources can be located by unique IP addresses. However, they are hard to remember. Consequently, *domain names* are used instead in most cases. Figure 4-1 shows the relationship between a domain name and a URL; `www.example.com` is a subdomain of the node `example.com`, which is the subdomain of the `com` domain. The domain name syntax rules are defined by RFC 1035 [67], RFC 1123 [68], and RFC 2181 [69].

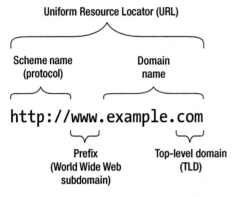

Figure 4-1. The domain within the URL

The tree of subdomains can contain a maximum of 127 levels. Each label may contain up to 63 characters. According to RFC 2181, the full length of a domain name is 253 characters.

Conventional domain names cannot contain Latin alphabet-based characters with diacritics, non-Latin characters, or scripts. With the introduction of Internationalized Domain Names (IDN), it is possible to represent names and words in several languages in native alphabets and scripts.

Domain names should be thought over before they are registered. They should be easy to remember and easy to spell [70]. There are also SEO considerations. While the name of a person generally remains the same over the years, a product or technology name can change. For example, the owner of a DVD store has probably changed from DVD sales to Blu-ray sales with the beginning of the HD era. However, the domain name containing the word *DVD* still represents the old technology. If the word *movie* or *films* would have been used, the domain name would not have become obsolete. Finding an appropriate domain name, which is still free and contains popular keywords, can be a real challenge, though.

No WWW

Although the `www.` subdomain is very common on the Web, some webmasters consider it outdated or inappropriate [71]. Similar to mail servers that do not use the `request@mail.example.com` format, web servers can allow access to web pages though the main domain.

On Apache servers, the `www.` can be removed from the URIs within the domain by adding the code in Listing 4-11 to the `.htaccess` file. Its name stands for hypertext access. This file provides directory-level access control that can be used for authorization, authentication, redirection, blocking, customized error response, and cache control.

Listing 4-11. Removing www. *from URIs with* .htaccess *Configuration*

```
RewriteEngine On
RewriteCond %{HTTP_HOST} ^www\.example\.com$ [NC]
RewriteRule ^(.*)$ http://example.com/$1 [R=301,L]
```

This code makes it unnecessary to remove the www. from every hyperlink of the web site one by one. However, a large share of webmasters disagrees with removing the www. from URIs [72]. According to their reasoning, www. is a reminder that the World Wide Web (WWW) is just one of the many services on the internet.

■ **Tip** The previous code is not really required since an unlimited number of subdomains are generally included in the domain registration price. It is a common practice that domain owners point both the main domain and the www subdomain to the same directory of the web server. In other words, www.domain.com is the preferred URI, and users retrieving domain.com are redirected to www.domain.com. Doing so, users can access the same content with and without www.

Base href

The previous sections discussed absolute URLs. Since many web page components are located in the subdirectories of the root directory associated with the domain, relative URLs can also be used. They are shorter, however, and not always convenient. For example, if the hierarchy is too deep and the style sheets are located in a styles directory three directories above a web page, the path becomes rather long (Listing 4-12).

Listing 4-12. A Long Path in a Complex Web Site

```
<link rel="stylesheet" type="text/css" href="../../../styles/main.css" />
```

The situation would be different if all locations were declared according to the root directory (Listing 4-13).

Listing 4-13. Setting a Base Directory for a Web Site

```
<base href="http://example.com/" />
```

The specified URL is used as the base for all relative URLs in the document. By adding the base element to the document head, the original example can be simplified (Listing 4-14).

Listing 4-14. A Short Path According to the Base Directory

```
<link rel="stylesheet" type="text/css" href="styles/main.css" />
```

Eliminating File Extensions

One of the key techniques for creating permanent URIs is to remove file extensions. On a file-based web server such as Apache, it can be done by *content negotiation* [73]. We used content negotiation earlier in the chapter to set the precedence between MIME types; now we will use it for creating a precedence order for file types. As a result, file extensions can be kept on the files but can safely be removed from links [74].

Using a type map file, Apache servers can check the directory for all files with the given name and any extension and select the appropriate one (the one with the highest precedence). A type map file takes precedence over the extension of the file (even if the special search for implicit file name pattern match, *Multiviews*, is enabled). The precedence of a higher-quality image file variant can be set by the qs parameter. In Listing 4-15, the file logo.svg will be used for all URIs that refer to the file without extension. If there is no SVG version of that file in the directory, the PNG version will be used.

Listing 4-15. Precedence Order of File Types Set by the qs Parameter

```
URI: logo

URI: logo.svg
Content-type: image/svg+xml; qs=0.8

URI: logo.png
Content-type: image/jpeg; qs=0.5
```

The qs value varies from 0.000 to 1.000. Variants with a qs value of 0.000 will never be chosen. Entries of the different variants are separated by blank lines that cannot be used within entries.

Explicitly setting paths to specific file variants is not feasible for larger sites with hundreds or thousands of files. The second option for content negotiation on Apache servers is to use the MultiViews search feature, where the server performs an implicit file name pattern match within directories and chooses from the results. MultiViews is a fine option for eliminating file extensions that contributes to easy maintenance (in case new file versions will be used) and optimal markup (because of shorter links). MultiViews can be enabled in the server configuration or .htaccess file (Listing 4-16).

Listing 4-16. MultiViews Enabled

```
<Directory /home/www/example/htdocs>
Options + MultiViews
</Directory>
```

Now when the server receives a request for /images/logo and /images/logo does not exist, the server searches inside the images directory looking for all files named logo.*, assigning MIME types based on the extension of each file. The server then chooses the best match based on the preferences and delivers that resource. For example, let's assume that the images directory contains the following file variants: logo.svg, logo.png, and logo.gif. When there is a query for /images/logo, the precedence order will be considered in the answer to the query (Listing 4-17).

Listing 4-17. The Precedence Order of Image File Formats

```
Accept: image/svg+xml; q=.8, image/png; q=.5, image/gif;q=0.2, */*;q=0.1
```

When MultiViews is enabled, the server would search the referenced directory and deliver the image with the highest quality (thanks to the highest precedence), in other words, logo.svg. This is achieved in a way that URIs in HTML/XHTML files do not need to contain the file extension, which makes maintenance easier and reduces file size. URIs can now omit the technology behind the resource. Since `example.com/images/logo.svg` becomes `example.com/images/logo`, the logo embedding used throughout the site becomes `<img src="logo" alt="Company logo">` instead of `<img src="logo.svg" alt="Company logo">`.

While a URI ending in `.html` or `.php` will probably remain the same in the near future, even widely used file types might soon become obsolete or less frequently used within a few years. A Flash animation (`.swf`) might be changed to HTML5 markup (`.html`), a PNG image (`.png`) to its SVG version (`.svg`), and so on. As a consequence, all currently created internal links of the site as well as the external links on other sites will be invalid.

The World Wide Web Consortium has mastered eliminating extensions in links. Even images of the site are provided without extension in links (the files have extensions), so the links pointing to the file in hundreds of web documents should not be modified if the image will be changed, as, for example, from `logo.png` to `logo.svg`.

References with extensions remain usable; however, they do not allow the server to select the best of currently available and future formats. With a *type map* declaration or with enabled *MultiViews search* [75], on the other hand, raster images used for ages can be updated to their new, SVG versions in no time. The file name without the extension is *content-type generic*, while file names with extensions are *content-type specific*.

There is a special file supported by all web servers, called `index.html`. When users do not specify a file in the address bar, browsers open this file by default (with content negotiation, the extension can be not only `.html` but also `.php`, `.jsp`, `.aspx`, and so on). This is the reason why web sites can be opened without typing the file name and extension to the end of the domain name such as `www.example.com/index.html`. This server behavior can also be used for creating permanent access to web pages within a site. Instead of adding the `about.html`, `services.html`, `portfolio.html`, and `contact.html` files to the root directory of the domain, they can be provided as `index.html` files within their own subdirectories. As a result, the pages of the site can be accessed as `www.example.com/about/`, `www.example.com/services/`, and so on, without file extensions. Naturally, original file names can also be kept if the default file of each directory is set on the server. However, in that case, server settings should also be migrated if the hosting provider of the web site is changed.

Namespace URIs

Namespace URIs are used to uniquely identify an XML application and separate it from other XML languages. The prefixes associated with a namespace URI are handy when you want to associate an element or an attribute with a particular XML namespace. Although a namespace URI does not necessarily point to a particular document, many do, such as the `http://www.w3.org/1999/xhtml` namespace used by XHTML 1.*x*/5 (discussed earlier in Chapter 3). The previous namespace URI will let the XML parser know that the elements and attributes used in the document are from the XHTML vocabulary.

■ **Note** Namespace URIs might reveal the corresponding specification or standard, but many are placeholders only.

Even if they are generally designed stable, namespaces might evolve over time [76]. To eliminate the problem, namespaces are often registered as *Persistent Uniform Resource Locators* at `purl.org`[77]. If the resource they point to changes, the URI can be modified in the profile settings on `purl.org`, which will provide the up-to-date URI with the persistent address.

The XML namespaces should be controlled by the corresponding W3C Recommendation [78].

Summary

In this chapter, you learned about the general structure of an HTTP header, which provides information about web documents sent by the server. You know the most common MIME types and their declaration by now, which can be used to ensure that browsers will properly handle your web site components. You also know how to use content negotiation on the server to eliminate file extensions, which makes future maintenance easier. Furthermore, you learned how to serve XHTML properly, which makes all the difference, because XHTML documents served as `application/xhtml+xml` will be parsed by an XML parser rather than a much less error-sensitive HTML parser. You know how to design URIs in order to maximize their persistence.

By now you are ready to create standard-compliant markup and use the proper settings for serving the files of your web sites. In the next chapter, you will learn techniques for separating web site content from its presentation by using Cascading Style Sheets (CSS).

References

1. Nottingham M, Mogul J (2005) HTTP Header Field Registrations. RFC 4229. The Internet Society. http://tools.ietf.org/html/rfc4229. Accessed 15 Aug 2011

2. IANA (2007) MIME Media Types. The Internet Assigned Numbers Authority. www.iana.org/assignments/media-types/. Accessed 01 January 2011

3. Murata M, Laurent S, Kohn D (2001) XML Media Types. The Internet Society. http://tools.ietf.org/html/rfc3023. Accessed 08 October 2010

4. Baker M, Stark P (2002) The 'application/xhtml+xml' Media Type. The Internet Society. http://tools.ietf.org/html/rfc3236. Accessed 08 October 2010

5. Masayasu I (2002) XHTML Media Types. W3C Note. World Wide Web Consortium. www.w3.org/TR/2002/NOTE-xhtml-media-types-20020801/. Accessed 08 October 2010

6. Nottingham M, Sayre R (eds) (2005) The Atom Syndication Format. The Internet Society. http://tools.ietf.org/html/rfc4287. Accessed 08 October 2010

7. IANA (2007) MIME Media Types. Internet Assigned Numbers Authority. www.iana.org/assignments/media-types/. Accessed 08 October 2010

8. IANA (2002) Application for Media Type. The Internet Assigned Numbers Authority. www.iana.org/cgi-bin/mediatypes.pl. Accessed 01 January 2011

9. Nottingham M, Sayre R (eds) (2005) The Atom Syndication Format. Proposed standard. The Internet Society. http://tools.ietf.org/html/rfc4287. Accessed 22 November 2010

10. Gregorio J, de Hora B (eds) (2007) The Atom Publishing Protocol. Proposed standard. The Internet Society. http://tools.ietf.org/html/rfc5023. Accessed 22 November 2010

11. Hoehrmann B (2006) Scripting Media Types. The Internet Society. http://tools.ietf.org/html/rfc4329. Accessed 01 January 2011

12. Crockford D (2006) The application/json Media Type for JavaScript Object Notation (JSON). RFC 4627. The Internet Society. http://tools.ietf.org/html/rfc4627. Accessed 01 January 2011

13. Carlisle D, Ion P, Miner R (eds) (2010) Selection of Media Types for MathML Instances. In: Mathematical Markup Language (MathML) Version 3.0. W3C Recommendation. World Wide Web Consortium. www.w3.org/TR/MathML3/appendixb.html. Accessed 02 January 2011

14. Freed N, Borenstein N (1996) Octet-Stream Subtype. In: Multipurpose Internet Mail Extensions (MIME) Part Two: Media Types. RFC 2046. The Internet Society. http://tools.ietf.org/html/rfc2046. Accessed 01 January 2011

15. Goncalves I, Pfeiffer S, Montgomery C (2008) Ogg Media Types. RFC 5334. The Internet Society. http://tools.ietf.org/html/rfc5334. Accessed 01 January 2011

16. Taft E, Pravetz J, Zilles S, Masinter L (2004) The application/pdf Media Type. RFC 3778. The Internet Society. http://tools.ietf.org/html/rfc3778. Accessed 01 January 2011

17. Freed N, Borenstein N (1996) Multipurpose Internet Mail Extensions (MIME) Part One: Format of Internet Message Bodies. RFC 2045. Internet Engineering Task Force. http://tools.ietf.org/html/rfc2045. Accessed 18 February 2011

18. Freed N, Borenstein N (1996) PostScript Subtype. In: Multipurpose Internet Mail Extensions (MIME) Part Two: Media Types. RFC 2046. The Internet Society. http://tools.ietf.org/html/rfc2046. Accessed 01 January 2011

19. Swartz A (2004) The application/rdf+xml Media Type Registration. RFC 3870. The Internet Society. www.ietf.org/rfc/rfc3870.txt. Accessed 02 January 2011

20. IANA (2007) Registration of the MIME type application/rtf. Internet Assigned Numbers Authority. www.iana.org/assignments/media-types/application/rtf. Accessed 03 January 2011

21. Levinson E (1995) SGML Media Types. Internet Assigned Numbers Authority. www.rfc-editor.org/rfc/rfc1874.txt. Accessed 03 January 2011

22. Hoschka P (2006) The application/smil and application/smil+xml Media Types. RFC 4536. The Internet Society. www.ietf.org/rfc/rfc4536.txt. Accessed 03 January 2011

23. Baker M, Nottingham M (2004) The "application/soap+xml" media type. RFC 3902. The Internet Society. http://tools.ietf.org/html/rfc3902. Accessed 01 January 2011

24. Prud'hommeaux E, Seaborne A (2007) Internet Media Type, File Extension and Macintosh File Type. In: SPARQL Query Language for RDF. World Wide Web Consortium. www.w3.org/TR/2007/CR-rdf-sparql-query-20070614/#mediaType. Accessed 03 January 2011

25. Beckett D, Broekstra J (eds) (2007) Internet Media Type, File Extension and Macintosh File Type. In: SPARQL Query Results XML Format. World Wide Web Consortium. www.w3.org/TR/2007/CR-rdf-sparql-XMLres-20070925/#mime. Accessed 03 January 2011

26. Baker M, Stark P (2002) The "application/xhtml+xml" Media Type. RFC 3236. The Internet Society. http://tools.ietf.org/html/rfc3236. Accessed 01 January 2011

27. Murata M, St.Laurent S, Kohn D (2001) XML Media Types. RFC 3023. The Internet Society. http://tools.ietf.org/html/rfc3023. Accessed 01 January 2011

28. Kay M (ed) (2007) The XSLT Media Type. In: XSL Transformations (XSLT) Version 2.0. W3C Recommendation. World Wide Web Consortium. www.w3.org/TR/2007/REC-xslt20-20070123/#media-type-registration. Accessed 03 January 2011

29. Paul Lindner (ed) (1993) Registration of the new MIME Content-Type/Subtype application/zip. Internet Assigned Numbers Authority. www.iana.org/assignments/media-types/application/zip. Accessed 01 January 2011

30. Ashbridge M (2006) Registration of the MIME type application/vnd.google-earth.kml+xml. Internet Assigned Numbers Authority. www.iana.org/assignments/media-types/application/vnd.google-earth.kml+xml. Accessed 03 January 2011

31. Ashbridge M (2006) Registration of the MIME type application/vnd.google-earth.kmz. Internet Assigned Numbers Authority. www.iana.org/assignments/media-types/application/vnd.google-earth.kmz. Accessed 03 January 2011

32. Lindner P (1993) Registration of the Media Type application/msword. Internet Assigned Numbers Authority. www.iana.org/assignments/media-types/application/msword. Accessed 02 January 2011

33. Gill SS (1996) Registration of the MIME type application/vnd.ms-excel. Internet Assigned Numbers Authority. www.iana.org/assignments/media-types/application/vnd.ms-excel. Accessed 03 January 2011

34. Gill SS (1996) Registration of the MIME type application/vnd.ms-powerpoint. Internet Assigned Numbers Authority. www.iana.org/assignments/media-types/application/vnd.ms-powerpoint. Accessed 03 January 2011

35. Schubert S (2009) The application/vnd.oasis.opendocument.graphics MIME type. Internet Assigned Numbers Authority. www.iana.org/assignments/media-types/application/vnd.oasis.opendocument.graphics. Accessed 02 January 2011

36. Schubert S (2009) The application/vnd.oasis.opendocument.presentation MIME type. Internet Assigned Numbers Authority. www.iana.org/assignments/media-types/application/vnd.oasis.opendocument.presentation. Accessed 02 January 2011

37. Schubert S (2009) The application/vnd.oasis.opendocument.spreadsheet MIME type. Internet Assigned Numbers Authority. www.iana.org/assignments/media-types/application/vnd.oasis.opendocument.spreadsheet. Accessed 02 January 2011

38. Schubert S (2009) The application/vnd.oasis.opendocument.text MIME type. Internet Assigned Numbers Authority. www.iana.org/assignments/media-types/application/vnd.oasis.opendocument.text. Accessed 02 January 2011

39. Nilsson M (2000) The audio/mpeg Media Type. RFC 3003. The Internet Society. http://tools.ietf.org/html/rfc3003. Accessed 01 January 2011

40. Barbato L (2008) RTP Payload Format for Vorbis Encoded Audio. RFC 5215. The Internet Society. http://tools.ietf.org/html/rfc5215. Accessed 01 January 2011

41. Microsoft Support (2003) MIME Type Settings for Windows Media Services. KB 288102. Microsoft Corporation. http://support.microsoft.com/kb/288102. Accessed 02 January 2011

42. Fleischman E (1998) WAVE and AVI Codec Registries. RFC 2361. The Internet Society. http://tools.ietf.org/html/rfc2361. Accessed 01 January 2011

43. Boutell T et al (1997) PNG (Portable Network Graphics) Specification Version 1.0. RFC 2083. Internet Engineering Task Force. http://tools.ietf.org/html/rfc2083. Accessed 01 January 2011

44. Randers-Pehrson G (2009) Registration of the Media Type image/png. Internet Assigned Numbers Authority. www.iana.org/assignments/media-types/image/png. Accessed 02 January 2011

45. Andersson O et al (2008) Media Type Registration for image/svg+xml. In: Scalable Vector Graphics (SVG) Tiny 1.2 Specification. W3C Recommendation. www.w3.org/TR/SVGTiny12/mimereg.html. Accessed 02 January 2011

46. Parsons G, Rafferty J (2002) Tag Image File Format (TIFF) – image/tiff MIME Sub-type Registration. RFC 3302. The Internet Society. http://tools.ietf.org/html/rfc3302. Accessed 01 January 2011

47. Butcher S (ed) (2003) Vendor Tree - vnd.microsoft.icon. Internet Assigned Numbers Authority. www.iana.org/assignments/media-types/image/vnd.microsoft.icon. Accessed 02 January 2011

48. Levinson E (1998) The MIME Multipart/Related Content-type. RFC 2387. The Internet Society. http://tools.ietf.org/html/rfc2387. Accessed 02 January 2011

49. Masinter L (1998) Returning Values from Forms: multipart/form-data. RFC 2388. The Internet Society. http://tools.ietf.org/html/rfc2388. Accessed 18 February 2011

50. Galvin J, Murphy S, Crocker S, Freed N (1995) Security Multiparts for MIME: Multipart/Signed and Multipart/Encrypted. RFC 1847. The Internet Engineering Task Force. http://tools.ietf.org/html/rfc1847. Accessed 02 January 2011

51. Lie H, Bos B, Lilley C (1998) The text/css Media Type. RFC 2318. The Internet Society. http://tools.ietf.org/html/rfc2318. Accessed 02 January 2011

52. Shafranovich Y (2005) Common Format and MIME Type for Comma-Separated Values (CSV) Files. RFC 4180. The Internet Society. http://tools.ietf.org/html/rfc4180. Accessed 02 January 2011

53. Connolly D, Masinter L (2000) The 'text/html' Media Type. RFC 2854. The Internet Society. http://tools.ietf.org/html/rfc2854. Accessed 02 January 2011

54. Hoehrmann B (2006) Scripting Media Types. RFC 4329. The Internet Society. http://tools.ietf.org/html/rfc4329. Accessed 02 January 2011

55. Gellens R (2004) The Text/Plain Format and DelSp Parameters. The Internet Society. http://tools.ietf.org/html/rfc3676. Accessed 02 January 2011

56. Lim Y, Singer D (2006) MIME Type Registration for MPEG-4. RFC 4337. http://tools.ietf.org/html/rfc4337. Accessed 02 January 2011

57. Goncalves I, Pfeiffer S, Montgomery C (2008) Ogg Media Types. RFC 5334. Internet Engineering task Force. http://tools.ietf.org/html/rfc5334. Accessed 02 January 2011

58. Lindner P (ed) (1993). Registration of the MIME content-type/subtype video/quicktime. Internet Assigned Numbers Authority. www.iana.org/assignments/media-types/video/quicktime. Accessed 02 January 2011

59. Microsoft Support (2003) MIME Type Settings for Windows Media Services. Microsoft Corporation. http://support.microsoft.com/kb/288102. Accessed 02 January 2011

60. Nottingham M, Mogul J (2005) HTTP Header Field Registrations. The Internet Society. http://tools.ietf.org/html/rfc4229. Accessed 08 October 2010

61. Fielding R, Irvine UC, Gettys J, Mogul J, Frystyk H, Masinter L, Leach P, Berners-Lee T (1999) Hypertext Transfer Protocol – HTTP/1.1. World Wide Web Consortium and The Internet Society. www.w3.org/Protocols/rfc2616/rfc2616-sec14.html. Accessed 08 October 2010

62. Berners-Lee T, Fielding R, Masinter L (1998) Uniform Resource Identifiers (URI): Generic Syntax. RFC 2396. The Internet Society. http://tools.ietf.org/html/rfc2396. Accessed 18 January 2011

63. Berners-Lee T, Masinter L, McCahill M (eds) (1994) Uniform Resource Locators (URL). RFC 1738. The Internet Engineering Task Force. http://tools.ietf.org/html/rfc1738. Accessed 18 January 2011

64. Mealling M, Denenberg R (eds) (2002) Report from the Joint W3C/IETF URI Planning Interest Group: Uniform Resource Identifiers (URIs), URLs, and Uniform Resource Names (URNs): Clarifications and Recommendations. RFC 3305. The Internet Society. http://tools.ietf.org/html/rfc3305. Accessed 18 January 2011

65. Berners-Lee T (1998) Cool URIs don't change. World Wide Web Consortium. www.w3.org/Provider/Style/URI. Accessed 13 December 2010

66. Sauermann L, Cyganiak R (eds), Ayers D, Völkel M (2008) Cool URIs for the Semantic Web. W3C Interest Group Note. World Wide Web Consortium. www.w3.org/TR/cooluris/. Accessed 18 February 2011

67. Mockapetris P (1987) Domain names – Implementation and specification. RFC 1035. The Internet Engineering Task Force. http://tools.ietf.org/html/rfc1035. Accessed 19 January 2011

68. Braden R (ed) (1989) Requirements for Internet Hosts – Application and Support. RFC 1123. The Internet Engineering Task Force. http://tools.ietf.org/html/rfc1123. Accessed 19 January 2011

69. Elz R, Bush R (1997) Clarifications to the DNS Specification. RFC 2181. The Internet Engineering Task Force. http://tools.ietf.org/html/rfc2181. Accessed 19 January 2011

70. Nielsen J (2007) URL as UI. Jakob Nielsen. www.useit.com/alertbox/990321.html. Accessed 19 January 2011

71. No WWW (2008) www. is deprecated. http://no-www.org/. Accessed 19 January 2011

72. Hampton M (2011) www. is not deprecated. Michael Hampton. www.yes-www.org/. Accessed 19 January 2011

73. Fielding R, Irvine UC, Gettys J, Mogul J, Frystyk H, Masinter L, Leach P, Berners-Lee T (1999) Content Negotiation. In: Hypertext Transfer Protocol – HTTP/1.1. The Internet Society. www.w3.org/Protocols/rfc2616/rfc2616-sec12.html. Accessed 08 October 2010

74. TASF (2011) Content Negotiation. Apache HTTP Server Version 2.0. The Apache Software Foundation. http://httpd.apache.org/docs/2.0/content-negotiation.html. Accessed 23 January 2011

75. TASF (2011) Apache Module mod_negotiation. The Apache Software Foundation. http://httpd.apache.org/docs/2.0/mod/mod_negotiation.html#typemaps. Accessed 23 January 2011

76. Berners-Lee T (ed) (2011) Namespace Changes over Time. In: URIs for W3C namespaces. World Wide Web Consortium. www.w3.org/2005/07/13-nsuri. Accessed 18 February 2011

77. OCLC, Zepheira (2011) Persistent Uniform Resource Locators (PURL). OCLC Online Computer Library Center Inc., Zepheira LLC. http://purl.org. Accessed 18 February 2011

78. Bray T, Hollander D, Layman A, Tobin R, Thompson HS (eds) (2009) Namespaces in XML 1.0 (Third Edition). W3C Recommendation. World Wide Web Consortium. www.w3.org/TR/xml-names/. Accessed 18 February 2011

CHAPTER 5

Style Sheets

A golden rule in web site standardization is to separate content from appearance. XHTML elements eliminate style attributes. Style sheets should be provided in external files. Style definitions provided in CSS have similar features to the ones applied in older HTML documents as inline styles. However, naming conventions and additional mechanisms are often confusing. Beyond code validity, there are other features such as scope, property value inheritance, and the order of separators, which should also be considered to obtain optimized CSS files.

In this chapter, you will learn frequently used standards for styling web sites, including general CSS grammar rules and selector syntaxes that are vital for every web site. After examining the differences between properties of different CSS versions, you will gain a solid understanding of standardization issues and the challenges of providing backward-compatibility. You will also become familiar with fundamental principles in CSS ruleset optimization. Furthermore, you will analyze the methods used by rendering engines for determining the styles to apply.

Cascading Style Sheets

Cascading Style Sheets (*CSS*) is a style sheets language (style language) introduced by W3C. *Cascading* refers to the process of determining the priority of styling rules. CSS is used to define the presentational semantics of structured documents. It provides control over visual as well as aural[1] characteristics of HTML and XHTML documents and their elements. Some typical features are, for example, fonts, colors, backgrounds, margins, borders, and layers. CSS provides a powerful feature to support more than just visual media and target special browsers running on different types of devices: media types. CSS supports not only the most commonly used visual media type but also other media types that can be grouped as follows:

- *Aural*: Properties for aural browsers. Examples: `pitch`, `pitch-range`, `play-during`, `richness`, `voice-family`.

- *Interactive*: Properties for devices that allow user interaction. Examples: `nav-down`, `nav-index`, `nav-left`, `nav-right`, `nav-up`.

---

[1] Although most styles associated with web documents are visual, CSS supports aural properties as well, including volume, speaking, pause, cue, spatial properties, and voice characteristics. They are used for aural presentation, such as when a document is converted to plain text and fed to a screen reader. Beyond improved accessibility, aural style sheets also have a potential in online education, entertainment, in-car use, and so on.

- *Paged and noncontinuous*: Properties for the content of documents split into one or more discrete pages, such as the pages of documents to print. Examples: image-orientation, page, page-break-before, page-break-inside, page-policy, size.

- *Speech*: Properties for styling speech. Examples: cue, cue-after, cue-before, mark, mark-after, mark-before, pause, speak-header, speak-numeral, speak-punctuation, speech-rate, stress.

As you will see later in the chapter, most CSS properties are visual properties or can be applied to all media, but there are many properties designed for a specific media type.

One of the major concepts of CSS is to separate HTML/XHTML content from appearance, in other words, to distinguish style from structure. Another aim is centralization, which means providing full control over the styles of multiple documents from a single location.

Although CSS is used primarily for styling (X)HTML web documents, it can also be applied to all kinds of XML documents, for example XUL or SVG [1]. In SVG, many CSS properties are reused for styling, such as font properties, text properties, and other visual properties. SVG also uses CSS features such as the CSS syntax, selectors, external style sheets, cascading, inheritance, and at-rules, each of which will be described later in detail. Since SVG is an XML application, internal CSS style sheets can be provided as CDATA sections (Listing 5-1).

Listing 5-1. Embedded CSS in SVG

```
<?xml version="1.0" standalone="no"?>
<!DOCTYPE svg PUBLIC "-//W3C//DTD SVG August 1999//EN"
 "http://www.w3.org/Graphics/SVG/SVG-19990812.dtd">
<svg>
  <defs>
    <style>
      <![CDATA[ main { font-size: 14; font-family: Georgia; } ]]>
    </style>
  </defs>
  <text class="main">Here is my title</text>
</svg>
```

CSS can even be used for mathematical notations with or without MathML, the markup language discussed in Chapter 3, which is especially designed for publishing equations and mathematical symbols on the Web [2, 3].

Levels, Profiles, and Modules

The various versions of CSS are often referred as *CSS levels*. Each CSS level is based on the previous level and adds new properties and features. The three most significant versions are CSS1, CSS 2.1, and CSS3.

Subsets of at least one level of CSS created for a particular device are called *CSS profiles*, such as the CSS Print Profile [4], the CSS TV Profile [5], and the CSS Mobile Profile [6].

The specifications that form CSS3 are called *CSS modules*.

■ **Caution** Profiles are not equal to media types, which were introduced in CSS2.

The three major CSS versions are described in the following sections.

CSS1

CSS Level 1, the first Cascading Style Sheet specification, was published in 1996. It is a W3C Recommendation, but its development has been closed by W3C [7]. CSS1 introduced styles for font properties, element color, alignment, tables, margin, border, padding, and positioning. CSS1 properties can be applied to uniquely identified elements or element groups.

CSS2 and CSS 2.1

CSS Level 2 was developed as a superset of CSS1 and has been extended with several new features. The most important ones are layer order (z-index), three types of element positioning (absolute, relative, and fixed), the aural media type, and bidirectional text.

CSS Level 2 Revision 1, often abbreviated as CSS 2.1 [8], has been the ultimate styling solution on the Web for many years. CSS 2.1 became a W3C Recommendation in 2011.

CSS3

The development of CSS Level 3 (CSS3) started in 2005. In contrast to further CSS specifications, CSS3 is modularized [9]. It is described by separate documents such as the modules Selectors, Media Queries, Text, Backgrounds and Borders, Colors, 2D Transformations, 3D Transformations, Transitions, Animations, and Multi-Columns. The modules are in different stages of development and browser implementation. Until recently, only a few modules had been standardized, such as the Color module [10].

A variety of new functions and features have been introduced in CSS3 such as border-radius, box-shadow, background-origin; color declaration in HSL, HSLA, and RGBA; text-shadow; text-overflow; word-wrap; box-sizing; attribute selectors; multicolumn layout; Web Fonts; and speech.

Grammar and Conventions

Parsing errors caused by nonexisting properties, incorrect values, malformed declarations, and so on, can be eliminated by following the proper *CSS syntax*. The grammar ensures syntactically correct CSS, which makes it possible for browsers to handle parsing rules, selector, property, value, and unit notations correctly. Although the fundamental rules are similar, each CSS version has its own syntax [11]. Being a superset of CSS 2.1, CSS3 introduced additional semantic constraints.

Identifiers and Classes

The ID and class identifiers should always start with a letter. Since these identifiers correspond to the id and class markup attributes and since an element with an id attribute is unique within a web page, ID identifiers can be used to style a unique element of a page. If the same styles are applied to multiple elements, class identifiers should be used. Identifier names are case sensitive. Using the letters a-z and the numbers 0-9 is highly recommended, although underscores and hyphens are also allowed. Names should be meaningful and semantic. Unique names should be applied.

Units

CSS supports several measurement values, which are summarized in Table 5-1.

Table5-1. CSS Units

Unit	Description
%	Percentage.
in	Inch.
cm	Centimeter.
mm	Millimeter.
em	1 em is equal to the current font size, which can be used to automatically adapt the font size proportions to the font size chosen by the user in the browser. The em unit defines the proportion of the width and height of a given letter with respect to the point size of a given font. This unit originates in typography.
ex	1 ex is the x-height of a font (approximately half the font size).
pt	1 point is equal to 1/72 inch.
pc	1 pica is equal to 12 points.
px	1 pixel is a dot on the screen.

■ **Note** In spite of this variety, only three of these units are used most of the time: %, em, and px.

Color Declarations

There are several notations in CSS for declaring colors. A brief overview is provided in the following sections, which is important because color declaration examples will be used intensively in the demonstrational rulesets throughout the chapter.

Hexadecimal Notation

Hexadecimal notation is by far the most commonly used notation for declaring colors in CSS. In the RGB color space used on the Web, any color can be represented by additive color mixing, using the different intensity variants of three colors: Red, Green, and Blue (RGB). Two hundred and fifty-six shades of the three base colors are adequate to mix any color, because any two adjacent shades of red, green, or blue with an intensity difference of 1/256 cannot be distinguished by the human eye. Since there are 256 shades for each channel, the values vary from 0 to 255 (00 to ff in hexadecimal notation) per channel; 0 is the darkest shade of the channel, and 255 is the lightest.

The hexadecimal numeral system applies the positional (also known as *place-value*) notation. In contrast to the 10 digits of the decimal numeral system, in the hexadecimal system there are 16 symbols from 0 to 9 and a to f (the letters represent the values from 10 to 15). The latest symbol corresponds to the value multiplied by the 0th power[2] of 16, the symbol preceding the last symbol represents the value multiplied by the 1st power of 16, and so forth.

Consequently, the symbols 0–9 in hexadecimal notation correspond to the identical numbers in decimal notation, while a in hex is equal to 10 in the decimal system, b to 11, c to 12, d to 13, e to 14, and f to 15. Further numbers can be computed by the place-value (starting from 0). For example, the hexadecimal value e8 corresponds to the decimal value 232, because $14 \cdot 16^1 + 8 \cdot 16^0 = 14 \cdot 16 + 8 \cdot 1 = 224 + 8 = 232$. Conversion from decimal to hexadecimal can be performed similarly, but with the reverse computation. For example, 86 in decimal notation is 56 in hexadecimal notation, because $86/16 = 5.375$, so the first digit is 5. $5 \cdot 16 = 80$, and the remainder is 6, which is the second digit, because $5 \cdot 16^1 + 6 \cdot 16^0 = 5 \cdot 16 + 6 \cdot 1 = 80 + 6 = 86$.

In CSS, hexadecimal color declarations begin with a number sign (#), followed by six hexadecimal (hex) values, two for each channel. They are used to mix colors arbitrarily. For example, pure red can be set by #ff0000. In other words, the intensity of the red channel is maximal (ff), while the intensity of green and blue are minimal (00). Similarly, pure green is #00ff00, while pure blue is #0000ff. If the values of each channel are set to 00, the result is black (#000000). If all values are maximal, you get white (#ffffff). If the values for each channel are identical, the result is a shade of gray (Listing 5-2).

Listing 5-2. A Gray Font Color Declared for All Paragraphs

```
p {
  color: #898989;
}
```

▪ **Tip** If the two digits of each channel are identical, they can be abbreviated by omitting the second digit. For example, #f00 represents red, #0f0 represents green, #00f represents blue, #000 represents black, #fff represents white, and so on.

The RGB and RGB(a) Notations

The saturation of each color channel in the RGB model can also be declared by either decimal numbers or percentages (Listing 5-3).

Listing 5-3. Simple RGB Notation

```
p {
  color: rgb(0, 255, 0) /*  equivalent to rgb(0, 100%, 0), #00ff00 and #0f0 */
}
```

---

[2] Any nonzero number raised to the power 0 is 1.

The previous notation is supported by CSS 2.1 but has been extended in CSS3 with the transparency (alpha channel) of the color. This notation is known as RGB(a). For example, the pure green with 75 percent transparency (which corresponds to 25 percent opacity) can be declared as shown in Listing 5-4. Note that the alpha is always a percentage (a value from 0 to 1) rather than running from 0–255 as the other colors do.

Listing 5-4. An RGB(a) Notation in CSS3

```
p {
   color: rgb(0, 255, 0, 0.25);
}
```

The HSL(a) Notation

In CSS, colors can also be denoted by the HSL(a) notation, where the colors are represented by their hue, saturation, and lightness. The first value can be a number from 0 to 360, while the second and third values can be declared as a percentage. The alpha channel works the same way as in RGB(a) (Listing 5-5).

Listing 5-5. A Transparent Color in HSL(a) Notation

```
#warning {
   background-color: hsl(240, 78%, 50%, 0.25);
}
```

■ **Tip** If you want to use a color seen on a photograph or on a web site, you can obtain the code in many ways. First, you can check the style sheet of the page or site for the color code. If it is not convenient, there are other techniques to get the color code. If there are no advanced image-processing applications installed on your computer, you should simply create a screenshot using the Print Screen button and copy and paste it to a basic image manipulation application, such as Microsoft Paint. Select the Color Picker tool, and click the color of your choice. Choose the Edit Colors option from the Color menu, and click Define custom colors.[3] You get the hue, lightness, and saturation of the color, along with the red, green, and blue components. Since they are provided in decimal, they need to be converted into hexadecimal with an application such as the Windows Calculator (in Scientific Mode). If you have a more advanced image manipulator than Paint, such as Adobe Photoshop, you can use the Color Picker tool on the pasted image to get the color code in different color spaces and notations, including decimal and hexadecimal.

---

[3] The version of Paint in Windows 7 has a ribbon interface instead of the conventional menu found in earlier versions.

Web-Safe Colors

In the first years of color computer screens, computers supported 256 different colors only. In that era, a list of 216 colors was referred to as *web-safe colors*. This cross-browser color palette was used to ensure that all computers, including the ones using a 256-color palette, would display the colors correctly. Web-safe colors consist of 00, 33, 66, cc, and ff values for each channel (for example, 00ff00, 663300, 993300, cc6600, and ff9966).

■ **Note** Web-safe colors are not interesting from the presentational point of view anymore, since all modern screens, monitors, and projectors are capable of representing any colors from the RGB color space.

Color Names

CSS supports the names of 16 basic colors. These keywords are easier to read than their corresponding hexadecimal values[4] (Table 5-2). Using hexadecimal notation, however, is strictly recommended (see Chapter 13).

Table 5-2. CSS Color Names Handled by All Browsers

Color	Hexadecimal Equivalent
aqua (= cyan)	#00ffff
black	#000000
blue	#0000ff
magenta (= fuchsia)	#ff00ff
gray	#808080
green	#008000
lime	#00ff00
maroon	#800000
navy	#000080
olive	#808000
purple	#800080

---

[4] After learning color mixing with hexadecimal notation, using values becomes a routine task.

Color	Hexadecimal Equivalent
red	#ff0000
silver	#c0c0c0
teal	#008080
white	#ffffff
yellow	#ffff00

Selector Syntaxes

A *CSS selector* identifies those markup elements to which the CSS style(s) will be applied. Specific element groups are styled by various types of selectors. The general structure of a *CSS rule* (or *CSS ruleset* for multiple declarations), as shown in Figure 5-1, can be written with the pseudocode shown in Listing 5-6.

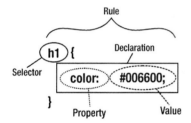

Figure5-1. CSS rule structure

Listing 5-6. Pseudocode of CSS Rulesets
```
selector [, selector2, …, selectorn] [:pseudo-class] {
   property: value;
   [property2: value2;

     …

   propertym: valuem;]
}
```

Multiple declarations of the same selector can be organized into groups separated by semicolons (;).

Tip Although it is legal to omit the semicolon after the last declaration in a ruleset, it is strongly recommended to always provide it. It makes maintenance and modifications easier and becomes handy when a declaration is moved to another location in the CSS.

For example, the rules in Listing 5-7 can be written as shown in Listing 5-8.

Listing 5-7. It Is Not Optimal to Declare Rules of the Same Element Separately

```
h1 { font-weight: bold }
h1 { font-size: 1.6em }
h1 { font-family: Verdana }
```

Listing 5-8. Rules of the Same Element Should Be Grouped

```
h1 {
  font-weight: bold;
  font-size: 1.6em;
  font-family: Verdana;
}
```

Although they are equivalent, the second version should be preferred for many reasons. First, it is shorter and thus contributes to code length optimality. Second, further declarations of other selectors might accidentally be inserted between the single lines, making the CSS file much harder to maintain. Finally, the second arrangement is easier to read, which makes development easier.

Element Selectors

If all paragraphs of a web site are intended to be written in Garamond with 1.2em font size, the ruleset looks like Listing 5-9.

Listing 5-9. A Ruleset for All Paragraphs

```
p {
  font-size: 1.2em;
  font-family: Garamond;
}
```

This applies to all paragraphs in the markup such as the ones in Listing 5-10.

Listing 5-10. Paragraphs to Be Styled by the Ruleset of Listing 5-9

```
<p>
 A paragraph.
</p>
<p>
 Another paragraph.
</p>
```

Naturally, a subset of paragraphs might have a different ruleset that partially or fully overrides the general rules (see the "Cascading" section later in the chapter).

In the previous example, the selector selects a markup element. Such selectors are called *element selectors* and apply the corresponding element names themselves. The curly braces contain the properties of the element to style, along with the values to which they should be changed. The curly braces and the content between them is the *declaration block*. The property-value pairs are separated from each other by semicolons. The properties are separated from their values by colons. Each line is called a *declaration* or *statement*.

The selectors are separated by *combinators*, that is, whitespace, **>** or **+**. Further whitespace characters might be present between the combinators and the simple selectors around them [12].

Selectors can also be grouped if the same CSS rules apply to them. The comma (**,**) should be used as the combinator. Grouping common rules contributes to CSS code optimality. For example, Listing 5-11 changes the color and font size of both div elements with the id attribute articles and relatedlinks, respectively.

Listing 5-11. Common Rules Can Be Grouped to Avoid Duplication

```
#articles, #relatedlinks {
  color: white;
  font-size: 1.8em;
}
```

Class Selectors

Class selectors, which begin with a period (.), select all elements with a class attribute identical to the value specified in them. Since the class attribute can be applied multiple times in a web page, class selectors can style any element within the document with the same class identifier. For example, the rule in Listing 5-12 is referred in the markup, as shown in Listing 5-13 and Listing 5-14.

Listing 5-12. Class Selector Example

```
.abstract {
  font-size: 1.1em;
 }
```

Listing 5-13. The Class Selector in Listing 5-12 Can Be Applied to Headings

```
<h3 class="abstract">Abstract</h3>
```

Listing 5-14. The Same Class Selector Can Also Be Applied to Paragraphs

```
<p class="abstract">
 The abstract of the first Chapter
</p>
```

If the ruleset should be applied for certain types of elements with the specified class name, a more specific rule can be written by providing the element name before the period. For example, if the previous rule should be valid exclusively for paragraphs, it should be extended by declaring the desired element type (Listing 5-15).

Listing 5-15. A Rule for All Paragraphs with the Class Name abstract

```
p.abstract {
  font-size: 1.1em;
 }
```

ID Selectors

Certain markup elements are intended to be unique throughout a web document; that is, they can occur only once per web page. They are identified by the identifier attribute id. Those selectors that select the unique element on the web page with the id attribute equal to the value specified in them are called *ID selectors* and begin with a hash mark (#). Listing 5-16 shows an example.

Listing 5-16. An ID Selector Example

```
#main {
  margin-left: 120px;
}
```

Listing 5-17 shows a markup example where the previous rule is applied.

Listing 5-17. Example Content for Which the ID Selector #main Can Be Applied

```
<div id="main">
  The main content has a left margin of 120 pixels.
</div>
```

Universal Selectors

A *universal selector* matches the name of any element type on a web page (any elements regardless of the type). The universal selector is referred to with an asterisk (*). Listing 5-18 shows an example.

Listing 5-18. A Universal Selector Example

```
*.caution {
  color: #ff2318;
}
```

The asterisk can be omitted if the universal selector is not the only component of a simple selector (Listing 5-19).

Listing 5-19. A Rule from Which the Asterisk Can Be Safely Omitted

```
.caution {
  color: #ff2318;
}
```

Considering the markup shown in Listing 5-20, the selector div * em will match most em elements and apply to the content of the em element in h1 (favorite), p (impressive), the first li element (hybrid electric), and the second li (fuel efficient). In the last two cases, the * matches the ul or the li.

Listing 5-20. A Demonstration Markup for the Universal Selector

```
<body>
  <div>
    <h1>My <em>favorite</em> car</h1>
    <p>The Lexus CT 200h is <em>impressive</em> due to the following reasons:</p>
    <ul>
      <li>It is a <em>hybrid electric</em> car.</li>
      <li>It is a <em>fuel efficient</em> car.</li>
    </ul>
    That's why it is a nice <em>entry-level luxury</em> hatchback.
  </div>
</body>
```

Since the em element with the content entry-level luxury is an immediate child of the div element, there is nothing for the * to match between div and em.

▦ **Caution** The implementation of universal selectors is imperfect in Internet Explorer 7 and earlier.

Attribute Selectors

Attribute selectors select every element with the attribute specified within square brackets. An attribute type or an attribute with a specific value can be styled with them. For example, all img elements with the title attribute within the document can have a yellow border by applying the rule shown in Listing 5-21.

Listing 5-21. An Attribute Selector Example with an Attribute

```
img[title] {
  border-color: #ff0;
}
```

Attribute selectors can be used not only for attributes but also for attribute-attribute value pairs. For example, a 10-pixel border can be added to all logo.png images within the web page with the CSS rule shown in Listing 5-22.

Listing 5-22. An Attribute Selector with an Attribute and an Attribute Value

```
img[src="logo.png"] {
  border: 10px;
}
```

This applies to multiple instances of the markup in Listing 5-23 throughout the web page.

Listing 5-23. A Markup Code Where Listing 5-22 Is Applied

```
<img src="logo.png" alt="logo" />
```

Child Selectors

Child selectors select the right-hand element in the selector if and only if it is a direct child of the left-hand element. The greater-than sign (>) is used between the child and the ancestor. Listing 5-24 shows an example.

Listing 5-24. Child Selector Example

```
td > a {
  font-weight: bold;
}
```

This is applied to all hyperlinks within table data cells, such as in Listing 5-25, but does not affect hyperlinks in general such as in Listing 5-26.

Listing 5-25. A Hyperlink Example for the Child Selector in Listing 5-24

```
<td><a href="http://www.nairobicity.go.ke/">Nairobi, Kenya</a></td>
```

Listing 5-26.The Child Selector Example Is Not Applied to Anchors That Are Not Children of a Data Cell

```
<a href="http://www.capital.sp.gov.br/">São Paulo, Brazil</a>
```

■ **Caution** Child selectors are not supported in Internet Explorer 6 and earlier.

Descendant Selectors

Styles of elements that are lower on the DOM tree can be provided by *descendant selectors* that use the element names separated by spaces. In contrast to child selectors, descendant selectors do not require the child element to be a direct child of the ancestor. Listing 5-27 shows an example.

Listing 5-27. Descendant Selector Example

```
td a {
  font-weight: bold;
}
```

This is applied to all hyperlinks within table data cells, for example to Listing 5-25 (similar to the child selector shown previously) or Listing 5-28. This rule does not affect hyperlinks in general, however.

Listing 5-28. An Anchor Example Where Listing 5-27 Is Applied

```
<td><p>One of the unique attractions of <a href="http://www.nairobicity.go.ke/">Nairobi,
Kenya</a> is the Nairobi National Park.</p></td>
```

Note the difference between the child selector and the descendant selector.

Adjacent Sibling Selectors

Adjacent sibling selectors select the element on the right-hand side of the selector if and only if it has an instance of the element on the left-hand side next to it. The **+** sign is applied as the combinator. Sibling elements are on the same level within the DOM hierarchy. Listing 5-29 shows an example.

Listing 5-29. Adjacent Sibling Selector Example

```
h2 + p {
  color: #0f0;
}
```

This selector applies to Listing 5-30, but neither to Listing 5-31 nor Listing 5-32.

Listing 5-30. Elements That Apply the Green Color from Listing 5-29

```
<h2>Heading</h2>
<p>A paragraph</p>
```

Listing 5-31. A Paragraph That Does Not Apply the Rule Shown in Listing 5-29

```
<p>A paragraph</p>
```

Listing 5-32. Because of the Missing Level 2 Heading Preceding the Paragraph, the Style Is Not Applied Here Either

```
<h1>Heading</h1>
<p>A paragraph</p>
```

■ **Caution** Adjacent sibling selectors are not supported in IE6 or earlier.

Pseudoclasses

Pseudoclasses, which use colons to separate an element from its state, are more sophisticated selectors. They are frequently used to determine the style of hyperlinks, depending on their states. For example, Listing 5-33 applies to all a elements but only when the mouse hovers over the link.

Listing 5-33. Link Color to Be Applied in Case an Anchor Is Being Hovered Over

```
a:hover {
  color: #000080;
}
```

Another example is Listing 5-34, which changes the color of all hyperlinks that have already been visited[5] to green.

---

[5] According to the current browser history

Listing 5-34. Link Color Set to Visited Hyperlinks

```
a:visited {
  color: #0f0;
}
```

Pseudoelements

Pseudoelements can be used to add style to specific element parts instead of whole elements. They can also be applied for inserting content before or after certain elements. The combinator is a colon (:). For example, the CSS rule in Listing 5-35 changes the font size of the first letter of all paragraphs within the web page to 2 em.

Listing 5-35. A Rule for the First Letter of Paragraphs

```
p:first-letter {
  font-size: 2em;
}
```

Property Value Types

CSS property values can be the following:

- Keywords (for example, auto)

- Basic data types (for example, %)

- Combination of keyword and custom data (for example, url('http://example.com/images/book.png')

Shorthand Notation

Certain CSS properties can be grouped into a single property declaration. The most common shorthand notations are described in the following sections.

Shorthand Notation for Font Properties

Font properties can be written either in the full form shown in Listing 5-36 or with the shorthand notation of Listing 5-37.

Listing 5-36. If Several Font Properties Should Be Set for the Same Element, the Ruleset Becomes Too Long

```
p {
  font-weight: bold;
  font-size: 1em;
  line-height: 1.2em;
  font-family: Garamond;
```

```
    font-style: normal;
}
```

Listing 5-37. Shorthand Notation for Font Properties

```
p { font: bold 1em/1.2em Garamond }
```

■ **Note** In the second case, the font-style property is not set and thus takes the value defined as the *default value* for that property in the CSS specification, which is normal.

Shorthand Notation for Background Properties

Separate background properties (Listing 5-38) have the shorthand property background (Listing 5-39).

Listing 5-38. Separate Background Properties That Can Be Shortened

```
body {
    background-color: #232323;
    background-image: url('images/bg.jpg');
    background-repeat: no-repeat;
    background-position: 100% 0%;
    background-attachment: fixed;
}
```

Listing 5-39. Background Properties Combined into a Single Background Property

```
body {
    background: #232323 url('images/bg.jpg') no-repeat 100% 0% fixed;
}
```

Shorthand Notation for List Properties

List styles, such as the ones in Listing 5-40, can also be shortened by the enumeration of the individual property values for the list-style shorthand property (Listing 5-41).

Listing 5-40. List Styles That Can Be Shortened

```
ul.tick {
    list-style-image: url('tick.png');
    list-style-type: none;
    list-style-position: inside;
}
```

Listing 5-41. A One-Line Rule for Three List Styling Property Values

```
ul.tick {
  list-style: url('tick.png') none inside;
}
```

Shorthand Notation for Padding, Border, and Margin Properties

There are five properties for setting the top, right, bottom, and left padding (`padding-top`, `padding-right`, `padding-bottom`, `padding-left`, respectively) or all of them together with the shorthand property `padding`. Similar conventions exist for borders (`border-top`, `border-right`, `border-bottom`, `border-left`, `border`) and margins (`margin-top`, `margin-right`, `margin-bottom`, `margin-left`, `margin`). There are various options for shortening the enumeration of property values in a certain order:

- Four values set the padding of each side: the top, the right, the bottom, and finally the left padding (clockwise, starting from top) (Listing 5-42).

■ **Tip** This order is worth memorizing, because it can be used not only for padding but also for borders and margins.

Listing 5-42. Padding Shorthand Property with Four Values

```
#decor {
  padding: 10px 5px 20px 30px;
}
```

- Three values set the top, right, and left (equally), and the bottom padding (Listing 5-43).

Listing 5-43. Padding Shorthand Property with Three Values

```
#decor {
  padding: 10px 20px 15px;
}
```

- Two values set an equal padding for the top and bottom sides, and then an equal padding for the right and left sides (Listing 5-44).

Listing 5-44. Padding Shorthand Property with Two Values

```
#decor {
  padding: 30px 20px;
}
```

- One value sets an equal padding for all sides (Listing 5-45).

Listing 5-45. Padding Shorthand Property with One Value

```
#decor {
   padding: 10px;
}
```

Similar shorthand notations can be used for setting border and margin property values with the border and margin shorthand properties. Further padding, border, and margin properties can also be written in shorthand notation. Listing 5-46 shows an example.

Listing 5-46. Border Properties That Can Be Shortened

```
.book {
   border-width: 1px;
   border-style: solid;
   border-top-color: #000;
   border-right-color: #000;
   border-bottom-color: #000;
   border-left-color: #000;
}
```

Since the border color of each side is the same in this example, the properties in the third, fourth, fifth, and sixth lines can be written as border-color (Listing 5-47).

Listing 5-47. The border-color Shorthand Property Sets the Border Color of Each Side of the Element

```
.book {
   border-width: 1px;
   border-style: solid;
   border-color: #000;
}
```

Even if the border colors are different, they can be declared by the border-color shorthand property by simply enumerating the desired colors in the top, right, bottom, left order (clockwise, starting from top).

All the previous properties can still be shortened to a single line, as shown in Listing 5-48.

Listing 5-48. The Shortest Border Declaration for Multiple Properties

```
.book {
   border: 1px solid #000;
}
```

Implementation

There are three ways to implement CSS. The chosen method determines the scope of styling.

- *Inline style:* Styling with the most limited scope. An inline style is embedded in an (X)HTML tag to which it exclusively applies. This CSS fragment is defined by the style attribute that can be provided on most markup elements. The attribute value has the same syntax as the contents of a CSS declaration block except that the delimiting braces are omitted [13]. Listing 5-49 shows an example.

  Listing 5-49. Inline Style Declaration Example

```
<img src="logo.png" style="margin: 10px;" alt="logo" />
```

- *Embedded (internal) style*. A code block usually located in the document head. Embedded styles are used for styling rules unique to that web page (the element to style does not occur in other pages on the site). Listing 5-50 shows an example.

Listing 5-50. An Example for Embedded Styles

```
<head>
    …
    <style type="text/css">
      #disclaimer {
        text-align: center;
        margin-top: 30px;
        margin-bottom: 60px;
      }
    </style>
    …
<head>
```

- *External style sheet*. An external style sheet is a separate file with the .css extension that contains style rules for multiple web documents, such as an entire web site. This is a plain-text file usually encoded in US-ASCII. CSS files cannot contain the style element, just the CSS style rules themselves. Each page refers to that file with the link element in the (X)HTML head section. Listing 5-51 shows an example.

Listing 5-51. Link to an External Style Sheet File in XHTML

```
<link rel="stylesheet" type="text/css" href="main.css" />
```

In XML documents (XML, XUL, SVG, and so on), external style sheets can be provided by the *XML processing instruction* xml-stylesheet in the first document section [14] (Listing 5-52).

Listing 5-52. Link to an External Style Sheet File in XML

```
<?xml-stylesheet type="text/css" href="default.css" title="Default style" ?>
```

Embedded styles override the corresponding styles declared in an external CSS file, which makes it possible to use the main styling rules of the web site while declaring some specific ones for a single web page. Inline styles are even more specific and locally override the styles of the external style sheet as well as the embedded styles (if any).

Style sheets can also import CSS rules from other style sheet files with the @import rule. It should be provided after the @charset rules (if any) but before all other rules. If the additional CSS files are in the same directory structure, the path is adequate (Listing 5-53).

Listing 5-53. Reusing an External Style Sheet

```
@import "styles/alter.css";
```

The rulesets of the file containing this rule will override the corresponding rules of the imported styles (if any). For example, if different pages of a site have the same styles except background-color, which is modified as part of the design, then all the styles can be imported and the background-color property is overwritten (alter.css in Listing 5-54). Similarly, a style sheet designed for mobile devices can reuse the main styles but remove the background image[6] and set the maximum width of the document body to the largest screen width available on smartphones today (mobile.css in Listing 5-54). All other styles are imported, including the color and the font-family.

Listing 5-54. Reusing and Extending Styles of the Main CSS File of a Site

main.css	alter.css	mobile.css
body {	@import ("main.css");	@import ("main.css");
background: url('http://example.com/ images/bg.jpg') no-repeat 100% 0% fixed;	body {	body {
background-color:#004c25;	background-color:#00254c;	background-image: none;
color: #fff;	}	max-width: 640px;
font-family: Garamond, serif;		}
}		
…		

A more robust declaration provides not the path but the URL of the file. Listing 5-55 shows an example.

Listing 5-55. Importing a Style Sheet File by Providing a Full URL

```
@import url("http://www.example.com/alter.css");
```

One of the applications of importing style sheets is to provide alternate styles for web sites that can serve several purposes. For example, accessibility can be improved by providing different style sheets for different media. The media-specific CSS files of a site can be controlled in the markup by the media attribute on the link element, as discussed earlier in Chapter 3. The rulesets of such CSS files have an intersection defined by the main CSS file of the site. The files of media-specific rules rely on each other and often import rules from each other (Listing 5-56). Multiple CSS files can also be used for site design.

---

[6] In the example, the background-image property is set using the shorthand property background in the main.css file.

Listing 5-56. Importing Media-Specific Styles

```
@import url("print.css") print;
@import url("mobile.css") handheld and (max-width: 480px);
```

Display and Visibility

The element levels of HTML and XHTML documents have already been discussed. In CSS, (X)HTML elements can generally be displayed in the following ways:

- *Block:* Uses the full width available, along with a new line before and after (Listing 5-57)

    Listing 5-57. Rule for Elements to Be Displayed As Block

    ```
    display: block;
    ```

- *Inline:* Uses only as much width as needed without breaking the row (Listing 5-58)

    Listing 5-58. Rule for Elements to Be Displayed Inline

    ```
    display: inline;
    ```

- *Not displayed:* Removes the element completely from the document so it does not take up any space, even though its corresponding markup is still in the source code (Listing 5-59)

    Listing 5-59. Rule for Elements to Hide Without Spaceholder

    ```
    display: none;
    ```

- *Hidden:* Hides the element but still takes up space in the layout (Listing 5-60)

    Listing 5-60. Rule for Elements to Hide with Spaceholder

    ```
    visibility: hidden;
    ```

Cascading

The *C* in CSS stands for *Cascading*. It is a mechanism that determines one declaration among a set of styling rules that should be applied for a certain element-property pair. Browsers consider three features in the following order to choose that declaration [15]:

1. *Weight:* The declaration with the highest weight is chosen. In CSS3, the weight of a declaration is based on the *origin of the declaration* and its *level of importance.* The origin can be of three kinds: *author, user,* and *user agent.* CSS declarations have two levels of importance: *normal* and *important* (the first one is the default level; the second one is optional and should be marked). An important declaration looks like Listing 5-61.

Listing 5-61. A Rule with the Highest Level of Importance

```
#menu {
   margin-top: 12px !important;
}
```

■ **Tip** The proper exploitation of the cascading mechanism eliminates the need for !important rules.

The weight of style sheets derived from the different origins, in descending order, is as follows:

a. User style sheets (important)

b. Author style sheets (important)

c. Author style sheets (normal)

d. User style sheets (normal)

e. Default style sheets of rendering engines

As a result, declarations written by developers generally have more weight than that of user style sheets, which have more weight than the default styles of the browser. This is the reason why links are generally rendered in the font color defined by the web site developer rather than the default anchor color (Listing 5-62).

Listing 5-62. A Rule in a CSS File That Has More Weight Than the Corresponding Rule in the Default Style Sheet of Browsers

```
a {
   font-color: #12ee12;
}
```

2. *Specificity.* The declaration with the highest specificity is chosen. The specificity of selectors can be calculated as follows [16]:

   •   The number of ID attributes in the selector is counted.

   •   The number of other attributes and pseudoclasses in the selector is counted.

   •   The number of element names in the selector is counted.

   •   The concatenation of these numbers is the specificity.

   •   Negative selectors are counted similar to their simple selectors argument.

   •   Pseudoelements are ignored.

In Listing 5-63, the specificity of the first declaration is the lowest, and the specificity of the last one is the largest. The font color of all paragraphs is the same (black), except those paragraphs that are included in a division, which have a different font color (green). The `div` elements with the `tip` value declared for the `class` attribute have an even more specific rule, which makes their font color distinctive (red, which is different from the color of any other paragraphs).

Listing 5-63. Declarations with Increasing Specificity

```
p {
    color: #000;
}


div p {
    color: #0f0;
}


.tip p {
    color: #00f;
}
```

3. *Declaration order.* If two declarations have the same weight, origin, and specificity, the last declaration is chosen (imported style sheets should also be considered). Imported style rules are processed prior to the rules of the style sheet. The rules of further imported style sheets are taken into account in the order of the `@import` rules.

Inheritance

In web markup languages and style sheets, certain codes are automatically reused. In CSS, property values of parent elements can be set to their children. The specified value of an element-property combination is copied from the corresponding computed value of the parent element. This procedure is called *inheritance*. It eliminates the need for defining properties that are straightforward. If, for example, the background color of a web document is defined, all container elements, divisions, and paragraphs within the document will inherit that property. Certainly, any of them can be arbitrarily overridden.

Certain CSS property values are defined as *inherited*. Unless a value is specified for these element-property combinations, the value is determined by inheritance.

The `inherit` value can be used for all properties to be determined by inheritance. For example, color is an inheritable property. However, the color of anchor elements is commonly set to blue by the user agent style sheet. By using the value `inherit`, the declaration of the user agent style sheet can be overridden: all child anchor elements inherit the value of the foreground color from the parent element (Listing 5-64).

Listing 5-64. Inherited Property Value

```
#warning {
   color: #000;
}
#warning a:link {
   color: inherit;
}
```

■ **Note** It should be taken into account that the more specific a property, the fewer elements it can be applied to. As you will see in the overview of CSS properties, a large share of CSS properties are not inherited at all.

Scopes and Structure

In contrast with the underlined blue hyperlinks used in the first years of the Web, modern web sites often apply different colors and decorations to accommodate the overall design. When using a dotted underline for hyperlinks, however, it is rather frustrating that linking images share the same style. To solve the problem, image borders should be removed and more specific styles set. Listing 5-65 shows an example.

Listing 5-65. Specific Rules to Eliminate the Underline for Links Declared by General Rules

```
img {
   border: 0;
}

a.nounder {
   border-bottom: none;
}
```

The *scope* of rules has a large impact on their application. The rules that apply to more (most) elements within the same category should be identified in an early stage of web site development. For example, if the vast majority of paragraphs have the same indent, that value should be applied as a general CSS rule to all p elements (for example, p { text-indent: 3em; }), and another rule should be written to the class of paragraphs that are different (for example, p.morein { text-indent: 5em; }).

In the optimal case, both the scope and the inheritance are considered for those properties that can be used as the basis for the entire web site, such as the default font size (Listing 5-66).

Listing 5-66. The Default Font Size of the Entire Web Site Can Be Inherited from the Document Body

```
body {
   font-size: 0.8em;
}
```

For those elements that require a different font size, such as headings, the property can be set specifically (Listing 5-67), and all the other elements inherit the default font size set for the document body. Consequently, there is no need to declare the font size for, say, all p and div elements, if the desired font size for them is the default one, because the property is inherited from the body element.

Listing 5-67. Specific Declarations That Override the Default Font Size Set in the Previous Listing

```
h1 {
  font-size: 1.4em;
}
h2 {
  font-size: 1.2em;
}
h3 {
  font-size: 1em;
}
```

The Box Model

The actual markup content of block elements is wrapped around by optional *paddings, borders,* and *margins,* called the *CSS box model* (Figure 5-2) [17]. These rectangular boxes are generated for certain markup elements in the document tree.

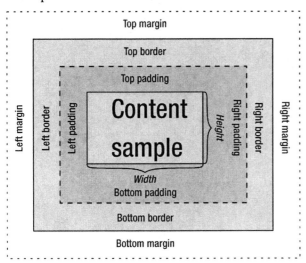

Figure5-2. The CSS box model

Text and images appear in the content. The padding clears the area around the content. The padding is affected by the background color of the box similar to the border area around the padding. The margin is the outermost area around the border. It has no background color and is transparent. The size of each area can be determined by CSS properties. Since they are optional, they can also be collapsed to 0 (that is, totally eliminated).

The margins of two vertically adjacent block elements normally collapse into one another; that is, a margin is rendered according to the size of the larger bottom margin of the first box and that of the top margin of the other below it.

The IE Box Model Bug

From the first version of CSS, the width and height of all block-level elements specified explicitly determine only the width or height of the visible element, and the padding, borders, and margins are applied afterward. In earlier versions of Internet Explorer, the CSS specifications were implemented incorrectly, which is often referred to as the *Internet Explorer box model bug*. For example, Internet Explorer 5 included the content, padding, and borders within a specified width or height, resulting in a narrower or shorter rendering of the box [18] (Figure 5-3).

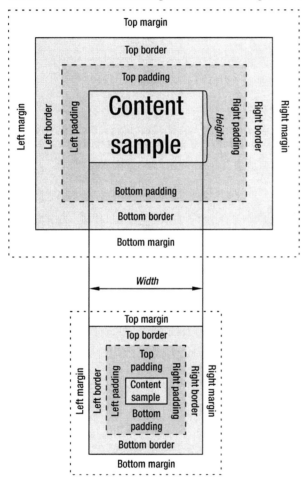

Figure 5-3. *Comparison of the W3C and the IE5 box model. Note the different interpretation of the width.*

Internet Explorer 6 and newer IE versions[7] apply the correct implementation in their standards-compliant mode, but for compatibility reasons, the bug still exists when a page is rendered in Quirks Mode.

Overview of CSS Properties

Table 5-3 summarizes the rich selection of CSS properties. There are 53 properties in CSS1, 120 in CSS2, 115 in CSS 2.1, and more than 200 (and counting) in CSS3.

Table 5-3. Overview of CSS Properties

Property	CSS1	CSS2	CSS 2.1	CSS3	Applicability	Inherited	Media
alignment-adjust	–	–	–	+	Inline elements	–	V
alignment-baseline	–	–	–	+	Inline elements	–	V
animation	–	–	–	+	Block and inline elements	–	V
animation-delay	–	–	–	+	Block and inline elements	–	V
animation-direction	–	–	–	+	Block and inline elements	–	V
animation-duration	–	–	–	+	Block and inline elements	–	V
animation-iteration-count	–	–	–	+	Block and inline elements	–	V
animation-name	–	–	–	+	Block and inline elements	–	V
animation-play-state	–	–	–	+	Block and inline elements	–	V
animation-timing-function	–	–	–	+	Block and inline elements	–	V
appearance	–	–	–	+	All elements	–	V, I
azimuth	–	+	+	?	All elements	+	A
backface-visibility	–	–	–	+	Block and inline elements	–	V
background	+	+	+	+	All elements	–	V

---

[7] The bug was not present in Internet Explorer for Mac (discontinued in 2006).

Property	CSS1	CSS2	CSS 2.1	CSS3	Applicability	Inherited	Media
background-attachment	+	+	+	+	All elements	–	V
background-break	–	–	–	+	All elements	–	V
background-clip	–	–	–	+	All elements	–	V
background-color	+	+	+	+	All elements	–	V
background-image	+	+	+	+	All elements	–	V
background-origin	–	–	–	+	All elements	–	V
background-position	+	+	+	+	All elements	–	V
background-repeat	+	+	+	+	All elements	–	V
background-size	–	–	–	+	All elements	–	V
baseline-shift	–	–	–	+	Inline elements	–	V
binding	–	–	–	+	All elements (but not pseudoelements)	–	All
bookmark-label	–	–	–	+	All elements	–	All
bookmark-level	–	–	–	+	All elements	–	All
bookmark-target	–	–	–	+	All elements	–	All
border	+	+	+	+	All elements	–	V
border-bottom	+	+	+	+	All elements	–	V
border-bottom-color	–	+	+	+	All elements	–	V
border-bottom-left-radius	–	–	–	+	All elements	–	V
border-bottom-right-radius	–	–	–	+	All elements	–	V

Property	CSS1	CSS2	CSS 2.1	CSS3	Applicability	Inherited	Media
border-bottom-style	−	+	+	+	All elements	−	V
border-bottom-width	+	+	+	+	All elements	−	V
border-collapse	−	+	+	?	Table and inline-table elements	−	V
border-color	+	+	+	+	All elements	−	V
border-image	−	−	−	+	Depends on individual properties	−	V
border-image-outset	−	−	−	+	All elements except internal table elements when border-collapse is set to collapse	−	V
border-image-repeat	−	−	−	+	All elements except table elements when border-collapse is set to collapse	−	V
border-image-slice	−	−	−	+	All elements except internal table elements when border-collapse is set to collapse	−	V
border-image-source	−	−	−	+	All elements except internal table elements when border-collapse is set to collapse	−	V
border-image-width	−	−	−	+	All elements, except internal table elements when border-collapse is set to collapse	−	V
border-left	+	+	+	+	All elements	−	V
border-left-color	−	+	+	+	All elements	−	V
border-left-style	−	+	+	+	All elements	−	V
border-left-width	+	+	+	+	All elements	−	V
border-length	−	−	−	+	@footnote areas	−	V

Property	CSS1	CSS2	CSS 2.1	CSS3	Applicability	Inherited	Media
border-radius	−	−	−	+	All elements except table elements when border-collapse is set to collapse	−	V
border-right	+	+	+	+	All elements	−	V
border-right-color	−	+	+	+	All elements	−	V
border-right-style	−	+	+	+	All elements	−	V
border-right-width	+	+	+	+	All elements	−	V
border-spacing	−	+	+	?	Table and inline-table elements (also frameset elements in certain document types)	+	V
border-style	+	+	+	+	All elements	−	V
border-top	+	+	+	+	All elements	−	V
border-top-color	−	+	+	+	All elements	−	V
border-top-left-radius	−	−	−	+	All elements	−	V
border-top-right-radius	−	−	−	+	All elements*	−	V
border-top-style	−	+	+	+	All elements	−	V
border-top-width	+	+	+	+	All elements	−	V
border-width	+	+	+	+	All elements	−	V
bottom	−	+	+	?	Positioned elements	−	V
box-align	−	−	−	+	Box elements	−	V
box-decoration-break	−	−	−	+	All elements	−	V
box-direction	−	−	−	+	Box elements	−	V

Property	CSS1	CSS2	CSS 2.1	CSS3	Applicability	Inherited	Media
box-flex	–	–	–	+	In-flow children of box elements	–	V
box-flex-group	–	–	–	+	In-flow children of box elements	–	V
box-lines	–	–	–	+	Box elements	–	V
box-ordinal-group	–	–	–	+	Children of box elements	–	V
box-orient	–	–	–	+	Box elements	–	V
box-pack	–	–	–	+	Box elements	–	V
box-shadow	–	–	–	+	All elements	–	V
box-sizing	–	–	–	+	All elements that accept width or height	–	V
caption-side	–	+	+	?	Table-caption elements	+	V
clear	+	+	+	+	Block-level elements	–	V
clip	–	+	+	?	Absolutely positioned elements	–	V
color	+	+	+	+	All elements	+	V
color-profile	–	–	–	+	All elements	+	V
column-break-after	–	–	–	+	Block-level elements	–	V
column-break-before	–	–	–	+	Block-level elements	–	V
column-count	–	–	–	+	Nonreplaced block-level elements (except table elements), table cells, and inline-block elements	–	V
column-fill	–	–	–	+	Multicolumn elements	–	N
column-gap	–	–	–	+	Multicolumn elements	–	V

Property	CSS1	CSS2	CSS 2.1	CSS3	Applicability	Inherited	Media
column-rule	–	–	–	+	Multicolumn elements	–	V
column-rule-color	–	–	–	+	Multicolumn elements	–	V
column-rule-style	–	–	–	+	Multicolumn elements	–	V
column-rule-width	–	–	–	+	Multicolumn elements	–	V
columns	–	–	–	+	Nonreplaced block-level elements (except table elements), table cells, and inline-block elements	–	V
column-span	–	–	–	+	Static, nonfloating elements	–	V
column-width	–	–	–	+	Nonreplaced block-level elements (except table elements), table cells, and inline-block elements	–	V
content	–	+	+	+	All elements, ::before, ::after, ::alternate, ::marker, ::line-marker, margin areas, and @footnote areas	–	All
counter-increment	–	+	+	+	All elements, ::before, ::after, ::alternate, ::marker, ::line-marker, margin areas, @footnote areas, and @page context	–	All
counter-reset	–	+	+	+	All elements, ::before, ::after, ::alternate, ::marker, ::line-marker, margin areas, @footnote areas, and @page context	–	All
crop	–	–	–	+	Replaced elements	–	V
cue	–	+	+	+	All elements	–	S
cue-after	–	+	+	+	All elements	–	S
cue-before	–	+	+	+	All elements	–	S

Property	CSS1	CSS2	CSS 2.1	CSS3	Applicability	Inherited	Media
cursor	–	+	+	+	All elements	+	V, I
direction	–	+	+	?	All elements*	+	V
display	+	+	+	+	All elements	–	V[8]
dominant-baseline	–	–	–	+	Inline-level elements*	–	V
drop-initial-after-adjust	–	–	–	+	::first-letter pseudoelement	–	V
drop-initial-after-align	–	–	–	+	::first-letter pseudoelement	–	V
drop-initial-before-adjust	–	–	–	+	::first-letter pseudoelement	–	V
drop-initial-before-align	–	–	–	+	::first-letter pseudoelement	–	V
drop-initial-size	–	–	–	+	::first-letter pseudoelement	–	V
drop-initial-value	–	–	–	+	::first-letter pseudoelement	–	V
elevation	–	+	+	?	All elements	+	A
empty-cells	–	+	+	?	Table-cell elements	+	V
fit	–	–	–	+	Replaced elements	+	V
fit-position	–	–	–	+	Replaced elements	+	V
float	+	+	+	+	All elements*	–	V
float-offset	–	–	–	+	Floated elements	–	V, P
font	+	+	+	+	All elements	+	V
font-family	+	+	+	+	All elements	+	V

[8] The value none applies to all media.

Property	CSS1	CSS2	CSS 2.1	CSS3	Applicability	Inherited	Media
font-size	+	+	+	+	All elements	+	V
font-size-adjust	–	+	–	+	All elements	+	V
font-stretch	–	–	–	+	All elements	+	V
font-style	+	+	+	+	All elements	+	V
font-variant	+	+	+	+	All elements	+	V
font-weight	+	+	+	+	All elements	+	V
grid-columns	–	–	–	+	All elements	–	V, P
grid-rows	–	–	–	+	All elements	–	V, P
hanging-punctuation	–	–	–	+	Block and inline-block elements, table cells	+	V
height	+	+	+	+	All elements except nonreplaced inline elements, table columns, and column groups	–	V
hyphenate-after	–	–	–	+	All elements	+	V
hyphenate-before	–	–	–	+	All elements	+	V
hyphenate-character	–	–	–	+	All elements	+	V
hyphenate-lines	–	–	–	+	All elements	+	V
hyphenate-resource	–	–	–	+	All elements	+	V
hyphens	–	–	–	+	All elements	+	V
icon	–	–	–	+	All elements	–	All

Property	CSS1	CSS2	CSS 2.1	CSS3	Applicability	Inherited	Media
image-orientation	–	–	–	+	Images	?	P
image-resolution	–	–	–	+	Replaced elements and background images	+	V
inline-box-align	–	–	–	+	Inline block-level elements	–	V
left	–	+	+	?	Positioned elements	–	V
letter-spacing	+	+	+	+	All elements	+	V
line-height	+	+	+	+	All elements	+	V
line-stacking	–	–	–	+	Block-level elements	+	V
line-stacking-ruby	–	–	–	+	Block-level elements	+	V
line-stacking-shift	–	–	–	+	Block-level elements	+	V
line-stacking-strategy	–	–	–	+	Block-level elements	+	V
list-style	+	+	+	+	All elements with display: list-item	N	V
list-style-image	+	+	+	+	All elements with display: list-item	+	V
list-style-position	+	+	+	+	All elements with display: list-item	+	V
list-style-type	+	+	+	+	All elements with display: list-item	+	V
margin	+	+	+	+	All boxes except certain table boxes and certain inline-level boxes	–	V
margin-bottom	+	+	+	+	All boxes except certain table boxes and certain inline-level boxes	–	V

Property	CSS1	CSS2	CSS 2.1	CSS3	Applicability	Inherited	Media
margin-left	+	+	+	+	All boxes except certain table boxes and certain inline-level boxes	–	V
margin-right	+	+	+	+	All boxes except certain table boxes and certain inline-level boxes	–	V
margin-top	+	+	+	+	All boxes except certain table boxes and certain inline-level boxes	–	V
mark	–	–	–	+	All elements	–	S
mark-after	–	–	–	+	All elements	–	S
mark-before	–	–	–	+	All elements	–	S
marks	–	+	–	+	Page context	–	V, P
marquee-direction	–	–	–	+	Nonreplaced block-level elements and nonreplaced inline-block elements	+	V
marquee-play-count	–	–	–	+	Nonreplaced block-level elements and nonreplaced inline-block elements	–	V
marquee-speed	–	–	–	+	Nonreplaced block-level elements and nonreplaced inline-block elements	–	V
marquee-style	–	–	–	+	Non-replaced block-level elements and nonreplaced inline-block elements	–	V
max-height	–	+	+	+	All elements except nonreplaced inline elements, table rows, and row groups	–	V

Property	CSS1	CSS2	CSS 2.1	CSS3	Applicability	Inherited	Media
max-width	–	+	+	+	All elements except nonreplaced inline elements, table rows, and row groups	–	V
min-height	–	+	+	+	All elements except nonreplaced inline elements, table rows, and row groups	–	V
min-width	–	+	+	+	All elements except nonreplaced inline elements, table rows, and row groups	–	V
move-to	–	–	–	+	All elements, ::before, ::after, ::alternate	–	All
nav-down	–	–	–	+	All enabled elements	–	I
nav-index	–	–	–	+	All enabled elements	–	I
nav-left	–	–	–	+	All enabled elements	–	I
nav-right	–	–	–	+	All enabled elements	–	I
nav-up	–	–	–	+	All enabled elements	–	I
opacity	–	–	–	+	All elements	–	V
orphans	–	+	+	+	Block-level elements	+	V
outline	–	+	+	+	All elements	–	V
outline-color	–	+	+	+	All elements	–	V
outline-offset	–	–	–	+	All elements	–	V
outline-style	–	+	+	+	All elements	–	V
outline-width	–	+	+	+	All elements	–	V

Property	CSS1	CSS2	CSS 2.1	CSS3	Applicability	Inherited	Media
overflow	–	+	+	+	Nonreplaced block-level elements and nonreplaced inline-block elements	–	V
overflow-style	–	–	–	+	Nonreplaced block-level elements and nonreplaced inline-block elements	+	V
overflow-x	–	–	–	+	Nonreplaced block-level elements and nonreplaced inline-block elements	–	V
overflow-y	–	–	–	+	Nonreplaced block-level elements and nonreplaced inline-block elements	–	V
padding	+	+	+	+	All elements	–	V
padding-bottom	+	+	+	+	All elements	–	V
padding-left	+	+	+	+	All elements	–	V
padding-right	+	+	+	+	All elements	–	V
padding-top	+	+	+	+	All elements	–	V
page	–	+	–	+	Block-level elements	+	P
page-break-after	–	+	+	–	Block-level elements	–	V, P
page-break-after	–	+	+	+	Block-level elements	–	P
page-break-before	–	+	+	+	Block-level elements	–	V, P
page-break-before	–	+	+	+	Block-level elements	–	P
page-break-inside	–	+	+	+	Block-level elements	+	P
page-policy	–	–	–	+	@counter and @string blocks	?	P

Property	CSS1	CSS2	CSS 2.1	CSS3	Applicability	Inherited	Media
pause	−	+	+	+	All elements	−	S
pause-after	−	+	+	+	All elements	−	S
pause-before	−	+	+	+	All elements	−	S
perspective	−	−	−	+	Block-level and inline-level elements	−	V
perspective-origin	−	−	−	+	Block-level and inline-level elements	−	V
phonemes	−	−	−	+	All elements	−	S
pitch	−	+	+	?	All elements	+	A
pitch-range	−	+	+	?	All elements	+	A
play-during	−	+	+	?	All elements	−	A
position	−	+	+	?	All elements	−	V
presentation-level	−	−	−	+	All elements	+	All
punctuation-trim	−	−	−	+	All elements	+	V
quotes	−	+	+	+	All elements, ::before, ::after, ::alternate, ::marker, ::line-marker, margin areas, and @footnote areas	−	V
rendering-intent	−	−	−	+	All elements	+	V
resize	−	−	−	+	Elements with overflow other than visible	−	V
rest	−	−	−	+	All elements	−	S
rest-after	−	−	−	+	All elements	−	S

Property	CSS1	CSS2	CSS 2.1	CSS3	Applicability	Inherited	Media
rest-before	–	–	–	+	All elements	–	S
richness	–	+	+	?	All elements	+	A
right	–	+	+	?	Positioned elements	–	V
rotation	–	–	–	+	Block-level elements, inline-table elements, and inline-block elements	–	V
rotation-point	–	–	–	+	Block-level elements	–	V
ruby-align	–	–	–	+	All elements and generated content	–	V
ruby-overhang	–	–	–	+	The parent of elements with display: ruby-text	+	V
ruby-position	–	–	–	+	The parent of elements with display: ruby-text	+	V
ruby-span	–	–	–	+	Elements with display: ruby-text	–	V
size	–	+	–	+	Page context	?	P
speak	–	+	+	+	All elements	+	S
speak-header	–	+	+	?	Elements that have table header information	+	A
speak-numeral	–	+	+	?	All elements	+	A
speak-punctuation	–	+	+	?	All elements	+	A
speech-rate	–	+	+	?	All elements	+	A
stress	–	+	+	?	All elements	+	A
string-set	–	–	–	+	All elements	–	All

Property	CSS1	CSS2	CSS 2.1	CSS3	Applicability	Inherited	Media
table-layout	–	+	+	?	Table and inline-table elements	–	V
tab-side	–	–	–	+	Elements with display: stack	+	V
target	–	–	–	+	Hyperlinks	–	I, V
target-name	–	–	–	+	Hyperlinks	–	I, V
target-new	–	–	–	+	Hyperlinks	–	I, V
target-position	–	–	–	+	Hyperlinks	–	I, V
text-align	+	+	+	+	Block containers	+	V
text-align-last	–	–	–	+	Block containers	+	V
text-decoration	+	+	+	?	All elements	–	V
text-emphasis	–	–	–	+	All elements	+	V
text-height	–	–	–	+	Inline elements and parents of element with display: ruby-text	+	V
text-indent	+	+	+	+	Block containers	+	V
text-justify	–	–	–	+	Block containers, inline elements	+	V
text-outline	–	–	–	+	All elements	+	V
text-replace	–	–	–	+	All elements	+	V
text-shadow	–	+	–	+	All elements	+	V
text-transform	+	+	+	?	All elements	+	V
text-wrap	–	–	–	+	All elements	+	V
top	–	+	+	?	Positioned elements	–	V

Property	CSS1	CSS2	CSS 2.1	CSS3	Applicability	Inherited	Media
transform	–	–	–	+	Block and inline elements	–	V
transform-origin	–	–	–	+	Block and inline elements	–	V
transform-style	–	–	–	+	Block and inline elements	–	V
transition	–	–	–	+	All elements, :before and :after pseudoelements	–	I
transition-delay	–	–	–	+	All elements, :before and :after pseudoelements	–	I
transition-duration	–	–	–	+	All elements, :before and :after pseudoelements	–	I
transition-property	–	–	–	+	All elements, :before and :after pseudoelements	–	V
transition-timing-function	–	–	–	+	All elements, :before and :after pseudoelements	–	I
unicode-bidi	–	+	+	?	All elements*	–	V
vertical-align	+	+	+	+	Inline-level elements	–	V
visibility	–	+	+	+	All elements	+	V
voice-balance	–	–	–	+	All elements	+	S
voice-duration	–	–	–	+	All elements	–	S
voice-family	–	+	+	+	All elements	+	S
voice-pitch	–	–	–	+	All elements	+	S
voice-pitch-range	–	–	–	+	All elements	+	S
voice-rate	–	–	–	+	All elements	+	S
voice-stress	–	–	–	+	All elements	+	S

Property	CSS1	CSS2	CSS 2.1	CSS3	Applicability	Inherited	Media
voice-volume	–	–	–	+	All elements	+	S
volume	–	+	+	?	All elements	+	A
white-space	+	+	+	+	All elements	+	V
white-space-collapsing	–	–	–	+	All elements	+	V
widows	–	+	+	+	Block-level elements	+	V
width	+	+	+	+	All elements except nonreplaced inline elements, table rows, and row groups	–	V
word-break	–	–	–	+	All elements	+	V
word-spacing	+	+	+	+	All elements	+	V
word-wrap	–	–	–	+	All elements	+	V
z-index	–	+	+	?	Positioned elements	–	V

Legend
*   Special rules might apply
n   Not defined for shorthand properties
?   Not finalized yet
V   Visual media
I   Interactive media
A   Aural media
P   Paged media
N   Noncontinuous media (continuous media only if column length is constrained)
S   Speech media

The browser support of CSS properties varies and is gradually improving. However, even the CSS 2.1 properties gained a more or less complete and correct implementation only recently. Consequently, old browsers do not support all properties and have incorrect implementation for many properties. This was the major reason for the huge difference in rendering the same site under different browsers for years. With the proper, if not full, implementation of CSS properties in modern browsers, this difference has been decreased to a minimum.

> ■ **Tip** It is highly recommended to apply CSS3 rules with caution, because most modules of CSS3 are not standardized yet, and browser support varies. Styling is not an "everything or nothing" proposition. For example, fundamental CSS properties—that are also supported by CSS 2.1 and thus most browsers—can be used to position a div element and provide styles such as background color, font size, and margins for it. Although the rounded corners declared by using the CSS3 property border-radius are not rendered by older browsers, the general layout and styling provide a similar appearance in old browsers as with modern browsers with CSS3 support. Similarly, if Web Fonts embedding—that is not supported by older browsers—is used on a site, a common font and at least a generic font family should be declared as a fallback mechanism (see Chapter 9 for details).

Initial Property Values

All CSS properties have their *initial values* that are applied when the property values are set neither by cascading nor by inheritance. The initial value of each property is defined by the CSS specifications. An initial value is one of the allowed values of the corresponding CSS property. For example, a color declaration (in any of the allowed formats, typically in hexadecimal notation), transparent, and inherit are all legal values of the background-color property, from which transparent is the initial value that can be easily overridden by declaring the desired value in your CSS file (Listing 5-68).

Listing 5-68. The Declared Value Overrides the Initial Value Defined by the CSS Specification

```
body {
  background-color: #198c00;
}
```

This is the reason why the background of all paragraphs, divisions, and other elements is transparent. Another example is the bullet type of lists, which is often used without override. If the value of the property list-style-type is not set by the developer, the initial value is used for rendering, which is disc. However, it can be overridden by any other allowed values of that property, including circle, square, decimal, decimal-leading-zero, lower-roman, upper-roman, lower-greek, lower-latin, upper-latin, armenian, georgian, lower-alpha, upper-alpha, none, and inherit. The last value, inherit, can be applied not only to list-style-type but also to any other CSS property in order to explicitly apply the initial value of the corresponding property.

Since the root element has no parent element, its value is set to the initial property value by default.

Default Styles of Rendering Engines

Since the default style sheet of rendering engines contains different property values for certain properties, the property values that are not declared by the web site developer might look different under various browsers. Because of the different line heights, margins, font sizes, and other properties, the overall appearance of a web site is typically not uniform. Although some of the default property values differ slightly only, developers cannot rely on the default styles of rendering engines.

▪ **Tip** The inconsistencies between the CSS implementations of browsers can be minimized by overriding the CSS property values of the default style sheet of rendering engines. This technique is called *CSS reset*. One of the most well-known CSS reset files was written and maintained by Eric A. Meyer (Listing 5-69) and can be used on your web site for free [19].

Listing 5-69. A CSS Reset

```
/* http://meyerweb.com/eric/tools/css/reset/
   v2.0 | 20110126
   License: none (public domain)
*/
html, body, div, span, applet, object, iframe, h1, h2, h3, h4, h5, h6, p, blockquote, pre, a,
abbr, acronym, address, big, cite, code, del, dfn, em, img, ins, kbd, q, s, samp, small,
strike, strong, sub, sup, tt, var, b, u, i, center, dl, dt, dd, ol, ul, li, fieldset, form,
label, legend, table, caption, tbody, tfoot, thead, tr, th, td, article, aside, canvas,
details, embed, figure, figcaption, footer, header, hgroup, menu, nav, output, ruby, section,
summary, time, mark, audio, video {
  margin: 0;
  padding: 0;
  border: 0;
  font-size: 100%;
  font: inherit;
  vertical-align: baseline;
}
/* HTML5 display-role reset for older browsers */
article, aside, details, figcaption, figure, footer, header, hgroup, menu, nav, section {
  display: block;
}
body {
  line-height: 1;
}
ol, ul {
  list-style: none;
}
blockquote, q {
  quotes: none;
}
blockquote:before, blockquote:after, q:before, q:after {
  content: '';
  content: none;
}
table {
  border-collapse: collapse;
  border-spacing: 0;
}
```

XSL

Although it is not widely used and only a limited number of web developers are familiar with it, since 1999 a technology other than CSS can also be used for styling certain web documents [20]. *Extensible Stylesheet Language* (*XSL*) is a language family that can be used for styling, manipulation, and transformation of XML files. There are three XSL languages; however, only one of them is a style sheet language:

- *XSL Transformations* (XSLT): An XML style sheet language that can be used for transforming XML documents into other XML documents or other formats such as HTML or plain text. The original document remains unchanged, and a new document is created based on the existing one.

- *XSL Formatting Objects* (XSL-FO): An XML markup language applied for specifying the visual formatting of XML documents. Several software support XSL-FO that can provide various output formats, including plain text, PDF, PS, SVG, PCL, and MIF.

- *XML Path Language* (XPath): A non-XML query language that can also be used by XSLT.

XSLT Style Sheets

XSLT style sheets consist of one or more style sheet modules that are part of XML documents or form entire XML documents by themselves. The typical file extensions of XSLT are `.xsl` and `.xslt`. XSLT style sheets use the media type `application/xslt+xml`.

Namespaces

The XSLT namespace is `http://www.w3.org/1999/XSL/Transform`. However, further (reserved) namespaces are also recognized by XSLT processors [21], including the following:

- The standard function namespace, `http://www.w3.org/2005/xpath-functions`

- The XML namespace, `http://www.w3.org/XML/1998/namespace`

- The schema namespace, `http://www.w3.org/2001/XMLSchema`

- The schema instance namespace, `http://www.w3.org/2001/XMLSchema-instance`

Structure

The structure of XSLT style sheets looks like Listing 5-70.

Listing 5-70. XSLT Style Sheet Structure

```
<xsl:stylesheet version="1.0"
xmlns:xsl="http://www.w3.org/1999/XSL/Transform">
  <xsl:import href="…"/>
  <xsl:include href="…"/>
```

```
<xsl:strip-space elements="…"/>
<xsl:preserve-space elements="…"/>
<xsl:output method="…"/>
<xsl:key name="…" match="…" use="…"/>
<xsl:decimal-format name="…"/>
<xsl:namespace-alias stylesheet-prefix="…" result-prefix="…"/>
<xsl:attribute-set name="…">
  …
</xsl:attribute-set>
<xsl:variable name="…">…</xsl:variable>
<xsl:param name="…">…</xsl:param>
<xsl:template match="…">
  …
</xsl:template>
<xsl:template name="…">
  …
</xsl:template>
</xsl:stylesheet>
```

Note that the previous example shows all allowed element types; however, style sheets might contain zero or more of these elements.

Elements

XSLT style sheets are represented by the xsl:stylesheet or xsl:transform element in XML documents. An xsl:stylesheet element must have a version attribute. The xsl:stylesheet element may contain the following types of elements: xsl:import, xsl:include, xsl:strip-space, xsl:preserve-space, xsl:output, xsl:key, xsl:decimal-format, xsl:attribute-set, xsl:param, xsl:variable, xsl:namespace-alias, and xsl:template. Table 5-4 provides an overview of XSLT 1.0 elements.

Table 5-4. Overview of XSLT Elements

Element	Description
apply-imports	Applies a template rule from an imported style sheet
apply-templates	Applies a template rule to the current element or to the child nodes of the current element
attribute	Adds an attribute
attribute-set	Defines a named attribute set
call-template	Calls a named template
choose	Multiple conditional test (used with when and otherwise)
comment	Creates a comment node

Element	Description
copy	Creates a copy of the current node
copy-of	Creates a copy of the current node (with child nodes and attributes)
decimal-format	Defines the format to be used for converting numbers into strings with the `format-number` function
element	Creates an element node in the output document
fallback	Declares an alternate code for XSLT elements
for-each	Provides a loop within a node set
if	Provides a template to be applied in case of a specified condition
import	Imports an external style sheet (with lower precedence)
include	Includes an external style sheet (with same precedence)
key	Declares a key to be used with the key function
message	Writes a message (typically error message)
namespace-alias	Replaces a namespace in the style sheet to another one in the output
number	Determines the position of the current node
otherwise	Specifies a default action for the choose element
output	Defines the format of the output document
param	Adds a (local or global) parameter
preserve-space	Defines elements with preserved whitespace
processing-instruction	Writes a processing instruction to the output
sort	Sorts the output
strip-space	Defines the elements from which whitespace should be removed
stylesheet	Defines the root element of a style sheet
template	Applies a template when a specified node is matched

Element	Description
text	Writes text to the output
transform	Defines the root element of a style sheet
value-of	Extracts the value from the selected node
variable	Declares a (local or global) variable
when	Specifies an action for the choose element
with-param	Defines the parameter value to be passed into a template

The application of XSLT elements is straightforward and follows general XML authoring principles. Listing 5-71 shows an example.

Listing 5-71. XSLT Elements and Attributes Correspond to XML Guidelines

```
<xsl:param name="page-header-margin">20px</xsl:param>
```

Standard Attributes

Several standard attributes are associated with XSLT elements, including version, exclude-result-prefixes, extension-element-prefixes, xpath-default-namespace, default-collation, and use-when. To distinguish them from attributes defined by authors, they should be written with the namespace notation as xsl:version, xsl:exclude-result-prefixes, xsl:extension-element-prefixes, xsl:xpath-default-namespace, xsl:default-collation, and xsl:use-when.

Combining CSS and XSL

XSL can also be used as a bridge between complex XML-based documents and the CSS formatting model. Since CSS has no XML syntax, CSS properties become XML attributes in the XSL syntax. The main CSS object is chunk. Additional objects might also be required. Usually they are other chunk objects with functionality such as anchor, or further objects such as switch. For example, the CSS ruleset in Listing 5-72 can be written in XSL syntax, as shown in Listing 5-73.

Listing 5-72. CSS Ruleset Example to Be Converted into XSL

```
{
  font-size: 1.2em;
  text-indent: 1em;
}
```

Listing 5-73. The XSL Equivalent of Listing 5-72

```
<css:chunk
```

```
font-size="1.2em"
text-indent="1em">
```

Summary

In this chapter, you learned how to separate presentation from content, which is imperative in web site standardization. You know the syntax of Cascading Style Sheets, the language used by virtually every web site. You have mastered the use of CSS selectors and can apply them in your daily work to control the appearance of exactly those elements or sets of elements that need to be styled. By now you know how to use the cascading feature of CSS with confidence, which makes it possible to create CSS files that are optimal in length and easy to maintain. You also know how to ensure backward-compatibility by applying a fallback mechanism and properties supported even by older browsers. You learned that XML files can be styled not only by CSS but also by using XSL.

In the next chapter, you will learn about the standardization issues of server-side scripting and web applications.

References

1.   Dahlström E, Dengler P, Grasso A, Lilley C, McCormack C, Schepers D, Watt J, Ferraiolo J, Jun F, Jackson D (eds) (2011) Styling with CSS. In: SVG 1.1 (Second Edition). World Wide Web Consortium. www.w3.org/TR/SVG/styling.html#StylingWithCSS. Accessed 18 Aug 2011

2.   Chavchanidze G (2004) Formatting Mathematical Articles with Cascading Style Sheets. Andrea Razmadze Mathematical Institute. www.princexml.com/samples/math.pdf. Accessed 09 October 2010

3.   Bos B, Carlisle D, Chavchanidze G, Ion PDF, Miller BR (2011) A MathML for CSS Profile. W3C Recommendation. World Wide Web Consortium. www.w3.org/TR/mathml-for-css/. Accessed 18 August 2011

4.   Grant M (ed) (2006) CSS Print Profile. World Wide Web Consortium. www.w3.org/TR/css-print/. Accessed 17 Aug 2011

5.   Hayes S, Adams G, Çelik T, Lie HW (2003) CSS TV Profile 1.0. World Wide Web Consortium. www.w3.org/TR/css-tv. Accessed 17 Aug 2011

6.   Schubert S (ed) CSS Mobile Profile 2.0. World Wide Web Consortium. www.w3.org/TR/css-mobile/. Accessed 17 Aug 2011

7.   Lie HW, Bos B (2008) Cascading Style Sheets, level 1. W3C Recommendation (revised version). World Wide Web Consortium. www.w3.org/TR/CSS1/. Accessed 09 October 2010

8.   Bos B, Çelik T, Hickson I, Lie HW (eds) (2011) Cascading Style Sheets Level 2 Revision 1 (CSS 2.1) Specification. World Wide Web Consortium. www.w3.org/TR/CSS21/. Accessed 18 August 2011

9.   Meyer EA, Bos B (eds) (2001) Module Descriptions and Related Information. In: Introduction to CSS3. W3C Working Draft. World Wide Web Consortium. www.w3.org/TR/css3-roadmap/#module. Accessed 09 October 2010

10. Çelik T, Lilley C, Baron LD, Pemberton S, Pettit B (eds) (2011) CSS Color Module Level 3. World Wide Web Consortium. www.w3.org/TR/css3-color/. Accessed 18 Aug 2011

11. Bos B, Çelik T, Hickson I, Lie HW (eds) (2011) Grammar of CSS 2.1. In: Cascading Style Sheets Level 2 Revision 1 (CSS 2.1) Specification. W3C Recommendation. World Wide Web Consortium. www.w3.org/TR/CSS21/grammar.html. Accessed 18 August 2011

12. Bos B, Çelik T, Hickson I, Lie HW (eds) (2011) Selector syntax. In: Cascading Style Sheets Level 2 Revision 1 (CSS 2.1) Specification. W3C Recommendation. World Wide Web Consortium. www.w3.org/TR/CSS21/selector.html#selector-syntax. Accessed 18 August 2011

13. Çelik T, Etemad EJ (eds) (2010) Syntax and Parsing. In: CSS Style Attributes. World Wide Web Consortium. www.w3.org/TR/2010/CR-css-style-attr-20101012/#syntax. Accessed 16 October 2010

14. Clark J, Pieters S, Thompson HS (eds) (2010) Associating Style Sheets with XML documents 1.0 (Second Edition). W3C Recommendation. World Wide Web Consortium. www.w3.org/TR/xml-stylesheet/. Accessed 02 November 2010

15. Lie HW (ed) (2005) Cascading. In: CSS3 module: Cascading and inheritance. W3C Working Draft. World Wide Web Consortium. www.w3.org/TR/2005/WD-css3-cascade-20051215/#cascading. Accessed 10 October 2010

16. Glazman D, Çelik T, Hickson I, Linss P, Williams J (eds) (2001) Calculating a selector's specificity. In: Selectors. World Wide Web Consortium. www.w3.org/TR/2001/CR-css3-selectors-20011113/#specificity. Accessed 10 October 2010

17. Bos B, Çelik T, Hickson I, Lie HW (2010) Box model. In: Cascading Style Sheets Level 2 Revision 1 (CSS 2.1) Specification. W3C Working Draft. World Wide Web Consortium. www.w3.org/TR/CSS21/box.html. Accessed 12 December 2010

18. Silver L (2006) Fix the Box Instead of Thinking Outside It. In: CSS Enhancements in Internet Explorer 6. Microsoft Corporation. http://msdn.microsoft.com/en-us/library/bb250395.aspx#cssenhancements_topic3. Accessed 19 Aug 2011

19. Meyer EA, Meyer KS (2011) CSS Tools: Reset CSS. Eric A. Meyer, Kathryn S. Meyer. http://meyerweb.com/eric/tools/css/reset/. Accessed 19 Aug 2011

20. Clark J (ed) (1999) XSL Transformations (XSLT) Version 1.0 W3C Recommendation. World Wide Web Consortium. www.w3.org/TR/xslt. Accessed 12 October 2010

21. Kay M (ed) (2007) XSL Transformations (XSLT) Version 2.0. W3C Recommendation. World Wide Web Consortium. www.w3.org/TR/xslt20/. Accessed 12 October 2010

CHAPTER 6

Scripting and Applications

Many modern web pages are meant to be dynamic. They have much more than just syntactic structure and semantics. Various web site sections can behave differently and might react to user interactions. Larger sites require databases that need to be handled. Small pieces of programs can be run on remote servers or local computers. However, content generated by server-side languages is often incorrect. Although content authors cannot affect the hard-coded parts of content management systems, templates often provide hand-coding options that involve standardization potential.

In this chapter, you will learn why the standardization of dynamic content is more challenging than that of static pages. Becoming familiar with the basic syntax of the most widely used client-side and server-side scripting languages is crucial, because small programs written in these languages are often embedded into the markup. Consequently, script embedding might have an impact on the standards compliance of a whole web page. You will also learn how to provide alternate content for scripts. Although the standard compliance of the markup generated on the server side using web programming languages, frameworks, and development platforms to provide web applications is constantly improving, there are still many cases when the resulting pages contain errors. Many of these development technologies are not standardized yet but still are in worldwide use. As a consequence, some of them are considered *de facto* standards. Many technologies rely on a number of other technologies and some on standards. This chapter provides a quick overview of some of the most common scripting and application development technologies; however, the list is not complete by any means.

Client-Server Architectures

The distributed application structure that divides tasks and/or workloads between resource or service providers, called *servers*, and service requesters, called *clients*, is known as the *client-server model*. Clients and servers communicate over the Web to exchange data and perform tasks.

The *client-server* architecture represents relationships between cooperating programs in a web application. For example, a contact form can be evaluated on the client side and processed on the server side.

The general syntax and grammar conventions of the most popular client-side and server-side scripting and programming languages, technologies, and frameworks are discussed in the following sections. Note that a detailed description of scripts and applications is beyond the scope of the book. Web programming is analyzed from the standardization point of view. The scripts directly embedded into the markup have a considerable effect on standard compliance, so standardistas should focus on valid embedding. Although the core of content management systems (CMSs) are in many cases hard-coded, their templates can be modified by their users, which makes it possible to provide standard-compliant code fragments.

Scripting and Standards Implementation

A *script* is program code that does not require preprocessing (such as compiling) before being run [1]. Small dynamic components of web documents such as the current date or interactive content and behavior can be added by *scripting languages*. Modifications can be performed on the web page content without reloading the new version of the page. Content can be added to or sent from a web page with *Asynchronous JavaScript and XML (Ajax)*, also without reloading the new page version.

Client-side scripts have constant content that, if provided carefully, can produce valid markup. Server-side scripting, on the other hand, provides *content generated on the fly*. The source code of the program serving as the basis for this task is quite complicated when checking for markup errors. Moreover, the templates used in the markup generated by server-side scripting technologies are hard-coded in many cases and cannot be modified by content authors. Validating and standardizing large web sites with hundreds of thousands of web pages can be practically impossible.

The major problem with web sites relying on data stored in databases and processed by server-side scripts is the higher complexity and the lack of full control. Templates used by CMSs are not always standards-compliant. As a consequence, all errors of such templates are present in thousands of sites applying the templates. Moreover, a single problem of either the script or the database can result in an error message instead of the web page content (Figure 6-1).

Figure 6-1. Content replaced by error message

There is a huge difference between small programs running on web pages and programs created for generating web pages. Server-side scripting languages are powerful and provide features that cannot be achieved by static content. There is nothing wrong with small contact forms, for example. However, server-side scripts should be used wherever appropriate. Large web sites with a database requirement should definitely apply these technologies. Furthermore, server-side scripts can provide the same headers, footers, and so on, as templates for identical markup fragments throughout the web site that can be easily maintained from a single location (in contrast to static web pages). However, the application of server-side scripting should be minimized on web sites that do not rely on databases and dynamically generated content, such as small-scale, brochure-style web sites. This is the most direct way to obtain and ensure full standards compliance. Undoubtedly, a large share of invalid markup code on the Web is generated by server-side scripting languages. In many cases, additional practices are required to obtain valid markup, such as to handle the ampersand characters used as an argument separator in URLs of PHP sessions [2].

Client-Side Development

Client-side development refers to those web programs that run on the client side, generally a web browser, instead of being executed on the server side (on a web server). Client-side programs can be used to provide different and changing content on a web page, depending on user input and other variables. For example, "dynamic" greetings can be added to a web page according to the current time of day.

Ajax

Ajax is an acronym for *Asynchronous JavaScript and XML.* It is not a programming language but a group of web development technologies related to each other, such as HTML, CSS, DOM, JavaScript, XML, and XSLT. Ajax can be used on the client side to create interactive web applications. Web site applications empowered with Ajax can send data to and retrieve data from servers asynchronously (which is the reason for the name). Ajax is suitable for avoiding full-page reloads when exchanging data asynchronously. This approach ensures that the display and behavior of the current page won't be interfered with. Despite the name, Ajax does not require XML; the JavaScript Object Notation (JSON), a lightweight text-based open standard [3], is often used instead. The requests are not necessarily asynchronous either. Ajax usually retrieves data using the XMLHttpRequest object [4]. The DOM is used along with JavaScript to dynamically display information and allow the user to interact with the information presented. The data interchanged using Ajax can be manipulated using XSLT.

■ **Note** Modern browsers have a built-in XMLHttpRequest object. Before IE7, Internet Explorer provided an object called ActiveXObject.

To demonstrate Ajax, the code in Listing 6-1 creates a link that will replace the content of a div element with the content of a text file. The Document Object Model is used to manipulate the object. The XMLHTTPRequest object is used to make the HTTP request load the file ajaxdemo.txt and display its content.

Listing 6-1. Ajax Demonstration

```
<script type="text/javascript">
  var http = false;
  if (navigator.appName == "Microsoft Internet Explorer") {
    http = new ActiveXObject("Microsoft.XMLHTTP");
    } else {
      http = new XMLHttpRequest();
    }

    function replace() {
      http.open("GET", "ajaxdemo.txt", true);
      http.onreadystatechange=function() {
        if (http.readyState == 4) {
          document.getElementById('repdiv').innerHTML = http.responseText;
        }
```

```
    }
    http.send(null);
  }
</script>
```

In the document body, we need a function call and a div with the text to replace (Listing 6-2).

Listing 6-2. The Function Call and the div with the Original Text

```
<p>
  <a href="javascript:replace()">Click here to replace text</a>
</p>

<div id="repdiv">
  Original text in the markup
</div>
```

The http.open() argument is the asynchronous argument that sends the request in the background.

Flex

Adobe Flex is a software development kit (SDK) for cross-platform, rich Internet applications based on the Adobe Flash technology [5]. The user interface layout and behavior are described by a declarative XML-based language, MXML, while the client logic is created by using the ActionScript 3.0 programming language.

■ **Note** ActionScript is an object-oriented language and a dialect of ECMAScript. Consequently, ActionScript is a superset of the syntax and semantics of JavaScript. Most frequently, ActionScript is embedded in SWF files.

As an example, let's create a simple RSS news feed reader! First, we need to write a common XML declaration, followed by an MXML declaration (Listing 6-3).

Listing 6-3. The XML and MXML Declaration

```
<?xml version="1.0" ?>
<mx:Application xmlns:mx="http://www.macromedia.com/2003/mxml">

</mx:Application>
```

Within the mx:Application, our HTTPService should be defined, and the custom controls (DataGrid, TextArea, and Button) are prepared for the panel (Listing 6-4).

Listing 6-4. The HTTPService and the Panel for the Custom Controls

```
<mx:Application xmlns:mx="http://www.macromedia.com/2003/mxml">
  <mx:HTTPService id="httpRSS" url="http://www.example.com/rss/" resultFormat="object" />
  <mx:Panel id="reader" title="Simple RSS Reader" width="600">
```

216

```
    </mx:Panel>
</mx:Application>
```

Now it is time to define the DataGrid. The horizontal dimension of the panel should be set by the `width` parameter. Each item tag of the RSS file is bound to a DataGrid row by the `dataProvider` attribute. Next we create an event handler to display the contents of the description tags inside the RSS items selected by the user. The `entries.selectedIndex` variable is used to determine which item was clicked. The description of the corresponding item is retrieved by `httpRSS.result.rss.channel.item[entries.selectedIndex].description`. The value of the RSS description is assigned to the `htmlText` property of the TextArea (Listing 6-5).

Listing 6-5. Creating the DataGrid for the RSS Reader

```
<mx:DataGrid id="entries" width="{reader.width-15}" ↵
 dataProvider="{httpRSS.result.rss.channel.item}" ↵
  cellPress= ↵
  "{body.htmlText=httpRSS.result.rss.channel.item[entries.selectedIndex].description}">
  <mx:columns>
    <mx:Array>
      <mx:DataGridColumn columnName="title" headerText="Title" />
      <mx:DataGridColumn columnName="pubDate" headerText="Date" />
    </mx:Array>
  </mx:columns>
</mx:DataGrid>
```

Finally, a TextArea needs to be created using the `mx:TextArea` tag, and a button needs to be created with a `click` event handler to call the `send()` method on the `HTTPService` object (Listing 6-6).

Listing 6-6. The TextArea and the Button

```
<mx:TextArea id="body" editable="false" width="{reader.width-15}" height="400" />
<mx:Button label="Load
RSS channel items" click="{httpRSS.send()}" />
```

HTML5 APIs

HTML5 provides much more than just new structuring elements. HTML5 supports many features that were available originally through plug-ins or sophisticated code only [6]. Beyond markup elements and attributes, HTML5 specifies scripting application programming interfaces (APIs) as well [7]. A native drawing API, native sockets, and so on, eliminate the problems associated with plug-ins, such as missing or disabled support to vulnerability issues.

Some HTML5 APIs are under W3C standardization, while others are under WHATWG development. Some of the most frequently used APIs are discussed in the following sections.

The HTML5 Canvas API

The canvas markup element has been introduced in HTML5. It allows dynamic, scriptable rendering of 2D shapes and bitmap images.

░ **Note** The HTML5 canvas has no built-in scene graph, which is a general data structure to arrange the logical (and often spatial) representation of a graphical scene. The scene graph is commonly used by vector-based graphical systems, including SVG. In SVG, all drawn shapes are stored as an object in the scene graph or the DOM and then rendered as bitmap graphics. Consequently, if the SVG object attributes are changed, the browser can automatically rerender the scene, which is not possible on the canvas. From this point of view, SVG graphics are more advanced than shapes on the HTML5 canvas.

In Listing 6-7, you can see how to draw a simple triangle on the HTML5 canvas. First, a custom-size canvas is declared with alternate textual content for older browsers that do not support the HTML5 canvas. Second, a script element specifies two variables to shorten the code, a two-dimensional canvas, an emerald fill color, the coordinates of the three corners of a triangle, and the triangle with the fill color.

Listing 6-7. Drawing on the HTML5 Canvas

```
<canvas id="samplecanvas" width="200" height="200">
  A triangle (requires HTML5 Canvas support)
</canvas>
<script>
  var mycanvas = document.getElementById("samplecanvas"),
  context2d = mycanvas.getContext("2d");
  context2d.fillStyle = "#2ad3a8";
  context2d.beginPath();
  context2d.moveTo(100, 0);
  context2d.lineTo(0, 55);
  context2d.lineTo(165, 100);
  context2d.fill();
</script>
```

The HTML5 canvas is supported by IE9+, Firefox 3.0+, Chrome 1.0+, Safari 3.0+, and Opera 9.5+.

The HTML5 File and DnD APIs

The HTML5 File API provides easy-to-use file control in web browsers. The File API is being standardized by the World Wide Web Consortium [8]. The Drag & Drop (DnD) API specification defines an event-based mechanism that adds additional markup for declaring elements to be draggable on web pages. The DnD API is being developed by the Web Hypertext Application Technology Working Group [9].

The code in Listing 6-8 creates an interface to choose files either through browsing the directories on your computer or by using drag and drop. The name, size, and MIME type of the selected files will be retrieved using the HTML5 File API.

Listing 6-8. File API Demonstration

```
<h1>Choose file(s)</h1>
<p>
```

```
     <input id="upload" type="file" multiple="multiple">
</p>
<div id="drop">
  You can also drag and drop your files here
</div>
<h1>Retrieved file information</h1>
<ul id="fileList">
  <li class="no-items">&lt;no files uploaded yet&gt;</li>
</ul>
<script>
  (function () {
     var filesUpload = document.getElementById("upload"),
     dropArea = document.getElementById("drop"),
     fileList = document.getElementById("fileList");
     function fileTransfer (files) {
       var li,
       file,
       fileInfo;
       fileList.innerHTML = "";
       for (var i = 0, fl = files.length; i < fl; i++) {
         li = document.createElement("li");
         file = files[i];
         fileInfo = file.name; // Name
         fileInfo += " (" + file.type + "), "; // Type
         fileInfo += file.size + " bytes"; // Size
         li.innerHTML = fileInfo;
         fileList.appendChild(li);
       };
     };
       filesUpload.onchange = function () {
         fileTransfer(this.files);
       };
       dropArea.ondragenter = function () {
         return false;
       };
       dropArea.ondragover = function () {
         return false;
       };
       dropArea.ondrop = function (evt) {
         fileTransfer(evt.dataTransfer.files);
       return false;
     };
  })();
</script>
```

The division representing the drop area in the previous example (<div id="drop">) should be styled either with a border or with a background color to make it visible (Listing 6-9).

Listing 6-9. CSS Ruleset for the Previous Example

```
#drop {
  border: 2px dashed #f00;
```

```
  padding: 10px;
}
```

Next, create a very simple drag-and-drop example with five words that can be dragged from one division to another and back. First, declare the div items and make them draggable with the draggable attribute. Then, put them into a container div and create the second div (the target) (Listing 6-10).

Listing 6-10. The Markup for the DnD Example

```
<section>
  <header>
    <h3>Drag the word "DnD" to the other box and back</h3>
  </header>
  <div id="leftDiv" ondragover="dragOver(event)" ondrop="dragDrop(event)">
   <div id="word1" class="dragbox" draggable="true" ondragstart="return ↵
   dragDefine(event)" ondragend="dragEnd(event)">My</div>
   <div id="word2" class="dragbox" draggable="true" ondragstart="return ↵
   dragDefine(event)" ondragend="dragEnd(event)">dog</div>
   <div id="word3" class="dragbox" draggable="true" ondragstart="return ↵
   dragDefine(event)" ondragend="dragEnd(event)">is</div>
   <div id="word4" class="dragbox" draggable="true" ondragstart="return ↵
   dragDefine(event)" ondragend="dragEnd(event)">called</div>
   <div id="word5" class="dragbox" draggable="true" ondragstart="return ↵
   dragDefine(event)" ondragend="dragEnd(event)">Bobby</div>
</div>
  <div id="rightDiv" ondragover="return dragOver(event)" ondrop="dragDropped(event)"></div>
</section>
```

In the document head, declare a script element, and create the functions to be called (Listing 6-11) when the following happens:

- The item starts to be dragged

- The item being dragged is over another item

- The drag is complete

- The item being dragged is dropped

Listing 6-11. The Functions for Handling Drag and Drop

```
<script>
  function dragStarted(evt) {
    evt.dataTransfer.effectAllowed = 'move';
    evt.dataTransfer.setData("text/plain", evt.target.getAttribute('id'));
    evt.dataTransfer.setDragImage(evt.target, 0, 0);
    return true;
}
```

```
function dragOver(evt) {
  evt.preventDefault();
}

function dragEnded(evt) {
  return true;
}

function dragDropped(evt) {
  var idDrag = evt.dataTransfer.getData("Text");
  evt.target.appendChild(document.getElementById(idDrag));
  evt.preventDefault();
}
</script>
```

Finally, declare styles, including the layout and colors for the boxes, in the document head or an external file (Listing 6-12).

Listing 6-12. The Styles for the Boxes

```
body {
  width: 800px;
  margin: 100px auto;
}

#leftDiv, #rightDiv {
  float: left;
  width: 200px;
  height: 100px;
  margin: 50px;
  background-color: #bbdeee;
  border: 1px solid #000;
}

.word {
  width: 60px;
  height: 20px;
  margin: 5px;
  text-align: center;
  font-weight: bold;
  background-color: #ff6;
  display: inline-block;
  cursor: move;
}
```

The File API is supported by Firefox 3.6+ and Chrome 6.0+. Opera 11.5 supports the File API but not the Drag & Drop API. IE9 supports the Drag & Drop API but not the File API. Safari partially supports the File API from version 4.0 and will support fully in version 6.

The HTML5 Forms API

HTML5 introduced new attributes for the input element (autocomplete, autofocus, form, formaction, formenctype, formmethod, formnovalidate, formtarget, height, list, max, min, multiple, pattern, placeholder, required, step, and width) and new attribute values for the type attribute of the input element (including email, url, number, range), search, color, and date pickers (date, month, week, time, datetime, and datetime-local), as well as form validation [10].

As an example, create an (X)HTML5 form for a registration page of a web site (Listing 6-13).

Listing 6-13. A Registration Form

```
<form action="newaccount.php" method="post">
  <fieldset title="Create account">
    <p>
      <label for="mailadd">E-mail address:</label>
      <input id="mailadd" type="email" required="required" name="mail"
        placeholder="email@example.com" />
    </p>
    <p>
      <label for="passwd1">Password:</label>
      <input id="passwd1" type="password" required="required" name="pwd" />
    </p>
    <p>
      <label for="passwd2">Confirm password:</label>
      <input id="passwd2" type="password" required="required" name="pwd2" />
    </p>
    <p>
      <label for="website">Website:</label>
      <input type="url" name="website" placeholder="http://www.example.com" />
    </p>
    <p>
      <label for="number">Number:</label>
      <input type="number" name="number" min="0" max="10" placeholder="0-10" />
    </p>
    <p>
      <label for="range">Range:</label>
      <input type="range" name="range" min="0" max="10" step="2" />
    </p>
    <p>
      <input type="submit" value="Create account" />
    </p>
  </fieldset>
</form>
```

The HTML5 Geolocation API

The Geolocation API provides an interface to retrieve information on the geographical location for a client-side device. In other words, it can be used in web browsers to find the current position of the user. The location of the user is not shared until the user confirms the request. The Geolocation API is being standardized by the W3C [11].

Listing 6-14 shows an example for the application of the Geolocation API. In the example, the `setOnLoadCallback` function is used to create a map. The `if-then` construct is used to check whether the Geolocation API is supported, get the current position, and, in case it is successfully retrieved, mark it on the map. If necessary, we inform the user to accept the Geolocation request, or the location cannot be determined. The location is hard-coded to Garden Island in Adelaide, Australia, which is used until the user enables geolocation. In the `else` branch, a nice location is set for users that use a browser without geolocation support.

Listing 6-14. *Retrieving the Location of the User*

```
<div id="map">
</div>
<script src="http://www.google.com/jsapi?key=ABQIAAAAlJFc1lrstqhgTl3ZYo38bBQcfCcww1WgMTx ↵
 EFsdaTsnOXOVOUhTplLhHcmgnaYOu87hQyd-n-kiOqQ">
</script>
<script>
  (function () {
    google.load("maps", "2");
    google.setOnLoadCallback(function () {
      var map = new google.maps.Map2(document.getElementById("map")),
      markerText = "<h2>You are here</h2><p>This is your current position</p>",
      markOutLocation = function (lat, long) {
        var latLong = new google.maps.LatLng(lat, long),
        marker = new google.maps.Marker(latLong);
        map.setCenter(latLong, 15);
        map.addOverlay(marker);
        marker.openInfoWindow(markerText);
        google.maps.Event.addListener(marker, "click", function () {
          marker.openInfoWindow(markerText);
        });
      };
      map.setUIToDefault();
      if (navigator.geolocation) {
        navigator.geolocation.getCurrentPosition(function (position) {
          markOutLocation(position.coords.latitude, position.coords.longitude);
        },
        function () {
          markerText = "<p>You should accept the Geolocation request, otherwise your ↵
            position cannot be determined.</p>";
          markOutLocation(59.3325215, 18.0643818);  // Garden Island, Adelaide, Australia
        });
      }
      else {
        markerText = "<p>Geolocation is not supported. Welcome to my favourite location.</p>";
        markOutLocation(-34.928621, 138.599959);  // Rundle Mall, Adelaide, Australia
      }
    });
  })();
</script>
```

■ **Tip** The position is approximate only. In the previous example, we get a marker that does not necessarily mark the exact location of the user. More sophisticated interfaces, such the "Location-Aware Browsing" test page of Firefox [12], provide a semitransparent circle above the map rather than a marker pointing to an exact position.

The HTML5 Geolocation API is supported by IE9+, Firefox 3.5+, Chrome 5.0+, Opera 10.6+, and Safari running on the iPhone.

The HTML5 Web Storage API

Web Storage is an API for persistent data storage of key-value pair data (similar to cookies) in browsers (sessionStorage) and window-local storage saved between sessions (localStorage). The Web Storage API is being standardized by the World Wide Web Consortium [13].

Table 6-1 summarizes the methods of localStorage and sessionStorage.

Table 6-1. Web Storage Methods

Method with Parameters	Description
setItem(string name, string value)	Adds or updates a value in the store
getItem(string name)	Retrieves a named value from the stored name-value pairs
removeItem(string name)	Removes a named value from the stored name-value pairs
length	Number of values stored
key(long index)	Name of the key at the index
clear()	Clears the store

As an example, create two input fields for the local storage of name-value pairs, as well as a push button to let the user set the items entered (Listing 6-15). Display the name-value pairs in a table. Create a text field where the user can add the item to remove from the stored pairs after clicking the associated button. Add a push button that can be used to clear the stored items. Provide another text field where the item name can be typed to retrieve its value. Since the table is created by the displayItems function, that function should be loaded by the onload attribute on the body element as <body onload="displayItems()">.

Listing 6-15. A localStorage Example

```
<form name="lsform">
  <fieldset title="WebStorage">
    <legend>Local storage of name-value pairs</legend>
    <p>
```

```
  <label>Value:</label>
  <input name="data">
</p>
<p>
  <label>Name:</label>
  <input name="name">
</p>
<p>
  <input type="button" value="Set item" onclick="setTheItem()">
</p>
<table id="pairs"></table>
<p>
  Enter name to remove item:
  <input name="remove">
  <input type="button" value="Remove item" onclick="removeTheItem()">
  <input type="button" value="Clear items" onclick="clearItems()">
</p>
<p>
  Enter name to retrieve value:
  <input name="retrieve">
  <input type="button" value="Get value" onclick="getTheItem()">
</p>
<script type="text/javascript">
  function setTheItem() {
    var name = document.forms.lsform.name.value;
    var data = document.forms.lsform.data.value;
    localStorage.setItem(name, data);
    displayItems();
  }
  function getTheItem() {
    var name = document.forms.lsform.retrieve.value;
    window.alert('The value associated with the name ' + name + ' is ' + ↵
      localStorage.getItem(name));
    displayItems();
  }
  function removeTheItem() {
    var name = document.forms.lsform.remove.value;
    document.forms.lsform.data.value = localStorage.removeItem(name);
    displayItems();
  }
  function clearItems() {
    localStorage.clear();
    displayItems();
  }
  function displayItems() {
    var key = "";
    var pairs = "<tr><th>Name</th><th>Value</th></tr>\n";
    var i = 0;
    for (i = 0; i <= localStorage.length-1; i++) {
      key = localStorage.key(i);
      pairs += "<tr><td>" + key + "</td>\n<td>" + localStorage.getItem(key) + ↵
        "</td></tr>\n";
```

```
      }
      if (pairs == "<tr><th>Name</th><th>Value</th></tr>\n") {
        pairs += "<tr><td><em>&lt;not set&gt;</em></td>\n<td><em>&lt;not ↵
        set&gt;</em></td></tr>\n";
      }
      document.getElementById('pairs').innerHTML = pairs;
    }
  </script>
  </fieldset>
</form>
```

The Web Storage API is supported by IE 8+, Firefox 3.5+, Google Chrome 4+ (sessionStorage from 5+), Safari 4+, and Opera 10.50+.

The HTML5 Web Workers API

Web Workers is an API that can be used to execute scripts in the background independent from any user interface scripts. Consequently, the user interface is not affected, and all browser tasks are performed without any delay.

The "worker" in Web Workers refers to a script stored in an external file, which is loaded and executed in the background (Listing 6-16).

Listing 6-16. Creating a "Worker"

```
new Worker("worker.js");
```

While complex JavaScript codes might hang your browser (such as giving an "unresponsive script" warning), the Web Workers API makes it possible to avoid user interruption, while the browser performs tasks such as event handling, DOM manipulations, queries, and processes.

■ **Note** Since JavaScript was originally designed to run in a single-threaded environment—that is, multiple scripts cannot be run simultaneously—Web Workers can be considered as an API that brings threading to JavaScript.

In our example, we create a "worker" that counts up from 0 to 10,000 in the background. First, two push buttons are needed in the document body to start and stop counting (two input elements with unique identifiers), and a paragraph is needed with an identifier (<p id="result">) where the result will be displayed (Listing 6-17).

Listing 6-17. Markup of a Web Worker Example

```
<h1>Start/Stop the Worker</h1>
<p>
  <input id="start" type="button" value="Start">
  <input id="stop" type="button" value="Stop">
</p>
```

```
<h1>The results</h1>
<p id="result">Click Start to start the Worker</p>
<script>
  (function () {
    function createWorker () {
      worker = new Worker("webworker.js");
    }
    document.getElementById("start").onclick = function () {
      createWorker();
      worker.postMessage(0);  // initial value
      worker.onmessage = function (evt) {
        document.getElementById("result").innerHTML = evt.data;
      };
      worker.onerror = function (evt) {
        document.getElementById("result").innerHTML = "Error";
      };
    };
    document.getElementById("stop").onclick = function () {
      if (worker) {
        worker.terminate();
      }
    };
  })();
</script>
```

We also need a function for the Start button, an error event handler, and a function for the Stop button. The function that actually performs the counting takes place in an external .js file (Listing 6-18).

Listing 6-18. The webworker.js *File*

```
onmessage = function (evt) {
  for (var i = evt.data, t = 10000; i < t; i++) {
    postMessage(i);
  };
};
```

The Web Workers API is supported by IE10+, Firefox 3.5+, Chrome 5.0+, Safari 4.0+, and Opera 10.6+.

The HTML5 WebSocket API

The WebSocket API can be used for bidirectional, full-duplex communication over a Transmission Control Protocol (TCP) socket.

The WebSocket API is being standardized by the World Wide Web Consortium [14].

After building a WebSocket connection with the web server, data can be retrieved from the server using the onmessage event handler and can be sent from the client to the server by the send() method.

A new WebSocket object can be created as shown in Listing 6-19.

Listing 6-19. A New WebSocket *Object*

```
var Socket = new WebSocket(http://example.com/ws/);
```

Optionally, the protocol can also be specified after the URI.

The WebSocket object has two read-only attributes: `Socket.readyState` and `Socket.bufferedAmount`. The first one represents the connection state (0 is no connection yet, 1 is connection has been built, 2 is closing handshake, 3 is connection closed or cannot be established). The second attribute gives the number of bytes queued using the `send()` method.

The WebSocket API supports four events: open (socket connection established), message (client receives data from server), error (error in communication), and close (the connection is closed). They can be handled by the `Socket.onopen`, `Socket.onmessage`, `Socket.onerror`, and `Socket.onclose` event handlers, respectively.

The two methods of WebSocket are `Socket.send()` (the `send()` method transmits data through the connection), and `Socket.close()` (the `close()` method is used to terminate the existing connection).

As an example, we create a bidirectional TCP socket between the client and the server in the document head (Listing 6-20).

Listing 6-20. Creating a WebSocket

```
<script type="text/javascript">
  function myWS() {
    if ("WebSocket" in window) {
      alert("WebSocket is supported by your Browser!");
      var ws = new WebSocket("ws://localhost:9998/echo");
      ws.onopen = function() {
        ws.send("Message to send");
        alert("Message sent…");
      };
      ws.onmessage = function (evt) {
        var received_msg = evt.data;
        alert("Message received…");
      };
      ws.onclose = function() {
        alert("Connection closed…");
      };
    }
    else {
      alert("WebSocket is not supported by your browser!");
    }
  }
</script>
```

In the document body, the `myWS()` function should be called to start the WebSocket (Listing 6-21).

Listing 6-21. An Anchor to Start the WebSocket

```
<p>
  <a href="javascript:myWS()">Start WebSocket</a>
</p>
```

The client program is now ready, but we also need a server with WebSocket support to test it. For example, pywebsocket, which can be used as a WebSocket stand-alone server and a WebSocket extension for Apache HTTP servers, is suitable for testing [15].

After the HTTP handshake, the TCP socket is ready for use, and the connection is live; both the server and the client can send data.

On the client side, the WebSocket API is supported by Firefox 4+, Google Chrome 4+, Safari 5+, and Opera 11+.

Offline Web Applications

The offline web application feature in HTML5 allows online applications to work without interruption even when the Internet connection is not available. For example, users can compose a message in their webmail client when they cannot find a Wi-Fi hotspot.

Since the browser has no access to web site files when it is offline, the first step is to specify the required resources (a simple list of fundamental files) for caching in a file called `offline.manifest` (Listing 6-22).

Listing 6-22. An offline.manifest File

```
CACHE MANIFEST
index.html
styles.css
main.js
```

This file should be provided as the attribute value of the `manifest` attribute on the `html` element (Listing 6-23). The file should be served with the MIME type `text/cache-manifest`.

Listing 6-23. Using the Manifest File

```
<html manifest="offline.manifest">
```

Users will be requested to allow caching on their computer.

The online/offline state of the browser can be determined by JavaScript using `navigator.onLine`.

When the browser is offline, the data can be easily stored locally using the Web Storage API discussed earlier, that is, the `sessionStorage` to retrieve data during a session or the `localStorage` to retain values for longer periods.

Offline web applications are supported by Firefox 3.5+, Chrome 1.0+, Safari 4.0+, and Opera 10.6+.

Java Applets

Java is an object-oriented, structured, imperative, cross-platform programming language. Java was originally developed by Sun Microsystems, which is now owned by Oracle Corporation. Java can be used in a variety of contexts on the client side as well as the server side, including applets, servlets, Swing applications, and JavaServer Pages (JSP).

Java applets are small applications for performing a specific task and are provided on web sites in a format called Java bytecode, which can be executed by the Java Virtual Machine (JVM). Although Java applets can be substituted by alternate technologies such as Flash, Curl, or Microsoft Silverlight, they are still present on the Web.

A Java applet should be provided by two `object` elements and self-closing parameters. The inner object is used by Trident and the outer object by Gecko. Listing 6-24 shows an example.

Listing 6-24. Java Applet Embedding with object

```
<object classid="java:bookflip.class"
 type="application/x-java-applet"
```

```
      archive="bookflip.jar"
      height="120" width="120">
       <param name="res" value="1" />
       <param name="image1" value="01.jpg" />
       <param name="link1" value="NO" />
       <param name="flip1" value="0" />
       <param name="image2" value="02.jpg" />
       <param name="link2" value="NO" />
       <param name="flip2" value="0" />
       <param name="speed" value="4" />
       <object classid="clsid:8AD9C840-044E-11D1-B3E9-00805F499D93" height="120" width="120" >
         <param name="code" value="bookflip" />
         <param name="archive" value="bookflip.jar" />
         <param name="res" value="1" />
         <param name="image1" value="01.jpg" />
         <param name="link1" value="NO" />
         <param name="flip1" value="0" />
         <param name="image2" value="02.jpg" />
         <param name="link2" value="NO" />
         <param name="flip2" value="0" />
         <param name="speed" value="4" />
       </object>
      </object>
```

Objects must be rendered only once per page. As you will see, a similar approach exists for Flash objects too (Chapter 9).

ECMAScript and JavaScript

A widely used scripting language is ECMAScript, which is standardized by Ecma International (ECMA-262 [16], ECMA-290 [17], ECMA-327 [18], ECMA-357 [19]) and the International Organization for Standardization (ISO/IEC 16262 [20]). The Internet media type of ECMAScript is application/ecmascript, and the file extension is .es.

The three best-known dialects of ECMAScript are JavaScript, JScript, and ActionScript. The first one, JavaScript, is the primary client-side scripting language on the Web. It is used by millions of web sites to add interaction and functionality.

▪ **Caution** JavaScript should not be confused with Java. Although both languages have a C-like syntax, JavaScript is a scripting language, while Java is general programming language. JavaScript has dynamic typing, while Java has static typing. JavaScript is a weakly typed language, while Java is strongly typed. JavaScript is loaded from human-readable source code, while Java is retrieved from a compiled bytecode. In contrast to JavaScript objects, which are prototype-based, Java objects are class-based.

JScript is the Microsoft implementation of ECMAScript [21]. The major implementations of JScript are Windows Script, and JScript .NET. The typical file extensions of JScript are .js, .jse, .wsf, .wsc, and, if embedded, .htm, .html, and .asp.

ActionScript is an object-oriented language originally developed by Macromedia, which is now owned by Adobe Systems. It is implemented in Adobe Flash and, as mentioned earlier, Adobe Flex. The typical file extension of external ActionScript files is .as. ActionScript reuses the MIME type of ECMAScript.

Embedding and Loading JavaScript

JavaScript codes applied to a whole web page are usually declared in the (X)HTML head. JavaScript can also be used locally in the body section of web documents. Those JavaScript codes that are used throughout the entire web site are written in external files.

Generally, there are three ways to use JavaScript on web sites. They are discussed in the following sections.

Loading JavaScript from an External File

This technique is used when the same script applies to multiple documents. The file extension of external JavaScript files is .js. The character encoding of these files is usually US-ASCII. JavaScript files encoded in other encoding schemes might have interoperability problems. While UTF-8 is the perfect choice for (X)HTML web documents and can be applied as the default character encoding in the text editor of any developer, care must be taken to encode JavaScript files (similar to CSS files) in US-ASCII whenever possible.

External JavaScript files should contain JavaScript code exclusively (Listing 6-25). The script tags must also be avoided (Listing 6-26)!

Listing 6-25. JavaScript Code in the Markup

```
<script type="text/javascript">
  document.write("Nice coding");
</script>
```

Listing 6-26. The Same Code in an External .js File

```
document.write("Nice coding");
```

External JavaScript files can be loaded with the src attribute on the script element.[1] Listing 6-27 shows an example.

Listing 6-27. Loading JavaScript from an External File

```
<script type="text/javascript" src="scripts/click.js"></script>
```

This embedding is commonly used for the scripts loaded in the document head and any scripts that are too long to write directly into the markup. Alternate style selectors, font resizers, and hidden layer controller scripts are some examples for this approach.

---

[1] In the early days of Web, the language="javascript" attribute-value pair was used on the script element and later was deprecated in favor of type="text/javascript".

Inline JavaScript

JavaScript can also be written directly in the markup as the content of the script element. Assume we have the JavaScript function shown in Listing 6-28 and variables in Listing 6-29 either in the document head or in an external .js file.

Listing 6-28. A Short JavaScript Function

```
function fourdigits(number) {
  return (number < 1000) ? number + 1900 : number;
}
```

Listing 6-29. Variables

```
var now = new Date();
var year = fourdigits(now.getYear());
```

This code provides the current year, which can be used for a "dynamic" copyright content as Listing 6-30.

Listing 6-30. Inline JavaScript Example

```
Copyright © <script type="text/javascript">document.write(year);</script> John Smith
```

This is an inline JavaScript code. In this case, it will represent the current year between the copyright sign and the name, as shown in Listing 6-31.

Listing 6-31. The result of Listings 6-28, 6-29, and 6-30

```
Copyright © 2011 John Smith
```

Note that if the JavaScript code cannot run for whatever reasons, the other parts of the document are still rendered (Listing 6-32).

Listing 6-32. The Result of the Same Code with JavaScript Disabled or Without JavaScript Support

```
Copyright © John Smith
```

Event Handlers

JavaScript is often used to provide control over document elements or the browser window according to user interaction such as clicking an element with the mouse.

Assume three images on a web page intended to modify the font size of the layer main when the user clicks them. Listing 6-33 shows a possible solution.

Listing 6-33. Functions to Manipulate the Font Size

```
function normal() {
  var esize = document.getElementById('main').style;
  esize.fontSize = "1.1em";
}
```

```
function larger() {
  var esize = document.getElementById('main').style;
  esize.fontSize  = "1.4em";
}

function huge() {
  var esize = document.getElementById('main').style;
  esize.fontSize = "1.8em";
}
```

These three functions can be written either within the script tags in the document or in the external file font.js. In the latter case, they can be loaded with the src attribute of the script element as discussed earlier in Listing 6-27 (the file path and name can be arbitrarily modified).

Now the appropriate event handler function can be loaded with the onclick attribute (Listing 6-34).

Listing 6-34. Event Handlers That Load the Appropriate Function Upon User Click

```
<a href="#" onclick="javascript:normal();">
  <img src="images/normal.png" alt="Normal font" title="Normal" />
</a>
<a href="#" onclick="javascript:larger();">
  <img src="images/larger.png" alt="Larger font" title="Larger" />
</a>
<a href="#" onclick="javascript:huge();">
  <img src="images/huge.png" alt="Huge font" title="Huge" />
</a>
```

Which function will be run depends on which image link the user clicks.

Determining JavaScript Support

JavaScript support can be easily determined by a script with an alternate content such as in Listing 6-35.

Listing 6-35. JavaScript with Alternate Content

```
<script type="text/javascript">
  document.write("If this text is displayed, your browser supports scripting, and ↵
  JavaScript is enabled!")
</script>
<noscript>JavaScript is NOT enabled!</noscript>
```

Browsers that do not support JavaScript will show the content of the noscript element.

Silverlight

Silverlight is a freeware application framework created by Microsoft Corporation for developing rich Internet applications [22]. The runtime environment for Silverlight is available as a web browser plug-in. Silverlight provides many features similar to those of Adobe Flash, such as animations, drawing objects, reflection effects, glyphs, and so on.

Silverlight uses the Extensible Application Markup Language (XAML) instead of Scalable Vector Graphics (SVG). XAML is a declarative, XML-based user interface markup language developed by Microsoft and used extensively in .NET.

Similar to Flash, a common embedding option for Silverlight is using the object tag (Listing 6-36).

Listing 6-36. Silverlight Embedding with Alternate Content (Determining Support)

```
<object id="SilverlightPlugin1" width="300" height="300" ↵
 data="data:application/x-silverlight-2," ↵
 type="application/x-silverlight-2" >
  <param name="source" value="SilverlightApplication1.xap" />
  <a href="http://go.microsoft.com/fwlink/?LinkID=149156&v=4.0.60310.0">
    <img src="http://go.microsoft.com/fwlink/?LinkId=161376" alt="Get Silverlight" />
  </a>
</object>
```

Silverlight can be written not only in your text editor but also in the Microsoft Visual Studio software development platform, which makes it easier to create graphical interfaces displayed simultaneously with the source code.

Server-Side Development

Although static content is adequate for many web site components, advanced web site features, such as web applications, content management, online banking, form submission, database management, and so on, require server-side programming.

▪ **Note** The main difference between client-side and server-side programming is that client-side scripts are downloaded, interpreted, and executed by the browser, while server-side scripts and applications run on the server.

▪ **Tip** In contrast to client-side technologies, where the support either is embedded in most browsers (such as for JavaScript) or can be set easily by installing a free plug-in (such as for SilverLight), the support for server-side technologies should be provided by the hosting service provider. While widely adopted technologies such as PHP and MySQL are supported by most hosting services, it is strongly recommended that you ask the provider about the support for special technologies before selecting and paying for a service, because hosting companies usually refuse to install any software components not included in, or supported by, one of their packages (for example, FFMPEG, ionCube PHP Loader, Apache Ant, Ivy, JTA, JAXP). Some technologies rely on others, and there might be a prerequisite to install certain software components.

There is a wide variety of server-side scripting and programming languages used to create server-side applications. Some of the most widely adopted ones are described in the following sections.

ColdFusion

ColdFusion is an application server offered by Adobe [23] to process the ColdFusion Markup Language (CFML). CFML is a scripting language that uses tags with a structure similar to that of HTML (which is the reason for the name) [24]; it has a functionality similar to that of PHP. CFML has several implementations beyond Adobe ColdFusion, such as the .NET Framework, the Java Virtual Machine, and the Google App Engine. Because of its scalability, ColdFusion is ideal not only for desktop environments but also for the increasingly popular mobile web applications.

The most significant technologies that compete with ColdFusion are BlueDragon [25], Coral Web Builder [26], IgniteFusion [27], Railo [28], and SmithProject [29].

Java

The Java programming language was already mentioned earlier in the chapter regarding Java applets. However, Java is also used on the server side.

JavaServer Pages (JSP) is a Java technology for dynamically generated web pages. The syntax of JSP combines scriptlet elements and markup (typically HTML or XML) [30]. The content of scriptlet elements is Java code that might be mixed with the markup.

The Java Platform, Enterprise Edition (Java EE) is a popular platform for server-side programming in Java. The platform and the associated APIs are defined in separate specifications [31, 32].

WebObjects is a Java web application server and web application framework for Mac OS X developed by Apple. WebObjects is described by Apple specifications [33, 34, 35].

The .NET Framework

Microsoft .NET is a popular software framework with a wide-ranging library [36]. The .NET Framework supports several programming languages (C#, J#, VB .NET, and so on). Any of these languages can use code written in other languages, which provides a high level of interoperability. A fundamental part of the framework architecture is the application virtual machine called *Common Language Runtime (CLR)*, which is Microsoft's implementation of the *Common Language Infrastructure (CLI)*. CLI is an ECMA standard (ECMA 335 [37]).

Some applications of the .NET Framework, such as ADO.NET, ASP.NET, and Windows Forms, are not parts of the previously mentioned standards.

ASP.NET

Active Server Pages, often referred to as ASP or ASP Classic, was a web application framework developed by Microsoft for creating interactive and dynamic web pages. It has been superseded by ASP.NET, which provides powerful features for web applications and services [38]. The typical file extensions are `.asp` for ASP and `.aspx` for ASP.NET files.

As you can see in Listing 6-37, an ASP script can be embedded in the document body of a web page by delimiting the script with `<%` and `%>`.

Listing 6-37. ASP Script in the Markup

```
<!DOCTYPE html>
<html>
  <head>
    <title>Simple ASP embedding example</title>
```

```
    <meta charset="UTF-8">
  </head>
  <body>
    <%
    response.write("Hello, World!")
    %>
  </body>
</html>
```

Before introducing HTML5 support in Visual Studio and ASP.NET in 2011, ASP.NET generated error-free XHTML markup in most cases. Since ASP.NET does not modify static text and nonserver markup elements, however, the final markup was not necessarily standards-compliant per XHTML 1.0 Strict. According to Microsoft, some markup controls providing optional functionality, especially those with a target attribute for specifying their client-side behavior (AdRotator, BulletedList, HyperLink, HyperLinkColumn, ImageMap, MenuItem, TreeNode), might result in markup code that is not standard compliant [39].

C#

A popular programming language often used in .NET is C# (pronounced *See Sharp*), which has been standardized by ECMA [40] and ISO [41, 42]. C# is a multiparadigm programming language, which is declarative, generic, functional, and imperative, and it has strong typing. C# applies object-oriented (class-based) as well as component-oriented disciplines.

Perl

Perl is a high-level, interpreted, general-purpose, dynamic programming language. The specification of the language is available at Perl.org [43]. In the late 1990s, Perl became popular as a CGI scripting language because of its parsing abilities. The core syntax of Perl is summarized in the "Perl style guide" [44]. A very impressive text-processing feature of Perl is that it can handle text files of arbitrary length if enough memory is available.

PHP

PHP: Hypertext Preprocessor is one of the most popular open source server-side scripting languages. It is a cross-platform, general-purpose language originally designed for generating dynamic web pages. Some programmers have tried to introduce "standardized" best practices for PHP over the years [e.g., 45, 46, 47, 48], none of which gained an official status yet. The major specification of PHP is being maintained by the PHP Group [49], which is considered as the *de facto* standard of the language, because there is no formal specification.

PHP is the widely used, free, and efficient alternative to competitors such as ASP.NET.

Embedding and Loading PHP

While some PHP code is embedded in (X)HTML documents and mixed with markup elements, complex PHP applications are provided in external files.

PHP in the Markup

PHP code is usually delimited by `<?php` and `?>` or `<script language="php">` and `</script>`. The less portable short tags `<?` and `<?=` and ASP-style tags such as `<%` and `<%=` should not be used. PHP parsers parse code only within the delimiters. In XML documents (thus also in XHTML), the first embedding method provides well-formed XML processing instructions. Since they are not part of the character data in the document, there is the potential that the combination of markup and PHP code provides valid markup on the server before PHP parsing.

The simplest example for embedding PHP in the markup is a "Hello World" script such as `hello.php` (Listing 6-38).

Listing 6-38. "Hello World" in PHP

```
<!DOCTYPE html>
<html xmlns="http://www.w3.org/1999/xhtml" xml:lang="en" lang="en">
  <head>
    <title>Hello World in PHP</title>
    <meta charset="UTF-8" />
  </head>
  <body>
    <?php echo '<p>Hello World</p>'; ?>
  </body>
</html>
```

Depending on the proper server configuration, the PHP code should be parsed, and the output in Listing 6-39 will be sent to the browser.

Listing 6-39. The Output with Parsed PHP

```
<!DOCTYPE html>
<html xmlns="http://www.w3.org/1999/xhtml" xml:lang="en" lang="en">
  <head>
    <title>Hello World in PHP</title>
    <meta charset="UTF-8" />
  </head>
  <body>
    <p>Hello World!</p>
  </body>
</html>
```

The resulting markup validates as HTML5. Note that structural elements and additional contents are omitted for the sake of understanding.

PHP in External Files

The typical file extensions of external PHP files are `.php`, `.phtml`, `.php5`, and `.phps`. External PHP files usually contain the PHP code between the opening and closing delimiters. In other words, they start with `<?php` and end with `?>`. However, many PHP files, such as the ones used for settings, do not necessarily have a closing delimiter.

The `include` command can be used to insert the content of a specified external PHP file into the markup (Listing 6-40).

Listing 6-40. Embedding a PHP File

```
<?php include("copyright.php"); ?>
```

An external PHP file might contain PHP code, markup, or a combination of the two.

■ **Tip** It is a common practice to collect the markup fragment of common—frequently repeated—web page contents, such as menus and legal information, and embed them from an external PHP file. This approach eliminates the redundancy of common scripting requirements of a site.

Python

Python is a general-purpose high-level programming language [50]. Python, similar to other dynamic languages, is often used as a scripting language as well. Multiple programming paradigms are supported by Python. Although Python is mainly object-oriented, it also involves functional programming styles. The capabilities of the language can be extended by third-party tools; for example, Python code can be provided as stand-alone executables. Python interpreters are available for a variety of operating systems, which makes Python a cross-platform language.

Ruby

Ruby is a general-purpose, dynamic, and reflective object-oriented programming language. One of the most common Ruby implementations is the open source web application framework called *Ruby on Rails*. The major documentation of Ruby includes the Ruby Core Reference [51], the Ruby Standard Library Reference [52], the Ruby C API Reference [53], and the document on Rails Searchable APIs [54].

SSJS

Although JavaScript is used primarily on the client side, it has server-side implementations as well. Server-side JavaScript (SSJS) was first implemented in 1996 in the Netscape Enterprise Server 2.0 and Netscape LiveWire. The common specifications for SSJS development are provided by the CommonJS community [55]. The Server-Side JavaScript Google Group makes efforts to create cross-platform SSJS standard APIs [56].

Combinations of Client-Side and Server-Side Technologies

Not all programming environments are purely client-side or server-side technologies. For example, the *Google Web Toolkit* has tools for programming JavaScript front-end applications in Java. Ajax applications and rich Internet applications can be developed in Python using the development tool and framework *Pyjamas*. An open source platform for developing rich Internet applications with client-side functionality and server-side processing is *Tersus*.

Database Technologies

A large share of server-side applications and services rely on data stored in databases. One of the most commonly used databases on the Web is the cross-platform relational database management system *MySQL* [57]. It is considered as a *de facto* standard and also used by the highest-traffic web sites in the world. Although it is very popular, languages such Ruby and Python often apply database servers other than MySQL. Some other frequently used database technologies on the Web are Apache Derby [58], IBM DB2 [59], Firebird [60], Microsoft SQL Server [61], Oracle [62], PostgreSQL [63], SQLite [64], and Sybase [65].

Alternate Content and Fallback Mechanism for Scripts

In web site standardization, it is vital to provide alternate content for scripts and also design web documents for user agents that do not support scripting. You can provide the alternate content by using the noscript element. A script is not executed, and user agents render the content of noscript elements only if the browser configuration eliminates scripting or in rare cases when the scripting language used in the script element is not supported. Browsers without client-side scripting support must render the contents of noscript elements.

For example, if dynamically created data is provided by the script element, a direct link to the resource can be used if scripting is not supported (Listing 6-41).

Listing 6-41. Useful Alternate Content

```
<noscript>
  <p><a href="http://example.com/news/">Latest News</a></p>
</noscript>
```

There is a practice of commenting out script written in the markup to eliminate rendering element content by browsers that cannot handle the script element. Advanced rendering engines recognize that scripts in comments should be executed. This could eliminate the need for comments if external script files are used.

As you learned earlier in the chapter, a properly embedded script does not break page layout or content flow when JavaScript is not supported. Still, this approach usually cannot provide the same functionality or behavior as the script would (the provided information should be similar). The importance of alternate content or fallback mechanism for JavaScript code can be best demonstrated by "dynamic" menus that should not rely on JavaScript alone, since the functionality of the site will be lost if JavaScript is disabled or the script cannot be loaded.

Let's assume that you have a special Help screen, contained by a layer, that is hidden by default (Listing 6-42) and displayed only when the user clicks the menu "Help".

Listing 6-42. A Help div Hidden by Default

```
#help {
  display: none;
}
```

Since the help is displayed using JavaScript (Listing 6-43), it will be not available if JavaScript is disabled or not supported.

Listing 6-43. The Function That Displays the Hidden div

```
function display_help() {
  document.getElementById("help").style.display = 'block';
}
```

A good fallback mechanism is to provide a conventional hyperlink—which looks the same as the link calling the JavaScript code that displays the special Help layer above the page—as an alternate content (Listing 6-44). If the layer cannot be displayed because of the lack of JavaScript support, the link opens another web document with the same content the Help div would provide. Although the visual appearance of the "Help screen" and the Help document is different, the content is the same. One of them is always available.

Listing 6-44. An Advanced Menu Item with Fallback Mechanism

```
<li>
  <script type="text/javascript">
    <a href="javascript:display_help();" title="Guide and access keys" accesskey="h" ↵
    tabindex="22">Help</a>
  </script>
  <noscript>
    <a href="http://example.com/help/" title="Guide and access keys" accesskey="h" ↵
    tabindex="22">Help</a>
  </noscript>
</li>
```

Summary

In this chapter, you learned about client-side and server-side scripting and programming languages used to create scripts, applets, and web applications. Using these technologies on a daily basis is inevitable, and you know by now that they are vital in web application and service development. However, many of them are vendor-specific and have not been standardized yet. You also know that a large share of incorrect markup is generated by server-side applications, even though more and more provide standard-compliant web documents.

In the next chapter, you will learn about emerging Semantic Web technologies and machine-readable metadata annotations.

References

1. Dominique Hazaël-Massieux D (2010) What is scripting? In: Scripting and Ajax. World Wide Web Consortium. www.w3.org/standards/webdesign/script. Accessed 24 January 2011

2. Dorward D (2005) Ampersands, PHP Sessions and Valid HTML. World Wide Web Consortium. www.w3.org/QA/2005/04/php-session. Accessed 24 January 2011

3. Crockford D (2006) The application/json Media Type for JavaScript Object Notation (JSON). The Internet Society. http://tools.ietf.org/html/rfc4627. Accessed 20 August 2011

4. van Kesteren A (2010) XMLHttpRequest. World Wide Web Consortium. www.w3.org/TR/XMLHttpRequest/. Accessed 20 August 2011

5. Adobe (2011) Adobe Flex – Build expressive, cross-platform mobile, web, and desktop applications. Adobe Systems Inc. www.adobe.com/products/flex/. Accessed 22 August 2011

6. Lubbers P, Albers B, Salim F (2010) Pro HTML5 programming – Powerful APIs for Richer Internet Application Development. Apress Media LLC, New York

7. van Kesteren A, Pieters S (2011) APIs. In: HTML5 differences from HTML4. World Web Web Consortium. http://dev.w3.org/html5/html4-differences/#apis. Accessed 22 August 2011

8. Ranganathan A, Sicking J (2010) File API. World Wide Web Consortium. www.w3.org/TR/FileAPI/. Accessed 22 August 2011

9. Hickson I (ed) (2011) Drag and drop. In: HTML. Web Hypertext Application Technology Working Group. www.whatwg.org/specs/web-apps/current-work/multipage/dnd.html. Accessed 22 August 2011

10. Hickson I (2011) Forms. In: HTML. Web Hypertext Application Technology Working Group. www.whatwg.org/specs/web-apps/current-work/multipage/forms.html. Accessed 23 August 2011

11. Popescu A (2010) Geolocation API Specification. World Wide Web Consortium. www.w3.org/TR/geolocation-API/. Accessed 20 August 2011

12. Mozilla (2011) Location-Aware Browsing. www.mozilla.com/en/firefox/geolocation/. Mozilla Corporation. Accessed 21 August 2011

13. Hickson I (2011) Web Storage. World Wide Web Consortium. www.w3.org/TR/webstorage/. Accessed 20 August 2011

14. Hickson I (2011) The WebSocket API. World Wide Web Consortium. www.w3.org/TR/websockets/. Accessed 20 August 2011

15. Google (2011) pywebsocket - WebSocket server and extension for Apache HTTP Server for testing. Google Inc. http://code.google.com/p/pywebsocket/. Accessed 23 August 2011

16. ECMA (2009) The ECMA 262 standard, 5th edition. Ecma International. www.ecma-international.org/publications/files/ECMA-ST/ECMA-262.pdf. Accessed 21 January 2011

17. ECMA (1999) ECMAScript Components Specification. The ECMA-290 standard. ECMA International. www.ecma-international.org/publications/files/ECMA-ST/ECMA-290.PDF. Accessed 23 August 2011

18. ECMA (2001) ECMAScript 3rd Edition Compact Profile. The ECMA-327 standard. ECMA International. www.ecma-international.org/publications/files/ECMA-ST/Ecma-327.pdf. Accessed 23 August 2011

19. ECMA (2005) ECMAScript for XML (E4X) Specification, 2nd edition. The ECMA-357 standard. ECMA International. www.ecma-international.org/publications/files/ECMA-ST/Ecma-357.pdf. Accessed 23 August 2011

20. ISO (2002) ISO/IEC 16262:2002. International Organization for Standardization. www.iso.org/iso/catalogue_detail.htm?csnumber=33835. Accessed 21 January 2011

21. Microsoft (2011) JScript (ECMAScript3) – Windows Scripting 5.8. Microsoft Corporation. http://msdn.microsoft.com/en-us/library/hbxc2t98%28v=VS.85%29.aspx. Accessed 23 August 2011

22. Microsoft (2011) Silverlight. Microsoft Corporation. www.silverlight.net. Accessed 23 August 2011

23. Adobe (2011) Adobe ColdFusion 9 family. Adobe Systems Inc. www.adobe.com/products/coldfusion-family.html. Accessed 23 August 2011

24. Brooks-Bilson R (2009) Core CFML Tags. CFML Advisory Committee. www.opencfml.org/display/cfmladvisory/Core+CFML+Tags. Accessed 23 August 2011

25. New Atlanta (2009) Upgrading from ColdFusion. In: BlueDragon 7.1 User Guide. New Atlanta Communications LLC. www.newatlanta.com/products/bluedragon/self_help/docs/7_1/BlueDragon_71_User_Guide.pdf. Accessed 24 August 2011

26. rave7 (2011) Coral Web Builder. rave7. www.pcaonline.com/index.cfm?DocID=10082&fkb=y. Accessed 24 August 2011

27. FindMySoft (ed) (2011) IgniteFusion CFML engine. www.findmysoft.com/scripts/IgniteFusion-CFML-engine-download.html. Accessed 24 August 2011

28. Railo (2011) Railo Technologies. Railo Technologies GmbH. www.getrailo.com. Accessed 24 August 2011

29. Placona M (2011) Yet another free ColdFusion engine. Marcos Placona Blog. www.placona.co.uk/52/coldfusion/yet-another-free-coldfusion-engine/. Accessed 24 August 2011

30. Sun (2001) JAVASERVER PAGES (JSP) SYNTAX version 1.2. Sun Microsystems, Inc. http://java.sun.com/products/jsp/syntax/1.2/card12.pdf. Accessed 23 August 2011

31. Oracle (2011) Your First Cup: An Introduction to the JavaTM EE Platform. Oracle Corporation. http://download.oracle.com/javaee/6/firstcup/doc/firstcup.pdf. Accessed 23 August 2011

32. Oracle (2011) Java Platform, Enterprise Edition 6 – API Specification. Oracle Corporation. http://download.oracle.com/javaee/6/api/. Accessed 23 August 2011

33. Apple (2007) WebObjects Overview. Apple Inc. http://developer.apple.com/legacy/mac/library/documentation/WebObjects/WebObjects_Overview/WebObjects_Overview.pdf. Accessed 23 August 2011

34. Apple (2007) WebObjects Web Applications Programming Guide. Apple Inc. http://developer.apple.com/legacy/mac/library/documentation/WebObjects/Web_Applications/Web_Applications.pdf. Accessed 23 August 2011

35. Apple (2007) WebObjects Enterprise Objects Programming Guide. Apple Inc. http://developer.apple.com/legacy/mac/library/documentation/WebObjects/Enterprise_Objects/EnterpriseObjects.pdf. Accessed 23 August 2011

36. Microsoft (2011) Microsoft .NET Framework. Microsoft Corporation. www.microsoft.com/net. Accessed 24 August 2011

37. ECMA (2010) Common Language Infrastructure (CLI), 5th edition. ECMA-335 Standard. ECMA International. www.ecma-international.org/publications/files/ECMA-ST/ECMA-335.pdf. Accessed 24 August 2011

38. Microsoft (2011) The Official Microsoft ASP.NET Site. Microsoft Corporation. www.asp.net. Accessed 23 August 2011

39. Microsoft (2010) XHTML Standards in Visual Studio and ASP.NET. Microsoft Corporation. http://msdn.microsoft.com/en-us/library/exc57y7e.aspx. Accessed 23 August 2011

40. ECMA (2006) C# Language Specification, 4th edition. ECMA-334 Standard. ECMA International. www.ecma-international.org/publications/files/ECMA-ST/Ecma-334.pdf. Accessed 24 August 2011

41. ISO (2006) Information technology – Programming languages – C#. ISO/IEC 23270:2006. International Organization for Standardization. www.iso.org/iso/iso_catalogue/catalogue_ics/catalogue_detail_ics.htm?csnumber=42926. Accessed 24 August 2011

42. ISO (2006) Information technology – Common Language Infrastructure (CLI) Partitions I to VI. ISO/IEC 23271:2006. International Organization for Standardization. www.iso.org/iso/iso_catalogue/catalogue_ics/catalogue_detail_ics.htm?csnumber=42927. Accessed 24 August 2011

43. Allen J (ed) (2011) Perl 5 version 14.1 documentation – Full version. Official documentation for the Perl programming language. Perl5 Porters. http://perldoc.perl.org/perldoc.tar.gz. Accessed 23 August 2011

44. Allen J (ed) (2011) Perl version 5.14.1 documentation – Perl style guide. http://perldoc.perl.org/perlstyle.pdf. Accessed 24 August 2011

45. Hoff T, Kristiansen F (2003) PHP Coding Standard. Todd Hoff, Fredrik Kristiansen. www.dagbladet.no/development/phpcodingstandard/. Accessed 24 August 2011

46. Google (2011) PHP Standards Working Group. Google Inc. http://groups.google.com/group/php-standards. Accessed 24 August 2011

47.   Icontem (2011) PHP standards discussion group opens to the world - PHP Classes. Icontem. www.phpclasses.org/blog/post/96-PHP-standards-discussion-group-opens-to-the-world.html. Accessed 24 August 2011

48.   Donat J (ed) (2011) PHP Standards. http://phpstandards.net. Accessed 24 August 2011

49.   Olson P (ed), Achour M, Betz F, Dovgal A, Lopes N, Magnusson H, Richter G, Seguy D, Vrana J, et al (2011) PHP Manual. PHP Documentation Group. www.php.net/manual/en/. Accessed 24 August 2011

50.   PSF (2011) Python Programming Language – Official Web site. Python Software Foundation. www.python.org. Accessed 23 August 2011

51.   Britt J, Neurogami (2010) Ruby Core Reference. James Britt, Neurogami. www.ruby-doc.org/core/. Accessed 24 August 2011

52.   Britt J, Neurogami (2011) Ruby Standard Library Reference. James Britt, Neurogami. www.ruby-doc.org/stdlib/. Accessed 24 August 2011

53.   Britt J, Neurogami (2006) Ruby C API Reference. James Britt, Neurogami. www.ruby-doc.org/doxygen/current/. Accessed 24 August 2011

54.   Kolesnikov V (2009) Rails Searchable API Doc. Vladimir Kolesnikov. http://railsapi.com. Accessed 24 August 2011

55.   Dangoor K *et al* (2009) CommonJS: JavaScript Standard Library. The CommonJS community. www.commonjs.org. Accessed 24 August 2011

56.   Google (2011) The CommonJS Google Group. Google Inc. http://groups.google.com/group/commonjs. Accessed 24 August 2011

57.   Oracle (2010) MySQL: The world's most popular open source database. Oracle Corporation. www.mysql.com. Accessed 24 August 2011

58.   ASF (2011) Apache Derby. Apache Software Foundation. http://db.apache.org/derby/. Accessed 24 August 2011

59.   IBM (2011) DB2 database software. International Business Machines. www-01.ibm.com/software/data/db2/. Accessed 24 August 2011

60.   Firebird Project (2011) Firebird: The true open source relational database for Windows, Linux, Mac OS X and more. Firebird Foundation Incorporated. www.firebirdsql.org. Accessed 24 August 2011

61.   Microsoft (2011) Microsoft SQL Server. Microsoft Corporation. www.microsoft.com/sqlserver/en/us/default.aspx. Accessed 24 August 2011

62.   Oracle (2011) Oracle Database. Oracle Corporation. www.oracle.com. Accessed 24 August 2011

63.   PostgreSQL GDG (2011) PostgreSQL: The world's most advanced open source database. PostgreSQL Global Development Group. www.postgresql.org. Accessed 24 August 2011

64.   Hipp DR (2011) SQLite. http://sqlite.org. Accessed 24 August 2011

65.   Sybase (2011) Database Management. Sybase Inc. www.sybase.com/products/databasemanagement. Accessed 24 August 2011

Metadata and the Semantic Web

The basic structure of web documents provides the desired appearance and functionality. By default, however, the content is human-readable only. You can use additional technologies to provide meaning to web documents, making them machine-readable and part of the Semantic Web. Many terms have been recently introduced for emerging Semantic Web technologies, but because of the lack of formal definitions, many of the definitions are somewhat fuzzy. For example, because of the potential to perform actions automatically, a new era of the Web has begun, which is denoted as Web 2.0. After gaining popularity on online community portals, some features of the Semantic Web, together with personalization, are now referred to as Web 3.0. There is a wide choice of metadata available, along with microformats and various annotations that can significantly extend the possibilities of web documents. They can also considerably improve the effectiveness of web searches. RDF should be used to add structure to the Web and change conventional search engines that apply brute-force approaches.

In this chapter, you will learn machine-readable metadata annotations and semantically meaningful attributes. You will also become familiar with the Resource Description Framework, the fundamental standard behind Semantic Web technologies. After reading the chapter, you will be able not only to apply a variety of metadata annotations but also to create new vocabularies, schemes, and ontologies, including but not limited to the following:

- *General metadata in the markup*: Conventional meta tags

- *Microformats*: Metadata provided as attribute values of markup elements

- *Microdata*: A metadata annotation for general metadata embedding in HTML5

- *RDF*: A standardized framework for Semantic Web data models

- *OWL*: A knowledge representation language for describing and sharing web ontologies that formally represent knowledge as a set of concepts within a domain and the relationships between those concepts

- *FOAF and DOAC*: Machine-readable ontologies for people and their professional capabilities

- *XMP, Rich Snippets, SearchMonkey RDFa*: Metadata formats for images and video clips

The Semantic Web

Until recently, software agents could not handle many kinds of information that could have been associated with files. Although file structure and extensions provided some information about files, much information could not be expressed. For example, a file with a `.jpg` extension has always represented a JPEG image but provided no information about the shutter speed, exposure program, f-stop, aperture, ISO speed rating, or focal length until the introduction of metadata formats such as Exif and XMP (see Chapter 9). However, sharing metadata stored in binary files is still not the most efficient way to share metadata, especially if it is much more generic. In the digital era, electronic files are being sold (e-books, MP3 files, and so on) that might be retrieved or played on many types of devices. A variety of metadata technologies can be used to express arbitrary information and represent any kind of knowledge associated with electronic documents in a machine-readable format. Machine-readable data (automated data) is data stored in a machine-readable format, making it possible for automated software agents to access and process it without human intervention.

To browsers, web documents consisted of human-readable data only. In fact, information was confused with the containers that contained them. In contrast to the conventional Web (the "Web of documents"), the Semantic Web is the "Web of data" [1]. The Semantic Web provides machine-processable data, making it possible for software agents to "understand" the meaning of information (in other words, semantics) presented by web documents. This feature can be used for a variety of services [2], such as museums [3], community sites [4], or podcasting [5].

■ **Caution** The word *semantic* is used on the Web in other contexts as well. For example, in HTML5 there are semantic (in other words, meaningful) structuring elements, but this expression refers to the "meaning" of elements. In this context, the word *semantic* contrasts the "meaning" of elements, such as that of `section` (a thematic grouping), with the generic elements of older HTML versions, such as the "meaningless" `div`. The semantics of markup elements should not be confused with the semantics (in other words, machine-processability) of metadata annotations and web ontologies used on the Semantic Web. The latter can provide far more sophisticated data than the meaning of a markup element.

Conventional web documents can be extended with additional data that add meaning to them rather than structure alone. *Semantic Web* is a new approach that is going to change the world of the Web. Surprisingly, as early as 2001, Tim Berners-Lee described the reason for the existence of the Semantic Web [6]. On the Semantic Web, data can be retrieved from seemingly unrelated fields automatically in order to combine them, find relations, and make discoveries [7]. The Semantic Web should be considered an extension of the conventional Web [8].

Two terms are frequently associated with the Semantic Web, although neither of them has a clear definition: *Web 2.0* and *Web 3.0*.

Web 2.0 is an umbrella term used for a collection of technologies that form the second generation of the Web, such as Extensible Markup Language (XML), Asynchronous JavaScript and XML (Ajax), Really Simple Syndication (RSS), and Session Initiation Protocol (SIP). They are the underlying technologies and standards behind instant messaging, Voice over IP, wikis, blogs, forums, and syndication.

The next generation of web services is more and more frequently denoted as Web 3.0, which is an umbrella term usually referring to customization and semantic contents and more sophisticated web applications toward artificial intelligence, including computer-generated contents [9].

The Semantic Web is a major aspect of Web 2.0 [10] and Web 3.0 [11]. Web 3.0 can be considered a superset of the Semantic Web that features social connections and personalization.

Several technologies contribute to the sharing of such information instead of web pages alone, and the number of Semantic Web applications is constantly increasing.

All data controlled by conventional web applications are kept by the applications themselves, making a significant share of data and their relationships virtually unavailable for automated processing. Semantic Web applications, on the other hand, can access this data through the general web architecture and transfer structured data between applications and web sites [12]. Semantic web technologies can be widely applied in a variety of areas, such as data integration, resource discovery and classification, cataloging, intelligent software agents, content rating, and intellectual property right descriptions [13]. A much wider range of tasks can be performed on semantic web pages than on conventional ones; for example, relationships between data and even sentences can be automatically processed (see the next sections). Additionally, the efficiency is much higher. For example, a very promising approach provides direct mapping of relational data to RDF, making it possible to share data of relational databases on the Semantic Web [14]. Since relational databases are extremely popular in computing, databases that have been stored on local hard drives up to now can be shared on the Semantic Web. Commercial RDF database software packages are already available on the market (5Store, AllegroGraph, BigData, Oracle, OWLIM, Talis Platform, Virtuoso, and so on) [15]. Semantic tools can also be used in a variety of other areas, including business process modeling or diagnostic applications [16].

Along with these benefits, there are several open issues that need further investigation and, in some cases, the development of new approaches. The largest challenge of Semantic Web applications is to resolve semantic data quality problems and identify useful and meaningful information [17]. There are more and more promising approaches; however, they have a common feature: all rely on standard annotations, taxonomies, vocabularies, and ontologies. We analyze these essential technologies and their features throughout the chapter from a standardization point of view.

Structured Data

Data should be structured to support advanced processability and searchability by data type. Structured data is data organized in a structure to become identifiable. Such data has been used for decades in computing, such as in the form of Access and SQL databases, where queries can be performed to retrieve information (for example, a ZIP code). In contrast to relational databases, most data on the Web is stored in (X)HTML documents that contain unstructured data.

Conventional web documents contain large amounts of unstructured data that can be rendered in web browsers. This approach works satisfactorily for publishing purposes; however, a large amount of data stored in, or associated with, web documents cannot be processed this way. According to Berners-Lee, the data used to describe social connections between people is a good example for that kind of data [18]: "The Web is more a social creation than a technical one. I designed it for a social effect—to help people work together—and not as a technical toy. The ultimate goal of the Web is to support and improve our weblike existence in the world. We clump into families, associations, and companies. We develop trust across the miles and distrust around the corner. What we believe, endorse, agree with, and depend on is representable and, increasingly, represented on the Web. We all have to ensure that the society we build with the Web is of the sort we intend."

On the Semantic Web, there is a variety of structured data, usually expressed in, or based on, the Resource Description Framework, which will be described later in detail. Similar to conventional conceptual modeling approaches, such as class diagrams and entity relationships, the RDF data model is based on statements that describe and feature resources, especially web resources, in the form of subject-predicate-object expressions. The subject corresponds to the resource. The predicate expresses a relationship between the subject and the object. Such expressions are called *triples*.

For example, the statement "The grass is green" can be expressed in an RDF triple as follows:

- Subject: "The grass"

- Predicate: "is"

- Object: "green"

RDF is an abstract model that has several serialization formats. Consequently, the syntax of the triple varies from format to format (see later in the section "Resource Description Framework").

■ **Caution** RDF is a concept, not a syntax.

The authors of the "conventional" Web usually publish unstructured data, because they do not know about the power of structured data, find RDF too complex, or do not know how to create and publish RDF in any of its serialization formats. The following are solutions to the problem that add structured data to conventional (X)HTML markup, which can be extracted by appropriate software and converted to RDF:

- Microformats, which reuse markup attributes

- Microdata, which extends HTML5 markup with structured metadata

- RDFa, which expresses RDF in markup attributes that are not part of (X)HTML vocabularies

Linked Open Data

Linked Data (also known as *Linking Data*) can be applied to improve the exploitation of the "Web of data." The expression refers to the publishing of structured data in a way that typed links are created between data from different sources [19] to provide a higher level of usability. By using Linked Data, it is possible to find other, related data. Structured data should meet four requirements to be called Linked Data [20]:

- URIs should be assigned to all entities of the dataset.

- HTTP URIs are required to ensure that all entities can be referenced and cited by users and user agents.

- Entities should be described using standard formats such as RDF/XML.

- Links should be created to other, related entity URIs.

All data that fulfill these requirements and are released for the public are called *Linked Open Data* (LOD). The variety of datasets published as Linked Data is represented by the LOD cloud diagram (Figure 7-1) [21].

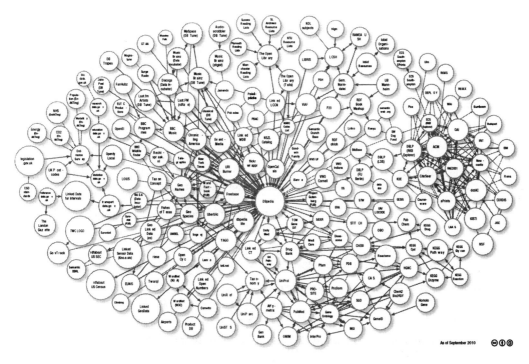

Figure 7-1. The LOD cloud diagram (courtesy of Richard Cyganiak and Anja Jentzsch)

The image collects the datasets published according to the Linked Data principles and represents links between them. The size of the bubbles corresponds to the number of triples stored in each dataset. Contributors include the Linking Open Data community project, individuals, and organizations.

Wide Variety of Annotations and Syntaxes

Metadata is structured data describing information about features and content of web sites. The `meta` *tags* written in (X)HTML head sections, which do not require additional technologies, can be used to describe general data about web pages (as mentioned earlier in Chapter 3 and will be described in detail in the next section). Semantic, machine-readable labels can be provided as attribute values of (X)HTML or XML elements by microdata, microformats, or RDFa.

There are several metadata technologies; many apply different annotations. For example, the description of a person can be expressed in RDFa, microdata, the vCard microformat, and further vocabularies such as FOAF or DOAC.

Special metadata such as licensing can be provided with different notations. Licensing information of images and of the web pages containing them can be different. Providing license metadata can be beneficial to every web site, especially the ones that have different copyright than the user content, such as image-sharing portals like Flickr [22]. Image licenses can be provided in basic markup, microdata, `rel="license"` microformat, and RDFa.

Several metadata technologies can be written in a variety of syntaxes. In the case of microformats, for example, there are differences between the markup languages they can be embedded into. In other cases, reducing complexity is desired (for example, RDF syntaxes).

The meta Tags

In the 1990s, meta elements had a large effect on web search results. Since then, their significance has been decreasing, partly because of the unethical tricks that have been used to manipulate search engine rankings. A good example is *keyword stuffing*, which was used to load a web page with popular keywords that were not necessarily relevant to the page content, either in the meta tags or in the content. In the latter case, the keywords were often hidden, but the web page that contained them was indexed by search engines. Such tricks made it possible for developers to achieve higher ranking on search results but significantly increased the number of irrelevant links on search result lists. Although they are less important nowadays, meta tags still should be used to provide information on web page contents for search engines.

The meta tags in HTML/XHTML can define a variety of metadata, for example, content type, author, publication date, keywords, page content description, character encoding, and so on. These tags were introduced in HTML 2.0 and are still current.

Four attributes can be used on the meta element: content, http-equiv, name, and scheme. The first one is the only required attribute. The meta element attributes can specify the following:

- *Alternatives to HTTP headers* that are sent by web servers prior to the web page content. Listing 7-1 shows an example.

  Listing 7-1. *Document Expiry Date Provided by the meta Tag*

  ```
  <meta http-equiv="expires" content="Fri, 15 October 2010 14:15:00 GMT" />
  ```

- *Names and associated content attributes* describing aspects of (X)HTML pages. Listing 7-2 shows an example.

  Listing 7-2. *Keyword Declaration with the meta Tag*

  ```
  <meta name="keywords" content="standardization, accessibility" />
  ```

  Schemes specify a semantic framework defining the meaning of the key and its value. They can also prevent potential ambiguity. Listing 7-3 shows an example.

  Listing 7-3. *A Meta Scheme*

  ```
  <meta name="foo" content="bar" scheme="DC" />
  ```

  In this case, the foo element in the meta element has the value bar from the Dublin Core (DC) Resource Description Framework (RDF).

The language, keywords, description, and robots attributes contribute to more precise web searches by defining document language, the most relevant keywords, and a short description. The value of the last attribute, robots, provides control over search engine behavior for a limited extent [23]. Web pages can be prevented from being indexed (noindex), crawled (nofollow), cached (noarchive), described (nosnippet), or described according to the *Open Directory Project* (noodp) [24]. The combination of the noindex, nofollow values can be substituted by the value none [25]. This setting can be used, for example, for confidential documents whose content and links should not be considered by search engines.[1] Web page descriptions retrieved from ODP used by search engines Google, Yahoo!, and Bing

---

[1] There are other techniques to achieve similar results. For example, web documents contained by a directory that is disallowed in robots.txt will not be included in the search results.

can be disallowed specifically. The meta name to be applied is Googlebot for Google, Slurp for Yahoo!, and msnbot for Bing (Listing 7-4).

Listing 7-4. meta Tags for Different Crawlers

```
<meta name="Googlebot" content="noodp" />
<meta name="Slurp" content="noodp" />
<meta name="msnbot" content="noodp" />
```

If you want to prevent the descriptions and titles retrieved from the Yahoo! Directory from being displayed in search results, you can use the noydir value [26] (Listing 7-5).

Listing 7-5. Using the noydir Attribute Value

```
<meta name="robots" content="noydir" />
```

It is important to keep in mind that in spite of the variety of attribute values, using meta tags for preventing search engine indexing or crawling is not the best solution. The robots.txt file should be used instead for this purpose.

The typical general metadata provided in the head section of web documents looks like Listing 7-6.

Listing 7-6. A Complete Example for meta Tags of a Web Document

```
<meta http-equiv="Content-Type" content="application/xhtml+xml; charset=utf-8" />
<meta http-equiv="Content-Style-Type" content="text/css" />
<meta name="robots" content="index, follow" />
<meta name="content-language" content="en" />
<meta name="author" content="John Smith" />
<meta name="keywords" content="My Darling, pet shop, pet accessories, dog, collar, ↵
   harness, dog lead, dog kennel, dog bowl, dog coats" />
<meta name="description" content="The website of the pet shop My Darling in Tauranga, ↵
   New Zealand." />
```

Since the attribute value of the name attribute on the meta element is robots, the value of the content attribute (index, follow) is applied to all search engines rather than a specific one.

Schemas, Vocabularies, and Ontologies

Taxonomies or *vocabularies* are structured collections of terms that can be used as metadata element values. They are parts of conceptual data *schemas* (conceptual data models) that map concepts and their relationships. The *namespaces* reveal the meaning of tags and attributes and form *vocabularies*. Formalized conceptual structures can be defined as *ontologies*, in other words, knowledge representations of sets of concepts in a domain and the relationships between them. Web ontologies make it possible to describe complex statements in any topic in a machine-readable format.

Namespaces provide a mechanism to extend the vocabulary of markup languages. To use external vocabularies and ontologies of various metadata technologies, the XML namespace facility is applied in order to associate all properties with the appropriate schema that defines them. Specific metadata can be provided this way such as friends of the author, the nearest airport to the author, GPS coordinates of the office, and so on. User-defined namespaces (schemas) can be created for additional classes and instances of resources.

Shorthand notations are used throughout the Semantic Web to reduce document length. A popular mechanism is called the *qualified name* (*Qname*), which is applied in XML, XML Schema, RDF, RDF Schema, OWL, Dublin Core, and so on. The following are the most common Qnames:

- dc

  Refers to the namespace URI `http://purl.org/dc/elements/1.1/`

- owl

  Refers to the namespace URI `http://www.w3.org/2002/07/owl#`

- rdf

  Refers to the namespace URI `http://www.w3.org/1999/02/22-rdf-syntax-ns#`

- rdfs

  Refers to the namespace URI `http://www.w3.org/2000/01/rdf-schema#`

- xsd

  Refers to the namespace URI `http://www.w3.org/2001/XMLSchema#`

The selection of Semantic Web applications is increasing. For example, OntosMiner runs ontology-driven multilingual information extraction and provides the output in various formats, including RDF(S), XML, OWL, and N3 [27]. Clinical archetypes can be represented and managed as web ontologies in OWL. OWL can also be applied for e-government representations. Web ontologies can be applied for considering viewpoints of learning resources such as online programming courses [28]. Financial headline news can also be represented by ontologies [29]. The following is a short list of some of the more established ontologies:

- *Functional Requirements for Bibliographic Records*, often abbreviated as *FRBR*, can be used to express bibliographic records with properties such as creator, part, embodiment, successor, and subject. FRBR has four classes: Work, Expression, Manifestation, and Item [30].

- Licenses of creative works can be denoted by *Creative Commons*. The Creative Commons Rights Expression Language is ideal to describe copyright in RDF. It has properties such as permits, requires, prohibits, jurisdiction, legalcode, and deprecatedOn, as well as the classes Work, License, Jurisdiction, Permission, Requirement, and Prohibition [31].

- The *Open Digital Rights Language* is an open standard for policy expressions and is being developed and promoted by the ODRL Initiative [32]. The digital management of rights performed using ODRL has also caught attention, and ODRL is also described as a W3C Note [33].

- Thesauruses and taxonomies can be described by the W3C standard *SKOS*, the *Simple Knowledge Organization System*. It has properties such as broader, narrower, subject, and related [34], that correspond to the properties of taxonomies, thesauri, classification schemes, and further structured, controlled vocabularies.

- Geographic positions can be precisely annotated in *Geo*. It has the lat, long, and alt properties and the SpatialThing and Point classes [35].

- Biographical information can be expressed by the *Bio* vocabulary [36].

- In education, the IMS/IEEE *Learning Object Metadata* (*LOM*) can do a service [37].

- Math-Net can be applied to standardize the presentation of information on mathematical departments and research institutes [38].

- People and their social networks can be precisely described in RDF/XML or OWL by Friend of a Friend (FOAF) properties such as name, homepage, knows, weblog, and interest (see the section "FOAF") [39]. FOAF should be used on all social networking sites.

- Professional capabilities and achievements can be described by Description of a Career (DOAC) (see the section "DOAC") [40]. DOAC is compatible with the European Curriculum (Europass) that can be generated from a FOAF+DOAC file.

- Software projects, in particular open source ones, can be expressed in Description of a Project (DOAP) [41].

These schemas, vocabularies, and ontologies are just demonstrations for the endless variety. The list is not complete by any means. Schemaweb.info [42], vocab.org [43], and other libraries collect further specific and sophisticated vocabularies, schemas, and ontologies such as the Beer Ontology [44], the Music Vocabulary [45], or the VidOnt ontology [46]. You can also find many vocabularies with a Google search.

Web ontologies have their limitations and open issues, however. For example, the verification of OWL ontologies with rule extensions is rather complex. However, they can be verified at the symbolic level by using a declarative approach (a new language called Datalog) [47]. The semantic differences between various ontologies should be resolved. The effort to achieve that goal is known as *ontology alignment*. Storing and retrieving data from large RDFs can be performed by advanced techniques only [48].

Microformats

A special approach to metadata is a set of simple open data formats called *microformats* (μF). They are highly correlated with the Semantic Web by applying and reusing features of existing technologies (for example, the (X)HTML rel attribute) and by introducing new ones with the simplest approaches possible—based on *Plain Old Semantic HTML* (*POSH*) (for example, hCard). They can be applied not only in (X)HTML markup but also in XML, RSS, Atom, and so on.

Microformats can express site structure, link weight, content type, and human relationships with the class, rel, and rev attribute values [49]. They are very easy to write, and the number of software supporting them is increasing (for example, the Operator [50] and Tails Export [51] add-ons for Firefox, the Google Chrome extension Michromeformats [52], the microformats transformer Optimus [53], or the Microformats Bookmarklet for Safari, Firefox, and IE [54]).

However, there are still some open issues. For example, applying various microformats as multiple values on the a element should be avoided (for example, rel="nofollow" and rel="friend"). The rev attribute used by the Vote Links microformat cannot be used in HTML5.

Profile URIs provided by the profile attribute cannot be used on the head element in HTML5, where the profile attribute values can be declared for the rel attribute on anchors (a) or link elements (link). As an example, a profile URI is presented for the hCalender microformat with all the three options. The hCalendar microformat is based on the iCalendar standard (RFC 2445 [55]). All contents that use hCalendar notation should refer to the hCalendar XMDP profile, in other words, `http://microformats.org/profile/hcalendar`, as shown in Listing 7-7 or Listing 7-8 for the document head or in Listing 7-9 as part of the document body. These methods can also be combined.

Listing 7-7. Providing the hCalendar Head Profile in the Document Head (Cannot Be Used in HTML5)

```
<head profile="http://microformats.org/profile/hcalendar">
```

Listing 7-8. Linking to the hCalendar Profile in the Document Head

```
<link rel="profile" href="http://microformats.org/profile/hcalendar">
```

Listing 7-9. Using the hCalendar Profile in the Document Body

```
<a rel="profile" href="http://microformats.org/profile/hcalendar">hCalendar</a>
```

New structural elements introduced by HTML5, such as `article`, `nav`, and `section`, are not recognized by certain microformat parsers.

In the next sections, we will give you an overview of some of the most popular microformats, namely, hCalendar, hCard, `rel="license"`, `rel="nofollow"`, `rel="tag"`, Vote Links, and XFN.

hCalendar

You can use the hCalendar microformat to create calendar entries for sport events, anniversaries, reminders, meetings, workshops, conferences, and other events. The root class name for hCalendar is `vcalendar`. The root class name for events is `vevent`, which is required for all event listings.

The properties are represented by the elements of hCalendar. The required properties are `dtstart`, which should be provided in the ISO date format,[2] and `summary`.

Listing 7-10 shows an hCalendar example.

Listing 7-10. A Three-Day Conference Represented in hCalendar

```
<div class="vevent">
  <h1 class="summary">Semantic Web Conference '11</h1>
  <div class="description">The Semantic Web Conference 2011 will take place in Pretoria, ↵
  South Africa.</div>
  <div>Posted on: <abbr class="dtstamp" title="20110825T080000Z">Aug 25, 2011</abbr></div>
  <div class="uid">uid1@host.com</div>
  <div>Organized by: <a class="organizer" href="mailto:js@expl.com">js@expl.com</a></div>
  <div>Dates: <abbr class="dtstart" title="20111012T093000Z">October 12, 2011, 09:30 ↵
  UTC</abbr> - <abbr class="dtend" title="20111014T200000Z">October 14, 2011, 20:00 ↵
  UTC</abbr></div>
  <div>Status: <span class="status">Confirmed</span></div>
  <div>Filed under:</div>
  <ul>
    <li class="category">Conference</li>
```

---

[2] Beyond microformats such as hAtom, hCalendar, hCard, and hReview, several web technologies apply the ISO 8601 date format for date-time representation, such as XML, XML schema datatypes, RDF, and Atom.

```
  </ul>
</div>
```

Optional properties include, but are not limited to, location, url, dtend (in ISO date format), duration (in ISO date duration format), rdate, rrule, category, description, uid, geo, attendee, contact, organizer, attach, and status. The geo property has the subproperties latitude and longitude, while attendee has the subproperties partstat and role. According to the specification, the property list is not final and is being extended [56].

Those who have to publish new events regularly might find the hCalendar generator hCalendar-o-matic useful [57].

hCard

The hCard microformat standard can be used to represent contact data of people, companies, and organizations by semantic markup [58]. hCard metadata should be provided on the contact pages of web sites. In summer 2010, hCard crossed the 2 billion mark according to Yahoo! Search Monkey, making it the most popular metadata format for people and organizations on the Web.

hCard is based on the vCard standard (RFC 2426 [59]). In fact, existing vCards can be easily converted to hCard.[3]

■ **Tip** The vCard standard is widely used for storing electronic business cards. For example, Microsoft Outlook uses this format for the business cards available under Contacts.

The hCard class names should be in lowercase.

■ **Caution** The root class name for an hCard is vcard. An element with a class name vcard is itself called an hCard.

The two required attributes in hCard are fn and n. However, the second one is optional if any *implied "N" optimization rules* are in effect.[4] The property n might have the subproperties family-name, given-name, additional-name, honorific-prefix, and honorific-suffix.

All other properties are optional, including adr, agent, bday, category, class, email, geo, key, label, logo, mailer, nickname, note, org, photo, rev, role, sort-string, sound, tel2, title, tz, uid, and url. Allowed subproperties are post-office-box, extended-address, street-address, locality, region, postal-code, country-name, type, and value for adr; type and value for email; latitude and longitude for geo; organization-name and organization-unit for org; and type and value for tel2.

A typical hCard code looks like Listing 7-11.

---

[3] The vCard notation BEGIN:VCARD is class="vcard" in hCard, N: is class="n", FN: is class="fn", and so on.
[4] If n is omitted but fn is present, the value of n will be equal to the value of fn.

Listing 7-11. A Typical hCard

```
<div id="hcard-John-Smith" class="vcard">
  <img src="http://www.example.com/jsmith.jpg" alt="Photo of John Smith" class="photo" />
  <a class="url fn" href="http://www.example.com">John Smith</a>
  <div class="org">Smith and Sons</div>
  <a class="email" href="mailto:smith@example.com">smith@example.com</a>
  <div class="adr">
    <div class="street-address">123 Nice Street</div>
    <span class="locality">Vancouver</span>,
    <span class="region">BC</span>,
    <span class="postal-code">V5K</span>
    <span class="country-name">Canada</span>
  </div>
  <div class="tel">+12345678</div>
</div>
```

The following hCard elements are singular and can be provided just once: fn, n, bday, tz, geo, sort-string, uid, class, and rev. All other properties are allowed to have multiple instances.

Generally, the visible property values of markup elements represent the value of the hCard property. However, there are some exceptions.

For hyperlinks that are represented by the a element for one or multiple hCard properties, the href attribute provides the property value for all properties with a URL value (for example, photo). In case the img element is used, the src attribute holds the property value for all properties with a URL value. For object elements, the data attribute provides the property value. The content of the element is the property value for all other properties.

If the title attribute is provided for abbr elements with hCard notation, its value is considered as the hCard property instead of the element contents used otherwise.

Although it is easy to create it manually, hCard metadata can be generated by the hCard creator *hCard-o-matic* on the web site of the authors of the specification [60]. You simply fill in a form about the name, organization, country, e-mail, and other contact data, and the software generates the hCard.

To provide additional information, microformats can also be nested. For example, a sport event review might contain not only the review but also personal information (hCard) at the same time (Listing 7-12).

Listing 7-12. A Combination of hReview and hCard

```
<div class="hreview">
  <span class="item"><strong class="item"><span class="fn">The winner takes it all</span>
Review</strong></span>
  <span class="reviewer vcard">
  By <span class="fn">John Smith</span>, <span class="title">Editor</span> ↵
at <span class="org">Consumer Reviews</span>
  </span>
  Rating: <span class="rating">4.5</span> out of 5.
  <span class="description">A fascinating performance.</span>
</div>
```

The review is described by the hReview microformat (class="hreview"). The name of the reviewer is revealed by span class="reviewer". The hCard microformat is nested inside the hReview microformat in order to provide additional information about him (a space-separated list of attribute values in <span

`class="reviewer vcard">`). The hCard properties describe the name (`fn`), job title (`title`), and organization (`org`) of the reviewer.

rel="license"

There are millions of web resources with some or all rights reserved. Many licenses associated with documents and objects are sophisticated, and users cannot be expected to know them.

The `rel="license"` microformat can be added to hyperlinks that point to the description of the license. This is especially useful for images but can be used for any resources.

Basic image embeddings apply only the `src` and `alt` attributes on the `img` element, such as in Listing 7-13.

Listing 7-13. A Basic Image Embedding

```
<img src="hotel.jpg" alt="The Palace Hotel" />
```

To declare the image license, the `rel` and `href` attributes should also be used. In the case of the *Creative Commons Attribution-ShareAlike license*, for example, it should be in the form shown in Listing 7-14.

Listing 7-14. Declaring an Image License

```
<img src="hotel.jpg" alt="The Palace Hotel" rel="license" ↵
 ref="http://creativecommons.org/licenses/by-sa/3.0/" />
```

The value of the `href` attribute provides the associated URI of the resource where the license is described. Some of the most commonly used *license deeds* are [61] as follows:

- Creative Commons Attribution (cc by)

  `http://creativecommons.org/licenses/by/3.0/`

- Creative Commons Attribution Share Alike (cc by-sa)

  `http://creativecommons.org/licenses/by-sa/3.0`

- Creative Commons Attribution No Derivatives (cc by-nd)

  `http://creativecommons.org/licenses/by-nd/3.0`

- Creative Commons Attribution Non-Commercial (cc by-nc)

  `http://creativecommons.org/licenses/by-nc/3.0`

- Creative Commons Attribution Non-Commercial Share Alike (cc by-nc-sa)

  `http://creativecommons.org/licenses/by-nc-sa/3.0`

- Creative Commons Attribution Non-Commercial No Derivatives (cc by-nc-nd)

  `http://creativecommons.org/licenses/by-nc-nd/3.0`

You should select a license that matches what you let others do with your work (distribute commercially or noncommercially, remix, tweak, share with proper crediting, alter, and so on).

The profile of this microformat is `http://microformats.org/profile/rel-license` [62], which can be specified on the head (X)HTML tag as shown in Listing 7-15.

Listing 7-15. The Head Profile of "rel=license"

```
<head profile="http://microformats.org/profile/rel-license">
```

rel="nofollow"

One value of the `rel` attribute deserves extended attention, because it is often used in *search engine optimization* (SEO). When `rel="nofollow"` is added to a hyperlink, the link destination should not be considered for additional ranking by search engines. This attribute value can be applied if document owners need hyperlinks without affecting the ranking of their web pages or links to external web sites. For example, if a hyperlink is vital on the web page but its destination page has a very low PageRank, the hyperlink should be provided with `rel="nofollow"` to avoid endorsement.

▪ **Note** PageRank (PR) is a link analysis algorithm used to assign a numerical weighting to each web document in order to express its relative importance on a 0–10 scale.

For example, if `lowprsite.com` has a low PR but you have to link to it because of the content presented there, you can use the `rel="nofollow"` microformat as shown in Listing 7-16.

Listing 7-16. A Link That Will Be Not Considered by Search Engines While Indexing a Page

```
<a href="http://www.lowprsite.com" rel="nofollow">Low PR site</a>
```

Listing 7-17 shows the profile URI of this microformat.

Listing 7-17. The Profile URI of rel="nofollow"

```
<link rel="profile" href="http://microformats.org/profile/rel-nofollow">
```

Although it is widely used, there are several open issues about this microformat [63]. The `rel="nofollow"` microformat indicates a behavior rather than a relationship, so the definition is illogical. The name of the microformat does not reflect the real meaning. It is not a noun. It does not affect spamming. Finally, many legitimate nonspam links might be ignored or given reduced weight, which is an unfortunate side effect that should be eliminated [64].

rel="tag"

The `rel="tag"` is still a draft specification since 2005 [65]. Unlike other microformats and general `meta` keywords, this microformat can be used for visible links. It can be applied on hyperlink elements to indicate that the destination of the link is a general author-designated tag (keyword) for the current page.

Within this microformat, spaces can be provided either as + or as %20. Unicode characters are encoded according to the generic syntax rules of URIs described by the Internet Society (RFC 3986 [66]).

Vote Links

Vote Links is an elemental microformat with three possible values on the rev attribute of the a element: vote-for, vote-against, and vote-abstain. The values are mutually exclusive. Optionally, visible rollovers can be provided by the title attribute. Listing 7-18 shows an example.

Listing 7-18. A Vote Links Example

```
<a rev="vote-for" href="http://example.com/thumbsup/" ↵
 title="HTML should be the primary markup language">HTML5</a>
<a rev="vote-against" href="http://example.com/thumbsdown/" ↵
 title="XHTML should be the primary markup language">XHTML5</a>
```

Initially, the draft specification applied Vote Links on the rel attribute, which is now deprecated [67].

Listing 7-19 shows the URI profile reference.

Listing 7-19. The URI Profile for Vote Links

```
<link rel="profile" href="http://microformats.org/profile/vote-links">
```

XFN

The very first HTML microformat, XHTML Friends Network (XFN), was introduced in December 2003 [68]. XFN was designed by Global Multimedia Protocols Group to express human relationships with simple hyperlinks [69]. XFN is especially useful for brochure-style home pages and blog entries.

The name of the person should be provided as the text of the hyperlink (between <a> and </a>). The personal web site is the target of the hyperlink, in other words, the value of the href attribute. All relationship data can be provided by the rel attribute on a elements. Multiple values are allowed and should be separated by spaces. The friendship type can be contact, acquaintance, or friend. If the person is known personally, it can be expressed by the met attribute value of the rel attribute. For example, a friend of Leslie Sikos whom he knows personally can publish that relationship on his web site by XFN, as shown in Listing 7-20.

Listing 7-20. Link to the Web Site of a Friend

```
I am an old friend of <a href="http://lesliesikos.com" rel="friend met">Leslie Sikos</a>.
```

The distance between the residence of the person and that of his friend can be expressed by the co-resident and neighbor values. Relatives can set to child, parent, sibling, spouse, or kin. The professional relationships co-worker and colleague are also supported. Feelings can also be expressed (muse, crush, date, sweetheart) [70].

CSS styles can also be added to XFN metadata. For example, friends can be provided in bold and colleagues in italic with the CSS rules shown in Listing 7-21.

Listing 7-21. Styling XFN

```
a[rel~="friend"] {
  font-weight: bold;
}

a[rel~="colleague "] {
  font-style: italic;
}
```

Although it is easy to create XFN from scratch, XFN creators such as XFN Creator [71] or Exefen [72] might speed up development.

XMDP

XHTML MetaData Profiles (XMDP) metadata is an XHTML-based format for defining metadata profiles that are both machine- and human-readable. XMDP consists of a property definition list, an optional description, and then, if applicable, one or more definition list items. The profile definition list is identified by the class (Listing 7-22).

Listing 7-22. XMDP Profile Definition

```
<dl class="profile">
```

The definition term is identified by the id (Listing 7-23).

Listing 7-23. Definition Term and Data for XMDP

```
<dt id="property1">property1</dt>
<dd>propertydesc</dd>
```

The informatively used meta properties author and keywords, for example, can be defined by XMDP as shown in Listing 7-24 [73].

Listing 7-24. A Complete XMDP Example

```
<dl class="profile">
  <dt id="author">author</dt>
  <dd>A person who wrote (at least part of) the document.</dd>
  <dt id="keywords">keywords</dt>
  <dd>A comma and/or space separated list of the keywords or keyphrases of the document.</dd>
</dl>
```

Listing 7-25 shows the structure of an XMDP profile URI.

Listing 7-25. An XMDP Profile URI

```
<link rel="profile" href="http://gmpg.org/xmdp/samplehtmlprofile.html">
```

Drafts and Future Microformats

The number of newly developed microformats is increasing. You can apply them to provide specific metadata on a wide variety of resources.

Address information can be described by adr [74]. Geographic coordinates (latitude-longitude pairs) can be provided according to the *World Geodetic System* (WGS) with the geo microformat [75]. hAtom can be used for web syndication [76]. Information about audio recordings can be embedded by using the hAudio microformat [77]. The hListing microformat can be applied for open, distributed listings [78]. Image, video, and audio media components can be described by hMedia [79]. hNews is a microformat to provide news content on web sites [80]. Product descriptions can be expressed in hProduct [81]. Cooking and baking recipes can be described on the Web with hRecipe [82]. Resumes and CVs can be published with hResume [83]. Document reviews can be written in hReview [84]. The rel-directory microdata can indicate that a link destination is a directory listing that refers to the current page [85]. File attachments provided for downloading can be indicated by the rel-enclosure microformat [86]. rel-home provides a hyperlink to the home page of the web site [87]. The rel-payment microformat is an online payment mechanism [88]. The reworking of the robots meta tag is the robots-exclusion microformat [89]. The xFolk microformat (stands for xFolksomony) was designed for publishing collections of bookmarks [90].

The Microformats Community welcomes metadata enthusiasts to create new microformats [91].

Microdata

The concept of *microdata* has been introduced in HTML5 for labeling content to describe a specific type of information [92]. HTML5 microdata can be used for semantical descriptions of people, organizations, events, products, reviews, and links.

■ **Note** Many descriptions provided in HTML5 microdata can also be expressed in microformats (discussed earlier), as well as in RDFa (as you will see later). However, each format has its strengths and weaknesses, as will be described later in detail.

People

A variety of metadata can be used to describe a person on the Web. One of the options to express properties such as name, job title, or address is microdata. A person can be described with microdata as shown in Listing 7-26.

Listing 7-26. Describing a Person with Microdata

```
<div itemscope itemtype="http://data-vocabulary.org/Person">
  <span itemprop="name">John Smith</span> lives in Adelaide, Australia and works as a ↵
  <span itemprop="title">Senior Developer</span> at ↵
  <span itemprop="affiliation">LS Inc</span>.
</div>
```

Events

Events, such as workshops, conferences, sport events, and so on, can be described by the following microdata properties:

- description: A description of the event

- duration: The duration date of the event in ISO duration format

- endDate (dtend): The ending date and time of the event in ISO date format

- eventType (category): The category of the event, for example, Concert, Festival, Lecture

- geo: Geographical coordinates of the location with two elements: latitude and longitude

- location: Location or venue of the event

- photo: Hyperlink to a photo or image related to the event

- startDate (dtstart): The starting date and time of the event in ISO date format (required)

- summary: The name of the event (required)

- url: Hyperlink of the web page describing the details of the event

For example, a sport event can be described as shown in Listing 7-27.

Listing 7-27. Describing a Sport Event with Microdata

```
<div>
   <a href="http://www.example.com/news.htm">National flyball competition</a>
   <img src="flyball.jpg" alt="Flyball" />
   The national flyball competition is approaching.
   When: Nov 13, 9:00AM–12:00AM
   Where: Dog Park, 123 Arena Eve, Melbourne, VIC
   Category: Sport
</div>
```

Image Licensing with Microdata

One of the options to provide image licensing information is HTML5 microdata. Listing 7-28 shows an example.

Listing 7-28. Describing the Image License with Microdata

```
<figure itemscope itemtype="http://example.org/pics" itemref="licenses">
   <img itemprop="name" src="images/amdb9.jpg" alt="My Aston Martin DB9.">
   <figcaption itemprop="title">The DB9.</figcaption>
</figure>
<footer>
```

```
<p id="licenses">All images are licensed under the <a itemprop="license" ↵
href="http://creativecommons.org/licenses/by-sa/3.0/">Creative Commons ↵
Attribution Share Alike license</a>.
</p>
</footer>
```

It is strongly recommended you publish photographs on the Web with licensing metadata. This can eliminate copyright issues and licensing problems as well as contribute to advanced web searches.

FOAF

FOAF is a machine-readable ontology to describe people and their contact data, interests, and relationships with other people. In 2007, Berners-Lee defined a new Semantic Web concept known as the "Giant Global Graph" [93]. He stated that FOAF is an important part of the GGG: "I express my network in a FOAF file, and that is a start of the revolution" [94].

Unlike conventional online social networks developed in PHP or JSP, FOAF networks can be built without a centralized database. Additionally, FOAF content can be processed automatically. No one has to search for friends in FOAF networks because the system itself describes the connections.[5] According to the original FOAF project started in 2000, these systems are open networks [95].

There are more and more FOAF search engines, for example, QDOS FOAFNet [96], netEstate Friend Of A Friend (FOAF) Search Engine [97], the Semantic Web Search [98], or Quatuo [99]. The latter one, for example, can also be used for creating FOAF files. However, there are dedicated FOAF generators as well. The most well-known is FOAF-O-MATIC developed by Leigh Dodds. FOAF files can be generated by filling in a form (Figure 7-2) [100].

---

[5] However, anybody can provide their own FOAF file and search for others'.

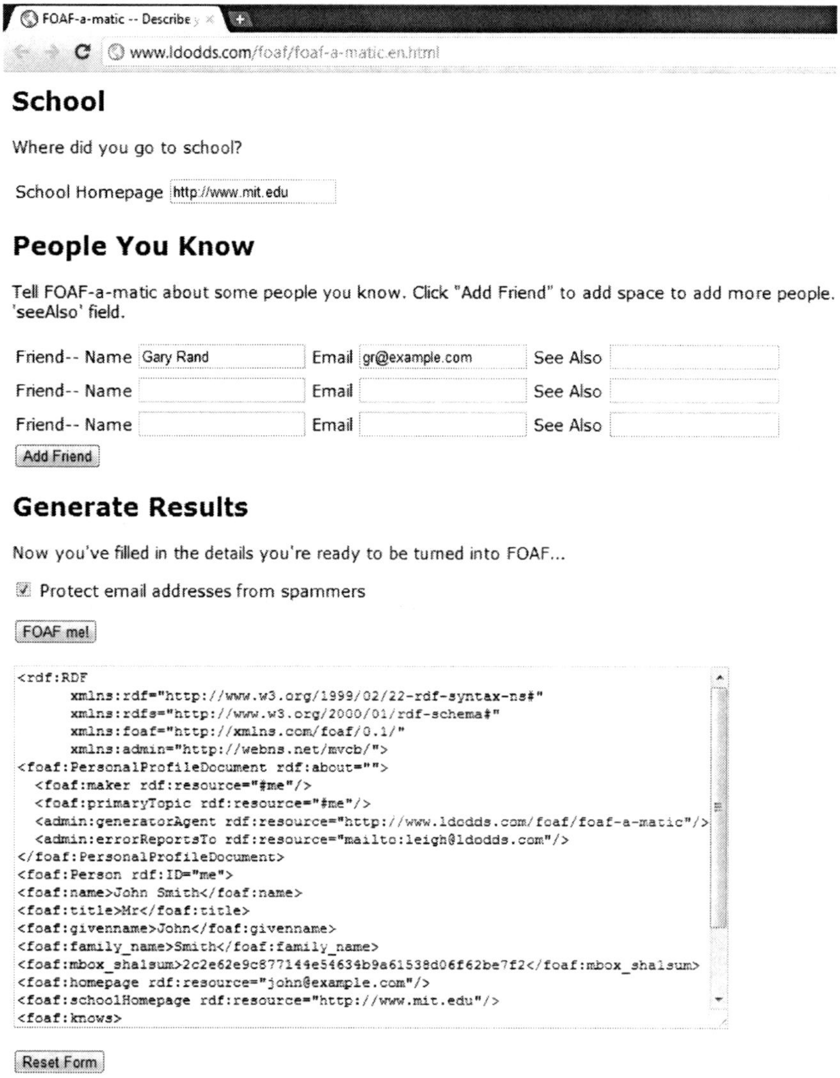

School

Where did you go to school?

School Homepage `http://www.mit.edu`

People You Know

Tell FOAF-a-matic about some people you know. Click "Add Friend" to add space to add more people. 'seeAlso' field.

Friend-- Name `Gary Rand` Email `gr@example.com` See Also

Friend-- Name Email See Also

Friend-- Name Email See Also

`Add Friend`

Generate Results

Now you've filled in the details you're ready to be turned into FOAF...

☑ Protect email addresses from spammers

`FOAF me!`

```
<rdf:RDF
      xmlns:rdf="http://www.w3.org/1999/02/22-rdf-syntax-ns#"
      xmlns:rdfs="http://www.w3.org/2000/01/rdf-schema#"
      xmlns:foaf="http://xmlns.com/foaf/0.1/"
      xmlns:admin="http://webns.net/mvcb/">
<foaf:PersonalProfileDocument rdf:about="">
  <foaf:maker rdf:resource="#me"/>
  <foaf:primaryTopic rdf:resource="#me"/>
  <admin:generatorAgent rdf:resource="http://www.ldodds.com/foaf/foaf-a-matic"/>
  <admin:errorReportsTo rdf:resource="mailto:leigh@ldodds.com"/>
</foaf:PersonalProfileDocument>
<foaf:Person rdf:ID="me">
<foaf:name>John Smith</foaf:name>
<foaf:title>Mr</foaf:title>
<foaf:givenname>John</foaf:givenname>
<foaf:family_name>Smith</foaf:family_name>
<foaf:mbox_sha1sum>2c2e62e9c877144e54634b9a61538d06f62be7f2</foaf:mbox_sha1sum>
<foaf:homepage rdf:resource="john@example.com"/>
<foaf:schoolHomepage rdf:resource="http://www.mit.edu"/>
<foaf:knows>
```

`Reset Form`

Figure 7-2. FOAF-a-matic in action

Some of the popular content management systems, such as Drupal, also support FOAF [101]. Prior to these tools, the lack of a graphical user interface could have been the major reason why this powerful technology has not come into general use until recently.

The FOAF vocabulary provides a variety of classes and properties to express personal data and relationships [26]:

- Basic information

  - Classes: Agent, Person

- Properties: name, nick, title, homepage, mbox, mbox_sha1sum, img, depiction (depicts), surname, family_name, givenname, firstName
- Personal information
  - Properties: weblog, knows, interest, currentProject, pastProject, plan, based_near, workplaceHomepage, workInfoHomepage, schoolHomepage, topic_interest, publications, geekcode, myersBriggs, dnaChecksum
- Online accounts
  - Classes: OnlineAccount, OnlineChatAccount, OnlineEcommerceAccount, OnlineGamingAccount
  - Properties: holdsAccount, accountServiceHomepage, accountName, icqChatID, msnChatID, aimChatID, jabberID, yahooChatID
- Projects and memberships
  - Classes: Project, Organization, Group
  - Properties: member, membershipClass, fundedBy, theme
- Documents and images
  - Classes: Document, Image, PersonalProfileDocument
  - Properties: topic (page), primaryTopic, tipjar, sha1, made (maker), thumbnail, logo

A complete FOAF description looks like Listing 7-29.

Listing 7-29. Describing Personal Metadata with FOAF

```
<foaf:Person>
  <foaf:name>Thomas Davis</foaf:name>
  <foaf:gender>Male</foaf:gender>
  <foaf:title>Mr</foaf:title>
  <foaf:givenname>Thomas</foaf:givenname>
  <foaf:family_name>Davis</foaf:family_name>
  <foaf:homepage rdf:resource="http://www.example.com"/>
  <foaf:weblog rdf:resource="http://www.example.com/blog/"/>
</foaf:Person>
```

As you will see, such descriptions can be embedded in XML and RDF files. In contrast to the profiles of conventional community portals, such as the ones driven by PHP and MySQL, the entire content of such files can be automatically processed. Anyone who publishes a FOAF or DOAC file on their web site can provide a machine-readable personal introduction, resources, and links to colleagues and friends.

DOAC

FOAF properties can be considered as the semantic equivalents of personal characteristics and relationships described on Facebook, and DOAC properties are the semantic counterparts of LinkedIn features. The DOAC vocabulary not only provides classes and properties to describe professional capabilities but also reapplies FOAF properties from the foaf:Person domain, including doac:summary, doac:experience, doac:education, doac:skill, doac:reference, and doac:publication [27].

Employment history and career experience can be described by the doac:title, doac:date-starts, doac:date-ends, doac:position, doac:activity, and doac:location properties of the doac:Experience class.

Education and training information can be provided by the doac:title, foaf:organization, doac:date-starts, doac:date-ends, doac:subject, and doac:level properties of the doac:Education class.

The doac:Skill class has the subclasses doac:Skill, doac:LanguageSkill, doac:SocialSkill, doac:OrganizationalSkill, doac:ComputerSkill, and doac:DrivingSkill.

A FOAF+DOAC file looks like Listing 7-30.

Listing 7-30. *A Complete FOAF+DOAC Example*

```
<foaf:Person>
  <foaf:name>John Smith</foaf:name>
  <foaf:mbox rdf:resource="mailto:john@jsmith.com" />
  <foaf:homepage rdf:resource="http://www.jsmith.com" />
  <doac:experience>
    <doac:VolunterExperience>
      <doac:title>CEO</doac:title>
      <doac:organization>ABC Company</doac:organization>
      <doac:start-date>2010-04-06</doac:start-date>
      <doac:end-date>2011-09-18</doac:end-date>
    </doac:VolunterExperience>
  </doac:experience>
  <doac:education>
    <doac:Degree>
      <doac:title>Information Management</doac:title>
      <doac:organization>Nanyang Technological University</doac:organization>
      <doac:start-date>2000-09-01</doac:start-date>
      <doac:end-date>2005-06-15</doac:end-date>
    </doac:Degree>
  </doac:education>
  <doac:skill>
    <doac:LanguageSkill>
      <doac:language>en</doac:language>
      <doac:reads rdf:resource="http://ramonantonio.net/doac/0.1/#nativelevel" />
      <doac:writes rdf:resource="http://ramonantonio.net/doac/0.1/#nativelevel" />
      <doac:speaks rdf:resource="http://ramonantonio.net/doac/0.1/#nativelevel" />
    </doac:LanguageSkill>
  </doac:skill>
</foaf:Person>
```

Such metadata is especially beneficial when someone is looking for a job or wants to describe the cornerstones of their career in a machine-processable format. Consequently, DOAC files could be used to enable software agents to make automatic job offers according to their qualification and experience.

Dublin Core

Dublin Core is a fundamental group of metadata elements developed and distributed by the Dublin Core Metadata Initiative (DCMI) and standardized by the International Organization for Standardization

(ISO 15836 [102]), the Internet Engineering Task Force (IETF) (RFC 5013 [103]), and the American National Standards Institute (ANSI/NISO Z39.85-2007 [104]). Dublin Core metadata is often used in (X)HTML document head sections (similar to general meta tags), in attributes of XHTML+RDFa documents, and in other files such as feed channels. It can be expressed using meta and link (X)HTML elements, RDFa, RDF/XML representation, and plain XML [105]. The Dublin Core syntax is provided in the reference model defined by the *Dublin Core Abstract Model* specification [106].

The *Dublin Core Metadata Element Set* defines the 15 fundamental elements of Dublin Core, including contributor, coverage, creator, date, description, format, identifier, language, publisher, relation, rights, source, subject, title, and type [107]. If these elements are used exclusively, we are talking about *Simple Dublin Core*. The extended set of elements is a higher level of Dublin Core called *Qualified Dublin Core*, which provides more specific elements. In addition to the general rules of Simple Dublin Core, further rules apply for Qualified Dublin Core. Qualified Dublin Core properties can be not only the 15 Dublin Core elements but also other elements recommended by the Dublin Core Metadata Initiative or DCMI element refinements. Optionally, Qualified Dublin Core values might have associated encoding schemes, each of which is identified by a name. Element refinements are handled similarly to properties (element refinement name associated with a Dublin Core namespace).

Dublin Core Namespaces

Dublin Core namespaces can be declared by the rel attribute on the (X)HTML link element or with the xmlns attribute in XML. The (X)HTML declaration consists of a prefix and a namespace URI (see Listing 7-31).

Listing 7-31. A Dublin Core Namespace Declaration

```
<link rel="schema.DC" href="http://purl.org/dc/elements/1.1/" />
```

The namespace URIs of all DCMI properties, classes, and encoding schemes are defined by the following DCMI namespace URIs [108]:

- http://purl.org/dc/dcmitype/

  Classes in the DCMI Type Vocabulary

- http://purl.org/dc/dcam/

  Terms used in the DCMI Abstract Model

- http://purl.org/dc/elements/1.1/

  The Dublin Core Metadata Element Set, Version 1.1 (the 15 original elements)

- http://purl.org/dc/terms/

  All other DCMI properties, classes, and encoding schemes

The DCMI Abstract Model also applies some semantic concepts of the Resource Description Framework and RDF Schema (RDFS), including resource, property/element, class, syntax encoding scheme, some relationships (has domain, has range, sub-property of, sub-class of), and the concept of plain and typed value strings [109].

Simple Dublin Core

Dublin Core records consist of one or more properties and their associated property values (Listing 7-32).

Listing 7-32. A DC Property (Creator) and a Value Associated with It (John Smith)

```
<meta name="DC.Creator" content="John Smith" />
```

Each property should be an element from the *Dublin Core Metadata Element Set*. All properties are optional and may be repeated [110]. The DC property values are considered as literal strings and might have an associated language (for example, en-US). Dublin Core records and the resources they are applied to are not linked; however, such a linkage can optionally be provided by the identifier element with the resource URI as the property value (Listing 7-33).

Listing 7-33. Dublin Core Metadata with identifier

```
<dc:title>
  Tutorials
</dc:title>
<dc:description>
  HTML5 and CSS3 tutorials.
</dc:description>
<dc:publisher>
  Dr. Leslie F. Sikos
</dc:publisher>
<dc:identifier>
  http://www.lesliesikos.com/tutorials/
</dc:identifier>
```

The Dublin Core Metadata Initiative recommends three general rules for Dublin Core implementation:

1. Dublin Core properties should be provided as XML elements. Property values should be the contents of those elements. Listing 7-34 shows an example.

    Listing 7-34. Dublin Core Properties as XML Elements

    ```
    <dc:title>Dublin Core in XML element format</dc:title>
    ```

2. All Dublin Core property names should be lowercase. Listing 7-35 shows an example.

    Listing 7-35. Dublin Core Property Names in Lowercase

    ```
    <dc:title>Dublin Core example</dc:title>
    ```

3. Multiple property values should be declared by repeating the XML element for that property (see Listing 7-36).

Listing 7-36. Repeated XML Elements for Multiple Dublin Core Property Values

```
<dc:creator>John Smith</dc:creator>

<dc:creator>Robert Johnson</dc:creator>
```

Qualified Dublin Core

Qualified Dublin Core makes more specific and advanced (meaningful) annotations possible than Simple Dublin Core. Using Qualified Dublin Core metadata is similar to adding Simple Dublin Core, except that Qualified Dublin Core properties can be not only from the set of the original 15 DC elements but also from additional elements or element refinements defined by the DCMI Metadata Terms recommendation [111]. Furthermore, all Qualified Dublin Core property values might have an associated encoding scheme with a unique name listed as the `Term name` in the DCMI Metadata Terms recommendation.

Beyond the general implementation guidelines, the following rules apply for Qualified Dublin Core:

1.   Similar to DC properties, the element refinement names should be XML
     qualified names (*QName*) that link to the associated DCMI namespace name
     (Listing 7-37).

     Listing 7-37. XML QName with Dublin Core

     ```
     <dcterms:available>2011-04</dcterms:available>
     ```

     In this example, the date or period when the resource became or will become
     available is expressed with Qualified Dublin Core.

     Element refinements might have further embedded element refinements.

2.   Encoding schemes should be declared by the `xsi:type` attribute on the XML
     element for the property. The name of the encoding scheme is provided as the
     attribute value in the form of a QName. Listing 7-38 shows an example.

     Listing 7-38. Encoding Scheme Declaration

     ```
     <dc:identifier xsi:type="dcterms:URI">
        http://www.example.com/
     </dc:identifier>
     ```

3.   The names of both the element refinements and the encoding schemes should
     be those that are specified in the DCMI Metadata Terms recommendation.
     The first letter of the element and element refinement names should always be
     in lowercase. The first letter of encoding scheme names should be in
     uppercase. Scheme names are often provided in all uppercase. Listing 7-39
     shows an example.

     Listing 7-39. Element Refinement and Encoding Scheme

     ```
     <dcterms:isPartOf xsi:type="dcterms:URI">
        http://www.example.com/
     </dcterms:isPartOf>
     ```

4. The language of the property value can optionally be provided by using the
    `xml:lang` attribute (Listing 7-40).

Listing 7-40. Setting the Natural Language for Dublin Core

```
<dc:subject xml:lang="en">
  website standardization
</dc:subject>
<dc:subject xml:lang="hu">
  weblap-szabványosítás
</dc:subject>
```

Dublin Core Expressed by (X)HTML Meta and Link Elements

A URI reference can be either a URI or a relative reference expressed in the RFC 3986 format [112]. URI references should be represented in full (Listing 7-41).

Listing 7-41. A Full URI Reference for the subject Metadata

```
<link rel="DCTERMS.subject" href="http://example.org/docs" />
```

Relative references are allowed only if they can be resolved by the base URI (`href` attribute on the base element or from the document URI). Listing 7-42 shows an example.

Listing 7-42. A Relative URI Reference for Dublin Core

```
<base href="http://example.org/docs/" />
<link rel="schema.DCTERMS" href="http://purl.org/dc/terms/" />
<link rel="DCTERMS.isReferencedBy" href="doc1" />
```

A *prefixed name* is an abbreviation for a URI used in the DC-HTML format [113]. A DC-HTML prefixed name consists of a *prefix* followed by a *period* (.) and a *local name*. For example, a DC-HTML prefixed name is expressed as attribute value in the form shown in Listing 7-43.

Listing 7-43. A DC-HTML Prefixed Name

```
<link rel="schema.DC" href="http://purl.org/dc/elements/1.1/" />
<meta name="DC.title" content="Smartphone descriptions" />
```

A Dublin Core statement is represented by either an (X)HTML `meta` or a `link` element, depending on the content of the statement (literal or nonliteral value surrogate). For example, the document title can be provided by the `meta` element as presented in Listing 7-44, while the subject is represented by the `link` element as in Listing 7-45.

Listing 7-44. Document Title Declared Using Dublin Core

```
<meta name="DC.title" content="Smartphone descriptions" />
```

Listing 7-45. Document Subject Declared Using Dublin Core

```
<link rel="DCTERMS.subject" href="http://example.org/topic" title="Topic" />
```

Dublin Core metadata on the document language, author, and so on, can be declared in the head section of XHTML documents, as shown in Listing 7-46.

Listing 7-46. Document Language and Creator Described with Dublin Core

```
<meta name="DC.language" content="en" />
<meta property="dc:creator" content="John Smith" />
```

Dublin Core Expressed in XML

Creating XML applications with Simple Dublin Core metadata according to XML schemas instead of XML DTDs is recommended. XML namespaces should be applied to identify Dublin Core elements, element refinements, or encoding schemes. Properties should be encoded as XML elements and values. The names of these XML elements should be XML qualified names (QNames). Property names should be all lowercase. The XML element should be repeated when providing multiple property values.

The xsi:type attribute of the XML element should be applied for implementing encoding schemes. Element refinements and encoding schemes use the names specified by the DCMI Metadata Terms. The xml:lang attribute should be applied to provide the language of Qualified Dublin Core values in XML [114]. Listing 7-47 shows a complex example.

Listing 7-47. Dublin Core in XML

```
<?xml version="1.0"?>
<metadata ↵
 xmlns="http://example.org/myapp/" ↵
 xmlns:xsi="http://www.w3.org/2001/XMLSchema-instance" ↵
 xsi:schemaLocation="http://example.com/xmlapp/ http://example.com/schemata/schema.xsd" ↵
 xmlns:dc="http://purl.org/dc/elements/1.1/">
  <dc:title>
    DC in XML sample document
  </dc:title>
  <dc:description>
    The description of the XML application.
  </dc:description>
  <dc:publisher>
    John Smith
  </dc:publisher>
  <dc:identifier>
    http://www.example.com
  </dc:identifier>
</metadata>
```

Dublin Core Description Sets (DC-DS-XML) can also be expressed in XML [115]. These sets consist of one or more descriptions containing zero or one described resource URI, and one or more statements. The statements contain one property URI and one value surrogate. Depending on the type of the value surrogate, it can be one value string (in case of literal value surrogates) or zero or one value URIs, zero or one vocabulary encoding scheme URI, and zero or more value strings (in case of nonliteral value surrogates). A value string can be a plain value string or a typed value string. The first one can optionally be associated with a value string language, while the latter one has a syntax encoding scheme URI. Nonliteral values can also be described by other descriptions.

A *description set element* has an expanded name with the pair of the XML namespace name http://purl.org/dc/xmlns/2008/09/01/dc-ds-xml/ and the local name descriptionSet (Listing 7-48).

Listing 7-48. A Description Set Element

```
<?xml version="1.0" encoding="UTF-8" ?>
<dcds:descriptionSet ↵
 xmlns:dcds="http://purl.org/dc/xmlns/2008/09/01/dc-ds-xml/">
  <dcds:description>
    <dcds:statement ↵
     dcds:propertyURI="http://purl.org/dc/terms/title">
      <dcds:literalValueString>
         Smith and Sons Inc Home Page
      </dcds:literalValueString>
    </dcds:statement>
  </dcds:description>
</dcds:descriptionSet>
```

Description elements are XML elements that are child elements of description set elements with the name dcds:description.

A statement element is a single Dublin Core statement represented by a child XML element of a description element. Statement elements have the name dcds:statement.

Value string elements are child elements of statement elements. Literal value surrogates, the value surrogates for literal values containing one value string representing a literal, can be encoded by the value string element dcds:literalValueString, which can be provided just once per statement element.

Nonliteral value surrogates optionally contain a value URI represented as the value of the XML attribute dcds:valueURI of the statement element (Listing 7-49).

Listing 7-49. Optional Value URI in a Nonliteral Value Surrogate

```
<dcds:statement ↵
 dcds:propertyURI="http://purl.org/dc/terms/publisher" ↵
 dcds:valueURI="http://example.com">
  <dcds:valueString>Smith and Sons Inc</dcds:valueString>
</dcds:statement>
```

For nonliteral value surrogates, the *vocabulary encoding scheme URI* can optionally be provided by the dcds:vesURI attribute.

The *value string language* of plain value strings can be provided by the xml:lang attribute of the value string element. Language identifiers of IETF RFC 4646 or later [116] should be applied. Listing 7-50 shows an example.

Listing 7-50. Value String Language Declaration

```
<?xml version="1.0" encoding="UTF-8" ?>
  <dcds:descriptionSet ↵
   xmlns:dcds="http://purl.org/dc/xmlns/2008/09/01/dc-ds-xml/">
```

```
  <dcds:description ↵
   dcds:resourceURI="http://example.com">
   <dcds:statement ↵
     dcds:propertyURI="http://purl.org/dc/terms/title">
     <dcds:literalValueString xml:lang="en-US">
       Example document
     </dcds:literalValueString>
   </dcds:statement>
  </dcds:description>
</dcds:descriptionSet>
```

For typed value strings, the syntax encoding scheme URI attribute dcds:sesURI should be used.

Dublin Core Expressed in RDF

Simple Dublin Core can be expressed also in RDF, including RDF/XML serialization[6] [117]. Listing 7-51 shows an example that includes an XML declaration, a reference to the XML DTD, an RDF declaration, and the resource descriptions.

Listing 7-51. Dublin Core in RDF/XML

```
<?xml version="1.0"?>
<!DOCTYPE rdf:RDF PUBLIC "-//DUBLIN CORE//DCMES DTD 2002/07/31//EN" ↵
 "http://dublincore.org/documents/2002/07/31/dcmes-xml/dcmes-xml-dtd.dtd">
<rdf:RDF xmlns:rdf="http://www.w3.org/1999/02/22-rdf-syntax-ns#" ↵
 xmlns:dc="http://purl.org/dc/elements/1.1/">
  <rdf:Description>
    <dc:title>Internet for everyone</dc:title>
    <dc:creator>Leslie Sikos</dc:creator>
    <dc:format>Book</dc:format>
    <dc:identifier>ISBN 963 9425 08 7</dc:identifier>
  </rdf:Description>
</rdf:RDF>
```

XML character-encoding rules apply. Optionally, the language of any element in these documents can be provided by the xml:lang attribute.

Expressing Qualified Dublin Core in RDF is described by another DCMI specification [118]. In contrast, properties such as dc:creator and dc:date are considered in this document as entities rather than names. Listing 7-52 shows an example.

Listing 7-52. Qualified Dublin Core in RDF

```
<http://www.example.com> dc:creator <http://www.example.org/pj>
```

The original specifications defining the RDF implementations of DC have been superseded by the 2008 specification [119] and notes [120]. For example, the RDF schemas for DCMI properties and classes have been removed from the specification.

---

[6] RDF will be described in the next sections.

Resource Description Framework

Although it was originally designed as a metadata data model, *Resource Description Framework* (*RDF*) has become a general web resource description and modeling language. It can be used for conceptual description or modeling of information stored in web resources. RDF can be used to create a machine-readable description about any kind of resource, because RDF files can be extended with an arbitrary number of external vocabularies. In contrast to many W3C standards, RDF has no single specification but is defined by a set of documents [121].

The RDF data model can be used for describing any kind of resources that can be identified by a URI. As mentioned earlier, an RDF document is a sequence of statements called *RDF triples* (resource–property–value or subject–predicate–object). The predicate (property) that denotes a relationship between the subject and the object can be binary only. Any expression in RDF is a collection of triples. A set of triples is called an *RDF graph*, which is a directed, labeled graph that represents information on the Web. The nodes of the RDF graph are the resources and values [122].

As shown earlier, a person can be described using the FOAF vocabulary. Such descriptions can be written either in XML or in RDF. Listing 7-53 shows how to write FOAF in RDF.

Listing 7-53. *Describing a Person in RDF*

```
<rdf:RDF ↩
  xmlns:rdf="http://www.w3.org/1999/02/22-rdf-syntax-ns#" ↩
  xmlns:foaf="http://xmlns.com/foaf/0.1/" ↩
  xmlns="http://www.example.com/johnsmith/contact.rdf#">
  <foaf:Person rdf:about="http://www.example.com/johnsmith/contact.rdf#johnsmith">
    <foaf:mbox rdf:resource="mailto:john.smith@example.com" />
    <foaf:homepage rdf:resource="http://www.example.com/johnsmith/" />
    <foaf:family_name>Smith</foaf:family_name>
    <foaf:givenname>John</foaf:givenname>
  </foaf:Person>
</rdf:RDF>
```

Figure 7-3 represents this file as an RDF graph.

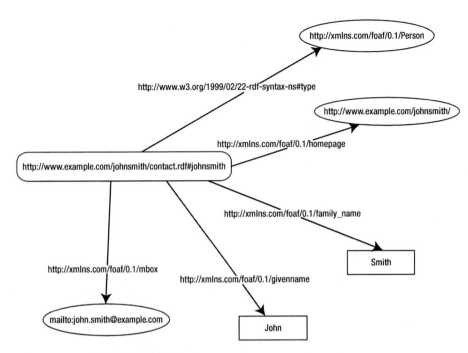

Figure 7-3. A simple RDF graph

As you will see, RDF can be expressed in a variety of formats. For example, Listing 7-54 is another notation of Listing 7-53. This notation, N3, will also be described later in detail.

Listing 7-54. The N3 Equivalent of the Previous Example

```
@prefix :     <http://www.example.org/~joe/contact.rdf#> .
@prefix foaf: <http://xmlns.com/foaf/0.1/> .
@prefix rdf:  <http://www.w3.org/1999/02/22-rdf-syntax-ns#> .

:joesmith a foaf:Person ;
  foaf:givenname "Joe" ;
  foaf:family_name "Smith" ;
  foaf:homepage <http://www.example.org/~joe/> ;
  foaf:mbox <mailto:joe.smith@example.org> .
```

The RDF namespace is `http://www.w3.org/1999/02/22-rdf-syntax-ns#`, which is conventionally associated with the namespace prefix `rdf:`.

The Unicode strings in URI references of RDF graphs cannot contain control characters (#x00–#x1F, #x7F–#x9F). These URIs should be absolute URIs with optional fragment identifiers.

RDF literals are used to identify values such as numbers and dates. RDF literals are Unicode strings containing one or two named components. They should be written in *UTF-8 normalized in Normalization Form C* (Canonical Decomposition followed by Canonical Composition [123]). RDF literals can be either plain or typed. Plain literals are strings combined with an optional language tag (normalized to lowercase). They correspond to plain text in a natural language. Typed literals are strings combined with a datatype URI for applying the lexical-to-value mapping to the literal string.

The Formal Grammar of the Resource Description Framework was introduced in 1999 [124]. RDF has the following vocabulary:

- rdf:Alt, rdf:Bag, rdf:Seq

  Containers of alternatives, unordered containers, and ordered containers (rdfs:Container is a superclass of the three)

- rdf:List

  The class of RDF lists

- rdf:nil

  An empty list (an instance of rdf:List)

- rdf:Property

  The class of properties

- rdf:Statement, rdf:subject, rdf:predicate, rdf:object

  Reification

- rdf:type

  A predicate that identifies the class that the resource is an instance of

- rdf:XMLLiteral

  The class of typed literals

This vocabulary is also used as the basis for the extensible knowledge representation language *RDF Schema* (see the section "RDF Schema").

There is a *query language* called *SPARQL* (pronounced "Sparkle") that can be used to retrieve and manipulate information stored in RDF or in any format that can be retrieved as RDF [125]. The output can be a results set or an RDF graph. It is also possible to update RDF graphs through a protocol known as the *SPARQL 1.1 Uniform HTTP Protocol* [126].

The Resource Description Framework technology is important from the standardization point of view for many reasons. First, the basic data model of RDF is a standard graph. Second, the naming system applies standard URLs. The data retrieval and composition mechanisms used by RDF are also standard technologies.

RDF can be provided in a variety of syntaxes/serialization formats, for example, RDF XML serialization (RDF/XML), RDFa, Turtle, Notation3, JSON-LD, N-Triples [127], TRiG [128], and TRiX [129]. The most common ones are described in the next sections.

RDF in XML Serialization Syntax

The recommended and most frequently used syntax for RDF applications is the XML serialization format, RDF/XML [130]. Although there are other notations of RDF that are easier to read and write (see the next sections), RDF/XML provides widely accepted XML documents. However, the fundamental problem with RDF/XML is the contradiction of representing a graph with a tree structure.

The Internet media type for RDF/XML is application/rdf+xml. The recommended file extension is .rdf.

The XML serialization of RDF provides well-formed XML documents (Chapter 1).

A person's Wikipedia page, for example, can be described in a machine-readable form in RDF/XML, as shown in Listing 7-55.

Listing 7-55. A Wikipedia Page Described in RDF/XML

```
<rdf:RDF ↵
 xmlns:rdf="http://www.w3.org/1999/02/22-rdf-syntax-ns#" ↵
 xmlns:dc="http://purl.org/dc/elements/1.1/">
  <rdf:Description rdf:about="http://en.wikipedia.org/wiki/Rowan_Atkinson">
    <dc:title>Rowan Atkinson</dc:title>
    <dc:publisher>Wikipedia</dc:publisher>
  </rdf:Description>
</rdf:RDF>
```

RDF in N3 Syntax

Notation 3, often abbreviated as *N3*, is a shorthand non-XML serialization of RDF. It is a superset of RDF and is more compact than the XML serialization of RDF. The grammar of N3 is defined by W3C in many formats [131], for example, in *Extended Backus-Naur Form* (*EBNF*)[7] [132].

The MIME type and character encoding of N3 should be declared as text/n3; charset=utf-8. The typical file extension is .n3. Tokenizing and whitespace handling are not specified in the grammar.

Base URIs to be used for the parsing of relative URIs can be set with the @base directive in the form @base <http://example.com/overview/>.

A prefix can be associated to a namespace URI by the @prefix directive.

Several rules for string escaping are derived from Python, namely, stringliteral, stringprefix, shortstring, shortstringitem, longstring, longstringitem, shortstringchar, and longstringchar. Additionally, the \U extension, also used in another RDF serialization (N-Triples), can be applied. Legal escape sequences are \newline, \\ (backslash, \), \' (single quote, '), \" (double quote, "), \n (ASCII Linefeed, LF), \r (ASCII Carriage Return, CR), \t (ASCII Horizontal Tab, TAB), \uhhhh (Unicode character in BMP), and \U00hhhhhh (Unicode character in plane 1–16 notation). The escapes \a, \b, \f, and \v cannot be used because the corresponding characters are not allowed in RDF.

Shorthand notation can be used for the following common predicates:

- a (stands for <http://www.w3.org/1999/02/22-rdf-syntax-ns#type>)

- = (stand for <http://www.w3.org/2002/07/owl#sameAs>)

- => (stands for <http://www.w3.org/2000/10/swap/log#implies>)

- <= (stands for <http://www.w3.org/2000/10/swap/log#implies>)

New classes and new properties can be defined in new vocabularies [133]. A class can be defined as Listing 7-56 because the rdf:type property is abbreviated as a in N3.

---

[7] EBNF is a family of metasyntax notations that can be used to express context-free grammars.

Listing 7-56. An RDF Class in N3

```
:Sport a rdfs:Class.
```

An object of the class can be defined as shown in Listing 7-57.

Listing 7-57. Declare an Object of a Class in N3

```
:Kayak a :Sport.
```

Objects can be in multiple classes. Relationships between classes can be written as shown in Listing 7-58.

Listing 7-58. Class Relationships in N3

```
:Watersport a rdfs:Class; rdfs:subClassOf :Sport .
```

A property can be defined as shown in Listing 7-59.

Listing 7-59. Property Declaration in N3

```
:paddle a rdf:Property.
```

Relationships between classes are not necessarily hierarchical relationships. You can see an example in Listing 7-60.

Listing 7-60. Nonhierarchical Relationships in N3

```
:paddle rdfs:domain :Sport;
        rdfs:range :Watersport.
```

The person's Wikipedia page described in the previous section can be written in N3 as shown in Listing 7-61.

Listing 7-61. A Wikipedia Page Description in N3

```
@prefix dc: <http://purl.org/dc/elements/1.1/>.

<http://en.wikipedia.org/wiki/Rowan_Atkinson>
  dc:title "Rowan Atkinson";
  dc:publisher "Wikipedia".
```

Notation3 has several subsets, including Turtle, N-Triples, N3 RDF, and N3 Rules. The most popular of them is discussed in the next section.

RDF in Turtle Syntax

A subset of N3 is the *Terse RDF Triple Language*, often referred to as *Turtle*. Turtle provides a syntax to describe RDF graphs in a compact textual form, which is easy to develop. It is a subset of Notation 3 (N3) and a superset of N-Triples. Turtle is popular among Semantic Web developers and considered as an easy-to-read alternative to RDF/XML. Turtle is being standardized by the World Wide Web Consortium [134]. The typical file extension of Turtle files is .ttl. The character encoding of Turtle files should be

UTF-8. The MIME type of Turtle is `text/turtle`. Turtle is supported by many software frameworks that can be used for querying and analyzing RDF data, such as Jena [135], Redland [136], and Sesame [137].

Turtle files consist of a sequence of directives, statements representing triples, and blank lines. Triples can be written in Turtle as a sequence of subject – predicate – object terms, separated by whitespace, and terminated by a period (`.`). URIs should be written in angle brackets (`<>`). Literals are delimited by double quotes (`""`). Listing 7-62 shows an example.

Listing 7-62. *A Basic Example for the Turtle Syntax*

```
<http://example.com/shop> <http://example.com/contact> "Text content" .
```

URI length can be reduced by the `@PREFIX` (Listing 7-63).

Listing 7-63. *A URI Prefix Declaration*

```
@PREFIX ex: <http://example.com/> .
```

In that case, the first example can be written as in Listing 7-64.

Listing 7-64. *Using a Prefix*

```
ex:shop ex:contact "Text content" .
```

where `ex:shop` declares the concatenation of `http://example.com/` with `shop`, revealing the original URI `http://example.com/shop`.

RDFa

The power of RDF, which was demonstrated earlier, can be exploited through external files written in rather complex syntax. However, there is a nice exception: RDFa. RDFa (RDF in attributes) adds attribute-level extensions to any markup language (from this point of view, the host language, as discussed earlier in Chapter 3) in order to describe structured data. In other words, RDFa notations can be declared in attributes, rather than elements (which is the approach used by other RDF serialization formats). Although many attributes are defined by RDFa, some markup attributes (such as `href` and `rel`) are reused. Wherever possible, the textual content is also reused. RDFa can serve as a bridge between the "human and data Webs," since RDFa makes it possible to write RDF triples in the (X)HTML markup [138]. Structured information can be extracted and utilized from web documents via an RDFa application programming interface (RDFa API) [139]. The mechanism of the RDF data model mapping allows RDF triples to be embedded within web documents as well as the extraction of RDF model triples by compliant software.

RDFa provides the option to embed rich metadata within certain attributes of web documents [140]. The set of attributes to be used for this purpose is as follows:

- `about`, `src`

  The Unified Resource Identifier (URI) or compact URI (CURIE) [141] of the resource that describes the metadata

- `rel`, `rev`

  Relationship with another resource

- href, resource

  The partner resource

- property

  A property for the content of an element

- content

  Element content override when using the property attribute (optional)

- datatype

  The datatype of text specified for use with the property attribute (optional)

- typeof

  The RDF type(s) of the subject (optional)

RDFa makes it possible to arbitrarily mix multiple independently developed vocabularies. It can be parsed without analyzing the specific vocabularies being applied. This is one of the most advanced technologies to provide different types of machine-readable structured data in the markup.

Since the "a" in RDFa stands for attributes whose styles are provided most commonly in Cascading Style Sheets, it is straightforward to use CSS selectors to style the code [142]. For example, if the name of the creator and the book title of the previous example appear throughout the site, all instances can be styled using universal selectors (Listing 7-65).

Listing 7-65. Styling RDFa

```
* [property="dc:creator"]  {
  color: #2a56d3;
  font-style:italic;

 }
* [property="dc:title"] {
  font-size: 2em;
  font-family:
 Georgia;
}
```

The latest news on RDFa can be tracked on the web site of the RDFa Working Group of W3C at www.w3.org/2010/02/rdfa/ [143].

For example, let's describe a person with RDFa notation using the FOAF vocabulary! First we need to declare the FOAF namespace (either in the document head or on the body element). The about attribute of RDFa can be used to express the subject, while the RDFa attribute property sets the predicate (Listing 7-66).

Listing 7-66. An RDFa Annotation Using FOAF

```
<body xmlns:foaf="http://xlmns.com/foaf/0.1/">
  <p about="#smith" property="foaf:name">John Smith</p>
</body>
```

The content of the p element is both a human- and machine-readable text that will be rendered on the web page.

Now extend the previous example with another person and express a relationship between the two persons (Listing 7-67)! The class of the entity can be declared by the typeof attribute. In this case, we use the Person class from the FOAF vocabulary to "let the browser know" that John Smith is a person. The second person is declared exactly the same way. Finally, we use the term knows from the FOAF vocabulary and pass it as the value of the rel attribute to express that John Smith knows Peter Johnson (declared by the resource attribute).

Listing 7-67. Two People and the Relationship Between Them Expressed Using FOAF in RDFa

```
<body xmlns:foaf="http://xmlns.com/foaf/0.1">
  <p>
    <span about="#john" typeof="foaf:Person" property="foaf:name">John Smith</span> is ↵
    interested in smartphones. <span about="#jane" typeof="foaf:Person" ↵
    property="foaf:name">Peter Johnson</span> is an Android developer. <span ↵
    about="#john" rel="foaf:knows" resource="#peter">John and Peter knows each other. ↵
    </span>
  </p>
</body>
```

Compare this machine-readable statement with MySQL database records displayed using PHP, and you have a glimpse of the power of the Semantic Web!

Other vocabularies can be similarly used with RDFa. For example, Dublin Core metadata can be embedded to the markup using RDFa, as shown in Listing 7-68.

Listing 7-68. An RDFa Annotation Using DC

```
<p xmlns:dc="http://purl.org/dc/elements/1.1/" ↵
 about="#standardweb" property="dc:title">
 Web standardista <span about="#sikos" property="dc:creator">Dr. Sikos</span> describes ↵
 Web standardization, accessibility, and Web semantics in his latest book ↵
 <cite about="#webstandards" property="dc:title">Web standards</cite>. The first press ↵
 release has been published on <span about="#webstandards" property="dc:date" ↵
 content="2011-11-16">16 November 2011</span>.
</p>
```

Microformats vs. Microdata vs. RDFa

You should have noticed that there are similar concepts defined by certain microformats and HTML5 microdata to describe people, events, or licenses. RDFa, on the other hand, is not limited to such concepts and can be used to annotate any kind of resource.

As discussed earlier, microformats reuse HTML attributes (for example, class, title) and have separate vocabularies that are difficult to combine, because microformats do not use the namespace mechanism. Last but not least, microformats do not define an RDF representation.[8]

HTML5 microdata, as also presented earlier, provides news attributes for the HTML5 markup. HTML5 microdata is easy to write and works well in documents that use a single external vocabulary.

---

[8] It is possible to transform microformats to RDF using technologies such as XSLT and GRDDL, but such transformations depend on the vocabularies being used.

Combining different vocabularies is rather complex in HTML5 microdata. Some vocabulary mappings, such as that of Dublin Core elements, are supported by the technology by default. A missing feature is the concept of data types and namespaces. Fortunately, however, HTML5 microdata defines a generic mapping to RDF, so it can be used to express triples.

In contrast to microformats and microdata, RDFa is a complete serialization of RDF and hence provides the most advanced annotation of them all. RDFa defines new markup attributes and uses URIs and namespaces by default. Consequently, combining vocabularies is very easy (similar to RDF). RDFa is completely flexible regarding literals and URI resources.

RDF Schema

According to the W3C Metadata Activity, *RDF Schema* (*RDFS*) is "a declarative representation language influenced by ideas from knowledge representation" [144]. RDF Schema extends RDF with structure (classes, properties of properties, and so on). It can be used to formalize metadata exchange between human-readable and machine-processable vocabularies. Beyond the basic RDF vocabulary discussed earlier, RDFS has several additional constructs [145]:

- Classes
    - `rdf:Property`
    - `rdf:XMLLiteral`
    - `rdfs:Class`
    - `rdfs:Datatype`
    - `rdfs:Literal`
    - `rdfs:Resource`
- Properties
    - `rdf:type`
    - `rdfs:comment`
    - `rdfs:domain`
    - `rdfs:isDefinedBy`
    - `rdfs:label`
    - `rdfs:range`
    - `rdfs:seeAlso`
    - `rdfs:subClassOf`
    - `rdfs:subPropertyOf`

These classes and properties provide a more advanced level of knowledge representation than RDF does and can be used for basic description of web ontologies. This is the reason why the more expressive language Web Ontology Language (OWL) reuses many RDFS components (see next section).

For example, the resource "macaw" can be declared as a subclass of the class "birds," as shown in Listing 7-69.

Listing 7-69. *A Simple RDFS Example*

```
<?xml version="1.0"?>
<rdf:RDF ↵
 xmlns:rdf="http://www.w3.org/1999/02/22-rdf-syntax-ns#" ↵
 xmlns:rdfs="http://www.w3.org/2000/01/rdf-schema#" ↵
 xml:base="http://www.example.com/birds#">
  <rdf:Description rdf:ID="bird">
    <rdf:type rdf:resource="http://www.w3.org/2000/01/rdf-schema#Class"/>
  </rdf:Description>
  <rdf:Description rdf:ID="macaw">
    <rdf:type rdf:resource="http://www.w3.org/2000/01/rdf-schema#Class"/>
    <rdfs:subClassOf rdf:resource="#bird"/>
  </rdf:Description>
</rdf:RDF>
```

This notation can also be shortened by using `rdfs:Class` instead of `rdf:Description` and omitting `rdf:type` (Listing 7-70).

Listing 7-70. *An Optimized Version of the Previous Example*

```
<?xml version="1.0"?>
<rdf:RDF ↵
 xmlns:rdf="http://www.w3.org/1999/02/22-rdf-syntax-ns#" ↵
 xmlns:rdfs="http://www.w3.org/2000/01/rdf-schema#" ↵
 xml:base="http://www.example.com/birds#">
  <rdfs:Class rdf:ID="bird" />
    <rdfs:Class rdf:ID="macaw">
    <rdfs:subClassOf rdf:resource="#bird"/>
  </rdfs:Class>
</rdf:RDF>
```

OWL

Web Ontology Language is a knowledge representation language with the primary purpose of creating *web ontologies*. Web ontologies can be used for a variety of purposes, such as searching, query formation, indexing, and agent or service metadata management, or to improve application and database interoperability. Web ontologies are especially useful for knowledge-intensive applications, where text extraction, decision support, or resource planning are common tasks, as well as in knowledge repositories used for knowledge acquisition.

The abbreviation of the Web Ontology Language, OWL, is not straightforward on purpose [146]. OWL ontologies are RDF graphs, in other words, sets of RDF triples. Similar to RDF graphs, OWL ontology graphs can be expressed in various syntactic notations. There are three variants of OWL: *OWL Lite*, *OWL DL*, and *OWL Full* [147]. OWL is a higher-level language than RDF; in fact, it is a vocabulary extension of RDF. Consequently, RDF graphs are OWL Full ontologies.

The default OWL namespace is `http://www.w3.org/2002/07/owl#`, which defines the OWL vocabulary. There is no MIME type defined specifically for OWL. Using the `application/rdf+xml` or the application/xml MIME type for OWL documents is recommended. The recommended file extension is either .rdf or .owl.

The development of the first version of OWL was started in 2002, and the second version, OWL2, in 2008. OWL became a W3C Recommendation in 2004 [148], and OWL2 became one in 2009 [149, 150].

Syntaxes

At the high level, the OWL abstract syntax [151] and the OWL2 functional syntax [152] can be used. OWL also supports several exchange syntaxes, including RDF syntaxes [153] (RDF/XML [154], RDF/Turtle [155]), the OWL2 XML syntax [156], and the Manchester syntax [157]. RDF/XML is the normative syntax [158].

For example, a class declaration for a smartphone ontology can be written in various syntaxes, as shown in Listings 7-71 to 7-75.

Listing 7-71. OWL2 Functional Syntax Example

```
Ontology(<http://example.com/smartphone.owl>
  Declaration( Class( :Smartphone ) )
)
```

Listing 7-72. OWL2 XML Syntax Example

```
 <Ontology ontologyIRI="http://example.com/smartphone.owl">
   <Prefix name="owl" IRI="http://www.w3.org/2002/07/owl#"/>
   <Declaration>
     <Class IRI="Smartphone"/>
   </Declaration>
 </Ontology>
```

Listing 7-73. RDF/XML Syntax Example

```
<rdf:RDF>
  <owl:Ontology rdf:about=""/>
  <owl:Class rdf:about="#Smartphone"/>
</rdf:RDF>
```

Listing 7-74. RDF/Turtle Example

```
<http://example.com/smartphone.owl> rdf:type owl:Ontology .
:Smartphone   rdf:type            owl:Class .
```

Listing 7-75. Manchester Syntax Example

```
Ontology: <http://example.com/smartphone.owl>
Class: Smartphone
```

Properties

In OWL, the following types of properties exist:

- *Object properties* that link individuals to other individuals

- *Datatype properties* that link individuals to data values (subclasses of object properties)

- *Annotation property* (owl:AnnotationProperty)

- *Ontology property* (owl:OntologyProperty)

Property features are defined by the property axioms. The basic form expresses the existence only. For example, in a smartphone ontology, the property hasKeyboard can be declared to express a major feature of mobile phones (see Listing 7-76). Most entry-level mobile phones have a phone keyboard, while many smartphones have a touchscreen only, but some have a full QWERTY keyboard.

Listing 7-76. A Property Declaration in OWL

```
<owl:ObjectProperty rdf:ID="hasKeyboard"/>
```

OWL property axioms can also define additional characteristics. OWL supports RDF Schema constructs such as rdfs:subPropertyOf, rdfs:domain, and rdfs:range. Relations to other properties can be expressed by owl:equivalentProperty and owl:inverseOf (Listing 7-77).

Listing 7-77. Two Equivalent Smartphone Properties (Accelerometer and G-sensor)

```
<owl:ObjectProperty rdf:ID="hasAccelerometer">
  <owl:equivalentProperty>
    <owl:ObjectProperty rdf:ID="hasGsensor"/>
  </owl:equivalentProperty>
</owl:ObjectProperty>
```

Global cardinality constraints are defined by owl:FunctionalProperty and owl:InverseFunctionalProperty. Logical property features are defined by owl:SymmetricProperty and owl:TransitiveProperty [159] (Listing 7-78).

Listing 7-78. A Symmetric Property in OWL

```
<owl:SymmetricProperty rdf:ID="hasLiveConnection">
  <rdfs:domain rdf:resource="#Smartphone"/>
  <rdfs:range rdf:resource="#Smartphone"/>
</owl:SymmetricProperty>
```

OWL provides precise declarations for expressing relationships, even if they are evident. For example, the *property hierarchy* of two smartphone features can be expressed in functional syntax, as presented in Listing 7-79.

Listing 7-79. Property Hierarchy in OWL

```
SubObjectPropertyOf( :hasGeotagging :hasCamera )
```

Classes

Similar to RDF, OWL provides classes to group resources. There are six different *class descriptions* in OWL:

- Class identifier (URI reference). A named instance of owl:Class, a subclass of rdfs:Class.[9] Listing 7-80 shows an example.

Listing 7-80. A Class Identifier in OWL

```
<owl:Class rdf:ID="Handheld"/>
```

- Set of individuals (instances of a class) defined by the owl:oneOf property. For example, the class of smartphones can be declared in the RDF/XML syntax with the RDF construct rdf:parseType="Collection", as shown in Listing 7-81.

Listing 7-81. Class Instances in OWL

```
<owl:Class>
  <owl:oneOf rdf:parseType="Collection">
    <owl:Thing rdf:about="#Touch"/>
    <owl:Thing rdf:about="#Type"/>
    <owl:Thing rdf:about="#TouchType"/>
    <owl:Thing rdf:about="#Business"/>
  </owl:oneOf>
</owl:Class>
```

- Property restriction: a value constraint or a cardinality constraint (for example, Listing 7-82).

Listing 7-82. Property Restrictions in OWL

```
<owl:Restriction>
  <owl:onProperty rdf:resource="hasGPS" />
  <owl:allValuesFrom rdf:resource="#Smartphone" />
</owl:Restriction>
```

- Intersection of two or more class descriptions. For example, the intersection of two Brochures enumerations can be described by the statement owl:intersectionOf, as presented in Listing 7-83.

Listing 7-83. Intersection in OWL

```
<owl:Class>
  <owl:intersectionOf rdf:parseType="Brochures">
    <owl:Class>
      <owl:oneOf rdf:parseType="Brochures">
        <owl:Thing rdf:about="#Manual" />
        <owl:Thing rdf:about="#Guide" />
        <owl:Thing rdf:about="#Prospectus" />
      </owl:oneOf>
    </owl:Class>
    <owl:Class>
      <owl:oneOf rdf:parseType="Brochures">
        <owl:Thing rdf:about="#Specs" />
```

---

[9] In OWL Lite and OWL DL. In OWL Full they are equivalent.

```
            <owl:Thing rdf:about="#Overview" />
            <owl:Thing rdf:about="#Guide" />
          </owl:oneOf>
        </owl:Class>
      </owl:intersectionOf>
    </owl:Class>
```

where the intersection is a class with the only common individual Guide.

- Union of two or more class descriptions. For example, the union of the previous example contains the individuals Manual, Guide, Prospectus, Specs, and Overview (if they are all different).

- Complement of a class description. The class extension contains exactly those individuals who do not belong to the class extension of the class description that forms the object of the statement. The complement can be described by the owl:complementOf property.

Class descriptions can be combined into *class axioms*. Class hierarchy can be expressed by *subclass axioms* (Listing 7-84).

Listing 7-84. Class Hierarchy in OWL

```
SubClassOf( :Slide :Smartphone )
```

The equivalence of two classes express that the individuals contained by them are identical. Listing 7-85 shows an example.

Listing 7-85. Equivalent Classes in OWL

```
EquivalentClasses( :Virtualkeyboard :Softquerty )
```

Although individuals can be members of several classes in general, in many cases memberships are exclusive. For example, a smartphone belongs to either the bar or the slide form factor. This *class disjointness* can be expressed as shown in Listing 7-86.

Listing 7-86. Class Disjointness in OWL

```
DisjointClasses( :Bar :Slide )
```

Combining Metadata

Schemas are often combined on the Semantic Web in order to apply all those specific vocabularies that are designed to express metadata on the topic of the web pages being described. The longest lists of namespaces occur in web documents that provide a significant amount of additional metadata, most commonly, in (X)HTML+RDFa. Listing 7-87 shows an example.

Listing 7-87. A Long List of Namespaces in an XHTML+RDFa Document

```
<html version="XHTML+RDFa 1.0" xmlns="http://www.w3.org/1999/xhtml" ↵
 xmlns:air="http://www.daml.org/2001/10/html/airport-ont#" ↵
 xmlns:bio="http://vocab.org/bio/0.1/" ↵
 xmlns:bibo="http://purl.org/ontology/bibo/" ↵
```

```
  xmlns:cc="http://creativecommons.org/ns#" ↵
  xmlns:contact="http://www.w3.org/2000/10/swap/pim/contact#" ↵
  xmlns:dbp="http://dbpedia.org/property/" ↵
  xmlns:dbr="http://dbpedia.org/resource/" ↵
  xmlns:dc="http://purl.org/dc/elements/1.1/" ↵
  xmlns:dcterms="http://purl.org/dc/terms/" ↵
  xmlns:fb="http://www.facebook.com/2008/fbml" ↵
  xmlns:foaf="http://xmlns.com/foaf/0.1/" ↵
  xmlns:geo="http://www.w3.org/2003/01/geo/wgs84_pos#" ↵
  xmlns:ical="http://www.w3.org/2002/12/cal/icaltzd#" ↵
  xmlns:og="http://opengraphprotocol.org/schema/" ↵
  xmlns:openid="http://xmlns.openid.net/auth#" ↵
  xmlns:owl="http://www.w3.org/2002/07/owl#" ↵
  xmlns:rdf="http://www.w3.org/1999/02/22-rdf-syntax-ns#" ↵
  xmlns:rdfa="http://www.w3.org/ns/rdfa#" ↵
  xmlns:rdfs="http://www.w3.org/2000/01/rdf-schema#" ↵
  xmlns:rel="http://vocab.org/relationship/" ↵
  xmlns:rss="http://web.resource.org/rss/1.0/" ↵
  xmlns:sioc="http://rdfs.org/sioc/ns#" ↵
  xmlns:smap="http://purl.org/net/ns/sitemap#" ↵
  xmlns:vcard="http://www.w3.org/2006/vcard/ns#" ↵
  xmlns:wot="http://xmlns.com/wot/0.1/" ↵
  xmlns:xhv="http://www.w3.org/1999/xhtml/vocab#" ↵
  xmlns:xsd="http://www.w3.org/2001/XMLSchema#">
```

These *vocabulary prefixes* allow the use of terms defined by the listed external vocabularies in the current document. It is highly recommended to list only those namespaces that are actually used in the document, which contributes to code optimality and easier maintenance. Although unnecessary namespaces do not cause any error messages in the browser, they make the markup more complex.

Because of the different features of vocabularies, the combined application is not always straightforward. For example, many terms are included in various vocabularies, and choosing one of them is often driven by personal preference only. In fact, you should consider the specification of the candidate properties in order to choose the most suitable one for a given scenario.

Combining Vocabularies in RDF

The easiest way to mix properties from any vocabulary is to create an RDF file. For example, a completely machine-readable personal profile uses FOAF terms to describe the title, name, gender, IM accounts, home page, phone number, and relationships of a person. The nearest airport to the office of the person can be expressed with a term from the Contact vocabulary, the date when the file has been created can be declared by Dublin Core, and so on (Listing 7-88).

Listing 7-88. Several Vocabularies Used for a Personal Profile Written in RDF

```
<?xml version="1.0" encoding="UTF-8"?>
<rdf:RDF ↵
  xmlns:contact="http://www.w3.org/2000/10/swap/pim/contact#" ↵
  xmlns:dc="http://purl.org/dc/terms/" ↵
  xmlns:foaf="http://xmlns.com/foaf/0.1/" ↵
  xmlns:google="http://rdf.data-vocabulary.org/#" ↵
```

```
xmlns:owl="http://www.w3.org/2002/07/owl#" ↵
xmlns:rdf="http://www.w3.org/1999/02/22-rdf-syntax-ns#" ↵
xmlns:rdfs="http://www.w3.org/2000/01/rdf-schema#" ↵
xmlns:wot="http://xmlns.com/wot/0.1/" ↵
xmlns:xhv="http://www.w3.org/1999/xhtml/vocab#"
>
  <rdf:Description rdf:about="http://www.example.com/metadata/foaf.rdf">
    <foaf:title>Dr</foaf:title>
    <foaf:givenname>John</foaf:givenname>
    <foaf:surname>Smith</foaf:surname>
    <foaf:gender>male</foaf:gender>
    <foaf:depiction rdf:resource="http://www.example.com/images/jsmith.jpg"/>
    <foaf:based_near rdf:resource="http://dbpedia.org/resource/New_York "/>
    <contact:nearestAirport rdf:resource=" http://www.panynj.gov/airports/jfk.html"/>
    <foaf:phone rdf:resource="tel:+1123456789"/>
    <foaf:homepage rdf:resource="http://www.example.com"/>
    <google:url rdf:resource="http://www.example.com"/>
    <foaf:holdsAccount rdf:resource="http://www.linkedin.com/in/jsmith"/>
    <foaf:holdsAccount rdf:resource="http://www.facebook.com/jsmith"/>
    <foaf:holdsAccount rdf:resource="http://www.twitter.com/jsmith"/>
    <foaf:interest rdf:resource="http://dbpedia.org/resource/Photography"/>
    <foaf:interest rdf:resource="http://dbpedia.org/resource/Semantic_Web"/>
    <foaf:interest rdf:resource="http://dbpedia.org/resource/Classical_music"/>
    <rdfs:seeAlso rdf:resource="http://www.example.com/metadata/foaf.rdf"/>
    <rdfs:seeAlso rdf:resource="http://www.example.com/metadata/doac.rdf"/>
    <rdf:type rdf:resource="http://xmlns.com/foaf/0.1/Person"/>
    <rdf:type rdf:resource="http://rdf.data-vocabulary.org/#Person"/>
    <rdf:type rdf:resource="http://purl.org/dc/terms/Agent"/>
    <owl:sameAs rdf:resource="http://www.example.com/about/"/>
    <foaf:publications rdf:resource="http://www.example.com/metadata/doac.rdf"/>
    <foaf:knows rdf:resource="http://www.1stfriendsweb site.net/foaf.rdf"/>
    <foaf:knows rdf:resource="http://www.2ndfriendssite.com/foaf/"/>
    <dc:date rdf:datatype="http://www.w3.org/2001/XMLSchema#date">2010-08-22</dc:date>
    <dc:creator>John Smith</dc:creator>
    <rdf:type rdf:resource="http://xmlns.com/foaf/0.1/PersonalProfileDocument"/>
    <xhv:stylesheet rdf:resource="http://www.example.com/styles.css"/>
    <wot:assurance rdf:resource="http://www.example.com/signature.asc"/>
    <foaf:primaryTopic rdf:resource="http://www.example.com/about/"/>
    <dc:title>Dr. John Smith associate professor</dc:title>
  </rdf:Description>
</rdf:RDF>
```

Microdata and Microformats

As mentioned earlier, overlapping features can be described by both microdata and microformats, as well as arbitrary features using RDFa. Microformats can also be used simultaneously with (X)HTML5 microdata. For example, hCard can be applied simultaneously with microdata, as shown in Listing 7-89.

Listing 7-89. Combining hCard with Microdata

```
<dl class="vcard" itemscope itemtype="http://data-vocabulary.org/Person">
  <dt class="fn" itemprop="name"><a href="http://example.com" ↵
   itemprop="url">John Smith</a></dt>
  <dd class="title" itemprop="title">Photographer</dd>
  <dd class="adr" itemprop="address" itemscope ↵
   itemtype="http://data-vocabulary.org/Address"><span class="locality" ↵
   itemprop="locality">Memphis</span>, <abbr title="Tennessee" class="region" ↵
   itemprop="region">TN</abbr>
  <span class="postal-code" itemprop="postal-code">38145</span></dd>
</dl>
```

Dublin Core and vCard in RDF

The flexibility of the Resource Description Framework makes it simple to use more than one kind of metadata from external namespaces at the same time. Consequently, rich semantics can be added to documents from a variety of vocabularies simultaneously (Listing 7-90).

Listing 7-90. Dublin Core and vCard in RDF

```
<?xml:namespace ns="http://www.w3.org/RDF/RDF/" prefix="RDF" ?>
<?xml:namespace ns="http://purl.oclc.org/DC/" prefix="DC" ?>
<?xml:namespace ns="http://person.org/BusinessCard/" prefix="CARD" ?>
<RDF:RDF>
  <RDF:Description RDF:HREF="http://uri-of-Document-1">
    <DC:Creator RDF:HREF="#Creator_001"/>
  </RDF:Description>
  <RDF:Description ID="Creator_001">
    <CARD:Name>John Smith<CARD:Name>
    <CARD:Email>jsmith@example.net<CARD:Email>
    <CARD:Affiliation>ABC Ltd.<CARD:Affiliation>
  </RDF:Description>
</RDF:RDF>
```

Dublin Core, vCard, and Math-Net

The introduction of a person on a brochure-style home page can be described in many ways. One of them is the combination of Dublin Core and vCard. Indexing and processing such data can be enhanced by providing them in RDF. Listing 7-91 shows an example.

Listing 7-91. Combining DC and vCard with Math-Net

```
<?xml version="1.0"?>
<rdf:RDF xmlns:rdf="http://www.w3.org/1999/02/22-rdf-syntax-ns#" ↵
 xmlns:dc="http://purl.org/dc/elements/1.1/" ↵
 xmlns:rdfs="http://www.w3.org/2000/01/rdf-schema#" ↵
 xmlns:vCard="http://www.w3.org/2001/vcard-rdf/3.0#">
  <rdf:Description>
```

```
  <dc:creator>
    <rdf:Description rdf:about="http://jsmith.com/about.htm">
      <rdfs:label>John Smith</rdfs:label>
      <vCard:FN>John Smith</vCard:FN>
      <vCard:N rdf:parseType="Resource">
        <vCard:Family>Smith</vCard:Family>
        <vCard:Given>John</vCard:Given>
        <vCard:Prefix>Dr</vCard:Prefix>
      </vCard:N>
      <vCard:BDAY>1976-05-12</vCard:BDAY>
    </rdf:Description>
  </dc:creator>
  </rdf:Description>
</rdf:RDF>
```

It is important to keep in mind that Dublin Core element name conventions and XML element nestings do not consequently apply to all the other metadata schemas.

Some vocabulary from the Math-Net schemes can be used to extend descriptions of persons expressed by other vocabularies, including Dublin Core and vCard [160].

DC, IMS, and ODRL

When using the XML or RDF/XML syntax, Dublin Core can be used in combination with external metadata vocabularies such as IEEE Learning Object Metadata (IMS) [161] or Open Digital Rights Language (ODRL) metadata [162]. For example, the storage, preservation, and retrieval of digital learning materials at universities can be properly provided by the combination of Dublin Core, LOM, and local labels describing learning materials when using the Greenstone digital library software [163].

For example, an online educational system can be described accurately by three different types of metadata (Listing 7-92).

Listing 7-92. A Combination of DC, IMS, and ODRL

```
<record ↵
 xmlns="http://www.example.org/virtualtutor/" ↵
 xmlns:xsi="http://www.w3.org/2001/XMLSchema-instance" ↵
 xsi:schemaLocation="http://www.example.org/virtualtutor/ ↵
 http://www.example.org/virtualtutor/schema.xsd" ↵
 xmlns:dc="http://purl.org/dc/elements/1.1/" ↵
 xmlns:dcterms="http://purl.org/dc/terms/" ↵
 xmlns:oex="http://odrl.net/1.0/ODRL-EX" ↵
 xmlns:odd="http://odrl.net/1.0/ODRL-DD" ↵
 xmlns:ims="http://www.imsglobal.org/xsd/imsmd_v1p2">
  <dc:title>
    Virtual Tutor
  </dc:title>
  <dc:identifier xsi:type="dcterms:URI">
    http://www.example.org/virtualtutor/
  </dc:identifier>
  <dc:description>
    Online educational system.
  </dc:description>
```

```
<ims:typicallearningtime>
  <ims:datetime>
    2011-08-02T08:00
  </ims:datetime>
</ims:typicallearningtime>
<dc:rights>
  All rights reserved.
</dc:rights>
<oex:rights>
  <oex:asset>
    <oex:context>
      <odd:uid idscheme="URI">
        http://www.example.org/virtualtutor/
      </odd:uid>
    </oex:context>
  </oex:asset>
</oex:rights>
</record>
```

Special Applications

There are metadata approaches that are specialized for images or a given media content type such as YouTube video. Some of them are provided in the markup, while others are embedded into binary files such as images.

Image Metadata and XMP

Digital photographs and custom images form integral parts of web sites. Various types of metadata can be provided with them, including descriptive, technical, and administrative metadata.

An advanced approach is to provide image metadata by markup. The alt attribute is vital for validity. Properly provided attribute values can improve accessibility too (see Chapter 10). The longdesc attribute, however, which could be used to provide a link to a long description for images and other nontext contents, has poor software support and is obsoleted in (X)HTML5.

Beyond the image descriptions provided in markup and the descriptions or image licensing written in RDFa discussed earlier, advanced and professional image manipulation software such as Adobe Photoshop can be used to add or modify metadata contained in the image files themselves (Figure 7-4). To a limited extent, file explorers of modern operating systems can also perform this task.

Depending on the image format, a wide variety of metadata can be applied, including, but not limited to, title, author, copyright holder, keywords, orientation, point of view, color space, photographer's contact data, camera data, origin, advanced metadata, and more.

░ **Note** Several types of metadata about the exposition are embedded in JPEG files taken by digital cameras that can be retrieved in image viewer and processing applications.

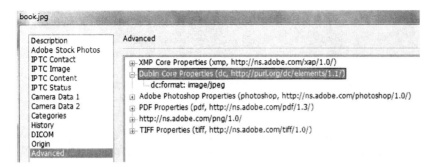

Figure 7-4. Manipulating image file metadata in Photoshop

Behind the scenes, Adobe Photoshop applies the Extensible Metadata Platform (XMP) standard created by Adobe Systems. The serialization of XMP can be embedded into several popular file formats, including GIF, JPEG, JPEG 2000, PNG, and TIFF images, as well as PDF files[10] [164]. GIF supports XMP embedding as an *application extension* with the identifier XMP Data and authentication code XMP. In JPEG files, the XMP metadata is embedded at *application segment 1* (0xFFE1) with segment header http://ns.adobe.com/xap/1.0/\x00. In JPEG 2000 images, the XMP metadata can be located at the uuid atom identified by the UID 0xBE7ACFCB97A942E89C71999491E3AFAC. In PNG files, XMP is embedded inside an iTXt text block with the keyword XML:com.adobe.xmp. XMP is located at *Tag 700* in TIFF images. The Portable Document Format supports XMP embedding in a metadata stream within a PDF object.

```
<x:xmpmeta xmlns:x="adobe:ns:meta/" x:xmptk="Adobe XMP Core 4.1-c036 46.276720, Fri Oct 15 2010 09:16:05      ">
   <rdf:RDF xmlns:rdf="http://www.w3.org/1999/02/22-rdf-syntax-ns#">
      <rdf:Description rdf:about="" xmlns:xap="http://ns.adobe.com/xap/1.0/" xmlns:dc="http://purl.org/dc/elements/1.1/"
xmlns:photoshop="http://ns.adobe.com/photoshop/1.0/" xmlns:Iptc4xmpCore="http://iptc.org/std/Iptc4xmpCore/1.0/xmlns/"
xmlns:xapMM="http://ns.adobe.com/xap/1.0/mm/" xmlns:tiff="http://ns.adobe.com/tiff/1.0/" xmlns:exif="http://ns.adobe.com/exif/1.0/"
xap:CreateDate="2010-10-15T08:51:07+02:00" xap:ModifyDate="2010-10-15T09:12:35+02:00"
xap:MetadataDate="2010-10-15T09:12:35+02:00" xap:CreatorTool="Adobe Photoshop CS3 Windows" dc:format="image/jpeg"
photoshop:ColorMode="3" photoshop:History="" xapMM:InstanceID="uuid:CA5BF9872BD8DF11AB8EF78C7944688B" tiff:Orientation="1"
tiff:XResolution="720000/10000" tiff:YResolution="720000/10000" tiff:ResolutionUnit="2"
tiff:NativeDigest="256,257,258,259,262,274,277,284,530,531,282,283,296,301,318,319,529,532,306,270,271,272,305,315,33432;6966157B8
458EA730AB07D7DBE4" exif:PixelXDimension="213" exif:PixelYDimension="174" exif:ColorSpace="-1"
exif:NativeDigest="36864,40960,40961,37121,37122,40962,40963,37510,40964,36867,36868,33434,33437,34850,34852,34855,34856,37377,
8,37379,37380,37381,37382,37383,37384,37385,37386,37396,41483,41484,41486,41487,41488,41492,41493,41495,41728,41729,41730,419
986,41987,41988,41989,41990,41991,41992,41993,41994,41995,41996,42016,0,2,4,5,6,7,8,9,10,11,12,13,14,15,16,17,18,20,22,23,24,25,26,
,30;CD88C06C74D97B1DDDDC1F0AA87E0AAB">
         <Iptc4xmpCore:CreatorContactInfo Iptc4xmpCore:CiUrlWork="http://www.example.com"/>
      </rdf:Description>
   <rdf:Description xmlns:dc="http://purl.org/dc/elements/1.1/"><dc:creator><rdf:Seq
xmlns:rdf="http://www.w3.org/1999/02/22-rdf-syntax-ns#"><rdf:li>John Smith</rdf:li></rdf:Seq>
      </dc:creator></rdf:Description><rdf:Description xmlns:tiff="http://ns.adobe.com/tiff/1.0/"><tiff:artist>John
Smith</tiff:artist></rdf:Description></rdf:RDF>
</x:xmpmeta>
<?xpacket end='w'?>
```

Figure 7-5. Textual RDF metadata in a binary JPEG image file

The major problem with images from this aspect is that they are binary files (Figure 7-5) that need different approaches to be indexed or searched than text files do. For example, in *Google Image Search* there are additional aspects, including the techniques applied for eliminating very small (for example, 1x1 pixel) images, scams, and so forth. Textual metadata used on top of the metadata stored in the image files themselves always provides an advanced level of processing and sharing options.

---

[10] External .xmp sidecar files can be provided for all other file formats that do not support embedded XMP metadata.

Metadata for YouTube Videos

The popular video-sharing web site YouTube provides a convenient option to embed videos stored on YouTube servers to custom web pages. RDFa notation can be used to improve the effectiveness of web searches on such videos.

The details on how to create standard-compliant markup from the YouTube embedding code by eliminating the embed tag and moving the required attributes to the object tag will be described later in Chapter 13.

There are two video metadata formats to be written in the markup that are recognized by Google: Facebook Share and Yahoo! SearchMonkey RDFa [165]. They can be used alternately or simultaneously. They should be written directly into the markup in a way that they can be read without JavaScript or Flash.

Facebook Share and RDFa Rich Snippets

The image and video resource URLs are required for Facebook Share (image_src and video_src). The medium property supports the values audio, image, video, news, blog, and mult. Video size can be provided using the video_width and video_height properties. The MIME type of videos can be identified by video_type (with the value application/x-shockwave-flash). A brief description of up to 200 characters can be written by using the description property. The title of the video, which can be a maximum of 60 characters long, can be added by the title property. These properties are also recognized by Google.

A complete Facebook Share example looks like Listing 7-93.

Listing 7-93. A Facebook Share Example

```
<meta name="title" content="Smith plays BWV543" />
<meta name="description" content="Organist John Smith plays Praeludium and Fuge in A minor ↵
 by J. S. Bach" />
<link rel="image_src" href="http://example.com/543thumb.jpg" />
<link rel="video_src" href="http://example.com/bach/543vid.swf" />
<meta name="video_width" content="640" />
<meta name="video_height" content="385" />
<meta name="video_type" content="application/x-shockwave-flash" />
```

Yahoo! SearchMonkey RDFa

Yahoo! SearchMonkey metadata can be provided on the object tag as demonstrated in Listing 7-94.

Listing 7-94. A Yahoo! SearchMonkey Example

```
<object type="application/x-shockwave-flash" width="480" height="385" ↵
 data="http://www.youtube.com/v/a38-oj8VEXI&amp;hl=en_US&amp;fs=1&amp;" rel="media:video" ↵
 resource="http://www.youtube.com/v/a38-oj8VEXI&amp;hl=en_US&amp;fs=1&amp;" ↵
 xmlns:media="http://search.yahoo.com/searchmonkey/media/" ↵
 xmlns:dc="http://purl.org/dc/terms/">
  <a rel="media:thumbnail" href="http://example.com/preview.jpg" />
</object>
```

The SearchMonkey media namespace `xmlns:media` is required, and the only acceptable value is `"http://search.yahoo.com/searchmonkey/media/"`. The GIF, JPEG, or PNG image with a resolution of 105x93 pixels that previews the video before the user clicks the Play button should be defined by the URI as the `href` attribute value of `media:thumbnail`. The video to be played when the user clicks the Play button should be defined by the resource of `media:video`.

All other tags are optional, including the Dublin Core namespace (`xmlns:dc`) and Dublin Core metadata (`dc:contributor`, `dc:creator`, `dc:date`, `dc:description`, `dc:identifier`, `dc:license`, `dc:subject`), the media metadata (`media:duration`, `media:height`, `media:player`, `media:region`, `media:title`, `media:type`, `media:views`, `media:width`), as well as `review:rating` [166].

Metadata in SEO

Although there is no strict correlation between higher page ranking or better search list positions and standardized web sites, several technologies contribute to better, higher-quality web documents. Semantic content adds meaning to web documents, making information indexing, searching, and processing easier. Metadata annotations considerably extend the potential of web searches.

The potential in web documents enriched with RDFa is increasing since major search engines have begun to process these annotations while indexing. More and more of this metadata is being indexed and considered by search engines. Google, for example, started to apply the hCard, hProduct, and hReview microformats as well as RDFa in 2009 on search result pages as what it calls *Rich Snippets* [167]. Yahoo! has indexed RDFa and microformats since 2008 [168]. Web site content enriched with RDFa or microformats can enhance web searches by providing useful structured data [169].

Google indexes microdata, microformats, and RDFa contact properties derived from the hCard microformat, including `name`, `nickname`, `photo`, `title`, `role`, `url`, `affiliation`, `friend`, `contact`, `acquaintance`, and `address`. The microformats properties `fn`, `org`, and `adr` that stand for name, affiliation, and address, respectively, are also displayed on web search pages.[11] Additionally, Google recognizes the XFN microformats `friend`, `contact`, and `acquaintance` [170]. Relationships and connections expressed in XFN and FOAF are also processed by Google [171].

As discussed earlier, the `nofollow` attribute value of the `rel` attribute on anchor elements can be used to ensure that the web page will gain no PageRank from the destination link. Such links are followed by Google, but PageRank is not added. Bing does not follow the link, and the page is not indexed. Yahoo! follows the link and indexes the page. Listing 7-95 shows an example.

Listing 7-95. Applying the nofollow Attribute on a Link

```
<a href="http://www.lowprsite.com" rel="nofollow">External site</a>
```

Yahoo! SearchMonkey supports the following metadata [172]:

- Microformats, including hCard, hCalendar, hReview, hAtom, hResume, adr, geo, tag, and XFN

- RDFa

- eRDF (embedded RDF)

---

[11] Google displays human-readable content only. Machine-readable metadata is not displayed. For example, the date declared as the content of the span element `<span class="value-title" title="2011-12-06T20:00-08:00" /> 06 December, 8 PM</span>` is the human-readable content, which is specified independently from the machine-readable attribute value of the `title` attribute in the ISO date format (`2011-12-06T20:00-08:00`).

Microformat searches in Yahoo! can be performed easily with queries in the form shown in Listing 7-96.

***Listing 7-96.** Microformat Search Syntax used by Yahoo!*

```
searchmonkeyid:com.yahoo.page.uf.metadata_name
```

where `metadata_name` is the name of the metadata in lowercase. RDFa and eRDF searches are similar. The only difference is that the string `uf` should be changed to `rdf`. For example, the hCard microformat can be searched with the query `searchmonkeyid:com.yahoo.page.uf.hcard`, RDF in attributes with `searchmonkeyid:com.yahoo.page.rdf.rdfa`, and so on.

Metadata annotations such as RDFa can effectively contribute to better search results. The more semantic content that is provided on the Web, the more reasonable and relevant search results that can be expected from search engines.[12] Properly set metadata can help search engines better process and provide personal introductions, contact data, and full descriptions of persons and human relationships in search results. The indexing of brochure-style business cards and personal information described in (X)HTML markup, XML, RDF, FOAF, and DOAC is straightforward. However, semantic contents embedded in conventional markup can be processed only if they are supported by the mechanisms used by web crawlers. Fortunately, the number of metadata types with meaning processable by search engines is constantly increasing.

In spite of the considerable potential of metadata applications in search engine optimization, there are several limitations as well. For example, image metadata cannot be fully exploited since a large share of social media and photo-sharing web sites either remove all embedded metadata during upload or apply a new, on-the-fly generated file without them (even in another file format). Images uploaded to the Internet by anonymous Wikipedia editors, on the other hand, can be found by their embedded metadata indexed by Google (if available). It is arguable whether this feature is advantageous.

Similar to any other data, it is important to decide wisely what to publish on the Web. It is no problem at all to publish the ISBN number of a book or a link to the DBpedia description of a web site item; however, several types of metadata are risky to publish since they can be abused. Especially e-mail addresses, phone numbers, and instant messenger screen names should be provided with extreme precaution.

Metadata embedding goes hand in hand with accessibility. Accessibility guidelines can ensure that alternate content is provided for objects and that the document structure is well organized (Chapter 10).

It is also important to note that SEO and user experience (UX) do not necessarily coincide. For example, frequently repeated keywords can decrease human readability [173].

Summary

In this chapter, you learned the fundamental concepts of the Semantic Web. You know by now how to create machine-readable metadata annotations and external metadata files at the source level. You are familiar with the most common schemas, vocabularies, and ontologies; the major serializations of the Resource Description Framework; and the basics of creating ontologies with OWL. You know how to combine annotations derived from different vocabularies, describe licenses and images in machine-readable formats, and use this metadata to boost the searchability of the files of your web site.

The next chapter will show you how to create standard-compliant news feed channels from scratch and maximize their interoperability.

---

[12] It is important to keep in mind, however, that markup is only one thing considered by search engines. For example, comprehensive and unique site content is becoming more and more important for gaining better positions on search results.

References

1. Herman I (ed) (2009) How would you define the main goals of the Semantic Web? In: W3C Semantic Web FAQ. World Wide Web Consortium. www.w3.org/2001/sw/SW-FAQ#swgoals. Accessed 05 June 2011

2. Sbodio LM, Martin D, Moulin C. Discovering Semantic Web services using SPARQL and intelligent agents. Web Semantics: Science, Services and Agents on the World Wide Web 2010, 8(4):310–328

3. Hyvönen E, Mäkelä E, Salminen M, Valo A, Viljanen K, Saarela S, Junnila M, Kettula S. MuseumFinland — Finnish museums on the semantic web. Web Semantics: Science, Services and Agents on the World Wide Web 2005, 3(2–3):224–241

4. Bojārs U, Breslin JG, Finn A, Decker S. Using the Semantic Web for linking and reusing data across Web 2.0 communities. Web Semantics: Science, Services and Agents on the World Wide Web 2008, 6(1):21–28

5. Celma Ò, Raimond Y. ZemPod: A semantic web approach to podcasting. Web Semantics: Science, Services and Agents on the World Wide Web 2008, 6(2):162–169

6. Berners-Lee T (2001) Business Model for the Semantic Web. World Wide Web Consortium. www.w3.org/DesignIssues/Business. Accessed 16 November 2010

7. Murphy T (2010) Lin Clark On Why Drupal Matters. Socialmedia. http://socialmedia.net/2010/09/07/lin-clark-on-why-drupal-matters. Accessed 09 September 2010

8. Hausenblas M, Adida B, Herman I (2008) RDFa – Bridging the Web of Documents and the Web of Data. Joanneum Research, Creative Commons, World Wide Web Consortium. www.w3.org/2008/Talks/1026-ISCW-RDFa/. Accessed 19 November 2010

9. Kobie N (ed) (2011) Q&A: Conrad Wolfram on communicating with apps in Web 3.0. Dennis Publishing Ltd. www.itpro.co.uk/621535/q-a-conrad-wolfram-on-communicating-with-apps-in-web-3-0. Accessed 25 August 2011

10. Ankolekar A, Krötzsch M, Tran T, Vrandečić, D. The two cultures: Mashing up Web 2.0 and the Semantic Web. Web Semantics: Science, Services and Agents on the World Wide Web 2008, 6(1):70–75

11. Shannon V (2006) A "more revolutionary" Web. International Herald Tribune. The New York Times Company. www.nytimes.com/2006/05/23/technology/23iht-web.html?scp=1&sq=A+%27more+revolutionary%27+Web&st=nyt. Accessed 25 August 2011

12. Adida B, Birbeck M, McCarron S, Herman I (eds) (2010) Abstract. In: RDFa Core 1.1. Syntax and processing rules for embedding RDF through attributes. W3C Working Draft. World Wide Web Consortium. www.w3.org/TR/rdfa-core/. Accessed 22 November 2010

13. Herman I (2009) W3C Semantic Web Frequently Asked Questions. World Wide Web Consortium. www.w3.org/RDF/FAQ. Accessed 16 November 2010

14. Arenas M, Prud'hommeaux E, Sequeda J (eds) (2010) A Direct Mapping of Relational Data to RDF. World Wide Web Consortium. www.w3.org/TR/rdb-direct-mapping/. Accessed 19 November 2010

15. Clark K (2010) The RDF Database Market. Clark & Parsia, LLC. http://weblog.clarkparsia.com/2010/09/23/the-rdf-database-market/. Accessed 21 November 2010

16. Oinonen K (2005) On the road to business application of Semantic Web technology. Semantic Web in Business – How to proceed. In: Industrial Applications of Semantic Web: Proceedings of the 1st IFIP WG12.5 Working Conference on Industrial Applications of Semantic Web. International Federation for Information Processing. Springer Science+Business Media Inc., New York

17. Nagy M, Vargas-Vera M (2010) Towards an Automatic Semantic Data Integration: Multi-agent Framework Approach. In: Semantic Web. In-Teh, Vukovar

18. Dertouzos LM, Berners-Lee T, Fischetti M (1999) Weaving the Web: The Original Design and Ultimate Destiny of the World Wide Web by Its Inventor. Harper San Francisco, San Francisco

19.   Bizer C, Heath T, Berners-Lee T. Linked data — The story so far. Semantic Web and Information Systems 2009, 5(3):1–22

20.   Berners-Lee T (2009) Linked Data. World Wide Web Consortium. www.w3.org/DesignIssues/LinkedData.html. Accessed 25 August 2011

21.   Cyganiak R, Jentzsch A. Linking Open Data cloud diagram. http://lod-cloud.net. Accessed 20 July 2011

22.   Yahoo (2010) Flickr – Photo sharing. Yahoo! Inc. www.flickr.com. Accessed 15 October 2010

23.   Google Webmaster Central Team (2007) Using the robots meta tag. Google Inc. http://googlewebmastercentral.blogspot.com/2007/03/using-robots-meta-tag.html. Accessed 16 October 2010

24.   AOL Inc. (2010) ODP – Open Directory Project. Netscape. www.dmoz.org/. Accessed 16 October 2010

25.   TWRP (2007) About the Robots <META> tag. The Web Robots Pages. www.robotstxt.org/meta.html. Accessed 02 November 2010

26.   Sullivan D (2007) Yahoo Provides NOYDIR Opt-Out Of Yahoo Directory Titles & Descriptions. Search Engine Land. Third Door Media. http://searchengineland.com/yahoo-provides-noydir-opt-out-of-yahoo-directory-titles-descriptions-10631. Accessed 16 October 2010

27.   Ontos (2010) OntosMiner. Ontos AG. www.ontos.com/o_eng/index.php?cs=3-2. Accessed 25 August 2011

28.   Wu G (ed) (2010) Semantic Web. In-Tech, Vukovar

29.   Mellouli S, Bouslama F, Akande A (2010) An ontology for representing financial headline news. doi:10.1016/j.websem.2010.02.001

30.   Davis I, Newman R, D'Arcus B (2005) Expression of Core FRBR Concepts in RDF. Richard Newman, Ian Davis. http://vocab.org/frbr/core.html. Accessed 21 February 2011

31.   Creative Commons (2011) Describing Copyright in RDF. Creative Commons Rights Expression Language. Creative Commons. http://creativecommons.org/ns. Accessed 21 February 2011

32.   ODRL (2011) The Open Digital Rights Language (ODRL) Initiative. http://odrl.net. Accessed 25 August 2011

33.   Iannella R (2002) Open Digital Rights Language (ODRL) Version 1.1. World Wide Web Consortium. www.w3.org/TR/odrl. Accessed 21 February 2011

34.   Miles A, Bechhofer S (eds) (2009) SKOS Simple Knowledge Organization System Reference. World Wide Web Consortium. www.w3.org/TR/skos-reference/. Accessed 21 February 2011

35.   Brickley D (ed) (2006) WGS84 Geo Positioning: an RDF vocabulary. World Wide Web Consortium. www.w3.org/2003/01/geo/wgs84_pos.rdf. Accessed 21 February 2011

36.   Davis I, Galbraith D (2010) BIO: A vocabulary for biographical information. Ian Davis, David Galbraith. http://vocab.org/bio/0.1/. Accessed 21 February 2011

37.   IMS (2006) IMS Meta-data Best Practice Guide for IEEE 1484.12.1-2002 Standard for Learning Object Metadata. Version 1.3 Final Specification. IMS Global Learning Consortium. http://www.imsglobal.org/metadata/mdv1p3/imsmd_bestv1p3.html. Accessed 21 February 2011

38.   Universität Osnabrück (2002) Math-Net RDF Collection. Universität Osnabrück. www.iwi-iuk.org/material/RDF/1.1/. Accessed 21 February 2011

39.   Brickley D, Miller L (2007) FOAF Vocabulary Specification 0.9. Dan Brickley, Libby Miller. http://xmlns.com/foaf/0.1/. Accessed 21 February 2011

40.   Parada RA (2008) DOAC Vocabulary Specification. Ramon Antonio Parada. http://ramonantonio.net/doac/0.1/. Accessed 21 February 2011

41.   Dumbill E (2011) DOAP. Edd Dumbill. http://trac.usefulinc.com/doap. Accessed 22 February 2011

42.   Lindesay V (2011) Schemaweb. RDF schema directory. VicSoft Ltd. www.schemaweb.info. Accessed 21 February 2011

43.   Davis I (2006) vocab.org - A URI space for vocabularies. Ian Davis. http://vocab.org. Accessed 21 February 2011

44.   Aumueller D (2006) Beer Ontology. David Aumueller. www.purl.org/net/ontology/beer.owl. Accessed 17 November 2010

45.   Kanzaki M (2007) Music Vocabulary. The Web KANZAKI. www.kanzaki.com/ns/music.rdf. Accessed 17 November 2010

46.   Sikos LF (2011) VidOnt – the video ontology. http://vidont.org/. Accessed 30 May 2011

47.   Baumeister J, Seipel D (2010) Anomalies in ontologies with rules. Web Semant, doi:10.1016/j.websem.2009.12.003

48.   Khan L (2009) Semantic Web and Cloud Computing. In: Research of Dr. Latifur Khan. The University of Dallas. www.utdallas.edu/~lkhan/research.html. Accessed 13 November 2010

49.   Smarty A (2010) How to Use Various REL Attributes – Learning Microformats. Search Engine Journal. www.searchenginejournal.com/how-to-use-various-rel-attributes-learning-microformats/16144/. Accessed 11 November 2010

50.   Kaply M (2010) Operator Add-on for Firefox. Michael Kaply. https://addons.mozilla.org/en-US/firefox/addon/4106/. Accessed 17 November 2010

51.   De Bruin R (2010) Tails Export Add-on for Firefox. Robert de Bruin. https://addons.mozilla.org/en-US/firefox/addon/2240/. Accessed 17 November 2010

52.   Ryckbost B (2010) Michromeformats Google Chrome extension. Brian Ryckbost. https://chrome.google.com/extensions/detail/oalbifknmclbnmjlljdemhjjlkmppjjl. Accessed 17 November 2010

53.   Baranovskiy D (2010) Optimus – Microformats Transformer. Dmitry Baranovskiy. http://microformatique.com/optimus/. Accessed 17 November 2010

54.   Left Logic (2010) Microformats Bookmarklet. Left Logic Ltd. http://leftlogic.com/projects/microformats_bookmarklet. Accessed 17 November 2010

55.   Dawson F, Stenerson D (1998) Internet Calendaring and Scheduling Core Object Specification (iCalendar). The Internet Society. www.ietf.org/rfc/rfc2445.txt. Accessed 12 November 2010

56.   Çelik T, Suda B (2010) hCalendar 1.0. The Microformats Community. http://microformats.org/wiki/hcalendar. Accessed 12 November 2010

57.   King R, Çelik T, Mullenweg M (2008) hCalendar Creator. The Microformats Community. http://microformats.org/code/hcalendar/creator. Accessed 11 November 2010

58.   Çelik T, Suda B (2010) hCard 1.0. The Microformats Community. http://microformats.org/wiki/hcard. Accessed 11 November 2010

59.   Dawson F, Howes T (1998) vCard MIME Directory Profile. The Internet Society. www.ietf.org/rfc/rfc2426.txt. Accessed 11 November 2010

60.   Çelik T (2005) hCard Creator. The Microformats Community. http://microformats.org/code/hcard/creator. Accessed 11 November 2010

61.   Casserly C, Domicone A, Green L, Heung A, Kinkade N, Linksvayer M, Park J, Peters D, Rees J, Roberts A, Rose T, Ruttenberg A, Schultz AJ, Steuer E, Vollmer T, Webber C, Wilbanks J, Yergler N, Yip J et al (eds) (2010) Licenses. Creative Commons. http://creativecommons.org/about/licenses/. Accessed 17 October 2010

62.   Çelik T (2005) rel="license". http://microformats.org/wiki/rel-license. The Microformats Community. Accessed 12 November 2010

63.   Olbertz D (2010) No to rel="nofollow". Fight Spam not Blogs. Dirk Olbertz. http://nonofollow.net. Accessed 13 November 2010

64.   Çelik T, Marks K (eds), Cutts M, Shellen J (2005) rel="nofollow". The Microformats Community. http://microformats.org/wiki/rel-nofollow. Accessed 12 November 2010

65.   Çelik T, Marks K, Powazek D (2010) rel="tag". The Microformats Community. http://microformats.org/wiki/rel-tag. Accessed 12 November 2010

66.   Berners-Lee T, Fielding R, Masinter L (2005) Uniform Resource Identifier (URI): Generic Syntax. The Internet Society. www.ietf.org/rfc/rfc3986.txt. Accessed 25 August 2011

67.   Çelik T, Marks K (2010) Vote Links. The Microformats Community. http://microformats.org/wiki/vote-links. Accessed 13 November 2010

68.   Paul A (2003) Social networking beginning to take shape on the Web. The Seattle Times. http://community.seattletimes.nwsource.com/archive/?date=20031229&slug=paul29. Accessed 10 November 2010

69.   GMPG (2010) XFN – XHTML Friends network. Global Multimedia Protocols Group. http://gmpg.org/xfn/. Accessed 10 November 2010

70.   Lewis EP (2008) Getting Semantic With Microformats, Part 2: XFN. Emily P. Lewis. http://ablognotlimited.com/index.php/articles/getting-semantic-with-microformats-part-2-xfn/. Accessed 11 November 2010

71.   Mullenweg M, Çelik T (2004) XFN 1.1 Creator. Global Multimedia Protocols Group. http://gmpg.org/xfn/creator. Accessed 11 November 2010

72.   Mullenweg M (2010) Exefen. Matthew Mullenweg. http://ma.tt/tools/exefen.php/. Accessed 11 November 2010

73.   Çelik T (2003) XMDP: Introduction and Format Description. Global Multimedia Protocols Group. http://gmpg.org/xmdp/description. Accessed 13 November 2010

74.   Çelik T (2010) The adr microformat Draft Specification. The Microformats Community. http://microformats.org/wiki/adr. Accessed 13 November 2010

75.   Çelik T (2009) The geo microformat Draft Specification. The Microformats Community. http://microformats.org/wiki/geo. Accessed 13 November 2010

76.   Janes D, Carlyle B, Tantek Çelik T (2010) The hAtom microformat Draft Specification. The Microformats Community. http://microformats.org/wiki/hatom. Accessed 13 November 2010

77.   Sporny M, McEvoy M et al (2010) The hAudio microformat Draft Specification. The Microformats Community. http://microformats.org/wiki/haudio. Accessed 13 November 2010

78.   Çelik T, Khare R (eds), Arkin A, Donato C, King R (2010) The hListing microformat Draft Specification. The Microformats Community. http://microformats.org/wiki/hlisting. Accessed 13 November 2010

79.   McEvoy M, Çelik T, Marks K, Hodder M, Begbie R, Kinberg J, Messina C, Rein L, Newell C, Sporny M, Johnson M, McEvoy M (2010) The hMedia microformat Draft Specification. The Microformats Community. http://microformats.org/wiki/hmedia. Accessed 13 November 2010

80.   Malek J, Myles S, Moore M, Ng M, Martin TB (2010) The hNews microformat Draft Specification. The Microformats Community. http://microformats.org/wiki/hnews. Accessed 13 November 2010

81.   Lee P, Myers J, Cook C, Gustafson A (2010) The hProduct microformat Draft Specification. The Microformats Community. http://microformats.org/wiki/hproduct. Accessed 13 November 2010

82.   Lörtsch T (ed), Berriman F, Ward B, Inkster T (2010) The hRecipe microformat Draft Specification. The Microformats Community. http://microformats.org/wiki/hrecipe. Accessed 13 November 2010

83.   King R, Çelik T, Levine J, Marks K (2010) The hResume microformat Draft Specification. The Microformats Community. http://microformats.org/wiki/hresume. Accessed 13 November 2010

84.   Çelik T, Diab A, McAllister I, Panzer J, Rifkin A, Sippey M (2010) The hReview microformat Draft Specification. The Microformats Community. http://microformats.org/wiki/hreview. Accessed 13 November 2010

85.   King R, Cook B, Çelik T, Marks K (2009) The rel-directory microformat Draft Specification. The Microformats Community. http://microformats.org/wiki/rel-directory. Accessed 14 November 2010

86. Marks K (2009) The rel="enclosure" microformat Draft Specification. The Microformats Community. http://microformats.org/wiki/rel-enclosure. Accessed 14 November 2010

87. Ayers D (2009) The rel="home" microformat Draft Specification. The Microformats Community. http://microformats.org/wiki/rel-home. Accessed 14 November 2010

88. Pedersen AH, Kinberg J, Dedman J, Van Dijk P (2010) The rel-payment microformat Draft Specification. The Microformats Community. http://microformats.org/wiki/rel-payment. Accessed 14 November 2010

89. Janes P (2009) The Robot Exclusion Profile. Draft Specification. The Microformats Community. http://microformats.org/wiki/robots-exclusion. Accessed 14 November 2010

90. Gibson B (2010) The xFolk microformat. Draft Specification. The Microformats Community. http://microformats.org/wiki/xfolk. Accessed 14 November 2010

91. 4K Associates (2009) So you wanna develop a new microformat? The Microformats Community. http://microformats.org/wiki/process. Accessed 13 November 2010

92. Hickson I (2010) HTML Microdata. World Wide Web Consortium. http://www.w3.org/TR/microdata/. Accessed 17 October 2010

93. Berners-Lee T (2007) Giant Global Graph. Massachusetts Institute of Technology. http://dig.csail.mit.edu/breadcrumbs/node/215. Accessed 23 September 2010

94. Berners-Lee T (2007) Giant Global Graph. Massachusetts Institute of Technology. http://dig.csail.mit.edu/breadcrumbs/node/215. Accessed 23 September 2010

95. Brickley D (2010) FOAF Project web site. The Friend Of A Friend (FOAF) Project. www.foaf-project.org/. Accessed 23 September 2010

96. QDOS (2010) FOAFNet. QDOS. http://foaf.qdos.com/. Accessed 23 September 2010

97. NetEstate (2010) Friend Of A Friend (FOAF) Search Engine. NetEstate. www.foaf-search.net. Accessed 23 September 2010

98. Intellidimension (2010) Semantic Web Search. Intellidimension. www.semanticwebsearch.com/query/. Accessed 23 September 2010

99. Quatuo (2010) Search FOAF profiles / Create, manage, store and publish your Friend of a Friend (FOAF) profile – A Semantic Web project. Quatuo. www.quatuo.com. Accessed 23 September 2010

100. Dodds L (2010) FOAF-a-matic. www.ldodds.com/foaf/foaf-a-matic.en.html. Leigh Dodds. Accessed 23 September 2010

101. Walker J (2010) The Drupal FOAF module. http://drupal.org/project/foaf. Dries Buytaert. Accessed 23 September 2010

102. ISO (2009) Information and documentation — The Dublin Core metadata element set. ISO 15836:2009. International Organization for Standardization. www.iso.org/iso/iso_catalogue/catalogue_ics/catalogue_detail_ics.htm?csnumber=52142. Accessed 26 August 2011

103. Kunze J, Baker T (2007) The Dublin Core Metadata Element Set. The IETF Trust. www.ietf.org/rfc/rfc5013.txt. Accessed 27 August 2011

104. ANSI, NISO (2007) The Dublin Core Metadata Element Set. ANSI/NISO Z39.85. National Information Standards Organization. www.niso.org/kst/reports/standards/kfile_download?id%3Austring%3Aiso-8859-1=Z39-85-2007.pdf&pt=RkGKiXzW643YeUaYUqZ1BFwDhIG4-24RJbcZBWg8uE4vWdpZsJDs4RjLz0t90_d5_ymGsj_IKVa86hjP37r_hFEijh12LhLqJw52B-5udAaMy22WJJl0y5GhhtjwcI3V. Accessed 26 August 2011

105. Hillmann D (2005) Syntax Issues. In: Using Dublin Core. Dublin Core Metadata Initiative. http://dublincore.org/documents/usageguide/#whichsyntax. Accessed 02 November 2010

106. Powell A, Nilsson M, Naeve A, Johnston P, Baker T (2007) DCMI Abstract Model. DCMI Recommendation. Dublin Core Metadata Initiative. http://dublincore.org/documents/abstract-model/. Accessed 25 October 2010

107. DCMI (2010) Dublin Core Metadata Element Set, Version 1.1. DCMI Recommendation. Dublin Core Metadata Initiative. http://dublincore.org/documents/dces/. Accessed 22 October 2010

108. Powell A, Wagner H (eds), Weibel S, Baker T, Matola T, Miller E, Johnston P (2007) Namespace Policy for the Dublin Core Metadata Initiative (DCMI). Dublin Core Metadata Initiative. http://dublincore.org/documents/dcmi-namespace/. Accessed 26 October 2010

109. Powell A, Nilsson M, Naeve A, Johnston P, Baker T (2007) DCMI Abstract Model semantics. In: DCMI Abstract Model. Dublin Core Metadata Initiative. http://dublincore.org/documents/2007/02/05/abstract-model/#sect-5. Accessed 26 October 2010

110. Hillmann D (2005) Using Dublin Core – The Elements, Dublin Core Metadata Initiative. Dublin Core Metadata Initiative. http://dublincore.org/documents/usageguide/elements.shtml. Accessed 11 September 2010

111. DCMI Usage Board (2010) DCMI Metadata Terms. DCMI Recommendation. Dublin Core Metadata Initiative. http://dublincore.org/documents/dcmi-terms/. Accessed 22 October 2010

112. Berners-Lee T, Fielding R, Masinter L (2005) RFC 3986: Uniform Resource Identifier (URI): Generic Syntax. Internet Engineering Task Force. http://www.ietf.org/rfc/rfc3986.txt. Accessed 26 October 2010

113. Johnston P, Powell A (2008) Expressing Dublin Core metadata using HTML/XHTML meta and link elements. Dublin Core Metadata Initiative. http://dublincore.org/documents/dc-html/. Accessed 09 November 2010

114. Powell A, Johnston P (2003) Guidelines for implementing Dublin Core in XML. Dublin Core Metadata Initiative. http://dublincore.org/documents/dc-xml-guidelines/. Accessed 06 November 2010

115. Johnston P, Powell A (2008) Expressing Dublin Core Description Sets using XML (DC-DS-XML). Dublin Core Metadata Initiative. http://dublincore.org/documents/dc-ds-xml/. Accessed 07 November 2010

116. Phillips A, Davis M (2006) Tags for Identifying Languages. The Internet Society. www.ietf.org/rfc/rfc4646.txt. Accessed 08 November 2010

117. Beckett D, Miller E, Brickley D (2002) Expressing Simple Dublin Core in RDF/XML. Dublin Core Metadata Initiative. http://dublincore.org/documents/dcmes-xml/. Accessed 31 October 2010

118. Kokkelink S, Schwänzl R (2002) Expressing Qualified Dublin Core in RDF / XML. Dublin Core Metadata Initiative. http://dublincore.org/documents/dcq-rdf-xml/. Accessed 02 November 2010

119. Nilsson M, Powell A, Johnston P, Naeve A (2008) Expressing Dublin Core metadata using the Resource Description Framework (RDF). Dublin Core Metadata Initiative. http://dublincore.org/documents/dc-rdf/. Accessed 02 November 2010

120. Nilsson M, Baker T (2008) Notes on DCMI specifications for Dublin Core metadata in RDF. Dublin Core Metadata Initiative. http://dublincore.org/documents/dc-rdf-notes/. Accessed 02 November 2010

121. Beckett D, McBride B (eds) (2004) Introduction. In: RDF/XML Syntax Specification. W3C Recommendation. World Wide Web Consortium. www.w3.org/TR/rdf-syntax-grammar/#section-Introduction. Accessed 21 November 2010

122. Klyne G, Carroll JJ, McBride B (eds) (2004) Resource Description Framework (RDF): Concepts and Abstract Syntax. W3C Recommendation. World Wide Web Consortium. www.w3.org/TR/rdf-concepts/. Accessed 21 November 2010

123. Davis M, Whistler K (eds) (2010) Unicode Standard Annex #15. Unicode Normalization Forms. The Unicode Consortium. www.unicode.org/reports/tr15/#Norm_Forms. Accessed 15 November 2010

124. Ora Lassila O, Swick RR (eds) (1999) Formal Grammar for RDF. In: Resource Description Framework (RDF) Model and Syntax Specification. World Wide Web Consortium. www.w3.org/TR/1999/REC-rdf-syntax-19990222/#grammar. Accessed 21 November 2010

125. Prud'hommeaux E, Seaborne A (eds) (2008) SPARQL Query Language for RDF. World Wide Web Consortium. www.w3.org/TR/rdf-sparql-query/. Accessed 22 February 2011

126. Ogbuji C (ed) (2010) SPARQL 1.1 Uniform HTTP Protocol for Managing RDF Graphs. World Wide Web Consortium. www.w3.org/TR/sparql11-http-rdf-update/. Accessed 22 February 2011

127. Grant J, Beckett D, McBride B (eds) (2004) N-Triples. In: RDF Test Cases. W3C Recommendation. World Wide Web Consortium. www.w3.org/TR/rdf-testcases/#ntriples. Accessed 21 November 2010

128. Chris Bizer C, Cyganiak R (2007) The TriG Syntax. Freie Universität Berlin. http://www4.wiwiss.fu-berlin.de/bizer/TriG/Spec/. Accessed 21 November 2010

129. Carroll JJ, Stickler P (2004) RDF Triples in XML. HP Laboratories. www.hpl.hp.com/techreports/2003/HPL-2003-268.pdf. Accessed 21 November 2010

130. Beckett D, McBride B (2004) RDF/XML Syntax Specification. World Wide Web Consortium. www.w3.org/TR/rdf-syntax-grammar/. Accessed 15 November 2010

131. Berners-Lee T, Connolly D (2008) Notation3 (N3): A readable RDF syntax. W3C Team Submission. World Wide Web Consortium. www.w3.org/TeamSubmission/n3/. Accessed 15 November 2010

132. Berners-Lee T, Connolly D (2008) Grammar of N3 in EBNF as used in XML 1.1 format. World Wide Web Consortium. www.w3.org/2000/10/swap/grammar/n3-ietf.txt. Accessed 15 November 2010

133. Berners-Lee T (2005) Primer: Getting into RDF & Semantic Web using N3. World Wide Web Consortium. www.w3.org/2000/10/swap/Primer. Accessed 15 November 2010

134. Prud'hommeaux E, Carothers G (ed), Beckett D, Berners-Lee T (2011) Terse RDF Triple Language. World Wide Web Consortium. www.w3.org/TR/2011/WD-turtle-20110809/. Accessed 25 August 2011

135. Epimorphics (2010) Jena – A Semantic Web Framework for Java. Epimorphics Ltd. http://openjena.org. Accessed 26 August 2011

136. Beckett D (2011) Redland RDF Libraries. Dave Beckett. http://librdf.org. Accessed 26 August 2011

137. Aduna (2011) openRDF.org – home of Sesame. Aduna. www.openrdf.org. Accessed 26 August 2011

138. Zeldman J, Marcotte E (2009) Designing with Web standards, 3rd edn. New Riders, Berkeley

139. Sporny M, Adrian B, Birbeck M (eds), Herman I (2010) RDFa API. An API for extracting structured data from Web documents. World Wide Web Consortium. www.w3.org/TR/rdfa-api/. Accessed 22 February 2011

140. Adida B, Birbeck M, McCarron S, Herman I (eds) (2010) RDFa Core 1.1. Syntax and processing rules for embedding RDF through attributes. World Wide Web Consortium. www.w3.org/TR/rdfa-core/. Accessed 22 February 2011

141. Birbeck M, McCarron S (2009) CURIE Syntax 1.0. A syntax for expressing Compact URIs, W3C Candidate Recommendation. World Wide Web Consortium. www.w3.org/TR/curie/. Accessed 11 September 2010

142. Lewis JR, Moscovitz M (2009) AdvancED CSS. Friends of ED, Berkeley

143. Adida B, Herman I (eds) (2011) W3C RDFa Working Group. World Wide Web Consortium. www.w3.org/2010/02/rdfa/. Accessed 22 February 2011

144. Swick R (ed) (2002) Metadata Activity Statement. World Wide Web Consortium. www.w3.org/Metadata/Activity.html. Accessed 28 October 2010

145. Brickley D, Guha RV, McBride B (eds) (2004) RDF Vocabulary Description Language 1.0: RDF Schema. World Wide Web Consortium. www.w3.org/TR/rdf-schema/. Accessed 22 February 2011

146. Herman I (2010) "Why OWL and not WOL?". Tutorial on Semantic Web Technologies. World Wide Web Consortium. www.w3.org/People/Ivan/CorePresentations/RDFTutorial/Slides.html#%28114%29. Accessed 28 October 2010

147. Smith MK, Welty C, McGuinness DL (eds) (2004) The Species of OWL. In: OWL Web Ontology Language Guide. W3C Recommendation. www.w3.org/TR/2004/REC-owl-guide-20040210/#OwlVarieties. Accessed 15 November 2010

148. Dean M, Schreiber G (eds), Bechhofer S, van Harmelen F, Hendler J, Horrocks I, McGuinness DL, Patel-Schneider PF, Stein LA (2004) OWL Web Ontology Language Reference. W3C Recommendation. World Wide Web Consortium. www.w3.org/TR/owl-ref/. Accessed 26 August 2011

149. Hitzler P, Krötzsch M, Parsia B, Patel-Schneider PF, Rudolph S (eds) (2009) OWL 2 Web Ontology Language – Primer. W3C Recommendation. World Wide Web Consortium. www.w3.org/TR/owl-primer/. Accessed 26 August 2011

150. Motik B, Grau BC, Horrocks I, Wu Z, Fokoue A, Lutz C (eds), Calvanese D, Carroll J, De Giacomo G, Hendler J, Herman I, Parsia B, Patel-Schneider PF, Ruttenberg A, Sattler U, Schneider M (2009) OWL 2 Web Ontology Language - Profiles. W3C Recommendation. World Wide Web Consortium. www.w3.org/TR/owl2-profiles/. Accessed 26 August 2011

151. Patel-Schneider PF, Horrocks I (eds) (2004) Abstract Syntax. In: OWL Web Ontology Language. Semantics and Abstract Syntax. World Wide Web Consortium. www.w3.org/TR/2004/REC-owl-semantics-20040210/syntax.html. Accessed 28 October 2010

152. Motik B, Patel-Schneider PF, Parsia B (eds), Bock C, Fokoue A, Haase P, Hoekstra R, Horrocks I, Ruttenberg A, Sattler U, Smith M (2009) OWL 2 Web Ontology Language. Structural Specification and Functional-Style Syntax. W3C Recommendation. World Wide Web Consortium. www.w3.org/TR/owl-syntax/. Accessed 28 October 2010

153. Patel-Schneider PF, Motik B (eds), Grau BC, Horrocks I, Parsia B, Ruttenberg A, Schneider M (2009) OWL 2 Web Ontology Language. Mapping to RDF Graphs. W3C Recommendation. World Wide Web Consortium. www.w3.org/TR/2009/REC-owl2-mapping-to-rdf-20091027/. Accessed 29 October 2010

154. Beckett D, McBride B (eds) (2004) RDF/XML Syntax Specification. W3C Recommendation. World Wide Web Consortium. www.w3.org/TR/rdf-syntax-grammar/. Accessed 28 October 2010

155. Beckett D, Berners-Lee T (2008) Turtle - Terse RDF Triple Language. W3C Team Submission. World Wide Web Consortium. www.w3.org/TeamSubmission/turtle/. Accessed 28 October 2010

156. Motik B, Parsia B, Patel-Schneider PF (eds), Bechhofer S, Grau BC, Fokoue A, Hoekstra R (2009) OWL 2 Web Ontology Language. XML Serialization. W3C Recommendation. World Wide Web Consortium. www.w3.org/TR/owl-xml-serialization/. Accessed 28 October 2010

157. Horridge M, Patel-Schneider PF (2009) OWL 2 Web Ontology Language. Manchester Syntax. W3C Working Group Note. World Wide Web Consortium. www.w3.org/TR/2009/NOTE-owl2-manchester-syntax-20091027/. Accessed 28 October 2010

158. W3C OWL Working Group (eds) (2009) Syntaxes. In: OWL 2 Web Ontology Language. Document Overview. W3C Recommendation. World Wide Web Consortium. www.w3.org/TR/owl2-overview/#Syntaxes. Accessed 28 October 2010

159. Dean M, Schreiber G (eds), Bechhofer S, van Harmelen F, Hendler J, Horrocks I, McGuinness DL, Patel-Schneider PF, Stein LA (2004) Properties. In: OWL Web Ontology Language Reference. W3C Recommendation. World Wide Web Consortium. www.w3.org/TR/owl-ref/#Property. Accessed 30 October 2010

160. Kokkelink S, Schwänzl R (2002) DC in collaboration with other vocabularies and DumbDown. In: Expressing Qualified Dublin Core in RDF / XML. Dublin Core Metadata Initiative. http://dublincore.org/documents/dcq-rdf-xml/#sec3. Accessed 02 November 2010

161. Barker P, Campbell LM, Roberts A, Smythe C (eds) (2006) IMS Meta-data Best Practice Guide for IEEE 1484.12.1-2002 Standard for Learning Object Metadata. Final Specification. IMS Global Learning Consortium. www.imsglobal.org/metadata/mdv1p3/imsmd_bestv1p3.html. Accessed 23 October 2010

162. Iannella R (ed) (2002) ODRL 1.1 Expression Language Schema. Open Digital Rights Language Initiative. http://odrl.net/1.1/ODRL-EX-11-DOC/index.html. Accessed 23 October 2010

163. Rivera-Aguilera AB, Vega-López M, Pozo-Marrero A (2010) Metadata Application Profile: Integrating Different Metadata Schemes for Cataloguing the Digital Learning Materials Collections. In: Proceedings of the International Conference on Dublin Core and Metadata Applications. Dublin Core Metadata Initiative, Pittsburgh

164. Adobe Systems Inc. (2010) Embedding XMP metadata in application files. In: XMP specification, Part 3 – Storage in files. www.adobe.com/content/dam/Adobe/en/devnet/xmp/pdfs/XMPSpecificationPart3.pdf. Accessed 17 November 2010

165. Sikos LF (2011) Advanced (X)HTML5 metadata and semantics for Web 3.0 videos. DESIDOC Journal of Library and Information Technology 2011, 31(4):247–252; http://publications.drdo.gov.in/ojs/index.php/djlit/article/viewFile/1105/434. Accessed 20 July 2011

166. Yahoo! Inc. (2009) SearchMonkey – Video. Yahoo! Developer Network. Inc. http://developer.search.yahoo.com/help/objects/video. Accessed 15 October 2010

167. Goel K, Guha RV, Hansson O (2009) Introducing Rich Snippets. Google Inc. http://googlewebmastercentral.blogspot.com/2009/05/introducing-rich-snippets.html. Accessed 21 October 2010

168. Birbeck M (2009) Introduction to RDFa. A List Apart Magazine. www.alistapart.com/articles/introduction-to-rdfa. Accessed 09 September 2010

169. Goel K, Gupta P, Hansson O (2009) Help us make the web better: An update on Rich Snippets. Google Inc. http://googlewebmastercentral.blogspot.com/2009/10/help-us-make-web-better-update-on-rich.html. Accessed 21 October 2010

170. Google Webmaster Central (2010) People. About contact information. Google Inc. www.google.com/support/webmasters/bin/answer.py?answer=146646. Accessed 10 November 2010

171. Google (2010) Social Graph API. Google Code Labs. http://code.google.com/intl/hu/apis/socialgraph/. Accessed 11 November 2010

172. Yahoo! Developer Network (2008) Monkey Finds Microformats and RDF. Yahoo! Inc. http://developer.yahoo.com/blogs/ydn/posts/2008/12/monkey_finds_microformats_and_rdf/. Accessed 13 November 2010

173. Anderson E, DeBolt V, Featherstone D, Gunther L, Jacobs DR, Jensen-Inman L, Mills C, Schmitt C, Sims G, Walter A (2010) Web writing that works (or doesn't). In: InterACT With Web Standards – A Holistic Approach to Web Design. New Riders, Berkeley

CHAPTER 8

Web Syndication

The amount of up-to-date information shared on the Internet is constantly growing. Web syndication provides news feed channels in order to publish a summary of recently updated web site contents, latest news, or forum posts. These web feeds make it possible for users to stay informed without browsing web sites. Moreover, the same feed can also be shared among multiple web sites. Although the two popular web syndication formats, RSS and Atom, have relatively easy vocabularies, news feed channels are desired to conform to strict standards, first of all XML.

In this chapter, you will learn how to create standard-compliant news feed channels by hand and update them frequently while maintaining standard compliance. You will be familiarized with the pros and cons of the two major rivals, RSS and Atom. Moreover, you will learn about the data formats used for news feed elements, along with the default and legal property values. You will also become familiar with the required channel and item elements, as well as the ones that should be provided to maximize interoperability.

News Feeds

Web syndication makes web site components available to multiple sites without logging in or downloading irrelevant components of other sites. The phrase often refers to *web news feeds* (*news channels*) that provide an up-to-date summary of recently added contents and the latest changes of web sites. Most commonly news feeds are used for the latest news, news headlines, blog entries, and forum posts.

The first technologies for web syndication appeared in 1997, including the *Channel Definition Format* [1], *Meta Content Framework* [2], and *scriptingNews* [3]. The first version of *Really Simple Syndication* (*RSS*), which later became the most widely used web feed format, was published by Netscape in 1999 [4]. The first part of the specification of *Atom*, the other popular news feed, was introduced in 2005.

Since feed readers and aggregators run on a variety of software platforms and devices including, but not limited to, web browsers, Windows news feed reader gadget, Microsoft Outlook, and news feed readers on smartphones, interoperability is vital.

Really Simple Syndication

Really Simple Syndication (RSS) is the most widely used web syndication format. Since RSS is an XML application, it can be extended through XML namespaces. Beyond its conventional use of representing news and press releases, RSS also has special applications such as providing up-to-date exchange rates for banks [5].

The typical file extensions for RSS are `.rss` and `.xml`. The Internet media type associated with RSS is `application/rss+xml`, which is not standardized yet [6].

RSS describes lightweight syndication channels with the properties `title`, `link`, `description`, `channel`, and `item`.

RSS has the following versions: RSS 0.90, RSS 0.91, RSS 0.92, and RSS 2.0. In 2000, the name RDF Site Summary was in use, which referred to the extensibility with RDF-based modularization [7]. Version 0.91 was called Rich Site Summary, which dropped the RDF structure and imported elements from the scriptingNews syndication format developed by Dave Winer for his news site "Scripting News." The current acronym is Really Simple Syndication. The latest version of the RSS Specification has a permanent URI at the RSS Advisory Board web site [8].The most widely used and most advanced version, RSS 2.0.11 [9], is discussed in the next sections.

Creating an RSS File

To create an RSS file, you first need an XML declaration and an `rss` element. The `rss` element is the root element of RSS files and is the container of a `channel` element, which provides information about the file and contains `item` elements (news feed entries). Listing 8-1 shows the general structure of an RSS file. The `version` attribute on the `rss` element is required, and its value must be `2.0` for RSS 2.0.11 (without indicating the subversion).

Listing 8-1. General Structure of an RSS File with Maximized Interoperability

```
<?xml version="1.0" encoding="utf-8" ?>
<rss version="2.0" ↵
 xmlns:content="http://purl.org/rss/1.0/modules/content/" ↵
 xmlns:dc="http://purl.org/dc/elements/1.1/" ↵
 xmlns:sy="http://purl.org/rss/1.0/modules/syndication/" ↵
 xmlns:atom="http://www.w3.org/2005/Atom">
   <channel>
   <title>An RSS news feed example</title>
   <link>http://www.example.com</link>
   <pubDate>Mon, 08 Aug 2011 08:03:00 +0200</pubDate>
   <image>
     <url>http://www.example.com/images/logo.png</url>
     <title>An RSS news feed example</title>
     <link>http://www.example.com</link>
   </image>
   <dc:creator>John Smith</dc:creator>
   <description>The news feed of rock star John Smith. Concerts, CDs, and more.</description>
   <language>en</language>
   <sy:updatePeriod>daily</sy:updatePeriod>
   <sy:updateFrequency>1</sy:updateFrequency>
   <atom:link href="http://www.example.com/rss.xml" rel="self" type="application/rss+xml" />
   <item>
     <title>News item 2</title>
     <link>http://www.news2link.com</link>
     <pubDate>Mon, 08 Aug 2011 08:03:00 +0200</pubDate>
     <dc:creator>John Smith</dc:creator>
     <category>CDs</category>
     <guid>http://www.news2link.com</guid>
     <description>Description of news item 2</description>
     <content:encoded>The full content of News #2.</content:encoded>
   </item>
```

```
  <item>
    <title>News item 1</title>
    <link>http://www.news1link.com</link>
    <pubDate>Sun, 07 Aug 2011 08:48:00 +0200</pubDate>
    <dc:creator>John Smith</dc:creator>
    <category>Concerts</category>
    <guid>http://www.news1link.com</guid>
    <description>A bit more about news 1</description>
    <content:encoded><![CDATA[ The full content of News #1. In CDATA sections, ↩
      <a href="http://examp.com">markup code</a> can also be included. ]]></content:encoded>
  </item>
  </channel>
</rss>
```

Naturally, RSS files generally contain many more item elements.

■ **Tip** Theoretically, an RSS channel can contain an arbitrary number of items. However, some RSS readers (such as the news feed reader gadget in Windows) do not support RSS files larger than approximately 150KB or 2,800 lines, which corresponds to approximately 7 months if you update your RSS file daily. It is recommended that you keep the file size under this limit to maximize interoperability.

Some of the presented elements are required, while others are optional but highly recommended. First we'll examine the required elements.

Required Elements

As shown in the previous section, the rss element contains the channel element with all its contents. The required elements of the channel element in RSS 2.0 are title, link, and description.

The title Element

The title element represents the name of the channel. It often coincides with the title of the web site it is associated with. Listing 8-2 shows an example.

Listing 8-2. The Title of an RSS Channel

```
<title>John Smith Headlines</title>
```

The link Element

The link element is a URI representing the domain where the news feed is located. Listing 8-3 shows an example.

Listing 8-3. A Link in RSS

```
<link>http://example.com/</link>
```

The description Element

The description element contains a sentence or sentence fragment that describes the channel, as demonstrated in Listing 8-4.

Listing 8-4. A Channel Description in RSS

```
<description>The latest news about rock star John Smith.</description>
```

Optional Elements

In RSS 2.0 news feeds, the channel element has 16 optional subelements, including category, cloud, copyright, docs, generator, image, language, lastBuildDate, managingEditor, pubDate, rating, skipDays, skipHours, textInput, ttl, and webMaster. We'll look at all of these subelements in more detail here.

A common feature of all RSS 2.0 elements providing a URL is that they should begin with a URI scheme defined by IANA [10], for example, http://, https://, news://, mailto://, or ftp://. Note that the http:// and ftp:// schemes cannot be used in RSS versions before RSS 2.0.

The category Element

One or more categories can be specified for RSS channels, which can be used for classification and filtering. For example, an RSS news feed of a web site dedicated to Semantic Web events might contain categories such as conferences, workshops, specifications, and so on. Another example might be a bookseller who uses categories to indicate the category of the latest book releases so that potential customers can easily track the latest books of a certain category (for example, the ones who are interested in Romans are not necessarily involved in technical books). The category element can be used for not only the entire channel but also for each item separately. Listing 8-5 shows an example.

Listing 8-5. A category Element in RSS

```
<category>Workshops</category>
```

The element has an optional domain attribute that is a URI identifying a taxonomy (Listing 8-6).

Listing 8-6. Category with Domain

```
<category domain="http://www.example.com/vocab">WS</category>
```

The value of the category element declared for the channel can be used by portals for classifying RSS news feed channels, while the values of category elements specified for item elements are displayed by certain news feed readers as hyperlinks, which can be used as filters (for example, in feed readers implemented in modern browsers). By clicking one of these links, the feed reader hides news entries from all other categories.

The cloud Element

To be immediately notified of updates of an RSS channel, a publish-subscribe protocol can be written for RSS feeds with the cloud element. It specifies a web service that supports the rssCloud interface (which can be implemented in HTTP-POST, XML-RPC, or SOAP 1.1). Two request methods are supported: a client-to-cloud call to request notification and a cloud-to-client call to perform notification. A client request has five required parameters, including the name of the remote procedure to be called by the cloud when an update occurred, the TCP port of the client, the remote procedure call path of the client, the string xml-rpc (in case the client uses XML-RPC) or soap (in case SOAP is used), and the URLs of RSS files. It is a prerequisite for the IP address used for the request for notification to coincide with the IP address that will receive notifications. Listing 8-7 shows an example.

Listing 8-7. Using the cloud Element in RSS

```
<cloud domain="rpc.example.com" port="80" path="/RPC2" registerProcedure="pingMe" ↵
 protocol="soap"/>
```

The update notification sent by the cloud to the client contains one parameter: the URL of the RSS file that changed. As a response, the client must return the Boolean value TRUE.

The copyright Element

Copyright notice of RSS channels can be provided by the copyright element. Listing 8-8 shows an example.

Listing 8-8. Providing Copyright Information in RSS

```
<copyright>Copyright © 2011 John Smith. All rights reserved.</copyright>
```

The docs Element

A hyperlink to the documentation of the RSS format being used can be provided by the docs element. The typical element value is http://www.rssboard.org/rss-specification.

The generator Element

RSS feeds generated by software tools can easily be recognized from the value of the generator element, where the generator software usually identifies itself (Listing 8-9).

Listing 8-9. An RSS News Feed Generated by Movable Type

```
<generator>Movable Type 4.34-en</generator>
```

If the element is omitted or contains a simple text editor, it usually shows that the feed is written by a hand-coder at the source level (as we do in this chapter). In such cases, the author provides a text editor such as Notepad++ and typically identifies himself or herself as the creator using the Dublin Core vocabulary. However, most people apply feed generators.

The image Element

An optional subelement of the channel element is image, which can be used to provide an image for the RSS feed. It has three required and three optional subelements:

- The URL of the image representing the channel is expressed by the url subelement. The image format can be GIF, JPEG, or PNG. Required.

- The alternate text of the image is defined by title. When the RSS is embedded into (X)HTML, this string is forwarded as the text for the alt attribute. The value of the title subelement should coincide with the value of the title element of the channel. Required.

- The image hyperlink to the site of the channel is determined by the link subelement. The value of the link subelement should coincide with the value of the link element of the channel. Required.

- The image width can be determined in pixels by the width subelement. The default value is 88, and the maximum is 144. Optional.

- The image height can be determined in pixels by the width subelement. The default value is 31, and the maximum is 400. Optional.

- The description of the image to be included in the title attribute of the hyperlink of the image in (X)HTML can be provided by the description subelement. Optional.

Listing 8-10 shows an example.

Listing 8-10. A Logo Image Specified for an RSS File

```
<image>
  <url>http://www. bigprofitconsulting.com/images/logo.png</url>
  <title>Big Profit Consulting</title>
  <link>http://www.bigprofitconsulting.com</link>
</image>
```

▨ **Note** The image declared for an RSS file is displayed in RSS readers such as the ones implemented in browsers but not used by feed readers such as the feed reader in Outlook or the Windows feed reader gadget.

The language Element

The natural language of the news feed content can be declared by the language element. For example:

```
<language>en</language>
```

Table 8-1 summarizes the allowed values.

Table 8-1. RSS-Specific Language Codes

Language	Language Code
Afrikaans	af
Albanian	sq
Basque	eu
Belarusian	be
Bulgarian	bg
Catalan	ca
Chinese (Simplified)	zh-cn
Chinese (Traditional)	zh-tw
Croatian	hr
Czech	cs
Danish	da
Dutch	nl
Dutch (Belgium)	nl-be
Dutch (Netherlands)	nl-nl
English	en
English (Australia)	en-au
English (Belize)	en-bz
English (Canada)	en-ca
English (Ireland)	en-ie
English (Jamaica)	en-jm
English (New Zealand)	en-nz

Language	Language Code
English (Philippines)	en-ph
English (South Africa)	en-za
English (Trinidad)	en-tt
English (UK)	en-gb
English (USA)	en-us
English (Zimbabwe)	en-zw
Estonian	et
Faeroese	fo
Finnish	fi
French	fr
French (Belgium)	fr-be
French (Canada)	fr-ca
French (France)	fr-fr
French (Luxembourg)	fr-lu
French (Monaco)	fr-mc
French (Switzerland)	fr-ch
Galician	gl
Gaelic	gd
German	de
German (Austria)	de-at
German (Germany)	de-de
German (Liechtenstein)	de-li

Language	Language Code
German (Luxembourg)	de-lu
German (Switzerland)	de-ch
Greek	el
Hawaiian	haw
Hungarian	hu
Icelandic	is
Indonesian	in
Irish	ga
Italian	it
Italian (Italy)	it-it
Italian (Switzerland)	it-ch
Japanese	ja
Korean	ko
Macedonian	mk
Norwegian	no
Polish	pl
Portuguese	pt
Portuguese (Brazil)	pt-br
Portuguese (Portugal)	pt-pt
Romanian	ro
Romanian (Moldova)	ro-mo
Romanian (Romania)	ro-ro

Language	Language Code
Russian	ru
Russian (Moldova)	ru-mo
Russian (Russia)	ru-ru
Serbian	sr
Slovak	sk
Slovenian	sl
Spanish	es
Spanish (Argentina)	es-ar
Spanish (Bolivia)	es-bo
Spanish (Chile)	es-cl
Spanish (Colombia)	es-co
Spanish (Costa Rica)	es-cr
Spanish (Dominican Republic)	es-do
Spanish (Ecuador)	es-ec
Spanish (El Salvador)	es-sv
Spanish (Guatemala)	es-gt
Spanish (Honduras)	es-hn
Spanish (Mexico)	es-mx
Spanish (Nicaragua)	es-ni
Spanish (Panama)	es-pa
Spanish (Paraguay)	es-py
Spanish (Peru)	es-pe

Language	Language Code
Spanish (Puerto Rico)	`es-pr`
Spanish (Spain)	`es-es`
Spanish (Uruguay)	`es-uy`
Spanish (Venezuela)	`es-ve`
Swedish	`sv`
Swedish (Finland)	`sv-fi`
Swedish (Sweden)	`sv-se`
Turkish	`tr`
Ukrainian	`uk`

All RSS versions support these language codes except the original Netscape version (0.91), which does not contain the codes et (Estonian) and haw (Hawaiian). The language codes allowed in HTML language tags, defined in the HTML 4.01 specification [11], can also be used. W3C refers to RFC 1766 [12]. Two-letter primary codes are reserved for ISO 639 [13] language abbreviations, including fr (French), de (German), it (Italian), nl (Dutch), el (Greek), es (Spanish), pt (Portuguese), ar (Arabic), he (Hebrew), ru (Russian), zh (Chinese), ja (Japanese), hi (Hindi), ur (Urdu), and sa (Sanskrit). Two-letter subcodes are ISO 3166 country codes [14].

The managingEditor Element

The `managingEditor` element can be used to provide the e-mail address of the news feed editor. Listing 8-11 shows an example.

Listing 8-11. Declaring the RSS Editor

```
<managingEditor>john@example.com (John Smith)</managingEditor>
```

The pubDate and lastBuildDate Elements

The publication date of the channel content can be provided by the `pubDate` element. The element value changes every time the news feed is updated. RSS applies the date and time specification RFC 822 [15] except that the year can be expressed either in two or four characters (the latter one is preferred). Offsets should be provided according to the difference from Greenwich mean time (GMT)/Coordinated Universal Time (UTC). For example, an RSS channel updated on 24 November, 2010, at 08:04 a.m. in London, England (in other words, in the GMT time zone), can state the publication date shown in Listing

8-12, while another news feed published in Suva, Fiji (time zone 1200 GMT or UTC+12), at the same time can be written as shown in Listing 8-13.

Listing 8-12. A Publication Date in the GMT Time Zone

```
<pubDate>Wed, 24 Nov 2010 08:04:00 GMT</pubDate>
```

Listing 8-13. A Publication Date in the UTC+12 Time Zone

```
<pubDate>Wed, 24 Nov 2010 08:04:00 +1200</pubDate>
```

■ **Caution** In countries where jurisdiction observes daylight saving time (summer time), the offset changes twice a year.

The date of the last modification of the news feed can be expressed by the lastBuildDate element in the same format as pubDate.

The skipHours and skipDays Elements

Periods without updates can be provided by the skipHours element and days by the skipDays element. Allowed values for skipHours are the integer numbers between 0 and 23 (the time in GMT) (Listing 8-14).

Listing 8-14. An RSS Channel That Should Be Checked for Updates During Business Hours Only

```
<skipHours>
  <hour>0</hour>
  <hour>1</hour>
  <hour>2</hour>
  <hour>3</hour>
  <hour>4</hour>
  <hour>5</hour>
  <hour>6</hour>
  <hour>7</hour>
  <hour>17</hour>
  <hour>18</hour>
  <hour>19</hour>
  <hour>20</hour>
  <hour>21</hour>
  <hour>22</hour>
  <hour>23</hour>
</skipHours>
```

The skipDays element has seven day subelements (the days of the week in full). They can be used to specify those days when the news feed channel is not updated and thus unnecessary to check for updates (Listing 8-15).

Listing 8-15. An RSS Feed That Is Not Updated on Weekends

```
<skipDays>
  <day>Saturday</day>
  <day>Sunday</day>
</skipDays>
```

■ **Note** The declared hours or days are hints only. RSS feed readers *may not* read the channel during the listed periods.

The textInput Element

Another optional subelement of the channel element is textInput, which can be used to specify a search box. It has four required subelements:

- The label of the Submit button is determined by the title subelement.

- The text input area can be described by the description subelement.

- The name subelement identifies the text object.

- The link subelement provides the URL of the CGI script used for processing requests.

The textInput element is ignored by many RSS readers.

The ttl Element

The duration of caching before refreshing from the source can be expressed in minutes with the ttl element (which stands for "time to live"). In the case of three hours, for example, it can be written as Listing 8-16.

Listing 8-16. 180-Minute Caching in RSS

```
<ttl>180</ttl>
```

The webmaster Element

The e-mail address of the webmaster responsible for the technical issues of the RSS channel can be expressed with the webMaster element.

Subelements of the item Element

The item element has ten subelements: author, category, comments, description, enclosure, guid, link, pubDate, source, and title. All subelements are optional; however, at least a title or a description should be provided for each **item** element.

The author Subelement

The e-mail address of the author of the news feed item can be provided by the author subelement. Listing 8-17 shows an example.

Listing 8-17. The RSS Author

```
<author>info@example.com (John Smith)</author>
```

The category and pubDate Subelements

The syntax of the category and pubDate subelements of the item element is the same as that of the corresponding subelements of the channel element (see the sections "0" and "0").

The comments Subelement

If there is a forum or blog that is related to a news entry (item element), a link to that page can be provided by the comments subelement of the item element. Listing 8-18 shows an example.

Listing 8-18. Comments of an RSS Item

```
<comments>http://example.com/blog/14352</comments>
```

The description Subelement

The texts of items (news summaries) are delimited by the description subelement, as shown in Listing 8-19.

Listing 8-19. An RSS Item Description

```
<description>
  Reports from workshop sessions
</description>
```

The enclosure Subelement

The enclosure subelement of the item element can be used to describe files (usually audio or video) related to the news feed item. It has three required attributes: url (URL of the file), length (file size in bytes), and type (media type), as demonstrated in Listing 8-20.

Listing 8-20. An Enclosure

```
<enclosure url="http://example.com/download/words.mp3" length="4875577" type="audio/mpeg"/>
```

The guid Subelement

Each RSS item might have a string that uniquely identifies it, called the *globally unique identifier*. The guid subelement has no specific syntax rules, but its content is usually a URL (Listing 8-21).

Listing 8-21. A guid Specifying a Permalink Related to the News Entry

```
<item>
  <title>New HTML5 and CSS3 tutorials</title>
  <link>http://www.lesliesikos.com/tutorials/</link>
  <pubDate>Mon, 06 Feb 2012 14:22:00 +0930</pubDate>
  <dc:creator>Dr. Leslie Sikos</dc:creator>
  <category>Website</category>
  <guid isPermaLink="true">http://www.lesliesikos.com/tutorials/</guid>
  <description>Tutorials on HTML5 video embedding and CSS3 transitions</description>
  <content:encoded>Several tutorials have recently been published on emerging ↩
    technologies such as HTML5 video embedding and CSS3 transitions.</content:encoded>
</item>
```

The guid subelement has an optional attribute, isPermaLink, that can be set to true or false. In the first case (which is the default), the attribute value must be a URL that points to the full article or story described by the item element). The false value is rarely used. In fact, the whole isPermaLink attribute is often omitted.

░ **Caution** The guid subelements, if provided, should be unique throughout the RSS file. This criterion might be difficult to meet if the frequent updates of the same web site are described multiple times in the file.

The value of a guid subelement is considered a string by RSS readers.

░ **Tip** Although the guid subelement is optional, it is recommended to provide it for all item elements in order to maximize interoperability.

The link Subelement

The URL of an item can be provided by the link subelement. Listing 8-22 shows an example.

Listing 8-22. A Link Declared for an RSS Item

```
<link>http://example.com/news</link>
```

The source Subelement

If the item content comes from an external RSS channel, it can be provided by the source subelement. The value is the title of the resource channel. The source element has one required attribute, url, which is the URL of the resource (Listing 8-23).

Listing 8-23. *The Source of an RSS Item*

```
<source url="http://www.example.com/news.xml">John Smith Headlines</source>
```

The title Subelement

The titles of RSS channel items can be declared by the title subelement of the item element. Listing 8-24 shows an example.

Listing 8-24. *The Title of an RSS Item*

```
<title>A new W3C standard</title>
```

Namespaces

The default namespace for RSS is http://purl.org/rss/1.0/, which is the *permanent URL* form of the RDF Site Summary (RSS) 1.0 namespace, http://web.resource.org/rss/1.0/. The namespace can be provided in the form presented in Listing 8-25.

Listing 8-25. *Declaring the RSS Namespace*

```
<rss version="2.0" xmlns:rss="http://purl.org/rss/1.0/">
```

Additional data on channel updates can be provided by the *web syndication namespace of RSS* (http://purl.org/rss/1.0/modules/syndication/). It extends the RSS channels with three elements:

- The period over which the news channel is updated can be described by the sy:updatePeriod element. Allowed values are hourly, daily, weekly, monthly, and yearly. If omitted, daily is assumed.

- The frequency of updates can be expressed in relation to the update period with the sy:updateFrequency element. Its value is a positive integer.

- To calculate the publishing schedule, a base date can be defined by the sy:updateBase element. It should be a #PCDATA date in one of the W3C date and time formats [16].

By default, news feed entries are plain-text contents. However, news aggregators often support (X)HTML markup that are not allowed in XML. Entity-encoded and CDATA-escaped contents can be provided with the content:encoded element defined by the http://purl.org/rss/1.0/modules/content/ namespace. The content:encoded element is especially useful if the hyperlink delimited by the link element is not enough and additional hyperlinks are needed (in the news item content). Although text formatting and other markup codes can also be written this way, they are ignored by many RSS readers.

There is an element, `atom:link`, that can be used from another syndication format (Atom[1]) to provide the self-link of the news feed channel. To apply this element, the Atom namespace `http://www.w3.org/2005/Atom` should be declared.

Advanced news feeds typically contain at least the namespace declarations presented in Listing 8-26.

Listing 8-26. Typical Namespace Declarations in RSS

```
<rss version="2.0" ↵
  xmlns:content="http://purl.org/rss/1.0/modules/content/" ↵
  xmlns:dc="http://purl.org/dc/elements/1.1/" ↵
  xmlns:sy="http://purl.org/rss/1.0/modules/syndication/" ↵
  xmlns:atom="http://www.w3.org/2005/Atom" ↵
>
```

Doing so, elements can be used from these namespaces in the channel as shown in Listing 8-27 or in item elements such as in the example in Listing 8-28.

Listing 8-27. Elements from External Namespaces in an RSS Channel

```
<dc:creator>Dr. Leslie Sikos</dc:creator>
<sy:updatePeriod>daily</sy:updatePeriod>
<sy:updateFrequency>1</sy:updateFrequency>
<sy:updateBase>2011-01-01T12:00+00:00</sy:updateBase>
<atom:link href="http://www.lesliesikos.com/sikos.xml" rel="self" ↵
 type="application/rss+xml" />
```

Listing 8-28. An Element from an External Namespace in an RSS Item

```
<content:encoded><![CDATA[ An escaped RSS item can contain markup elements such as ↵
 <a href="http://www.example.com/">hyperlinks</a> that work in all major news feed ↵
 readers. ]]></content:encoded>
```

Styling RSS Feeds

The browsers that support news feeds usually provide a basic styling or no styling at all (rendering a tree structure instead). Developers who are not satisfied with that or want to ensure an advanced look (which is also similar in all browsers) can format RSS channels using CSS or XSLT.

In the first case, a CSS reference is required in the form presented in Listing 8-29.

Listing 8-29. Using a CSS File for Styling RSS

```
<?xml version="1.0" encoding="utf-8" ?>
<?xml-stylesheet type="text/css" href="css/feed.css" ?>
<rss version="2.0">
```

Writing the CSS rules is straightforward. For example, the font size of the main title can be increased by the CSS rule presented in Listing 8-30.

---

[1] The Atom format will be described later in the chapter.

Listing 8-30. Setting the Font Size for the RSS Channel and Title

```
channel title {
  font-size: 1.4em;
}
```

The font of the document can be set as shown in Listing 8-31.

Listing 8-31. A CSS Rule for the Entire RSS Document

```
rss {
  font-family: Verdana, Helvetica, sans-serif;
}
```

Similarly, further styles can be set for other RSS elements. Much information is not necessarily relevant and can be omitted, as for example in Listing 8-32.

Listing 8-32. Hiding RSS Elements with CSS

```
channel link, channel language, channel copyright, channel managingEditor, ↵
 channel webMaster, channel docs, channel lastBuildDate {
  display: none;
}
```

The second approach applies XSL Transformation, which provides more control. For example, hyperlinks can be activated, and node order can be changed. The XSL file can be linked as shown in Listing 8-33.

Listing 8-33. Using XSLT for Styling RSS

```
<?xml version="1.0" encoding="utf-8" ?>
<?xml-stylesheet type="text/xsl" href="css/feed.xsl" ?>
<rss version="2.0">
```

■ **Note** Additional functionality such as searching or category listings provided by the built-in RSS reader of certain browsers are not available when custom style sheet are applied to a news feed.

Atom

The Atom news feed specification consists of two standards: the *Atom Syndication Format* and the *Atom Publishing Protocol* (AtomPub or APP). The first one is a web feed format in XML syntax defined by an IETF proposed standard (RFC 4287 [17]). The second one is an HTTP-based protocol that can be used for creating and updating web resources. It is also a proposed standard (RFC 5023 [18]). This section focuses on the Atom Syndication Format.

The file extensions of Atom feeds are .atom and .xml. The Internet media type of Atom is application/atom+xml.

The Atom namespace is http://www.w3.org/2005/Atom.

Creating an Atom File

Atom files begin with an XML declaration. The root element of Atom files and the container of news feed entries (entry elements) is the feed element. Listing 8-34 shows the general structure of an Atom file.

Listing 8-34. General Structure of an Atom File

```
<?xml version="1.0" encoding="utf-8"?>
<feed xmlns="http://www.w3.org/2005/Atom">
  <title>An Atom news feed example</title>
  <link rel="alternate" type="text/html" href="http://www.example.com/" />
  <link rel="self" type="application/atom+xml" href="http://www.example.com/News/atom.xml" />
  <id>tag:www.example.com,2008-09-29://4</id>
  <updated>2011-08-08T08:03:00Z</updated>
  <entry>
    <title>News item 2</title>
    <link rel="alternate" type="text/html" href="http://www.expl.com/2011.html#entry-9167" />
    <id>tag:www.expl.com,2011://4.9167</id>
    <published>2011-08-08T08:03:00Z</published>
    <updated>2011-08-08T08:03:00Z</updated>
    <summary>Summary of news entry 2</summary>
    <author>
      <name>John Smith</name>
    </author>
    <category term="Home Page Stories" />
    <category term="Web of Services" />
    <content type="html" xml:lang="en" xml:base="http://www.example.com/">The full content ↵
    of News #2.</content>
  </entry>
  <entry>
    <title>News item 1</title>
    <link rel="alternate" type="text/html" href="http://www.example.com/news/#entry-9165" />
    <id>tag:www.example.com,2011://4.9165</id>
    <published>2011-08-07T08:48:00Z</published>
    <updated>2011-08-07T08:48:00Z</updated>
    <summary>Summary of news entry 1</summary>
    <author>
      <name>John Smith</name>
    </author>
    <category term="Publication" />
    <category term="Web design" />
    <category term="Press releases" />
    <content type="html" xml:lang="en" xml:base="http://www.example.com/">
      <![CDATA[ The full content of News #1. In CDATA sections, ↵
      <a href="http://example.com/markup/">markup code</a> can also be included. ]]>
    </content>
  </entry>
</feed>
```

These elements and attributes are described in the following sections in detail.

Text Constructs

Text constructs of Atom contain language-sensitive, human-readable texts. An optional attribute of text constructs is the `type` attribute. If provided, the attribute must have one of the following values: `text`, `html`, or `xhtml`. If omitted, Atom feed readers consider text constructs as if they were specified with the default value `text`. MIME types cannot be declared as attribute values for the `type` attribute.

Person Constructs

There are three person constructs in Atom that describe an entity such as a person or a corporation: `name`, `uri`, and `email`.

Atom news feeds must contain exactly one `name` element that provides the name of the author. The element content is language-sensitive.

The `uri` element is optional, and a maximum one can be provided to link to the web site of the author. The content of the `uri` element is an Internationalized Resource Identifier (IRI) in the form defined by RFC 3987 [19].

The e-mail address of the author can be declared by the optional `email` element of which no more than one can be used in an Atom file. The content of the `email` element should conform to the standard Internet Message Format defined by RFC 2822 [20].

Date Constructs

The contents of date construct elements should be declared according to the date-time format defined in RFC 3339 [21]. Date and time should be separated by an uppercase T, while an uppercase Z should be used when the numeric time zone offset is omitted (Listing 8-35).

Listing 8-35. *Some Valid Timestamps in Atom*

```
<updated>2012-12-13T08:15:01Z</updated>
<updated>2012-12-13T08:15:01.25Z</updated>
<updated>2012-12-13T08:15:01+01:00</updated>
<updated>2012-12-13T08:15:01.25+01:00</updated>
```

All date values of Atom new feeds should comply with the ISO standard on date and time representation (ISO 8601:2004 [22]) and the W3C date and time format [23] specifications, as well as the ISO 8601 Conventions in the W3C Recommendation "XML Schema Part 2: Datatypes Second Edition" [24].

Containers

There are three container elements in Atom:

- The `feed` element, which contains the entire feed

- The `entry` element, which contains a simple news entry

- The `content` element, which contains a full story (the content of a news entry)

The next sections describe these containers in detail.

The feed Element

As mentioned earlier, the top-level element of Atom feeds is feed; it contains the news feed metadata and contents (all other Atom elements). One or more author elements are required for feed elements, except all child entry elements of the feed element contain at least one author element. Exactly one id element must be provided for all feed elements. The feed elements must contain exactly one updated element. Exactly one title element is required for all feed elements. The feed elements should contain one link element with a rel attribute value set to self.

An arbitrary number of category as well as contributor elements can be included in feed elements. Only one generator is allowed for each feed. The same is for icon and logo elements as well.

The feed elements can contain a maximum of one link element with a rel attribute value set to alternate that has the same type and hreflang attribute values. Beyond such link elements, additional link elements might be included in the feed elements.

Only one rights and subtitle element is allowed for each feed element.

All Atom elements are described in the next sections.

The entry Element

Atom news can be provided by the entry element. It can be a child of the feed element or a stand-alone, top-level element within the feed. The entry elements must have a minimum of one author element except when a source element is provided in the entry that has an author element or the feed element contains an author element. Optionally, entry elements have any number of category elements. The entry elements might have a maximum of one content element. Another optional subelement of the entry element is the contributor. An arbitrary number of contributors can be provided.

The entry elements must have an id element.

The entry elements without content must provide a minimum of one link element with the rel attribute and the alternate attribute value.

The entry elements cannot contain more than one link element with the rel attribute and the alternate attribute value with exactly the same type and hreflang attribute values. Optionally, additional link elements can also be provided for the entry elements.

The entry elements can contain a maximum of one published, rights, source, and summary element.

The summary subelement should be provided for entry elements if the entry contains a content element with the src attribute or the entry content is Base64 encoded.[2]

The entry elements must contain exactly one title and one updated element.

The content Element

The Atom news content can be provided by the content element. The content of this element is language-sensitive. The content element has two attributes: type and src.

The value of the type attribute on the content element might be text, html, or xhtml. If it is omitted, text is considered the default value by Atom readers. Another option is to provide a MIME media type (but not a composite type).

The content element has an optional src attribute. The value of this attribute should be an Internationalized Resource Identifier that conforms to RFC 3987. If the src attribute is provided, the

---

[2] Although the type attribute of the atom:content element is an Internet media type, it neither is an XML media type nor begins with text/ or ends in /xml or +xml.

content must be empty. The type attribute should also be provided with a MIME type along with the src attribute.

Metadata and Content Elements

Similar to RSS, there are several elements in Atom to express metadata and describe the contents of news entries, such as author, category, contributor, generator, icon, id, link, logo, published, rights, source, subtitle, summary, title, and updated. Those elements whose specification assigns meaning to the content and the ones with special restrictions are described in the following sections.

The author Element

The author in Atom feeds can be provided in three levels. If the author element is not provided as a subelement of an entry element, the author is derived from the author subelement of the source element. Otherwise, the author declared by the author of the feed element is considered (Listing 8-36).

Listing 8-36. Declaring the Author of an Atom Feed

```
<author>
    <name>John Smith</name>
</author>
```

The category Element

The category element has three attributes: the required term and the optional scheme and label (Listing 8-37).

Listing 8-37. A Category Declaration in Atom

```
<category term="Publication" />
```

The value of the label attribute is language-sensitive. Character entities used in the attribute values are considered characters instead of markup.

The contributor Element

The person or company that contributed to an entry or the whole feed can be indicated by the contributor element (Listing 8-38).

Listing 8-38. A Feed Contributor

```
<contributor>
  <name>Alex Sikos</name>
</contributor>
```

The generator Element

If a software tool is used to generate the Atom news feed, it can be identified by the generator element. The generator element has two optional attributes. The value of the uri attribute should be an Internationalized Resource Identifier according to RFC 3987. The other optional attribute is version that represents the version of the Atom generator (Listing 8-39).

Listing 8-39. An Atom Generator Identified in the Feed

```
<generator uri= "http://www.sixapart.com/movabletype/" ver="4.34-en">Movable Type</generator>
```

The icon Element

Similar to the contents of the uri element and that of the uri attribute of the generator element, the content of the icon element should also be an IRI reference that conforms to RFC 3987. This element specifies an image file for the Atom news feed. Image resolution should be provided (Listing 8-40).

Listing 8-40. An Icon for the Atom Feed

```
<icon>http://example.com/images/ icon.gif</icon>
```

The id Element

The id element is a permanent identifier provided in lowercase (Listing 8-41). It is used as a subelement of both the feed element and the entry elements.

Listing 8-41. An Atom Identifier

```
<id>tag:example.org,2003:3</id>
```

Percent-encoding, the mechanism that encodes certain characters of a URI using a string that begins with a percent sign (%),[3] should be eliminated whenever possible.[4] Dots should be avoided in URIs. The Internationalized Resource Identifier should be NFC normalized, or NFKC normalized. Empty fragment identifiers should be preserved. The URIs in id elements are case-sensitive. Identifiers that apply percent-escaping are considered different from the ones that do not when comparing id instances.

The link Element

External hyperlinks related to an Atom entry or the whole feed can be provided by the link element. This element has six attributes: href, rel, type, hreflang, title, and length. The required href attribute contains the Internationalized Resource Identifier of the link. The optional rel attribute must have a nonempty string as a value according to either the *IRI* or the *isegment-nz-nc* syntax rules of RFC 3987. Allowed values are alternate, related, self, enclosure, and via. The type attribute, which is optional,

---

[3] One of the most well-known examples for percent encoding is the %20 string that appears in place of space characters in poorly designed URIs.
[4] If percent encoding is essential and cannot be eliminated, letters should be uppercase characters A–F.

must have a MIME media type as its value. The `hreflang` attribute is also optional. When provided, it must have an RFC 3066 language tag. The optional `title` attribute is language-sensitive. Character entities used in the title are considered characters instead of markup. A hint on the advisory length of the linked content can be provided by the optional `length` attribute in octets. Listing 8-42 shows a typical `link` element.

Listing 8-42. A link Element in Atom

```
<link rel="self" type="application/atom+xml" href="http://example.net/ atom.xml" />
```

The logo Element

An image that visually identifies your Atom news feed can be provided by the `logo` element (Listing 8-43). Its content is an IRI reference (RFC 3987). The aspect ratio of the logo image should be 2:1 (horizontal to vertical).

Listing 8-43. A Logo Image of an Atom Feed

```
<logo>http://example.com/images/ icon.gif</logo>
```

The published Element

The time when the first version of a news entry has been written can be specified by a date construct of the `published` element (Listing 8-44).

Listing 8-44. A published Element

```
<published>2011-09-18T16:35:24Z</published>
```

Such timestamps might coincide with the content of the `updated` element in the entry.

The rights Element

Custom copyright information can be written as a text construct and added to your Atom news feed using the `rights` element (Listing 8-45).

Listing 8-45. Copyright Information in Atom

```
<rights>Copyright © 2012 John Smith. All rights reserved.</rights>
```

The source Element

If an entry is derived from an external Atom news feed, the metadata of the original entry can optionally be used as the subelements of the `source` element. The elements `author`, `contributor`, `rights`, and `category` should be preserved in all cases.

The subtitle Element

Atom feeds can be described by a string provided as the content of a subtitle element, which provides a longer description than the title element (Listing 8-46).

Listing 8-46. The Description of an Atom News Feed

```
<title type="text">Steven Johnson News</title>
<subtitle>
 The news feed of poet Steven Johnson. New booklets, press releases, readings, and more.
</subtitle>
```

The summary Element

A short description can be added to each Atom entry with the summary element (Listing 8-47).

Listing 8-47. A Summary of an Atom Entry

```
<summary>The latest book of S. Johnson, "My Darling", has been released.</summary>
```

RSS or Atom?

Both RSS and Atom are widely supported in all major consumer feed readers. **RSS** seems to be more popular than Atom, though. From the standards points of view, however, the RSS 2.0 specification is copyrighted by Harvard University and is considered finalized. Significant changes cannot be expected, although the specification has been released under the Creative Commons license. In contrast, Atom 1.0 is a more feature-rich syndication format by default and can be extended.

The Internet media type application/rss+xml is unregistered while application/atom+xml is registered by IANA.

In contrast to RSS 2.0, which supports the RSS document format only, the Atom Entry documents of the Atom news feeds can apply any network protocol. As a result, the aggregation and extraction of Atom news feeds have more possibilities.

Although the namespace of RSS 2.0 is not an XML namespace, it can optionally contain elements from external XML namespaces (as discussed earlier). The namespace of Atom 1.0 is an XML namespace itself and might also have elements and attributes from other XML namespaces. The implementation of these external elements and attributes is clearly defined by specification guidelines. It can be concluded that Atom is more extensible than RSS.

RSS does not support relative URIs, while Atom reuses the xml:base attribute, which allows relative references.

There is no schema defined in RSS 2.0. Atom 1.0 applies the RelaxNG schema, which is the non-normative ISO-standard ISO/IEC 19757-2:2008 [25]. It can be used to validate the data provided in the Atom news feed. Optionally, further schemas can be generated from RelaxNG.

Practically, both formats are supported by most news feed readers. Correctly written RSS and Atom files are well-formed XML files that can be processed in many ways and can be extended using the namespace mechanism. Users usually do not notice the difference between the two formats when using a feed reader application.

Summary

This chapter took you through the RSS and Atom new feed formats with all the background information and practices required to not only create standard-compliant feed channels but also maintain them manually without interrupting the XML serialization format, the RSS or Atom format requirements, or the highest level of interoperability.

In the next chapter, you will learn how to secure the layout of your web sites, use advanced typography features on the Web, and optimize image files to maximize user experience. You will also learn standard-compliant, cross-browser video and multimedia embedding techniques.

References

1. Ellerman C (1997) Channel Definition Format (CDF). Microsoft Corporation. www.w3.org/TR/NOTE-CDFsubmit.html. Accessed 23 November 2010

2. Guha RV, Bray T (eds) (1997) Meta Content Framework Using XML. www.w3.org/TR/NOTE-MCF-XML/. Accessed 23 November 2010

3. Winer D (1997) Scripting News in XML. Dave Winer. http://scripting.com/davenet/1997/12/15/scriptingnewsinxml.html. Accessed 23 November 2010

4. RAB (2008) RSS 0.90 Specification. Transferred from original specification of Netscape published in 1999. RSS Advisory Board. www.rssboard.org/rss-0-9-0. Accessed 23 November 2010

5. Asman P, Cannon S, Sommo C (2010) Extending RSS to Meet Central Bank Needs. In: Proceedings of the International Conference on Dublin Core and Metadata Applications. Dublin Core Metadata Initiative, Pittsburgh

6. Cadenhead R, Smith G, Hanna J, Kearney B (2006) The application/rss+xml Media Type. The Internet Society. www.rssboard.org/rss-mime-type-application.txt. Accessed 22 November 2010

7. Beged-Dov G, Brickley D, Dornfest R, Davis I, Dodds L, Eisenzopf J, Galbraith D, Guha RV, MacLeod K, Miller E, Swartz A, van der Vlist E, et al (2008) RDF Site Summary (RSS) 1.0. RSS-DEV Working Group. http://web.resource.org/rss/1.0/spec. Accessed 23 November 2010

8. RAB (2008) The current version of the RSS Specification. RSS Advisory Board. www.rssboard.org/rss-specification. Accessed 23 November 2010

9. RAB (2010) Specification History. RSS Advisory Board. www.rssboard.org/rss-history. Accessed 28 August 2011

10. The Internet Corporation for Assigned Names and Numbers (2010) Permanent URI Schemes. Internet Assigned Numbers Authority. www.iana.org/assignments/uri-schemes.html. Accessed 26 November 2010

11. Raggett D, Le Hors A, Jacobs I (eds) (1999) Language codes. In: HTML 4.01 Specification. World Wide Web Consortium. www.w3.org/TR/REC-html40/struct/dirlang.html#langcodes. Accessed 24 November 2010

12. Alvestrand H (1995) Tags for the Identification of Languages. Internet Engineering Task Force. www.ietf.org/rfc/rfc1766.txt. Accessed 24 November 2010

13. ISO (2002) ISO 639-1:2002. International Organization for Standardization. www.iso.org/iso/iso_catalogue/catalogue_ics/catalogue_detail_ics.htm?csnumber=22109. Accessed 24 November 2010

14. ISO (2006) ISO 3166-1:2006. International Organization for Standardization. www.iso.org/iso/iso_catalogue/catalogue_tc/catalogue_detail.htm?csnumber=39719. Accessed 24 November 2010

15.   Crocker DH (ed) (1982) Standard for the format of ARPA internet text messages. University of Delaware. http://asg.web.cmu.edu/rfc/rfc822.html. Accessed 24 November 2010

16.   Wolf M, Wicksteed C (1997) Date and Time Formats. World Wide Web Consortium. www.w3.org/TR/NOTE-datetime. Accessed 27 November 2010

17.   Nottingham M, Sayre R (eds) (2005) The Atom Syndication Format. Proposed standard. The Internet Society. http://tools.ietf.org/html/rfc4287. Accessed 22 November 2010

18.   Gregorio J, de Hora B (eds) (2007) The Atom Publishing Protocol. Proposed standard. The Internet Society. http://tools.ietf.org/html/rfc5023. Accessed 22 November 2010

19.   Duerst M, Suignard M (2005) Internationalized Resource Identifiers (IRIs). The Internet Engineering Task Force. http://tools.ietf.org/html/rfc3987. Accessed 01 December 2010

20.   Resnick P (ed) (2001) Internet Message Format. The Internet Society. http://tools.ietf.org/html/rfc2822. Accessed 01 December 2010

21.   Klyne G, Newman C (2002) Date and Time on the Internet: Timestamps. The Internet Society. http://tools.ietf.org/html/rfc3339. Accessed 02 December 2010

22.   ISO (2004) Data elements and interchange formats – Information interchange – Representation of dates and times. ISO 8601:2004. International Organization for Standardization. www.iso.org/iso/iso_catalogue/catalogue_tc/catalogue_detail.htm?csnumber=40874. Accessed 02 December 2010

23.   Wolf M, Wicksteed C (1998) Date and Time Formats. World Wide Web Consortium. www.w3.org/TR/NOTE-datetime. Accessed 02 December 2010

24.   Biron PV, Malhotra A (eds) (2004) ISO 8601 Conventions. In: XML Schema Part 2: Datatypes Second Edition. W3C Recommendation. World Wide Web Consortium. www.w3.org/TR/xmlschema-2/#isoformats. Accessed 02 December 2010

25.   ISO (2008) ISO/IEC 19757-2:2008. Information technology – Document Schema Definition Language (DSDL) – Part 2: Regular-grammar-based validation – RELAX NG. International Organization for Standardization. www.iso.org/iso/iso_catalogue/catalogue_tc/catalogue_detail.htm?csnumber=52348. Accessed 07 December 2010

CHAPTER 9

Optimized Appearance

Design has always been an important factor in web site development, partly because appearance is responsible for the first impression. If the design of a web site catches the eye, it is more likely that visitors will become customers or clients. Web typography has recently started to attract attention, especially though proper whitespace handling and the introduction of web fonts. Images that are fundamental parts of web sites should be optimized for web publishing in order to achieve a reasonable quality to file size ratio and minimize download time. Since high-speed Internet connections have become widespread, the need for sharing multimedia content has increased enormously. Until the new elements introduced in HTML5, general objects have been used to embed audio and video content. Although design and multimedia are extremely popular, the basic usability principle should always be kept in mind: functionality over design.

In this chapter, you will learn how to create multiple-column layouts and fixed menus without the now-obsolete approaches, such as the ones that applied tables and frames. This chapter also describes a CSS property, called z-index, that provides full control over the appearance of layers above each other.

Until recently, most web sites used one or more fonts from a small list, resulting in a kind of monotony. There have been many methods for using a greater variety of fonts over the years, but not one was very satisfactory or dependable. You can now improve the appearance of text by declaring that font files be used for rendering textual content, which makes it possible to display web pages with carefully selected fonts in superior quality. However, web sites can contain not only text. You will learn how to optimize images for web publishing and embed multimedia files such as Flash content, audio, and video.

Layout

The layout of web content determines the overall appearance and has a large impact on functionality, usability, accessibility, and design. Web layout should be reliable and browser- and resolution-independent.

Positioning and Floating

Some web page components are placed on the page in relation to a corner of the browser window, such as the top-left corner (the 0, 0 position), while the position of others depends on the position of their parent elements (*containers*). There are various options including relative, absolute, and fixed positioning. Beyond the appropriate positioning, you must be careful to provide browser- and resolution-independent solutions.

On your web site, perhaps certain components should "float" on the web page, and the content should appear next to, rather than above or below, the main text. Typical examples are images, which frequently apply the float property to wrap text around images.

Absolute and Fixed Positions

Depending on the design and site structure, some page components (logo, menu, header, footer, and so on) are intended to be fixed and should not move when the page is being scrolled.

The CSS rule `position: fixed;` is very similar to `position: absolute;`, but the first one prevents element scrolling when the user scrolls the page while the second does not. The `position: fixed;` rule is not supported by Internet Explorer 6 or earlier, which has been a major layout problem in web site development for years. Instead of reverting it to `position: absolute;` to provide a similar effect, `position: fixed;` has been considered as `position: static;`, which results in no positioning at all. Consequently, a layer at the bottom of a web page with `position: fixed;`, which is intended to be a footer that remains intact when the user scrolls the page, appears on the page according to the DOM structure in older browsers, resulting in an unaesthetic or even unusable appearance. The problem does not exist from IE7 and onward or in other browsers.

Tableless Web Layout

Until recently, a significant number of web sites applied presentational markup rather than semantic code. (X)HTML tables have been used for arranging web site elements and ensuring pixel-by-pixel layout. This easy and quick "development" was also encouraged by WYSIWYG development tools. However, it has many drawbacks. Web sites whose layout relies on tables waste bandwidth and take longer to download and render. The document structure is illogical, making semantic data harder or impossible to retrieve. These web sites are not accessible and are difficult to maintain.

Tableless web layout eliminates the use of tables for page layout and web page element positioning [1]. This does not mean that tables are not allowed on web pages, but tables should be used exclusively for tabular data.

The positioning and layout of web page components can be fully controlled by layers that are represented as `div` elements in the markup.

The following sections describe two very common types of layout. Naturally, developers can create other layouts, too, but the point is that arbitrary layouts can be described by `div` elements.

Multiple-Column Layouts

A typical web page arrangement is the *multiple-column layout with floating divisions* [2]. Multiple-column sites usually have a header at the top of each page. The menu is often provided on the left (or right). Additionally, a footer is a frequently used component on the bottom of each page. The usual number of columns is one, two, or three. Figure 9-1 shows a typical three-column layout.

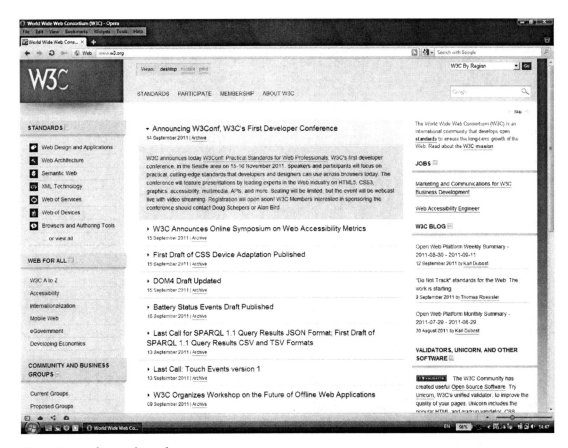

Figure 9-1. A three-column layout

You can see the main menu on the top of the page. Underneath the main menu there is the main content. On the left there are submenus, while on the right there are additional functions, such as a search box and blog entries.

Centralized-Column Layouts

Another typical arrangement applies *a centralized column with a width of approximately 700–900 pixels*—ideally not wider than 800 pixels to guarantee that the main content remains visible on small resolutions back to 800×600 (SVGA).[1] Such sites usually have the header and the main menu on the top.

---

[1] The next standard resolution, 1024×768 (XGA), is larger than many screen resolutions of modern mobile devices with Internet browsing features such as netbooks or small laptops with wide-screen display. Since the typical resolution is constantly growing, the latest models might support 1024×600 (WSVGA), or higher, resolution, which has adequate width for XGA optimization. The resolution of smartphone screens is smaller, and web sites can be optimized for them with alternate style sheets, as discussed earlier in Chapter 5.

Optionally, there might be a secondary or submenu on the left (or right) within the main column. If required, there could be a footer at the bottom.

There are various possibilities to horizontally center page content. A frequently used method applies the attribute value auto to the left and right margins of the container (Figure 9-2). This technique was introduced in the errata of the CSS2 specification [3]. Listing 9-1 shows an example.

Listing 9-1. *Centralizing with Autowidth Margins*

```
#content {
  width: 720px;
  margin: 0px auto;
}
```

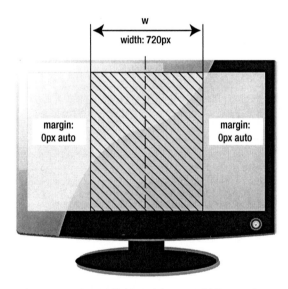

Figure 9-2. *Centralizing with autowidth margins*

This method works on all browsers that support CSS2.

Another method for centralizing the content, introduced by Simon Coggins, is to use offsets and negative margins. After declaring the width of the container element (similar to the previous method), its left edge is horizontally centered within the page by the combination of absolute positioning and a 50 percent left offset. Since the content begins on the second half of the page, the left margin of the layer should be set to the opposite of half the width of the layer. For example, if the width of the layer to be centralized is 780px, the left margin should be set to -390px (Figure 9-3).

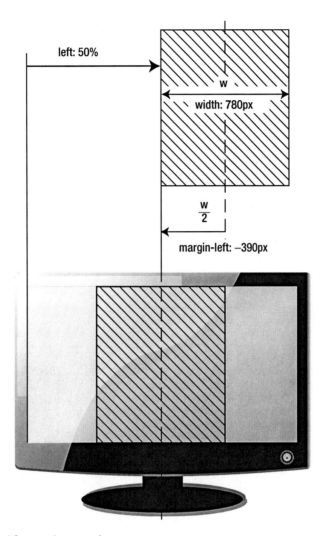

Figure 9-3. Centralizing with negative margins

The corresponding CSS ruleset can be written as shown in Listing 9-2.

Listing 9-2. Centralizing with Negative Margins

```
#main {
  position:absolute;
  width: 780px;
  left: 50%;
  margin-left: -390px;
}
```

Text Around Objects

In many cases, web page text should "wrap around" an object or image. You can achieve this effect by using the float property; in other words, the image (or its container) should float (Listing 9-3).

Listing 9-3. Styles for Containers of Floating Images

```
#onleft {
  float: left;
}

#onright {
  float: right;
}
```

Figure 9-4 shows an image without styling and two floating images that use the previous rules. Without floating, the text does not wrap around the image: only the first line of the text appears next to the image (top photo). The second image applies the first rule of Listing 9-3 and is rendered on the left, surrounded by text on the right. The third image uses the second rule of Listing 9-3 and thus appears on the right, while the text surrounds the image on the left.

My Favourite Animals

I like animals, especially birds. One of my favourite parrot species is the **macaw**. The largest one of all is the Hyacinth Macaw *(Anodorhynchus hyacinthinus)*, also known as the Hyacinthine Macaw, which is mainly blue (top).

However, many macaw species are colourful. Some species are known for their impressive size. These creatures are native to certain parts of Latin America (Central and South America). There are six different parrots in the *Psittacidae* genera classified as macaws: Ara, Anodorhynchus, Cyanopsitta, Primolius, Orthopsittaca, and Diopsittaca.

I really admire the Blue-and-Yellow Macaw *(Ara ararauna)*, also known as the Blue-and-Gold Macaw, which is one of the most beautiful animals in the world (left). The Blue-and-Gold Macaw is native to Paname in Central America, and the tropical South America from Trinidad and Venezuela south to Peru, Brazil, Bolivia, and Paraguay. I also like the Scarlet Macaw *(Ara macao)*, which is one of the most colorful macaws (red-yellow-green-blue, see the picture on the right). The Scarlet Macaw is native to the Central and South American tropics, including south-eastern Mexico, and the rainforests of Peru, Bolivia and Brazil.

Figure 9-4. Floating images

Since the text would be rendered right next to the floating images, you should declare margins to get the final result shown in Listing 9-3. If you intend to display all images of a page on the right side, you can specify the float:right; rule on images without identifiers or classes as img { float:right; }.

If you want to ensure that the next paragraph is displayed below a floating image, you can use the clear property to stop the float on the left (clear: right;), on the right (clear: left;), or on both sides of the image (clear:both;).

Layers Above Each Other

Web site components can also be considered in a virtual space where the component order can be set by a CSS property that represents depth (the third dimension). This property is called z-index. It is frequently used for setting layer order. The larger the value, the higher the elements in the stack order. The element with the largest z-index appears above all other elements of the page. This property works on positioned elements only (elements that have a position rule). For example, the rulesets in Listings 9-4 and 9-5 put the layer with the logo above the main content.

Listing 9-4. The Lower Layer (Compared to Listing 9-5)

```
#main {
  position:absolute;
  width: 780px;
  left: 50%;
  margin-left: -390px;
  z-index: 1;
}
```

Listing 9-5. The Upper Layer (Compared to Listing 9-4)

```
#logo {
  position: absolute;
  width: 146px;
  height: 120px;
  margin-top: 20px;
  margin-left: 20px;
  z-index: 2;
}
```

■ **Caution** Flash content requires an additional parameter that allows the developer to override the default setting that renders Flash content in front of other elements (see the section "Embedding Flash in XHTML").

Typography

Text has always been a fundamental web component. The first web documents contained mainly (if not exclusively) text with black fonts over a white background. In the next few years, the Web gradually transformed to a full multimedia platform. At the same time, more sophisticated whitespace handling and character encoding have appeared.

In contrast to books and other printed media where proper type arrangements and type design have always been ensured by typography, until recently the Web lacked these features.

After the introduction of TFT monitors and the ClearType fonts designed for them, characters have become really clear on the screen. With the increasing popularity of web fonts, an endless variety of fonts appeared on the Web.

You must be careful to provide not only eye-catching fonts and type but also legible text. The technique required to achieve that aim is known as *web typography*, which should also guarantee the proper appearance of characters and whitespace.

Misused Characters

According to the World Wide Web Consortium, you should be careful to apply the proper punctuation marks on the Web instead of their misused equivalents (Table 9-1) [4]. Which punctuation marks are typographically correct depends on the natural language of the web page. For example, in British English, single quotes are often preferred to double quotes, and commas generally park outside rather than inside the closing mark. In other languages, the quotation marks might be inverted. Similar differences exist in the use of en and em dashes.

Table 9-1. Frequently Applied Punctuation Marks and Their Misused Equivalents

Character	Name	Entity/Entities	Misused Equivalent(s)
"	Opening quote	&#8220;	"
"	Closing quote	&#8221;	"
'	Apostrophe	&#8217;	'
–	En dash (ranges)	– or –	-
—	Em dash (change of thought)	— or —	- or --
…	Horizontal ellipsis (an omission or a pause)	… or …	...

The opening and closing quotation marks appear identical in certain typefaces, known as the straight, vertical, or typewriter quotation marks, which should not be used in the text flow. On the other hand, these characters are used in the markup as the delimiters of attribute values.

■ **Tip** Many text editors do not support typographic (curly) quotation marks and insert their misused equivalents. One of the options for getting the proper quotation marks is to insert them in a word processor (usually by pressing Shift+2) and then copy the characters to the source code through the clipboard.

Even if the proper quotation marks are used in the markup, browsers might render them incorrectly. Although it is a straightforward idea to apply the q tag for short quotations,[2] browsers render it differently. Firefox 3.6.6 renders both the opening and the closing quotes correctly. However, IE8 incorrectly applies the character „ for opening the quote (the closing is correct). In Safari 5 and Opera 10.6, the misused equivalent " is used for rendering. However, rendering quotes also depends on the language being used and relies on proper language settings in the markup.

Web Fonts

Originally, the Web was developed as a text-based medium. Initially, the selection of fonts available to web designers was limited to the intersection of fonts natively installed on all major platforms. In 1998,

---

[2] If the quotation spans multiple lines, the blockquote tag should be used instead.

the CSS2 specification introduced a font matching and downloading mechanism (which has been dropped in CSS 2.1). In CSS3, external fonts can be applied, along with the declaration of multiple (similar) fonts as a fallback option if the specific fonts cannot be downloaded or are not installed on the user's computer. The technique has both legal and technical issues, however.

Fonts are generally copyrighted; thus, their font files cannot be stored and used on web sites. Even the ones that are advertised as free fonts cannot be used for web sites in many cases [5]. Since a standard font pack has been released under the "Core fonts for the Web" program by Microsoft, the fonts Arial, Georgia, and Verdana (among others) have become *de facto* fonts on the Web.

■ **Caution** The character repertoire of typefaces varies greatly. While the English alphabet and the common punctuation marks are supported by most font files, the list of supported characters should be a major concern for sites written in a natural language other than English. Multilingual sites should not apply font files that do not support the full range of required characters, which makes it possible to apply the same fonts for the different language versions. One of the options to avoid nonsupported characters is to apply Unicode fonts. However, not all fonts presented on font collection sites as "Unicode fonts" support a really wide range of Unicode characters. In fact, the ones that do are typically 20MB to 25MB in size (compared to the typical font file size of 50KB to 300KB), which is inadequate for web publishing: the fonts won't appear while the font files are being downloaded, and this would take much more time than downloading the entire page with all of its components, including images.

From the technical point of view, the browser support for font embedding and downloading varies from browser to browser. However, the differences are decreasing because of standardization and the growing popularity of implementations. *Embedded OpenType* (*EOT*) font embedding is supported by Internet Explorer from version 4. Other browsers have introduced font linking for *TrueType* (TT) and *OpenType* (OT) fonts (Firefox 3.5+, Opera 10+, Safari 3.1+, Google Chrome 4.0+). Internet Explorer 9+ also supports TT/OT fonts but only those that have embedded permissions set to installable. TT has been extended to support additional metadata and gzip compression, known as the Web Open Font Format (WOFF). WOFF is a cross-browser, web-only format being standardized by the W3C [6] and supported by Internet Explorer 9+, Mozilla Firefox 3.6+, and Google Chrome 5+.

■ **Note** The semistructural details appearing on the ends of certain strokes of letters and symbols are known as *serifs* in typography. The typefaces that use serifs, such as Times New Roman, Cambria, Garamond, and Georgia, are known as *serif typefaces*. The typefaces that do not have these small projecting features are the *sans-serif typefaces*,[3] for example, Verdana, Tahoma, and Helvetica. Declaring one of the generic font families (serif, sans-serif, cursive, fantasy, monospace) is an excellent fallback mechanism [7].

---

[3] The word *sans* means "without" in French.

Two different fonts (or the same font in two different formats[4]) can be declared with a fallback mechanism, as shown in Listing 9-6, and can be applied as demonstrated in Listing 9-7.

Listing 9-6. Using Fonts Stored in Different Formats

```
@font-face {
  font-family: "Csuff";
  src: url("http://example.com/fonts/csuff.ttf");
  src: url("http://example.com/fonts/csuff.eot");
}
```

Listing 9-7. Applying Web Fonts with a Fallback Mechanism

```
p {
  font-family: "Csuff", "Helvetica", sans-serif;
}
```

Note that a widely available font is also provided, along with the font family declaration that always works, in case neither of the external fonts can be used.

■ **Tip** Serif fonts are easy to read[5] and adequate for long text blocks published on web pages in medium or large font size, as well as for printer style sheets. Sans-serif typefaces are more suitable for short texts in small font size, such as copyright information in the page footer, which is often written in Verdana or a similar font. Monospace fonts like Courier and DejaVu Sans Mono are ideal for preformatted text, computer codes, and typewriter effects. Cursive fonts, such as Comic Sans MS and Brush Script, are used for cursive handwriting such as signatures. Fantasy fonts are best used for headings and artistic texts (for example, Impact and Copperplate).

The normal, bold, and italic versions, as well as the bold and italic fonts, of a typeface are generally stored in separate files. Consequently, multiple declarations are needed to download and apply the appropriate font styles of the selected typeface (Listing 9-8). Without that, the content of headings and strong elements will be rendered using normal fonts rather than bold ones, em elements will be displayed with normal rather than italic fonts, and so on.

Listing 9-8. Multiple Declarations for the Same Typeface

```
@font-face {
  font-family: Calluna;
  src: url('fonts/Calluna-Regular.otf');
}
```

---

[4] Although there are tools for converting fonts from one format to another, it is legally prohibited in many cases.
[5] This is the reason for their widespread application in books, newspapers, and magazines.

```css
@font-face {
  font-family: Callunab;
  src: url('fonts/Calluna-Bold.otf');
}

@font-face {
  font-family: Callunai;
  src: url('fonts/Calluna-It.otf');
}

body {
  font-family: "Calluna", "Helvetica", serif;
}

h1, h2, h3, strong {
  font-family: "Callunab";
}

em {
  font-family: "Callunai";
}
```

There are also some alternatives for web fonts. A technique called *image replacement*, which is considered legal by many, is applied by some web designers to use rendered images of fonts. However, image replacement prevents text selection, has searchability and accessibility issues, and increases bandwidth use.

Another approach applies the Flash-based solution *Scalable Inman Flash Replacement* (*sIFR*). It is similar to image replacement, but the text is selectable and rendered as a vector graphic. A big disadvantage is that this method relies on a Flash plug-in on the client side.

The text can also be replaced by SVG or VML[6] (for Internet Explorer up to version 8) with JavaScript.

In SVG 1.1, fonts can be created within the SVG document. SVG fonts can improve the semantics of graphics that represent texts, such as logos. SVG fonts are partly supported by Safari 3+ and Opera 8+.

Similar to (X)HTML documents, CSS can also be applied in SVG documents. Consequently, the `@font-face` rule can be used for SVG texts too [8]. Listing 9-9 shows an example.

Listing 9-9. An Example for Using the @fontface CSS Rule in SVG

```xml
<?xml version="1.0" encoding="UTF-8" standalone="no"?>
<!DOCTYPE svg PUBLIC "-//W3C//DTD SVG 1.1//EN"
  "http://www.w3.org/Graphics/SVG/1.1/DTD/svg11.dtd">
<svg xmlns="http://www.w3.org/2000/svg" version="1.1">
  <defs>
    <style>
      <![CDATA[
        @font-face {
          font-family: Calluna;
          src: url('fonts/Calluna-Regular.otf');
```

---

[6] SVG was not supported by earlier versions of Internet Explorer, which supported the Vector Markup Language (VML) instead, which is now obsoleted.

```
        }
      ]]>
    </style>
  </defs>
  <text x="20"  y="40" style="font-family: Calluna, serif; font-size: 1.2em; stroke: #0f0;
  fill: #0f0;">SVG text with Web Fonts</text>
</svg>
```

Embedding External Content

The majority of web sites contain not only formatted texts but also graphics and multimedia content, audio and video clips, and Flash animations. In contrast to formatted text content described by markup languages in text files, this type of content is retrieved from binary files. Although its optimal format and features are not standardized for web publishing, its optimization has a huge impact on overall appearance, look and feel, file size, and download time.

Raster Graphics

Bitmap graphics (also known as raster images), which are stored in a mapped array of bits and represent a grid of pixels, are common web site components. On the Web, bitmap file formats are used mainly for storing photographs and other images that are not line art. There are several image file features to be optimized for web publishing, such as pixel density, color depth, and resolution. You should choose the file format according to the content and the desired quality.

The Golden Rule of image processing and retouching for the Web is that whatever will be modified, the original master file should not be overwritten (even if it has a large file size). For example, a title in a compound image created on multiple layers in Photoshop cannot be modified later if you don't preserve the .psd file. Similarly, a heavily retouched or compressed photograph cannot be restored to its original state (which might be useful in many cases) if you haven't saved the original file.

Note The following sections describe the major features and possibilities; however, a detailed description of image processing is beyond the scope of this book.

Pixel Density

Not just text content but also graphics can and should be optimized for web publishing. The measure of *spatial dot density* is dots per inch (dpi), which means the number of individual dots represented in a line within the span of 1 inch (2.54 cm). Although dot density correlates with image resolution, it is related indirectly. Instead of the dots that are used for printing, however, computer screens apply pixels to build up images. Their density can be expressed in pixels per inch (ppi). Although confusing, pixel densities standardized for computer screens are often expressed incorrectly in dpi rather than ppi (72, 96, and 120 dpi). The lowest value, 72 ppi, derives from typography where 1 point (pt) is defined to be 1/72 inch ($\approx$ 0.0139 inch or 352.8 µm). An image displayed on a 72 ppi screen has the same physical dimensions as the printed version in 72 dpi; in other words, 1 pt on paper is equal to 1 px on the screen. However, this is just a theoretical approach; it is not accurate and has lost its significance. Since the pixel density affects not only the quality of image rendering but also text readability, higher values provide better user experience. Modern operating systems and computer screens usually support 96–120 ppi. The pixel density of a screen can be calculated by the ratio of the diagonal resolution in pixels (using the Pythagorean theorem) and the diagonal size in inches:

$$PPI = \frac{d_p}{d_i} = \frac{\sqrt{w_p^2 + h_p^2}}{d_i}$$

where

d_p is diagonal resolution in pixels,

w_p is width resolution in pixels,

h_p is height resolution in pixels, and

d_i is diagonal size in inches.

For example, a 10.1-inch netbook with a WSVGA (1024x600) screen provides 117.51 ppi, a 20-inch monitor with a WSXGA+ (1680x1050) screen provides 99.06 ppi, and a 23-inch HD (1920x1080) monitor provides 95.78 ppi.

Smartphones are very competitive from this aspect. The 4.3-inch HTC Evo 4G has a WVGA (800x480) screen that corresponds to a pixel density of 216 ppi. In 2010, the Apple iPhone 4 featured the largest resolution screen, called the *Retina display* (960x640), which gives an incredibly high 326 ppi[7] for the 3.5-inch screen. As of 2011, high-end smartphones introduced the HD display with a resolution of 1280x720 on a typical screen size of 4.3", making pixel density even higher.

Although the optimal pixel density for web publishing is not standardized, it should be taken into account that computer screens and settings generally support 120 ppi as a maximum and apply an average of 96 ppi. Larger pixel densities needlessly increase the file size.

Resolution

On the screen, resolution determines image size, not quality in general (printing is the opposite). As a general rule, the smallest image size that provides the desired details should be applied. The usual 8–10 MP photos taken by modern digital cameras should be resized to a smaller resolution for web publishing in most cases. It should be kept in mind that huge-resolution photographs are large in size (a few megabytes depending on compression ratio and file format) and thus take too long to download. Moreover, they have too much detail that might cause legal issues considering faces, number plates, and so on, in the background. The high-resolution depiction of a human face can be used for fraudulent purposes because it can be easily retouched and printed (especially in passport size).

Providing width and height attributes on img elements for faster rendering of web page images is highly recommended. However, these attributes should not be used for resizing photos. Online galleries and albums should apply small thumbnails linking to the original or full-size version of images.

---

[7] At a distance of 12 inches from one's eye, this is the maximum amount of detail the human retina can process (hence the name).

Aliasing

Resizing digital images can result in distortions and quality loss. A high-resolution image represented at a lower resolution, for example, might cause distortion artifacts called *aliasing*. *Anti-aliasing* allows the edges of objects to be rendered smoothly. On the Web, anti-aliasing is often applied for fonts and curved web graphics such as rounded corners.

Anti-aliasing requires additional colors with gradually decreasing intensity that merge with the background (Figure 9-5).

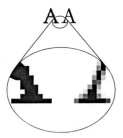 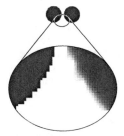

Figure 9-5. Aliased vs. anti-aliased fonts and circles. The original images are shown above, the magnification below. Note the pixelated edges on the left images.

Using anti-aliased fonts on the Web has pros and cons. The most important advantages are smoother fonts, many of which are easier to read because of reduced blurring, the similarity with printed types (depending on the font being used), and in many cases the more aesthetic appearance. However, small fonts become too fuzzy to read, and sharp edges are not always precise.

▪ **Caution** The readability of different web fonts is very different, and even the same typeface might look gorgeous in medium size but becomes unreadable when used with a small font size. There is often a transition between the two states: some parts of the font curves disappear, while others remain visible. Moreover, the rendering of the same web fonts is different in various browsers.

Color Depth

The number of bits required for representing the color of a single pixel in a bitmap image or video frame buffer typically varies from 1 to 2^{32} and is known as *color depth*. Consequently, the higher the color depth, the larger the file size, which is an important factor in image optimization.

Monochrome (binary) images such as line art with black lines should be stored with 1 bit color depth, in other words, two possible values for each pixel.

Black-and-white photographs, which are composed exclusively of 256 shades of gray, should be represented as 8-bit grayscale images ($2^8 = 256$).

24-bit color depth (*true color*) applies red, green, and blue colors with various intensity values between 0 and 255 per channel (RGB color model) to reproduce $2^8 \cdot 2^8 \cdot 2^8 = 2^{24} = 16,777,216$ different colors with additive color mixing. Since the human eye cannot distinguish any two adjacent intensity values of these channels, this color depth is adequate for storing photographs.

Photorealistic images with partially transparent parts can be represented in 32 bits with an additional channel called the *alpha channel*[8] (that is, RGBA color space).

The color depth of logos, pictograms, and icons varies, depending on the complexity and image content.

Compression

To reduce file size, digital bitmap images are usually compressed. Compressed images are popular not only for storage but also for web publishing because of the smaller bandwidth requirement.

Image compression can be lossy or lossless. In the case of *lossy compression*s, part of the original information is lost and cannot be restored, which might affect image quality. *Lossless compression* algorithms allow the reconstruction of the original data from the compressed data, which is a nice feature but not always needed. The resulting files of lossy compression algorithms are generally smaller in size than the ones using lossless compression; however, their quality might be lower if the compression ratio is too high. As you will see, JPEG is the most popular lossy image format, and PNG is the most popular lossless image format on the Web.

Image-processing software tools usually provide the option to adjust the degree of compression, making it possible to select a trade-off between storage size and image quality. For example, Adobe Photoshop has a scale for a JPEG compression ratio with values 0–12. The supported quality ranges are Low (0–4), Medium (5–7), High (8–9), and Maximum (10–12). The settings are available after determining the name and destination of the file in the File Save As… dialog window (Figure 9-6).

---

[8] There are also other approaches to provide transparency, but for partially transparent photographs, it is the common solution.

Figure 9-6. Excellent quality with small file size

JPEG typically achieves 10:1 compression with hardly perceptible loss in image quality.

Interlacing

Certain bitmap formats such as GIF and PNG have the option to provide a degraded copy of an image before it is fully downloaded. The method is known as *interlacing.* Advanced image-processing software applications support interlacing and offer the choice to save such files either as *interlaced* or as *noninterlaced.* A similar effect can be achieved in photographs by applying a *frequency decomposition hierarchy* in *progressive JPEG* files. In the era of slow, dial-up connections, interlacing was a useful feature but lost most of its significance after the widespread application of high-speed Internet connections.

Transparency

The popularity of partially transparent images is increasing. They can be used not only for design effects but also to provide images that can be used on different background colors or textures (Figure 9-7).

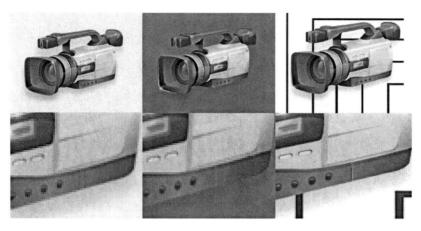

Figure 9-7. An image on three different backgrounds (first row). The second row is magnified to 600 percent. The transparent shadow perfectly fits to all backgrounds

Not all raster image formats support transparency, though. GIF is generally a good (sometimes the best) option for partially transparent geometric shapes and cartoon-style images, while PNG is ideal for more complex partially transparent images. With the exception of really simple shapes with relatively large areas of the same color, PNG is the better option.

Raster File Formats

The most common raster image file formats on the Web are JPEG, GIF, and PNG.

Joint Photographic Experts Group (JPEG) is a common lossy compression format for digital photographs. Part 1 has been standardized in ISO/IEC 10918-1:1994 [9] and ITU-T T.81 (09/92) [10], Part 2 in ISO/IEC 10918-2:1995 [11] and ITU-T T.83 (11/94) [12], Part 3 in ISO/IEC 10918-3:1997 [13] and ITU-T T.84 (07/96) [14], Part 4 in ISO/IEC 10918-4:1999 [15] and ITU-T T.86 (06/98) [16], and Part 5 in ISO/IEC FCD 10918-5 [17].

The original version of the Graphics Interchange Format, GIF87a, was introduced in 1987 [18], and the enhanced version with transparency and interlacing support, GIF89a, was introduced in 1989 [19].

The Portable Network Graphics (PNG) format was standardized by IETF RFC 2083 in 1997 [20] and ISO/IEC 15948 in 2004 [21]. However, the PNG format has not gained full support until recently. Although Internet Explorer supports PNG images from version 4.01b, the implementation was neither complete nor correct until IE9 (for example, IE6 had a buggy support for alpha-channel transparency). There were color inconsistencies between various browsers, partly because of the different handling of gamma correction (for example, colors of PNG images were displayed incorrectly on Safari running under Windows). Fortunately, modern browsers overcame these issues.

To choose the right file format for a given image, the main features of file types and compression algorithms should be considered (Table 9-2).

Table 9-2. Quick Comparison of JPEG, GIF, and PNG

	JPEG	GIF	PNG
Maximum color depth	24-bit	8-bit	48-bit
Palette	Full	Restricted	Optional
Compression	Lossy (in most cases)	Lossless	Lossless
Transparency	–	+	+
Interlaced mode	+ (progressive JPEG)	+	+
Animation	–	+	–[9]
Optimal usage	Photographs	Icons, logos, diagrams (geometric shapes), clipart, cartoon-style images, and small animations	Photographs, partially transparent photographs, icons, and logos

For example, a simple image such as a solid circle can be stored with two colors in GIF with a very small file size compared to other formats such as JPEG. For images that have no complex content, the color depth can be reduced with color palettes (selected/indexed colors) in file formats such as GIF, TIF, and PNG. Certainly, an anti-aliased version needs a larger color depth resulting in a larger file size. Although GIF and PNG formats are usually better than JPEG for storing icons and logos, the SVG vector format should be preferred for such content (see the section "Vector Graphics").

Although it is very efficient on photographs, the JPEG compression algorithm adds additional pixels to the whole image, including solid areas. As a result, simple images become more complex than they were originally. This is the main reason why a solid circle stored in JPEG has several times larger file size than a GIF file with the same content even if the compression is high. Moreover, if the compression ratio is high, JPEG artifacts become noticeable, resulting in lower image quality. On the other hand, JPEG works perfectly on complex images. If the compression is set properly, the image quality to file size ratio is excellent.

File Size Optimization

Pixel density, resolution, dimensions, color depth, compression ratio, image complexity, and file format all have a large impact on file size.

---

[9] There is an extension called Animated Portable Network Graphics (APNG) that supports animation. APNG is natively supported by Firefox 3+, by Opera 9.5+, and with an add-on by Google Chrome.

The width and height should be optimized by cropping useless or unnecessary parts of the image. It is a typical task for scanned and high-resolution images where image parts can often be removed without losing information.

The required color depth must be used; 24-bit color depth is the default setting in many software tools, which can be reduced in many cases without affecting image quality. For example, black-and-white drawings should not be stored with 16 million colors.

The proper compression ratio must be used for all images.

The size-quality ratio can be effectively optimized with the File ▸ Save For Web & Devices… function of Photoshop (Figure 9-8).

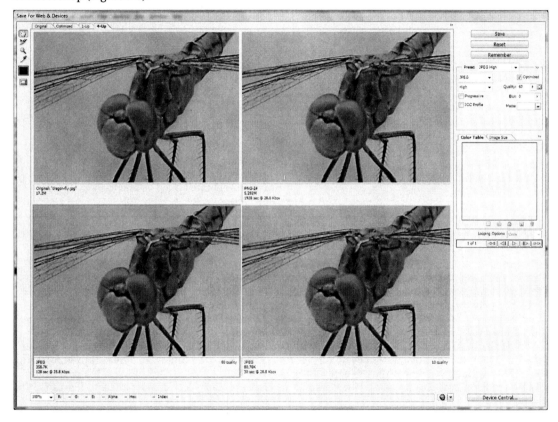

Figure 9-8. Comparison of file formats and settings for web publishing in Photoshop

Photoshop also offers optimization to a desired file size, but it should be kept in mind that image content and complexity determine the reasonable level of compression.

Beyond the compression settings of JPEG files available in Photoshop or GIMP, some software tools (such as JPEG Optimizer [22]) are capable of optimizing the file size to quality ratio by applying different compression ratios to various image areas.

The major aim of file size optimization is to achieve the perfect balance between file size and picture quality. A fast web page with low-quality images is pointless.

Small, highly compressed versions (thumbnails) should be provided with links to a larger, high-quality version in online photo galleries and albums. This approach allows users to determine whether the image is relevant for them and, thus, reasonable to download the larger version, which will naturally take more time.

Vector Graphics

Vector and bitmap images have different application areas. Bitmaps are best suitable for photographs and photorealistic images, while vector images can be applied for artwork and illustrations that consist of lines and curves. Nonetheless, bitmaps are still used widely on the Web for all kinds of images, including the ones that should be provided in a vector format instead, partly because of the lack of native support for a single standard vector format across all major browsers. The situation has started to change with the widespread support of SVG.

Scalable Vector Graphics should be preferred for all images that require basic shapes such as circles and polygons, Bézier paths and curves, text, opacity, transformations (rotation, skew, scale, and so on),[10] gradients, and animations. SVG content can also be combined with bitmap graphics such as with a PNG file.

Similar to PNG, the browser support of SVG should be considered for the sake of backward compatibility. It should be kept in mind that the browser support of SVG is different for inline SVG, and the SVG should be embedded via the `img` or the `object` element. Additionally, SVG has several versions, and the support of the different versions varies. The Gecko layout engine has had incomplete SVG 1.1 Full support since 2005 and WebKit since 2006. Opera supports SVG 1.1 Tiny from version 8, SVG 1.1 Basic and partially SVG 1.1 Full from version 9, and partially SVG Tiny 1.2 (including compressed SVG) from version 9.5.

Flash

Flash is one of the most popular technologies for publishing active content on the Web. However, the standard embedding code provided by Flash development tools is often not standard-compliant and has some browser-dependent issues. Moreover, alternate content should be supported that is automatically activated if the Flash content cannot be displayed for whatever reasons.

Embedding Flash in XHTML

The first Flash implementations applied the `embed` element, which was deprecated in HTML 4 and XHTML in favor of the `object` element but then was added back into the HTML 5 specification (see next section). Consequently, in XHTML documents Flash content should be provided by the `object` element.

To avoid browser- and vendor-specific code, various implementation methods have been introduced, including duplication (the *twice-cooked method*), the *nested objects method*, and *Flash Satay*. The latter one, Flash Satay, provides robust and standard-compliant Flash implementation by including an additional `movie` parameter. W3C also suggests this method [23]. Listing 9-10 shows an example.

---

[10] Similar effects are also supported by CSS3.

Listing 9-10. Embedding Flash Using Flash Satay

```
<object type="application/x-shockwave-flash" data="australia.swf" width="735" height="677" ↵
 id="flash">
  <param name="movie" value="australia.swf" />
</object>
```

Note that the same Flash file is specified both as a data attribute value on the object element and as a movie parameter value. It is also important to realize that the classid and codebase parameters used by older methods have been eliminated. If the codebase parameter is left in the code when modifying a traditional Flash embedding code, it prevents Firefox from rendering the Flash content, and the optionally provided alternate content appears instead (or nothing at all).

Even this method has some known issues, however. For example, using the Flash Satay method, the Flash movie is not streamed by some browsers such as Internet Explorer. Waiting for the whole file to download and start to play afterward works fine for small files and fast Internet connections only.

If you develop a web page with layers above each other, it might be rather frustrating that Flash content appears above all other web site elements by default. To provide the possibility of setting the layer order within pages containing Flash content, an additional parameter (wmode) should be set (Listings 9-11 and 9-12).

Listing 9-11. Setting the wmode for Nontransparent Flash Content

```
<param name="wmode" value="opaque" />
```

The parameter value opaque indicates that the content is not transparent. If it is transparent, the attribute value should be changed to transparent (Listing 9-12).

Listing 9-12. Setting the wmode for Transparent Flash Content

```
<param name="wmode" value="transparent" />
```

Although it seems that there is no correlation between the transparency of Flash content and the stack position of the Flash content in the layer order, the wmode parameter should be used for setting both. Either the opaque or the transparent attribute value is used on the wmode parameter; Flash content can be sent behind any layers within the web page (or in any desired position in the layer order). The only problem associated with wmode is that the Flash content becomes inaccessible to users with screen readers and is therefore best avoided whenever possible.

Similar to (X)HTML markup, Flash content should be accessible and search engine friendly. The version of the installed Flash plug-in of the user should be detected to determine whether it is up-to-date. Outdated plug-ins might encounter functionalities that are supported in higher plug-in versions only. This should be considered to eliminate broken and missing content.

As for the version dilemma, Adobe provides the Flash Player Detection Kit [24]; however, the codes provided by the kit are not standard-compliant.

DOM scripting can address these issues. An open source example is the *SWFObject* by Geoff Stearns et al [25]. SWFObject provides a cross-browser method to embed SWF files into web pages using a very small JavaScript code. This JavaScript code detects Flash Player, declares alternate content, improves search engine indexing, assists Flash Player downloading if it is not installed, includes Adobe Express Install, and offers an API for JavaScript developers. However, version detection with JavaScript relies on scripting, results in longer code, and overcomplicates Flash embedding. As a conclusion, there is no better standard-compliant, cross-browser Flash embedding method than Flash Satay.

Embedding Flash in (X)HTML5

HTML5 has an embed element for embedded content that requires plug-ins. It supports all the standard attributes and event attributes of HTML5. Additionally, it has the specific attributes src, type (which specifies MIME type), height, and width. You can use it as shown in Listing 9-13.

Listing 9-13. Basic Flash Embedding in (X)HTML5

```
<embed src="australia.swf" />
```

The embed tag also supports the global and event attributes of HTML5, which have already been discussed in Chapter 3.

Audio

Prior to HTML5, there has never been native markup support for playing audio on web pages. Most audio content is played through a plug-in such as Flash. The major problem with this approach is that not all browsers have the same plug-ins.

HTML5 specifies a standard way to include audio content by the audio element. It can be used to play sound files as well as audio streams. Three major audio formats are supported by the audio element: MP3, Ogg Vorbis, and WAV. However, the browser support of these formats varies (Table 9-3). Note that the audio element is not supported at all in IE8 and earlier.

Table 9-3. Audio Format Support for the audio Element in Different Browsers

Format	IE	Firefox	Chrome	Opera	Safari
MP3	9+	–	3.0+ – 3.0+		
WAV	–	3.5+	3.0+	10.5+	3.0+
Ogg Vorbis	–	3.5+	3.0+	10.5+	3.0+

The basic use of the audio element is straightforward (Listing 9-14).

Listing 9-14. Basic Audio Embedding in (X)HTML5

```
<audio src="valerie.mp3">
</audio>
```

Beyond the src attribute that specifies the source URL of the audio content to play, there are further attributes for automatic playing (autoplay="autoplay"), control buttons (controls="controls"), repeating (loop="loop"), and loading at page load (preload="preload"). The last one is ignored if autoplay is present.

To achieve a higher level of accessibility, alternate content should be provided (Listing 9-15).

Listing 9-15. Alternate Content for Audio

```
<audio src="valerie.mp3" controls="controls">
  <p><a href="valerie.mp3">Valerie by Joy</a></p>
</audio>
```

Since certain formats supported by a browser cannot be played in another, the audio element allows multiple source declarations that link to different audio files. Listing 9-16 shows an example.

Listing 9-16. Multiple Source Declaration for Different Formats

```
<audio controls="controls">
  <source src="valerie.mp3" type="audio/mpeg" />
  <source src="valerie.ogg" type="audio/ogg" />
  <p><a href="valerie.mp3">Valerie by Joy</a></p>
</audio>
```

Browsers can play the first supported format from the different audio formats.

Video

For many years, publishing videos was possible through general object embedding only. Because of the variety of video and audio codecs and the varying browser support, there is still no ultimate solution for publishing videos on the Web.

Embedding Video in XHTML

Content from video-sharing services such as YouTube or Google Video, which serve movies through the Flash Player,[11] can be embedded using the Flash Satay method discussed earlier. Listing 9-17 shows an example.

Listing 9-17. Embedding a Flash Sdeo Using Flash Satay

```
<object type="application/x-shockwave-flash" ↵
 data="http://video.google.com/videoplay?docid=4226784084458819393#" width="400" ↵
 height="326" id="VideoPlayback">
  <param name="movie" value="http://video.google.com/videoplay?docid=4226784084458819393#" />
  <param name="allowFullScreen" value="true" />
  <param name="allowScriptAccess" value="always" />
</object>
```

Window Media Video files (.wmv) can be embedded by using the MIME type video/x-ms-wmv (Listing 9-18).

---

[11] Adobe Flash Player is widely used to embed video on web sites because of the native support found in many browsers.

Listing 9-18. Embedding a WMV Video File

```
<object type="video/x-ms-wmv" ↩
 data="http://www.example.com/dreamcar.wmv" ↩
 width="320" height="260">
  <param name="src" value="http://www.example.com/dreamcar.wmv" />
  <param name="autostart" value="true" />
  <param name="controller" value="true" />
</object>
```

For QuickTime videos, there are dedicated MIME types: the video/quicktime and the application/x-quicktime. IE tends to open such videos through an ActiveX control. To embed QuickTime videos in a browser-independent way that also validates, you can use the method presented in Listing 9-19.

Listing 9-19. Embedding a QuickTime Video File

```
<object classid="clsid:02BF25D5-8C17-4B23-BC80-D3488ABDDC6B" ↩
 codebase="http://www.apple.com/qtactivex/qtplugin.cab" width="352" height="288">
  <param name="src" value="http://www.example.com/video/dreamcars.mov" />
  <param name="controller" value="true" />
  <param name="autoplay" value="false" />
  <!--[if !IE]>-->
    <object type="video/quicktime" data="http:// www.example.com/video/dreamcars.mov" ↩
      width="352" height="288">
    <param name="autoplay" value="false" />
    <param name="controller" value="true" />
  </object>
  <!--<![endif]-->
</object>
```

The code provided as IE-style conditional comments[12] is used by all browsers except Internet Explorer, from which it is hidden and applies the outer object.

Embedding Video in (X)HTML5

In contrast to the complexity of video embedding with the object element in XHTML, (X)HTML5 provides the video element, which is easy to use and has full control over the video being embedded. The video element is supported in IE9+, Firefox 3.5+, Chrome 3.0+, Opera 10.5+, and Safari 3.0+. However, its usability depends also on the supported codecs. If you just think of DivX, Xvid, WMV, FFmpeg, 3ivx, Sorenson, or Flash Video from the enormous variety of video file formats, the video codec support of web browsers is undoubtedly in its infancy (Table 9-4).

---

[12] The method was suggested by Lachlan Hunt.

Table 9-4. Overview of Video Format Support for the video Element in Different Browsers

Format	IE	Firefox	Chrome	Opera	Safari
H.264	9+	–	*Dropped*	–	3.1+
Ogg Theora	*Installable*	3.5+	3.0+	10.5+	*Installable*
WebM	*Installable*	4.0+	6.0+	10.6+	*Installable*

Certainly, there is no need to maximize the number of natively supported video formats on the Web, but the reliable support for the most widely used, advanced formats would be desirable.

■ **Note** Many video files are stored in container formats that are not restricted to one kind of video and audio codec. Consequently, the full support for a video container should include the support for all kinds of video and audio codecs allowed in that container format. For example, if browser vendors would like to introduce support for .flv Flash videos, it would require support for the H.264/MPEG-4 AVC, Sorenson, Screen Video, and VP6 video codecs, as well as the AAC, ADPCM, Linear PCM, Nellymoser, MP3, and Speex audio codecs. Moreover, many codecs have proprietary licenses or are encumbered by patents (this is the main reason why Chrome dropped the H.264 support). Evidently, the different associations of audio and video codecs along with the licensing issues make it rather complex to standardize video implementations on the Web. Different formats are suitable for different purposes and application areas, and there is no ultimate choice for video publishing: it depends on the scenario.

Listing 9-20 shows the basic code for the video element.

Listing 9-20. Basic Video Embedding in (X)HTML5

```
<video src="sample.ogv">
</video>
```

Features such as height or width can be added optionally. An image representing a frame from the video can also be defined in case the video cannot be rendered. Additionally, alternate content can also be given between the opening and closing video tags (Listing 9-21).

Listing 9-21. Additional Properties and Alternate Content for (X)HTML5 Video Embedding

```
<video src="sample.ogv" width="320" height="240" poster="sample.jpg">
    <p>Download the <a href="video.ogv">sample video</a> (OGV, 5.34 MB)</p>
</video>
```

Video controls can be shown or hidden in the browser by using the controls attribute on the video element (Listing 9-22).

Listing 9-22. Controls Set to Be Displayed for (X)HTML5 Video Embedding

```
<video src="xyz.mov" controls="controls">
</video>
```

Since the video codec support is different in each browser, the same video can be provided in various formats, avoiding the need to download videos that cannot be played on the system. Listing 9-23 shows an example.

Listing 9-23. The Same Video in Different Formats

```
<video>
  <source src="video.mp4" type="video/mp4" />
  <source src="video.ogv" type="video/ogg" />
  <p>Download the <a href="video.ogv">sample video</a> (OGV)</p>
</video>
```

However, the MIME type cannot reflect the codecs of videos stored in container formats (for example, H.264 in MPEG-4). They can be provided by the codecs parameter (Listing 9-24).

Listing 9-24. Declaring Video Codecs in (X)HTML5

```
<video controls="controls">
  <source src="video.mp4" type='video/mp4; codecs="avc1.42E01E, mp4a.40.2"' />
  <source src="video.ogv" type='video/ogg; codecs="theora, vorbis"' />
  <p>Download the <a href="video.ogv">sample video</a></p>
</video>
```

Care must be taken to apply single and double quotes alternately for the type attribute values.

The video element of (X)HTML5 provides playback support detection, including the canPlayType() method on the media element or the onerror event listener. Listing 9-25 is an example of the second method.

Listing 9-25. Video Plackback Support Detection in (X)HTML5

```
<video controls="controls">
  <source src="video.mp4" type='video/mp4; codecs="avc1.42E01E, mp4a.40.2"' />
  <source src="video.ogv" type='video/ogg; codecs="theora, vorbis"' ↵
  onerror="fallback(this.parentNode)" />
  <p>Download the <a href="video.ogv">sample video</a> (OGV)</p>
</video>
```

The major problem is that video support in browsers is not standardized yet. Thus, there is no ultimate cross-browser video-embedding code.

Although one of the major advantages of the video element is the avoided object element and plug-in declaration, they can still be useful in some cases. If plug-ins are preferred to simple error messages, the object element can be embedded into the video element. Flash supports MPEG-4/H.264/AAC playback, so an .mp4 file can usually be played by the code presented in Listing 9-26.

Listing 9-26. MPEG-4 Plackback

```
<video controls="controls">
  <source src="video.mp4" type='video/mp4; codecs="avc1.42E01E, mp4a.40.2"' ↵
  onerror="fallback(this.parentNode)" />
  <object data="videoplayer.swf">
    <param name="flashvars" value="video.mp4" />
    <p>Download the <a href="video.ogv">sample video</a> (OGV)</p>
  </object>
</video>
```

Certain browsers cannot stream the video or automatically download the whole video file even if playback has not been started yet. One of the exceptions is Firefox 3.6+, which downloads only a fragment necessary to determine duration and render a frame from the video. This behavior can be overridden by the preload attribute. The attribute value none forces the browser to avoid downloading. The metadata attribute value hints that enough data should be downloaded only to show a frame and determine duration. The value auto downloads the whole video if possible. The effect of preload="none" can be simulated in browsers that do not support it by omitting the src attribute and source elements that are provided only if the user clicks a button (Listing 9-27).

Listing 9-27. Loading Video on User Click

```
<video controls="controls">
  Video not supported
</video>
<input type="button" value="Load video" ↵
  onclick="document.getElementsByTagName('video')[0].src = 'video.mp4';" />
```

Additionally, customized controls can also be added to the video embedding since the DOM API for video in (X)HTML5 supports several events that can be handled through JavaScript. Listing 9-28 shows an example.

Listing 9-28. Customized Video Controls

```
<script>
  var video = document.getElementsByTagName('video')[0];
</script>
<input type="button" value="Play" onclick="video.play()" />
<input type="button" value="Pause" onclick="video.pause()" />
```

Playback can be started automatically by the autoplay attribute of the video element (Listing 9-29).

Listing 9-29. Video Playback to Be Started Automatically

```
<video src="abc.mp4" autoplay="autoplay"></video>
```

However, not all users want to download the video, and a start button is usually preferred. Additionally, if there are multiple videos on the same page, automatic playing is out of the question, especially if there are at least two that are not mute.

Currently, the src attribute value of the video tag should be a physical file, which makes it impossible to embed your favorite Aston Martin video from YouTube. For example, the code in Listing 9-30 cannot be used.

Listing 9-30. A YouTube Video Cannot Be Played Using the video *Tag (Illegal Example)*

```
<video src="http://www.youtube.com/watch?v=wKhEpifPTlY"></video>
```

(X)HTML5 videos can be dynamically drawn on a canvas with JavaScript using the drawImage method, such as in Listing 9-31.

Listing 9-31. Video Drawn on the Canvas Using JavaScript

```
<video src="video.mp4" controls="controls">
  Video not supported
</video>
<canvas id="canvas">
  Canvas not supported
</canvas>
<script>
  var ctx = document.getElementById('canvas').getContext('2d');
  var video = document.getElementsByTagName('video')[0];
  video.onloadeddata = function(e) {
  ctx.canvas.width = video.videoWidth;
  ctx.canvas.height = video.videoHeight;
  ctx.drawImage(video, 0, 0);
  }
</script>
```

Summary

In this chapter, you learned how to provide an advanced user experience through optimized appearance using standards. You became familiar with many web site components that contribute to user impression and affect web site usability and functionality. You know that it is a real challenge to ensure proper appearance on the variety of devices, which can be achieved by creating browser- and resolution-independent web sites with robust layout. You are well aware that many of the once popular techniques are obsolete, and tables should be used for representing tabular data, not for layout. CSS provides full control over the appearance of web site components, and multicolumn layouts should be used in place of frameset documents. You also know how to optimize images for your web sites and embed Flash and video files in a browser-independent, standard-compliant manner.

In the next chapter, you will learn accessibility techniques that maximize user access to your web sites. By following the accessibility guidelines, you will be capable of supporting not only people with disabilities and mobile users but also all the others, because everyone benefits from an advanced level of web accessibility.

References

1.   Hazaël-Massieux D (2005) Tableless layout HOWTO. World Wide Web Consortium. www.w3.org/2002/03/csslayout-howto. Accessed 07 December 2010

2.   Cederholm D (2009) CSS layouts. In: Web standards solutions, Special edn. Friends of ED, Berkeley

3.   W3C (2003) Errata in REC-CSS2-19980512. World Wide Web Consortium. www.w3.org/Style/css2-updates/REC-CSS2-19980512-errata.html. Accessed 14 December 2010

4. W3C (2010) English Typography. W3C Cheat Sheet. World Wide Web Consortium. www.w3.org/2009/cheatsheet/#typo. Accessed 07 December 2010

5. Mason B (2009) When Free Fonts Aren't Free. Small Batch Inc. http://blog.typekit.com/2009/06/11/when-free-fonts-arent-free/. Accessed 24 January 2011

6. Kew J, Leming T, van Blokland E (2011) WOFF File Format 1.0. World Wide Web Consortium. www.w3.org/TR/WOFF/. Accessed 07 September 2011

7. Bos B, Çelik T, Hickson I, Lie HW (2011) Generic font families. In: Cascading Style Sheets Level 2 Revision 1 (CSS 2.1) Specification. W3C Recommendation. World Wide Web Consortium. www.w3.org/TR/CSS2/fonts.html#generic-font-families. Accessed 08 September 2011

8. Dahlström E, Dengler P, Grasso A, Lilley C, McCormack C, Schepers D, Watt J, Ferraiolo J, Jun F, Jackson D (eds) The 'font-face' element. In: Scalable Vector Graphics (SVG) 1.1 (Second Edition). W3C Recommendation. World Wide Web Consortium. www.w3.org/TR/SVG/fonts.html#FontFaceElement. Accessed 07 September 2011

9. ISO (1994) Information technology – Digital compression and coding of continuous-tone still images: Requirements and guidelines. ISO/IEC 10918-1:1994. International Organization for Standardization. www.iso.org/iso/iso_catalogue/catalogue_tc/catalogue_detail.htm?csnumber=18902. Accessed 26 February 2011

10. ITU-T (1992) T.81: Information technology – Digital compression and coding of continuous-tone still images - Requirements and guidelines. International Telecommunication Union. www.itu.int/rec/T-REC-T.81. Accessed 26 February 2011

11. ISO (1995) ISO/IEC 10918-2:1995 Information technology – Digital compression and coding of continuous-tone still images: Compliance testing. International Organization for Standardization. www.iso.org/iso/iso_catalogue/catalogue_tc/catalogue_detail.htm?csnumber=20689. Accessed 26 February 2011

12. ITU-T (1994) T.83: Information technology – Digital compression and coding of continuous-tone still images: Compliance testing. International Telecommunication Union. www.itu.int/rec/T-REC-T.83. Accessed 26 February 2011

13. ISO (1997) ISO/IEC 10918-3:1997 Information technology – Digital compression and coding of continuous-tone still images: Extensions. International Organization for Standardization. www.iso.org/iso/iso_catalogue/catalogue_tc/catalogue_detail.htm?csnumber=25037. Accessed 26 February 2011

14. ITU-T (1996) T.84: Information technology - Digital compression and coding of continuous-tone still images: Extensions. International Telecommunication Union. www.itu.int/rec/T-REC-T.84. Accessed 26 February 2011

15. ISO (1999) ISO/IEC 10918-4:1999 Information technology – Digital compression and coding of continuous-tone still images: Registration of JPEG profiles, SPIFF profiles, SPIFF tags, SPIFF colour spaces, APPn markers, SPIFF compression types and Registration Authorities (REGAUT). International Organization for Standardization. www.iso.org/iso/iso_catalogue/catalogue_tc/catalogue_detail.htm?csnumber=25431. Accessed 26 February 2011

16. ITU-T (1998) T.86: Information technology – Digital compression and coding of continuous-tone still images: Registration of JPEG Profiles, SPIFF Profiles, SPIFF Tags, SPIFF colour Spaces, APPn Markers, SPIFF Compression types and Registration authorities (REGAUT). International Telecommunication Union. www.itu.int/rec/T-REC-T.86. Accessed 26 February 2011

17. ISO (2011) ISO/IEC FDIS 10918-5 Information technology – Digital compression and coding of continuous-tone still images: JPEG File Interchange Format (JFIF). International Organization for Standardization. www.iso.org/iso/iso_catalogue/catalogue_tc/catalogue_detail.htm?csnumber=54989. Accessed 26 February 2011

18.   CompuServe (1987) GIF – Graphics Interchange Format. A standard defining a mechanism for the storage and transmission of raster-based graphics information. CompuServe Incorporated. www.w3.org/Graphics/GIF/spec-gif87.txt. Accessed 26 February 2011

19.   CompuServe (1990) Graphics Interchange Format Version 89a. CompuServe Incorporated. www.w3.org/Graphics/GIF/spec-gif89a.txt. Accessed 16 February 2011

20.   Boutell T et al (1997) PNG (Portable Network Graphics) Specification Version 1.0. RFC 2083. Internet Engineering Task Force. http://tools.ietf.org/html/rfc2083. Accessed 26 February 2011

21.   ISO (2004) ISO/IEC 15948:2004 Information technology – Computer graphics and image processing – Portable Network Graphics (PNG): Functional specification. International Organization for Standardization. www.iso.org/iso/catalogue_detail.htm?csnumber=29581. Accessed 26 february 2011

22.   xat.com (2011) JPEG Optimizer: The JPEG Image Compressor for Windows. xat.com Internet Technology. http://xat.com/jpegopt/. Accessed 26 February 2011

23.   W3C (2010) How can I include flash in valid (X)HTML Web pages? In: Help and FAQ for the Markup Validator. World Wide Web Consortium. http://validator.w3.org/docs/help.html#faq-flash. Accessed 15 December 2010

24.   Adobe (2010) Flash Player Detection Kit. Adobe Systems Incorporated. www.adobe.com/products/flashplayer/download/detection_kit/. Accessed 07 December 2010

25.   Google Inc (2010) Swfobject. Google Project Hosting. http://code.google.com/p/swfobject/. Accessed 07 December 2010

CHAPTER 10

Accessibility

With the rapid evolution of web services and technologies, the number of Internet users is constantly increasing. Since many people suffer from various temporary or permanent disabilities and deficiencies, advanced web development practices should be applied to provide content that is accessible for all. The importance of web accessibility is being recognized by an increasing number of web designers and developers. W3C provides useful guidelines to ensure content accessibility. The accessibility support implemented in modern software tools and web sites should be clearly indicated so people living with disabilities can easily identify them. HTML5 markup also supports accessibility through advanced structuring elements, metadata, and Accessible Rich Internet Applications (ARIAs). Web accessibility techniques are not limited to the visually impaired or people with other disabilities. In fact, they also ease mobile access to web content and improve overall web page quality.

In this chapter, you will learn the criteria of accessible web sites, along with the techniques to fulfill them. You will understand the concept of web accessibility and become familiar with the most widely adopted official guidelines. The corresponding guidelines provide access to your web sites for the disabled and improve the user experience for people using devices with limited hardware capabilities, such as mobile users. The content of your web sites should remain legible even if the style sheets are turned off, can be read out loud effectively by screen readers, and rendered also in text-based browsers such as Lynx. Moreover, the techniques that support accessibility have a nice side effect: they contribute to web site usability; thus, you can further improve the overall quality of any web site.

Defining Web Accessibility

By default, web sites containing a variety of components, especially the ones with nontextual content such as videos, cannot be used by all people. Even common web site components like text might be difficult, and sometimes impossible, for some people to read. Not all users can see colors or move the mouse. Everybody knows how frustrating a web site can be when it does not work or has functionality that is very difficult to use for whatever reasons. Now imagine that feeling magnified by a factor of ten or a hundred, which is what people with disabilities suffer from when using inaccessible web sites. The degree of frustration varies from person to person, because some people live with visual impairment, while others with mobility, dexterity, auditory, or cognitive impairment.

More and more countries have introduced legislation addressing the need for web sites to be accessible to people with disabilities or the requirement to be nondiscriminative against people with disabilities. Some examples are the *Disability Discrimination Act 1992* in Australia [1], the *Disability Act 2005* in Ireland [2], the *Disability Discrimination Act* 1995 in the United Kingdom [3], or *Section 508 Amendment to the Rehabilitation Act of 1973* in the United States [4].

Web accessibility covers those web site development practices that provide web content usable ("accessible") for everybody, including people with disabilities. W3C director Tim Berners-Lee announced the launch of the International Program Office (IPO) for the Web Accessibility Initiative

(WAI) [5] at W3C in 1997 by defining accessibility as follows: "The power of the Web is in its universality. Access by everyone regardless of disability is an essential aspect" [6].

While the brightly contrasting colored strips on the steps of buses provide improved visibility for the visually impaired, such strips can be useful to other people too (for example, in poor light conditions or when someone is in a hurry). Many ramps might be useful not only for people in a wheelchair but also for parents with children, skateboarders, in-line skaters, or people moving heavy goods. Similarly, the improved accessibility of web content is useful not only for people with disabilities but for any user in general. For example, web accessibility contributes to a higher level of user experience in mobile browsing, and mobile devices are used by everybody, not only people with disabilities.

There are several software tools and hardware devices used by people with disabilities for web browsing (and using the computer in general). Such tools and devices are referred to as *assistive technology* (AT).[1] This umbrella term covers screen readers, screen magnifiers, switch mechanisms, alternative and adaptive keyboards such as large key keyboards with simplified keyboard layout and approximately four-times bigger (and often colored) keys than the keys on standard keyboards, high-contrast keyboards, keysets (chorded keyboards), keyboards with mousepads or keyguards, trackballs, mouthsticks, handsticks (keyboard aids, type aids), head pointers (head wands), and so on (Figure 10-1).

Figure 10-1. *Examples for assistive technology*

According to the 2010 World Standards Day Message, at least 650 million people around the world are affected by some kind of disability. Consider that as the world population ages, the need for accessibility is constantly growing. Moreover, accessibility is not only an issue for the elderly or disabled. Anybody at any stage in life might experience temporarily reduced accessibility [7].

In contrast to the common misbelief, web accessibility authors address much more than just visual impairment. Many people have motor, mobility, auditory, or cognitive problems. The Web is just as, if not more, important to people with disabilities than it is to anyone. The reason is that the Web provides access to services and/or information that cannot be obtained easily without it (for example online ordering) [8]. However, badly designed web sites create barriers that exclude people from using the Web [9].

The World Wide Web Consortium provides accessibility guidelines and techniques for web content (*WCAG*), authoring tools (*ATAG*) [10], and user agents (*UAAG*) [11]. Accessibility test results can be expressed in a special language called *Evaluation Language* (*EARL*) [12].

The accessibility of dynamic contents and advanced user interfaces developed in a combination of HTML, JavaScript, Ajax, and other technologies is defined by the collection of specifications released by

---

[1] Sometimes the term Adaptive Technology is also used.

the Web Accessibility Initiative (WAI) at the W3C. This collection is known as the *Accessible Rich Internet Applications Suite*, which includes the following documents [13]:

- *WAI-ARIA technical specification:* Accessibility tips for the authors and editors of web standards, as well as developers of user agents and accessibility evaluation tools [14]

- *WAI-ARIA Primer:* The technical approach of WAI-ARIA with detailed descriptions of accessibility problems that can be solved applying WAI-ARIA [15]

- *WAI-ARIA Authoring Practices:* A practical guideline for developers about accessible rich Internet applications developed using WAI-ARIA [16]

- *WAI-ARIA User Agent Implementation Guide:* Accessibility requirements for user agents [17]

Standards such as Synchronized Multimedia Integration Language (SMIL), which is an XML markup for describing multimedia presentations [18], or the Timed Text Markup Language (TTML), which provides text in synchrony with media such as video [19], can also be used to improve site accessibility.

WCAG 1.0

The first version of the Web Content Accessibility Guidelines (WCAG 1.0) became a W3C Recommendation in 1999 with the slogan "how to make web content accessible to people with disabilities." WCAG 1.0 consists of fourteen guidelines [20]:

1. Equivalent alternatives must be provided for auditory and visual content.

2. Information expressed in colors must also be available and perceivable without colors.

3. Markup and style sheets must be applied properly.

4. The natural language(s) of web documents must be declared.

5. Tables must be created in a way that they transform gracefully.

6. Pages that apply new technologies must transform gracefully.

7. User control must be provided for time-sensitive content changes.

8. Direct accessibility of embedded user interfaces must be ensured.

9. Web site design must be device-independent.

10. Interim solutions must be used.

11. W3C technologies and guidelines must be applied.

12. Information must be provided on context and orientation.

13. Navigation must be easy-to-understand.

14. Documents must be clear and simple.

Each guideline is subdivided into checkpoints that serve as the basis for checking WCAG conformance. There are 65 of them. Each of these checkpoints has a priority, from 1 to 3. As you will see in the next section, they are very similar to the conformance levels introduced in WCAG 2.0. The three priority levels are the following:

- *Priority 1* (cf. *Level A conformance*): Developers *must* satisfy these requirements, or else one or more groups cannot access the content.

- *Priority 2* (cf. *Level AA (Double-A) conformance*): Developers *should* satisfy these requirements; otherwise, the content will be difficult to access for some groups. This level removes significant barriers.

- *Priority 3* (cf. *Level AAA (Triple-A) conformance*): Developers *may* address these checkpoints in order to maximize accessibility.

WCAG 2.0

The second version of the Web Content Accessibility Guidelines (WCAG 2.0) became a W3C Recommendation in 2008 [21]. WCAG 2.0 can be summarized with twelve guidelines following four principles [22]:

Principle 1: User interface components and published information perceivable to anyone.

1. Alternate text must be provided for nontext contents, making it possible to change it into other forms.

2. Time-based media must have alternatives.

3. Web content must be available through different presentations without losing information or structure.

15. Both visual and aural contents must be easy to distinguish.

Principle 2: Operable user interface and usable navigation.

16. All functionality must be available from the keyboard.

17. Users cannot be forced to perform actions within time limits.

18. Designs that might cause seizures must be avoided.

19. Guidance and help must be provided for users to navigate through the site.

Principle 3: Understandable content and operation of the user interface.

20. Text content must be convenient to read and easy to understand.

21. Content appearance and operation must be predictable.

22. Assistance must be provided for users to avoid, find, and correct mistakes.

Principle 4: Robust content with high interoperability that can be used reliably on any kind of user agent, including assistive technology.

23. Compatibility must be maximized with current and future user agents and assistive technology, including the ones running on limited resources [23].

These guidelines contain 61 *success criteria*. WCAG 2.0 conformance can be achieved by applying a series of techniques [24]. Some of them are required to meet success criteria (*sufficient techniques*), while others are optional only (*advisory techniques*). W3C claims that none of the accessibility techniques can be referred to as *required* or *mandatory* [25]. They are recommended only, and developers may choose to apply them.

In contrast to WCAG 1.0, which has three priority levels, WCAG 2.0 success criteria are organized into three *levels of conformance*. The *conformance requirements* of all levels of WCAG 2.0 are summarized in the following sections. Generally, the word *must* in the following sections—similar to the word use of the WCAG specifications published by the W3C—corresponds to Level A conformance, which is the minimum level of accessibility in WCAG 2.0 (for example, text alternative for nontext content). The word *should* corresponds to Level AA conformance (for example, captions for live synchronized media). The words *may* and *can* correspond to Level AAA conformance (for example, optional sign-language interpreters).

The higher the accessibility conformance level, the more requirements or higher restrictions apply. For example, Guideline 1.4 describes distinguishable color use and the requirements for separating foreground from background. To meet level A, you should not rely on color alone for conveying information. Level AA has a stricter requirement and prescribes a minimum contrast ratio of 4.5:1 (3:1 for large text), while Level AAA demands an even higher-contrast ratio of 7:1 (4.5:1 for large text).

Note that some requirements are general, while others are technology-specific and apply to a certain technology only, such as Flash. Some techniques can be used either alone or in combination with a similar technique, such as short and long descriptions, but the corresponding requirements regarding their application depend on the desired level of accessibility.

It is important to keep in mind that Level AAA conformance is not recommended as a general policy, because there are content types that cannot be published in a way that the document meets all AAA criteria because of the nature of the content or special technology features and limitations. In other words, using certain content types might limit the maximum achievable level of accessibility to WCAG 2.0 AA, while WCAG 2.0 AAA cannot be met if certain content types are present. For example, section headings can contribute to AAA conformance; however, they cannot be added to all kinds of documents (for example, a long letter [26]). Naturally, site structure or markup elements should be reorganized, added, or modified when creating an accessible web site or redesigning a nonaccessible site to become accessible, but there is no reason for a content author to modify the textual content of a web page just to make the site accessible or more accessible. Another example is Flash, which had known accessibility barriers at the time the WCAG specifications were formed, and generally it was infeasible to provide Flash content and achieve level AAA conformance at the same time.

Additionally, WCAG conformance can be limited to a *conforming alternate version* instead of the whole web site. For example, if the complex design of a web site makes it infeasible to meet WCAG requirements, the site can still be accessible by providing an alternate style sheet or, in the case of more sophisticated design, an alternate, accessible version of each page within the site. Consequently, determining WCAG conformance requires deep site analysis and cannot be judged by simply opening the home page [27].

■ **Note** In contrast to documents with tag soup and bad markup, well-structured, standard-compliant web sites with properly written content provide a basic level of accessibility by default, which can be further extended to achieve the desired (advanced) level of accessibility.

Site Structure Requirements

All web pages (not only the home page) must have descriptive titles provided by the `title` element. In the optimal case, page titles identifying the subject are short as well as reasonable and understandable without context. Moreover, they should be unique and identify the page within the site. Table 10-1 shows an example.

Table 10-1. Unique and Short, but DescriptiveWeb Page Titles Within a Site

URI	Page	Title Example
http://www.example.com	Index page	Professional consultants
http://www.example.com/about/	About page	Professional consultants: About
http://www.example.com/contact/	Contact page	Professional consultants: Contact

A hyperlink pointing to the main content page must be provided at the top of each web page within a site.

⬛ **Tip** This requirement can be easily provided without interrupting the content or design by adding the link to the web site logo as `<a href="http://www.example.com"><img src="images/logo.png" alt="Pro Consultants" /></a>`.

Links to all other pages of the site must be available directly or indirectly from the home page. The relationship between the currently visited web page and other parts of the web site can be clearly indicated with properly selected web site components and well-written element content (descriptive URIs, descriptive titles, metadata provided with link rel, breadcrumb trails, chapters added using headings, and so on).

Breadcrumb trails may be applied to help the user visualize content structure, ease navigation, and identify the current location within the site structure as well as within the current web page. This can be obtained by displaying locations in the path or the location of the current web page within the site structure. Breadcrumb trails might provide links to previously visited web pages. They are placed in the same location within each web page. Typical separators used for breadcrumb trailing are ▼, ▶, >, |, ::, and /. For example, it can be clearly indicated that the web store user is browsing LCD monitors with a screen size equal to or larger than 22 inches as Electronics > Computers & Accessories > Monitors > LCD > 22 Inches & Up (Figure 10-2).

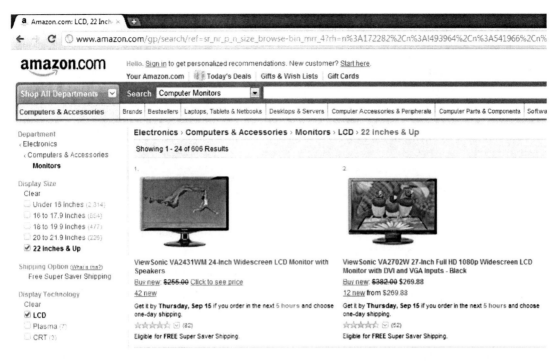

Figure 10-2. Breadcrumb trails to ease navigation

The current location may be presented within navigation bars too. The list of all other pages of the site as well as links to related web pages can also ease navigation. The `link` element may be applied for clearly indicating multiple relationships between the current web page and other web pages within the web site (with values of the rel attribute such as Start, Next, Prev, Contents, and Index). Listing 10-1 shows an example.

Listing 10-1. Declaring Web Page Relationships in the Document Head

```
<head>
  <title>Chapter 4</title>
  ...
  <base href="http://www.example.com/" />
  <link rel="prev" href="chapter3/">
  <link rel="next" href="chapter5/">
  ...
</head>
```

A logical tab order must be added to web sites that allows the user to easily navigate through links, objects, and form controls (Listing 10-2).

Listing 10-2. Tab Order Declared for the Menu, Search Box, and Flash Header of a Web Page

```
...
   <base href="http://www.example.com/" />
...
<ul>
  <li>
    <a href="http://www.example.com/" title="Home" accesskey="h" tabindex="1">↵
      <span class="ak">H</span>ome</a>
  </li>
  <li>
    <a href="about/" title="Introduction" accesskey="a" tabindex="2"> ↵
      <span class="ak">A</span>bout</a>
  </li>
  <li>
    <a href="services/" title="Wedding photography" accesskey="s" tabindex="3"> ↵
      <span class="ak">S</span>ervices</a>
  </li>
  <li>
    <a href="portfolio/" title="Samples and testimonials" accesskey="p" tabindex="4"> ↵
      <span class="ak">P</span>ortfolio</a>
  </li>
  <li>
    <a href="contact/" title="Address, mail, and phone" accesskey="c" tabindex="5"> ↵
      <span class="ak">C</span>ontact</a>
  </li>
</ul>
...
<form method="get" action="http://www.google.com/search">
  <fieldset>
    <label for="q">Search query</label>
    <input type="text" name="q" id="q" size="19" maxlength="255" value="Type to search" ↵
      tabindex="6" />
    <input type="submit" name="btnG" value="Search" tabindex="7" />
    <input type="hidden" name="domains" value="http://www.example.com/" />
    <input type="hidden" name="sitesearch" value="http://www.example.com/" />
  </fieldset>
</form>
...
<object type="application/x-shockwave-flash" data="flash/header.swf" width="720" ↵
 height="300" id="flash" tabindex="8">
  <param name="movie" value="flash/header.swf" />
  <param name="wmode" value="transparent" />
  <div>
    <a href="longdesc/"><img src="images/alter.jpg" alt="The image alternative for the ↵
    flash header." /></a>
  </div>
</object>
```

A search function is vital for all web sites because it might help users find content. A popular approach for providing a search function to web sites is to create a site-specific Google search field (also shown in the previous example). The Search button should be adjacent to the search field.

Content sections must begin with a heading element to provide structure (h1–h6). Descriptive headings and labels must be provided that allow users to select the information relevant to them. Pages can be organized efficiently with headings. In (X)HTML5, document introductions should apply the header element.

Content Requirements

The order of content in the source code must coincide with the visual presentation of the content; in other words, the DOM order must match the visual order. Dynamic content inserted into the Document Object Model right after the element used to activate the dynamic content insertion ensures a correct tab order (and thus a correct reading order for screen readers) through the exploitation of the default tab order of user agents. Web page content must be ordered in a meaningful sequence. This also holds for interactive elements. Page section reordering must be performed by using the DOM. Repeated components should always be presented in the same order. Users must be allowed to skip repeated menu items through expandable and collapsible menus. Flash contents must apply the tabIndex property in order to specify a logical reading order and a logical tab order.

User Assistance

A site map and a table of contents also contribute to accessibility. A help link may be added to every web page. A dedicated help page can be used to collect information that can be helpful for less experienced users but omitted from the main content, because they are evident (and perhaps annoying) for most users. Moreover, a help page might provide information about special web site features that are not common on the Web. For example, a user of a highly accessible web site can be informed about the option to control the menu with keyboard buttons, which is not available on every site. Help may also be provided in the form of an assistant who gives a tour to new visitors on the functionality and content of the site. Such an assistant can be presented as an animation with a digital character (also known as a multimedia avatar) or a video clip with a real person, who gives instructions or a service overview or explains concepts related to the company portfolio (Figure 10-3).

Figure 10-3. An assistant (video clip with a real person) [28]

Ensured Readability

In the optimal case, text is easy to read. Complex text content may be summarized in a form that requires a reading ability less advanced than the upper secondary education level. For example, a technical article can be too complex to read for some people, and a text summary containing shorter sentences and more common words might be helpful for them. To achieve AAA conformance, text lines may not exceed an average of 80 characters even if the browser window is resized.

People with certain cognitive disabilities who have trouble tracking single-spaced lines might find a spacing of 1.5–2 more convenient to read. Web pages may have buttons to improve readability by increasing line spaces and paragraph spaces (Listing 10-3).

Listing 10-3. Sample Buttons for Manipulating Line Space and Paragraph Space

```
...
<script type="text/javascript">
  function inclineh() {
    document.getElementById('main').style.lineHeight="200%";
  }

  function incpars() {
    var get_ps = document.getElementsByTagName("p");
    for (var i = 0; i < get_ps.length; i++) {
      get_ps[i].style.marginBottom="40px";
    }
  }
</script>
...
<div>
  <a href="javascript:inclineh();"><img src="images/lineh.png" alt="Line height" ↵
  title="Increased line height" /></a>
  <a href="javascript:incpars();"><img src="images/pspacing.png" alt="Paragraph spacing" ↵
  title="Increased paragraph spacing" /></a>
</div>
...
<div id="main">
  <p>
    This is the first paragraph of the main content.
  </p>
  <p>
    This is the second paragraph of the main content.
  </p>
</div>
```

Additionally, the `letter-spacing` CSS property must be used to control spacing within words (whitespace between characters) that can further increase readability. Font sizes are best provided in relative units (% or em). The em unit is preferred for text sizes of containers such as tables where percent-based fonts might cause a font size that is too large when resizing. Information presented by text formatting such as font face, font size, or text decoration must also be accessible without formatting. Basic text formatting should apply not only for (X)HTML documents but also for plain-text files. Text files must have text formatting that represents paragraphs, lists, and headings.

The visual presentation of texts should be controlled with CSS properties such as `font-family`, `font-size`, `font-style`, `font-weight`, `color`, `letter-spacing`, `line-height`, `text-align`, `text-transform`, and background-image and the pseudoclasses :first-line, :first-letter, :before and :after. These properties and pseudoclasses avoid the need for image text.

Color Use

Web content must be accessible without the ability of sensory perception required for recognizing locations, shapes, sizes, or sounds.

Justified text aligned to both the left and right margins can be hard to read for people with certain cognitive disabilities. Consequently, text aligned to one side only contributes to the highest level of accessibility. If it is not feasible because of layout purposes, a mechanism may be added to remove full justification upon request.

If users are allowed to use the default colors of their browsers, that is, no background color, text color, or text background color is specified by CSS rules, users with vision disabilities can override certain colors that they have trouble seeing. This technique guarantees text readability presented over a background. It is allowed to specify container layout and border colors, though.

A cross-browser color selector solution may be applied that allows users to change the foreground and background colors of text sections.

The text-background contrast ratio should be 4.5:1 to achieve AA conformance (3:1 for large text) and may be a minimum of 7:1 (4.5 for large text) for AAA conformance (including images of text). A high-contrast control should always be provided that allows users to switch to a presentation with sufficient contrast. You can easily calculate the contrast ratio between arbitrarily selected colors by considering the differences in luminosity.

The relative luminance is defined by the WCAG 2.0 specification as "the relative brightness of any point in a colorspace, normalized to 0 for darkest black and 1 for lightest white." In case of the sRGB color space, the relative luminance of a color is defined as L = 0.2126 × R + 0.7152 × G + 0.0722 × B, where the R, G, and B components are defined as follows [29]:

$$R_{sRGB} = \frac{R_{8bit}}{255} \qquad \text{If } R_{sRGB} \leq 0.03928 \text{ then } R = \frac{R_{sRGB}}{12.92} \text{ else } R = \left(\frac{R_{sRGB} + 0.055}{1.055}\right)^{2.4}$$

$$G_{sRGB} = \frac{G_{8bit}}{255} \qquad \text{If } G_{sRGB} \leq 0.03928 \text{ then } G = \frac{G_{sRGB}}{12.92} \text{ else } G = \left(\frac{G_{sRGB} + 0.055}{1.055}\right)^{2.4}$$

$$B_{sRGB} = \frac{B_{8bit}}{255} \qquad \text{If } B_{sRGB} \leq 0.03928 \text{ then } B = \frac{B_{sRGB}}{12.92} \text{ else } B = \left(\frac{B_{sRGB} + 0.055}{1.055}\right)^{2.4}$$

If you don't want to calculate the color contrast, there are many useful tools that can check it for you, for example the WebAIM Color Contrast Checker [30], the Luminosity Colour Contrast Ratio Analyser of Juicy Studio [31], or the Luminosity Contrast Ratio Analyser 1.1 of WAT-C [32].

Information expressed in colors must also be available and perceivable without colors. Additional visual cues must be available when text color differences are used to convey information. Semantic markup must be added whenever color cues are used to convey information.

An optional multicolor selection tool added to pages to change the foreground and background colors arbitrarily allows users to specify colors according to their personal preference (Figure 10-4).

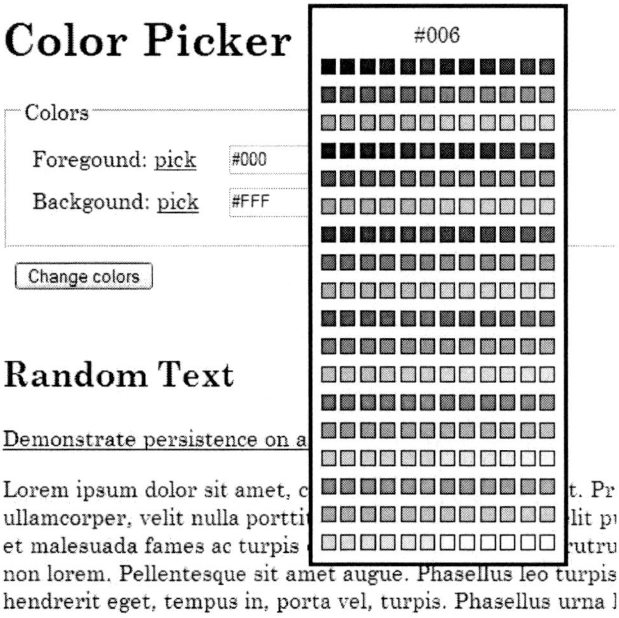

Color Picker

Colors

Foregound: <u>pick</u>   #000

Backgound: <u>pick</u>   #FFF

[Change colors]

Random Text

<u>Demonstrate persistence on a</u>

Lorem ipsum dolor sit amet, c ... t. Pr
ullamcorper, velit nulla porttit ... lit p
et malesuada fames ac turpis ... rutru
non lorem. Pellentesque sit amet augue. Phasellus leo turpis
hendrerit eget, tempus in, porta vel, turpis. Phasellus urna l

Figure 10-4. *A color picker example suggested by W3C [33]*

Information and structure must be separated from presentation to enable different presentations. Various color combinations can be provided for the text and background of the main content along with component groups within the web page.

Abbreviations, Definitions, and Foreign Words

The full form of words may precede their shortenings. Abbreviations might have an inline expansion or explanation they are associated with the first time they occur within a web page. Definitions may be provided by the abbr and acronym elements for all abbreviations. Defined words can be enclosed by the dfn element. Terms, abbreviations, initialism, and acronyms can be linked to their definitions in order to provide the highest level of accessibility. Terms and phrases written as definition list items are the most accessible. They may be collected on a glossary page available through a simple hyperlink provided by the link element. Alternatively, a search function can be embedded that provides the definitions through an external online dictionary. Beyond abbreviations, all words or phrases used in an unusual way or restricted manner can be made more accessible with a definition.

The pronunciation of a special or foreign word provided immediately after the word at least the first time it occurs within a web page contributes to AAA conformance. Other instances can alternatively provide a link to a list of pronunciations.

The default language of web documents must be identified in the HTTP header as well as by the lang and/or xml:lang attribute on the html element in the markup. This is also vital for web pages with Flash content because embedded Flash objects inherit the language settings provided by the lang and/or xml:lang attributes. Document sections written in a language other than the default language must be clearly identified on their containing elements.

To ensure text direction for bidirectional inline content, the Unicode right-to-left marks (‏, ‏, or U+200F), and left-to-right marks (‎, ‎ or U+200E) must be applied.

Text direction of inline content must apply the dir attribute to clearly indicate text direction.

In many languages, such as Arabic, Hebrew, or East Asian languages, text meaning largely depends on pronunciation. Web content written in such languages may apply Ruby annotation with ruby, rt, and rp elements in order to provide information about the pronunciation and meaning of text fragments.

▨ **Note** Ruby annotations were introduced a long time ago in Far Eastern textbooks to provide hints for students about complex characters. For example, Japanese texts written in the Kanji syllabary (writing system) often contain characters that are known only by those Japanese who have at least a high school graduation. Ruby texts written in Hiragana, which is a syllabary all Japanese are familiar with, can make the text clearer. Similarly, traditional Chinese texts can be displayed in simplified Chinese using Ruby annotations.

Using Ruby, a base text can be declared within the Ruby markup (the content of the ruby element), along with the associated Ruby text (the rt element), and optionally the Ruby parentheses (rp), that can be declared for browsers that cannot render Ruby text correctly. For example, pronunciation hints can be provided for words on an educational portal, while foreign words or unusual names can be transliterated into English (Listing 10-4) or represented using the International Phonetic Alphabet (IPA) (Listing 10-5).

Listing 10-4. Ruby Annotation for Tokyo

```
<ruby>
  東京
   <rp> (</rp>
   <rt>Tō kyō</rt>
     <rp>)</rp>
</ruby>
```

In the case of simple Ruby markup, user agents should render the Ruby text above the base text at approximately half the font size. In our case, the result should look like Figure 10-5.

Figure 10-5. The Ruby annotation for the word Tokyo rendered in IE9

■ **Note** Ruby annotations are rendered most accurately by Internet Explorer.

Browsers that do not support Ruby annotations will render the previous code inline without interrupting the text flow (Figure 10-6).

東京 (Tō kyō)

Figure 10-6. The fallback mechanism of the Ruby annotation in action

Listing 10-5. The IPA Representation of an Eastern-European Name Using Ruby Annotation

```
<p>
  Count
  <ruby>
    István Széchenyi
    <rp>(pronounced: </rp>

    <rt>ˈiʃtvaːn ˈseːtʃeːɲi</rt>
    <rp>)</rp>
  </ruby>
  was one of the greatest statesmen of Hungarian history.
</p>
```

Listing 10-5 is rendered in compliant browsers as presented in Figure 10-7.

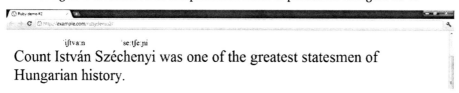

Figure 10-7. Pronunciation hint provided by Ruby annotation

In browsers that do not recognize Ruby markup, the same example would be rendered inline (Figure 10-8).

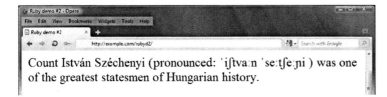

Figure 10-8. Pronunciation hint rendered inline in browsers that do not support Ruby annotations

More complex Ruby annotations can specify not only the default display and fallback mechanism shown earlier but also positioning offsets, alignment, spacing, and overhang. The Ruby annotation was introduced as an XHTML 1.1 module and can also be used in HTML5.[2] The Ruby annotations can also be styled using the corresponding CSS3 module, which provides precise positioning and line breaking, defines the Ruby box model, and supports the vertical-ideographic layout mode [34].

The most accessible documents apply standard diacritical marks in a way that users are allowed to turn them on and off upon request.

Properly selected positioning and units should be applied that support the zooming and text resizing features of browsers.

Accessible web sites have controls that allow users to incrementally change the size of all text (up to 200 percent). There must be no loss of content or functionality when the text resizes while the dimensions of text containers remain the same.

User Interface

Content must be accessible through alternate user interfaces. Properly written markup must be provided that allows assistive technology to understand the content, expose information such as form control IDs, and control certain elements through an API (for example, the DOM).

Standard DOM functions must be applied to dynamically add content to web pages instead of scripting, which provide contents not necessarily read by screen readers.

░ **Note** Screen readers may not automatically read dynamically added content. Reading of dynamically added new content can be ensured by setting the focus to the new element or adding it below the current location where it will be encountered as the user continues browsing.

Liquid layout should be used on all web sites to present content without introducing unnecessary horizontal scroll bars. Page content should adapt to the available horizontal space. Layout regions should be resized with text and reflow as needed to display the page section. Highly accessible web sites eliminate horizontal scrolling even if the user resizes the browser window. One of the techniques to achieve such a foolproof layout is to specify the width of text containers in %. If it is not feasible on the default screen, an alternate layout may be provided that does not require horizontal scrolling.

---

[2] There is a difference between the XHTML 1.1 and HTML5 implementations. As of 2011, the rb (ruby base) element of the original specification cannot be used in HTML5, however, its reintroduction is still an open question. The examples in the listings show HTML5 examples.

Content positioning should be based on structural markup. The appearance can be enhanced with CSS, but the content structure must also remain meaningful without style sheets.

If the content of the default version of a web page is not accessible but an alternate, WCAG-conforming version is, that web page must be linked at the beginning of the nonconforming page. If nonaccessible objects cannot be eliminated from the content, a link must be added adjacent to or associated with these objects that link to an alternate, WCAG-compliant version. User preference must be saved in a cookie. The accessibility of the alternate version must always be ensured with `.htaccess` or the HTTP referrer header. A style switcher must be provided to ensure an alternate version with WCAG-compliant styles.[3] Three different types of style sheets are required to create a style switcher:

1. *Persistent CSS file:* The base styles that are used to share common styles throughout the site. The `rel` attribute is set to `stylesheet`, while the `title` attribute is omitted (Listing 10-6).

   Listing 10-6. *A Persistent CSS File*

   ```
   <link rel="stylesheet" type="text/css" href="styles/main.css" />
   ```

24. Preferred CSS file: Styles enabled by default when the page is loaded. The attribute value of the rel attribute is stylesheet, and the title attribute is provided (Listing 10-7).

    Listing 10-7. *A Preferred CSS File*

    ```
    <link rel="stylesheet" type="text/css" href="styles/main.css" title="Preferred" />
    ```

25. Alternate CSS files: CSS files designed for alternate versions of the site that reuse the styles declared in the main style sheet file but overwrite some of them (for example, set the font size to a larger value, or modify the font color to achieve higher contrast) or add new ones on top of the reused ones (for example, define a maximum width for mobile devices). They can be used not only for increasing accessibility but also for design or media-specific versions of the site (as hinted earlier in Chapter 3). Alternate CSS files have the rel attribute value alternate stylesheet instead of stylesheet, and they have a title attribute that identifies them (Listing 10-8).

    Listing 10-8. *Alternate Style Sheets*

    ```
    <link rel="alternate stylesheet" type="text/css" href="styles/large.css" ↵
      title="Large" />
    <link rel="alternate stylesheet" type="text/css" href="styles/contrast.css" ↵
      title="Contrast" />
    ```

First, create three CSS files, one for the main styles (Listing 10-9) and two for alternate styles that will provide large font size (Listing 10-10) or huge font size with high contrast (Listing 10-11), respectively.

---

[3] Since not all functionalities can be provided through CSS, a conforming alternate version of a web site cannot always be provided by simply creating additional style sheets.

Listing 10-9. The Main CSS File (main.css)

```
body {
  background-color:#004c25;
  color: #cff;
  font-family: Garamond, serif;
  font-size: 1.2em;
}

#wrapper {
  width: 800px;
  margin: auto;
}

#wrapper a:link {
  color: #ff0;
}

#wrapper a:hover {
  color: #ffa000;
}

#wrapper a:visited {
  color: #fff;
}

#colorswitch a:link {
  padding: 10px;
}
```

Listing 10-10. The CSS File for the Large Font Version (large.css)

```
@import ("main.css");

body {
  font-size: 1.8em;
}
```

Listing 10-11. The CSS File for the High-Contrast Version (contrast.css)

```
@import ("main.css");

body {
  background-color: #000;
  font-size: 2em;
}

#wrapper a:hover {
  color: #ff2121;
}
```

383

Next, we need a script that sets the styles from the selected CSS file and stores the choice in a cookie that can be read if the user returns to the page (Listing 10-12). Without cookies, the alternate styles would be applied for the current page of the current session only, which is almost useless. If a visually impaired user selects the "high-contrast theme," he or she would probably like to read all the pages of the site with the same setting.

Listing 10-12. The styleswitcher.js *[35]*

```
function setActiveTheme(title) {
  var i, a, main;
  for (i = 0; (a = document.getElementsByTagName("link")[i]); i++) {
    if (a.getAttribute("rel").indexOf("style") != -1 && a.getAttribute("title")) {
      a.disabled = true;
      if (a.getAttribute("title") == title) a.disabled = false;
    }
  }
}

function getActiveTheme() {
  var i, a;
  for(i = 0; (a = document.getElementsByTagName("link")[i]); i++) {
    if(a.getAttribute("rel").indexOf("style") != -1 && a.getAttribute("title") && ↵
      !a.disabled) return a.getAttribute("title");
  }
  return null;
}

function getPreferredTheme() {
  var i, a;
  for (i = 0; (a = document.getElementsByTagName("link")[i]); i++) {
    if (a.getAttribute("rel").indexOf("style") != -1
        && a.getAttribute("rel").indexOf("alt") == -1
        && a.getAttribute("title")
      ) return a.getAttribute("title");
  }
  return null;
}

function createCookie(name,value,days) {
  if (days) {
    var date = new Date();
    date.setTime(date.getTime() + (days*24*60*60*1000));
    var expires = "; expires=" + date.toGMTString();
  }
  else expires = "";
  document.cookie = name + "=" + value + expires + "; path=/";
}

function readCookie(name) {
  var nameEQ = name + "=";
  var ca = document.cookie.split(';');
  for (var i = 0; i < ca.length; i++) {
```

```
    var c = ca[i];
    while (c.charAt(0)==' ') c = c.substring(1, c.length);
    if (c.indexOf(nameEQ) == 0) return c.substring(nameEQ.length, c.length);
  }
  return null;
}

window.onload = function(e) {
  var cookie = readCookie("style");
  var title = cookie ? cookie : getPreferredTheme();
  setActiveTheme(title);
}

window.onunload = function(e) {
  var title = getActiveTheme();
  createCookie("style", title, 365);
}

var cookie = readCookie("style");
var title = cookie ? cookie : getPreferredTheme();
setActiveTheme(title);
```

Finally, we put all the components together and get the style switcher functionality on our site (Listing 10-13).

Listing 10-13. The Markup Code Featuring the Style Switcher

```html
<!DOCTYPE html>
<html>
  <head>
    <title>Style switcher demo</title>
    <meta charset="UTF-8" />
    <link rel="stylesheet" type="text/css" href="styles/main.css" />
    <link rel="stylesheet" type="text/css" href="styles/main.css" title="Preferred" />
    <link rel="alternate stylesheet" type="text/css" href="styles/large.css" title="Large" />
    <link rel="alternate stylesheet" type="text/css" href="styles/contrast.css" ↵
      title="Contrast" />
    <script type="text/javascript" src="scripts/styleswitcher.js"></script>
  </head>
  <body>
    <div id="wrapper">
      <h1>Style switcher demo</h1>
      <p>This is the content.</p>
      <div id="colorswitch">
        <a href="javascript:void(0);" onclick="javascript:setActiveTheme('Preferred'); ↵
          return false;" id="default">Default CSS</a>
        <a href="javascript:void(0);" onclick="javascript:setActiveTheme('Large'); ↵
          return false;" id="larger">Large fonts</a>
        <a href="javascript:void(0);" onclick="javascript:setActiveTheme('Contrast'); ↵
          return false;" id="contrast">High contrast</a>
      </div>
    </div>
```

```
    </body>
</html>
```

Content scrolled with scripts, such as banners, must have a mechanism to pause or stop scrolling.

Web pages that apply image replacement for text fragments from CSS should have an interface that allows users to switch between the two versions.

Web content structure should contain appropriate semantic markup elements. The elements must be used according to their meaning rather than their (default) appearance. Semantically meaningful markup such as em or strong must be used for emphasized and special texts. The ol, ul, and dl elements must be applied for both lists and link groups. Links must be grouped using the map element.

Keyboard users must not be stopped by a web site section accessible exclusively with a mouse. The same holds for Flash objects that are not keyboard accessible by default.

■ **Note** Duplicated attributes on the same element might cause key errors for assistive technology and must be eliminated.

The appearance of elements receiving focus or being hovered over with a pointing device should be changed (for example, highlighted) to provide visual feedback to the user (such as changed background or border color). Flash content should also provide highly visible focus indication.

Alternate texts, labels, and names should be shared among components with the same functionality.

An optional sign language version provided for all information required to use the content can improve accessibility for people who are deaf or have certain cognitive disabilities. It can be either a multimedia avatar using a technology such as Flash or a video clip of an animated or real sign language interpreter (Figure 10-9).

Figure 10-9. A signing avatar [36]

Web site components such as markup, style sheets, and XML files must be validated to guarantee the proper use of formal specifications, grammar, syntax, and vocabulary. Opening and closing tags must be used according to the markup specification. All web pages must be well-formed.

Markup Requirements for Nontext Content

Images, photos, graphics, and symbols can be applied to improve user experience and help the user understand the content. However, all nontext content, such as images, embedded objects (Flash content, applets, audio, video, and so on), *ASCII arts*, *emoticons*, and *leetspeaks* must have alternate texts.

All images must have an `alt` attribute. For those images that can be safely ignored by assistive technology, the `title` attribute must be omitted and the `alt` text set to null (`alt=""`). If an image and its associated text have the same link, they must be combined in order to avoid unnecessary duplication.

Spacer images such as 1x1 pixel GIF files should be totally eliminated in favor of CSS margins and padding.

For those images and objects where a short description is not adequate, a long description must be added. For years, the `longdesc` attribute was used for that purpose. However, the `longdesc` attribute is obsoleted in (X)HTML5, and a regular a element with a link to the description must be used instead.

Nontext content represented in colors must also be available with patterns that can be understood without colors.

Alternate text must be provided for nontext content that identifies its purpose (even for the content that requires sensory experience). Additionally, both a short and a long description must be provided for nontext content with an identical purpose that presents the same information.

If the original nontext content is too long or the same information cannot be achieved with text alone, short alternate text must be written that briefly summarizes the nontext content.

Images used exclusively for decoration, such as background images, image rollovers, or tab images, must be provided using CSS. Since there is no additional markup, assistive technology can ignore this nontext content.

Alternate text must be written for all `area` elements within image maps.

A text or nontext alternative must be provided for all objects. Alternate texts can be written directly in the content of the `object` element. Nontext alternatives can be provided by nested objects.

Adjacent nontext content sharing information or functionality must be described by alternate text in order to avoid unnecessary duplication.

Blinking and Flashing Content

Photoepileptic seizures caused by strobing or flashing effects should be eliminated. A link or button must always be added to web pages with blinking content that loads equivalent pages without blinking content. Blinking contents can be included on web pages only by using a technology that provides the option to turn off blinking with a browser feature. Blinking content must be minimized below 5 seconds using scripts and, if possible, totally eliminated. The same holds for animated GIF images.

Flashing content must also be minimized. A maximum of three flashes is allowed within 1 second. If it is not feasible because of the content features, the flashing area must be less than 25 percent of 10 degrees of the visual field. The content is not allowed to violate the general flash threshold or red flash threshold, which avoids photosensitive seizures. There are tools, such as the Photosensitive Epilepsy Analysis Tool (PEAT) [37], that can be used to evaluate flashing content to reduce the risk of seizure.

Flash Objects

The dimensions of embedded Flash objects may be specified in relative units (em or %).

Nontext objects marked with the name property must be applied in Flash to allow assistive technology to access them. A long text alternative must be provided by the description property for nontext objects in Flash. Text alternatives must be provided for clickable image hotspots that serve the same purpose. The accessible description of DataGrids has been used for years to provide information readable by screen readers.

Flash graphics must be marked in a way that they can be ignored by assistive technology if needed. This can be accomplished by directly exploiting the accessibility features of Flash objects or by applying textual alternatives using ActionScript.

If adjacent text and image buttons (icons) serve the same purpose, they must be combined into a single button symbol instance.

Forms written in markup are preferred to Flash forms. However, if you have to use Flash forms on your site, the following guidelines should be considered. Flash controls must be understood out of context. To achieve this, control labels can be changed via scripting to provide additional information. Similar to their markup equivalents, the required fields of Flash forms must be clearly indicated. Related Flash form controls must be grouped together to provide semantic meaning. Flash forms must be validated on the client side. If errors are found, a description must be added to the controls containing invalid data. Flash form controls must have an associate text label (for example, via auto labeling). Only CheckBox and RadioButton components get labels by default.

Users must be allowed to pause scrolling Flash contents controlled by a script.

Blinking of Flash contents must be controlled by scripts to stop within a maximum of five seconds.

Link Requirements

Hyperlink anchors must always have a text description that clearly identifies the purpose of the link. Links must apply the title attribute to provide additional link text. Hyperlinks must have a descriptive alternate text that clearly indicates the purpose of the link.

Additional link text added for advanced screen reader and Braille display support can be hidden using CSS selectors (without visibility:hidden or display:none). This link text can also be applied in combination with a style switcher. Repetitive content must be avoided.

A control must be added to the top of each web page providing an alternate page version with link texts that are sufficient to determine their purpose even without context.

The purpose of a link must be clear even without context (applying a descriptive link text), but the container context (paragraph, preceding heading, list item, table cell, and its associated table heading) must also be written in a way that further improves the clarity of the purpose of the link.

The minimum contrast ratio of 3:1 should be ensured between link colors and text colors. Moreover, additional visual cues must be provided on focus for links and controls where color alone is used to identify them.

Destination URIs are generally not sufficiently descriptive. The link text Read more… is, for example, not sufficient to understand a link. However, if the description precedes the link in the same sentence, it can be understandable. The link purpose must be identified using the combination of link text and the text of the enclosing sentence to ensure a logical text flow for screen readers. Link text changed dynamically upon context must be provided whenever reasonable.

Links should be added for all web page elements and objects that do not support long descriptions on the attribute level. The links must be next to the nontext content. The location of the long description must be indicated in the short description (if applicable). For example, the short description of an image provides the text "Comparison of smartphone operating systems—see details below," while the long description below the image states "In Figure 1, you can see the market share of smartphone operating systems, including Android, BlackBerry OS, iOS, Microsoft Windows Mobile, Symbian, and webOS."

If a web page contains blocks of repeated content such as navigation links or table of contents, a link must be added to the beginning of the blocks that allows users to bypass them. The top of the web page must contain links to the different sections of the content.

Dialog messages must be device-independent. Pop-up windows should be eliminated whenever possible. If a new window cannot be eliminated, advanced warning may be provided. To avoid confusion, new windows opened on user request with the `target` attribute may have a proper link text clearly indicating that the content will be opened in a new window. As a general rule, however, links should be opened in the same window rather than a new window or tab. While this approach contributes to accessibility, it has the drawback that it might lead to loss of visitors (if they forget to return to your site).

User Input and Form Requirements

Form controls and links must be provided using (X)HTML elements rather than other technologies such as Flash.

Text inputs of forms must have a `title` attribute that can be used for providing context-sensitive help.

An accessible name must be applied for labeling Flash form controls. Flash buttons must always have an accessible label that describes the purpose of the link. Flash image buttons must have accessible names that provide information about the function of the buttons but do not describe the images in general.

The `label` property must be set for the `Button`, `CheckBox`, and `RadioButton` Flash form components explicitly. As a result, the label text appears next to the component and becomes available for assistive technology.

Groups of form controls must have a description provided by the `legend` element and must be grouped with `fieldset`.

A button must be applied along with `select` elements to perform an action. The `option` elements must be grouped with `optgroup` within `select` elements.

To keep proportions, textual form elements such as input boxes and buttons should be resized when text size is significantly changed in the browser.

Beyond enumerated options, forms sometimes allow user-defined values (typically with the text `other, please specify`) for which text descriptions must be provided.

Text instructions must be added to the beginning of forms and fieldsets that clearly indicate the required input. Text input elements may have a spell checker. Required fields must be clearly indicated, for example with an asterisk (*) character. The user must be informed through a text description if the input is a prohibited value, falls outside the allowed limits, or is provided in a nonsupported format.

When using technologies that support Accessible Rich Internet Applications (WAI-ARIA), the allowed range of entry fields should be identified with the `aria-valuemin` and `aria-valuemax` properties. User agents typically do not permit users to enter values outside the specified range and generate a validation error if users do so.

Expected data formats presented with examples reduce the probability of inadequate user input. The same holds for review and correction options offered before form submitting. A mechanism should be provided for web applications to recover information deleted in error upon request.

Multipart forms must provide a checkbox on the first page that gives users more time upon request or totally eliminates session time limits.

User input should be validated by means of client-side scripting. If errors are found, an alert dialog must be used to inform the user. Error messages can also be added via the DOM. Additionally, a mechanism should be provided that helps users find the location of input errors. If the information supplied by the user is not adequate and cannot be accepted, correct text should be suggested (if available).

If a CAPTCHA is applied, alternate text must be added that describes its purpose. Additionally, another CAPTCHA should be generated upon request.

A checkbox provided in addition to Submit buttons encourages users to review their input before submitting. If confirmation is required to continue a selected action, form submission problems can be minimized or eliminated. After submission, a stated time period should be provided when the order/request can be updated or canceled by the user. A success feedback should always be provided when data is submitted successfully.

The `aria-describedby` WAI-ARIA property can be applied to attach descriptive information to one or more elements. Form controls must be associated with text labels by the `label` element. When the `label` element cannot be used, the `title` attribute must be applied. Labels must be positioned immediately before the field (with text direction taken into account) except the labels of radio buttons and checkboxes that are positioned after the field. Form fields and the buttons that clearly indicate their purpose must be adjacent.

A text cue must be added to colored form control labels to combine color and text or character cues to convey information. For example, required field labels represented in red can be quickly recognized by most people, but not all people can see colors. However, they can still read text cues or listen to them.

A description must be associated with form controls indicating context changes in advance. A `submit` button must be used in order to allow users to explicitly request changes of context. The `aria-required` WAI-ARIA property can be used to indicate that user input is required before submission. Text descriptions must be provided to identify required fields that were not completed.

Table Requirements

Tabular information must be presented with the `table` element. Table captions must be associated with tables by using the `caption` element. Data cells and header cells must be associated with the `id`, `header`, and `scope` attributes in tables. In Flash, the `DataGrid` component must be used to associate column headers with cells. These components must have a caption text. The `summary` attribute must be applied on the `table` element to give an overview of the table.

User Control Requirements

All web site functionalities must be accessible not only with pointing devices such as a mouse but also with the keyboard. This also holds for Flash contents (using the `click` event on standard components).

A control must be provided on all web pages that allows users to stop moving, blinking, or autoupdating contents.

Both a pausing and a restarting option must be provided for all automatically refreshing or disappearing contents such as banners or flash headers. A link to the alternative for time-based media must be placed immediately next to the nontext content. Users should not be forced to complete any activities within time limits. Users must always be warned by a script if the time limit is about to expire. This also holds for Flash content.

Users must always have the option of setting time limits to ten times the default value. The option for extending the default time limit also applies for Flash contents. Moreover, users must be allowed to turn off time limits.

The actions of markup elements such as anchors and form elements must be keyboard-accessible. Event handlers must be device-independent and allow not only the mouse but also keyboard access to full content functionality (for example, drag and drop). This can be achieved using redundant keyboard and mouse event handlers. The same holds for Flash contents as well as all scripting functions.

Web servers that require user authentication often terminate sessions for security reasons after a certain period of time spent without user activity. If the user cannot provide the input quickly enough, the session times out before data submission, and reauthentication is required. Servers should store such data in a temporary cache and retain them after a successful user reauthentication, so the user can continue filling in the form rather than starting it all over again, because all previously entered data is restored. Reauthorization pages may hide and encrypt user data.

Context changes must apply predictable actions. For example, if data entries of a form cannot be presented on a single page, the second page should not be loaded automatically after the user presses the Tab key on the last entry of the first page, because it can confuse screen reader users, which must be avoided.

Automatic redirections should be eliminated whenever possible. Both client-side (`meta refresh`) and server-side (HTTP response) redirections have accessibility issues that can confuse users.

Certain user interface components are highlighted by some browsers when they receive focus. For example, a form input is slightly highlighted in Google Chrome and strongly highlighted in Safari by default but not highlighted at all in IE, Firefox, and Opera (Figure 10-10).

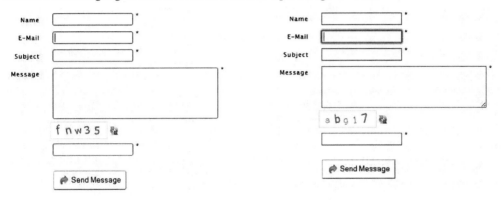

Figure 10-10. Default browser highlighting of the same input field in Firefox and Safari (the second text input is selected)

Since highlighting varies from component to component and from browser to browser, the high visibility of focus indicators should be ensured by web developers.

Form components, links, and all elements with a `tabindex` attribute greater than 0 can receive focus. However, the default focus indicator of some platforms is not highly visible and may be difficult to see against certain backgrounds. The visibility of focus indicators should always be ensured.

Nonessential alerts are optional. In the ideal case, users are not disturbed with unnecessary modal pop-up windows (dialog windows that require the user to click the OK button to disappear).

Time-based media such as presentations must always have an alternate textual version or description. Automatically updated contents may be eliminated and a mechanism provided to postpone automatic content update. Moving and scrolling texts must also be available in a static page section or window.

Live Media, Audio, and Video Requirements

Prerecorded synchronized media such as video clips must have captions. Sounds can be played on user request only. Sound effects must automatically be turned off within three seconds. Additionally, an easily discoverable control must be located near the beginning of the page for turning sound on/off. Flash contents must also have a control for the same purpose.

In Flash movies, screen reader detection with the `flash.accessibility.Accessibility.active` property can be used to turn off sounds that are played automatically if assistive technology is used (by default, the sound can still be played automatically).

Nonspeech sounds in audio files may be at least 20 dB lower than the speech audio content.

An additional, user-selectable audio track must be provided with audio descriptions.

A spoken version of the text can significantly improve site accessibility because it is more accurate and perceivable than the speech of screen readers.

Live audio-only contents may have text alternatives. This can be achieved by a *real-time caption service* with a trained human operator who can type the text with small delay. Note that such services are very rarely used in practice.

A link to a text transcript of a prepared statement or script may be provided for scripts followed by live audio contents. These scripts can be more accurate and complete than live transcriptions; however, care must be taken to ensure correct synchronization.

Accessible alternatives must be provided for time-based media presenting audio-only or video-only contents.

A descriptive label must be provided for live audio-only and live video-only content.

Videos must be provided with extended audio comments that fully describe the video content. Additionally, a second version of video content must always be provided with audio descriptions to maximize accessibility. This also holds for Flash audio-visual materials. Gaps of dialogue must be filled with extended audio descriptions using SMIL.

Video-only content, which is inaccessible to blind and certain visually impaired people, must have an audio alternative in a common audio format such as MP3. Video stream accessibility can be maximized with sign language interpreters through a synchronized video whose display can be selected by the user.

Captions must be added for video contents that can be turned on and off upon request because they maximize availability. Captions must provide information for the hearing impaired not only about the dialogue but also the sound descriptions (unlike conventional subtitles).

Migrating from WCAG 1.0 to WCAG 2.0

Some projects require web site upgrade from WCAG 1.0 to WCAG 2.0. Several WCAG 1.0–compliant sites require little or no changes at all to meet WCAG 2.0. WCAG 2.0 is based on WCAG 1.0; however, there are some differences in the approach and requirements.

Sites that meet WCAG 1.0 partly fulfill WCAG 2.0 by default. The two versions of WCAG are compatible. Consequently, it is possible to meet both WCAG 1.0 and WCAG 2.0 requirements at the same time. Because of the advanced flexibility of the second version, however, a WCAG 2.0–compliant site does not automatically meet the requirements of WCAG 1.0. Some WCAG 2.0 success criteria are very similar to WCAG 1.0 checkpoints. On the other hand, there are WCAG 1.0 requirements that are not needed in WCAG 2.0. Some WCAG 2.0 requirements are more specific than the related requirements in WCAG 1.0 [38].

WCAG 1.0 is technology-specific [39], while WCAG 2.0 applies to W3C and non-W3C technologies as long as they provide accessibility [40].

WCAG 1.0 uses interim solutions ("until user agents…"), while WCAG 2.0 success criteria compliance assumes user agent support.

In WCAG 1.0, JavaScript is considered a technology with accessibility problems [41]. In fact, JavaScript can be accessible, depending on the application and functionality being used (which we'll discuss in more detail later). Scripting techniques successfully tested with screen readers are considered in WCAG 2.0.

The major steps of migrating from WCAG 1.0 to 2.0 can be summarized as follows [42]:

1. Conformance parameters should be determined.

2. Applied technologies should be determined.

3. The application potential of technical requirements should be analyzed.

4. WCAG 1.0 checkpoints should be checked related to WCAG 2.0 requirements.

5. WCAG 2.0 success criteria should be checked.

Finally, strange as it sounds, not everyone is enthused over the highest level of web accessibility. Although WCAG 2.0 is very impressive from the accessibility point of view, it is still being criticized for many reasons. For example, the specifications are very long and complex, the technology-neutral descriptions are rather difficult to implement for developers, very special requirements are included (especially for AAA conformance, like the real-time caption service), some definitions are difficult to understand, inaccessible page versions are tolerated when an accessible version is present, testing is far too complex, and not all content can be written in a way that conforms to the strictest requirements [43].

U.S. Section 508

Beyond W3C standards, there are country-specific standards and/or legislations on web accessibility around the world. In the United States, a basic requirement for government web sites is Section 508 compliance. Subpart B of the Amendment describes technical standards. The most important part for web developers is §1194.22 (Web-based Intranet and Internet Information and Applications) [44].

The web-based technology and information criteria defined by Section 508 are based on W3C WAI guidelines. Consequently, §1194.22 and WCAG 1.0 checkpoints are consistent [45].

There are no limitations on graphic or animation use, but they must be provided in an accessible form. Beyond the text labels and descriptions provided for graphics, this section also addresses usability of style sheets, forms, scripting, multimedia contents, image maps, languages, and plugins.

An alternate text should be written for all nontext elements. Multimedia presentations should be synchronized with their equivalent alternatives. Information cannot be expressed in color alone.

Information representation cannot rely exclusively on associated style sheets.

Row and column headers should be declared for data tables.

Data cells and header cells of data tables should be associated.

Client-side image maps should be preferred to server-side image maps except where the regions cannot be defined with an available geometric shape.

Redundant text links should be provided for all active regions of server-side image maps.

Frames should have unique titles.

Screen flickering with a frequency of 2–55 Hz should be eliminated.

A text-only page should be provided with equivalent information and functionality.

Assistive technology must be able to access content provided by scripting.

Web content that requires third-party software such as plug-ins must provide a link to the plug-in web site.

Forms should provide access for assistive technology.

Users should be allowed to skip repetitive navigation links.

Users should be notified on timed response requirements and allowed to extend time limits.

Semantic (X)HTML5 Elements and WAI-ARIA

The new semantic markup elements introduced in the HTML5 specification such as header, hgroup, footer, article, section, aside, and nav involve accessibility potential. It is important to keep in mind, however, that browser support for these elements varies.

The support for ARIA roles is also increasing. ARIA roles can be applied as additional markup to improve accessibility potential; in other words, their presence does not cause any problems on systems without ARIA support. ARIA roles are added as attributes to elements such as banner, complementary, contentinfo, form, main, navigation, or search. Several ARIA roles describe document structure, namely, article, columnheader, definition, directory, document, group, heading, img, list, listitem, math, note, presentation, region, row, rowheader, separator, and toolbar.

The role of structuring elements can be provided by the role attribute. Listing 10-14 shows an example.

Listing 10-14. Using the role Attribute

```
<header role="banner" />
```

Certain roles must be unique within a page. The banner header code shown is a good example. While developers can use an unlimited number of headers, only one header can be a banner header.

JavaScript Accessibility

Hidden content, navigation, and strange user control behavior provided by scripting can cause confusion and accessibility problems. For example, the onblur event used for checking user input can override the default behavior of user agents and maintains focus until the correct answer is given, which makes it impossible for screen readers to access any other parts of the page (including the feedback text provided elsewhere) without entering the correct answer. Not all event handlers are device-independent, and some rely on the mouse (onmouseover, onmouseout, ondblclick) or keyboard (for example, onkeydown, onkeyup), and cannot be triggered on all devices. If device-independent event handlers are used (such as onfocus, onblur, onselect, or onchange), content and functionality provided through scripting are accessible, full keyboard control is provided, and the scripts do not cause confusion by modifying or overriding normal browser functionality, then scripts can be accessible [46]. When JavaScript cannot be made natively accessible, an accessible alternative must be provided.

Drop-down and fly-out menus are commonly used throughout the Web. However, the onmouseover and onmouseout event handlers cannot be made directly accessible to keyboard users. Thus, an alternative must be provided.

The onfocus and onblur event handlers can be inconvenient or inaccessible for keyboard users to trigger.

The onclick event handler is a device-independent event handler; however, some applications rely on the mouse. In contrast to links or form controls, where the onclick event handlers can be triggered by pressing the Enter key, plain text and table cells cannot gain focus while navigating with the keyboard. Consequently, keyboard users cannot activate the onclick event for elements other than links or form controls. If this event is used with a form element (for example, for form validation), it is not a problem, and the Submit button using the onclick event can be activated by both pointing devices and keyboards.

The ondblclick event handler is generally mouse-dependent, because it is associated with the double-click of the mouse, and there is no equivalent event on all input devices such as on keyboards.

Drop-down selection lists such as language selectors usually apply the onchange event handler. Going directly to the corresponding version by selecting an option from the list with a single click is very convenient for mouse users. However, these lists are not accessible for keyboard users who cannot select anything else but the first option (after pressing the cursor down key on the keyboard, the first option is selected immediately). One possible solution for the problem is to add a button to be the trigger of the `onclick` event handler. However, in this case all users should press the button after selecting the desired option to trigger the event handler.

The `onselect` event handlers can also be applied in a device-independent way.

Certain event handlers such as `onkeydown` and `onkeyup` can be triggered exclusively by the keyboard. The actions associated with them cannot be accessed by the mouse.

Dynamic content, such as the current time presented by `document.write`, cannot be read by screen readers.

Note Some features of dynamic web pages can also be achieved by pure CSS (especially CSS3); thus, certain JavaScript code can be eliminated in favor of CSS (for example, transitioning effects or transforming menu items). However, screen readers can handle certain CSS features poorly, for example, elements hidden by `display: none;` or `visibility: hidden;`.

PDF Accessibility

Adobe Acrobat and Acrobat Reader provide accessibility (Figure 10-11) as well as screen reader options. They are available under Edit Preferences or directly with the shortcut Ctrl+K. You can find the screen reader option under View Read out loud.

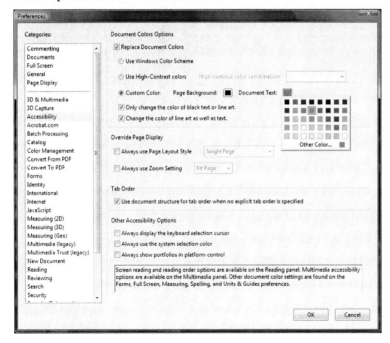

Figure 10-11. Accessibility preferences in Adobe Acrobat/Acrobat Reader

Special features such as the Setup Assistant can be set under Advanced Accessibility (Figure 10-12).

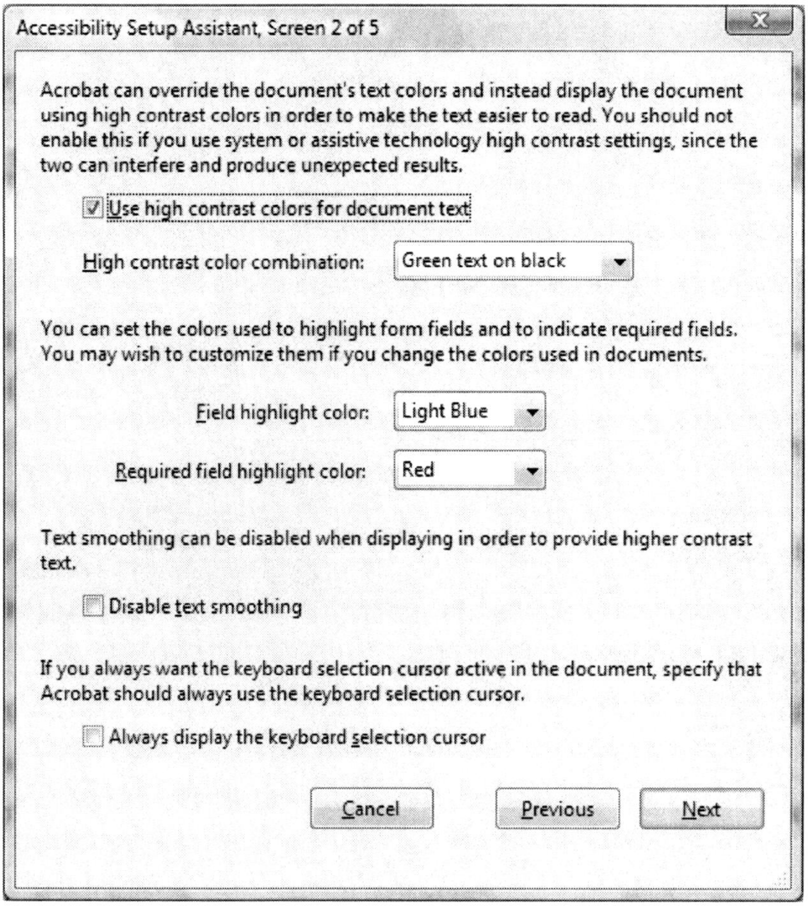

Figure 10-12. *Accessibility Setup Assistant*

Image-only PDF files, which are usually created by scanning paper documents, have accessibility issues. Text cannot be searched. Colors cannot be adjusted. Screen readers cannot read the image only PDF files. Authors should use the OCR capabilities of Acrobat to provide text documents as text and preserve structure at the same time.

The accessibility of *unstructured PDF files* varies. Their reading order can be changed. They provide automatic tagging and authors can optionally use manual tagging. Protected files cannot be saved to accessible formats.

Texts of *structured PDF files* are completely accessible. Hyperlinks are functional. The alternate text of images is accessible (if present). Page numbers are correct. Screen readers can read basic data tables correctly. If provided, the optional bookmarks can further improve accessibility. Protected files are also accessible. However, even structured PDF files have some known accessibility issues. Paragraphs, for example, cannot be located perfectly. Font attribute information is not available.

Flash Accessibility

Although accessibility was a weak point of the Flash technology for ages, both the developer environment and the free player have been improved in this aspect. Adobe Flash Professional and Adobe Flash Player have several features to support assistive technology [47].

The layout and structure can be rather complex in Flash movies, making it very difficult for screen readers to read the content. A description added for the entire movie can give hints for screen readers about the movie structure.

Text equivalents must be added for graphic elements such as names for graphic icons or descriptions for gesturing animations. Element groups must have a single text equivalent.

Movies that never stop moving cause screen readers to refresh frequently. Even on web pages that contain a movie at the bottom, screen readers might interpret motion as a page update and return to the top to start reading again. This behavior can be eliminated by making the child objects of movie clips or entire movies inaccessible [48].

To allow users to control motion, Next buttons must be added to movies instead of displaying information for a limited time.

Several user interface components are accessible in Flash that automate common accessibility tasks such as labeling or providing keyboard access. The accessibility object can be enabled with the class `enableAccessibility()`.

The FLVPlayback component provides the option to include a video player in Flash applications to play downloaded Adobe Flash Video (FLV) files and streaming FLV files. The FLVPlaybackCaptioning component makes it possible to associate captions to your video. The captioning component supports the Timed Text Markup Language (TTML) W3C standard, along with multiple captioning and toggle control.

There are various approaches for providing control over reading order in Flash such as limiting stage size, providing an additional, linear version of the content or specifying reading order via ActionScript.

User controls must be accessible through the keyboard. Keyboard shortcuts must be added to buttons. In order to consider the limitations of screen readers, scripts must be kept within frames and empty movie clips used as buttons must be avoided.

In Flash Professional CS5, a new component was introduced to display audio captions contained either in Timed Text format (DFXP) or integrated with the FLV file as cue points. Flash Professional CS5 also provides native support for accessible video player skins.

User control is a must for audio playback such as the Play and Pause button.

For all controls, it is important to provide the user with feedback on the control as it changes.

The general rules for color selection described earlier in the WCAG requirements also apply for Flash contents.

Accessibility of Mathematical Notations

Mathematical equations provided in GIF images can be hard to read for the visually impaired and, if provided without a textual description, are inaccessible for screen readers.

In contrast, MathML equations are accessible. The accessibility potential of MathML is clearly demonstrated by the accessibility features of a free MathML plug-in for Internet Explorer,[4] Design Science MathPlayer [49]. The software provides audio or Braille descriptions for mathematical notations

---

[4] Since Internet Explorer has native MathML support from version 9, a MathML plugin is required for earlier versions only. The company also provides tools for creating mathematical notations such as MathType (see section "MathType").

to screen readers. MathPlayer also has native speech capabilities (speak expression from the local menu). It allows keyboard navigation. MathPlayer 2 also contains MathZoom that allows users to magnify individual expressions. The matching algorithm ensures that the font size of mathematical notations is increased when the surrounding text is zoomed. Additionally, MathPlayer supports line breaks, which can improve readability if the font size is zoomed. It provides synchronized highlighting of subexpressions that are being read out loud, which helps people with certain learning disabilities such as dyslexia or dyscalculia.

Summary

In this chapter, you learned the accessibility guidelines to be applied in the markup, style sheets, client- and server-side scripting, and multimedia content. You are now capable of creating web sites with the desired level of accessibility that can be used by anyone, regardless of user disability or browsing device limitations.

In the next chapter, you will learn about the tools of a web standardista. You will become familiar with the requirements to be taken into account when selecting your advanced text editor, specific editor, or markup corrector that can ease your work significantly.

References

1.   AustLII (1992) Disability Discrimination Act. Australasian Legal Information Institute. www.austlii.edu.au/au/legis/cth/consol_act/dda1992264/. Accessed 06 January 2011

2.   Office of the Houses of the Oireachtas (2005) Disability Act. The National Parliament of Ireland. www.oireachtas.ie/documents/bills28/acts/2005/a1405.pdf. Accessed 06 January 2011

3.   OPSI (1995) Disability Discrimination Act. The UK Statue Law Database. www.statutelaw.gov.uk/content.aspx?activeTextDocId=3330327. Accessed 06 January 2011

4.   U.S. Access Board (2010) Section 508 Homepage: Electronic and Information Technology. United States Access Board. www.access-board.gov/508.htm. Accessed 06 January 2011

5.   Henry SL (ed) (2011) Web Accessibility Initiative (WAI). World Wide Web Consortium. www.w3.org/WAI/. Accessed 04 February 2011

6.   W3C (1997) World Wide Web Consortium Launches International Program Office for Web Accessibility Initiative. World Wide Web Consortium. www.w3.org/Press/IPO-announce. Accessed 14 October 2010

7.   Régis J, Morrison A, Touré H (2010) World Standards Day Message. International Organization for Standardization. www.iso.org/iso/wsd2010/wsd2010_message.htm. Accessed 14 October 2010

8.   Paciello MG (2000) Web Accessibility for People with Disabilities. CMP Books, Lawrence

9.   Henry SL, McGee L (eds) (2010) Accessibility. In: Web Design and Applications. World Wide Web Consortium. www.w3.org/standards/webdesign/accessibility. Accessed 14 October 2010

10.   Richards J, Spellman J, Treviranus J, May M (eds) (2010) Authoring Tool Accessibility Guidelines (ATAG) 2.0. World Wide Web Consortium. www.w3.org/TR/ATAG20/. Accessed 02 February 2011

11.   Allan J, Ford K, Richards J, Spellman J (eds) (2010) User Agent Accessibility Guidelines (UAAG) 2.0. World Wide Web Consortium. www.w3.org/TR/UAAG20/. Accessed 02 February 2011

12.   Abou-Zahra S, Squillace M (eds) (2009) Evaluation and Report Language (EARL) 1.0 Schema. World Wide Web Consortium. www.w3.org/TR/EARL10-Schema/. Accessed 02 February 2011

13.   Henry SL (ed) (2011) The WAI-ARIA Documents. In: WAI-ARIA Overview. World Wide Web Consortium. www.w3.org/WAI/intro/aria.php#is. Accessed 09 September 2011

14.   Craig J, Cooper M, Pappas L, Schwerdtfeger R, Seeman L (2011) Accessible Rich Internet Applications (WAI-ARIA) 1.0. World Wide Web Consortium. www.w3.org/TR/wai-aria/. Accessed 02 February 2011

15. Pappas L, Schwerdtfeger R, Cooper M (2010) WAI-ARIA 1.0 Primer – An introduction to rich Internet application accessibility challenges and solutions. www.w3.org/TR/wai-aria-primer/. Accessed 09 September 2011

16. Scheuhammer J, Cooper M (2010) WAI-ARIA 1.0 Authoring Practices – An author's guide to understanding and implementing Accessible Rich Internet Applications. World Wide Web Consortium. www.w3.org/TR/wai-aria-practices/. Accessed 09 September 2011

17. Snow-Weaver A, Cooper M (2010) WAI-ARIA 1.0 User Agent Implementation Guide – A user agent developer's guide to understanding and implementing Accessible Rich Internet Applications. World Wide Web Consortium. www.w3.org/TR/wai-aria-implementation/. Accessed 09 September 2011

18. Bulterman D, Jansen J, Cesar P, Mullender S, Hyche E, DeMeglio M, Quint J, Kawamura H, Weck D, Pañeda XG, Melendi D, Cruz-Lara S, Hanclik M, Zucker DF, Michel T (eds) (2008) Synchronized Multimedia Integration Language (SMIL 3.0). W3C Recommendation. World Wide Web Consortium. www.w3.org/TR/SMIL/. Accessed 13 September 2011

19. Adams G (ed) (2010) Timed Text Markup Language (TTML) 1.0. W3C Recommendation. World Wide Web Consortium. www.w3.org/TR/ttaf1-dfxp/. Accessed 13 September 2011

20. Chisholm W, Vanderheiden G, Jacobs I (eds) (1999) Web Content Accessibility Guidelines 1.0. World Wide web Consortium. www.w3.org/TR/WAI-WEBCONTENT/. Accessed 24 January 2011

21. Caldwell B, Cooper M, Reid LG, Vanderheiden G, Chisholm W, Slatin J, White J (eds) (2008) Web Content Accessibility Guidelines (WCAG) 2.0. World Wide Web Consortium. www.w3.org/TR/WCAG20/. Accessed 25 January 2011

22. Vanderheiden G, Reid LG, Caldwell B, Henry SL, Lemon G (eds) (2010) How to Meet WCAG 2.0. A customizable quick reference to Web Content Accessibility Guidelines 2.0 requirements (success criteria) and techniques. World Wide Web Consortium. www.w3.org/WAI/WCAG20/quickref/. Accessed 14 January 2011

23. Vanderheiden G, Reid LG, Caldwell B, Henry SL (2008) How to meet WCAG 2.0. A customizable quick reference to Web Content Accessibility Guidelines 2.0 requirements (success criteria) and techniques. World Wide Web Consortium. www.w3.org/WAI/WCAG20/quickref/20081211/. Accessed 23 September 2010

24. Cooper M, Reid LG, Vanderheiden G, Caldwell B, Chisholm W, Slatin J (eds) (2010) Techniques for WCAG 2.0. Techniques and Failures for Web Content Accessibility Guidelines 2.0. World Wide Web Consortium. www.w3.org/TR/WCAG20-TECHS/. Accessed 24 January 2011

25. Cooper M, Reid LG, Vanderheiden G, Caldwell B, Chisholm W, Slatin J (eds) (2010) Appendix A. How to refer to WCAG 2.0 from other documents. In: Understanding WCAG 2.0. A guide to understanding and implementing Web Content Accessibility Guidelines 2.0. World Wide Web Consortium. www.w3.org/TR/UNDERSTANDING-WCAG20/appendixA.html. Accessed 02 February 2011

26. Cooper M, Reid LG, Vanderheiden G, Caldwell B (eds) (2010) Section Headings: Understanding SC 2.4.10. In: Understanding WCAG 2.0. World Wide Web Consortium. www.w3.org/TR/UNDERSTANDING-WCAG20/navigation-mechanisms-headings.html. Accessed 10 September 2011

27. Abou-Zahra S et al (eds) (2005) Conformance Evaluation of Web Sites for Accessibility. World Wide Web Consortium. www.w3.org/WAI/eval/conformance.html. Accessed 02 February 2011

28. WebsynergiDesign (2011) Accessibility – Our Experience & Accessible web site Design Portfolio. WebsynergiDesign Ltd. www.websynergi.com/accessibility/accessibility-bobby-w3c.aspx. Accessed 10 September 2011

29. Caldwell B, Cooper M, Reid LG, Vanderheiden G (eds) (2008) Relative luminance. In: Web Content Accessibility Guidelines (WCAG) 2.0. W3C Recommendation. World Wide Web Consortium. www.w3.org/TR/2008/REC-WCAG20-20081211/#relativeluminancedef. Accessed 11 September 2011

30. WebAIM (2011) Color Contrast Checker. Utah State University. http://webaim.org/resources/contrastchecker/. Accessed 11 September 2011

31. Juicy Studio (2011) Luminosity Colour Contrast Ratio Analyser. Juicy Studio. http://juicystudio.com/services/luminositycontrastratio.php. Accessed 11 September 2011

32. WAT-C (2005) Luminosity Contrast Ratio Analyser 1.1. Web Accessibility Tools Consortium. http://www.wat-c.org/tools/CCA/LCRA/index.html. Accessed 11 September 2011

33. Cooper M, Reid LG, Vanderheiden G, Caldwell B, Chisholm W, Slatin J (eds) (2010) Color Picker. Working example. In: Techniques for WCAG 2.0. Techniques and Failures for Web Content Accessibility Guidelines 2.0. World Wide Web Consortium. www.w3.org/TR/WCAG20-TECHS/working-examples/G175/index.php. Accessed 28 January 2011

34. Ishida R (ed) (2011) CSS3 Ruby Module. World Wide Web Consortium. www.w3.org/TR/css3-ruby/. Accessed 11 September 2011

35. Sowden P (2001) Alternative Style: Working With Alternate Style Sheets. A List Apart Magazine. www.alistapart.com/d/alternate/styleswitcher.js. Accessed 12 September 2011

36. W3C (2004) Demonstration of Signing Avatar Technology as used in the Signing Science Project. TERC. www.w3.org/2004/Talks/0628-rdig-sims/vcom3d-signsci.mov. Accessed 12 September 2011

37. Trace Center (2011) Photosensitive Epilepsy Analysis Tool (PEAT). The University of Wisconsin.http://trace.wisc.edu.peat/. Accessed 11 September 2011

38. EOWG, WCAG WG (eds) (2009) Comparison of WCAG 1.0 Checkpoints to WCAG 2.0, in Numerical Order. World Wide Web Consortium. www.w3.org/WAI/WCAG20/from10/comparison/. Accessed 03 February 2011

39. Chisholm W, Vanderheiden G, Jacobs I (eds) (1999) Guideline 11. Use W3C technologies and guidelines. In: Web Content Accessibility Guidelines 1.0. World Wide Web Consortium. www.w3.org/TR/WAI-WEBCONTENT/#gl-use-w3c. Accessed 03 February 2011

40. Cooper M, Reid LG, Vanderheiden G, Caldwell B, Chisholm W, Slatin J (2008) Understanding Accessibility Support. In: Understanding WCAG 2.0. A guide to understanding and implementing Web Content Accessibility Guidelines 2.0. World Wide Web Consortium. www.w3.org/TR/2008/NOTE-UNDERSTANDING-WCAG20-20081211/conformance.html#uc-accessibility-support-head. Accessed 03 February 2011

41. Chisholm W, Vanderheiden G, Jacobs I (eds) (1999) Guideline 6. In: Web Content Accessibility Guidelines 1.0. World Wide Web Consortium. www.w3.org/TR/WCAG10/wai-pageauth.html#tech-scripts. Accessed 03 February 2011

42. Swan H, Henry S (2010) How to Update Your Web Site from WCAG 1.0 to WCAG 2.0. World Wide Web Consortium. www.w3.org/WAI/WCAG20/from10/websites.html. Accessed 02 February 2011

43. Clark J (2006) To hell with WCAG2. A List Apart. www.alistapart.com/articles/tohellwithwcag2. Accessed 23 September 2010

44. The United States Government (2010) § 1194.22 Web-based intranet and Internet information and applications. In: Section 508 Standards Guide. The United States Government. www.section508.gov/docs/Section%20508%20Standards%20Guide.pdf. Accessed 04 February 2011

45. The United States Government (2010) Note to §1194.22. In: Section 508 Standards Guide. The United States Government. www.section508.gov/index.cfm?fuseAction=stdsdoc. Accessed 04 February 2011

46. WebAIM (2011) Creating Accessible JavaScript. Overview of Creating Accessible JavaScript. Web Accessibility in Mind. http://webaim.org/techniques/javascript/. Accessed 03 February 2011

47. Adobe (2011) Adobe Flash accessibility design guidelines. Adobe Systems Incorporated. www.adobe.com/accessibility/products/flash/best_practices.html. Accessed 04 February 2011

48. Adobe (2011) Accessibility best practices overview. In: Adobe Flash accessibility design guidelines. Adobe Systems Inc. www.adobe.com/accessibility/products/flash/best_practices.html. Accessed 12 September 2011

49. Design Science (2011) MathPlayer Can Speak! MathPlayer: Speech instructions and examples. Design Science. www.dessci.com/en/products/mathplayer/tech/accessibility.htm. Accessed 04 February 2011

PART 2

Developing with Standards

After learning the specifications required for creating standard-compliant web site components, you have to combine and implement them to create complex web sites ready to publish. In this part of the book, you will analyze those errors that occur most frequently in standard-based web site development, and you will master techniques and best practices through step-by-step guides to be able to plan and create standards-compliant web sites with confidence. You will get useful tips to achieve full standards compliance, robust functionality, optimal code length, and interoperability, as well as meaningful, structured, and accessible content, and proper settings at the same time. You will also learn the features of development and evaluation software to consider when selecting tools for web site development, standardization, and optimization.

CHAPTER 11

Development Tools

Since modern markup elements and attributes are becoming more and more sophisticated, complex development software is used to generate web pages. However, certain web content such as descriptive metadata can be so complex that it often requires human decisions. Advanced text editors always have a top priority in the software list of every web standardista. Although they can be used for a variety of tasks, specific editors should be applied such as semantic editors and markup correctors. Advanced text editors can also be integrated with SFTP clients. WYSIWYG editors and content management systems can be useful for rapid development; however, they often produce invalid code. Consequently, their application should be minimized in web site standardization and optimization.

In this chapter, you will learn about software tools that can help you develop standard-compliant web sites. You will become familiar with those vital features that should be considered when selecting your development tools, optimizers, and testing environments.

Feature Requirements

Although experienced web standardistas can write valid code in any text editor, the software tools to be selected should provide some advanced features that are vital for efficient hand-coding:

- Comprehensive character encoding support, including full Unicode support

- Whitespace character support

- Control character support, for example, CR+LF (Windows), LF only (UNIX), and Apple (CR only) break rows

- Multifile editing with tabs

- Customizable color schemas for *syntax highlighting* (XHTML, CSS, XML, scripts, and so on)

- Undo/redo

- Forced word wrap

- Line numbering

- Auto indent

- Guides for tag pairs and element nesting

- OS integration (adds application to right-click menu)

The selected editor should be integrated with at least one of your browsers as the default source code editor, which you can use to open the currently rendered web document for editing with a button or hotkey.

There are additional features of text editors that are not vital but can be useful:

- Customized color and font settings

- Customizable toolbars

- Spell checker

- Templates

- Bookmarks

- Full drag-and-drop support

- Built-in FTP client or integration with an (S)FTP client

- Conversions (uppercase, lowercase, invert case, and initial caps)

- International versions (can be convenient for some developers)

- Support for double-byte character systems (DBCS) used in Far East languages such as Chinese or Japanese (if required)

- Browser preview[1] (launching the default or selected web browser for debugging and testing)

Text Editors

In contrast with word processors such as Microsoft Word or OpenOffice.org Writer, *plain-text editors* cannot be used for document formatting. These basic text editors can be used for creating web pages, though. However, they are not convenient, and some vital features are missing from them. For example, many of them do not handle all control and whitespace characters correctly. The most well-known examples are Notepad under Windows and vi under Linux.

Advanced text editors such as WordPad provide text formatting and other additional features. *Source code editors* are advanced text editors with additional tools specifically designed for hand-coders and programmers. The most common feature of them is syntax highlighting for a variety of markup languages, style sheets, and programming languages. These full-featured editors are comprehensive tools suitable for hand-coding web pages. The following are some examples:

Linux

- BlueFish [1]

- Komodo Edit [2]

Mac OS

- BBEdit [3]

---

[1] Some developers do not use this feature and open the desired browser(s) manually.

- TextWrangler [4]

Windows

- EditPad Lite (free [5] and low-cost versions [6] are available)

- EditPlus [7]

- NotePad++ (free, open source [8])

- TextPad (low cost, free evaluation [9])

Cross-platform

- Arachnophilia (available for Windows, Linux, Unix, FreeBSD, and Mac OS [10])

As an example, let's look at the major features of Notepad++. It is a multifile editor with convenient file manager options. For example, the editor saves multiple files with a single click, opens recently edited files, and provides tabs for each opened file. It has a fully customizable interface with advanced features such as line markers, guides for opening and closing tag pairs, structuring guides to collapse or reveal the currently edited level of the DOM tree, and syntax highlighting (Figure 11-1).

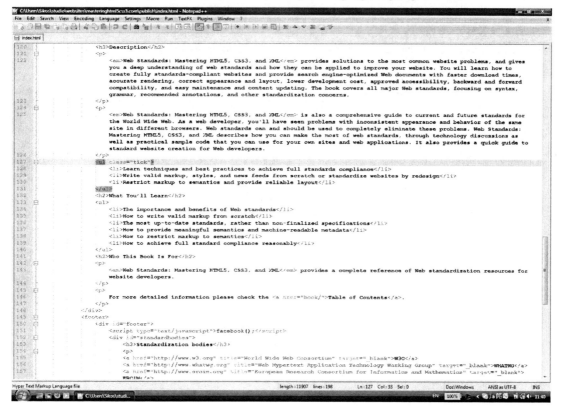

Figure 11-1. Syntax highlighting and tag pair guides in Notepad++

There are a variety of programming and web development languages supported in syntax highlighting from HTML to XML and from PHP to Ruby. There are several predefined color themes you can select from, or you can create and apply new ones if you want. The different document components (indent guidelines, marks, carets, whitespaces, tag pairs, active and inactive tabs, and so on) can be styled individually. Notepad++ can change text direction of documents. It also supports a variety of character encodings, can add and remove byte-order marks, supports big-endian and little-endian Unicode files, and converts files from one encoding to another.[2] The documents opened in the application can be previewed in any installed browsers.

Notepad++ also provides advanced text transformation functionalities, such as escaping certain characters, transforming lowercase characters to uppercase (or vice versa), searching for matching strings, converting decimal numbers to their hexadecimal equivalents, inserting the current date and time, sorting lists ascending or descending, automatically converting leading spaces to tabs, and so on. Notepad++ also supports macros, which you can run multiple times. The list of features can be extended through additional plug-ins, such as the MIME tools for Base64 encoding and decoding.

WYSIWYG Editors

Graphical authoring tools can be comfortable, but standard compliance is not guaranteed in all cases. They have features that can be useful even for advanced developers, and they provide an interface with markup window, instant preview, and advanced debugging tools. Still, not all developers apply them, and some use an advanced text editor exclusively. The graphical developing environments usually require only a basic knowledge of markup and CSS (and sometimes no technical background whatsoever), which is the major reason for their extreme popularity. Because of the large number of features, however, there might be usability issues. For example, the interface can be confusing and intimidating to some users, especially the ones without a few years' expertise. In spite of the graphical interface, some systems are difficult to master. Moreover, all of them have a different interface, and someone who is an expert in one of them is not necessarily familiar with other systems, which is a limitation, especially if the editor is available for one platform only. In contrast, hand-coders can work in pretty much any environment, because text editors are available for all platforms, and their major functionalities are very similar.

It is important to note that most WYSIWYG editors have a built-in source editor. Consequently, WYSIWYG editors can be applied as source code editors as well. Additionally, some features of graphical editors can be useful for any web developers, such as for database management, web servers, and frameworks. Moreover, there are WYSIWYG editors that are dedicated to web standardistas such as XStandard XHTML and W3C Amaya (Figure 11-2).

---

[2] This feature can be used for certain encodings that can be reasonably converted to another, more advanced encoding without sacrificing certain characters (for example, ANSI to UTF-8).

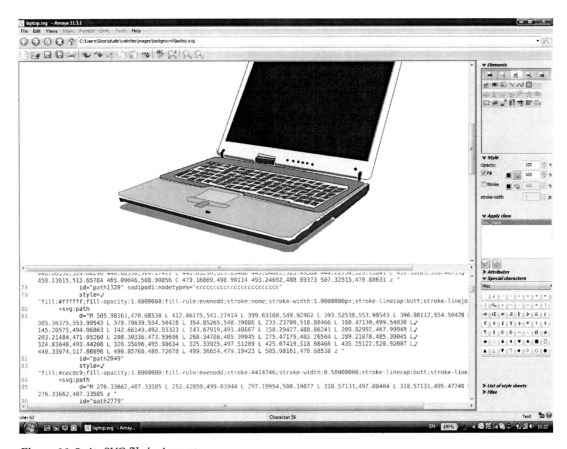

Figure 11-2. An SVG file in Amaya

Many commercial and free editing tools exist [11]. Compared to advanced text editors and source code editors, however, many commercial WYSIWYG editors are expensive. On the other hand, there are several graphical developers that are not only free but also open source. Here are some examples:

Windows

- Microsoft Expression Web [12] (commercial)
- Microsoft WebMatrix [13] (freeware)

Cross-platform

- Adobe Dreamweaver, available for Windows and Mac OS (commercial) [14]
- W3C Amaya, a free, open source (X)HTML, MathML, and SVG editor [15]
- XStandard XHTML, the standards-compliant XHTML editor, available for Windows and Mac OS (free lite version) [16]

407

The standard compliance of the industry-leading authoring application Dreamweaver is constantly evolving. However, it took several years for web standards to attract attention.

The latest versions support HTML, CSS, XSLT, JavaScript, ActionScript, XML, ASP, ColdFusion, JSP, and PHP. Some features and tools in Dreamweaver are useful not only for development in general but also for standard-compliant development. Some examples are invalid code highlighting, syntax error alerts displayed in the info bar, the list of CSS properties associated with the currently selected element, and syntax highlighting. The program interface is highly customizable and features different modes for displaying the code, the result, or both at the same time (Figure 11-3).

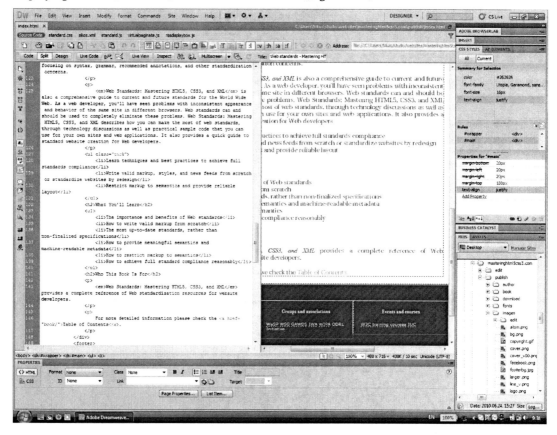

Figure 11-3. Code and design can be displayed simultaneously in Adobe Dreamweaver.

Content Management Systems and Bloggers

Content management systems (CMSs) are WYSIWYG tools developed mainly for web content authoring and blog publishing. Many of them are driven by PHP. The most well-known content management systems are cross-platform, such as Drupal [17], Joomla! [18], and WordPress [19]. Beyond the common tasks of web publishing, they provide modern functionalities such as semantic content support. However, the standard support of CMSs varies. Undoubtedly, they are responsible for a large share of invalid markup on the Web. Figure 11-4 shows a typical example.

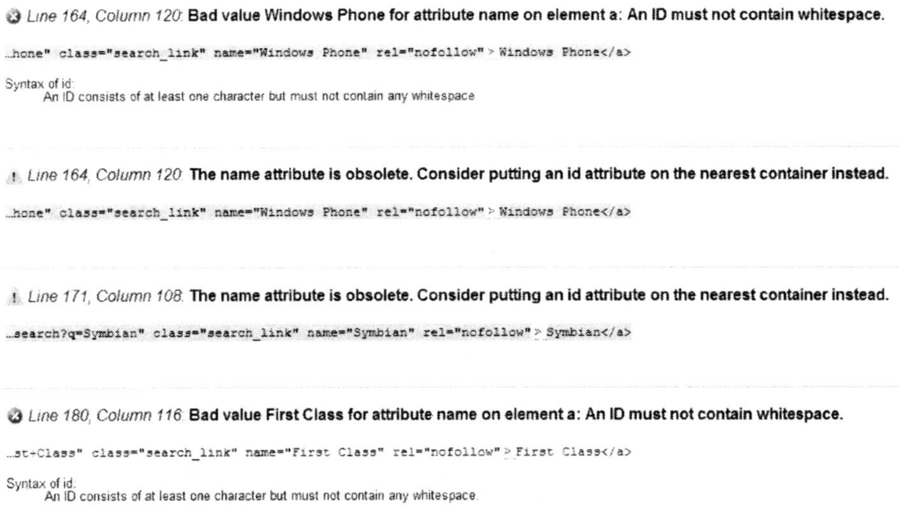

😕 *Line 164, Column 120:* **Bad value Windows Phone for attribute name on element a: An ID must not contain whitespace.**

```
…hone" class="search_link" name="Windows Phone" rel="nofollow" > Windows Phone</a>
```

Syntax of id:
  An ID consists of at least one character but must not contain any whitespace

⚠ *Line 164, Column 120:* **The name attribute is obsolete. Consider putting an id attribute on the nearest container instead.**

```
…hone" class="search_link" name="Windows Phone" rel="nofollow" > Windows Phone</a>
```

⚠ *Line 171, Column 108:* **The name attribute is obsolete. Consider putting an id attribute on the nearest container instead.**

```
…search?q=Symbian" class="search_link" name="Symbian" rel="nofollow" > Symbian</a>
```

😕 *Line 180, Column 116:* **Bad value First Class for attribute name on element a: An ID must not contain whitespace.**

```
…st-Class" class="search_link" name="First Class" rel="nofollow" > First Class</a>
```

Syntax of id:
  An ID consists of at least one character but must not contain any whitespace.

Figure 11-4. *Errors and warnings in every tenth row of the markup generated by a CMS*

Since they are designed for rapid development without source editing, experienced web standardistas avoid using them whenever possible. Although there are more and more CMSs that claim to produce standard-compliant code (LiveStoryboard [20], WebDandy [21], sNews [22], and so on), most of them do not provide a holistic approach to standards implementation; however, some produce a reasonable markup code that is close to optimal.

Web Standards Support

The standards support of editors varies. Several tools know certain markup versions or variants, while others have partial CSS support only (Table 11-1). No ultimate solution exists, but any comprehensive tools could be a good choice for hand-coders. For example, BlueFish supports not only all (X)HTML versions and variants but also RSS, Atom, MathML, CSS2, frames, JavaScript, Java, XSLT, XForms, and XPath.

Table 11-1. *Markup Language Support of Some Editors with Validation Feature*

	HTML 4.01			XHTML			1.1	2	HTML 5
				1.0					
	S	T	F	S	T	F			
Amaya	−	+ −		+	+	−	+	−	−
BlueFish	+	+	+	+	+	+	+	+	+
Dreamweaver	+	+	−	+	+	−	+	−	+

	HTML 4.01			XHTML						HTML 5
					1.0			1.1	2	
	S	T	F	S	T	F				
Freeway	+	+	–	+	+	–	–	–	–	–
KompoZer	+	+	–	+	+	–	–	–	–	–
Expression Web	+	+ +		+	+	+	+	–	+	

Specific Editors

Beyond advanced text editors, there are special tools that cannot be missed from the tool set of web standardistas. Such tools are semantic editors, markup correctors, special editors, SFTP clients, and browser plug-ins.

Semantic Editors and Reasoners

Along with the increasing popularity of OWL, more and more tools are appearing on the market for OWL development. Web ontologies are machine-processable, and *semantic reasoners* (also known as reasoning engines or rules engines) can be used to infer logical consequences from facts or axioms described by the ontologies. Some of the most useful *semantic editors* and *reasoners* are described next.

Protégé is a free open source framework [23] and one of the most widely used OWL editors. It is an efficient tool for developing and testing ontologies. Protégé supports several file formats and syntaxes, including OWL, OWL in functional syntax, OWL in Manchester syntax, RDF/XML, OBO flat file, KRSS2, Latex, and Turtle. It can directly open not only saved files but also online ontologies.

HermiT is an OWL Reasoner that can be used to determine ontology consistency, identify relationships between classes, and further tasks. It can be used from the command line, in Java applications, or as a Protégé plug-in (Figure 11-5).

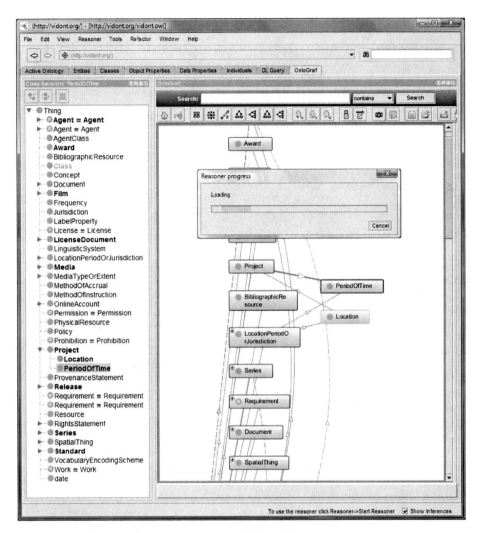

Figure 11-5. The HermiT reasoner running in Protégé

HermiT is released under the LGPL license [24]. *TopBraid Composer* is a graphical development tool for data modeling and semantic data processing that supports standards such as RDF, OWL, and SPARQL [25]. *Pellet* is an OWL 2 Reasoner for Java [26]. *RacerPro 2.0* supports standards such as RDF, RDFS, OWL Lite, OWL DL, and SPARQL. Connectivity with external software is also possible [27]. FaCT++ is a Description Logic reasoner compatible with OWL DL and OWL 2 [28].

MathType

MathType is an advanced editor for mathematical notations developed by Design Science. The equations and annotations can be edited through a powerful graphical user interface (Figure 11-6).

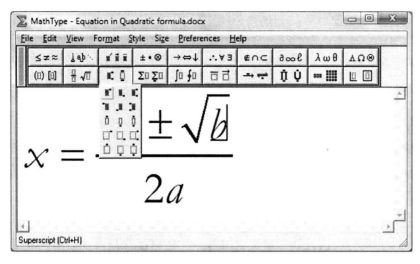

Figure 11-6. *Equation editing in MathType*

The software is available for Windows and Mac OS [29]. The editor is often embedded into Microsoft Word to replace the Equation Editor (either as a new menu or as a new ribbon, depending on the Word version), but it can also be used in other word processors such as OpenOffice, Google Docs, or Apple Pages. The mathematical annotations edited in MathType can also be exported to MathML and LaTeX. In fact, using MathType is one of the easiest ways to generate MathML. Beyond MathType, the W3C browser/editor Amaya can also be used to generate MathML.

Markup Correctors

Although sophisticated markup components such as metadata require human decision, conventional (X)HTML markup elements and attributes can be reliably corrected automatically. They can be useful in many cases; however, markup correctors do not replace hand-coder web standardistas. In contrast with developers, software tools do not always support the latest standards; some of them are discontinued or will be updated several years later than the date of standard release.

HTML Tidy

HTML Tidy is a markup corrector that fixes invalid HTML and improves the layout and indent style of the markup. The tool was developed by *Dave Raggett*, the coauthor and editor of several markup specifications at W3C. Since it is written in ANSI C, precompiled binaries are available for a variety of platforms and can be compiled for further ones. HTML Tidy is available under the W3C license at Sourceforge.net (both as a downloadable binary and as the source code) [30] or as an online service at W3C [31].

The software can identify and correct missing or mismatched end tags, mixed-up tags, and quotes, as well as change markup layout according to predefined styles [32].

Tidy for PHP

The HTML markup generated by PHP scripts can be checked and corrected by the PHP extension *Tidy*. As an example, functions can be written to take HTML markup fragments as strings and run them through HTML Tidy. The output is a valid markup. This approach makes automatic page processing and standardization possible. If there are errors in the code, the location (line, column) and the error cause are clearly indicated or automatically corrected [33].

Log Validator

W3C Log Validator "combines a Server Log analysis engine with batch validation, link checking, and other quality-oriented processing, for step-by-step improvement and maintenance of Web Site Quality" [34]. It finds the most frequently downloaded invalid documents, broken links, other errors, and inconsistencies, and it sets a priority list for fixing them. This feature is designed for standardizing large-scale invalid web sites step by step by correcting only a certain amount of documents at a time. Eventually, the whole site will be fixed, but the standardista can determine how to schedule development time and effort.

Log Validator applies processing modules that validate the latest server logs against markup and style sheet recommendations (according to W3C HTML and CSS Validation Services). The SurveyEngine module creates a summary of errors for the most popular documents that might affect the overall quality of the site. The basic processing module generates only a list of documents by popularity. Log Validator supports three types of output: raw, mail, and HTML.

Browsers as Development Tools

Although the primary aim of web browsers is to process and render web documents, they can also be used in development and standardization. Accessibility can be effectively evaluated by turning off style sheets and nontext content or by applying a text-based browser.

Debugging and Add-ons

There are various built-in debugging features in browsers such as the Developers Tools in Internet Explorer (Tools Developer Tools or F12) [35], the Developer Tools in Safari (Edit Preferences Show Developer Menu in menu bar) [36], or the Developer Mode in Opera (View Developer Tools) [37].

Browsers can also be extended with additional functionality by installing developer plug-ins, many of which are freely available.

There are numerous add-ons for Firefox that can be useful for developers [38]. For example, HTML Validator is an extension that adds HTML validation inside Firefox [39]. It clearly indicates the number of markup errors as an icon in the status bar when browsing. Live HTTP Headers displays HTTP headers of a page and while browsing [40]. FireFTP is a free, secure, cross-platform (S)FTP client for the browser [41]. The User Agent Switcher extension adds a menu and a toolbar button to switch the user agent of the browser [42]. The IE Tab extension supports Internet Explorer rendering from IE6 to IE9, which can be useful for testing purposes [43]. The Web Developer extension adds various web developer tools to a browser, such as the option to disable certain styles or display CSS by media type [44]. One of the most comprehensive developer add-ons for Firefox is Firebug [45]. It integrates several development tools to the browser to directly edit, debug, and monitor HTML, CSS, and JavaScript (Figure 11-7).

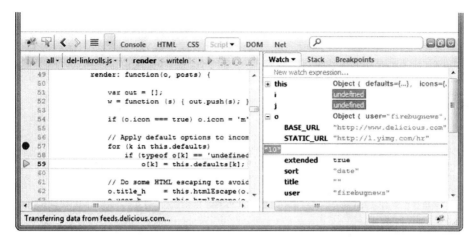

Figure 11-7. Firebug in action

Some of these Firefox tools are also available under Chrome (for example, Firebug [46], Web Developer [47]), and the ones that do not have a Chrome version have their equivalents for Chrome (such as IE Tab [48]). There are many other developer tools under Chrome 49], such as W3C HTML5 & CSS3 Validator [50], Validity that validates the markup from the address bar (or with hotkeys) [51], colorPicker [52], XML Tree [53], Resolution Test [54], just to mention a few.

Testing Web Pages in Text Browsers

Testing a web site in text browsers such as Lynx [55] is the best method to check information availability without styles and graphics[3] as well as accessibility. Properly designed web content remains usable in text browsers (Figure 11-8), while a large share of web sites do not.

---

[3] Lynx cannot display nontext contents by default, but external programs can be launched from Lynx such as image viewers or video players.

Figure 11-8. Browsing an accessible site in Lynx

View the Source Code

Web browsers provide the option to view the source code of the currently opened web page (usually by selecting View   Source or Page Source, selecting a similar menu item from the local menu, or pressing Ctrl/Cmd+U or in Safari Ctrl/Cmd+Alt+U). This feature can be used to analyze the markup and other components of the site. Although it can be very useful to learn from other developers, it is crucial to keep in mind that a large amount of web sites are not standard-compliant and should not be considered as a reference or best practice.

There is a difference between the copyright of the web site content and that of the markup code that produces it. As a general rule, code derived from other web pages without permission is not allowed to be published.

Summary

In this chapter, you learned how to select development tools, independent from the platform of your preference. By now you should know the vital features that are needed for effective work, such as support for control characters and special characters like the BOM. The most fundamental tool of a web standardista is an advanced text editor, and a carefully selected combination of software tools can expedite your web site standardization efforts, both for redesign and for start-from-scratch projects.

After you have acquired the standards, approaches, and knowledge described in the previous chapters, it is time to apply the theory in practice. In the next chapter, all these things will be used together in step-by-step guides to improve your standardization skills.

References

1. Sessink O (2011) BlueFish. The Bluefish Project Team. http://bluefish.openoffice.nl/. Accessed 05 February 2011

2. ActiveState Software (2011) Komodo. ActiveState Software. www.activestate.com/komodo-ide. Accessed 05 February 2011

3. Bare Bones Software (2011) BBEdit. Bare Bones Software, Inc. www.barebones.com/products/bbedit/. Accessed 05 February 2011

4. Bare Bones Software (2011) TextWrangler. Bare Bones Software, Inc. www.barebones.com/products/textwrangler/index.html. Accessed 05 February 2011

5. Goyvaerts J (2011) EditPad Lite. Just Great Software Co. Ltd. www.editpadlite.com. Accessed 05 February 2011

6. Goyvaerts J (2011) EditPad Pro. Just Great Software Co. Ltd. www.editpadpro.com. Accessed 05 February 2011

7. ES-Computing (2011) EditPlus – Text editor, HTML Editor, PHP Editor and Java Editor for Windows. ES-Computing. www.editplus.com. Accessed 05 February 2011

8. Ho D et al (2011) Notepad++. Don Ho. http://notepad-plus-plus.org. Accessed 05 February 2011

9. HELIOS (2011) TextPad. Helios Software Solutions. www.textpad.com/products/textpad/index.html. Accessed 05 February 2011

10. Lutus P (2009) Arachnophilia Home Page. www.arachnoid.com/arachnophilia/. Paul Lutus. Accessed 13 October 2010

11. htmlArea (2011) WYSIWYG editor directory. htmlArea. www.htmlarea.com. Accessed 05 February 2011

12. Microsoft (2011) Microsoft Expression Web. Microsoft Corporation. www.microsoft.com/expression/products/Web_Overview.aspx. Accessed 05 February 2011

13. Microsoft (2011) Microsoft Corporation. www.microsoft.com/web/webmatrix/. Accessed 05 February 2011

14. Adobe (2011) Adobe Dreamweaver. Adobe Systems Incorporated. www.adobe.com/products/dreamweaver/. Accessed 05 February 2011

15. Quint V (ed) (2010) Amaya. World Wide Web Consortium. www.w3.org/Amaya/. Accessed 05 February 2011

16. Belus Technology (2011) XStandard XHTML (Strict or 1.1) WYSIWYG Editor. The standards-compliant XHTML editor. Belus Technology Inc. http://xstandard.com/. Accessed 05 February 2011

17. Buytaert D (2011) Drupal. Dries Buytaert. http://drupal.org. Accessed 05 February 2011

18. Moffatt S et al (2011) Joomla! Open Source Matters, Inc. www.joomla.org. Accessed 05 February 2011

19. Mullenweg M, Boren R, Jaquith M, Ozz A, Westwood P (2011) WordPress. http://wordpress.org/. Accessed 05 February 2011

20. liveSTORYBOARD (2011) liveSTORYBOARD web content management. Web standards save time, decrease costs, increase flexibility - don't ignore them. liveSTORYBOARD, Inc. www.livestoryboard.com/Benefits/CMS-standards-compliant.html. Accessed 16 September 2011

21. Web Dandy (2011) Web Dandy Content Management System - Accessbility Comes As Standard. www.webdandy-cms.co.uk/w3c-standards.htm. Accessed 16 September 2011

22. sNews (2011) sNews – Lightweight Content Management System. http://snewscms.com. Accessed 16 September 2011

23. Stanford University (2010) The Protégé Ontology Editor and Knowledge Acquisition System. Stanford Center for Biomedical Informatics Research. http://protege.stanford.edu/. Accessed 29 October 2010

24. Motik B, Shearer R, Glimm B, Stoilos G, Horrocks I (2011) Hermit OWL Reasoner. University of Oxford. http://hermit-reasoner.com/. Accessed 01 march 2011

25. TopQuadrant (2011) TopBraid Composer. TopQuadrant Inc. www.topquadrant.com/products/TB_Composer.html. Accessed 01 March 2011

26. Clark & Parsia (2010) Pellet: The Open Source OWL 2 Reasoner. Clark & Parsia LLC. http://clarkparsia.com/pellet. Accessed 29 October 2010

27. Haarslev V, Hidde K, Möller R, Wessel M et al (2011) RacerPro. Racer Systems GmbH & Co. www.racer-systems.com. Accessed 01 March 2011

28. Tsarkov D et al (2011) FaCT++. Dmitry Tsarkov et al. http://code.google.com/p/factplusplus/. Accessed 01 March 2011

29. Design Science (2011) MathType – equation editor. Design Science. www.dessci.com/en/products/mathtype/. Accessed 01 March 2011

30. Raggett D, Paehl D, Nelson C, Hennecke C, Teague T (2008) HTML Tidy Library Project. SourceForge.net: Find, Create, and Publish Open Source software for free.http://tidy.sourceforge.net. Accessed 15 September 2011

31. Connolly D, Hazaël-Massieux D (2011) Tidy your HTML. World Wide Web Consortium. http://services.w3.org/tidy/tidy. Accessed 15 September 2011

32. Raggett D (2003) Clean up your Web pages with HTML TIDY. Dave Raggett. www.w3.org/People/Raggett/tidy/. Accessed 01 March 2011

33. The PHP Group (2011) PHP: Tidy – manual. The PHP Group. http://php.net/manual/en/book.tidy.php. Accessed 01 March 2011

34. Thereaux O, Dubost K, Bless T, Skytta V, Cope AS, Rezic S et al (2007) LogValidator. World Wide Web Consortium. www.w3.org/QA/Tools/LogValidator/. Accessed 01 March 2011

35. Microsoft (2010) Debugging HTML and CSS with the Developer Tools. Microsoft Corporation. http://msdn.microsoft.com/en-us/library/dd565627(v=VS.85).aspx. Accessed 02 March 2011

36. Apple (2011) Safari Developer Tools. Apple Inc. http://developer.apple.com/technologies/safari/developer-tools.html. Accessed 16 September 2011

37. Bovens A (2010) Opera extensions developer workflow. Opera Software ASA. http://dev.opera.com/articles/view/opera-extensions-developer-workflow/. Accessed 02 March 2011

38. Mozilla (2011) Web development :: Add-ons for Firefox. Mozilla Foundation. https://addons.mozilla.org/en-US/firefox/extensions/web-development/. Accessed 02 March 2011

39. Gueury M (2011) Html Validator. Mozilla Corp. https://addons.mozilla.org/en-us/firefox/addon/html-validator/. Accessed 16 September 2011

40. Savard D, Coukouma N (2011) Live HTTP Headers. Mozilla Corp. https://addons.mozilla.org/en-us/firefox/addon/live-http-headers/. Accessed 16 September 2011

41. Čuvalo M (2011) FireFTP. Mozilla Corp. https://addons.mozilla.org/en-US/firefox/addon/fireftp/. Accessed 16 September 2011

42. Pederick C (2011) User Agent Switcher. Mozilla Corp. https://addons.mozilla.org/en-US/firefox/addon/user-agent-switcher/. Accessed 16 September 2011

43. Mozilla (2011) IE Tab V2. Mozilla Corp. https://addons.mozilla.org/en-US/firefox/addon/ie-tab-2-ff-36/. Accessed 16 September 2011

44. Pederick C (2011) Web Developer. Mozilla Corp. https://addons.mozilla.org/en-US/firefox/addon/web-developer/. Accessed 16 September 2011

45. Hewitt J, Odvarko J, et al (2011) Firebug. Mozilla Corp. http://getfirebug.com/. Accessed 16 September 2011

46. Simonetti P (2011) Firebug Lite for Google Chrome. Mozilla Corp. http://getfirebug.com/releases/lite/chrome/. Accessed 16 September 2011

47. Pederic C (2011) Web Developer. Mozilla Corp. https://chrome.google.com/webstore/detail/bfbameneiokkgbdmiekhjnmfkcnldhhm. Accessed 16 September 2011

48. Blackfish (2011) IE Tab. Blackfish Software. https://chrome.google.com/webstore/detail/hehijbfgiekmjfkfjpbkbammjbdenadd. Accessed 16 September 2011

49 Google (2011) Google Chrome Developer Tools page. Google Inc. https://chrome.google.com/webstore?category=ext%2F11-web-development. Accessed 16 September 2011

50. Cebeci G (2011) W3C HTML5 & CSS3 Validator. https://chrome.google.com/webstore/detail/idofkioidbjjebcdefblbikkojgdknfp. Accessed 16 September 2011

51. Renyard I (2011) Validity. Ian Renyard. https://chrome.google.com/webstore/detail/bbicmjjbohdfglopkidebfccilipgeif. Accessed 16 September 2011

52. Dematte P (2011) colorPicker. Peter Dematte. https://chrome.google.com/webstore/detail/jegimleidpfmpepbfajjlielaheedkdo. Accessed 16 September 2011

53. Stroop A (2011) XML Tree. Alan Stroop. https://chrome.google.com/webstore/detail/gbammbheopgpmaagmckhpjbfgdfkpadb. Accessed 16 September 2011

54. Beckford B (2011) Resolution Test. Ben Beckford. https://chrome.google.com/webstore/detail/idhfcdbheobinplaamokffboaccidbal. Accessed 16 September 2011

55. Dickey T et al (2011) Lynx source distribution and potpourri. Internet Software Consortium. http://lynx.isc.org/. Accessed 02 March 2011

CHAPTER 12

Putting It All Together

Being familiar with certain technologies and standards is not sufficient for standardizing invalid sites and developing valid sites from scratch. Web site standardization is always a complex project, and it takes into account a variety of needs simultaneously. The list includes, but is not limited to, full standard compliance; optimal code length; interoperability; meaningful, structured, and accessible content; adequate metadata; and proper settings. Creating valid code can be learned most efficiently through the collection of step-by-step guidelines provided in this chapter.

After becoming familiar with web standards, it is time to learn how to create fundamental standard-compliant web site components from scratch in a text editor and extend them for your web pages. Most XHTML 1.0 Strict code fragments you will learn can be used as the basis for XHTML projects and HTML5 markup for new HTML projects. You will see how to use indentations to create clear, easy-to-maintain markup and provide the end tags immediately after the opening tags to avoid tags to be missed. The presented guidelines also demonstrate the proper, logical use of structural elements from paragraphs to lists and from tables to forms. After mastering the basic structure of lists, tables, objects, and forms, you will be able to extend, modify, and standardize the corresponding markup elements and never get lost in the details even if the markup is rather long and complex.[1]

Choosing the Relevant Standards

In web site standardization, there is no ultimate choice. The browser support and the concerns of developers are constantly changing. Most developers have at least a notion about W3C Recommendations; however, there are standards released by other standardization bodies as well, such as ERCIM, IETF, WaSP, or WSG (as discussed in Chapter 1). Even developers with a thorough grasp of standards do not necessarily apply them appropriately.

The choice of standards has a serious impact on each process of web site standardization and future possibilities. When considering the similarities and differences between the various markup languages and their variants, the choice should be made before the design and development stage.

Switching Between Standards

It is a common misconception that applying the latest technologies immediately at all costs is the key to developing modern web sites. In fact, the latest technologies without finalized specification are not recommended for use. The latest standards (with the W3C status "Recommendation") should be applied exclusively, and the Working Drafts, which are subject to change, should not be used. For example, there

---

[1] Each step-by-step guide in this chapter focuses on a certain element or element group and the corresponding markup elements. The complexity of the markup will increase drastically when adding additional contents and attributes, but the basic structure always remains the same.

is no reason to update a web site using valid XHTML markup to XHTML5 (not to mention HTML5) unless the new elements introduced in that specification are required on the site. The major reason is that these technologies are at varying degrees of adoption and standardization. Moreover, web sites applying these technologies cannot be validated (or validators provide this feature as an experimental tool only). Users of such web sites might face nonworking components, be prompted to download files of unknown types, and so on. Functionality and usability are more important than the incorrect use of the latest, nonfinalized specifications (Figure 12-1).

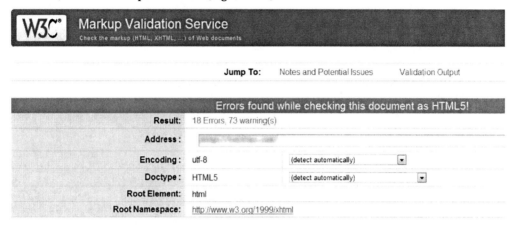

Figure 12-1. Modern markup applied incorrectly. What is the point?

On the other hand, web developers should not fall behind if they want to remain competitive. Additionally, they should keep making their clients or bosses believe in the importance of quality code and development time, which is often in competition with direct business interests.

Step-by-Step Development

Creating a standard-compliant web site with valid markup, styles, semantic content, and accessible code should be the preferable way to develop a web site. You can verify whether individual technologies are standard-compliant by validating the markup, the style sheet, and further components such as the feed channel during development. However, the full standards compliance of a whole web site is more complex than that. As discussed throughout this book, full standards compliance covers valid character encoding (preferably valid UTF-8), valid HTML or valid XHTML markup (the stricter, the better), valid CSS, valid RSS or valid Atom news feed, valid RDF, valid metadata, valid XML, valid object embedding, valid script embedding, WCAG 2.0 and Section 508 conformance, accessibility-friendliness, the application of Semantic Web technologies, browser- and resolution-independent code, and proper server settings, just to mention the most important ones.

Starting from Scratch

Typically, you should perform the following core tasks when creating a web site from scratch:

- Determine the document type.

- Create the index.html file. All required elements must be provided, along with the ones that are highly recommended for structuring.[2] As a general rule, the html element should be used as the root element for all HTML and XHTML documents. Markup documents should contain a document head (between <head> and </head>) and a document body (delimited by <body> and </body>). Beyond the general container div and paragraph p used in HTML 4.01 and XHTML, or the more specific HTML5 structuring elements header, article, and section, the cohesive parts of web page content should have headings. In (X)HTML, there are six levels of headings: h1, h2, h3, h4, h5, and h6 (from the largest to the smallest). Levels should not be skipped (for example, applying h4 in a document in which there is no h3 but just h1 and h2).

- Multiply files. Carefully applied copying and pasting reduces development time for hand-coders. It provides integrity throughout the site; however, modifications should be done on all files if the initial file has been modified. Such modifications are often easier on dynamic sites, which typically store the identical sections centrally.

- Create the primary style sheet file (for example, main.css) with an initial design for basic layout, colors, and font styles (they will be updated later). The main designing concepts should be determined in advance.

- Provide optional elements. Which optional elements are reasonable depends on the project. The various meta elements are recommended in most cases. Several link elements are also frequently applied including, but not limited to, links to external files such as the Atom or RSS news feed (atom.xml, rss.xml), the web site icon (favicon.ico), or optional metadata (metadata.rdf, foaf.rdf, doac.rdf).

- Add useful extensions. The number of useful—and free—web site extensions and APIs is constantly increasing. Some are Google Analytics tracking code (JavaScript), interactive Google Maps for contact details, or the Like and Tweet buttons for social networking. Although they are popular and used by millions, most of them are not standardized. The golden rule is that you must be careful to avoid invalid embedding codes provided by third-party software developers.

■ **Note** This doesn't mean you have to sacrifice third-party content, because many invalid embedding codes can be rewritten in a standard-compliant manner.

- Do additional tasks depending on client needs.
- Set up hosting on a web server.

---

[2] Development tools often provide templates and skeleton documents to begin your work with. Even text editors have options to insert markup elements, which might be faster than typing.

- Beyond the simplest static sites, all web sites apply server-side scripting and applications with prerequisite technology support and configuration. These depend on the user needs.

- Upload and install.

  - Static files can be directly uploaded to the web server.

  - Server-side applications usually have some installation files that should be uploaded to the server. These files can be executed on the server to install and configure the application.

- Share the web site through a domain.

Note that there is no fixed order for these tasks, although some always precede others. Furthermore, these steps apply for static web pages. If the site relies on server-side scripting, the steps depend on the type of the system.

Following the basic principles discussed in the next sections can be good starting points for developing standard-compliant code from scratch. The list of web site components is not complete by any means. However, most of these samples can be applied in a variety of markup languages and style sheets and are frequently applied in web site development.

▨ **Note** The order of the step orders is a suggestion only.

XHTML

XHTML 1.0 Strict documents can be developed with the following steps. Other XHTML documents can be authored similarly by applying the desired document type.

1. Create XML declaration.

```
<?xml version="1.0" encoding="UTF-8"?>
```

2. Add document type declaration.

```
<?xml version="1.0" encoding="UTF-8"?>
<!DOCTYPE html ↵
  PUBLIC "-//W3C//DTD XHTML 1.0 Strict//EN" ↵
  "http://www.w3.org/TR/xhtml1/DTD/xhtml1-strict.dtd">
```

3. Add root element with default namespace and language setting.

```
<?xml version="1.0" encoding="UTF-8"?>
<!DOCTYPE html ↵
  PUBLIC "-//W3C//DTD XHTML 1.0 Strict//EN" ↵
  "http://www.w3.org/TR/xhtml1/DTD/xhtml1-strict.dtd">
<html xmlns="http://www.w3.org/1999/xhtml" xml:lang="en" lang="en">

</html>
```

4. Additional namespaces can also be added upon request.

5. Add document head and body.

```
<?xml version="1.0" encoding="UTF-8"?>
<!DOCTYPE html ↵
 PUBLIC "-//W3C//DTD XHTML 1.0 Strict//EN" ↵
 "http://www.w3.org/TR/xhtml1/DTD/xhtml1-strict.dtd">
<html xmlns="http://www.w3.org/1999/xhtml" xml:lang="en" lang="en">
<head>

</head>
<body>

</body>
</html>
```

6. Add document title.

```
<?xml version="1.0" encoding="UTF-8"?>
<!DOCTYPE html ↵
 PUBLIC "-//W3C//DTD XHTML 1.0 Strict//EN" ↵
 "http://www.w3.org/TR/xhtml1/DTD/xhtml1-strict.dtd">
<html xmlns="http://www.w3.org/1999/xhtml" xml:lang="en" lang="en">
<head>
<title>XHTML Document Sample</title>
</head>
<body>

</body>
</html>
```

7. Add head content, including metadata, base URI, links, and scripts. Although they are optional elements, many of them are used frequently. The most common one of all is the link to an external CSS file:

- Create a basic link with the file path or URI. If XHTML syntax is used, self-closing is required.

```
<link href="styles/main.css" />
```

- Set the link type.

```
<link type="text/css" href="styles/main.css" />
```

- Identify the link role.

```
<link rel="stylesheet" type="text/css" href="styles/main.css" />
```

- Set the media type (optional).

```
<link rel="stylesheet" type="text/css" media="all" href="styles/main.css" />
```

8. Head content can be arbitrarily extended upon request, for example with metadata from external vocabularies such as DC. A typical head section with highly customized content looks like this:

423

```
<?xml version="1.0" encoding="UTF-8"?>
<!DOCTYPE html ↵
 PUBLIC "-//W3C//DTD XHTML 1.0 Strict//EN" ↵
 "http://www.w3.org/TR/xhtml1/DTD/xhtml1-strict.dtd">
<html xmlns="http://www.w3.org/1999/xhtml" xml:lang="en" lang="en">
  <head>
    <title>XHTML Document Sample</title>
    <meta http-equiv="Content-Type" content="application/xhtml+xml; charset=utf-8" />
    <meta http-equiv="Content-Style-Type" content="text/css" />
    <meta name="robots" content="noindex, nofollow" />
    <meta name="content-language" content="en" />
    <meta name="author" content="Dr. Leslie Sikos" />
    <meta name="keywords" content="Dr. Leslie F. Sikos, networking" />
    <meta name="description" content="Contact data of IT pro Dr. Leslie Sikos. ↵
      Website  standardization, semantic websites, accessability, professional ↵
      photography, videography, multimedia &amp; more." />
    <base href="http://www.lesliesikos.com/" />
    <link rel="alternate" type="application/rss+xml" title="Dr. Leslie Sikos IT ↵
      professional" href="http://www.lesliesikos.com/sikos.xml" />
    <link rel="author" href="http://www.lesliesikos.com/" />
    <link rel="shortcut icon" href="favicon.ico" />
    <link rel="stylesheet" type="text/css" media="all" href="styles/sikos.css" ↵
      title="Default style" />
    <link rel="stylesheet" type="text/css"  media="handheld" href="styles/mobile.css" ↵
      title="Styles for mobile devices" />
    <link rel="stylesheet" type="text/css"  media="print" href="styles/print.css" ↵
      title="Styles for printing" />
    <script type="text/javascript" src="js/help.js"></script>
    <script type="text/javascript" src="js/access.js"></script>
  </head>
  <body>

  </body>
</html>
```

9. Add body content.

```
<?xml version="1.0" encoding="UTF-8"?>
<!DOCTYPE html ↵
 PUBLIC "-//W3C//DTD XHTML 1.0 Strict//EN" ↵
 "http://www.w3.org/TR/xhtml1/DTD/xhtml1-strict.dtd">

<html xmlns="http://www.w3.org/1999/xhtml" xml:lang="en" lang="en">
  <head>
    <title>XHTML Document Sample</title>
    <meta http-equiv="Content-Type" content="application/xhtml+xml; charset=utf-8" />
    <meta http-equiv="Content-Style-Type" content="text/css" />
    <meta name="robots" content="noindex, nofollow" />
    <meta name="content-language" content="en" />
    <meta name="author" content="Dr. Leslie Sikos" />
    <meta name="keywords" content="Dr. Leslie F. Sikos, networking" />
```

```
    <meta name="description" content="Contact data of IT pro Dr. Leslie Sikos. ↩
      Website standardization, semantic websites, accessability, professional ↩
      photography, videography, multimedia &amp; more." />
    <base href="http://www.lesliesikos.com/" />
    <link rel="alternate" type="application/rss+xml" title="Dr. Leslie Sikos IT ↩
      professional" href="http://www.lesliesikos.com/sikos.xml" />
    <link rel="author" href="http://www.lesliesikos.com/" />
    <link rel="shortcut icon" href="favicon.ico" />
    <link rel="stylesheet" type="text/css" media="all" href="styles/sikos.css" ↩
     title="Default style" />
    <link rel="stylesheet" type="text/css"  media="handheld" href="styles/mobile.css" ↩
     title="Styles for mobile devices" />

    <link rel="stylesheet" type="text/css"  media="print" href="styles/print.css" ↩
     title="Styles for printing" />

    <script type="text/javascript" src="js/help.js"></script>
    <script type="text/javascript" src="js/access.js"></script>
  </head>
  <body>
    <p>
      An XHTML 1.0 Strict Document.
    </p>
  </body>
</html>
```

(X)HTML5

(X)HTML5 documents can be developed with the following steps:

1. Create document type declaration.

```
<!DOCTYPE html>
```

2. Add root element.

```
<!DOCTYPE html>
<html>

</html>
```

3. Add document head and body.

```
<!DOCTYPE html>
<html>
  <head>

  </head>
  <body>

  </body>
</html>
```

4. Add title. Similar to the example discussed in the previous section, metadata, base URI, links, and scripts can be added arbitrarily.

```
<!DOCTYPE html>
<html>
  <head>
    <title>Sample HTML5 document structure</title>
  </head>
  <body>
  </body>
</html>
```

5. Add character encoding declaration.

```
<!DOCTYPE html>
<html>
  <head>
    <title>Sample HTML5 document structure</title>
    <meta charset="UTF-8" />
  </head>
  <body>
  </body>
</html>
```

6. Create structure with a header, section, and footer.

```
<!DOCTYPE html>
<html>
  <head>
    <title>Sample HTML5 document structure</title>
    <meta charset="UTF-8" />
  </head>
  <body>
    <header>
      <h1>Document sample</h1>
    </header>
    <section>

    </section>
    <footer>
      Copyright © 2011 John Smith. All rights reserved.
    </footer>
  </body>
</html>
```

7. Provide content.

```
<!DOCTYPE html>
<html>
  <head>
    <title>Sample HTML5 document</title>
    <meta charset="UTF-8" />
  </head>
  <body>
```

```
<header>
  <h1>Document sample</h1>
</header>
<section>
  <article>
    <h2>Article1</h2>
      The first article of the document.
  </article>
  <article>
    <h2>Article2</h2>
      The second article of the document.
  </article>
</section>
<footer>
  Copyright © 2011 John Smith. All rights reserved.
</footer>
</body>
</html>
```

Links

Hyperlinks are fundamental elements of web pages that can be developed as follows:

1. Provide the basic anchor. It can be a URI of an external site such as the following:

```
<a href="http://www.example.com">
```

- or a path within your site such as the following:

```
<a href="gallery/">
```

- Hyperlinks can also point to a document segment (identified by the id attribute) with a *fragment identifier*. Here's an example:

```
<a href="gallery/canada.html#calgary">
```

2. Set the target (if required). External links are often intended to be opened in a new window. Here's an example:

```
<a href="http://www.example.com" target="_blank">
```

3. Add a tabbing index to improve accessibility (optional).

```
<a href="http://www.example.com" tabindex="5" target="_blank">
```

4. Ensure that external links won't affect the PageRank of your site (optional).

```
<a href="http://www.example.com" rel="nofollow" tabindex="5" target="_blank">
```

- Steps 2 and 4 apply for external links only.

Images

Images are embedded with the `img` element. If XHTML syntax is used, self-closing is required. The location of the image file is determined by the `src` (source) attribute.

1. Embed a basic image.

```
<img src="images/logo.png" />
```

2. Provide alternate content that can be rendered in case the image cannot be displayed (fundamental for accessibility).

```
<img src="images/logo.png" alt="The logo of Big Profit Company" />
```

3. Provide a text to be displayed when the user moves the mouse over the image (optional). It can be the same as the alternate text or different.

```
<img src="images/logo.png" alt="The logo of Big Profit Company" title="The logo of Big Profit
Company" />
```

Lists

List items of both ordered (`ol`) and unordered lists (`ul`) are delimited by `<li>` and `</li>` (Listing 12-1).

Listing 12-1. List Item Structure in Ordered and Unordered Lists

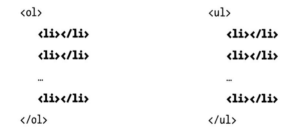

1. An unordered list can be created as follows:

```
<ul>

</ul>
```

2. The list items can be added arbitrarily.

```
<ul>
  <li>Apricot</li>
  <li>Cherry</li>
  <li>Peach</li>
</ul>
```

Definition lists define definition terms (`dt`) and their descriptions (`dd`) (Listing 12-2).

Listing 12-2. A Definition List Example

```
<dl>
  <dt>
    <label>Web site development</label>
  </dt>
  <dt>RDF</dt>
    <dd>A W3C acronym for Resource Description Framework, an XML specification for ↵
      metadata models.</dd>

  <dt>RSS</dt>
    <dd>Really Simple Syndication. An XML format for frequently updated content, e.g., ↵
    news headlines, blog entries.</dd>
</dl>
```

List Accessibility

You can improve the accessibility of lists by adding elements such as accesskey and tabindex. Here's an example:

```
<ul>
  <li>
    <a href="http://www.example.com/" title="Home" accesskey="h" tabindex="1">Home</a>
  </li>
  <li>
    <a href="about/" title="Introduction" accesskey="a" tabindex="2">About</a>
  </li>
  <li>
    <a href="gallery/" title="Gallery" accesskey="g" tabindex="4">Gallery</a>
  </li>
  <li>
    <a href="shop/" title="Webstore of oil paintings" accesskey="s"
tabindex="6">Shop</a>
  </li>
  <li>
    <a href="exhibition/" title="Exhibitions" accesskey="e" tabindex="7">Exhibitions</a>
  </li>
  <li>
    <a href="contact/" title="Address and phone" accesskey="c" tabindex="7">Contact</a>
  </li>
</ul>
```

Styling Lists

You can use unordered lists for more sophisticated purposes than simple lists. They are often used to build menus.[3] Typical horizontal menus override the default display style, as shown in Listing 12-3, in order to render the list items next to instead of below each other.

Listing 12-3. Styling of List Items to Be Displayed Inline

```
li {
  display: inline;
}
```

A simple style frequently applied for the hyperlinks of such list items are bottom borders (Listing 12-4).

Listing 12-4. Bottom Border for Menu Hyperlinks

```
a:hover {
  color: #949295;
  border-bottom: 1px solid #949295;
}
```

Naturally, this style is seldom applied globally. Instead, it is extended with the identifier of the list or its container parent element such as #main a:hover or #navtabs li a:hover.

A usual technique for creating custom navigation effects is to add a background image to the list items. Listing 12-5 shows an example.

Listing 12-5. Custom Navigation Effect with a Background Image

```
li {
  background: url('images/navbg.png') 5px no-repeat;
  padding-left: 16px;
}
```

If certain links, such as the first, the last, or the currently selected one, have different styles than all the others, unique identifiers should be provided for them (Listing 12-6).

Listing 12-6. More Specific Rules for the First and Last Items

```
<ul>
  <li id="first">
    <a href="http://www.example.com/" title="Home" accesskey="h" tabindex="1">Home</a>
  </li>
...
  <li id="last">
    <a href="contact/" title="Address and phone" accesskey="c" tabindex="7">Contact</a>
  </li>
</ul>
```

The first ruleset can be styled as shown in Listing 12-7.

---

[3] XHTML 2.0 also provides the more specific element nl for navigation lists.

Listing 12-7. A Specific Ruleset for the First List Items

```
li.first {
  background: none;
  padding-left: 0;
}
```

If the project is more than just a small web page, these styles should not be applied globally, simply because these specific styles would be applied to all lists throughout the document, most of which should be overridden (there would be more styling rules to override than the inherited rules that suit our needs). Instead, an identifier should be added to the list such as shown in Listing 12-8.

Listing 12-8. An Unordered List Used for Navigation Is Identified to Be Styled Differently

```
<ul id="navtabs">
  <li id="first">
    <a href="http://www.example.com/" title="Home" accesskey="h" tabindex="1">Home</a>
  </li>
  ...
  <li id="last">
    <a href="contact/" title="Address and phone" accesskey="c" tabindex="7">Contact</a>
  </li>
</ul>
```

From now on, all styles should begin with #navtabs (Listing 12-9).

Listing 12-9. A Specific Ruleset for Styling the First List Items of the Unordered List navtabs

```
#navtabs li.first {
  background: none;
  padding-left: 0;
}
```

Alternatively, the styles can be declared at the container level and use inheritance to style the list.[4] This approach is useful when multiple lists are used within the document that have the same styles or are slightly different only. Such differences can be easily overridden by more specific styling rules.

Additional styles can be declared for access keys and further features. For example, the markup in Listing 12-10 can be styled with the CSS rules shown in Listing 12-11.

Listing 12-10. A Span Used to Style an Access Key

```
S<span class="ak">i</span>temap
```

Listing 12-11. CSS Rules for Access Keys

```
span.ak {
  color: red;
  background-color: #ffffbb;
```

---

[4] Note that in this case the identifiers should be changed from id to class in the markup and from hash mark (#) to period (.) in the CSS.

```
    border-bottom: solid navy 1px;
}
```

The default bullets can be changed to arbitrary characters or images by CSS. Listing 12-12 shows an example, which applies to unordered lists such as the one presented in Listing 12-13.

Listing 12-12. Bullet Image

```
ul.tick {
  list-style-image: url('images/tick.png')
}
```

Listing 12-13. Application of the Custom Bullet Style Presented in Listing 12-12

```
<h1>The major benefits of standard compliance</h1>
<ul class="tick">
   <li>Resolution independence</li>
   <li>Browser independence</li>
   <li>Interoperability</li>
   <li>Robust functionality</li>
</ul>
```

The result is visually more appealing (and more specific) than a list with ordinary bullets (Figure 12-2).

The major benefits of standard compliance
- ✔ Resolution independence
- ✔ Browser independence
- ✔ Interoperability
- ✔ Robust functionality

Figure 12-2. Custom bullets with CSS

Tables

Let's assume that a 5x5 comparison table of iPhone models needs to be presented on a web page (Table 12-1).

Table 12-1. A Sample Table to Be Coded

Model	iPhone	iPhone 3G	iPhone 3GS	iPhone 4
Preinstalled OS	iPhone OS 1.0	iPhone OS 2.0	iPhone OS 3.0	iOS 4.0
Display resolution	480 x 320	480 x 320	480 x 320	960 x 640
CPU clockrate	620 MHz	620 MHz	833 MHz	1 GHz

Model	iPhone	iPhone 3G	iPhone 3GS	iPhone 4
Camera	2 MP	2 MP	3 MP	5 MP (rear), 0.3 MP (front)

1. All tables should have an opening and a closing tag.

```
<table>
</table>
```

2. Table rows should be delimited by `<tr>` and `</tr>`. The first row starts like this:

```
<table>
  <tr>
  </tr>
</table>
```

3. Table header cells should be written between `<th>` and `</th>`. Since the desired table has five columns, five header cell elements are required:

```
<table>
  <tr>
    <th></th><th></th><th></th><th></th><th></th>
  </tr>
</table>
```

4. A new row should be started for the first row of data cells.

```
<table>
  <tr>
    <th></th><th></th><th></th><th></th><th></th>
  </tr>
  <tr>
  </tr>
</table>
```

5. Data cells should be provided by td tags. Since the desired table has five columns, five data cell elements are required for each row.

```
<table>
  <tr>
    <th></th><th></th><th></th><th></th><th></th>
  </tr>
  <tr>
    <td></td><td></td><td></td><td></td><td></td>
  </tr>
</table>
```

6. Since the structure of rows is identical, the table row containing the five data cells can be copied three times with a simple copy and paste:

```
<table>
  <tr>
    <th></th><th></th><th></th><th></th><th></th>
  </tr>
```

```
<tr>
  <td></td><td></td><td></td><td></td><td></td>
</tr>
<tr>
  <td></td><td></td><td></td><td></td><td></td>
</tr>
<tr>
  <td></td><td></td><td></td><td></td><td></td>
</tr>
<tr>
  <td></td><td></td><td></td><td></td><td></td>
</tr>
</table>
```

7. Finally, the cells should be filled with data:

```
<table>
  <tr>
    <th>Model</th><th>iPhone</th><th>iPhone 3G</th><th>iPhone 3GS</th><th>iPhone 4</th>
  </tr>
  <tr>
    <td>Preinstalled OS</td><td>iPhone OS 1.0</td><td>iPhone OS 2.0</td><td>iPhone ↩
    OS 3.0</td><td>iOS 4.0</td>

  </tr>
  <tr>
    <td>Display resolution</td><td>480 x 320</td><td>480 x 320</td><td>480 x 320</td> ↩
    <td>960 x 640</td>
  </tr>
  <tr>
    <td>CPU clockrate</td><td>620 MHz</td><td>620 MHz</td><td>833 MHz</td><td>1 GHz</td>
  </tr>
  <tr>
    <td>Camera</td><td>2 MP</td><td>2 MP</td><td>3 MP</td><td>5 MP (rear), ↩
    0.3 MP (front)</td>

  </tr>
</table>
```

Table Accessibility

You can further improve the markup to increase accessibility. Processing and understanding tables can be challenging for nonvisual browsers. You can use the table header (th) and the caption (caption) markup elements as well as the summary attribute for increasing table accessibility. The first two are useful for visual browsers too, while the third one is valuable for screen readers.

The table header element th not only adds meaning to the first row but is repeated by screen readers when each row of the table is read. It helps the visually impaired understand the correlations between table cells.

While the data provided by the caption element is usually sufficient for small, easy-to-understand tables, more complex tables might provide a summary attribute (Listing 12-14). However, the summary attribute is considered obsolete in HTML5, where the details element can be used instead.[5] Consequently, it is recommended you describe the table structure either in a caption element or in a figcaption element within a figure element next to or containing the table. Alternatively, tables can also be described in conventional paragraphs surrounding the table. These methods can also be combined.

Listing 12-14. Table Caption

```
<table>
  <caption>
    A comparison table of iPhone models.
  </caption>
  <tr>
    <th>Model</th><th>iPhone</th><th>iPhone 3G</th><th>iPhone 3GS</th><th>iPhone 4</th>
  </tr>
  <tr>
    <td>Preinstalled OS</td><td>iPhone OS 1.0</td><td>iPhone OS 2.0</td><td>iPhone OS ⏎
      3.0</td><td>iOS 4.0</td>
  </tr>
  <tr>
    <td>Display resolution</td><td>480 x 320</td><td>480 x 320</td><td>480 x 320</td> ⏎
      <td>960 x 640</td>
  </tr>
  <tr>
    <td>CPU clockrate</td><td>620 MHz</td><td>620 MHz</td><td>833 MHz </td><td>1 GHz</td>
  </tr>
  <tr>
    <td>Camera</td><td>2 MP</td><td>2 MP</td><td>3 MP</td><td>5 MP (rear), 0.3 MP (front)</td>
  </tr>
</table>
```

You can also add access keys to the table cells if required.

Table Styling

Although table headers are usually rendered in bold by most browsers, the default styles of table cells, padding, and borders are different in each rendering engine, which is inadequate in many cases. All table features can be styled arbitrarily through CSS rulesets, however. For example, the default value of the border-collapse property, separate, can be overridden in order to make borders collapse into a single border whenever possible (Listing 12-15).

Listing 12-15. Set Borders to Collapse

```
table {
  border-collapse: collapse;
}
```

---

[5] As of 2011, the details element is not supported properly by browsers yet; thus, it is recommended to wait for implementations.

In this case, the `border-spacing` and `empty-cells` properties will be ignored. The padding and border of the header and data cells can be set as shown in Listing 12-16.

Listing 12-16. Padding and Border for Header and Data Cells

```
th, td {
  padding: 10px;
  border: 1px solid #13b141;
}
```

Drop-Down Selection Lists

Selection lists can provide options to choose from. Suppose a language selector is needed for a multilingual web site. It can be developed as follows:

1. Create a selection list with the select element.

```
<select>

</select>
```

2. Add the default option.

```
<select>
  <option value="http://www.example.com" selected="selected">English</option>

</select>
```

3. Add further options. Provide the URIs of each language version as the option values.

```
<select>

  <option value="http://www.example.com" selected="selected">English</option>
  <option value="http://de.example.com">Deutsch</option>
  <option value="http://fr.example.com">Français</option>
  <option value="http://es.example.com">Español</option>
  <option value="http://ja.example.com">日本語</option>
</select>
```

4. To load the appropriate web page, the subdomains provided as the option values can be used as target URIs through an event handler. Although the use of the onchange event handler would be logical, it would be inaccessible for keyboard users. One of the solutions is to provide a button with an onclick event handler, which is device-independent. For example, the following function

```
<script type="text/javascript">
  function goto_URL(object) {
    window.location.href=object.options[object.selectedIndex].value;
  }
</script>
```

5. declared in the document head or a linked external file can be used by the onclick event handler on the input element as follows:

```
<form>
  <select id="langsel">
    <option value="http://www.example.com" selected="selected">English</option>
    <option value="http://de.example.com">Deutsch</option>
    <option value="http://fr.example.com">Français</option>
    <option value="http://es.example.com">Español</option>

    <option value="http://ja.example.com">本語</option>
  </select>
  <input type="button" value="Go!" onclick="goto_URL(this.form.langsel);" />
</form>
```

6. Note that other methods can also be applied such as server-side redirection, which eliminates the need for JavaScript.

Forms

Basic forms can be created with the following steps:

1. Create an empty form.

<form>

</form>

2. Specify the location of the server-side script used to process data from the form.

<form **action="register.php"**>

</form>

3. Specify the method to be used for sending data. The form data can be sent as URL variables (method="get") or as an HTTP post (method="post").

• The get method appends the form data to the URL as name-value pairs, which makes it possible to bookmark the result of the form submission. Because of the length limitations of URLs, however, it cannot be ensured that all form data will be transferred. Moreover, the get method is inadequate for transforming sensitive information such as passwords, because the data will be visible in the address bar of the browser.

• The post method sends the form data as an HTTP post transaction. This method has no size limitations and is more secure than the get method.

<form **method="post"** action="register.php">

</form>

4. Create logical group(s) for form elements.

<form method="post" action="register.php">

437

```
<fieldset>

</fieldset>
<fieldset>

</fieldset>
</form>
```

5. Add the desired form controls such as text fields (text) and checkboxes (checkbox) and their attributes.

```
<form method="post" action="register.php">
  <fieldset>
    <input type="text" name="firstname" id="firstname" size="15" maxlength="255" />
    <br /><input type="text" name="lastname" id="lastname" size="20" maxlength="255" />
  </fieldset>
  <fieldset>
    <input type="checkbox" name="interests" value="1" id="photo" />
    <input type="checkbox" name="interests" value="2" id="video" />
    <input type="checkbox" name="interests" value="3" id="web" />
  </fieldset>
</form>
```

6. Improve accessibility. The label element adds a label to a form control. The legend element assigns a caption to a fieldset. The tabbing order can be set by tabindex attributes.

```
<form method="post" action="register.php">
  <fieldset>
    <legend>Personal data</legend>
    <label for="firstname">First name</label><br />
    <input type="text" name="firstname" id="firstname" size="15" maxlength="30" ↵
      tabindex="12" /><br />
    <label for="lastname">Last name</label><br />
    <input type="text" name="lastname" id="lastname" size="20" maxlength="50" ↵
      tabindex="13" />
  </fieldset>
  <fieldset>
    <legend>Main interests</legend>
    <input name="interests" type="checkbox" value="1" id="photo" tabindex="14" />
    <label for="photo">Photography</label><br />
    <input name="interests" type="checkbox" value="2" id="video" tabindex="15" />
    <label for="video">Videography</label><br />
    <input name="interests" type="checkbox" value="3" id="web" tabindex="16" />
    <label for="web">Web</label>
  </fieldset>
</form>
```

Flash Content

You can embed a Flash file with the general object tag in XHTML as follows:

1. Declare an `application/x-shockwave-flash` object.

```
<object type="application/x-shockwave-flash">

</object>
```

2. Add the source with cross-browser code.

```
<object type="application/x-shockwave-flash" data="flash/header.swf">
  <param name="movie" value="flash/header.swf" />

</object>
```

3. Provide attributes such as dimensions and an identifier (if required).

```
<object type="application/x-shockwave-flash" data="flash/header.swf" width="610" ↵
 height="224" id="flash">
  <param name="movie" value="flash/header.swf" />

</object>
```

4. If the Flash content has a transparent background, it should be declared as an optional parameter. This is also required for providing the possibility to set layer order within the web page.

```
<object type="application/x-shockwave-flash" data="flash/header.swf" width="610" ↵
 height="224" id="flash">
  <param name="movie" value="flash/header.swf" />
  <param name="wmode" value="transparent" />

</object>
```

5. Add alternate content such as a placeholder image and text descriptions to improve accessibility. If a short description is not adequate, a good practice is to add a hyperlink to a resource that describes the object.

```
<object type="application/x-shockwave-flash" data="flash/header.swf" width="610" ↵
 height="224" id="flash">
  <param name="movie" value="flash/header.swf" />
  <param name="wmode" value="transparent" />
  <a href="longdesc/"><img src="images/altheader.jpg" alt="The image alternative for ↵
  the Flash header." title="Our headquarters" /></a>
</object>
```

In (X)HTML5, the embed tag should be used instead of object.

6. Create an embed element. Since the parameters can be provided as attributes of embed, the self-closing tag can be applied in XHTML5 as follows:

```
<embed />
```

Evidently, the shorthand notation should be omitted in HTML5.

7. Add the path or URI of the file. It can be done by using the src attribute instead of data applied on object elements.

```
<embed src="flash/header.swf" />
```

8. Add dimension and optional parameters.

```
<embed src="flash/header.swf" width="550" height="400" wmode="transparent" />
```

RSS News Feeds

Creating RSS news feeds generally consists of the following steps:

1. Create the XML declaration. Since RSS 2.0 news feeds should be valid XML documents, the first line is the XML declaration:

```
<?xml version="1.0" encoding="utf-8"?>
```
The character encoding is optional but recommended.

2. Create the RSS channel. The contents of the RSS channel should be written within the rss and channel tags as follows:

```
<rss version="2.0">
<channel>

</channel>
</rss>
```

If additional namespaces are required, they should be added to the rss element. The widest interoperability possible can be achieved by providing escaped HTML markup, the creator with Dublin Core metadata, the update period and frequency defined by the syndication namespace, and the self-link from the Atom vocabulary. The following namespace declarations should be added:

```
<rss version="2.0" ↵
 xmlns:content="http://purl.org/rss/1.0/modules/content/" ↵
 xmlns:dc="http://purl.org/dc/elements/1.1/" ↵
 xmlns:sy="http://purl.org/rss/1.0/modules/syndication/" ↵
 xmlns:atom="http://www.w3.org/2005/Atom"
>
```

3. Provide feed information, including the required title, link, and description elements, as well as optional elements such as lastBuildDate and language.

```
<title>John Smith photography</title>
<link>http:// example.com/</link>
<description>The news feed of Alaskan photographer John Smith.</description>
<lastBuildDate>Fri, 10 Feb 2012 14:47:00 GMT-0900</lastBuildDate>
<language>en-US</language>
```

4. Provide news items. To create a valid RSS 2.0 feed channel with the highest level of interoperability, each item should have the following elements: title, link, description, pubDate, and guid.

```
<item>
```

```
<title>Photo exhibition</title>
<link>http://example.com/events/</link>
<pubDate>Fri, 10 Feb 2012 14:47:00 GMT-0900</pubDate>
<dc:creator>John Smith</dc:creator>
<category>Events</category>
<guid>http://example.com/events/</guid>
<description>Best shots of 2011</description>
<content:encoded><![CDATA[ My photo exhibition ↵
    <a href="http://example.com/events/">Best shots of 2011</a> takes place at the ↵
      Moose Hotel in Anchorage, AK, USA on 17-18 February 2012. ]]></content:encoded>
</item>
```

This is the section that can be copy and pasted and then modified each time the feed channel is updated with the latest news. The next news should be provided before the latest one, that is, earlier in the source code.

5. Validate.

6. Share. News feeds are usually used by linking to the XML file that contains them[6]. To use the built-in RSS reader of modern browsers, a link should be provided in the head section of (X)HTML documents. Here's an example:

```
<link rel="alternate" type="application/rss+xml" title="John Smith photography" ↵
href="http://www.example.com/rss.xml" />
```

This makes it possible for browsers to recognize that the current web page has an RSS news feed.

Making Web Sites Valid Through Redesign

The stricter the markup, the easier to upgrade to a newer version. However, in certain cases, migrating to another standard is not feasible without completely rewriting the site. Regarding style sheets, valid CSS 2.1 can be easily extended with CSS3 features in most cases. Still, standardizing an existing site can be a difficult task.

Generally, there are two possibilities: rewrite the whole site from scratch or manually standardize each page one by one. Both seem to need much more work than developers can afford. The first approach often results in broken links. The second approach requires lots of time and work (unless the site is very small) and can be performed in only a few cases.

The World Wide Web Consortium suggests a solution: carefully selected sections should be updated systematically [1]. The most frequently served (most popular) documents can be identified by the Log Validator, which also tries to find n invalid documents among the most popular ones (as discussed in the previous chapter). Certainly, the whole project is affected by the deadline and the affordable workload.

Summary

In this chapter, you saw a series of step-by-step guides for creating fundamental web site components from character to character by hand. By learning the semantic use of structural elements, you are now

---

[6] Another option is to retrieve the desired number of channel items with scripting. If you want to publish the latest news as part of a web page rather than a separate file, you need a script that opens the file, retrieves the contents of the news feed items, and generates the corresponding markup code.

capable of creating meaningful markup with a logical flow and a perfect DOM in the background. The core elements of XHTML 1.0 Strict can be used in most projects, naturally with or without self-closing tags (depending on the markup language of your choice). Such carefully created markup code provides a high level of interoperability and can be rendered in virtually any browser running on any kind of device without multiple site versions. Even if the CSS styles are disabled, the headings, paragraphs, lists, and other site components remain legible, and the content is accessible to not only the latest browsers but also to very old versions and mobile browsers with limited capabilities and standard support.

In the next chapter, you will learn widely used standard-compliant best practices that can be applied in your daily work.

References

1.   Thereaux O (2008) Making your web site valid: a step by step guide. World Wide Web Consortium. www.w3.org/QA/2002/09/Step-by-step. Accessed 09 January 2011

CHAPTER 13

Best Practices

Beyond optimal markup and styles provided by the appropriate use of web standards, there are designing conventions that are browser-independent, reliable, and satisfactory, which thus can be applied as ultimate solutions. Best practices should have top priority in web site development. Although they change over time, many can be applied for years. It is important to know the techniques that provide standard-compliant codes and distinguish them from those tricks and hacks that cause incorrect markup.

By now you should know the major web standards for markup, styles, news feeds, and other web site components. It is time to learn how to apply these standards in practice, which can be used in the daily work of any developer. Even standard-compliant web pages do not necessarily provide content in a meaningful, logical manner; thus, you should learn the purpose of markup elements and CSS properties to maximize web page quality. The ultimate aim is to find the right combination of structure, presentation, and behavior and to separate them in order to exploit the benefits of web standards.

Appropriately Used Elements

A vital point in web development is the application of appropriate elements. Always apply the more specific elements if applicable. Here are some examples:

- Tables for tabular data

- Floating elements instead of tables for positioned components (very bad practice)

- Headers instead of general paragraphs

- Paragraphs instead of separate lines with break rows (very bad practice)

- Paragraphs for text paragraphs instead of divisions

- Definition lists for terms and their descriptions instead of general paragraphs

- Headers, articles, and sections instead of general div containers (HTML5)

- The audio and video elements instead of general object embeddings (HTML5)

Most of these items are gross errors even if the web sites containing them validate.

Content in Logical Order

Even though CSS styling makes it possible to arbitrarily position document sections and elements, content should be written in a logical order. This approach has the following advantages:

- Easier development and maintenance

- Higher efficiency in text-based browsers

- Legible and usable content even without CSS (in case the `.css` file cannot be loaded or the style sheets are turned off)

- Improved accessibility through advanced support for aural browsers and screen readers that read pages without breaking continuity by default

Reliable Positioning

The Coggins method discussed in Chapter 9 can be extended to position the layer not just horizontally but also vertically. The *"dead center"* positioning is a technique that positions a container element to the very center of the screen, independently from resolution or aspect ratio. It is also browser-independent. In the case of an 800 × 600 layer, for example, the rules presented in Listing 13-1 can be applied.

Listing 13-1. "Dead Center" Positioning

```
#wrapper {
  position: absolute;
  left: 50%;
  top: 50%;
  margin-left: -400px;
  margin-top: -300px;
  width: 800px;
  height: 600px;
}
```

Certainly, if this technique is used for a logo on a loading screen, a proportion such as 2:3, $1 : \sqrt{3}$, or the Golden Section should be applied by decreasing the top offset to the desired value. You should take into account, however, that very small images or short text looks completely different on various screens. Moreover, if the positioned layer is larger than the resolution of the browser window, parts of the content will be truncated and become inaccessible for some users. Consequently, the positioned layer should not be larger than the smallest resolution currently used worldwide (which is constantly increasing). There are several alternate solutions such as resolution detection, media-specific style sheets (for example, maximized width for mobile devices), or browser-independent design with liquid layout. The latter one, liquid layout, is ideal in all cases where the design allows content positioning in a way that it spans the entire page width according to the available space (expands or contracts as required[1]).

Sizes and Proportions

Style sheet validity does not guarantee proper sizes and proportions. The selection of CSS units has a large impact on the overall appearance of web page components, as well as the usability and readability of the content.

---

[1] Liquid layout works not only for different resolutions, but also for resized windows on the same resolution.

Lengths in Relative Units

The relative units of CSS (em and %), which are computed with respect to a feature of another element, should be used for lengths.

The absolute units such as inches, centimeters, points, and pica can be used only if the physical characteristics of the target media are known. A typical example is a printing option of a web page where the default output for an official document can be in 12pt Times New Roman with 2.5 cm margins on a standard-sized paper, such as the North American letter paper (8.5 ×11") or standard A4 paper (210 × 297 mm, ISO 216 international standard [1]).

Combine Units Properly

The em unit can be used in CSS to provide scalable styles. It is a general unit for measuring lengths such as page margins or element paddings. It allows developers to specify several CSS properties relative to the current font size. Consequently, margins declared in this unit stay in proportion even if the user magnifies the font size.

To ease the calculation of font sizes expressed in em, user experience expert Richard Rutter introduced a technique that applies a font size of 62.5 percent on the body element (Listing 13-2) [2].

Listing 13-2. The Rutter Method

```
body {
    font-size: 62.5%;
}
```

Since 62.5 percent of the 16px default size used by many user agent style sheets is 10px, the previous rule makes the font size of the paragraphs styled by the rule in Listing 13-3 be 12 pixels because $1.2 \cdot 10 = 12$ px.

■ **Caution** Although widely implemented, this value is not completely reliable and might be different in some browsers.

Listing 13-3. Font Size Easily Calculated Using the Rutter Method

```
p {
    font-size: 1.2em;
}
```

Although em-based sizing could be used to ensure readable font sizes on any screen, this approach has a known issue. If the user changes the default font size or applies zooming in the browser, the text might become unreadable. On the other hand, font sizes set in pixels are robust in different environments but not proportional to other elements and the screen. The larger the resolution, the smaller the font size. Moreover, the built-in text zoom of browsers cannot be used in all cases for content with pixel-based font sizes.

■ **Note** Because of the differences between browsers, font sizing on the Web is challenging. Absolute positioned content is not scaled uniformly in all cases by the magnifier feature in IE7+ (sometimes they are scaled smaller). IE supports both zooming and text size changes for fonts set with %, em, or named sizes. In Firefox 2 and older, only text size changes are supported; however, changing the size of pt and px fonts is also possible beyond the ones set in %, em, or declared using named sizes. Firefox 3+ supports both zooming and text size changes. Opera 9+ also has a zooming feature. Zooming might give different results under different browsers, depending on the content and the styles associated with the page.

Embedding External Content Properly

Since the Web is a truly full multimedia platform, web pages often have embedded video clips, interactive objects, and other external components. Because of the incorrect embedding codes provided by the content resources, however, additional tasks are required in many cases to make them standard-compliant. Moreover, standardization cannot be performed sometimes because of the inadequate code provided along with the embedding code. Even if web developers standardize the invalid embedding code, they cannot correct the associated namespaces, scripts, and other components. A good example is the classic "Like" box of Facebook[2]. The namespace and vocabulary provided with the embedding code generated in the developers' section on Facebook.com are not consistent. One of the "solutions" developers use on the Web is to add the incorrect markup section to a JavaScript function such as the one in Listing 13-4, which writes the markup fragment delimited by apostrophes into the (X)HTML source.[3]

Listing 13-4. A Widely Used Trick to Embed Invalid Code

```
document.write('<script src="http://connect.facebook.net/en_US/all.js#xfbml=1"></script> ↵
<fb:like-box href="http://www.facebook.com/pages/Your-page/122946805997761" width="280" ↵
show_faces="true" stream="false" header="false"></fb:like-box>');
```

The same fragment gives error messages in validators if it is written directly in the markup. The iframe version of the button has problems too because it cannot be used in XHTML. It can be rewritten as an object (with the same parameters), but then it stops working. Users of APIs and third-party software components often apply the previous trick if they want their web page to validate.

■ **Caution** Providing markup code with document.write in JavaScript is a hack that you should not use. The same trick is applied for validating virtually any kind of otherwise incorrect markup that definitely cannot be accepted by real web standardistas even in cases where this markup code validates. It certainly does validate

---

[2] Fortunately, Facebook provides a valid HTML5 embedding code for "Like" buttons and boxes from fall 2011. However, the classic embedding code is still used on many websites.
[3] Assuming that JavaScript is enabled

because the content written in the external `.js` file is not considered by the validator. This code is still not valid! How to provide such content without sacrificing either functionality or validity is an open question in many cases, though.

Embedding YouTube Videos as Valid XHTML or HTML5

The popular video-sharing portal YouTube offers two types of embedding codes for YouTube videos:

- The older-style embed code applies the `object` element with parameters and an embed element. It supports Flash playback only.

- The new embed code uses an `iframe` and supports both Flash and HTML5 video content.

Under each video on YouTube, there is a Share button that provides a link to the current video with options such as long link, HD link, and declaring a starting position for playback. Below the link area, there is an Embed button. After clicking it, a text box appears with the selected new-type embedding code ready for copying to the clipboard. Below that text box there are further options for customizing the embedding code, such as declaring the size[4] or using the old-style embed code.

From the standardization point of view, both versions need some improvement.

In XHTML, the following issues should be addressed:

- The `embed` element contained by the older-style embedding code is invalid in XHTML.

- The `iframe` element used by the new-style embedding code cannot be used in XHTML 1.0 Strict or XHTML 1.1 (only in XHTML 1.0 Transitional, which should not be used). Moreover, the `data` and `type` attributes should be provided to maximize interoperability (without them, the embedding will not work under certain browsers). However, providing the `data` attribute while preserving the `movie` parameter from the suggested embedding code ensures browser-independence, because some rendering engines will use the outer declaration (the value of the `data` attribute on the `object` element), and others will use the inner declaration (the value of the `movie` parameter) to identify the URL to retrieve the video from (similarly to the Flash Satay method used for Flash embedding covered in Chapter 9).

In HTML5, the following issues should be addressed:

- If you prefer the new-style embedding code, the `frameborder` and `allowscreen` attributes should not be used on the `iframe` element.

- If you want to use the old-style code, the `data` and `type` attributes are missing from the `object` element. Moreover, the `param` elements as well as the `embed` element should be closed using the shorthand notation rather than the closing tags `</param>` and `</embed>`.

Suppose we want to embed the video with the embedding code presented in Listings 13-5 and 13-6.

---

[4] The size can also be modified arbitrarily later in the markup when using the embedding code.

Listing 13-5. New Embed Code for Example Video Suggested by YouTube

```
<iframe width="560" height="315" src="http://www.youtube.com/embed/L2tuL_2Q3vA?rel=0"
frameborder="0" allowfullscreen></iframe>
```

Listing 13-6. New-Style Embed Code for Example Video Suggested by YouTube

```
<object width="560" height="315"><param name="movie"
value="http://www.youtube.com/v/L2tuL_2Q3vA?version=3&amp;hl=en_US&amp;rel=0"></param><param
name="allowFullScreen" value="true"></param><param name="allowscriptaccess"
value="always"></param><embed
src="http://www.youtube.com/v/L2tuL_2Q3vA?version=3&amp;hl=en_US&amp;rel=0"
type="application/x-shockwave-flash" width="560" height="315" allowscriptaccess="always"
allowfullscreen="true"></embed></object>
```

In XHTML, the old-style embedding should be preferred and modified accordingly (Listing 13-7).

Listing 13-7. The Standardized Embedding Code in XHTML/HTML5

```
<p>
  <object type="application/x-shockwave-flash"
    data="http://www.youtube.com/v/L2tuL_2Q3vA?version=3&amp;hl=en_US&amp;rel=0" ↵
    width="560" height="315">
    <param name="movie" ↵
     value="http://www.youtube.com/v/L2tuL_2Q3vA?version=3&amp;hl=en_US&amp;rel=0" />
    <param name="allowFullScreen" value="true" />
    <param name="allowscriptaccess" value="always" />
  </object>
</p>
```

■ **Note** The nesting rules of the applied document type should not be forgotten. In XHTML 1.0 Strict, the `object` element should be wrapped in a container element such as `div` or `p`; otherwise, the code will not validate.

The same code can also be used in HTML5, where the `embed` element could also be preserved; however, it can be safely removed: the first two lines ensure browser-independence. In HTML5, the new-style embedding code can also be used. It can be standardized by removing the `frameborder` and `allowfullscreen` attributes (Listing 13-8).

Listing 13-8. A Standard-Compliant YouTube Embedding in HTML5

```
<iframe width="560" height="315" src="http://www.youtube.com/embed/L2tuL_2Q3vA?rel=0">
</iframe>
```

Embedding Google Maps as Valid XHTML or HTML5

A popular way of defining the position of offices, restaurants, and so on, is embedding interactive Google Maps objects.

The source code provided by Google Maps is something like Listing 13-9.

Listing 13-9. A Google Maps Embedding Code Provided by Google

```
<iframe width="425" height="350" frameborder="0" scrolling="no" marginheight="0"
marginwidth="0"
src="http://maps.google.com/maps?f=q&amp;source=s_q&amp;hl=en&amp;geocode=&amp;q=Honolulu,+HI,
+United+States&amp;sll=37.0625,-
95.677068&amp;sspn=50.557552,89.208984&amp;ie=UTF8&amp;hq=&amp;hnear=Honolulu,+Hawaii&amp;ll=2
1.306944,-157.858333&amp;spn=0.234454,0.479279&amp;t=h&amp;z=12&amp;output=embed"></iframe><br
/><small><a
href="http://maps.google.com/maps?f=q&amp;source=embed&amp;hl=en&amp;geocode=&amp;q=Honolulu,+
HI,+United+States&amp;sll=37.0625,-
95.677068&amp;sspn=50.557552,89.208984&amp;ie=UTF8&amp;hq=&amp;hnear=Honolulu,+Hawaii&amp;ll=2
1.306944,-157.858333&amp;spn=0.234454,0.479279&amp;t=h&amp;z=12" style="color:#0000FF;text-
align:left">View Larger Map</a></small>
```

However, this code is not standard-compliant. In HTML5, the `frameborder`, `scrolling`, `marginheight`, and `marginwidth` attributes should be removed (styling should be achieved through CSS). In XHTML, the embedding code should be modified as follows:

- Since the inline frame element (`iframe`) cannot be used in XHTML 1.0 Strict and XHTML 1.1, it should be replaced by the `object` tag.

- The `type` attribute should be defined with the value `text/html`; otherwise, the map will not appear even if the code is valid.

- The `src` attribute should be replaced by the `data` attribute.

- The `frameborder`, `scrolling`, `marginheight`, and `marginwidth` attributes should be removed.

- The `object` element should be enclosed by a `p` or `div` container element.

- Styles should be defined by CSS to fit into page design (if the default appearance is not adequate).

The result should be in the form presented in Listing 13-10.

Listing 13-10. A Standardized Version of the Embedding Code in Listing 13-9

```
<p>
  <object type="text/html" width="425" height="350" data="http://maps.google.com/maps?f= ↵
  q&amp;source=s_q&amp;hl=en&amp;geocode=&amp;q=Honolulu,+HI,+United+States&amp; ↵
  sll=37.0625,-95.677068&amp;sspn=50.557552,89.208984&amp;ie=UTF8&amp;hq=&amp; ↵
  hnear=Honolulu,+Hawaii&amp;ll=21.306944,-157.858333&amp;spn=0.234454,0.479279&amp; ↵
  t=h&amp;z=12&amp;output=embed">
  </object>

  <a href="http://maps.google.com/maps?f=q&amp;source=embed&amp;hl=en&amp;geocode=&amp; ↵
  q=Honolulu,+HI,+United+States&amp;sll=37.0625,-95.677068&amp;sspn=50.557552, ↵
```

```
    89.208984&amp;ie=UTF8&amp;hq=&amp;hnear=Honolulu,+Hawaii&amp;ll=21.306944, ↵
    -157.858333&amp;spn=0.234454,0.479279&amp;t=h&amp;z=12">View Larger Map</a>
</p>
```

This embedding code works on all modern browsers and validates as XHTML 1.0 Strict, XHTML 1.1, and HTML5. However, there is an issue with (X)HTML documents embedded with the object element: the layer order set by z-index in the CSS is ignored by older versions of Internet Explorer.

Semantic Web Best Practices

The Semantic Web Best Practices and Deployment Working Group at the World Wide Web Consortium provides documents for authoring semantic web sites [3]. The most important ones are the following:

- *Image Annotation on the Semantic Web* [4]: The document describes the importance and advantages of image metadata. It provides guidelines for Semantic Web–based image annotation and use cases. The related RDF and OWL vocabularies are mentioned, together with an overview of free tools.

- *Best Practice Recipes for Publishing RDF Vocabularies* [5]: The document provides RDF Schema and OWL best practices for vocabulary designers.

- *RDFa Primer—Bridging the Human and Data Webs* [6]: Techniques are shown for providing metadata with RDFa notation, along with techniques that turn existing human-visible text and links into machine-readable data without repeating content. There is also a live example for RDFa notation entitled "Alice in Semantic Wonderland" [7]. It can be used as a starting point for providing image, personal, and licensing metadata with external vocabularies.

- *Quick Guide to Publishing a Thesaurus on the Semantic Web* [8]: The document describes how RDF can be used to express the content and structure of a thesaurus, as well as the associated metadata.

- *Managing a Vocabulary for the Semantic Web—Best Practice* [9]: External vocabularies that identify, document, and publish vocabulary terms can be cited and reused in a wide range of applications. However, proper maintenance is inevitable.

WAI-ARIA Best Practices

The W3C WAI-ARIA Authoring Practices Guide describes best practices for developing rich Internet applications [10]. Approaches are recommended to create accessible widgets, keyboard navigation, form properties, drag-and-drop support, relationships, dialog boxes, and reusable component libraries.

Mobile Web Best Practices

More and more users browse the Internet on mobile phones, smartphones, or PDAs with smaller screen size and resolution, limited bandwidth and capacity, and a less convenient interface than desktop computers. Web pages optimized for them should be designed and served in the appropriate manner to provide a reasonable user experience. The specific features of mobile devices, PDAs, and smartphones should be considered when designing for mobile media [11]. The most important ones are as follows [12]:

- *Limited bandwidth*: Techniques such as compression, caching, and minimized data size can contribute to a better mobile user experience. Cookies and redirections should be eliminated whenever possible.

- *Limited processing capacity*: A large DOM, huge background images, a large number of scripts, and so on, can increase processing time. As a result, users will have to wait for relatively long periods of time, which should be avoided. Simple markup can be provided for mobile devices with XHTML Basic [13]. As for styles, CSS has a profile dedicated to mobile devices [14].

- *Limited technology support*: Do not rely on scripts, embedded objects, cookies, or style sheets. Tabular presentation should be minimized. Since mobile browsers usually support a small set of file types only, download sections should warn users of files provided in formats poorly supported by mobile devices.

- *Smaller interface*: The automatic sign-in feature and unchanged focus on dynamically updated pages can make the use of mobile applications more convenient. Preselected default values should be provided where possible. Default text entry mode, language, and/or input format should be specified [15]. The small screen size and resolution should be taken into account for sizing and positioning. Absolute units and pixel measures should be eliminated.

- *Harder navigation*: The simpler the top navigation, the easier to use on mobile devices. Link targets should be clearly identified. Access keys used for accessibility might also ease navigation.

- *Flexibility*: If devices are classified, the user experiencecan be boosted significantly. Providing alternate content for JavaScript is important.

- *Mobile-specific features*: Certain web page components can be exploited more on mobile devices than on computers. Telephone numbers, for example, should be provided with a direct calling feature.

Rendering web sites on mobile devices require optimization. Pop-up windows should be completely eliminated. Graphical components should not be used for spacing. The use of image maps should be reduced. Bad practices such as frames or table-based layouts that should be avoided can make web pages unusable on mobile devices

Providing Robustness

Web developers should ensure that the content can be used even if some expected technologies cannot be used or fail. Some common examples are discussed in the following sections.

Declaring Fallback Generic Fonts

Because of the endless variety of fonts available for computers, it cannot be guaranteed that a special font exists in each browser. One of the *generic font families* defined by the CSS specification, that is, `serif`, `sans-serif`, `cursive`, `fantasy`, and `monospace` [16], should always be specified. Let's look at an example of text provided in Gill Sans, which is not available for all users. The rule shown in Listing 13-11 can be applied; it ensures that the document text will be rendered with Gill Sans when available and any other sans-serif font when not. Depending on the browser and configuration applied, it might be Arial, Helvetica, or a similar font.

Listing 13-11. A Fallback Mechanism for Fonts

```
body {
    font-family: "Gill Sans", sans-serif;
}
```

Certainly, you can specify further (preferably similar) fonts of the same type as well (Listing 13-12), from which the first available will be applied, but the generic font family declaration will always work.

Listing 13-12. A List of Similar Fonts Preceding the Generic Font Family

```
body {
    font-family: "Gill Sans", "London", "Corinthian", sans-serif;
}
```

Declarations with Appropriate Specificity

Web developers often have to choose from a variety of settings and options. As a general rule, declarations should be defined in a way that obtains the desired effect or functionality on the widest range of devices and settings. For example, the color names reliably supported by CSS are limited to 16 colors (as discussed in Chapter 5). Although they are known by all browsers and seem developer-friendly, the hexadecimal notation should be preferred because there is no ultimate color list for the Web. Certain browsers support additional color names, but they are not standardized. There is no reason to mix the basic color names and other color notations in the CSS. After all, hexadecimal notation can produce virtually any color.

Testing

Since several web site features cannot be guaranteed by standardization, testing is vital in most cases.

Rendering in Multiple Browsers

Because of the differences of rendering engines, markup, and style, validity cannot ensure proper rendering under different user agents. Consequently, the legibility and functionality of web sites should be checked on all major browsers before publishing.[5] The more sophisticated the site design, the more complicated it is to provide similar rendering under different browsers. There are freely available, browser-independent style sheets that eliminate this time-consuming task. Good examples are the W3C Core Styles [17].

Readability Without Styles

An advanced method for testing web sites is to render them with the default style sheet of the browser. Properly structured, logically constructed web documents remain legible without the style sheet(s) developed for them. This test is also useful for checking content accessibility.

―――――――――――――――――――

[5] As discussed in the previous chapter, some browsers provide the option to render web pages with different rendering engines, and there are more and more plug-ins available for testing browser-independence on tabs.

Summary

In this chapter, you learned standardized best practices that should be differentiated from the trends introduced by enthusiastic content authors and developers. You can safely apply these time-proven techniques in almost all scenarios and improve the overall web page quality, from code optimality to robust rendering.

The standard compliance of web sites created using the techniques and standards presented so far should be approved by validation, which will be described in the next chapter.

References

1.   ISO (2007) Writing paper and certain classes of printed matter – Trimmed sizes – A and B series, and indication of machine direction. ISO 216:2007. International Organization for Standardization. www.iso.org/iso/iso_catalogue/catalogue_tc/catalogue_detail.htm?csnumber=36631. Accessed 18 September 2011

2.   Rutter R (2004) How to size text using ems. Richard Rutter. http://clagnut.com/blog/348. Accessed 25 January 2011

3.   Swick R, Schreiber G, Wood D (eds) (2006) Semantic Web Best Practices and Deployment Working Group. World Wide Web Consortium. www.w3.org/2001/sw/BestPractices/. Accessed 16 January 2011

4.   Troncy R, van Ossenbruggen J, Pan JZ, Stamou G (eds), Halaschek-Wiener C, Simou N, Tzouvaras V (2007) Image Annotation on the Semantic Web. World Wide Web Consortium. www.w3.org/2005/Incubator/mmsem/XGR-image-annotation/. Accessed 16 January 2011

5.   Berrueta D, Phipps J (eds) (2008) Best Practice Recipes for Publishing RDF Vocabularies. World Wide Web Consortium. www.w3.org/TR/swbp-vocab-pub/. Accessed 16 January 2011

6.   Adida B, Birbeck M (2008) RDFa Primer – Bridging the Human and Data Webs. World Wide Web Consortium. www.w3.org/TR/xhtml-rdfa-primer/. Accessed 16 January 2011

7.   Adida B, Birbeck M (2008) Alice in Semantic Wonderland. RDFa notation example. World Wide Web Consortium. www.w3.org/TR/xhtml-rdfa-primer/alice-example.html. Accessed 16 January 2011

8.   Miles A (ed) (2005) Quick Guide to Publishing a Thesaurus on the Semantic Web. World Wide Web Consortium. www.w3.org/TR/2005/WD-swbp-thesaurus-pubguide-20050517/. Accessed 16 January 2011

9.   Baker T (ed) (2005) Managing a Vocabulary for the Semantic Web – Best Practice. World Wide Web Consortium. http://esw.w3.org/VocabManagementNote. Accessed 16 January 2011

10.   Scheuhammer J, Cooper M (eds) (2010) WAI-ARIA 1.0 Authoring Practices. An author's guide to understanding and implementing Accessible Rich Internet Applications. World Wide Web Consortium. www.w3.org/TR/wai-aria-practices/. Accessed 16 January 2011

11.   Connors A, Sullivan B (eds) W3C (2010) Mobile Web Application Best Practices. W3C Recommendation. World Wide Web Consortium. www.w3.org/TR/mwabp/. Accessed 15 January 2011

12.   W3C (2010) Mobile Web Application Best Practices Cards. World Wide Web Consortium. www.w3.org/2010/09/MWABP/. Accessed 15 January 2011

13.   McCarron S, Ishikawa M (eds) (2010) XHTML Basic 1.1 - Second Edition. World Wide Web Consortium. www.w3.org/TR/xhtml-basic/. Accessed 15 January 2011

14.   Schubert S (ed) (2008) CSS Mobile Profile 2.0. World Wide Web Consortium. www.w3.org/TR/css-mobile/. Accessed 15 January 2011

15.   W3C (2010) Mobile Web Best Practices. W3C Cheatsheet. World Wide Web Consortium. www.w3.org/2009/cheatsheet/#mwbp. Accessed 15 January 2011

16.   Bos B, Çelik T, Hickson I, Lie HW (eds) (2010) Generic font families. In: Cascading Style Sheets Level 2 Revision 1 (CSS 2.1) Specification. World Wide Web Consortium. www.w3.org/TR/2010/WD-CSS2-20101207/fonts.html#generic-font-families. Accessed 15 January 2011

17.   Bos B (2009) W3C Core Styles. World Wide Web Consortium. www.w3.org/StyleSheets/Core/Overview.html. Accessed 16 January 2011

CHAPTER 14

Validation

The various computer languages used on the Web, including but not limited to (X)HTML, CSS, RDF, and RSS, provide structure, style, metadata, semantics, and other document features. Similar to natural languages, they have their own grammar, vocabulary, and syntax that need to be followed. However, just like the grammar, structural, or spelling errors that occur in documents written in natural languages, web documents might also have errors in them. Validation is the task of checking the source code of web documents against a DTD or schema. It contributes to error-free, clean code and increases overall web page quality.

Even a single character might affect your carefully created standard-compliant code, so it is important to regularly check your documents. After achieving the necessary routine, you are able to modify or extend web documents at the source level without destroying standard compliance. In this chapter, you will learn about the tools that help you locate and correct errors if they occur and can assure you whether your code is error-free.

Concepts

Markup language grammar rules are defined by Document Type Definitions (DTDs). Prior to HTML5/XHTML5, developers should have provided a reference to the DTD associated with the document type being used (as discussed in Chapter 3).

Web documents can be verified against these rules, which is called *validation*. The tools used to perform validation are called *validators*. Documents successfully passing validation are claimed to be *valid*; in other words, they are free of errors and do not contain incorrectly used elements or attributes. However, validation guarantees neither well-structuredness nor proper element use [1]. A valid document follows the grammar rules outlined in the corresponding DTD, which makes it possible for user agents to construct the DOM correctly and render the document accurately.

Applying the grammar rules defined in DTDs is described in *technical specifications*, most of which are published by W3C.

Standard conformance is the feature of those web documents that fulfill all the requirements described by the appropriate DTD and specification. A web document is valid when it is correctly written in accordance to the *formal grammar* included in the technical specification of the corresponding markup language, whereas conformance relates to the entire specification. Since some conformance requirements, such as the proper use of attribute values, cannot be described by the formal grammar, validity is only part of conformance. Consequently, validity and conformance might be identical, but the latter one is a wider term.

Valid documents are written according to the formal grammar of the language being used. Standard-compliant documents apply the technology the recommended way.

Validation should not be considered as the final step right before publication. Instead, it should be performed as an essential part of development. If new markup elements or attributes are used in large quantities and the developer cannot provide them with 100 percent certainty, validation can help identify potential errors and prevent invalid markup from being duplicated or multiplied. Even the most experienced web standardistas might find validation useful and consider it an assistance rather than a mandatory task. After inserting new structural elements to the source, for example, it can be more than inconvenient to identify the numerous—and often identical—closing tags (such as four to five or more consecutive </div> tags). While finding start tag–end tag pairs is very easy in a file containing 100–200 lines, the task can be overwhelming for larger files.[1]

No matter how experienced a developer is or how sophisticated development tools are used, errors are inevitable. This is where validators can help the work of developers. As you will see, validators provide error locations, along with hints for possible causes and potential solutions.

Since validation contributes to overall web page quality, validators and advanced specific checkers are also known as *web quality assurance* tools [2].

Markup Validation

The primary validator for HTML/XHTML documents is the W3C Markup Validation Service at http://validator.w3.org. In fact, Markup Validation Service v1.1 can be used to validate several types of markup [3], including the following:

- *HTML*: ISO/IEC 15445:2000 ("ISO HTML"), HTML 2.0, HTML 3.2, HTML 4.01 Frameset, HTML 4.01 Transitional, and HTML5

- *MathML*: MathML 2.0

- *SMIL*: SMIL 1.0, SMIL 2.0

- *SVG*: SVG 1.0, SVG 1.1, SVG 1.1 Basic, SVG 1.1 Tiny

- *XHTML*: XHTML Basic 1.0, XHTML Basic 1.1, XHTML 1.0 Frameset, XHTML 1.0 Strict, XHTML 1.0 Transitional, and XHTML 1.1, XHTML Mobile Profile 1.2, and XHTML Print 1.0

- *Mixed-namespace documents*: XHTML + RDFa[2], XHTML 1.1 + MathML 2.0, and XHTML 1.1 + MathML 2.0 + SVG 1.1

The W3C Markup Validation Service offers three options to validate web documents:

- *Validation by direct input*: Validation of the markup provided in a textbox. The code can be either typed directly or copied and pasted from an advanced text editor. This is suitable for testing. Since there is no physical file to validate, neither character encoding nor server settings can be checked by direct input.

- *Validation by file uploading*: Validation of a file uploaded to a temporary folder. Character encoding can also be checked. Experienced web standardistas do not use this option frequently because the file can be uploaded to the host (final destination) with the same effort (in the case of static files).

---

[1] Even if there are tools that represent the hierarchy with vertical dotted lines between the opening and closing tag pairs (e.g., Notepad++).
[2] The RDFa notation can be perfectly validated in XHTML documents. As of 2011, the Validator still does not recognize RDFa in HTML5, however, and gives errors.

456

- *Validation by URI*: Validation of an uploaded version on a web server. This is the ultimate validation that validates markup, character encoding, and server settings. It's ideal for final checking and the validation of web pages developed by others.

The W3C validator supports the following character encodings: UTF-8, UTF-16, ISO-8859-1, ISO-8859-2, ISO-8859-3, ISO-8859-4, ISO-8859-5, ISO-8859-6-i, ISO-8859-7, ISO-8859-8, ISO-8859-8-i, ISO-8859-9, ISO-8859-10, ISO-8859-11, ISO-8859-13, ISO-8859-14, ISO-8859-15, ISO-8859-16, US-ASCII, EUC-JP, Shift_JIS, ISO-2022-jp, EUC-kr, gb2312, gb18030, big5, Big5-HKSCS, tis-620, koi8-r, koi8-u, ISO-ir-111, Macintosh, Windows-1250, Windows-1251, Windows-1252, Windows-1253, Windows-1254, Windows-1255, Windows-1256, and Windows-1257.

Both document type and character encoding are detected automatically and used for validation accordingly. If detection is not possible, the validator assumes the document type and/or character encoding; however, the results might be unreliable. Properly served standard-compliant web documents always provide both data; thus, the validator performs validation accurately. The validator can also be forced manually to use certain document type and/or character encoding; however, this feature should not be used in general cases. It should be considered a fallback mechanism rather than an overriding feature.

If there are errors in the markup, they are clearly indicated by the red stripe and the number of errors (Figure 14-1). Even the favicon of the page becomes a red square.

Figure 14-1. The red stripe and the number of errors and warnings clearly show that the markup is invalid.

The consecutive errors/potential errors are listed under the summary sequentially by default, in other words, in the order of occurrence (location in the markup). This behavior can be overridden to group error messages by error type. However, since many errors can cause further ones (such as a missing closing tag), sequential checking is adequate in most cases.

> ■ **Tip** Because of the high potential of correlation between markup errors, it might be convenient to correct some errors only (especially if the document is full of errors) and then revalidate the document. The number of errors might decrease exponentially. Revalidation is also useful for testing implementations of special or new markup specifications as a direct input.

There are several advanced settings of the Markup Validation Service you can use for your standardization projects. The (X)HTML source code can be displayed with the error messages directly linking to the corresponding lines. This is a useful feature for developers. The tree structure of document headings can be visualized by the outline option, which makes it easier to realize which header is missed (if any). Custom 404 error pages sent by the server can be validated by ticking the checkbox "Validate error pages." Beyond the concise reports provided by default, more explanations and longer suggestions can be requested with the Verbose Output option. Another option of the W3C Markup Validation Service is to correct markup errors using the tool HTML Tidy discussed in Chapter 11.

Beyond the error location, the Markup Validation Service gives hints for corrections and links to the corresponding specifications and FAQs (Figure 14-2). Some of the characters might be highlighted, which is another aid, and sometimes makes the detection of invalid characters very easy.

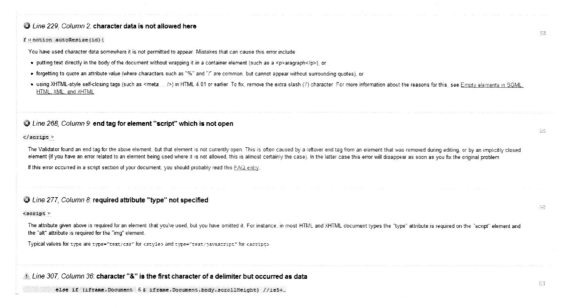

Figure 14-2. The W3C Markup Validation Service clearly indicates error locations and provides useful hints for correction.

The markup validation results and suggestions are useful not only for the less experienced developers but also for experts. Using the line numbers, it is fairly easy to find errors, which is a prerequisite step for correcting them even for those who do not rely on the correction tips.

After the necessary corrections and the final revalidation, the result should look like Figure 14-3.

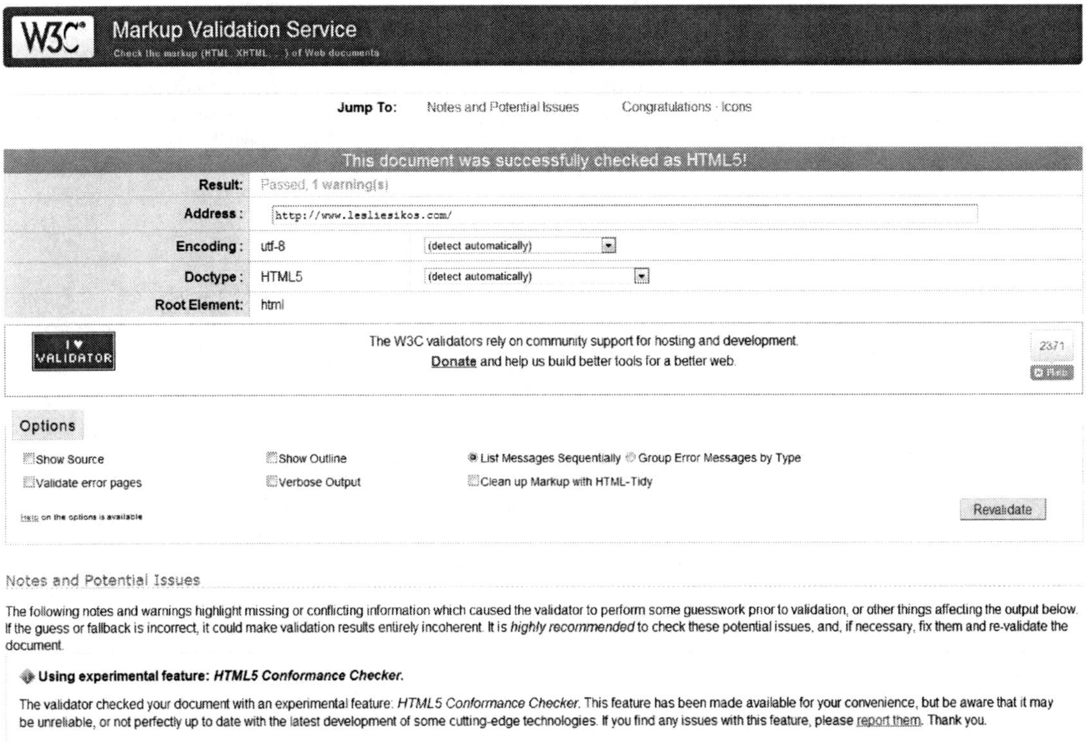

Figure 14-3. The green stripe and the result "Passed" indicate that the markup is valid.

▪ **Note** As of 2011, validating HTML5 is still only an experimental feature at the W3C Markup Validation Service. Consequently, the validator will give a warning (not error!) even if the web page being analyzed is valid. The validator does not recognize RDFa annotations in HTML5, nor XHTML5 documents.[3] Furthermore, in contrast to valid XHTML documents, the validator does not provide validation badges with hyperlinks for valid HTML5 documents. As will be discussed later, such badges can be downloaded from a separate site.

The W3C Markup Validator is not only free but also open source and available under the W3C Software License [4]. Anyone is allowed to set up mirrors of the service or contribute to its development.

---

[3] The XML declaration and all namespace declarations provided in XHTML5 result in an error message, even if they are valid. Moreover, the validation result of XHTML5 documents states HTML5 instead of XHTML5.

Although there are other markup validators on the Web, such as the WDG HTML Validator [5], or offline tools such as the Firefox plug-in *HTML Validator* [6], using the W3C Markup Validation Service is recommended. It is part of W3C Unicorn, which can be used if styles sheets and feed channels should also be checked (see later in section "W3C Unicorn").

Validating markup is more complicated for developers of dynamic web sites since markup validators generally cannot deal with scripts such as PHP. Checking the dynamically generated (X)HTML output, performing corrections, and revalidating documents are all real challenges. This is one of the major reasons why dynamically generated web pages are often invalid.

Validating XML

XML documents can be validated for conformance with a DTD, an XML schema, or the schema language RELAX NG. Syntactic well-formedness is a basic requirement, but it does not guarantee XML validity, which has several constraints, such as proper use of required and optional elements and attributes, correct document structure and syntax, and properly applied data types.

Although XML validation and parsing are logically independent tasks, both are often performed by XML parsers. Considering that even a single error can prevent the document from being parsed or its tree structure shown, XML parsers of web browsers can always be used as basic XML validators.

XML validity is not required by all XML parsers but by the XML parsers that check the document against its associated schema.

Batch validation of XML files can be performed by the xmlvalidate task of Apache Ant [7]. For example, the target in Listing 14-1 validates the .xml files in the directory specified by the dir attribute.[4]

Listing 14-1. Validating XML with xmlvalidate

```
<target name="validate-xml">
  <xmlvalidate lenient="no">
    <fileset dir="semweb/ont" includes="*.xml" />
    <attribute name="http://xml.org/sax/features/validation" value="true"/>
    <attribute name="http://apache.org/xml/features/validation/schema"  value="true"/>
    <attribute name="http://xml.org/sax/features/namespaces" value="true"/>
  </xmlvalidate>
</target>
```

Validating RDF/XML

RDF documents written in the XML serialization format (RDF/XML) can be checked with the W3C RDF Validation Service at www.w3.org/RDF/Validator [8]. Validations can be performed by URI or direct input. The Validator not only checks the RDF code but also represents RDF triples (Figure 14-4).

---

[4] Relative to the Ant build file

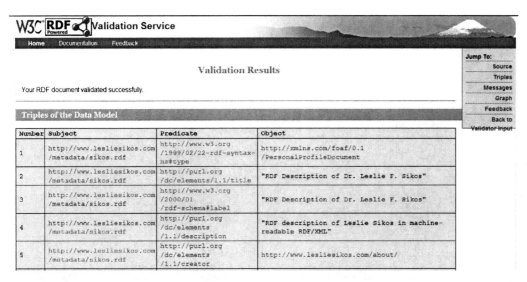

Figure 14-4. Subject–predicate–object triples retrieved from a valid RDF file

Optionally, the RDF graph can be generated in various formats, including embedded or linked PNG, SVG, GIF, PostScript, IsaViz/ZVTM, HPGL, and HPGL/2. Although the arcs look like hand-drawn curves and often overlap each other—which is not the most visually appealing representation—the image output can be useful for demonstrational or designing purposes (Figure 14-5). It is also important to keep in mind that there are only very few similar services available on the Web for generating graph images from RDF.

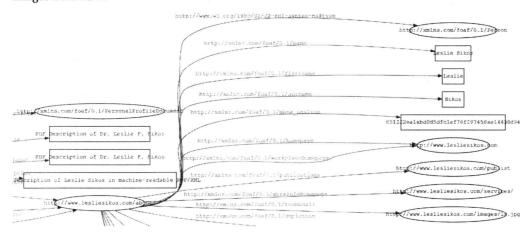

Figure 14-5. Detail of an RDF graph generated by the W3C RDF Validation Service

---

▪ **Note** In contrast to the raster (PNG) output, the SVG output not only has incomparable quality but also contains the URIs as hyperlinks.

Optionally, the triples can be displayed in N-Triples format. The colors of nodes, arcs, and text, as well as font size and orientation, can be set as advanced options.

Validating News Feeds

Since RSS and Atom news feeds should be valid XML documents, care must be taken to provide error-free elements and well-formed XML structure.

The World Wide Web Consortium runs the *W3C Feed Validation Service, for Atom and RSS* at `http://validator.w3.org/feed/` [9]. Similar to other W3C validators, it provides not just validation by URI but also validation by direct input. After successful validation, the service provides a "valid RSS" or "valid Atom" logo (depending on the validated feed), an embedding code, and a text link.

The *FEED Validator for Atom and RSS and KML* at `http://feedvalidator.org` can also be used to validate RSS 2.0 as well as Atom 1.0 feeds [10]. Additionally, it validates elements of the blogChannel, dc, itunes, mod_admin, mod_syndication, and mod_content[5] namespaces.

Validating CSS

Style sheet validations should be performed according to the CSS level being used. Although valid CSS1 style sheets are also valid CSS 2.1 style sheets, some CSS1 rulesets should be written with slightly different semantics in CSS 2.1 [11]. Since certain CSS2 features are omitted in CSS 2.1, not all CSS2 styles are valid in CSS 2.1 [12]. Similarly, the new properties introduced in CSS3 are invalid in earlier CSS versions. Valid CSS style sheets must conform to the grammar rules of the corresponding version and must contain only at-rules, properties, and property values defined in that specification.

In spite of the relatively wide selection of markup language versions and variants, the document type to be used for markup validation can be selected automatically in most cases because of the document type declaration. However, there is no similar mechanism in CSS, and determining the version of style sheets to be validated is not so straightforward. First, there is no version declaration in CSS, and second, there is a large overlap between the vocabularies, making automatic version detection impossible. Hence, the W3C CSS Validation Service at `http://jigsaw.w3.org/css-validator/` [13] validates style sheets against CSS 2.1 by default. However, the profile to be applied can be overridden manually as an advanced option. For example, if you want to validate a CSS3 file by URI, you should construct a URI[6] similar to the one shown in Listing 14-2.

Listing 14-2. Manual Override for CSS3 Validation

```
http://jigsaw.w3.org/css-validator/validator?uri=www.example.com/styles/main.css ↩
  &profile=css3&usermedium=all&warning=0&lang=en
```

---

[5] content:encoded only
[6] Naturally, you can select the profile "CSS level 3" from the drop-down list under "More Options." However, you need to construct a URI manually if you want to provide a validation link for your CSS3 button, because the default code assumes CSS 2.1.

Similar to the Markup Validation Service, the CSS validator can perform the validation by URI, file uploading, or direct input. The CSS validator can be used primarily to validate external CSS files, but internal styles can also be checked. However, in the latter case, the (X)HTML document should be validated first with the Markup Validation Service.

The CSS Validation Service supports CSS1, CSS2, CSS 2.1, and CSS3 style sheets, along with other document profiles. Media types can be selected manually, including `all`, `aural`, `Braille`, `embossed`, `handheld`, `print`, `projection`, `screen`, `TTY`, `TV`, or `presentation`. The default media type is `all`. Beyond errors, the validator might identify warnings as well. Since they might be false positives or the consequence of errors, warnings can be hidden.

The validation request applies parameters in conjunction with the base URI `http://jigsaw.w3.org/css-validator/validator`. The supported parameters are the following:

- `uri`: The URI of the document to be validated. It can be CSS or (X)HTML.

- `text`: The CSS document to validate.

- `usermedium`: The media type used for validation.

- `output`: `html` (HTML), `xhtml` (XHTML, default), `soap12` (SOAP 1.2), `text` (plain text).

- `profile`: `css1`, `css2`, `css21`, `css3`, `svg`, `svgbasic`, `svgtiny`, `mobile`, `atsc-tv`, `tv`, or `none`.

- `lang`: The report language such as `en` (default), `fr`, `it`, `ko`, `ja`, `es`, `zh-cn`, `nl`, `de`, `it`, or `pl`.

- `warning`: Warning level with possible values `no` (hidden warnings), `0` (less warnings), `1` or `2` (more warnings). `2` is the default.

The output of the W3C CSS Validation Service is similar to the result page of the W3C markup validator. A green stripe indicates a valid file, while a red stripe means that the CSS file is invalid.

Validating I18N

The Internationalization Activity Group at the World Wide Web Consortium runs the W3C Internationalization Checker [14]. The I18N checker can be used to check web pages for *internationalization-friendliness* according to the following factors:

- *Character encoding*: HTTP Content-Type, byte-order mark, XML declaration, the Content-Type metadata, and HTML5 `meta charset`

- *Language settings*: the `lang` and `xml:lang` attributes on the `html` element, the HTTP Content-Language, and the `content-language` metadata

- *Text direction*: `ltr` (default) or `rtl`

- *The `class` and `id` names*: Non-ASCII as well as non-NFC classes and identifiers

- *Request headers*: `Accept-Language`, `Accept-Charset`

Validating Hyperlinks

One of the most disappointing browser experiences is the broken hyperlink (dead link). W3C Link Checker at `http://validator.w3.org/checklink` is a useful tool for checking internal and external hyperlinks of web documents [15]. Linked documents can also be checked recursively throughout a maximum of 150 documents. URI fragments including a hash mark such as `index.html#about` are included in the test. Links forbidden by the *robots exclusion rules* declared in the `robots.txt` file are not checked (Figure 14-6).

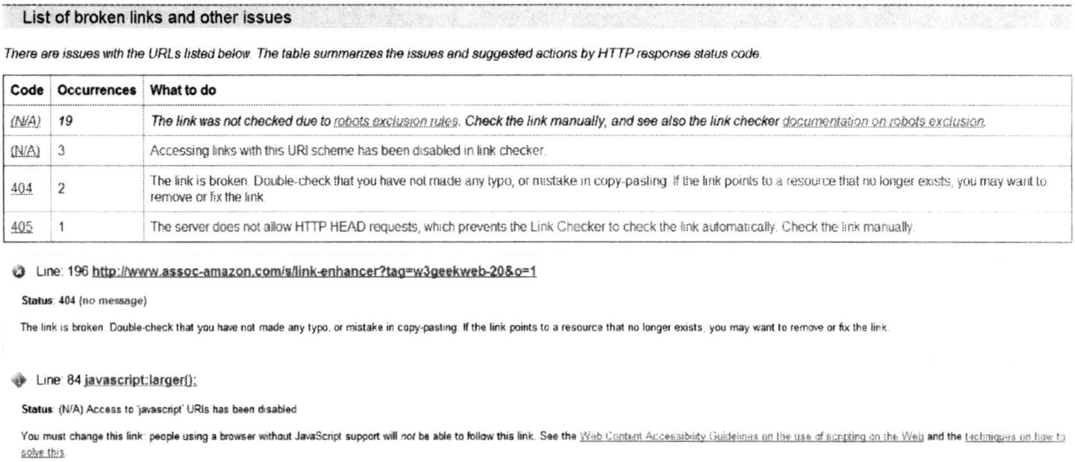

List of broken links and other issues

There are issues with the URLs listed below. The table summarizes the issues and suggested actions by HTTP response status code.

Code	Occurrences	What to do
(N/A)	19	*The link was not checked due to robots exclusion rules. Check the link manually, and see also the link checker documentation on robots exclusion.*
(N/A)	3	Accessing links with this URI scheme has been disabled in link checker.
404	2	The link is broken. Double-check that you have not made any typo, or mistake in copy-pasting. If the link points to a resource that no longer exists, you may want to remove or fix the link.
405	1	The server does not allow HTTP HEAD requests, which prevents the Link Checker to check the link automatically. Check the link manually.

◉ Line: 196 http://www.assoc-amazon.com/s/link-enhancer?tag=w3geekweb-20&o=1

Status: 404 (no message)

The link is broken. Double-check that you have not made any typo, or mistake in copy-pasting. If the link points to a resource that no longer exists, you may want to remove or fix the link.

◈ Line: 84 javascript:larger();

Status: (N/A) Access to 'javascript' URIs has been disabled

You must change this link: people using a browser without JavaScript support will not be able to follow this link. See the Web Content Accessibility Guidelines on the use of scripting on the Web and the techniques on how to solve this.

Figure 14-6. Link Checker results

Hyperlink validation is useful not only for checking entry points but also for important files such as style sheet files, scripts, or external URIs that might be modified by their administrators any time without notification. For example, permanent redirections (HTTP response status code 301) are also identified by Link Checker, and although they work, such links should be updated. The results can be useful for eliminating broken links and accessibility barriers associated with links of the analyzed web page.

Validating Accessibility

Unlike other web site features, accessibility cannot be validated by validators with 100 percent certainty. While markup errors, such as incorrect element use, missing tags, or structural errors, can be identified automatically, accessibility is too complex and sophisticated to be validated automatically [16]. Many potential issues require human decision, checking, or confirmation. The equivalent functionality of scripts and `noscript` contents, adequacy of text descriptions, script functionality and effects, visual lists represented by paragraphs and break rows, and pause options in objects are some of the features that cannot be checked automatically with full certainty.

Even so, there are useful tools that can make the work of accessibility developers easier [17]. Such tools should be used throughout the phases of web site development to prevent accessibility barriers, repair encountered barriers, and improve overall web page quality. The major task of accessibility tools is to identify accessible-friendly elements and attributes in the markup. Moreover, certain tools can assist developers in performing those checks that cannot be validated automatically [18]. Accessibility tools perform validation against W3C Web Accessibility Guidelines (WCAG 1.0 and/or WCAG 2.0) as well as Section 508.

A typical online accessibility checker is *AChecker* (`http://achecker.ca` [19]) that has been released by the Inclusive Design Research Centre at the University of Toronto, Canada. AChecker can test web sites for conformance to various accessibility guidelines, including WCAG 1.0/2.0 Level A/AA/AAA, Section 508, Stanca Act, and BITV. The interface provides accessibility checking by either URL or file upload. It identifies three types of errors: known, likely, and potential problems. Known problems are claimed to be errors that can be identified with certainty (for example, `img` element with missing `alt` attribute, missing label for the `input` element). Likely problems need human decisions (for example, misused elements, onchange event handler on the `select` element might cause extreme change in context). Potential problems are often not errors at all; however, they require human decision and confirmation (for example, `dir` attribute may be required to identify changes in text direction, data table may require th elements, script user interface may not be available from the keyboard). Unfortunately, not every suggestion would validate and some of them are incorrect (for example, the `lang` attribute on the `html` element is neither valid nor required in XHTML+RDFa if the natural language of the document is identified by the `xml:lang` attribute) (Figure 14-7).

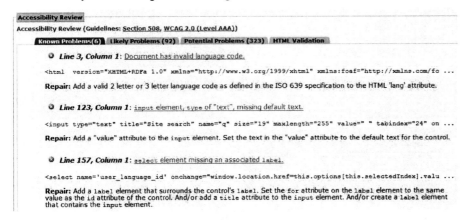

Figure 14-7. AChecker provides good suggestions; however, not all of them would be valid.

AChecker also supports HTML validation. It provides error descriptions and suggestions for corrections.

The online accessibility validation tool Cynthia can perform validations by URI according to Section 508 and WCAG 1.0 with all priority levels [20]. Advanced options are also available such as browser emulation or line exclusions. Reports are clear and useful for developers dealing with accessibility (Figure 14-8).

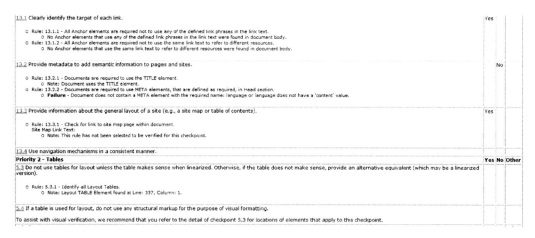

13.1 Clearly identify the target of each link. | Yes

  ○ Rule: 13.1.1 - All Anchor elements are required not to use any of the defined link phrases in the link text.
    ○ No Anchor elements that use any of the defined link phrases in the link text were found in document body.
  ○ Rule: 13.1.2 - All Anchor elements are required not to use the same link text to refer to different resources.
    ○ No Anchor elements that use the same link text to refer to different resources were found in document body.

13.2 Provide metadata to add semantic information to pages and sites. | No

  ○ Rule: 13.2.1 - Documents are required to use the TITLE element.
    ○ Note: Document uses the TITLE element.
  ○ Rule: 13.2.2 - Documents are required to use META elements, that are defined as required, in Head section.
    ○ **Failure** - Document does not contain a META element with the required name: language or language does not have a 'content' value.

13.3 Provide information about the general layout of a site (e.g., a site map or table of contents). | Yes

  ○ Rule: 13.3.1 - Check for link to site map page within document.
    Site Map Link Text:
    ○ Note: This rule has not been selected to be verified for this checkpoint.

13.4 Use navigation mechanisms in a consistent manner.

Priority 2 - Tables | Yes | No | Other

5.3 Do not use tables for layout unless the table makes sense when linearized. Otherwise, if the table does not make sense, provide an alternative equivalent (which may be a linearized version).

  ○ Rule: 5.3.1 - Identify all Layout Tables.
    ○ Note: Layout TABLE Element found at Line: 337, Column: 1.

5.4 If a table is used for layout, do not use any structural markup for the purpose of visual formatting.

To assist with visual verification, we recommend that you refer to the detail of checkpoint 5.3 for locations of elements that apply to this checkpoint.

Figure 14-8. Detailed accessibility report with explanations and links to W3C guidelines

One of the most comprehensive accessibility tools is WebAIM WAVE [21]. It is a free online tool at `http://wave.webaim.org` that renders web pages with accessibility errors, warnings, and information (Figure 14-9). It identifies accessible attribute values, inaccessible and potentially inaccessible content such as Flash or scripts, and device-dependent content such as keyboard traps.

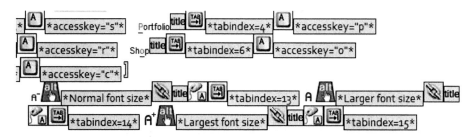

Figure 14-9. Section of an accessible menu rendered by WAVE

While WAVE is a general accessibility tool focusing on markup, there are much more specific tools as well. For example, there are several free online tools for evaluating the contrast between text color and background color, such as the Color Contrast Analyzer [22], the Luminosity Color Contrast Ratio Analyzer [23], or the index of color texts on white background provided by the University of Wisconsin [24].

It is important to keep in mind that no accessibility tools can perform a complete evaluation by any means.

With the introduction of new semantic elements in HTML5, care must be taken to apply the latest checkers available.

The final accessibility test is always a real-life test that involves evaluation performed by people with disabilities.

Validating Mobile-Friendliness

With the enormous popularity of mobile browsing, it is vital to test your web sites on mobile devices. However, it is practically infeasible to check web sites on all kinds of mobile devices. Fortunately, the W3C mobileOK Checker at http://validator.w3.org/mobile/ can help you analyze the suitability of your web pages for mobile browsing [25]. The mobileOK Checker applies the tests defined in the W3C Recommendation "W3C mobileOK Basic Tests 1.0" [26], categorizes failures, and gives useful error descriptions (Figure 14-10).

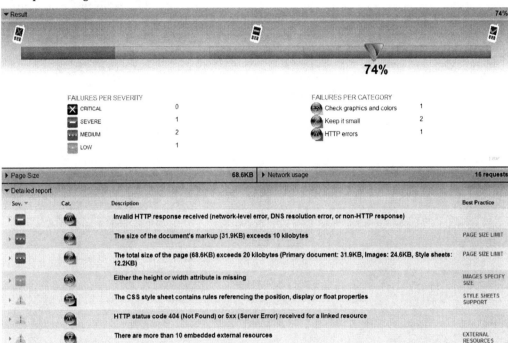

Figure 14-10. The W3C mobileOK checker gives useful hints when evaluating web site suitability for mobile browsing.

After correcting the flagged issues, the web site will fulfill the fundamental requirements for providing a reasonable mobile browsing experience.

Unified Validators

Although individual validators could be used in combination for validating full web sites, in the case of large projects, it would be inconvenient and slow. Developers can apply unified validators to perform multiple validations easily and effectively.

W3C Unicorn

On 27 July 2010, W3C released Unicorn, a unified validator available at `http://validator.w3.org/unicorn/` [27] with the slogan "Improve the quality of the Web." Unicorn is the ultimate markup, CSS, and news feed validator and mobileOK checker. Validations can be performed by URI, by file upload, or by direct input individually or simultaneously. The advanced options are identical to the ones provided by the individual W3C validation services discussed earlier. Unicorn is available in many languages [28].

Depending on the tests chosen, the output provides information about the validity of the markup, style sheets, and news feeds, as well as the mobile-friendliness of the web page (Figure 14-11).

Figure 14-11. The heaven of web standardistas: valid markup, valid style sheet, and valid news feed

Similar to the individual W3C validators, valid documents are indicated by a green stripe, while invalid documents are indicated by a red stripe. By clicking the stripes, the validation test results can be collapsed/uncollapsed by category (they are uncollapsed by default). On the right side, on each stripe you can see the number of errors, warning, and information (if any). These numbers are hyperlinks and can be used to jump to the corresponding section on the page. In case of a valid web page, the validators provide not only reassuring information but also W3C badges with evaluation links that can be embedded to your valid web page. In other words, the output of Unicorn is identical to the output of the separate validators.

Total Validator

Another unified validator is Total Validator, which once was an online service. In contrast, the current version is available exclusively as a desktop software tool for different platforms [29]. The basic version can be downloaded free of charge. Total Validator is available for different platforms, including Windows, OS X, and Linux.[7] Total Validator is a small and powerful tool that combines a markup validator, an accessibility validator, a spell-checker, and a link validator (Figure 14-12).

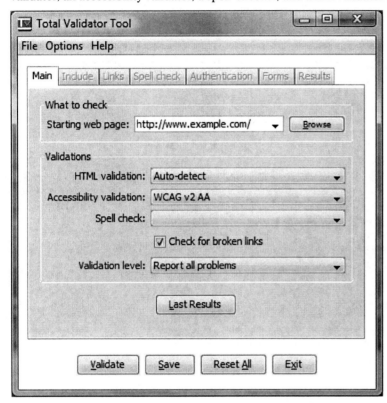

Figure 14-12. The configuration interface of Total Validator

This interface is used for starting the process only. After declaring the URI of the web page to validate, along with the parameters, Total Validator opens a browser window and displays the validation results. Errors and warnings are shown in the markup code with hyperlinks to the corresponding entries of the long description after the markup code (Figure 14-13).

---

[7] The basic tool is Java based and requires Java 1.5 or later.

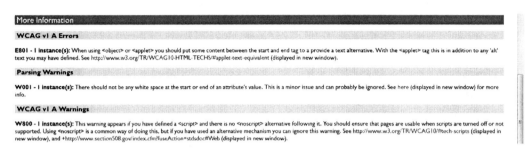

Figure 14-13. *Validation results with a segment of the markup code (top) and the long description at the bottom of the page*

Beyond common markup languages such as XHTML 1.0 Strict, XHTML 1.1, and HTML5 (and many older versions), Total Validator also supports HTML + RDFa 1.1, XHTML + RDFa 1.1, HTML5 used as a polyglot language, and even XHTML5. Accessibility can be checked at all levels of WCAG, as well as according to Section 508. The spell checker supports American and British English, French, Italian, Spanish, and German.

Total Validator provides screenshots for analyzing web page appearance in different browsers, including various versions of Firefox from version 1.5, Internet Explorer from version 5.5, Konqueror 3.5, Lynx 2.8, Opera, and Safari.

An interesting option is that the validation result can be saved as HTML and opened with a single click on the button Last Results the next time the tool is executed.

SortSite

A comprehensive commercial validator is SortSite, developed by PowerMapper [30]. Its main features can be summarized as follows:

- *Accessibility*: Check conformance against WCAG 1.0, WCAG 2.0, and Section 508.

- *Broken links*: Check for broken links and incorrect server configuration.

- *Compatibility*: Check for browser-specific code, scripts, and image formats.

- *Compliance*: Check for compliance with EU and U.S. law.

- *Markup and styles*: HTML, XHTML and CSS validation.

- *Search engine optimization*: Check Google, Yahoo!, and Bing content guidelines

- *Usability*: Check against Usability.gov guidelines.

Extracting Semantic Content

Semantic content of web sites can be checked with the W3C Semantic Data Extractor [31]. It can extract semantic data such as following:

- Generic metadata

    - Title, author, and description provided in the document head

    - RDFa metadata embedded in the document body (also generated in RDF/XML)

- Related resources

    - Linked files, for example, RSS or Atom news feeds

- Glossary, copyright, and bookmarkable points provided in the document head

- Outline of the document

- Quotes and citations

Menu points and URIs are provided with hyperlinks.

Another comprehensive semantic data extractor tool is the Sindice Web Data Inspector at `http://inspector.sindice.com` [32]. The tool can be used to extract RDF triples from markup, RDF/XML, Turtle, or N3 documents provided either by URI or by direct input. Sindice Web Data Inspector can be used exclusively for retrieving semantic data (Inspect button) or combined semantic data extraction and validation (Inspect + Validate button), as well as ontology analysis and reasoning (Figure 14-14).

Figure 14-14. Comprehensive options on the start screen of Sindice Web Data Inspector

As a result, the tool provides the full list of subject–predicate–object triples retrieved from the file (Figure 14-15). The output format can also be changed to N-triples or RDF/XML.

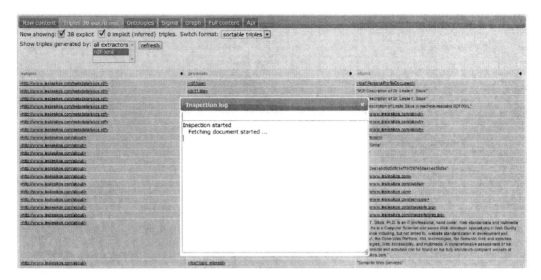

Figure 14-15. *Semantic data extraction is in progress*

The "Sigma" option is a really good demonstration of machine-readable metadata. Software tools can extract structured data from properly written semantic documents and display them arbitrarily (Figure 14-16). This is the true essence of the Semantic Web!

Figure 14-16. A personal description extracted from RDF and displayed in a visually appealing manner

A very nice feature of Sindice Web Data Inspector is that a scalable graph can be generated from the semantic document (Figure 14-17). The graph not only presents the triples but also provides a quick summary of the ontologies and vocabularies used in the file.

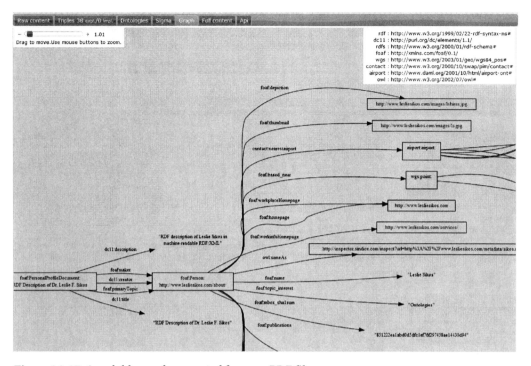

Figure 14-17. A scalable graph generated from an RDF file

The Sindice Web Data Inspector also has a validation feature with two different options. The first one, called "RDF syntax validation," performs an RDF syntax validation according to the W3C specification. The second option is the "Pedantic validator," which is a validation over the extracted triples. In case of a valid document, both validators give the result "Valid document."

Expressing Validity

Standard conformance of web sites can be expressed easily by the "valid" icons (also known as *validity badges* or *validity logos*). In addition to notifying readers, they can also be used as instant validation links if used appropriately. The expected hyperlink is listed in the sample code provided by W3C validators themselves when validating web documents (Figure 14-18).

W3C CSS Validator results for http://www.lesliesikos.com/styles/sikos.css (CSS level 3)

Jump to: Validated CSS

W3C CSS Validator results for http://www.lesliesikos.com/styles/sikos.css (CSS level 3)

Congratulations! No Error Found.

This document validates as CSS level 3 !

To show your readers that you've taken the care to create an interoperable Web page, you may display this icon on any page that validates. Here is the XHTML you could use to add this icon to your Web page:

```
<p>
    <a href="http://jigsaw.w3.org/css-validator/check/referer">
        <img style="border:0;width:88px;height:31px"
            src="http://jigsaw.w3.org/css-validator/images/vcss"
            alt="Valid CSS!" />
    </a>
</p>
```

```
<p>
    <a href="http://jigsaw.w3.org/css-validator/check/referer">
        <img style="border:0;width:88px;height:31px"
            src="http://jigsaw.w3.org/css-validator/images/vcss-blue"
            alt="Valid CSS!" />
    </a>
</p>
```

Figure 14-18. W3C validation icons with embedding code

Note that the codes are just suggestions. For example, the style attribute on the img element can be omitted in favor of external CSS rules. The recommended embedding code for XHTML [33] is presented in Listing 14-3.

Listing 14-3. Embedding Code for W3C Validation Icons

```
<p>
  <a href="http://validator.w3.org/check/referer">
  <img src="http://www.w3.org/Icons/valid-xhtml10" alt="Valid XHTML 1.0!" height="31" ↵
    width="88" />

  </a>
</p>
```

W3C Icons

The W3C "valid" icons represent a W3C logo on the left and the Recommendation on the right (Figure 14-19). In many cases, the version or the Recommendation is also shown.

Figure 14-19. Structure of conventional W3C validity icons

The default size of the icons is 88 × 31 pixels. The World Wide Web Consortium provides two versions for each icon: a gold one and a blue one. The content author is free to choose which one to use. The W3C Trademark License as well as the logo and icon usage policies apply to all W3C validity icons. Modifying icons is not allowed.

The W3C valid logos can be used exclusively on web pages that pass validation. They are designed for verification. The icons must provide a hyperlink that validates the web page according to the corresponding W3C technology or standard. Consequently, clicking a correctly set "valid markup button" should pass the URI of the page to the W3C Markup Validation Service, which gives the same result page as if the URI was used directly for validation on the validator web page. The same holds for CSS validation buttons. Consequently, these buttons can also be used by content providers and web developers to revalidate pages every time they are modified. Experts can use this facility to reassure themselves about the latest modifications without the need for loading the corresponding validator and adding the URI manually.

The World Wide Web Consortium does not verify the validity of web pages; thus, it is the developers and Web authors' responsibility to ensure consistency and conformance.

The full list of W3C validation icons is listed on the W3C Quality Assurance site [34] and includes the following:

- *Markup icons*: "HTML 2.0", "HTML 3.2", "HTML 4.0", "HTML 4.01", "ISO-HTML" for ISO/IEC 15445 (legacy missing), "XHTML 1.0", "XHTML 1.1", "XHTML Basic 1.0", "XHTML-Print 1.0", and "XHTML+RDFa"

- *CSS icons*: A general valid "CSS" icon and more specific icons for "CSS level 1" and "CSS level 2"

- *XML icons*: "XML 1.0", "XML 1.1"

- *SVG icons*: "SVG 1.0", "SVG 1.1", "SVG 1.2", "SVG Tiny 1.1", and "SVG Tiny 1.2"

- *MathML icon*: "MathML 2.0"

The validity icons are also available directly at the W3C Icon Repository (along with other images) [35].

Representing Technologies

Beyond validation, numerous icons are available that represent web technologies used by web sites. They can express not only underlying technologies but also dedication, initiatives the site developers agree with, or projects and organizations they sympathize with. They can also be used to proudly present rarely implemented but advanced features that can hardly be seen on other sites. The most frequently used W3C technology icons are the following:

- "HTML5"

  - "HTML5 Powered with CSS3/Styling"

  - "HTML5 Powered with Semantics"

  - "HTML5 Powered with Offline & Storage"

  - "HTML5 Powered with Connectivity/Realtime"

  - "HTML5 Powered with Multimedia"

  - "HTML5 Powered with Graphics, 3D, and effects"

  - "HTML5 Powered with Device Access"

  - "HTML5 Powered with Performance & Integration"

  Technology names are optional and can be combined (by adding the word "and" prior to the last technology selected). The badges can be generated with Badge Builder 5000 in both horizontal and vertical orientations. The HTML5 mark with or without wordmark, supporting elements, technology classes, and sticker templates are available as separate SVG and PNG files. The HTML5 logo is also available as a one-color version. All badges are released with the Creative Commons Attribution 3.0 License [36].

- "Made with Cascading Style Sheets".

- Accessibility icons: "WAI-A WCAG 1.0", "WAI-AA WCAG 1.0", "WAI-AAA WCAG 1.0" [37], "WAI-A WCAG 2.0", "WAI-AA WCAG 2.0", and "WAI-AAA WCAG 2.0" [38].

- Semantic Web technology buttons: "GRDDL", "OWL", "POWDER", "RDF", "RDFa", "RIF", "SKOS", and "SPARQL" [39].

However, W3C is not the only institution that releases technology icons and logos. Here are some examples:

- "Unicode encoded"

- "Dublin Core used here"

- "Java—Get it now"

- "HCARD", "XFN FRIENDLY", and icons and logos for other microformats [40]

- "Cynthia tested" [41]

- "SEO friendly"

- "NO popups, NO spyware"

- "Powered by PERL"

- PageRank n/10—PRchecker.info (where n is a number between 1 and 10) [42]

Summary

In this chapter, you learned that there are powerful, efficient tools to check your web documents for errors. They can be used during development and are very useful for redesign. Many of these validators are free tools and are available online. The most commonly used ones are markup validators and CSS validators, because the markup and style sheets are such fundamental web site components that can be validated automatically. Validating web site accessibility is a real challenge, because several aspects of WCAG often require human decision.

The last chapter will enumerate the most common errors that result in invalid markup, style sheets, news feed channels, and accessibility barriers.

References

1. Murphy C, Persson N (2009) Valid code is not necessarily well-structured code. In: HTML and CSS Web Standards Solutions – A Web Standardistas' Approach. Friends of ED, Berkeley

2. Thereaux O, Lacourba V et al (eds) (2010) Web Quality Assurance Tools. www.w3.org/QA/Tools/. Accessed 07 January 2011

3. W3C (2011) The W3C Markup Validation Service v1.1. World Wide Web Consortium. http://validator.w3.org. Accessed 04 January 2011

4. W3C (2011) Source code availability for the W3 Markup Validator. World Wide Web Consortium. http://validator.w3.org/source/. Accessed 04 January 2011

5. Quinn L (2007) WDG HTML Validator. Liam Quinn. www.htmlhelp.com/tools/validator/. Accessed 04 January 2011

6. Gueury M (2010) The HTML Validator add-on for Firefox. Marc Gueury. https://addons.mozilla.org/en-US/firefox/addon/249/. Accessed 08 January 2011

7. The Apache Ant Project (2010) XMLValidate. The Apache Software Foundation. http://ant.apache.org/manual/Tasks/xmlvalidate.html. Accessed 26 January 2011

8. Prud'hommeaux E (2007) W3C RDF Validation Service. www.w3.org/RDF/Validator. Accessed 05 January 2011

9. Thereaux O et al (2010) W3C Feed Validation Service, for Atom and RSS. World Wide Web Consortium. http://validator.w3.org/feed/. Accessed 30 November 2010

10. Ruby S, Pilgrim M, Walton J, Ringnalda P (2009) FEED Validator for Atom and RSS and KML. Sam Ruby, Mark Pilgrim, Joseph Walton, and Phil Ringnalda. http://feedvalidator.org. Accessed 30 November 2010

11. Bos B, Çelik T, Hickson I, Lie HW (eds) (2010) Grammar of CSS 2.1. In: Cascading Style Sheets Level 2 Revision 1 (CSS 2.1) Specification. W3C Working Draft. World Wide Web Consortium. www.w3.org/TR/CSS/grammar.html. Accessed 05 January 2011

12. Bos B, Çelik T, Hickson I, Lie HW (eds) (2010) Conformance: Requirements and Recommendations. In: Cascading Style Sheets Level 2 Revision 1 (CSS 2.1) Specification. W3C Working Draft. World Wide Web Consortium. www.w3.org/TR/CSS/conform.html. Accessed 05 January 2011

13. W3C QA (2011) CSS Validation Service. World Wide Web Consortium. http://jigsaw.w3.org/css-validator/. Accessed 05 January 2011

14. W3C I18N Activity Group (2010). World Wide Web Consortium. http://qa-dev.w3.org/i18n-checker/. Accessed 30 September 2010

15. W3C (2010) W3C Link Checker. World Wide Web Consortium. http://validator.w3.org/checklink. Accessed 05 January 2011

16. Abou-Zahra S (ed) (2010) Evaluating Web Sites for Accessibility: Overview. World Wide Web Consortium. www.w3.org/WAI/eval/Overview.html. Accessed 06 January 2011

17. Abou-Zahra S (ed) (2006) Complete List of Web Accessibility Evaluation Tools. World Wide Web Consortium. www.w3.org/WAI/ER/tools/complete.html. Accessed 06 January 2011

18. Abou-Zahra S (ed) (2010) Selecting Web Accessibility Evaluation Tools. World Wide Web Consortium. www.w3.org/WAI/eval/selectingtools.html. Accessed 07 January 2011

19. ATRC (2009) AChecker (Web Accessibility Checker). University of Toronto. http://achecker.ca. Accessed 19 September 2011

20. HiSoftware (2010) HiSoftware Cynthia Says Portal. HiSoftware Inc. www.cynthiasays.com/. Accessed 04 February 2011

21. Kasday L, Andersen A, Smith J, Hernandez D, Bohman P, Anderson S, Maturi N, Varanasi B, Parija J (2011) WAVE. Web accessibility evaluation tool. Web Accessibility in Mind. http://wave.webaim.org. Accessed 03 February 2011

22. Johansson D (2010) Color Contrast Analyzer. Donald Johansson. www.colorsontheweb.com/colorcontrast.asp. Accessed 03 February 2011

23. Lemon G (2011) Luminosity Colour Contrast Ratio Analyser. Juicy Studio. http://juicystudio.com/services/luminositycontrastratio.php. Accessed 03 February 2011

24. UoW (2011) Index of Color Contrast Samples. The University of Wisconsin. http://trace.wisc.edu/contrast-ratio-examples/index.htm. Accessed 03 February 2011

25. W3C (2010) W3C mobileOK Checker. Is your Web site mobile-friendly? World Wide Web Consortium. http://validator.w3.org/mobile/. Accessed 19 September 2011

26. Owen S, Rabin J (eds) (2008) W3C mobileOK Basic Tests 1.0. W3C Recommendation. World Wide Web Consortium. www.w3.org/TR/mobileOK-basic10-tests/. Accessed 19 September 2011

27. W3C (2011) Unicorn - unified validator. World Wide Web Consortium. http://validator.w3.org/unicorn/. Accessed 07 January 2011

28. W3C (2010) Translations of Unicorn. World Wide Web Consortium. http://validator.w3.org/unicorn/translations. Accessed 23 September 2010

29. Total Validator (2011) Total Validator. www.totalvalidator.com. Accessed 05 January 2011

30. Powermapper (2010) PowerMapper – Website Testing and Site Mapping Tools. Powermapper Software. www.powermapper.com/. Accessed 05 January 2011

31. Hazaël-Massieux D (ed) (2011) W3C Semantic Data Extractor. World Wide Web Consortium. www.w3.org/2003/12/semantic-extractor.html. Accessed 07 January 2011

32. Sindice (2011) Sindice Web Data Inspector. Sindice Ltd. http://inspector.sindice.com. Accessed 20 September 2011

33. W3C (2010) "Valid" icons. In: Help and FAQ for the Markup Validator. World Wide Web Consortium. http://validator.w3.org/docs/help.html#icon. Accessed 20 December 2010

34. Thereaux O (2010) List of all W3C Validation Icons. World Wide Web Consortium. www.w3.org/QA/Tools/Icons. Accessed 20 December 2010

35. W3C (2011) W3C Icon Repository. World Wide Web Consortium. www.w3.org/Icons/. Accessed 08 January 2011

36. W3C (2011) W3C HTML5 logo. World Wide Web Consortium. www.w3.org/html/logo/. Accessed 19 January 2011

37. W3C (2008) W3C Web Content Accessibility Guidelines 1.0 Conformance Logos. World Wide Web Consortium. www.w3.org/WAI/WCAG1-Conformance. Accessed 08 January 2011

38. W3C (2010) W3C Web Content Accessibility Guidelines 2.0 Conformance Logos. World Wide Web Consortium. www.w3.org/WAI/WCAG2-Conformance. Accessed 08 January 2011

39. Jacobs I (2009) W3C Semantic Web Logos and Policies. World Wide Web Consortium. www.w3.org/2007/10/sw-logos.html. Accessed 08 January 2011

40. Messina C, Baranovskiy D, Bartelme W (2010) Icons. Microformats Wiki. Microformats Community. http://microformats.org/wiki/icons. Accessed 08 January 2011

41. HiSoftware (2010) Cynthia Tested Button Guidelines – When, Why, and How to use. HiSoftware Inc. www.cynthiasays.com/org/cynthiatested.htm. Accessed 04 February 2011

42. Page Rank Checker (2011) Google Page Rank Checker. http://prchecker.info/. Accessed 08 January 2011

CHAPTER 15

Most Common Errors

Several factors should be considered to achieve web site validity. The code is written either manually or generated automatically, and errors are inevitable. This is also true for server settings. Errors occur in the markup, in the style sheet, in the XML files, in scripts, and so forth. By analyzing and learning the most common errors, many of them can be eliminated or at least minimized. As a result, they can be recognized, localized, and corrected quickly and efficiently.

Even the most carefully created web pages can contain errors. In this chapter, you will learn about the most common errors and their solutions. It is really beneficial to know them, because they occur rather frequently, and learning how to correct them will decrease the time required for corrections and ease your standardization efforts.

Common Serving Errors

One of the most common serving errors is to serve XHTML as `text/html`. For many years, web browsers handled XHTML markup as if it were HTML. This is known as the "dirty secret of XHTML." Self-closing tags and other XHTML specific notations have been ignored, and XHTML documents have been rendered by SGML parsers instead of XML parsers [1]. As a result, none of the beneficial features of XML has been used.

In contrast, modern browsers support the proper MIME type. XHTML documents should be served as `application/xhtml+xml` instead of `text/html`, as discussed in Chapter 4.

Common Markup Errors

Web standardistas should know all the common markup errors in order to easily identify, find, and correct them. Incorrectly used elements, wrong document structure, incorrectly closed tags, missing `alt` attributes, directly provided ampersand characters, ignored case sensitivity, nonunique identifiers, and misspelled keywords are among the most common markup errors. Many of them are clearly indicated by markup validators and can be corrected easily. Validators also provide useful hints on the correction. However, some errors can cause several others. For example, a missing end tag for a division makes not only the document collapse in the browser but also the nesting to become incorrect. Consequently, it might happen that an invalid document with 18 errors indicated by a validator has 2–3 errors only. So, do not be frightened by the initial number of errors!

Incorrectly Used Elements

As a golden rule, extended care must be taken to eliminate unnecessary containers in the markup. For example, images positioned to the right side of the page with the text "wrapping around" can be styled directly instead of putting them onto floating divisions. Another example is the p tag, which should be used for a paragraph container and not for carriage return. Look at the (really bad) example shown in Listing 15-1.

Listing 15-1. A Practice That Should Never Be Used

```
<p>This is a very bad practice
<p>dating back to the early days
<p>of the Web
<p>unfortunately it is still in use
<p>even if it has many drawbacks, e.g.,
<p>illogical
<p>hard to identify related content
```

The technique of omitting end tags should be forgotten. Although it is allowed in HTML, it is not a clean code and is invalid in XHTML. Beginners with a basic (X)HTML knowledge might think that br elements should be added to the end of each line instead of incorrectly forcing line break with paragraphs. They are wrong.

Web content should be logical. The first five rows should belong to a paragraph, and the last two should belong to an unordered list. The previous example should be written as shown in Listing 15-2.

Listing 15-2. The Correct Markup for Listing 15-1

```
<p>This is a very bad practice dating back to the early days of the Web. Unfortunately it ↩
   is still in use even if it has many drawbacks, e.g.,</p>
<ul>
  <li>Illogical</li>
  <li>Hard to identify related content</li>
</ul>
```

Text width can be set by external style sheets in order to achieve similar (or exactly the same) effect expected according to the original example. It all depends on the content and the publishing needs. In this case, the markup in Listing 15-3 with the appropriate style in the external CSS file shown in Listing 15-4 would be a standard solution.

Listing 15-3. A More Advanced Solution

```
<div id="thinbox">
  <p>This is a very bad practice dating back to the early days of the Web. Unfortunately it ↩
     is still in use even if it has many drawbacks, e.g.,</p>
  <ul>
    <li>Illogical</li>
    <li>Hard to identify related content</li>
  </ul>
</div>
```

Listing 15-4. CSS Ruleset for Listing 15-3

```
.thinbox {
  width: 400px;
  height: 600px;
```

```
   font-size: 14px;
}
```

Incorrect Structure

Incorrectly used elements often offend the DOM model. Required elements should be provided, and nesting rules should be followed. Moreover, the document structure should be maintained by using correct containers and elements in the proper manner. Take a look at the code in Listing 15-5.

Listing 15-5. *List Items Without Structure or Semantic Meaning (Incorrect)*

```
- first item <br />
- second item <br />
- third item <br />
```

Since the previous rows are items of a list, they evidently should be collected into an unordered list (Listing 15-6).

Listing 15-6. *The Correct Markup for Listing 15-5*

```
<ul>
  <li>first item</li>
  <li>second item</li>
  <li>third item</li>
</ul>
```

The default bullets provided by the li elements can be changed in CSS to an arbitrary character or image (see the section "Styling Lists"). CSS completely separates presentation from structure; thus, any elements can be arbitrary styled.

Misused Tables

Tableless layout: a Web standardista's phrase. Tables are for organizing data, not for controlling layout. For that purpose, div elements should be used instead. Their positions, sizes, colors, layer orders, transparencies, and many other features can be set via style sheets (Listing 15-8 instead of Listing 15-7).

Listing 15-7. *Fragment of a Misused Table*

```
<table border="1" bgcolor="#898989" width="400">
<td align="center" valign="top" spanning="2">  
<td>
```

Listing 15-8. *Correct Structure of Tabular Data in the Markup*

```
<table>
  <tr>
    <td>Meaningful content in data cell</td>
    <td>Content of other data cell</td>
  </tr>
</table>
```

The position of the table is determined by the content elements, text, and images as well as the container div element. The parameters should be given as CSS rulesets in the external style sheet associated with the document (see the section "Table Styling").

Nonoptimal Code Length

Analogously to the "tag soup" discussed in Chapter 1, the more specific "div soup" refers to the misuse and overuse of divisions (Zeldman calls it *divitis* [2]).Listing 15-9 shows an example.

Listing 15-9. *A Divitis*

```
<div class="maincontainer"><div class="nounderlineleftmargin"><div class="container"><div
class="topheadlinesleftalign">The Latest News</div><div
class="maintextthickborder"></div></div></div>
</div>
```

The major problem is that there is no structure at all (even if it might be valid). Unnecessary divisions should be removed. Moreover, the names are far too long (although descriptive). They should be kept within reasonable limits.

Remember that in (X)HTML5 other elements dedicated to structuring should be used as the main containers.

Element and Attribute Errors

A gross element error is when elements defined in another specification are used. Elements should be used according to the document type.

Incorrectly nested elements break the document structure and should be eliminated. The location and order of elements within (X)HTML documents are not arbitrary and should meet the criteria of nesting rules discussed in Chapter 3.

Both errors can cause the message "document type does not allow element here" in the W3C Markup Validation Service.

Similar problems are associated with attributes as well. The W3C Markup Validation Service gives the error "there is no attribute 'attrib_name'" message. The selection of allowed attributes depends on the document type being used. For example, several attributes defined in the specification of the Transitional variant of XHTML are not allowed in Strict XHTML documents, as described in detail in Chapter 3. Similarly, several HTML attributes are prohibited in XHTML. Styling attributes should be provided in the CSS rather than the markup. Applying vendor-specific extensions such as `marginheight` can also cause similar problems. If an element is undefined, its attributes are considered invalid too.

End Tag Errors

The W3C Markup Validation Service clearly indicates the missing end tags by the message "end tag for element omitted, but its declaration does not permit this." Additional (unnecessary) end tags are identified as "end tag for element which is not open" by the W3C Markup Validation Service.

One of the easiest ways to ensure proper element closing is to write the closing tags immediately after opening them, such as shown in Listing 15-10.

Listing 15-10. Closing Tag Provided Before Any Child Elements

```
<div>

</div>
```

Element content should not be written until the closing tag is provided. It might seem evident, but consider that there could be hundreds of code lines between the opening and closing tags. Moreover, there might be several identical subsequent closing tags whose opening pairs can be difficult to identify even if indentation is used.

Identifiers

Generally, there are two types of identifiers used in (X)HTML markup. Naturally, `class` identifiers used mainly for styling multiple elements can be applied several times within the same document—not so with the `id` attribute, which should be unique throughout the document (such as a fragment identifier).

Common Style Sheet Errors

Although CSS parsers have a mechanism for handling style sheet errors [3], they should be eliminated by proper authoring and confirmed by validation. Writing declarations with incorrect properties and nonexisting property values are among the most common errors in CSS.

Nonexisting Properties

One of the most common CSS errors is the application of nonexisting style properties. The W3C CSS Validator clearly indicates these errors with the message "Property doesn't exist."

CSS name convention differs from the ones used in (X)HTML markup. The less experienced might type a CSS property name that is logical and "should be correct." For example, the left margin can be set with the `margin-left` property, although `left-margin` (which does not exist) would be more logical. Even if it seems to be straightforward, the result would be incorrect. If somebody is not familiar with the whole vocabulary of Cascading Style Sheets, all properties should be checked in the appropriate CSS specification before applying them. Another good example is a table data cell with vertically centralized content. In the early days of the Web when many styles were provided on HTML attributes directly, the `valign` attribute was used on the `td` element for that. In CSS, however, there is no property with the name `valign`. The corresponding property has a different name: `vertical-align`.

Nonexisting or Incorrectly Used Property Values

To avoid errors caused by incorrect CSS property values, the allowed values as well as the associated data types should be known. Additionally, it is very useful to know the initial (default) value. For example, one of the three attribute values, `collapse`, `separate`, or `inherit`, can be set for the `border-collapse` property used to set whether table borders are collapsed into a single border or rendered detached. The ruleset `border-collapse: yes;` cannot be used, because the attribute value `yes` would be illegal. Since this is an inheritable property, a corresponding ruleset is needed only if the inherited value is not appropriate for our purposes and needs to be overridden (or ensured).

Ignored Inheritance

Redundancy often occurs in badly written CSS. Although such style sheets might even be standard-compliant, they are longer than necessary, use more bandwidth, and are harder to maintain. *Code optimality* can be achieved only if inheritance is considered properly. Assume the style rulesets presented in Listing 15-11.

Listing 15-11. Redundant Rulesets (Should Be Optimized)

```
body {
  font-family: Verdana, Arial;
  font-size: 1.2em;
  color: #351801;
}

p {
  font-family: Verdana, Arial;
  font-size: 1.2em;
  color: #351801;
}

div {
  font-family: Verdana, Arial;
  font-size: 1.2em;
  color: #351801;
}
```

The previous rules are obviously redundant. Some developers would write them in the form shown in Listing 15-12.

Listing 15-12. A Better Yet Still Redundant Solution

```
body, p, div {
  font-family: Verdana, Arial;
  font-size: 1.2em;
  color: #351801;
}
```

Since browsers apply the same styles for the child elements (p and div in this example) as defined for the parent element (body), the code is still redundant and should be written as shown in Listing 15-13.

Listing 15-13. The Correct Solution

```
body {
  font-family: Verdana, Arial;
  font-size: 1.2em;
  color: #351801;
}
```

In other words, the second and third rulesets of the original example aren't required and should be deleted. Note such identical, redundant rules are much more difficult to notice in long CSS files where there are tens of other rulesets between them. That's why it is important to think the major CSS rules over at the very beginning and later override those rules only where inherited values are not appropriate for the overall design and layout.

Descendant selectors (also known as *contextual selectors* [4]) should be used for optimum code length. Examine the markup shown in Listing 15-14 and CSS rules in Listing 15-15.

Listing 15-14. Standard-Compliant but Nonoptimal Markup (Classitis)

```
<div id="main">
  <p class="maintext">The is the main content of the site.</p>
  <p class="maintext">The second paragraph should look like the first one.</p>
  <p class="maintext">In fact, all paragraphs of the document have the same styles.</p>
</div>
```

Listing 15-15. Standard-Compliant but Nonoptimal Styling Rules

```
.maintext {
  margin-left: 15px;
  margin-right: 15px;
  margin-top: 10px;
  margin-bottom: 5px;
  font-size: 1.4em;
  color: #1d4c90;
}
```

Although both the markup and the style rules are presented in a standard form, the code is far from optimal. This kind of class overuse is called *classitis* [5]. A much shorter, easier to understand, optimal solution could be the markup presented in Listing 15-16 with the CSS rules shown in Listing 15-17.

Listing 15-16. The Correct Markup for Listing 15-14

```
<div id="main">
  <p>The is the main content of the site.</p>
  <p>The second paragraph should look like the first one.</p>
  <p>In fact, all paragraphs of the document have the same styles.</p>
</div>
```

Listing 15-17. The Optimal CSS Rules

```
#main p {
  margin: 10px 15px 5px;
  font-size: 1.4em;
  color: #1d4c90;
}
```

If this is not a unique section of the page, the id attribute could be omitted, and the CSS ruleset could be modified in order to be applied to p elements in general.

Color Errors

CSS validation often results in color warnings that indicate potential problems with foreground and background colors. For example, if a very light font color is used on a white background, it might be hard or even impossible to read the content. In such cases, the W3C CSS Validator gives the message "Same colors for color and background-color in two contexts."

However, some of these messages can be considered as false positives since there are cases when visibility is not a problem at all (transparent or overlapping layers, text on background image, and so on). To be on the safe side, the text must remain readable even if other components of the page (for example, background image) cannot be downloaded.

Incorrect Locations

Incorrect location errors are typically caused by not properly closed rulesets. They should be checked one by one near the line indicated by the W3C CSS Validation Service error message "The element can't appear here in the context CSS 2.1."

Transparent Backgrounds

Transparent surfaces are becoming more and more popular throughout the Web. The transparency of a div is usually set as shown in Listing 15-18.

Listing 15-18. A Typical but Nonstandard, Browser-Dependent Ruleset for Transparency

```
#transdiv {
  opacity: 0.7;
  filter: alpha(opacity=70);
  -moz-opacity: 0.7;
  -khtml-opacity: 0.7;
}
```

In modern browsers it works fine. However, when validating as CSS 2.1, the validator would give errors. Even in CSS3, only the first one (opacity) is valid, which works in Firefox, Opera, and Safari but not in IE (which requires the filter property). Thus, validity can be obtained by removing the last three properties; however, the result won't work under Internet Explorer and older versions of other browsers.

A valid, cross-browser solution could be the transparent background image such as the one shown in Listing 15-19.

Listing 15-19. A Transparent PNG Background File Is a Robust Solution

```
#transdiv {
  background-image: url('images/transpbg.png');
  background-repeat: repeat;
}
```

Miscellaneous Errors

Not all documents can be checked by validators. Incorrect serving or temporary server errors are the most common reasons. Without providing data required for automatic document type detection or character encoding detection, validation cannot be performed or provides unreliable results.

Common News Feed Errors

Valid news feed channels should be well-formed and meet all general XML criteria. Even so, some errors might occur in manually updated news feeds because of human error. One of the most common errors is an incorrect date. If the publication date is earlier than the date of updating, validators give an error. This is referred to as an *implausible date*. Care must be taken to apply the proper offset whose misuse can lead to the same problem.

Common Script Errors

Scripts are out of the scope of markup validators. Consequently, extended care must be taken to ensure correctness and proper functionality. It should be ensured that a web page remains usable even if the scripts cannot be executed for whatever reason. It is important to keep in mind that alternate content written for scripts cannot be checked by software tools, and their evaluation depends on human decision.

Common Accessibility Errors

In contrast with markup or CSS errors where errors depend on the language version being used, accessibility errors are determined by the version and level of guidelines considered. A comprehensive overview of accessibility errors and their solutions ("Failures of Success Criteria") is collected in the W3C group note describing techniques and failures for WCAG 2.0 [6]. The most common accessibility errors can be summarized as follows:

- Lack of structured markup or table layout
- Images that convey important information are embedded through CSS
- User control is missing to stop or pause blinking, scrolling, and automatically played sound files or videos
- Missing captions or labels for sound effects and synchronized media
- Inadequate user guidance for forms
- Difficult navigation and traps
- Time limits
- Information representation relies exclusively on color, shape, location, or graphics
- Inaccessible custom controls
- Nonunique identifiers (not only inaccessible but also invalid)
- Missing alternate content and long description for nontext content and scripts
- Functionality that might disturb the user with nonrequested features such as a new window
- Text is not legible or clear enough, too small font size, or insufficient contrast difference between foreground and background colors or images

- Missing document title
- Missing or inadequate text alternatives such as filenames or placeholder
- Missing labels
- Whitespace or control spacing used to create multiple columns in plain text or within words
- Automatic form submission without warning
- Missing or incorrect tab order declaration
- Missing header cells, captions, and summaries in tables
- Pointing device-specific event handlers
- Nonspecific links such as "Click here" or "More"

Summary

This chapter enumerated the most common errors you might face in your daily work as a web developer. You are well aware by now how to eliminate them when you develop from scratch and correct them when you redesign a site.

After thoroughly reading this book, you have learned the importance and benefits of web standards and techniques for writing valid markup from scratch. You know how to recognize standards and differentiate them from nonfinalized specifications. You now have all the skills required to provide meaningful semantics and machine-readable metadata, restrict markup to semantics, and achieve full standard compliance in your projects.

References

1. Hickson I (2009) Sending XHTML as text/html Considered Harmful. Ian Hickson. www.hixie.ch/advocacy/xhtml. Accessed 17 January 2011

2. Zeldman J, Marcotte E (2010) The Heartbreak of Divitis. In: Designing with Web standards, 3rd Ed., New Riders, Berkeley

3. Bos B, Çelik T, Hickson I, Wium Lie HW (eds) (2010) Rules for handling parsing errors. In: Cascading Style Sheets Level 2 Revision 1 (CSS 2.1) Specification. World Wide Web Consortium. www.w3.org/TR/CSS21/syndata.html#parsing-errors. Accessed 13 October 2010

4. Murphy C, Persson N (2009) HTML and CSS Web Standards Solutions – A Web Standardistas' Approach. Friends of ED, Berkeley

5. Zeldman J, Marcotte E (2010) Classitis: The Measles of Markup. In: Designing with Web standards, 3rd Ed. New Riders, Berkeley

6. Cooper M, Reid LG, Vanderheiden G, Caldwell B, Chisholm W, Slatin J (eds) (2010) Failures for WCAG 2.0. In: Techniques for WCAG 2.0. Techniques and Failures for Web Content Accessibility Guidelines 2.0. World Wide Web Consortium. www.w3.org/TR/WCAG20-TECHS/failures.html. Accessed 03 March 2011

Index

F

J

K

L

■ M

■ W

Y

 Z

CPSIA information can be obtained at www.ICGtesting.com
Printed in the USA
LVOW050230170512

282117LV00004B/3/P